GW00372791

HARDEN'S

UK
Restaurants
2004

IN ASSOCIATION WITH

RÉMY MARTIN

FINE CHAMPAGNE COGNAC

RÉMY MARTIN

FINE CHAMPAGNE COGNAC

A Taste for the Finest

Founded in 1724, Rémy Martin is renowned for producing Fine Champagne Cognacs of the highest quality. Each Rémy Martin cognac – ranging from VS Grand Cru and the world's best selling VSOP to XO Excellence, Extra and the "ultimate cognac" Louis XIII de Rémy Martin – reflects the brand's philosophy of balance, strength and character.

Rémy Martin has a heritage of creating exceptional taste experiences: the very best grapes are selected from the finest growing areas of Cognac and expensive, traditional methods of production are still used to ensure that Rémy Martin cognacs remain the finest in the world - whether you enjoy them neat, on ice as an aperitif, mixed in a long drink or as a delicious accompaniment to a meal.

Likewise, such dedication to creating excellence with talent, passion and good judgement of taste is what makes a truly outstanding chef. Great chefs are passionately committed to using the finest ingredients and the best methods in order to produce the ultimate taste experience for the diner.

These are the qualities that we seek in the second year of the Restaurant Rémy awards.

THE RESTAURANT RÉMYS

Paying Tribute to Excellence

Rémy Martin inaugurated the Restaurant Rémy awards in 2003 to recognise the emerging talent of the UK restaurant scene and give a voice to British diners who are passionate about sharing their quality dining experiences and acknowledging the truly outstanding.

In the second year of the Restaurant Rémy awards we are delighted to pay tribute to twenty establishments that have received consistently excellent independent reviews from both members of the public and Harden's experts and are setting new exacting standards for the whole industry.

As the epitome of quality dining, the twenty Restaurant Rémy 2004 winners form a fascinating snapshot of the changing landscape of the UK restaurant scene and the exciting diversity that diners can enjoy. In each and every winner - from local gastropubs to fine French restaurants - we are witness to a commitment to delivering quality and new taste experiences to our tables. Their geographical spread highlights how the highest levels of culinary expertise are accessible all over the country.

We hope you may have the opportunity to visit them and enjoy for yourself everything that they have to offer.

Excellence Award 2004
TOM AIKENS

While the Restaurant Rémys pay tribute to twenty quality dining establishments around the UK, this year we are delighted to present a special Excellence Award to Tom Aikens, based in the heart of London's Chelsea.

Since opening in Spring 2003, Tom Aikens has swiftly become a destination restaurant, thanks to its modern twist on French cuisine and its consistent and friendly service.

Tom Aikens was the youngest-ever recipient of two Michelin stars as Head Chef and co-proprietor at Pied à Terre in London. He subsequently went on to work as private chef to Andrew Lloyd Webber and Sir Anthony and Lady Bamford, before venturing out with his own eponymous opening.

Front of house is Tom's Finnish born wife Laura, who gained wide experience in restaurant management, at L'Escargot, Pied à Terre and The Capital. Laura says, "We hope that our customers will return time and again, and when they do we will welcome them by name, remember their favourite dishes and make them feel special. That is very important."

Regional Restaurant Rémy Winners 2004

AUBERGE DU LAC – Lemsford, Hertfordshire
Jean-Christophe Novelli has been applauded by reviewers for his lakeside restaurant in the beautiful grounds of Brocket Hall, where diners enjoy his modern take on French cuisine. Novelli says "I am now settled back on my feet and enjoying working with a great team in this most picturesque environment. We all share the same goal to be one of the top destination restaurants in Europe."

EDMONDS – Henley-in-Arden, Warwickshire
Andy Waters has a simple philosophy and it is to ensure that quality is what the customer receives in terms of both staff attitude and what's presented on the plate. "We buy quality and we employ quality. We use only the very best fresh ingredients and we cook them simply but well," says Andy. The busy, booked-out restaurant is testimony that the customer agrees.

L'ENCLUME – Cartmel, Cumbria
A modern and contemporary restaurant in a beautiful traditional, riverside setting, L'Enclume prides itself on offering the 'ultimate' dining experience. Using wild herbs, flowers and roots from the local valleys, Simon Rogan aims to help diners "rediscover forgotten flavours by presenting them in modern ways." His flagship 19-course menu demonstrates this dedication to developing unusual flavour combinations whilst pushing the boundaries of taste and texture. Simon affirms, "We would like to think we are cooking the most progressive food in the UK."

THE ENDEAVOUR – Staithes, North Yorkshire
Brian Kay and Charlotte Willoughby's seafood restaurant in a former fisherman's cottage aims to give a truly distinctive dining experience, and not just thanks to the excellence of the food served. "We set great store in the quality of the raw ingredients, and feel this allows us to keep the cooking simple and the flavours distinct," says Charlotte. All ingredients are sourced locally and everything is created in-house right down to the bread and chocolates.

FIVE NORTH STREET – Winchcombe, Gloucestershire

Kate and Marcus Ashenford had a dream when they met at catering college: one day to open a restaurant in the Cotswolds offering the highest quality cuisine and service at a value-for-money price. Today, the relaxed and comfortable surroundings at Five North Street have won their restaurant praise and acclaim, with customers returning time and again to this charming establishment for its perfectly executed cooking.

LE MONT – Manchester

A sleek and stylish restaurant at the top of the new Urbis museum, Le Mont's aim was to bring to Manchester a restaurant that delivered food living up to the menu's promise: "quality regional food with honest integrity." Robert Kisby emphasises that it is perceived value for money that is what pleases the clientèle at Le Mont – and judging by reports this approach is working!

THE OUTSIDER – Edinburgh

Malcolm Innes's informal atmosphere and a menu designed for sharing have won the Outsider many admirers. Innes claims that the "atmosphere is our most precious commodity", as his aim is for diners to have a "dramatic" dining experience. Innes believes his secret lies in the combination of an "exuberant, youthful staff and a great, innovative, eclectic menu from Head Chef Kenny Waugh."

RED LION – Stathern, Leicestershire

Passion for the traditional British country pub is what drives Ben Jones and the team at the Red Lion. Ben says, "our intention is to revitalise traditional pub values offering excellent food, beer and wine in a friendly and enjoyable atmosphere." Diners regularly praise the sheer quality of the produce used, thanks to the dedicated sourcing from local farmers, breweries and suppliers.

THE WILLOW TREE – Taunton, Somerset

Darren Sherlock's consistent high standards have earned rave reviews from customers. His aim is to offer top quality ingredients "cooked to achieve a real clarity of flavour." Sherlock's belief is that the whole dining experience should by far outshine anything that can be achieved at home. This philosophy paired with warm and comfortable surroundings has certainly had an extraordinary response from diners in the opening year.

THE YEW TREE – Lower Wield, Hampshire
The Yew Tree is well off the 'beaten track', so the team try to make the journey well worthwhile! They have succeeded in creating a homely and relaxed establishment renowned for delightfully fresh and beautifully cooked dishes that, according to owners Christopher and Donna Richards, are truly "cooked from the heart." Fresh herbs and salads picked from their very own garden, fish freshly caught on day boats off the Cornish coast and the fantastic earthy flavours of local game all contribute to a beautifully thought out and expertly created menu.

London Restaurant Rémy Winners 2004

FINO – Fitzrovia
"All food prepared with the minimum of fuss". It's difficult to get a clearer and – for a restaurant inspired by Spanish tapas bars – more authentic 'mission statement' than the one brothers Sam and Eddie Hart have set for themselves. In its first few months of operation their efficient Fitzrovia basement restaurant has already made itself a great hit.

MA CUISINE – Twickenham
John McClements first set up shop as a 'bistrotier' 17 years ago, but the quality of his cooking was such that his establishment soon moved 'upmarket'. Having a successful restaurant under his own name, he recently decided to let his young chef take over... and then discovered that he positively missed the kitchen! So much so that he decided to set up a real old-fashioned bistro next to his established restaurant to instant acclaim.

PAINTED HERON – Chelsea
Yogesh Datta's very individual Indian cooking has slowly been gathering a devoted following for this stylishly-furnished modern restaurant in a quiet Chelsea backstreet. Why? Because like very few other chefs offering the cuisine of the subcontinent, his menu is written freshly every day, to make best use of ingredients at their seasonal prime. It is chefs like Yogesh that keep London at the forefront of the evolution of subcontinental cuisine.

REAL GREEK SOUVLAKI – Farringdon
Street food from around the world is often delicious, and few people seemed more likely to bring Londoners the best of Greek street food than the team which had established The Real Greek to great acclaim four years ago. They have not disappointed, and this Farringdon souvlaki bar has taken the area by storm.

SUMOSAN – Mayfair

You can't make top-quality sushi without the very best fish, and head chef Bubker Belkhit has spent years developing relationships with top fish suppliers across the world for this Mayfair restaurant. His efforts are complemented by those of owner Janina Wolkow, who has created a suitably stylish setting for an establishment which is winning growing recognition.

THE SWAN – Chiswick

The Swan prides itself on its completely unpretentious charms, aiming to surprise (and hopefully delight) customers with the sheer quality of what it does, rather than by any 'fireworks'. In fact, it aims to offer "the charm you'd expect from a busy 'local'": this is a gastropub, where 'gastro' and 'pub' are treated with equal respect!

THYME – Clapham

Thyme's philosophy is about "time and space", which they endeavour to give customers by moving away from the traditional three-course meal concept towards a more European style of eating. The style perhaps took a little while to establish itself in the pysche of London diners-out, but – now it has – the place is an ever more recognised success.

TSUNAMI – Clapham

Ni Lenette and Ken Sam see the evolution of this Japanese restaurant (which, like Thyme, is also in emerging Clapham) as a "journey of becoming", and their establishment is certainly becoming one of the key destinations south of the river. The emergence of such a place emphasises how presumptions about 'suburban' London restaurants not matching West End standards are progressively becoming out-of-date.

THE WELLS – Hampstead

Can it survive? Hampstead has always frustrated local residents and visitors with its mystifying inability to sustain quality eating places. There's every hope, though, that this new gastropub – or really a pub with smart dining rooms above – is set to break the mould. With its menu changing twice-daily, its interesting and eclectic menu, and its use of top-quality ingredients, it emphasises just how far 'pub' eating has come in London over the past decade.

Discover Perfect Taste Matches with Rémy Martin

Harden's UK Restaurants offers practical guidance for anyone keen to try new taste experiences. So next time you eat out, why not embark on a true voyage of discovery by choosing a dish or type of cuisine with which Rémy Martin Fine Champagne cognacs can harmonise? There's no need to save  cognac until after dessert – Rémy Martin Fine Champagne cognac can make a delicious alternative to your traditional glass of wine as you dine.

Composed exclusively from eaux-de-vie from the two best Cognac crus, Grande and Petite Champagne, the Rémy Martin range features an amazing richness of aromas and nuances of flavour that can create some stunning partnerships with your food and release new levels of sensation, texture and taste on your palate.

Whichever restaurant you select for your evening out, Rémy Martin Fine Champagne cognac can offer a great match to your menu choice. Here are some suggestions for you to try:

Rémy Martin Grand Cru
Before beginning your meal, enjoy a refreshing Grand Cru as a long drink with ginger ale or tonic or try it in a cocktail as an aperitif.

Foie Gras and Rémy Martin XO Excellence
However the foie gras is served (gently fried, preserved in jelly, sliced, or fresh) a chilled glass of Rémy Martin XO Excellence is a perfect match. The prune, fig and candied orange notes of Rémy Martin XO Excellence subtly blend with the smoothness of the foie gras to unlock the cognac's spicy aromas. The textures harmonise beautifully, with the roundness of XO Excellence acting as a perfect foil to the softness of the foie gras in the mouth.

Sushi and Rémy Martin Grand Cru
At your favourite Japanese restaurant ask for a chilled glass of Rémy Martin Grand Cru with your meal. The fresh notes of lime blossom, apples and vanilla complement the gentle acidity of dishes such as tuna, sea bream, smoked eel, salmon and prawn, as well as sea urchin or caviar.

Game and Rémy Martin Extra
Game matches perfectly with a glass of Extra cognac as the deep flavours of the meat blend with the spicy notes of the Rémy Martin Extra for a real treat on your palate. Try with pigeon or partridge.

Chocolate and Rémy Martin XO Excellence
Really indulge yourself at the end of the meal and accompany your chocolate dessert with a glass of XO Excellence. The combination releases the richness of flavours to make a unique and delicious tasting experience. The cognac's fruity, floral and spicy notes marry wonderfully with chocolate's delicate bitter-sweet flavours.

The Cheese Board and Rémy Martin VSOP
The aromatic depth of flavour in a glass of Rémy Martin VSOP is a perfect complement to the cheese board. Fresh, strong flavoured cheeses such as Roquefort match well for a delicious taste experience.

RATINGS & PRICES

We see little point in traditional rating systems, which generally tell you nothing more than that expensive restaurants are 'better' than cheap ones because they use costlier ingredients and attempt more ambitious dishes. You probably knew that already. Our system assumes that, as prices rise, so do diners' expectations.

Prices and ratings are shown as follows:

£ Price
The cost of a three-course *dinner* for one person.
We include half a bottle of house wine, coffee and service (or a 10% tip if there is no service charge).

Food
The following symbols indicate that, ***in comparison with other restaurants in the same price-bracket***, the cooking at the establishment is:

★★ **Exceptional**
★ **Very good**

We also have a category for places which attract a notably high proportion of adverse comment:

✗ **Disappointing**

Ambience
Restaurants which provide a setting which is very charming, stylish or 'buzzy' are indicated as follows:

𝔸 **Particularly atmospheric**

Restaurant Rémy awards

 A bold restaurant Rémy symbol signifies this year's winners

 A faded restaurant Rémy symbol signifies last year's winners

Small print

Telephone number – *All numbers in the London section are (020) numbers. Dublin numbers are shown for dialling within the Republic (the international code for which is + 353).*

Sample dishes – *these dishes exemplify the style of cooking at a particular establishment. They are merely samples – it is unlikely that these specific dishes will be available at the time of your visit.*

Details – *the following information is given where relevant:*

Directions – *to help you find the establishment.*

Website – *if applicable.*

Last orders time – *at dinner (Sun may be up to 90 mins earlier).*

Opening hours – *unless otherwise stated, restaurants are open for lunch and dinner seven days a week.*

Credit and debit cards – *unless otherwise stated, Mastercard, Visa, Amex and Switch are accepted.*

Dress – *where appropriate, the management's preferences concerning patrons' dress are given.*

Smoking – *cigarette smoking restrictions are noted. Pipe or cigar smokers should always check ahead.*

Children – *if we know of a specified minimum age for children, we note this.*

Accommodation – *if an establishment has rooms, we list how many and the minimum price for a double.*

Publisher's announcements

At last... Hardens on your PDA

Harden's London Restaurants and *Harden's UK Restaurants* are now available for use on your PDA (both Pocket PC and Palm OS).

Other Harden's titles

Hotel Guide – NEW
London Restaurants
Good Cheap Eats in London
London Bars & Pubs
London Party Guide
London Food Shops
London Baby Book
London for Free

The ideal corporate gift

Harden's London Restaurants, Harden's UK Restaurants, Harden's Hotel Guide and *Harden's London Bars & Pubs* are available in a range of specially customised corporate gift formats.
For further information on any of the above, please call (020) 7839 4763 or visit www.hardens.com.

© Harden's Limited 2003

ISBN 1-873721-59-5 (paperback)
ISBN 1-873721-63-3 (bonded leather)

British Library Cataloguing-in-Publication data:
a catalogue record for this book is available from the British Library.

Printed and bound in Finland by
WS Bookwell Ltd

Production Manager: Elizabeth Warman
Research: Frances Gill

Harden's Limited
14 Buckingham Street
London WC2N 6DF

CONTENTS

HOW THIS BOOK IS ORGANISED

This guide begins in *London*, which, in recognition of the scale and diversity of its restaurant scene, has an extensive introduction and indexes, as well as its own maps. Thereafter, the guide is organised strictly alphabetically, without regard to national divisions – Ballater, Beaumaris, Belfast and Birmingham appear together under 'B'.

For *cities and larger towns*, you should therefore be able to turn straight to the relevant section. Cities which have significant numbers of restaurants also have a brief introductory overview, as well as entries for the restaurants themselves.

In *less densely populated areas*, you will generally find it easiest to start with the map of the relevant area at the back of the book, which will guide you to the appropriate place names.

HOW THIS BOOK IS RESEARCHED

This book is the result of a research effort involving thousands of 'reporters'. These are 'ordinary' members of the public who share with us summary reviews of the best and the worst of their annual dining experiences. This year, some 6500 people gave us approximately 80,000 reviews in total.

The density of the feedback on London (where many of the top places attract several hundred reviews each) is such that the ratings for the restaurants in the capital included in this edition are almost exclusively statistical in derivation. We have, as it happens, visited all the restaurants in the London section, anonymously, and at our own expense, but we use our personal experiences only to inform the standpoint from which to interpret the consensus opinion.

In the case of the more commented-upon restaurants away from the capital, we have adopted an approach very similar to London. In the case of less-visited provincial establishments, however, the interpretation of survey results owes as much to art as it does to science.

In our experience, smaller establishments are – for better or worse – generally quite consistent, and we have therefore felt able to place a relatively high level of confidence in a lower level of commentary. Conservatism on our part, however, may have led to some smaller places being under-rated compared to their more visited peers.

HOW YOU CAN JOIN THE SURVEY

Register on our mailing list at www.hardens.com and you will be invited, in the spring of 2004, to participate in our next survey. **If you take part you will, on publication, receive a complimentary copy of *Harden's UK Restaurants 2005*.**

FROM THE EDITORS

We have been in the business of publishing restaurant guides (to London) for the past thirteen years, but this is only the sixth edition of our guide to the UK as a whole.

To an extent that we believe is unique in the UK, this guide is written 'from the bottom up'. That is to say, its composition is driven by the restaurants which people across the country – as represented by our diverse reporter base – talk about. It does not, therefore, concentrate on hotel restaurants (as is the case with one of our 'independent' competitors, which does a big business in hotel inspections). Nor – unlike all the other major UK restaurant guides – does it (by their relative omission) give the impression that 'ethnic' cuisines are somehow second-rate, or of less interest than 'proper' European ones.

The effects of London's restaurant revolution of the '90s are now becoming apparent across the whole of the UK. The task of following the growing number of restaurants proper – as well as the gastropubs, the hotel dining rooms, the bistros and the quality café/bars – grows annually. We know – as any honest publisher must acknowledge – that all guide books are imperfect. There will be deserving places missing, and opinions will be repeated that the passing of time has rendered redundant. However, we believe that our system – involving the careful processing of tens of thousands of reports – is the best available.

Given the growing scale of our task, we are very grateful for the continuing support we have received from Rémy Martin in the publication of this guide. With their help, we hope to make this the most comprehensive, as well as the most diverse, guide available to the restaurants of the UK.

We are also very grateful to each of our thousands of reporters, without whose input this guide could simply not have been written.

All restaurant guides are the subject of continual revision. This is especially true when the restaurant scene is undergoing a period of rapid change, as at present.

Please help us to make the next edition even more comprehensive and accurate: sign up to join the survey by following the instructions opposite.

Richard Harden   **Peter Harden**

LONDON
INTRODUCTION
& SURVEY RESULTS

LONDON INTRODUCTION

Introduction

In practically every respect, London today is an incomparably more interesting city to eat out in than it was ten years ago. For quality *and* range, London now has only one serious competitor in the world, New York, and – as noted on previous pages – the 'scene' is currently changing faster than ever.

With its many maps and indexes – in particular the Survey results (pages 23-26) and Area overviews (pages 88-100) – this guide is designed to provide numerous ways of locating the restaurant you're seeking for any particular occasion. But, if you're new in town – or just an occasional visitor – you may find the following a handy introduction.

Which is London's best restaurant?

In the sense people usually mean this question – that is, money-no-object, probably French – the answer is clearly *Gordon Ramsay* (in Chelsea, not at Claridge's). Or, for a more traditional atmosphere, head for *Le Gavroche* – London's longest established 'temple of gastronomy'. *Pétrus* has been a strong performer in recent years, and opens in a new location shortly after this guide appears. *Tom Aikens* is a name not yet well known to London's restaurant-goers, but the eponymous chef has recently opened an establishment of very high ambition, in Chelsea.

For first-rate cooking, hotel dining rooms are rarely the best option, but three are of note. If you like fish, *Restaurant One-O-One*, in Knightsbridge, is well worth seeking out, mainly for the quality of the cooking. If you're looking for a more all-round 'classic' experience, *1837* in Mayfair would be the place: we hope it survives the recent sale of the hotel which houses it. Knightsbridge's *Capital Hotel* has consistently offered cooking of high quality for many years, but its dining room is not atmospheric.

What's 'in' at the moment?

The Ivy (if you can get a booking) and, to a lesser extent, its siblings *J Sheekey* and *Le Caprice* are always 'in' – they make a 'can't-go-wrong' choice for pretty much any occasion.

The hottest ticket of recent years has been *Nobu*, which has spawned a host of imitators, some of which (notably *Zuma*) now threaten to eclipse it. Among other recent arrivals, *Hakkasan* and *Locanda Locatelli* stand out. In Notting Hill, trustafarians still fall over themselves to get seats at *E&O* and the *Electric Brasserie*. The new *Balham Bar & Kitchen* is quickly establishing itself as a prime South London 'scene', in an area some might have thought unpromising.

As a star magnet, *San Lorenzo* has a timeless – and to the uninitiated, quite inexplicable – appeal. The new *Sketch* – part owned by the man behind the ever-fashionable *Momo* – is enjoying its 15 minutes of fame (though it is perhaps the bar which is really the trendy destination).

I'm not fussed about fashionable scenes – where can I find a really good meal without spending the earth?

The Ivy, *J Sheekey* and *Le Caprice* are not that expensive, and if you want a bit of glamour plus a decent meal in the heart of town, this trio of establishments is hard to beat. Though more remote, three places owned by Nigel Platts-Martin are top choices – *Chez Bruce* in Wandsworth, *La Trompette* in Chiswick and *The Glasshouse* in Kew. Do not be fooled by their suburban locations – these are serious restaurants! For French cooking of utmost quality, but without great formality, *Monsieur Max* in distant Hampton Hill is another name which stands out.

Other, more central names which have stood the test of time include *Clarke's* (Kensington) and *Zafferano* (Belgravia).

What if I want the best of British tradition?
Because Britain is a 'pub culture', there are very few traditional restaurants of note (and fewer which can be recommended). *The Dorchester Grill* is currently the grandest of the native flag bearers. The venerable *Rules* combines generally good (but recently rather variable) cooking with charming period style. The City preserves some extraordinary olde-worlde places such as *Sweetings* and *Simpson's Tavern*, and the famous pub *Ye Olde Cheshire Cheese*. Other ancient taverns include the *Grenadier*, the *Queen's Head*, the *Trafalgar Tavern* and the *Windsor Castle*. (For more on modern pubs see below.)

For afternoon tea, the *Basil Street Hotel* or *The Ritz* are best. Any light meal at *Fortnum's Fountain* is pleasant. For good old fish 'n' chips, the best chippies are *Faulkner's*, *Two Brothers*, *Seashell* and *Toff's* (though only the Seashell has a vaguely handy location so far as most visitors are concerned). Smithfield's *St John* has made quite a name for its exploration of traditional British cooking, including lots of offal: uncompromising food in an uncompromising setting.

Isn't London supposed to be a top place for curry?

There are – it is said – more Indian restaurants in London than in India. What's more, London is leading the way with a new style of Indian-fusion cooking that, for many, has taken the cuisine out of the 'ethnic' category altogether. Leading exponents are *Zaika*, *Vama*, *Tamarind* and *Chutney Mary*.

At the other end of the scale – but famous for the quality of its food – lies the legendarily scruffy *Lahore Kebab House*. In between, good places are legion – see page 24 for a comprehensive list. Note that many of the best names – *Rasa* and *Kastoori*, for example – are veggie. Good Indian restaurants are rare in the heart of the West End: useful exceptions to this rule include the budget duo *Chowki* and *Mela*, as well as the more upmarket *Veeraswamy*.

What are gastropubs?
In the past ten years, many pubs have re-invented themselves as informal restaurants – generally you order at the bar, and your meal is brought to you. *The Eagle* was the original, and is still often credited as the best.

The trend goes from strength to strength. There are now

almost no affluent suburbs (inner or outer) which lack pubs which serve food of a quality that even five years ago would have been inconceivable. Examples include *The Ealing Park Tavern, St Johns* and the *Oak.*

Some pubs are pushing so far upmarket that they have almost lost touch with their boozer origins, offering waiter service, linen napkins and tablecloths – whether these are really pubs any more becomes a question of semantics! Examples include the *Drapers Arms,* the *Perseverance* and the *Wells.*

You said diverse: what about other cuisines?

London has good representations of most major cuisines (with the possible exception of Latin American ones).

Italian cooking has long been a popular choice for relaxed neighbourhood dining, especially in the more affluent parts of town, and there is an enormous variety of trattorias and pizzerias. In recent years, some excellent high-level Italians have emerged – see the list on page 24.

Of the many traditional Chinese restaurants, the very best – with the exception of *Yming* – are not in or near Chinatown. The biggest concentration of very good restaurants is, in fact, in Bayswater – including *Royal China, Four Seasons* and *Mandarin Kitchen.* In the West End, *Hakkasan* can claim to have brought a revolutionary degree of style to the quality Chinese dining experience.

The capital was historically weak in other oriental cuisines, but there has been much activity in recent years, often combining quality Japanese (or Japanese fusion) cooking with innovative design. *Zuma* and *Sumosan* are good examples.

Thai cooking is also widespread but strongest in west London. Fulham's grand *Blue Elephant* has been amazingly consistent over the years, as has Notting Hill's *Churchill* – an example of that curious London creation: Thai in a pub.

A major hit of recent years has been the cuisines of North Africa and the Eastern Mediterranean. For quality and originality of cooking, *Moro*, part of the early wave, is still one of the best places, and the new *Aziz* is very promising. These cuisines also lend themselves well to good budget experiences – the *Tas* chain and the new *Haz* are among the good, less expensive places.

See the lists on page 25 for the top exponents of each type of cuisine by nationality.

Are there any sharp practices I should look out for?

Yes: the 'blank credit card slip trick' – a fraud practised to a shocking extent, even by many top places. It once seemed to be in decline, but we have noted it on numerous occasions this year, including at many establishments which ought to know better.

If you are presented with a credit card slip with a blank line for a gratuity, you should **not** assume that a tip is appropriate. Often, 10% or (more usually) 12.5% service has already been included in the sum you are being asked to pay, but the restaurant is hoping that you will inadvertently 'double up'.

SURVEY – MOST MENTIONED

These are the restaurants which were most frequently mentioned by reporters. (Last year's position is given in brackets.) An asterisk* indicates the first appearance in the list of a recently-opened restaurant.

1   J Sheekey (2)
2   The Ivy (1)
3   Gordon Ramsay (7)
4   Nobu (5)
5   Chez Bruce (9)
6   Hakkasan (20)
7   La Poule au Pot (12)
8   Mirabelle (3)
9   Locanda Locatelli*
10 Oxo Tower (4)

11 Gordon Ramsay at Claridge's (10)
12 Andrew Edmunds (17)
13 Pétrus (St James's Street) (6)
14 Bleeding Heart (11)
15 The Square (15)
16 Le Caprice (8)
17 The Cinnamon Club (26)
18 Blue Elephant (12)
19 La Trompette (28)
20 Club Gascon (14)

21 Le Pont de la Tour (24)
22 Le Gavroche (23)
23 The River Café (22)
24 Smiths (Dining Rm) (18)
25 Racine*
26 Moro (19)
27= Coq d'Argent (32)
27= Zafferano (16)
29 Connaught (Angela Hartnett)*
30 Zuma*

30= Orrery (-)
30= Café du Marché (-)
33 1 Lombard Street (37)
34 Chutney Mary (-)
35 Busaba Eathai (-)
36 Bibendum (-)
37 Assaggi (-)
38 The Don (-)
39 Sketch*
40 The Sugar Club (25)

LONDON – HIGHEST RATINGS

These are the restaurants which received the best average food ratings.

Where the most common types of cuisine are concerned, we present the results in two price-brackets. For less common cuisines, we list the top three, regardless of price.

For further information about restaurants which are particularly notable for their food, see the cuisine lists starting on page 214. These indicate, using an asterisk (*), restaurants which offer exceptional or very good food.

British, Modern

£40 and over
1 Chez Bruce
2 Clarke's
3 The Glasshouse
4 Lindsay House
5 Redmond's

Under £40
1 Thyme
2 The Stepping Stone
3 The Lord Palmerston
4 The Havelock Tavern
5 St John

French

£40 and over
1 Gordon Ramsay
2 Capital Hotel
3 Monsieur Max
4 Le Gavroche
5 Pied à Terre

Under £40
1 Soulard
2 Lou Pescadou
3 Racine
4 Chez Lindsay
5 Chez Max

Italian/Mediterranean

£40 and over
1 Zafferano
2 Locanda Locatelli
3 Assaggi
4 Toto's
5 Teca

Under £40
1 Oliveto
2 Pizzeria Castello
3 Aglio e Olio
4 Made in Italy
5 Osteria Basilico

Indian

£40 and over
1 Zaika
2 Vama
3 Tamarind
4 Chutney Mary
5 Red Fort

Under £40
1 Lahore Kebab House
2 Kastoori
3 Malabar Junction
4 Vijay
5 Sarkhel's

Chinese

£40 and over
1 Hakkasan
2 Dorchester Oriental
3 Ken Lo's Memories SW1
4 Ken Lo's Memories W8
5 Mr Chow

Under £40
1 Hunan
2 Royal China
3 Mandarin Kitchen
4 Yming
5 The Four Seasons

Japanese

£40 and over
1 Defune
2 Tatsuso
3 Nobu
4 Ubon
5 Sumosan

Under £40
1 Tsunami
2 K10
3 Jin Kichi
4 Café Japan
5 Tokyo Diner

British, Traditional
1 Dorchester Grill
2 Monkeys
3 Wilton's

Vegetarian
1 Blah! Blah! Blah!
2 The Gate
3 Food for Thought

Burgers, etc
1 Gourmet Burger Kit'
2 Eagle Bar Diner
3 Lucky Seven

Pizza
1 Pizza Metro
2 Basilico
3 Oliveto

Fish & Chips
1 Faulkner's
2 Two Brothers
3 Seashell

Thai
1 Amaranth
2 Talad Thai
3 Blue Elephant

Fusion
1 Nobu
2 Tsunami
3 Ubon

Fish & Seafood
1 Rest' One-O-One
2 Chez Liline
3 J Sheekey

Greek
1 Vriskai
2 The Real Greek
3 Lemonia

Spanish
1 Fino
2 Moro
3 Cambio de Tercio

Turkish
1 Gallipoli
2 Tas
3 Ozer

Lebanese
1 Ranoush
2 Fairuz
2 Noura

SURVEY – NOMINATIONS

Ranked by the number of reporters' votes.

Top gastronomic experience

   1   Gordon Ramsay (1)
   2   Chez Bruce (3)
   3   Gordon Ramsay at Claridge's (4)
   4   Nobu (2)
   5   Locanda Locatelli*
   6   The Ivy (6)
   7   Pétrus (St James's Street) (5)
   8   J Sheekey (-)
   9   La Trompette (-)
   10 Le Gavroche (10)

Favourite

   1   The Ivy (1)
   2   Chez Bruce (3)
   3   Gordon Ramsay (4)
   4   Le Caprice (2)
   5   J Sheekey (5)
   6   Nobu (8)
   7   Andrew Edmunds (-)
   8   Hakkasan (-)
   9   Moro (7)
   10 La Trompette (10)

Best for business

   1   The Square (3)
   2   1 Lombard Street (2)
   3   Coq d'Argent (5)
   4   Bleeding Heart (9)
   5   The Don (-)
   6   Oxo Tower (Brasserie) (6)
   7   Bank Aldwych (4)
   8   Smiths (Dining Rm) (-)
   9   The Ivy (8)
   10 Axis (-)

Best for romance

   1   La Poule au Pot (1)
   2   Andrew Edmunds (2)
   3   Bleeding Heart (4)
   4   The Ivy (3)
   5   Blue Elephant (10)
   6   Chez Bruce (8)
   7   Odette's (-)
   8   Julie's (7)
   9   Mirabelle (9)
   10 Oxo Tower (Brasserie) (6)

OPENINGS AND CLOSURES

Restaurants in **bold** are included in the London section of this guide – for the full selection, see *Harden's London Restaurants 2004* (£9.99), available in all good bookshops.

OPENINGS

Aaura
Abbeville
Allegro Con Brio
Allium
Anda
Apium
Assembly
Aura
Aziz
Balham Bar & Kitchen
Banquette
Bar Mezé *(group)*
The Barnsbury
Base *(NW1)*
The Belsize
Berkeley Square Café
Bermondsey Kitchen
Bibo
Bistro Aix
Black & Blue *(SW7, NW3)*
Blu
Bodean's
Bonchurch Brasserie
Boxwood Café
Brian Turner
The Bridge
Cafeteria
Cava
Cedar Lounge
Cheyne Walk Brasserie
Chez Max
Chez Moi *(W14)*
Chintamani
La Contenta
Cristini
The Curzon
Devonshire House
Dish Dash *(SW12)*
Ditto Grill
Don Pedro
Eagle Bar Diner
Earl Spencer
The Easton
Eat & Two Veg
The Ebury
Eight Over Eight
1802
The Endurance
Enigma
L'Etranger

Exotika
Farm
Fez
Figa
Fino
FireHouse
FishWorks
5 Cavendish Square
Fleur
Formosa Dining Room
Garanger Restaurant
Giá
The Green
Haandi *(NW10)*
Haz
Hazuki
The Hill
The House
Imperial China
The International
The Interval
Jaan
The Junction Tavern
Just India
Kaslik
Kazan
Khew
Kulu Kulu *(WC2, SW7)*
Lamberts
Little Basil
Locanda Ottoemezzo
Lonsdale
Ma Cuisine
The Mall Tavern
Matsuri
Mediterranean Kitchen
  (WC2, W8)
Michael Moore
Mim's *(SW6)*
Mint Leaf
Nicolas Bar à Vins
Osia
Osmani
Pappagallo
The Pepper Tree *(SW18)*
Pétrus (Berkeley Hotel)
The Phoenix
Plateau
Quirinale

OPENINGS (cont'd)

The Real Greek
  Souvlaki & Bar
Rhodes 24
River Walk
The Rivington Bar & Grill
Rocket *(SW15)*
The Royal Exchange
  Grand Café
Running Horse
Sausage & Mash Café
Saagar
Salt
Samphire
Santa Lucia
Sherlock's Grill
Shumi
Smithy's
Souk *(Adelaide St)*
So.uk *(W1)*

Il Sogno di Dante
St John Bread & Wine
Segafredo Zanetti
The Station
sticklebackpink
The Swan
Taro *(Old Compton St)*
Tas Pide
Thai Canteen
Tom Aikens
202
Utsav
The Wells
White's
The Wolseley
Yauatcha
Zimzun
Zinc *(SW6)*

CLOSURES

Alastair Little *(W11)*
Alfred
Amandier
Angel of the North
El Asado
Aykoku Kaku
Bar 107
Belgo *(W10)*
Bellamys
Bibo Cibo
Bice
Blythe Road
Bonjour Vietnam
Brasserie du Marché
  aux Puces
Bubb's
Café Spice Namaste *(SW11)*
Calzone
  (W11, N1, NW3)
Caravan Serai
Catch
La Chaumière
Che
Chelsea Mandarin
Chez Moi *(W11)*
Chin Chin
China City
China House
Chinon
Chiswick Restaurant

Chives
Christopher's *(SW1)*
City Rhodes
Coffee Republic
  (all branches)
Creelers
The Crinnigan Rooms
Dumela
Errays
Fabrizio
Field & Forest
Fish *(E14)*
Fishbar
500
Formula Veneta
Il Forno W1
Foxtrot Oscar *(SW11)*
Francofill
Fuego *(EC2)*
Fusion
Futures *(EC2)*
George II *(now a bar)*
Getti, *(Wardour St W1)*
Glaisters *(SW13)*
Goose
Harry's Social Club
The Honest Cabbage
House *(E14)*
Ibla
The Independence

* was a newcomer last year; † came and went during year

(now a bar)
Infuzion
Innecto
John Burton-Race
Kaspia
The Lane
Laurent
Maison Novelli
Maquis
The Marquee
Metrogusto *(SW8)*
Mims *(EN4)*
Need the Dough! *(SW11)*
New Soraya
Nine-Eleven Jamestown
Noho *(W1)*
One-Seven-Nine
Orsino
Palatino
Parade
Parisienne Chophouse
Le P'tit Normand
Petit Robert
Pétrus *(St James's St)*
Pizzeria Condotti
Il Posto
Purple Sage
Quiet Revolution *(EC1)*
Rhodes in the Square
Ristorante Italiano
Ruby in the Dust
  (all branches)
Rupee Room
Sabbia
Salon
San Frediano
Sans Culottes
Savoy Hotel, Upstairs
Shoeless Joe's *(all branches)*
Silks & Spice W1
Simply Nico SE1
Stream
Street Hawker *(NW6)*
Suntory
Sushi Wong
La Tante Claire
Tartuf *(SW4)*
Teatro
10
Touzai
Tuscan
Twentyfour
The Vestry
Village Bistro
Vong
Yellow River Café *(E14)*

Zaika Bazaar
Zilli *(W11)*

sign up for the survey at www.hardens.com

LONDON DIRECTORY

Abu Zaad W12 £16 ★

29 Uxbridge Rd   8749 5107
*"Eat yourself senseless for a fiver a head!" – it's not just low prices,
though, which inspire fans of this "very authentic" Syrian,
near Shepherd's Bush Market, but also a "huge choice of exciting
dishes"; the rear dining room is rather "opulent", too, at least by local
standards. / Sample dishes: goats cheese in pastry.grilled chicken baked with
pitta bread; Details: 11 pm; no Amex; no smoking area.*

Admiral Codrington SW3 £40

17 Mossop St   7581 0005   4–2C
*"More than a gastropub, but less than a restaurant", this "casual and
comfortable" Brompton Cross destination is always "buzzy", rather
"average" cooking notwithstanding. / Sample dishes: mussels with thyme &
shallots; honey & ginger chicken with kaffir lime rice; banana tarte Tatin.
Details: 11 pm.*

Aglio e Olio SW10 £29 ★

194 Fulham Rd   7351 0070   4–3B
*With its "yummy" pasta and its "accommodating" service,
this "cheap", "trendy" and "loud" Chelsea café deserves its continuing
success. / Sample dishes: beef carpaccio & rocket salad; spaghetti with lobster;
panna cotta. Details: 11.30 pm.*

Al Sultan W1 £37 ★

51-52 Hertford St   7408 1155   2–4B
*It still gets fewer reports than the nearby Al Hamra, but their
consistency is such as to support those who say that this "casual but
elegant" Shepherd Market spot is "London's best Lebanese".
/ Details: www.alsultan.co.uk; 11 pm.*

Alastair Little W1 £40 ★

49 Frith St   7734 5183   3–2A
*Is it "undergoing a mini-renaissance" or is it "a shadow of its earlier
days"? – conflicting signals continue to emanate from this "rather
austere" foodie shrine in Soho, but its "less-is-more" approach
is applauded by most reporters; (Mr Little himself is no longer involved).
/ Sample dishes: spring nettle & ricotta risotto; calves liver with button onions &
pancetta; apple tart with praline ice cream. Details: 11.30pm; closed Sat L & Sun.*

Alba EC1 £32 ★

107 Whitecross St   7588 1798   5–1B
*"Authentic" and "interesting" regional cooking has long made this
Piedmontese fixture something of a "gem" in the wastelands by the
Barbican; its "clinical" décor makes it more a lunch place, though,
and "slow" service was a problem this year. / Sample dishes: calamari with
aubergine caponata; braised rabbit wth olives & polenta; pannetone with chocolate
mousse. Details: 10.30 pm; closed Sat & Sun.*

Ali Baba NW1 £19 ★

32 Ivor Pl   7723 5805   1–1A
*"If you want authentic Egyptian, this is the place" – "home-cooked"
food is "served by the family" at this "quirky" BYO Marylebone dining
room (which feels like a living room, "complete with Al Jazeera on the
box"). / Sample dishes: koshari; lamb stew; rice pudding. Details: 11.30 pm;
no credit cards.*

Alloro W1 £46 ★

19-20 Dover St   7495 4768   2–3C
*"Good quality all round" is making this "polished" (but "no-nonsense")
modern Mayfair Italian a destination well worth knowing about;
its "spacious" quarters make it good for business (especially at lunch).
/ Sample dishes: scallop and asparagus salad; sea bass with salami; double
chocolate soufflé. Details: 10.30 pm; closed Sat L & Sun.*

The Almeida N1   **£ 41**
30 Almeida St   7354 4777
Fans of this "'70s-retro" Islington yearling say that – with its
"courteous" staff and "classic" Gallic cuisine – it "deserves to convert
the anti-Conran brigade"; critics might counter that the fact that (after
a promising start) its ratings are so quickly heading into
"unmemorable" territory provides yet more ammunition. / **Sample
dishes:** foie gras terrine; coq au vin; nougat glacé.
Details: www.almeida-restaurant.co.uk; 11 pm.

Andrew Edmunds W1   **£ 29**   𝔸 ★
46 Lexington St   7437 5708   2–2D
"A genuine delight" – this "special" and "intimate" ("squashed") Soho
townhouse enjoys a 'destination' status (especially for romance) totally
at odds with its modest size; the food is "straightforward",
but "amazingly reasonably priced", and the "unusual" wine list has
some "real bargains"; book well ahead. / **Sample dishes:** courgette & rocket
pesto cake; gnocchi with bacon & sausage; tarte Tatin. **Details:** 10.45 pm;
no Amex; booking: max 6.

The Anglesea Arms W6   **£ 29**   ★
35 Wingate Rd   8749 1291
"Arrive early as you can't book, and take it easy" – the service can
be "glacially slow" at this famous, no-frills boozer, near Ravenscourt
Park; it's "worth it in the end", though, for the "exemplary" but
"cheap", "restaurant-quality" cooking. / **Sample dishes:** goujons of sole &
scampi; papardelle with lamb's sweetbreads & lardons; Knickerbocker Glory.
Details: 10.45 pm; no Amex; no booking.

Antipasto e Pasta SW4   **£ 27**   ★
31 Abbeville Rd   8675 6260   6–2D
Given the "attentive" service and the "real" Italian cooking,
Claphamites find little to complain about at this "friendly" local.
/ **Sample dishes:** beef carpaccio; grilled squid; tiramisu. **Details:** 11.30 pm.

Archipelago W1   **£ 56**   𝔸
110 Whitfield St   7383 3346   1–1B
"Fascinatingly intimate and sexy", this "den" near the Telecom Tower
offers a "wild and wacky" menu of "exotic but elegantly presented
dishes"; the experience is undoubtedly "expensive", but romantics find
it "magical". / **Sample dishes:** peacock & tropical fruit satay; smoked open
lasagne; ginger brûlée with nashi pears. **Details:** 10.30 pm; closed Sat L & Sun;
no smoking area.

Armadillo E8   **£ 32**   𝔸 ★★
41 Broadway Mkt   7249 3633
"What a find!"; "cool Latino food" – "great tastes from combos you'd
never think would work" – have quickly put this "convivial" and
"very friendly" Hackney spot firmly on the map; "for less of a crush,
go upstairs". / **Sample dishes:** baked courgettes with sweetcorn & Parmesan
crust; salt cod, curly kale & potato stew; Mayan chocolate ice cream & almond
pastry. **Details:** www.armadillorestaurant.co.uk; 10.30 pm; no Amex or Switch.

Assaggi W2   **£ 47**   ★★
39 Chepstow Pl   7792 5501
"Fantastic" execution of "rustic" but "truly Italian" dishes (with notably
"solicitous" service) maintains the stellar reputation of this "excessively
noisy" room above a Bayswater pub; some reporters find the "hysteria"
about the place "unfathomable", but you still need to book weeks
ahead. / **Sample dishes:** pan-fried Pecorino with Parma ham; rack of lamb with
spring vegetables; fig & almond tart. **Details:** 11 pm; closed Sun; no Amex.

sign up for the survey at www.hardens.com   33

The Atlas SW6 £29 🄰★
16 Seagrave Rd   7385 9129   4–3A
"Generous portions of really good upmarket pub grub" win a widespread following for this *"oddly-situated"* boozer, near Earl's Court 2; *"it's a cosy place in winter, or in the summer you can sit in the garden"*. / *Sample dishes: broccoli & sweet onion soup with Parmesan crisps; Turkish style lamb with couscous salad; lemon polenta cake with poached pears.* **Details:** *10.30 pm; no Amex; no booking.*

Aubergine SW10 £65 ★
11 Park Walk   7352 3449   4–3B
William Drabble may not hog the headlines, but his "sumptuous" Gallic cuisine is the equal of many of the capital's more famous faces; with their Michelin-friendly style, however, these Chelsea premises can seem rather *"formal"* and *"nondescript"*. / *Sample dishes: crab & cauliflower salad with avocado purée; poached turbot with red wine sauce; cherry beignet soufflé.* **Details:** *10.45pm; closed Sat L & Sun; jacket required.*

Aurora W1 £34 🄰★
49 Lexington St   7494 0514   2–2D
"A good night out is guaranteed" at this *"lovely"*, *"low-key"* spot, whose *"good"* uncomplicated food and *"cosy"* ambience are attested to by all; it has *"a lovely small garden"*, too – *"in the middle of Soho"! / Sample dishes: yellow pepper soup; pork with spiced red cabbage & caramelised pears; sticky toffee pudding.* **Details:** *10.30 pm; closed Sun; no Amex.*

L'Aventure NW8 £42 🄰★★
3 Blenheim Ter   7624 6232
"A terrace with trees draped in fairy lights" (*"wonderful on a warm night"*) sets the ultra-*"romantic"* tone at this *"old-fashioned"* St John's Wood dining room; almost all reporters are blown away by its charm, its *"personal"* service and its *"first-rate"* Gallic cooking. / *Sample dishes: snail & oyster mushroom fricasée; rabbit confit with lemon & dried tomatoes; apricot compote with creme anglaise.* **Details:** *11 pm; closed Sat L & Sun.*

Axis WC2 £50
1 Aldwych   7300 0300   1–2D
"Efficient, impressive, perhaps slightly soulless" – this *"surprisingly airy"* Covent Garden-fringe basement is decorated in *"slick"* style and maintains high standards; it's most nominated as a business rendezvous, but is *"also a good bet pre-theatre"*. / *Sample dishes: crispy duck noodle salad; summer truffle risotto; crème caramel.* **Details:** *www.onealdwych.com; 11.30 pm; closed Sat L & Sun.*

Aziz SW6 £33 ★
24-32 Vanston Pl   7386 0086   4–4A
Ex-Momo chef Michel Giraud serves up some mouthwatering and creative Moroccan/Middle Eastern dishes at this excellent Fulham newcomer; service is charming too, so it's a shame that the setting is on the faceless side. / *Sample dishes: sweetcorn fritters; tuna steak with crushed peppercorns; mulhallabia (cardomom dessert).* **Details:** *10.30 pm.*

Babur Brasserie SE23 £28 ★
119 Brockley Rise   8291 2400
"Seasonally-changing menus" – which include many *"unusual"* and *"delicately cooked"* dishes – help make a visit to this *"fabulous curry house"* in Brockley *"a great and different dining experience"*. / **Details:** *www.babur-brasserie.com; 11 pm; closed Fri L; no smoking area.*

Back to Basics W1 £41 ★★
21a Foley St   7436 2181   1–1B
"Superb fish", *"great prices"* – four words say it all about this *"noisy"* and *"no-frills"* Fitzrovia bistro, where *"the food is always top-notch"*; nice outside seating for sunny days. / *Sample dishes: monkfish & spicy prawn couscous; deep-fried Dover sole with tartare sauce; bananas & rum baked in foil.* **Details:** *www.backtobasics.uk.com; 10.30 pm; closed Sun.*

Balans   **£32**

60 Old Compton St, W1   7439 2183   3–3A
239 Old Brompton Rd, SW5   7244 8838   4–3A
187 Kensington High St, W8   7376 0115   4–1A
The "best brunch in London" is the special attraction at these "buzzy
and upbeat" (but also "crowded and noisy") Miami Beach-style diners;
it's not just a gay-scene thing, either – male visitors are promised
"a good time, whether or not they fancy the waiters".
/ **Details:** www.balans.co.uk; midnight, SW5 2am Fri & Sat, W1 Mon-Fri 5 am,
Sat 6 am, Sun 2 am; W1 no booking, SW5 Sun L no booking.

Balham Kitchen & Bar SW12   **£30**   A★

15-19 Bedford Hill   8675 6900   6–2C
Grooviness Notting Hill-style – courtesy of the people from Soho House
– took root in sarf London in the summer of 2003; a visit just after
opening found an extraordinarily accomplished and friendly
bar/brasserie, already awash with Balham's beau monde. / **Sample
dishes:** oysters; hamburger & chips; crème brûlée. **Details:** www.sohohouse.com;
11 pm; booking: max 6.

Baltic SE1   **£33**   A★

74 Blackfriars Rd   7928 1111   5–4A
"A stunning interior" and a "dangerously good" vodka range help win
high acclaim for this "roomy" and "buzzy" bar/restaurant, near Tate
Modern; "never before has Polish cuisine been so enticing". / **Sample
dishes:** Polish black pudding with pickled cabbage & pear purée; paprika chicken
with garlic yoghurt; vodka-marinated berry compote.
Details: www.balticrestaurant.co.uk; 11 pm; closed Sat L.

Bam-Bou W1   **£37**   A★

1 Percy St   7323 9130   1–1C
"Plenty of dark oriental ambience" and "great cocktails" are the
traditional strengths of this "trendy" Fitzrovia townhouse; the "inventive
and original" Vietnamese food has greatly improved of late, however,
as has the "friendly" service. / **Sample dishes:** marinated squid with bitter
lemon dressing; pan-fried duck with crispy greens; banana spring rolls with chocolate
sauce. **Details:** www.bam-bou.co.uk; 11.30 pm; closed Sat L & Sun.

Bangkok SW7   **£30**   ★

9 Bute St   7584 8529   4–2B
"Say what you like, this is a great canteen" – this "cramped" Thai
(the UK's oldest) has been an "unchanging" South Kensington
"institution" for decades, and most reports say its cooking is "fast,
simple and consistently excellent". / **Details:** 10.45 pm; closed Sun; no Amex
or Switch.

Bank Aldwych WC2   **£44**

1 Kingsway   7379 9797   1–2D
This large and "noisy" – and perhaps rather "jaded" – '90s brasserie
on the City side of Covent Garden is a "reliable" suits' rendezvous,
and also has its fans for breakfast, brunch and pre-theatre; Conran
Restaurants – whose larger establishments achieve standards below
Bank's – took a shareholding in mid-2003, so it will be interesting
to see what happens next. / **Sample dishes:** tuna with miso dressing; calves
liver with bubble & squeak; honey nougat with iced cherries.
Details: www.bankrestaurants.com; 11 pm.

Bar Capitale   **£29**   ★

The Concourse, 1 Poultry, EC2   7248 3117   5–2C
Bucklersbury Hs, 14 Walbrook, EC4   7236 2030   5–3C
"Really good, authentic-style pizza" is a key attraction at these "loud"
and very popular Italian diners, in the heart of the City.
/ **Sample dishes:** pasta with clams & garlic; four cheese pizza; tiramisu.
Details: www.mithrasbars.co.uk; 10 pm; closed Sat & Sun.

sign up for the survey at www.hardens.com   35

Bar Estrela SW8 £ 20 ★

111-115 South Lambeth Rd 7793 1051 6–1D

"The biggest and best of the Portuguese places along South Lambeth Road", this *"thriving"* café (with pleasant tables outside) is simply *"wonderful"*; *"cheap and cheerful tapas"* are the highlight of a huge menu. / **Details:** 11 pm.

Bar Spice E14 £ 33 ★

145 Three Colts St 7093 1111

"Good-quality Anglo/Indian cooking" is the almost invariable theme of reports on this *"pleasant"* (but slightly *"clinical"*) Docklands yearling (near the Westferry DLR); it also boasts a champagne bar. / **Details:** www.barspice.com; 10.45 pm; closed Sat L & Sun L; no smoking area.

Basilico £ 29 ★★

690 Fulham Rd, SW6 0800 028 3531 6–1B
515 Finchley Rd, NW3 0800 316 2656
175 Lavender Hill, SW11 0800 389 9770 6–2C
178 Upper Richmond Rd, SW14 0800 096 8202 6–2B

"Very thin and crispy bases, with ultra-fresh toppings" put these *"designer"* pizzas amongst London's best; service, though – both in-house, and for the (more popular) take-away service – could be better. / **Sample dishes:** Caesar salad; smoked haddock & spinach pizza; bittersweet chocolate tart. **Details:** www.basilico.co.uk; 11pm; no Amex; no booking.

Beirut Express W2 £ 18 ★★

112-114 Edgware Rd 7724 2700

"Wonderful shwarmas and other Middle Eastern delights" at *"top-value"* prices win high praise for this *"small"* Maroush-group café. / **Sample dishes:** mezze; chicken & lamb kebabs; baklava. **Details:** www.maroush.com; 1.45 am; no credit cards.

Beiteddine SW1 £ 39 ★

8 Harriet St 7235 3969 4–1D

It never attracts much comment, but fans insist that the fare at this *"quiet"* Lebanese, just off Sloane Street, is *"just like home-cooking in Beirut"*. / **Details:** midnight.

Belvedere W8 £ 48 𝔸

Holland Park, off Abbotsbury Rd 7602 1238

"Indulgent décor" and an *"idyllic location"* – in the middle of Holland Park – makes this charming period building a *"perfect place for a date"*; the school-of-MPW Gallic cuisine *"isn't bad"* either, but there are those who think it *"very overpriced"*. / **Sample dishes:** tarte Tatin of endive & foie gras; smoked haddock with poached egg & colcannon; caramel soufflé. **Details:** www.whitestarline.org.uk; 10.45 pm.

Bengal Clipper SE1 £ 31 𝔸★

Shad Thames 7357 9001 5–4D

A white grand piano and a smart location *"set the scene"* for this (surprisingly) *"authentic"* and *"interesting"* South Bank Indian – a *"comfortable"* and *"spacious"* place, which is emerging as an ever more reliable destination. / **Details:** www.bengalrestaurants.co.uk; 11.30 pm.

Benugo £ 9 ★

14 Curzon St, W1 7629 6246
23-25 Great Portland St, W1 7631 5052
24 Berwick St, W1 7439 3233
116 St John St, EC1 7253 3499
82 City Rd, EC1 7253 1295

These *"friendly"* upmarket sandwich bars are unanimously praised by reporters for their *"good fast food"*, including *"delicious fresh soups"*. / **Details:** www.benugo.com; L & afternoon tea only; closed weekends; no credit cards.

Bermondsey Kitchen SE1 £30 Ⓐ★
194 Bermondsey St 7407 5719 5–4D
"A good addition to the area", this *"relaxed"* and *"lively"* local wins
nothing but praise for its *"ever-changing"* and *"well-executed"* menu
(with fish a highlight). / *Sample dishes:* carrot, pepper and harissa soup;
twice-baked goats cheese and marjoram soufflé; hot chocolate pudding with crème
fraîche. *Details:* 10 pm; no Amex; no smoking area.

Bibendum SW3 £60 Ⓐ
81 Fulham Rd 7581 5817 4–2C
"Still an impressive choice", this *"light"* and *"spacious"* first-floor dining
room (above Chelsea's Conran Shop) *"looks just like a restaurant
should"*; it comes complete with an *"encyclopaedic"* wine list
(plus *"helpful"* sommelier), and *"accomplished"* Gallic cooking. / *Sample
dishes:* sea bass tartare with dill crostini; steak with foie gras pithivier; tarte Tatin.
Details: www.bibendum.co.uk; 11.30 pm.

Bibendum Oyster Bar SW3 £38 Ⓐ★
81 Fulham Rd 7589 1480 4–2C
"Great for a champagne and lobster lunch" – if you're not counting the
pennies, this *"buzzy"* bar (off the foyer of the Chelsea Conran Shop)
is a *"wonderful"* spot for *"fabulous"*, *"fresh"* seafood (all cold); there's
"great people-watching", too. / *Sample dishes:* egg mayonnaise; seafood
platter; lemon tart. *Details:* www.bibendum.co.uk; 10.30 pm; no booking.

Black & Blue £39 ★
105 Gloucester Rd, SW7 7244 7466 4–2B
215-217 Kensington Church St, W8 7727 0004
205-207 Haverstock Hill, NW3 7443 7744
"Fine steaks and burgers" are making this emerging chain (from the
founder of Tootsies) a real success; some find its *"upscale diner"* look
a mite *"soulless"*, but *"friendly"* service and *"good-value"* prices provide
ample compensation. / *Sample dishes:* prawn cocktail; ribeye steak; lemon
tart. *Details:* 11 pm; no Amex; no smoking area; no booking.

Blah! Blah! Blah! W12 £25 ★★
78 Goldhawk Rd 8746 1337
"The best veggie food" – *"which you can enjoy with great wine, as it's
BYO"* – wins raves for this Shepherd's Bush fixture; some think its style
enjoyably *"unpretentious"* – others feel the décor *"could do with a re-
think"*. / *Sample dishes:* warm mushroom salad; pasta with asparagus;
blueberry & amaretti tart. *Details:* 11 pm; closed Sun D; no credit cards.

Blakes Hotel SW7 £96 Ⓐ
33 Roland Gdns 7370 6701 4–2B
"Soooo sexy" – this *"discreet, dark and decadent"* townhouse hotel
basement remains a key haunt for South Kensington *"schmoozers and
sugar daddies"*; even fans, though, concede that the *"extraordinarily
expensive"* cooking is *"hardly spectacular"*. / *Sample dishes:* ginger soup
with prawn gyoza; rack of lamb with rosemary; tamarillo sorbet with biscuits.
Details: www.blakeshotels.com; 11.30 pm.

Bleeding Heart EC1 £42 Ⓐ★
Bleeding Heart Yd, Greville St 7242 8238 5–2A
A *"tucked-away location"*, in a Holborn yard, adds to the *"cosy and
rustic"* charms of this rambling tavern/brasserie/restaurant (which has
"a special and intimate feeling, despite the number of suits"); a wide
array of *"good, honest"* French dishes is backed up by a *"fantastic"*
wine list. / *Sample dishes:* scallops with fennel & ginger; Welsh lamb with
rosemary jus; blueberry & blackberry mousse. *Details:* 10.30 pm; closed Sat &
Sun.

Blue Elephant SW6 £ 44 *A* ★
3-6 Fulham Broadway   7385 6595   4–4A
*"Naff as you like, but great fun"; this "magical retreat in the depths
of Fulham" has for many years attracted a huge following, thanks to its
"dramatic" jungle décor, its "attentive" service, and – perhaps
surprisingly – its "fantastic and authentic" Thai cuisine.* / **Sample
dishes:** *citrus fruit, chicken & prawn salad; sweet & sour pork with mushrooms &
baby corn; sour mango & roasted coconut.* **Details:** *www.blueelephant.com;
midnight; closed Sat L.*

Bluebird SW3 £ 49 ✗
350 King's Rd   7559 1000   4–3C
*Even by Conran's standards, this "characterless factory" of a place –
occupying the first floor of a Chelsea landmark – is simply "tragic";
in the summer of 2003, its manager was promoted to run the entire
group!* / **Sample dishes:** *spring pea soup; sautéed kidneys & bacon in mustard
sauce; apricot clafoutis.* **Details:** *www.conran.com; 11 pm.*

Bohème Kitchen & Bar W1 £ 37 *A*
19 Old Compton St   7734 5656   3–2A
*The "chilled-out, laid-back vibe" makes this "funky" Soho bar –
an offshoot of the fabulously successful Cafe Bohème – something of a
"haven" in these parts; the "simple" food is "not too bad".* / **Sample
dishes:** *asparagus & Gruyère tart; char-grilled tuna with couscous & salsa verde;
orange cheesecake.* **Details:** *www.bohemekitchen.co.uk; 11.45 pm.*

Boiled Egg & Soldiers SW11 £ 18 *A*
63 Northcote Rd   7223 4894   6–2C
*"If you don't mind screaming brats and pushchairs, the breakfasts are
great and not too greasy" at this celebrated Battersea café (which now
also offers a few more 'serious' dishes); "the wait for a table can be a
killer", though.* / **Sample dishes:** *egg, ham & cheese muffin; vegetable pie; carrot
cake.* **Details:** *6 pm; L & afternoon tea only; only Switch; no booking.*

Bombay Bicycle Club SW12 £ 35 *A* ★
95 Nightingale Ln   8673 6217   6–2C
*"A nice change from traditional curry houses"; this "upmarket"
Wandsworth fixture is still pronounced "brilliant after all these years",
by fans who laud its "fresh" and "un-greasy" curries and its "light" and
"airy" ambience; the take-aways offshoots are "great", too.* /
Details: *11 pm; D only, closed Sun.*

Bombay Brasserie SW7 £ 45 *A* ★
Courtfield Close, Gloucester Rd   7370 4040   4–2B
*Perhaps the "old colonial/Raj" look seems a fraction "dated" these
days, but this "grand and classy" Indian, by Gloucester Road tube, still
wins enthusiastic all-round praise for its "reliable" cooking and general
"attention to detail"; "book ahead to make sure you sit in the
conservatory".* / **Details:** *www.bombaybrasserielondon.com; 11.45pm.*

Bombay Palace W2 £ 37 ★★
50 Connaught St   7723 8855
*This Bayswater Indian is acclaimed for its "fantastic" food and its
"courteous" and "attentive" service; it really does deserve to be more
widely known.* / **Details:** *www.bombay-palace.co.uk; 11.30 pm; no smoking area.*

Il Bordello E1 £ 36 *A* ★
75-81 Wapping High St   7481 9950
*"Massive portions" of "tasty" fare – not least "pizzas that barely fit
on the table" – ensure that this "lively and noisy" Wapping Italian
is usually "packed".* / **Sample dishes:** *avocado & prawns wrapped in salmon;
seafood pizza; tiramisu.* **Details:** *www.ilbordello.com; 11 pm; closed Sat L.*

sign up for the survey at www.hardens.com 38

Boxwood Café
The Berkeley SW1   £45   ★
Wilton Pl 7235 1010 4–1D
Gordon Ramsay's new Knightsbridge 'diffusion' restaurant – why call it a
café? – has taken over the hotel basement vacated by Vong (RIP);
shame about the dark décor – which we found a touch claustrophobic
– as the cooking on our July 2003 visit was impressive, and service
relaxed and friendly. / **Sample dishes:** mushroom soup; seared salmon with red
onion and mint salad; black forest gâteau. **Details:** 11 pm.

Brady's SW18   £20   ★
513 Old York Rd 8877 9599 6–2B
"Excellent grilled and fried fish at knock-down prices" wins consistent
plaudits for this "cramped" but "prompt" Wandsworth chippy;
it's "usually full". / **Sample dishes:** salmon fishcakes; battered plaice with
chips & mushy peas; apple crumble. **Details:** 10.30 pm; D only, closed Sun;
no credit cards; no booking.

Brasserie St Quentin SW3   £35
243 Brompton Rd 7589 8005 4–2C
The stellar (post-relaunch) promise of this "elegant" Gallic brasserie
in Knightsbridge has not quite been fulfilled; standards have been
extremely "variable", but most reporters still find this a "civilised"
destination with "enjoyable" bourgeois cooking. / **Sample dishes:** Burgundy
snails in garlic butter; rabbit cassoulet with polenta; tarte Tatin.
Details: www.brasseriestquentin.co.uk; 10.30 pm.

Brian Turner
Millennium Hotel W1   £45   ★
44 Grosvenor Sq 7596 3444 2–2A
Good, simple British cooking, at modest prices – by local standards,
anyway – should make a success of TV-chef Brian Turner's spacious
new dining room; our only reservation is the blue 'n' beige décor, which
might look cool in, say, Miami Beach, but just looks plain chilly
in Mayfair. / **Sample dishes:** chicken liver pâté; roast salmon; steamed treacle
pudding. **Details:** 10.30 pm; closed Sat L.

Brick Lane Beigel Bake E1   £4   ★★
159 Brick Ln 7729 0616
"Many interesting conversations are to be had in the queue", at this
24/7 East End institution; it serves up "the best bagels in the UK,
and they're cheap too". / **Sample dishes:** cream cheese & tomato beigel;
salt beef sandwich; no puddings. **Details:** open 24 hours; no credit cards;
no smoking; no booking.

Brilliant UB2   £29   ★
72-76 Western Rd 8574 1928
"Worth the trek"; you get "authentic Punjabi home cooking"
(plus "Bollywood films on enormous TVs") at this famed Southall
institution – a large restaurant "in the heart of the Indian community".
/ **Details:** www.brilliantrestaurant.com; 11 pm; closed Mon, Sat L & Sun L;
no smoking area; booking: weekends only.

(The Court)
British Museum WC1   £36   𝔸✗
Great Russell St 7323 8990 1–1C
In the British Museum's Great Court, this mezzanine restaurant has
a "wonderful position" – "why is the food such an afterthought?"
/ **Sample dishes:** salmon with minted tabbouleh; chicken & artichokes with pesto
mash; mango & passion fruit crème brûlée. **Details:** www.digbytrout.co.uk; 5 pm,
Thu-Sat 9 pm; L only, Thu-Sat open L & D; no Amex; no smoking.

The Builder's Arms SW3   £29   𝔸
13 Britten St 7349 9040 4–2C
"A model for a relaxed London eating-place" – the attractions of its
"good, wholesome food" help make it "difficult to get a table" at this
"cosy", "younger-Chelsea" gastroboozer. / **Details:** 9.30 pm; no Amex;
no booking.

Busaba Eathai £ 23 A

106-110 Wardour St, W1   7255 8686   2–2D

22 Store St, WC1   7299 7900   1–1C

"Funky décor" ("sleek teak and low lighting") plus "fab fast fusion food" (mostly Thai) ensures there are "always queues" at this "Wagamama-style" duo; standards have slipped since the early days, though – service can be "slow" and the formula is increasingly "affordable, rather than cheap". / **Details:** 11 pm, Fri & Sat 11.30 pm; no smoking; no booking.

Café Bohème W1 £ 34 A

13 Old Compton St   7734 0623   3–2A

"Paris in London", say twentysomething fans of this "crowded", "buzzing" and "low-lit" bar/café/brasserie in the throbbing heart of Soho; the food is "on the mediocre side", but the place is still strongly tipped for romance, and for late-night sustenance. / **Sample dishes:** poached egg & smoked salmon salad; rabbit & pappardelle with mustard sauce; glazed strawberry crepes. **Details:** www.cafeboheme.com; 2.45 am, Sun 11.30 pm; booking: max 6, Fri & Sat.

Café du Marché EC1 £ 40 A★

22 Charterhouse Sq   7608 1609   5–1B

Decked out in "French farmhouse" style, this "beautiful" and "hidden-way" Smithfield fixture – "the City's least Citified restaurant" – is as popular for "dîner-à-deux" (or live jazz) as it is for a businesslike lunch; overall ratings drifted a fraction this year, but, all in all, standards remain very "consistent". / **Sample dishes:** fish soup; prawn & herb risotto; cherry sorbet. **Details:** 10 pm; closed Sat L & Sun; no Amex.

Café Laville W2 £ 30 A

453 Edgware Rd   7706 2620

"Great views over the canal" distinguish this small Little Venice café – "on a sunny Sunday, it's the place to be"; standards are otherwise "OK". / **Sample dishes:** goats cheese crostini; smoked haddock & salmon fishcakes with dill sauce; chocolate fudge cake. **Details:** www.cafelaville.co.uk; 10.30 pm; no Amex; no smoking area.

Café Spice Namaste E1 £ 32 ★★

16 Prescot St   7488 9242

"A tremendous range of flavours" ("tantalising fish dishes", in particular) wins continuing acclaim for Cyrus Todiwala's "innovative" and "accommodating" east-City Indian, whose "bright" ("Aztecy") premises are an oasis in a "culinary desert". / **Details:** 10.30 pm; closed Sat L & Sun.

Cambio de Tercio SW5 £ 42 A★

163 Old Brompton Rd   7244 8970   4–2B

A "reliably entertaining" South Kensington spot ("particularly cosy in winter"), whose "imaginative" and "authentic" cuisine still win it nominations as "the best Spanish restaurant in town"; this year's performance, however, has been more "variable" than usual. / **Sample dishes:** octopus with paprika & olive oil; roast suckling pig; gin & tonic sorbet. **Details:** 11.30 pm.

Capital Hotel SW3 £ 79 ★★

22-24 Basil St   7589 5171   4–1D

Eric Chavot's "serious" and "beautifully presented" cooking won particularly high acclaim this year for this "formal" and "very professional" Knightsbridge dining room; the set lunch menu has a reputation in some quarters as "London's best bargain". / **Sample dishes:** crab risotto; veal cutlet with gnocchi; black forest gâteau. **Details:** www.capitalhotel.co.uk; 11 pm.

Le Caprice SW1 £ 48 🄰★

Arlington Hs, Arlington St 7629 2239 2–4C

"Sophisticated, but unpretentious", this "chic" St James's brasserie "favourite" may not attract the massive attention it once did, but it remains "a class act" – "hugely enjoyable", and delivering "first-class food, service and hospitality"; "sometimes (unlike its sibling, The Ivy) you can even get a table!" / **Sample dishes:** Chinese crispy duck; squid with chorizo & figs; Scandinavian iced berries. **Details:** midnight.

Caraffini SW1 £ 36 🄰★

61-63 Lower Sloane St 7259 0235 4–2D

"Outstanding" staff "make any occasion special" at this "great" and "buzzy" ("noisy" and "crowded") trattoria, just south of Sloane Square; "good-value", "classic" cooking completes an extremely popular formula. / **Sample dishes:** antipasti; scallops with spinach & mushrooms; crème brûlée. **Details:** www.caraffini.co.uk; 11.30 pm; closed Sun.

Carnevale EC1 £ 29 ★

135 Whitecross St 7250 3452 5–1B

"Good enough to make me consider becoming a veggie" – this "intimate, if cramped" café near the Barbican does what it does very well. / **Sample dishes:** tagliatelle with Taleggio & wild garlic; okra & red pepper casserole with falafel; apple & date bread pudding.
Details: www.carnevalerestaurant.co.uk; 10.30 pm; closed Sat L & Sun; no Amex.

Chamberlain's EC3 £ 46 ★

23-25 Leadenhall St 7648 8690 5–2D

"A good fish restaurant for business lunches in the City" – even those who think it's "fantastic", though, say "it's definitely one for people with expense accounts". / **Sample dishes:** lobster chowder; seared tuna; passion fruit bavarois. **Details:** www.chamberlains.org; 9.30 pm; closed Sat & Sun; no smoking area.

Champor-Champor SE1 £ 37 🄰★★

62 Weston St

7403 4600 5–4C

"A magic carpet ride that starts in India and heads to all points east" is on offer at this "tiny" – but "theatrical" and "unique" – Borough dining experience, with its "brilliant" cooking and its "very attentive" service. / **Sample dishes:** chicken satay with steamed Indian bread; smoked cobra dumplings in vermicelli broth; black rice pudding with durian ice cream
Details: www.champor-champor.com; 10.30 pm; closed L (unless receive a booking for 6+), closed Sun; booking: max 8.

Chapter Two SE3 £ 29 🄰★

43-45 Montpelier Vale 8333 2666

"Much improved this year"; this "above-average local" in Blackheath – with its "good range of modern dishes" and smart-casual ambience – is praised by fans from across south London for its "West End standards". / **Sample dishes:** garlic soup with watercress purée; roast fillet of beef; hot chocolate fondant. **Details:** www.chaptersrestaurant.co.uk; 10.30 pm, Fri & Sat 11.30 pm; no smoking in dining room.

Chelsea Bun Diner £ 22

9a Lamont Rd, SW10 7352 3635 4–3B

70 Battersea Bridge Rd, SW11 7738 9009 4–4C

"Proof that hangovers can be assuaged by a good breakfast"; every variety – from "the Full Monty" to "American-style bacon and pancakes" – wins hearty support for this "basic" (but often "buzzing") World's End diner. / **Details:** SW10 10.45 pm, SW11 L only; SW10 closed Sun D; no Amex; no brunch bookings.

Chez Bruce SW17 £ 47 A★★

2 Bellevue Rd 8672 0114 6–2C

Bruce Poole's "sophisticated but unpretentious" food – complemented by "an extensive and reasonably-priced" wine list, and served by notably "knowledgeable and friendly" staff – has built a simply enormous following for this "cramped" and always "buzzy" dining room, by Wandsworth Common. / **Sample dishes:** asparagus frittata with ham & Manchego; rabbit with stuffed cabbage & polenta; cherry & almond tart. **Details:** 10.30 pm; no smoking area; booking: max 6 at D.

Chez Liline N4 £ 32 ★★

101 Stroud Green Rd 7263 6550

You'd never guess it from the "grim" location and décor, but this Crouch End Mauritian is an "oasis of seafood splendour" – for "excellent fish, exotically prepared", it is simply without peer. / **Sample dishes:** tuna & pesto with rocket salad; snapper in Creole sauce; coconut & passion fruit sorbet. **Details:** 10.30 pm; closed Mon & Sun L.

Chez Lindsay TW10 £ 30 ★

11 Hill Rise 8948 7473

"The perfect place for delicious crêpes and cider"; "it feels like you're in Brittany", at this "friendly" bistro – a "haven" of "real French food", near Richmond Bridge. / **Sample dishes:** mussels; seafood pancake; crepes Suzette. **Details:** 11 pm; no Amex.

Chez Max SW3 £ 34 A★

3 Yeoman's Row 7590 9999 4–2C

Max's "hammy" cod-French service can seem a trifle "overblown", but this Knightsbridge basement newcomer – where Monsieur Renzland acts as 'restaurateur' for Marco Pierre White – is a commendable place, offering "authentic" and "good-value" bistro fare. / **Sample dishes:** black pudding with mustard sauce; steak frites; tarte à la crème. **Details:** www.whitestarline.org.uk; 11 pm.

Chiang Mai W1 £ 31 ★

48 Frith St 7437 7444 3–2A

"The best Thai, you just have to ignore the grim décor" – the story's the same as ever at this "authentic" and "quirky" Soho fixture. / **Details:** 11 pm; closed Sun L; no smoking area.

Chowki W1 £ 23 ★

2-3 Denman St 7439 1330 2–2D

"Astonishing value, given the location and the constantly-changing menu" – this "novel", year-old Indian near Piccadilly Circus has won instant popularity as a "great central place to eat". / **Details:** www.chowki.com; 11.30 pm; no smoking area.

Churchill Arms W8 £ 17 A★

119 Kensington Church St 7792 1246

"It's hard to get a table" in the conservatory-annex of this Notting Hill "old favourite" – "a Thai pub food pioneer", where "the menu is limited but portions are large", and the dishes "incredibly cheap". / **Details:** 9.30 pm; closed Sun D; no smoking area; no booking at L.

Chutney Mary SW10 £ 50 A★

535 King's Rd 7351 3113 4–4B

"The million-pound revamp really worked", says one of the many fans of this grand distant-Chelsea subcontinental (whose former Raj-look has gone, well, the way of the Raj); its cooking – with "splashes of modern genius" adding lustre to "the best traditional Indian dishes" – remains as popular as ever. / **Details:** www.realindianfood.com; 11pm; closed weekday L; no smoking area.

Chutneys NW1 £ 22 ★

124 Drummond St   7388 0604

"Excellent, tasty, vegetarian food, even for carnivores" maintains the popularity of this 'Little India' fixture (by Euston); the *"great buffet lunch deal"*, especially on Sundays, is a key feature. / **Details:** 11 pm; no Amex; no smoking at L; need 4+ to book.

Cicada EC1 £ 35 ★

132-136 St John St   7608 1550   5–1B

"Thai-with-a-twist" cooking that's *"well thought-out"* and often *"perfectly executed"* is, perhaps surprisingly, the star attraction at this *"trendy"* and *"noisy"* Clerkenwell joint (which also does *"lethal but delicious cocktails"*). / **Details:** www.cicada.nu; 10.45 pm; closed Sat L & Sun; no smoking area.

The Cinnamon Club SW1 £ 52 ★

Great Smith St   7222 2555   1–4C

"Delicate and different" cuisine served in the *"spacious"* quarters that used to house a Westminster library has quickly won a very wide following for Iqbal Wahhab's *"stylish"* (if rather *"hushed"*) nouvelle Indian; ratings have slipped since the early days, though, and the place is certainly *"on the pricey side"*. / **Sample dishes:** smoked lamb kebabs; mustard tandoori prawns with saffron kedgeree; coconut cake with cumin yoghurt. **Details:** www.cinnamonclub.com; 11 pm; closed Sat L & Sun; no smoking area; booking: max 8.

City Miyama EC4 £ 38 ★★

17 Godliman St   7489 1937   5–3B

The place is *"drab"* and prices are *"silly"*, but this grand City Japanese serves *"about the best sushi in London"*; there's also *"excellent teppan-yaki"*. / **Details:** 9.30 pm; closed Sat D & Sun.

Clarke's W8 £ 60 𝔸★★

124 Kensington Church St   7221 9225

"How does she do it year in year out?" – Sally Clarke's *"simple but superb"* Kensington dining room (whose dinner menu offers no choice) remains one of the capital's most *"reliable"* gastronomic destinations; its *"intimate"* (but not in any way clichéd) setting strikes many as romantic too. / **Sample dishes:** onion puff pastry with tomatoes & Mozzarella; salmon with courgette flower fritters; vanilla cream pot with lemon thyme shortbread. **Details:** www.sallyclarke.com; 10 pm; closed Sat & Sun (open for Sat brunch); no smoking.

Club Gascon EC1 £ 48 𝔸★★

57 West Smithfield   7796 0600   5–2B

A *"sinfully delicious"* selection of *"foie gras and all good things from SW France"*, served tapas-style, has won a huge following for this Smithfield spot; other attractions include an *"exciting list of regional French wines"*, *"attentive and knowledgeable staff"* and an *"intimate"*, if *"slightly squashed"*, setting. / **Sample dishes:** foie gras consommé with oysters; steamed white fish with chorizo; French cheese selection. **Details:** 10 pm, Fri & Sat 10.30 pm; closed Sat L & Sun.

(Angela Hartnett's Menu)
The Connaught W1 £ 70

Carlos Pl   7592 1222   2–3B

Fans hail *"new life for an old classic"*, but the controversial revamp of this Mayfair stalwart has been an *"anticlimax"*; reporters rate Ramsay-protégée AH's *"Mediterranean-tinged"* cuisine a fraction less favourably than the old régime's, service (formerly extraordinary) has declined, and the revamped room has *"lost charm"*. / **Sample dishes:** chilled pea soup with langoustines; smoked pork belly with summer vegetables & thyme & garlic bouillon; apple tarte Tatin. **Details:** www.the-connaught.co.uk; 11 pm; booking: max 8.

Coq d'Argent EC3 £51

1 Poultry 7395 5000 5–2C

The gardens and terrace of Conran's "flash" top-floor vantage-point by the Bank of England may be "the City's best place for a summer drink", but the dining room's appeal is deeply dubious – the food is "boring" and "overpriced", and service can be "terrible". / *Sample dishes:* veal sweetbreads with pea purée; lamb with goat's cheese crust; peach gratin. *Details:* www.conran.com; 10 pm; closed Sat L & Sun D.

Coromandel SW11 £29 ★

2 Battersea Rise 7738 0038 6–2C

"Friendly", "helpful", "authentic" and "very enjoyable" it may be, but this south Indian in Battersea never seems to win the following it deserves. / *Details:* 11.30 pm; no smoking area.

The Cow W2 £32 A★

89 Westbourne Park Rd 7221 0021

Accorded "classic" status by its many fans, Tom Conran's "atmospheric" Irish boozer in Bayswater is "the top pub for Guinness and oysters" (plus a range of other seafood dishes); it's "often too full"; (upstairs, the separately-run restaurant inspires limited but generally favourable commentary). / *Sample dishes:* risotto nero with cuttlefish; grilled Dover sole with parsley & cockles; chocolate & Amaretto torte. *Details:* 10.30 pm; no Amex.

Cristini W1 £34 ★

13 Seymour Pl 7724 3446 1–2A

"Small, intimate and family-run", this new Italian – in a little street just north of Marble Arch – yielded few reports, and mainly about the "excellent-value lunch deal"; (it has, therefore, an Editors' rating based on our own dinner-time visit). / *Sample dishes:* crispy duck leg with caramelized onions; grilled loin of pork with asparagus & mushrooms; almond biscuits to dip in dessert wine. *Details:* www.cristini.co.uk; 10.30 pm; closed Sat L & Sun.

The Criterion Grill W1 £36 A

224 Piccadilly Circus 7930 0488 2–3D

Marco Pierre White's "Byzantine beauty" occupies a "breathtaking" chamber in the very heart of London; in spite of somewhat reduced prices, it can still seem "expensive", though, and still attracts a fair number of reports of "mediocre" food and "couldn't-care-less" service. / *Sample dishes:* vichysoisse; roast pheasant with quince purée; lemon tart. *Details:* www.whitestarline.org.uk; 11.30 pm; closed Sun L.

Cru N1 £38 ★

2-4 Rufus St 7729 5252 5–1C

This is quite a "grown-up" place ("by Hoxton standards"), and – as the name suggests – an "extensive" wine list is a key part of its appeal; the "very good" cooking is by no means incidental, though, and "friendly" staff add to the "buzzy" ambience. / *Sample dishes:* Tuscan bread salad; salmon with spiced lentils; spice, mango and pineapple crumble. *Details:* www.cru.uk.com; 11 pm; closed Sun D.

Deca W1 £54

23 Conduit St 7493 7070 2–2C

Often "delicious" Gallic cooking and "sophisticated" décor has – for many – made "a real hit" of this year-old establishment in a Mayfair townhouse; there were a few "very ordinary" meals this year, though, and many reporters complain of a "distinct lack of ambience". / *Sample dishes:* foie gras with oranges; John Dory with olive oil & thyme sauce; pear tart with crème anglaise. *Details:* 11 pm; closed Sun.

Delfina Studio Café SE1 £ 34 A★★

50 Bermondsey St   7357 0244   5–4D

*It's a shame this "spacious" and arty Bermondsey space (as seen in the BBC's 'Diners') isn't open for dinner, because it makes an "impressive venue", and "consistently delights" with its "original" cooking. / **Sample dishes:** pea & mint soup with feta croutons; cinnamon-crusted pork with fennel & orange salad; rhubarb streusel tart. **Details:** www.delfina.org.uk; L only, closed Sat & Sun.*

La Delizia SW3 £ 23 ★

63-65 Chelsea Manor St   7376 4111   4–3C

*"Authentic and delectable pizzas, pastas and salads" maintain the popularity of this tiny Chelsea spot – the sole survivor of what was once a fashionable small chain. / **Details:** midnight; no Amex.*

The Depot SW14 £ 33 A

Tideway Yd, Mortlake High St   8878 9462   6–1A

*"Great river views" are the undoubted plus at this "lively" Barnes "favourite" – a famously "child-friendly" weekend destination; the cooking seems to be on an up at present, but sceptics insist it's still "not as good as they think it is". / **Sample dishes:** poached langoustine with tomato consommé; roast duck with braised cabbage & berry jus; strawberry pavlova with raspberry coulis. **Details:** 10.30 pm; no smoking area.*

Diwana Bhel-Poori House NW1 £ 16 ★

121-123 Drummond St   7387 5556

*"Utilitarian" but "cheerful", this '70s BYO veggie, in the 'Little India' by Euston station, has long been known for its "excellent value for money"; the "fantastic lunchtime buffet" is a particular attraction. / **Details:** www.diwanarestaurant.com; 11.15 pm; no smoking area; need 6+ to book.*

The Don EC4 £ 45 A★

20 St Swithin's Ln   7626 2606   5–3C

*"Tucked away down an alley in the City", this "worthy sibling to the Bleeding Heart" is rapidly becoming a top (less formal) business venue; both restaurant and bistro offer "fantastic" Gallic cooking and notably "efficient" service – not least from a "knowledgeable" sommelier, who presides over a "well priced" list. / **Sample dishes:** scallops en croute with lime; venison with roasted figs & port mash; banana tarte Tatin. **Details:** 10 pm; closed Sat & Sun.*

(Grill Room)
Dorchester Hotel W1 £ 62 A★

53 Park Ln   7629 8888   2–3A

*"Luxurious and old-fashioned", this Spanish-Baronial grill still makes an "impressive" venue for a grand meal, offering "very good" cooking, matched by an "excellent" wine list; at the time of writing, this is London's best surviving traditional dining room – let's hope the forthcoming revamp doesn't wreck it! / **Sample dishes:** smoked Norfolk duck with onion compote; Aberdeen beef with sautéed goose liver; flambéed peppered peaches. **Details:** www.dorchesterhotel.com; 11 pm.*

The Drapers Arms N1 £ 34 A★

44 Barnsbury St
7619 0348

*"A real find", this "elegant restaurant above a pub in Georgian Islington" has quickly won a very large fan club, thanks to its "superb" and "technically precise" cooking ("even in the bar"), not to mention its "friendly" staff and its "intimate" atmosphere. / **Sample dishes:** smoked duck & beetroot with Brie croutons; chilli-roasted fish with Asian coleslaw; panna cotta with raspberries. **Details:** 10.30 pm; closed Sun D; no Amex.*

E&O W11 £34 A★★

14 Blenheim Cr

7229 5454

Will Ricker's "glitterati-infested" Notting Hill bar/restaurant yearling is not just "blisteringly trendy" – the "novel" menu of "oriental tapas" includes some "wonderful" dishes, and the staff are "really nice and unpretentious… considering". / **Sample dishes:** pan-fried squid with chilli & salt; black cod with sweet miso; chocolate pudding with green tea ice cream. **Details:** www.eando.nu; 10.30 pm; booking: max 6.

The Eagle EC1 £24 A★

159 Farringdon Rd 7837 1353 5–1A

"The original is still the best", says one of the legion of fans of London's first gastropub (1991)… "if you can get a seat", that is; it's the "the great rustic food" (Mediterranean) which is the attraction – not the "smoky" and "packed" setting or the "somewhat arrogant" staff. / **Sample dishes:** stuffed aubergine with cracked wheat salad; sea bass with fennel & orange salad; Portuguese custard tart. **Details:** 10.30 pm; closed Sun D; no Amex; no booking.

Ealing Park Tavern W5 £29 ★

222 South Ealing Rd

8758 1879

"What a delightful surprise in a barren area" – "top-quality food and attention to detail" win high praise for the "large dining room" of this tastefully modernised south Ealing pub; it's "very reasonably priced", too. / **Sample dishes:** apple, apricot & pigeon terrine; Toulouse cassoulet; apple & pear crumble. **Details:** 10.30 pm; closed Mon L; booking: max 10.

Earl Spencer SW18 £29 ★

260-262 Merton Rd 8870 9244 6–2B

"What Southfields has been waiting years for", say fans of this large, new gastropub sibling to the famed Havelock; the food is "always good, sometimes heroic", and service is "chirpy", too – perhaps they could learn a thing or two from it in Olympia? / **Sample dishes:** spaghetti with clams; pork belly with onion and cider cream; crème brûlée. **Details:** 10 pm; no Amex; no booking.

Eco £29 ★

162 Clapham High St, SW4 7978 1108 6–2D

4 Market Row, Brixton Mkt, SW9 7738 3021 6–2D

"Amazing", "well-priced" pizzas maintain the crush at this "loud" and "funky" Clapham rendezvous (and its Brixton Market offshoot); such is the pressure that service can prove "elusive". / **Details:** SW4 11 pm, Fri & Sat 11.30 pm; SW9 L only, closed Wed & Sun; SW9 no booking.

Eddalino W1 £45 ★

10 Wigmore St 7637 0789 2–1B

"A lack of atmosphere" is something of a refrain in reports on this "relaxing" Italian, north of Oxford Street – a shame, as the cooking "tries hard" (with pasta a top recommendation). / **Sample dishes:** monkfish carpaccio; veal with chestnut and cheese sauce; hot chocolate pudding. **Details:** www.eddalino.com; 10.30 pm; closed Sat L & Sun; no smoking area.

Edera W11 £30 ★

148 Holland Park Ave 7221 6090

It's a shame that bland décor, "slow" service and a slightly pretentious attitude undermine the appeal of this nearly-chic newcomer in Holland Park; though the straightforward Italian dishes don't quite seem to justify the reverential way in which they are served, they're deftly done and come at fantastic prices. / **Sample dishes:** Mozzarella, served in three styles; beef entrecote with sautéed potatoes & asparagus; crunchy chocolate mousse. **Details:** 11pm; closed Mon L.

1837
Brown's Hotel W1 **£ 65** ★
Albemarle St
7408 1837   2–3C
A "fantastic wine list" (with 250 choices by the glass) and often "exceptional" cooking are at last establishing the reputation this "formal" but "friendly" – and sometimes "under-utilised" – Mayfair dining room deserves; let's hope Rocco Forte (who recently bought the hotel) doesn't try to 'improve' it! / **Sample dishes:** Chilled gazpacho, langoustines and courgette; Roast breast and confit leg of challans duck with foie gras, green celery; Raspberry soufflé, bitter chocolate sorbet.
Details: www.raffles-brownshotel.com; 10.30 pm; closed Sat L & Sun.

El Rincón Latino SW4 **£ 25** *A*
148 Clapham Manor St   7622 0599   6–2D
"The best atmosphere in London" is claimed by fans of this "very friendly" and "fantastically entertaining" Clapham tapas bar, which serves some "great-value" scoff; "you must book at weekends". / **Sample dishes:** goats cheese croquettes; Colombian chorizo with fried plantain; Manchego with quince jelly. **Details:** 11.30 pm.

The Endurance W1 **£ 29** ★
90 Berwick St   7437 2944   2–2D
"Good British pub food" of a vaguely retro nature is the highlight at this newly converted but determinedly 'real' boozer (from the same team as The Perseverance), in the heart of a sleazy Soho market. / **Sample dishes:** foie gras terrine; chicken confit with mash; apple crumble. **Details:** L only; no Amex; need 12+ to book.

The Engineer NW1 **£ 36** *A*
65 Gloucester Ave   7722 0950
An "excellent brunch" is the forte of this still "super-cool" Primrose Hill gastropub of long standing; some reporters wonder if it's a touch "overhyped" nowadays, but its "lovely garden for the summer" is undoubtedly a major attraction. / **Sample dishes:** tequila cured salmon with blinis, horseradish cream & cucumber; pork tenderloin wrapped in chorizo served with saffron & pea paella; prune & armagnac créme brûlee.
Details: www.the-engineer.com; 11pm; no Amex.

English Garden SW3 **£ 46** ★
10 Lincoln St   7584 7272   4–2D
It now offers "surprisingly competent" cooking, but – since an ill-advised revamp a couple of years back – opinion is still divided as to whether this "quiet and intimate" Chelsea townhouse is "romantic" or just plain "dreary". / **Sample dishes:** celeriac remoulade with quince paste & Seranno ham; daube of organic pork; banana & toffee crumble . **Details:** 11 pm; closed Mon L; booking: max 8.

Enoteca Turi SW15 **£ 42** ★
28 Putney High St   8785 4449   6–2B
"An amazing list of mostly Italian wines" has helped win a wide following for this "unpretentious" spot, near Putney Bridge; it's also praised for its "robust" and "authentic" Italian fare and "helpful" service, but its premises can seem rather "clinical". / **Sample dishes:** Mozzarella with sardines & pine nuts; roast lamb; peach tart with lime sorbet. **Details:** 11 pm; closed Sun.

The Enterprise SW3 **£ 35** *A*
35 Walton St   7584 3148   4–2C
An "incredible buzz" has always been the real point of this "smart" but "fun" Chelsea boozer; it's not a foodie kind of place, but "a good range of dishes" is "well executed". / **Sample dishes:** Caesar salad; roast rump of lamb, aubergine blini & rosemary oil; chocolate mousse.
Details: www.sparkjumbo.co.uk; 10.30 pm; no booking, except weekday L.

L'Escargot W1 £42 ★

48 Greek St 7437 2679 3–2A

Under Marco Pierre White's management, this long-established and "impressive" Soho classic has re-established itself as a "reliable" Gallic destination (both in the ground-floor brasserie, and in the grander Picasso Room); gently ebbing ratings, however, support reporters who've found "a missing wow-factor" of late. / Sample dishes: foie gras & green peppercorn terrine; caramelised skate wing with winkles; Grand Marnier soufflé. Details: www.whitestarline.org.uk; 11.30 pm; closed Sat L & Sun (Picasso Room also closed Mon).

Faulkner's E8 £21 ★★

424-426 Kingsland Rd 7254 6152

"Fantastic fish and chips" (and "hand-made fishcakes to kill for") make this Dalston legend London's best chippy by some margin; a major refurb is planned for late-2003. / Sample dishes: fish soup; rock salmon & chips; pistachio ice cream. Details: 10 pm; no Amex; no smoking area; need 8+ to book.

Fez N1 £33 ★

70 Upper St 7359 1710

We were surprised by the high quality of the Moroccan cooking on our July 2003 visit to this Islington newcomer; other aspects of the operation are amateur, but endearing. / Details: www.fez-islington.co.uk; midnight; no Amex.

Fino W1 £40 A★★

33 Charlotte St
7813 8010 1–1C

"Fantastic" tapas have instantly won a big following for this "smart" new Fitzrovia basement; we didn't find its "canteenish" style particularly characterful (or authentic), but all reporters insist the place is "sure to be a hit". / Sample dishes: wild mushroom croquettes; escalivada (mixed vegetables, Catalan-style); crema catalana. Details: www.finorestaurant.com; 10.30 pm; closed Sat L & Sun.

Fish Hoek W4 £40 ★★

6-8 Elliott Rd 8742 0766

An "awesome" array of "esoteric" and "terrifically fresh" fish and seafood, "beautifully" cooked, has made a big name for this year-old South African yearling, off Chiswick's main drag; it's a "shame about the space", though – it's "way too cramped". / Sample dishes: giant prawns in garlic cream; grilled barracuda with seasonal vegetables; chocolate mealy meal pudding. Details: 10.30 pm; closed Mon (except Aug-Dec); no Amex; no smoking area.

Fleur SW1 £42 ★

33 St James's St 7930 4272 2–4C

High-quality dishes of deceptive simplicity come notably reasonably priced (especially for St James's) at Marcus Wareing's new 'diffusion' outlet; having inherited Pétrus's stiff décor, however, the creation of a suitably relaxed atmosphere is no small challenge. / Sample dishes: crab & salmon ravioli with pak choi & lemongrass bisque; roast partridge with caramelised chicory & port jus; coffee panna cotta with rum caramel sauce. Details: 10.45 pm; booking: max 6.

Foliage
Mandarin Oriental SW1 £61 A★

66 Knightsbridge 7201 3723 4–1D

"Exquisitely prepared" contemporary cuisine has made the name of this "stylish" Knightsbridge hotel dining room; its style can seem a bit "bland", but not if you visit for the "wonderful-value set lunch" (and book one of the tables with a "great view" of Hyde Park). / Sample dishes: cauliflower & spiced quail salad; roast bream with pumpkin ravioli; Cuban chocolate fondant. Details: www.mandarinoriental.com; 10.30 pm; no smoking area; booking: max 8.

Food for Thought WC2   £ 15   ★
31 Neal St   7836 0239   3–2C
*Serving "enormous portions" of "wholesome" veggie scoff
at "reasonable prices" ensues that this "friendly" but "cramped"
Covent Garden basement café is "still right on, even after all these
years"; unlicensed, but you can BYO.* / **Sample dishes:** *carrot & coriander
soup; Ethiopian vegetable wrap; strawberry crunch.* **Details:** *8.15 pm; closed Sun D;
no credit cards; no smoking; no booking.*

The Four Seasons W2   £ 22   ★
84 Queensway   7229 4320
*"Excellent roast duck" is the star attraction at this "dependable"
Bayswater Chinese... but then "the queues and the surly service need
some compensation".* / **Details:** *11.15 pm.*

The Fox EC2   £ 29   A ★
28 Paul St   7729 5708   5–1C
*"Honest" (and sometimes "innovative") cooking "using well-sourced
ingredients" – served "in the bar or, better, in the dining room above" –
makes Eagle founder Michael Belben's "quirky" Shoreditch boozer
a "promising" destination.* / **Sample dishes:** *Serrano ham & fig; rabbit with
cabbage & bacon; chocolate pudding.* **Details:** *11 pm; closed Sat & Sun; no Amex.*

Frederick's N1   £ 44   A ★
106 Camden Pas   7359 2888
*A "special" atmosphere distinguishes this "buzzy" Islington "favourite",
where the "beautiful conservatory" provides a "lovely" setting for
business or a celebration; no one makes exaggerated claims for the
Gallic cooking, but it's "always of good quality".* / **Sample dishes:** *smoked
haddock & new potato salad; roast duck with French beans; fruit crudités with Greek
yoghurt.* **Details:** *www.fredericks.co.uk; 11.30 pm; closed Sun; no smoking area.*

French House W1   £ 37   A ★
49 Dean St   7437 2477   3–3A
*"A wonderful bolt-hole" – this "lovely and intimate" room over
a (famous) pub has a real "old Soho" ambience (that makes it "great
for a date"); "genuinely helpful" staff and "simple and unpretentious"
cooking complete a very popular formula.* / **Sample dishes:** *chicken liver &
foie gras pâté; seared scallops with gazpacho sauce; nougat glacé with passion fruit
coulis.* **Details:** *11 pm; closed Sun D; booking: max 8.*

Fung Shing WC2   £ 34   ★
15 Lisle St   7437 1539   3–3A
*"A recent drop in standards" looks set to dent this grungy oriental's
long-held reputation as "the best Chinese in Chinatown"; it's still
"more interesting than most", though, with "adventurous dishes better
than the Westernised ones".* / **Details:** *www.fungshing.co.uk; 11.15 pm.*

Furnace N1   £ 25   ★
1 Rufus St   7613 0598   5–1D
*"Rustic-style pizzas which put most others to shame" win notably
consistent reports for this "always-buzzy" Hoxton Italian; there's "a nice
range of starters", too.* / **Details:** *11 pm; closed Sat L & Sun; no Amex.*

Gallipoli   £ 21   A ★
102 Upper St, N1   7359 0630
120 Upper St, N1   7226 8099
*"Wonderfully friendly", "cosy" and "cramped", these Islington Turks are
"packed out nightly" – testament to their "amazing-value" mezze and
their "outstanding" staff, who cope remarkably well, considering.*
/ **Details:** *11 pm, Fri & Sat midnight; no Amex.*

sign up for the survey at www.hardens.com   49

Garanger Restaurant Bar W1 £50 ★
114-115 Crawford St   7935 8447   1–1A
"Fantastic food" is the theme of all reports on this French/Mediterranean newcomer in Marylebone; its premises, however, are frankly underwhelming – let's hope that the eponymous chef soon finds a location to match his skills. / **Details:** www.garangers.com; 10.15 pm; closed Sun; no smoking area.

The Gate £31 ★★
51 Queen Caroline St, W6   8748 6932
72 Belsize Ln, NW3   7435 7733
There's "not a hessian skirt or 2CV in sight" at this (moderately) "stylish" veggie duo, rated by many as "the best in town"; the "church hall-like" Hammersmith original has "nice tables outside in summer", whereas Belsize Park is "modern and clean". / **Sample dishes:** courgette flower & feta salad; teriyaki aubergine with rice noodles; banana brûlée. **Details:** www.gateveg.co.uk; 10.45 pm; W6 closed Sun & Sat L, NW3 closed weekday L; smoking restrictions at NW3; W6 booking: max 10.

Gaucho £32 ★
88 Ifield Rd, SW10   7823 3333
Chelsea Farmers' Mkt, Sydney St, SW3   7376 8514
30 Old Brompton Rd, SW7   7584 8999
"The best meat in town at a reasonable price", says one of the fans of these basic Chelsea and (now) South Kensington Argentinians; for top atmosphere, sit outside at the original branch – a hut in Chelsea Farmers' Market. / **Details:** SW7 & SW10 11.30 pm; SW3 L only, SW10 & SW7 D only, SW10 closed Sun; SW3 no credit cards; SW3 no booking in summer.

Gaudi EC1 £44 ★
63 Clerkenwell Rd   7608 3220   5–1A
This "surreal" modern Spaniard is "even better in its new home" (still close to the all-hours Clerkenwell nightclub, Turnmills – "beware thumping bass notes"); it can seem "very expensive", but all reports about its "tasty and artistic" cooking are upbeat. / **Sample dishes:** clams with parsley sauce; grilled pork fillet marinated in paprika & cumin; selection of Spanish cheeses. **Details:** 10.30 pm; closed Sat L.

Le Gavroche W1 £91 Ⓐ★★
43 Upper Brook St   7408 0881   2–2A
For a "classic" Gallic meal, this "discreet" and "exceptionally accommodating" Mayfair "gastro-temple" is still hard to beat; Michel Roux Jr's "rich and traditional" cuisine is "everything it's cracked up to be" (and complemented by a "staggeringly extensive" wine list); there is of course a downside – "the price". / **Sample dishes:** artichoke heart with foie gras & chicken mousse; roast grouse with bread sauce; millefeuille with Mascarpone & mango. **Details:** www.le-gavroche.co.uk; 11 pm; closed Sat L & Sun; jacket required at D.

Geeta NW6 £15 ★★
57-59 Willesden Ln   7624 1713
It's "very ordinary-looking" and in a "grotty" bit of Kilburn, but "the food-quality never ceases to amaze" at this "utterly dependable" south Indian veteran (many of whose best dishes are veggie); its licensed, or you can BYO (corkage £2). / **Sample dishes:** hot lentil curry; prawn curry with lemon rice; gulab jamon. **Details:** 10.30 pm, Fri & Sat 11.30 pm; no Switch.

Ginger W2 £31 ★
115 Westbourne Grove   7908 1990
"Curry with a difference" – this "modern" Bayswater Bangladeshi is "better than your average subcontinental", and even reporters who find it "slightly expensive" say it's "well worth a trip". / **Details:** www.gingerrestaurant.co.uk; 11 pm, Fri & Sat midnight; no smoking area.

Giraffe £ 26

6-8 Blandford St, W1   7935 2333   1–1A
270 Chiswick High Rd, W4   8995 2100
7 Kensington High St, W8   7938 1221   4–1A
29-31 Essex Rd, N1   7359 5999
46 Rosslyn Hill, NW3   7435 0343
27 Battersea Rise, SW11   7223 0933   6–2C

"Massive, yummy breakfasts" (again the survey's most popular) and
"great brunches" ("including fruit shakes and pancakes") win consistent
praise for these "bright and cheery" "New World cafés"; they're
"family-friendly", too – excessively so, for some tastes. / **Details:** 11 pm;
no smoking.

The Glasshouse TW9 £ 45   A★★

14 Station Pde   8940 6777

Kew's "wonderful culinary outpost" – a sibling of the legendary Chez
Bruce – offers "sensational" modern British cooking and "superb"
service at "very reasonable prices"; the "smart but simple" setting
is "as airy as the name suggests", but the seating is "cramped".
/ **Sample dishes:** salt cod fishcake with pickled cucumber; roast pork with black
pudding & grainmustard; rhubarb & yoghurt ice creams. **Details:** 10.30 pm.

Good Earth SW3 £ 37   ★

233 Brompton Rd   7584 3658   4–2C

A "high-quality, traditional Chinese" not far from Harrods; it has long
offered "the best food of its type in the area", and "great service" too.
/ **Details:** 10.45 pm.

Goolies W8 £ 33   ★

21 Abingdon Rd   7938 1122   4–1A

A small but dedicated fan club hails "consistently good" and somewhat
"out-of-the-ordinary" cooking at this "friendly local", just off Kensington
High Street; the odd doubter can find its style "pretentious". / **Sample
dishes:** scallops with lemon & parsley; duck breast with blackberries; exotic sorbets.
Details: www.goolies-bar.com; 10.30 pm; D only.

Gordon Ramsay SW3 £ 91   A★★

68-69 Royal Hospital Rd   7352 4441   4–3D

"Devastatingly good" modern Gallic cooking remains the hallmark
of London's top chef's Chelsea flagship, which – despite the relentless
growth of his empire – remains "second to none"; service is "fabulous",
too (if sometimes "comically attentive"). / **Sample dishes:** hot foie gras with
lentils; lobster & langoustine tortellini in shellfish bisque; blood oranges in jelly.
Details: www.gordonramsay.com; 11 pm; closed Sat & Sun; jacket required;
booking: max 6.

**Gordon Ramsay at Claridge's
Claridge's Hotel W1** £ 72

55 Brook St   7499 0099   2–2B

A year into its new régime, this potentially great Art Deco dining room
is still "living off Ramsay's reputation"; many reporters (especially those
at the new chef's table) do praise "fabulous" cooking, but the number
of disappointments is so high that there can be only one overall
conclusion – "good, but not even close to outstanding". / **Sample
dishes:** scallops with cauliflower purée & beetroot crisps; roast duck with celeriac
fondant & confit leeks; chocolate savarin with champagne granita. **Details:** 11 pm;
booking: max 8.

Gordon's Wine Bar WC2 £ 25   A✗

47 Villiers St   7930 1408   3–4D

"It's annoying that the resident cat gets its own seat even when the
place is busy", but that's the kind of quirk which makes this ancient
wine bar by Embankment tube such a "wonderful" fixture (and one
where the food is incidental); great summer terrace. / **Sample
dishes:** duck pâté & French bread; sausages, mash & onion gravy; apple pie.
Details: 10 pm; no Amex; no booking.

Goring Hotel SW1   £ 59   A
15 Beeston Pl 7396 9000 1–4B
"A true bastion of Englishness", this "lovely" family-owned Victoria hotel boasts a "formal" and "discreet" dining room, to whose charms "old-fashioned and courteous" service makes no small contribution; as you might hope, breakfasts "approach perfection". / **Sample dishes:** watercress soup; Norfolk duck with caramelised apple; chocolate millefeuille with coffee ice cream. **Details:** www.goringhotel.co.uk; 10 pm; closed Sat L; no smoking area.

Gourmet Burger Kitchen   £ 21   ★
49 Fulham Broadway, SW6 7381 4242 4–4A
331 West End Ln, NW6 7794 5455
44 Northcote Rd, SW11 7228 3309 6–2C
333 Putney Bridge Rd, SW15 8789 1199 6–2B
"The best burgers in town" – full stop – are winning deserved success for this growing simple-thing-done-well chain; "shame they aren't on every corner" – well, not yet, anyway. / **Sample dishes:** chunky chips with salsa; Jamaican burger with mango & ginger sauce; no puddings. **Details:** www.gbkinfo.co.uk; 11 pm; no Amex; no smoking; no booking.

Govinda's W1   £ 9   ★
9 Soho St 7437 4928 3–1A
A seminal 'cheap eat'; this café below a Hare Krishna temple (off Soho Square) attracts an eclectic crowd with its great and plentiful veggie grub at prices that time forgot; Indian dishes are best. / **Details:** 8 pm; closed Sun; no Amex; no smoking.

Grenadier SW1   £ 35   A
18 Wilton Row 7235 3074 4–1D
This "gem of a pub", in an impossibly cute Belgravia mews, is on every tourist trail, and the "standard British fare" in the tiny rear dining room is priced accordingly; opt, instead, for a banger and one of their "good Bloody Marys" in the front bar. / **Sample dishes:** Stilton tart with red wine & port jam; beef Wellington; blackberry & apple crumble. **Details:** 9 pm.

Hakkasan W1   £ 63   A★
8 Hanway Pl 7927 7000 3–1A
"Achingly trendy, dark and atmospheric", this "slick", "NYC-nightclub"-style West End basement – "amazingly decorated" (and with lots of "eye-candy" too) – has been a huge success; the oriental fare is of course "pricey" – the surprise is that it's "innovative" and "delicious" too. / **Sample dishes:** steamed scallops with tobiko caviar; deep-fried Tienging bun stuffed with chicken & prawn; mango spring roll. **Details:** 11 pm Mon-Wed, midnight Thurs-Sat; no smoking area.

The Havelock Tavern W14   £ 29   A★★
57 Masbro Rd 7603 5374
"Pub grub at its best" – "delicious, hearty and well cooked" – has won a vast following for this backstreet Olympia boozer; it's "a nightmare to get a table", though, and, once ensconced, "you have to work quite hard to get attention" from the rather "snooty" staff. / **Sample dishes:** pork & duck terrine; lamb shank with mash; sticky toffee pudding. **Details:** 10 pm; no credit cards; no booking.

Haz E1   £ 26   ★
9 Cutler St 7929 7923 5–2D
"A great Turkish newcomer in the City"; it's already "overflowing", and you need to "book ahead" if you want to enjoy the "tasty" grills, kebabs and mezze on offer at this "stylish, light and airy" – but also "noisy" and "tightly-packed" – spot, off Houndsditch. / **Details:** 11.30 pm; no smoking area.

Hazuki WC2   **£ 26**   ★

43 Chandos Pl   7240 2530   3–4C

*It's early days for this simple and welcoming Japanese near Trafalgar Square; it's already tipped, though, for its "value-for-money sushi" and its reasonably-priced lunch deals. / **Details:** www.sushihazuki.co.uk; 10.30 pm; closed Sat L & Sun L.*

The Highgate NW5   **£ 33**   ★

79 Highgate Rd   7485 8442

*A "young and buzzy media-type crowd" is a defining feature of this "spacious" Kentish Town gastrobar, whose "original" dishes are widely praised; eat in the bar, or descend to the more "intimate" environment of the basement restaurant. / **Sample dishes:** pumpkin & parmesan ravioli; peppered tuna with white beans; chocolate brownie. **Details:** 10.30 pm; no Amex.*

The Hill NW3   **£ 36**   ★

94 Haverstock Hill   7267 0033

*Very charming service and 'junk shop'-style décor impart a cosy feel to this new gastropub between Chalk Farm and Belsize Park; even an early reporter who didn't actually like the setting conceded that the creative food is "very good". / **Sample dishes:** scallops; lamb shank with rosemary & garlic; apple crumble. **Details:** 10.30 pm; closed Sat L & Sun L.*

The House N1   **£ 37**   𝔸★

63-69 Canonbury Rd   7704 7410

*It's "slightly expensive", but this "formerly rough" Islington boozer is now a "bright" and "buzzy" gastropub, which – thanks to its "tasty" cooking – is already quite "crowded". / **Sample dishes:** deep-fried Stilton with pear chutney; spinach & ricotta gnocchi; treacle tart. **Details:** www.inthehouse.biz; 10.30 pm; closed Mon L; no Amex; no smoking area.*

Hunan SW1   **£ 36**   ★★

51 Pimlico Rd   7730 5712   4–2D

*"Just eat what Mr Peng tells you, and all will be well"; "fantastic varied and spicy food" – that's "just a little challenging, in a good way" – makes this inauspicious-looking Pimlico site simply "the best Chinese in the Western World"… well, almost. / **Details:** 11 pm; closed Sun; no smoking area.*

**Huong-Viet
An Viet House N1**   **£ 20**   ★★

12-14 Englefield Rd   7249 0877

*"Just like being back in Pnom-Penh"; "genuine, uncompromised Vietnamese food" wins the highest praise for this "buzzing", "BYO/licensed" canteen (whose cultural-centre premises were once De Beauvoir Town's public baths); it's "always busy", and the friendly service can struggle to keep up. / **Details:** 11 pm; closed Sun; no Amex.*

The Ifield SW10   **£ 29**   𝔸★

59 Ifield Rd   7351 4900   4–3A

*A following of "grubby trustafarians and 'It'-girls" seems to be the only snag at this "warm" and "vibey" pub-conversion on the fringes of Chelsea, where the food is "unusually satisfying". / **Details:** 11 pm; Mon-Thu D only, Fri-Sun open L & D.*

Ikkyu W1   **£ 28**   ★

67a Tottenham Court Rd   7636 9280   1–1C

*"Extraordinary, so friendly and peaceful"; this "unchanging" West End cellar "feels like somewhere in Tokyo", and is unanimously praised as a "great" place, whose "good cheap and cheerful" dishes include "very good sushi". / **Details:** 10 pm; closed Sat & Sun L; no Switch; no smoking area.*

Imperial City EC3 £36 ★

Royal Exchange, Cornhill 7626 3437 5–2C

"A great City stand-by"; oriental food that's "head and shoulders above the local competition" help make the cellars of the Royal Exchange a "reliable" and "discreet" destination. / **Details:** www.imperial-city.co.uk; 9.30 pm; closed Sat & Sun.

Inaho W2 £26 ★★

4 Hereford Rd 7221 8495

"The best sushi for miles around, and at very reasonable prices" – that's the theme of all reports on this tiny but "amazing" Bayswater shack; service is "sweet, but sometimes inept". / **Details:** 11 pm; closed Sat L & Sun; no Amex or Switch.

Incognico WC2 £35

117 Shaftesbury Ave 7836 8866 3–2B

The "very reasonably-priced menu for lunch and pre-theatre" is a particular plus at this popular "oasis" of "stylish French" dining, in the heart of Theatreland; it strikes some as a "posher but less relaxed" alternative to the celebrated Mon Plaisir, nearby. / **Sample dishes:** goat's cheese & roast pepper open ravioli; crispy salmon in ginger cream sauce; warm chocolate mousse. **Details:** midnight; closed Sun.

Indian Ocean SW17 £22 ★

216 Trinity Rd 8672 7740 6–2C

"Good, reliable food" puts this "friendly" Wandsworth subcontinental "streets ahead of the bog-standard local competition". / **Details:** 11.45 pm; no smoking area.

Indigo
One Aldwych WC2 £49 A★

1 Aldwych 7300 0400 1–2D

Reporters find "nothing to fault" at this "calm" mezzanine dining room, where the "sensible" food is of "good quality", and service is "impeccable"; the "comfortable" and "spacious" setting – looking down on the cocktail bar below – is particularly popular with business types. / **Sample dishes:** monkfish carpaccio woth mango salsa; roast lamb with vegetable caviar; crunchy chocolate praline tart. **Details:** www.onealdwych.com; 11.15 pm.

Itsu £25 ★

103 Wardour St, W1 7479 4790 2–2D
118 Draycott Ave, SW3 7590 2400 4–2C
Level 2, Cabot Place East, E14 7512 5790

"Fresh sushi and a constantly-evolving selection of pseudo-sushi" (including "salads, brochettes, etc" and a "good crême brûlée") make these "funky" conveyor belt operators "a great place to graze"; the Chelsea original branch is best. / **Details:** www.itsu.co.uk; 11 pm, W1 Fri & Sat midnight; E14 closed Sat & Sun; no smoking; no booking.

The Ivy WC2 £48 A★

1 West St 7836 4751 3–3B

"I can't help it – I love The Ivy"; for the 8th consecutive year, this "buzzy" Theatreland "classic" – where "comfort food of the highest order" is served by "impeccable" staff who "treat everyone like a celebrity" – was reporters' favourite; star-spotting is just "the icing on the cake of a great experience". / **Sample dishes:** rock shrimp linguine; braised beef in Guinness with carrot mash; chocolate pudding soufflé. **Details:** midnight; booking: max 6.

Iznik N5 £24 A

19 Highbury Park 7354 5697

"Beautiful décor" and "atmospheric lighting" make this "friendly" and "charming" Turkish restaurant a top budget destination for Highbury romantics; the food, though, "is not always reliable". / **Sample dishes:** courgette & feta fritters; lamb with stuffed aubergines; baklava. **Details:** 11 pm; no Amex.

Jenny Lo's Tea House SW1 £22 ★
14 Eccleston St 7259 0399 1–4B
"Delicious" noodles at *"reasonable"* prices – *"quickly served, and quickly devoured"* – is the gist of all reports on this *"bright and happy"* Belgravia canteen. / **Details:** 10 pm; closed Sun; no credit cards; no booking.

Joy King Lau WC2 £23 ★
3 Leicester St 7437 1132 3–3A
"Great food, dire surroundings" – that's the deal at this *"huge"* but *"better-than-average"* spot just off Leicester Square; it's *"always full"*. / **Details:** 11.30 pm.

Julie's W11 £45 A
135 Portland Rd 7229 8331
"It feels like you're having a secret rendezvous (even if you're not!)", at this *"sexy"* Holland Park fixture – a *"warren of interesting rooms"*, whose *"intimate nooks and crannies"* are *"perfect for romance"*; *"the food is very much hit-and-miss, but the prices aren't"*. / **Sample dishes:** prosciutto & Parmesan summer salad; rack of lamb with garlic bean mash; meringue with red berries. **Details:** www.juliesrestaurant.com; 10.45 pm; closed Sat L.

Just India SW15 £30 ★
193 Lower Richmond Rd 8785 6004 6–1A
"A refreshingly decent Indian in the suburbs" – this *"modern"* Putney newcomer provides *"clean and fresh"*-tasting food from an *"innovative"* menu; it *"doesn't burn a hole in your pocket"* either. / **Details:** 11 pm; D only, ex Sun open L & D; no Amex.

K10 EC2 £25 ★★
20 Copthall Ave 7562 8510 5–2C
"Divine conveyor sushi" – many think *"the best in town"* – and *"good tempura and hot dishes"* generate *"enormous queues"* for this *"buzzing"*, *"friendly and fast"* City operation, off Moorgate. / **Sample dishes:** courgette tempura; seared tuna with miso vinaigrette; ginger mousse. **Details:** www.k10.net; 9.45pm; closed Sat & Sun; no smoking; no booking.

Kai W1 £50 ★
65 South Audley Street 7493 8507 2–3A
A *"short but creative"* menu of *"refined"* dishes makes make this *"comfortable"* and *"classy"* Mayfair Chinese a destination of some note; it can seem *"incredibly expensive for what it is"*, though, and remains little-known – *"you can usually get a table"*. / **Sample dishes:** deep-fried soft shell crab; Szechuan chicken with cashews & crispy seaweed; green tea. **Details:** www.kaimayfair.com; 10.45 pm.

Kastoori SW17 £21 ★★
188 Upper Tooting Rd 8767 7027 6–2C
"Awesome" East African/Indian veggie food, *"extremely nice"* staff and *"incredibly cheap"* prices make the *"drab"* décor of this famous Tooting shop-conversion easy to bear – this is the only truly 'destination' restaurant hereabouts. / **Sample dishes:** samosas; mushroom & spinach curry; Indian cheesecake. **Details:** 10.30 pm; closed Mon L & Tue L; no Amex or Switch.

Ken Lo's Memories SW1 £49 ★
67-69 Ebury St 7730 7734 1–4B
"Only flying to China matches this", say fans of this eminent Belgravia veteran, which is almost unanimously judged *"expensive but worthwhile"*; despite a revamp in recent times, no one finds the décor wildly exciting. / **Sample dishes:** courgettes stuffed with prawns; stewed lamb with lemongrass; toffee apple & banana. **Details:** 11.30 pm; closed Sun L.

Khan's W2 £14 ★
13-15 Westbourne Grove 7727 5420
"Noisy and scruffy, but the food is great" – some reporters claim
to have found *"the best price/quality ratio in town"* at this *"large,
loud and atmospheric"* Bayswater subcontinental; since they banned
alcohol, it's much less of a zoo than it was.
/ **Details:** www.khansrestaurant.com; 11.45 pm; no smoking area.

Khan's of Kensington SW7 £27 ★
3 Harrington Rd 7581 2900 4–2B
"Very tasty" curries served in a pleasantly *"quiet"* environment, and at
very *"decent prices"* for the area, make this South Kensington Indian
a useful stand-by. / **Details:** 11.15 pm, Fri & Sat 11.45 pm; no smoking area.

Konditor & Cook SE1 £23 ★★
66 The Cut 7620 2700 5–4A
"Delicious and imaginative daytime food" – *"scrummy cakes and
sandwiches"*, *"super pasta"* and so on – make this café/take-away
by the Young Vic immensely popular; it's *"a bit pricey"*, but offers *"all-
round quality"*. / **Details:** 8 pm; closed Sun; no Amex; no smoking area.

Kulu Kulu £19 ★★
76 Brewer St, W1 7734 7316
51-53 Shelton St, WC2 7240 5687
39 Thurloe Pl, SW7 7589 2225
"The best conveyor belt sushi in London" at *"cheap"* prices wins the
highest praise for these *"uninspiring and functional"-looking 'Kaiten'
ventures*; having queued, be prepared to *"eat and go"*. / **Details:** 10 pm,
SW7 10.30 pm; closed Sun; no Amex; no smoking area; no smoking,
WC2; no booking.

The Ladbroke Arms W11 £33 ᵉ
54 Ladbroke Rd 7727 6648
"Restaurant-quality cooking" (and *"at reasonable prices"*, too) makes
this *"small"*, *"homely"* and *"traditional"* Notting Hill boozer consistently
popular; inside, it gets *"very crowded"* (and the outside tables are very
sought-after, too). / **Sample dishes:** pan fried salmon with red wine & olive
risotto; roast lamb with aubergine, red onion & potato; chocolate truffles.
Details: capitalpubcompany.co.uk; 9.45 pm; no Amex; no smoking area; no booking
after 7.30 pm.

Lahore Kebab House E1 £17 ★★
2 Umberston St 7488 2551
The décor *"may make a roadside burger van look appealing"*,
but *"the best kebabs this side of the Indian subcontinent"* have created
a vast reputation for this East End diner (where you BYO – no corkage);
somewhat improbably, a NYC branch is planned. / **Details:** 11.30 pm;
no Amex; need 12+ to book.

Lan Na Thai SW11 £43 ★
2 Lombard Rd 7924 6090 6–1C
This grand but *"authentic"* Battersea Thai is *"tragically under-visited"*,
insist its fans, who say *"it offers excellent service, a beautiful riverside
location, a stunning interior, and exquisite food"*. / **Details:** 10.30 pm.

The Langley WC2 £32 ᵉ
5 Langley St 7836 5005 3–2C
"Good, if basic, food" adds to the attractions of this *"excellent after-
work bar"*; located in an impressive series of Covent Garden cellars,
it's *"great for people-watching"*. / **Sample dishes:** smoked trout hash with
eggy bread; chicken & mushroom pie ; mango & white chocolate mousse.
Details: www.latenightlondon.co.uk; 1 am, Sun 10.30 pm.

Latymers W6   £ 22   ★

157 Hammersmith Rd   8741 2507

"Decent, cheap Thai food served unceremoniously in the back room of an unremarkable pub" – one reporter says it all about this Hammersmith destination. / **Details:** 10 pm; closed Sun D; no smoking; no booking at L.

Launceston Place W8   £ 46   𝔸 ★

1a Launceston Pl   7937 6912   4–1B

"In some ways like the Ivy, but without all the 'celeb' hassle", this *"discreet"*, *"comfortable"* and *"consistently good"* English restaurant, in a pretty Kensington backstreet, retains a loyal following; its *"elegant but not cold"* style makes it a particular romantic favourite. / **Sample dishes:** deep-fried oysters with tartare sauce; Dover sole with parsley butter; apple soufflé. **Details:** www.egami.co.uk; 11.30 pm; closed Sat L & Sun D.

Lemonia NW1   £ 25   𝔸

89 Regent's Park Rd   7586 7454

Always *"full to bursting"*, this large and *"buzzing"* Greek taverna has long been a Primrose Hill landmark; the food is *"not inspiring but dependable"*, and *"cheeky"* service adds to the *"fun"*. / **Sample dishes:** deep-fried aubergine; lamb baked with lemon & herbs; Greek yoghurt with honey & nuts. **Details:** 11.30 pm; closed Sat L & Sun D; no Amex.

Levant W1   £ 40   𝔸

Jason Court, 76 Wigmore St   7224 1111   2–1A

"Refreshing cocktails" and *"amazing belly-dancing"* create a *"permanent party atmosphere"* at this North African bar/restaurant, just north of Oxford Street; *"excellent mezze"* are the highlight of an otherwise *"uninspiring"* menu. / **Details:** www.levantrestaurant.co.uk; 11.30 pm.

The Light House SW19   £ 41   ★

75-77 Ridgway   8944 6338   6–2B

"Fusion food with a strong eastern flavour" generally *"lives up to expectations"* at this trendy Wimbledon venture – *"the best in the area by far"*; shame that *"detached"* or *"slow"* service can take the edge off the experience. / **Sample dishes:** Mozzarella & tomato salad; roast monkfish tail; chocolate mousse tart. **Details:** 10.45 pm; closed Mon L & Sun D; no smoking area.

Lightship E1   £ 37   𝔸

5a Katharine's Way, St Kath's Dock   7481 3123   5–3D

It's *"a very romantic and out-of-the-ordinary experience"* to dine on this *"cosy yet modern"* 19th-century lightship, now moored handily for the City; some find the Scandinavian cooking a bit *"strange"*, but it can be *"very good"*, too. / **Sample dishes:** mussels cooked in beer & wild garlic; Scandinavian meatballs; passion fruit crème brûlée. **Details:** www.lightshipx.com; 10 pm.

Lindsay House W1   £ 65   𝔸

21 Romilly St   7439 0450   3–3A

On a good day, Richard Corrigan's *"romantic"* Georgian Soho townhouse can still be a *"magical"* spot, with *"excellent"* food; service can be *"very slow"*, though, and cooking *"lacking the former 'wow'-factor"* is beginning to make this a place that's *"OK, but nothing special"*. / **Sample dishes:** crayfish gazpacho; stuffed guinea fowl with Madeira jus; banana soufflé. **Details:** www.lindsayhouse.co.uk; 11 pm; closed Sat L & Sun.

Lisboa Patisserie W10   £ 5   ★★

57 Golborne Rd   8968 5242

The *"most wonderful coffee and Portuguese custard tarts in town"* (and a few good savouries) ensure a constant crush at this *"basic"* North Kensington café; *"lovely cakes"*, too. / **Sample dishes:** cheese croissant; vegetable rissoles; custard tarts. **Details:** 7.30 pm; L + early evening only; no Amex; no booking.

sign up for the survey at www.hardens.com   57

LMNT E8   £ 26   A

316 Queensbridge Rd   7249 6727

This "weird and wonderful", "faux-Egyptian" Dalston pub-conversion
is almost universally hailed as "a good laugh"; given that it's
so "affordable", the food is pretty "decent" too. / *Sample dishes:* goats
cheese & beetroot terrine with walnut bread; baked sea bass with olive & lemongrass
dressing; tarte Tatin with green apple sorbet. *Details:* www.lmnt.co.uk; 11 pm;
no Amex.

Locanda Locatelli
Churchill
InterCont'l W1   £ 46   A ★★

8 Seymour St

7935 9088   1–2A

Giorgio Locatelli's "authentic and robust, but exquisitely refined" cooking
helps make his year-old Italian, near Portman Square, a "fabulous"
destination; with its "wonderful, personal service" and "chic" setting,
it's simply "hard to fault" – book well ahead. / *Sample dishes:* cabbage
stuffed with sausage & saffron risotto; sea bream with braised fennel & anchovies;
iced gingerbread mousse with mandarins. *Details:* www.locandalocatelli.com;
11 pm; closed Sun.

The Lord Palmerston NW5   £ 27   A ★

33 Dartmouth Park Hill   7485 1578

Food that's "good-quality and great value" wins nothing but praise for
this Dartmouth Park gastropub; it's "difficult to get a table, but always
worth the wait". / *Sample dishes:* leek & potato soup; pan-fried baby squid;
sticky toffee pudding. *Details:* 10 pm; no Amex; no booking.

Lou Pescadou SW5   £ 37   ★

241 Old Brompton Rd   7370 1057   4–3A

"Mad" service aside, there are few grumbles about this "charismatic"
Earl's Court Gallic fish veteran (now boasting a shiny new façade);
its performance has continually ebbed and flowed over the years,
but it's currently "on top of its game". / *Sample dishes:* seafood crêpe;
grilled brill; île flottante. *Details:* midnight.

Lucky Seven W11   £ 30   ★

127 Westbourne Park Rd   7727 6771

Tom Conran's "hip" retro diner – a study in "supercharged Americana"
– has been a smash hit with Notting Hill hipsters; "you struggle to get
a seat", "share cubicles", "wait forever" and service is "rotten"… but
fans still say it's worth it, as the "heavenly burgers", "ace chips" and
"fab gloopy shakes" are just "soooooo good". / *Sample dishes:* clam
chowder; cheeseburger & fries; triple chocolate fudge brownies. *Details:* 11 pm;
closed Sun D; no credit cards; no booking.

Lundum's SW7   £ 40   A ★

119 Old Brompton Rd   7373 7774   4–2B

"Excellent Danish dining" ("heavenly fish dishes" in particular) and
"very friendly service" are helping to establish quite a reputation for this
"charming" old-style South Kensington restaurant; some reporters find
it the "perfect venue for romance". / *Sample dishes:* marinated herrings;
cured duck with radishes & honey sauce; crème brûlée. *Details:* 11 pm; closed
Sun D.

Ma Cuisine TW1   £ 27   ★★

6 Whitton Rd

8607 9849

If every town had a tiny, no-frills bistro like John McClement's newcomer
(a few doors down from his main gaff), would anyone ever bother going
to France?; it offers wonderful, simple dishes, cheerily and efficiently,
and all at prices that would have seemed reasonable ten years ago!
/ *Sample dishes:* boudin of foie gras with mango salsa; bouillabaisse; crêpe suzette.
Details: 11.30 pm; closed Sun.

Ma Goa SW15 £29 ★
244 Upper Richmond Rd   8780 1767   6–2B
"Fresh, spicey and different" Goan "home cooking" ("more interesting than a standard Indian") attracts a huge local fan club to this "friendly", family-run Putney bistro; ratings drifted a little this year, though.
/ Details: www.ma-goa.com; 11 pm; closed Mon, Tue–Sat D only, Sun open L & D.

Made in Italy SW3 £32 ★
249 King's Rd   7352 1880   4–3C
"Awesome pizzas make up for any other shortcomings", at this "fun" (and very popular) Chelsea destination; just as well, as the "erratic" service can sometimes be "abysmal". / Sample dishes: ravioli with sage butter; seafood platter; cream-filled liqueur sponge. Details: 11.30 pm; closed L Mon-Thurs; no credit cards.

Madhu's UB1 £26 ★★
39 South Rd   8574 1897
It's "worth the trek" for the "fantastic food" served at this "extremely reasonably-priced" Southall subcontinental.
/ Details: www.madhusonline.com; 11.30 pm; closed Tue, Sat L & Sun L.

Maggie Jones's W8 £44 Ⓐ
6 Old Court Pl   7937 6462   4–1A
"Intimacy begins here", say fans of this "uniquely quirky" and "romantic" Kensington "hideaway", where "proper English comfort fare" is dispensed in "hearty" portions; service, though, can be "slow". / Sample dishes: haddock mousse; grilled chicken with cucumber hollandaise; bread & butter pudding. Details: 10.30 pm.

Maison Bertaux W1 £9 Ⓐ★
28 Greek St   7437 6007   3–2A
This "wondrous Soho relic" (1871, or thereabouts) is "a fabulous institution in these days of coffee shop homogeneity"; "and, oh those cakes!". / Sample dishes: no starters; ham & cheese croissant; plum & almond cake. Details: 8 pm; no credit cards; no smoking area; no booking.

Malabar W8 £28 ★
27 Uxbridge St   7727 8800
"Sympathetic spicing" and "original dishes" helps make for a "different take" on the usual curry house répertoire at this "professionally-run" Indian, near Notting Hill Gate – a "consistent" success since time immemorial. / Details: www.malabar-restaurant.co.uk; 11.15 pm; no Amex.

Malabar Junction WC1 £34 Ⓐ★
107 Gt Russell St   7580 5230   1–1C
"Very good south Indian cooking" and an "elegant" atmosphere (certainly by curry house standards) make it well worth seeking out this "reliable" Bloomsbury backstreet spot. / Details: 11.30 pm; no smoking area.

The Mall Tavern W8 £31 ★
71-73 Palace Gardens Ter   7727 3805
With its "good-value" cooking and its "consistently friendly" staff, this year-old gastropub, just off Notting Hill Gate, is an establishment which "deserves to be much busier". / Sample dishes: chargrilled quail with cous cous, pine nut & raisin salad; braised rabbit & thyme ravioli with snail butter; coconut panna cotta with papaya & mint salad. Details: 10.30 pm.

Mandalay W2 £18 ★★
444 Edgware Rd   7258 3696
"Tremendous-value" Burmese food (a cross between Indian and Chinese) plus "the friendliest service imaginable" makes it well worth enduring the "tatty" surroundings of this simple shop-conversion, north of Edgware Road tube. / Details: 10.30 pm; closed Sun; no smoking.

Mandarin Kitchen W2 £33 ★★

14-16 Queensway 7727 9012
It's certainly not the décor ("appalling") or the ambience ("mayhem")
which wins a huge following for this Bayswater Chinese; it must have
something to do with the "lip-smackingly good" dishes ("especially the
lobster with noodles"), which fans hail as "the best seafood in town".
/ **Details:** 11.15 pm.

Mangal E8 £15 ★★

10 Arcola St 7275 8981
"This is the real thing"; there's no menu at this "homely",
but "renowned" Turkish café in deepest Dalston – you choose from the
splendid array of kebabs at the counter and ask which salads and
mezze are 'on'; pricewise, don't sweat – you might get into double
figures; BYO. / **Details:** midnight; no credit cards; need 10+ to book.

Mango Room NW1 £30 Ⓐ★

10 Kentish Town Rd 7482 5065
"Surprisingly refined" food (as well as "fab cocktails") makes this
"very atmospheric" (and always-busy) Camden Town Caribbean more
of a 'culinary' destination than one might expect. / **Details:** 10.45 pm;
closed Mon L; no Amex.

Mango Tree SW1 £47 ★

46 Grosvenor Pl 7823 1888 1–4B
"Amazing" Thai cooking is beginning to win a name for this large, well-
spaced Belgravian – even if it does feel a bit like a "glamorous hotel
dining room"; "disinterested" service (and the odd "tasteless" dish),
however, can still lead to the occasional let-down.
/ **Details:** www.mangotree.org.uk; 10.45 pm; closed Sat L; no smoking area.

Mao Tai £40 ★

96 Draycott Ave, SW3 7225 2500 4–2C
58 New King's Rd, SW6 7731 2520 6–1B
Support for these "quality", "classic" Fulham and (more recently)
Chelsea Chineses remains impressive, although there is the odd
complaint that "complacency has set in" since the opening of the
second branch. / **Details:** www.maotai.co.uk; 11.30 pm; no smoking area.

Matsuri £59 ★

15 Bury St, SW1 7839 1101 2–3D
71 High Holborn, WC1 7430 1970 1–1D
"The skill of the chefs makes for excellent entertainment", at these
"very friendly" and "high-quality" teppan-yakis (which also do "some of
the freshest sushi in London"); the new Holborn branch is rather more
"polished" than the "calm" but "slightly unatmospheric" St James's
original. / **Details:** www.matsuri-restaurant.com.

McClements TW1 £56 ★

2 Whitton Road 8744 9610
No one doubts the quality of the "classic, ancien-régime" cooking
at this "really surprising" Twickenham fixture (which also boasts a wine
list of real note); however, its "formal" style – perhaps intended to catch
the eye of Michelin – does the place no favours. / **Sample dishes:** scallops
with cep risotto; roast pigeon & foie gras wrapped in spinach; baked lime & rhubarb
mousse. **Details:** www.mcclementsrestaurant.com; 10.30 pm; closed Sun D;
no smoking area.

Mediterraneo W11 £35 Ⓐ★

37 Kensington Park Rd 7792 3131
This "hugely popular" Notting Hill neighbourhood Italian – sibling to the
even busier Osteria Basilico – is a "cracking" place, with "fresh, honest"
food and a "lively" (if "cramped" and "noisy") setting; "appalling"
service, however, is not entirely unknown. / **Sample dishes:** pan-fried
mussels & clams; veal with deep-fried courgettes; tiramisu. **Details:** 11.30 pm;
booking: max 8.

Mela WC2 £31 ★
152-156 Shaftesbury Ave 7836 8635 3–2B
"Authentic and moderately-priced Indian food" makes this "interesting"
Theatreland venture one of the West End's best subcontinentals;
"it's rather tacky, but that's half the fun".
/ **Details:** www.melarestaurant.co.uk; 11.30 pm; no smoking area.

Memories of India SW7 £27 ★
18 Gloucester Rd 7581 3734 4–1B
"Reliable and good value" – this civilised curry house remains a useful
South Kensington stand-by. / **Details:** 11.15 pm.

Metrogusto N1 £40 ★
13 Theberton St 7226 9400
"Good modern Italian food" and "understanding service" have helped
make this "relaxed" spot something of an "oasis", just off Islington's
Upper Street; niggles include sometimes "microscopic" portions;
(the former Battersea branch is no more). / **Sample dishes:** grilled stuffed
baby squid with piquant sauce ; calf's liver with sweet balsamic sauce & fried
polenta; parfait of pear & grappa with passionfruit sauce. **Details:** 10.30 pm;
closed Mon; no smoking area; booking: max 6 at weekends.

Mezzo W1 £48 ✗
100 Wardour St 7314 4000 2–2D
Thanks to its "factory" cooking and it staff who "give you the feeling
of being processed", Conran's "loud" and "cavernous" Soho joint strikes
many reporters as "an unfailing disappointment". / **Sample
dishes:** tomato & basil gallete; honey glazed quail, pommes rosti, Muscat grape &
cognac jus; apple & rhubarb crumble. **Details:** www.conran.com; midnight, Thu-Sat
1 am (bar food until 3 am); closed Mon L, Tue L, Sat L & Sun; booking: max 12.

Mildred's W1 £25 ★
45 Lexington St 7494 1634 2–2D
Some still lament the move (a year ago) to "less homely" premises,
but this "veg-tastic" Soho spot still offers "a wide selection
of imaginative and mouthwatering dishes" (including for vegans).
/ **Sample dishes:** spring rolls with chilli jam; veggie burger with cheese; double
chocolate pudding with mocha sauce. **Details:** 11 pm; closed Sun; only Switch;
no smoking; no booking.

Mirabelle W1 £60 𝔸★
56 Curzon St 7499 4636 2–4B
Marco Pierre White's "beautiful" Mayfair flagship provides a haven
of "James Bond-style" sophistication for many reporters, and its "pricey
but marvellous" Gallic cooking still generally wins high approval;
an "endless" wine list plays a strong supporting rôle. / **Sample
dishes:** warm salad of smoked eel & bacon; steak & kidney pudding with swede
purée; peppered pineapple tarte Tatin. **Details:** www.whitestarline.org.uk;
10.45 pm; no smoking area.

Mirch Masala £16 ★★
1416 London Road, SW16 8679 1828 6–2C
213 Upper Tooting Rd, SW17 8672 7500 6–2C
"The food is dynamite", but "don't expect any frills" at these "bustly"
Punjabi canteens, in Norbury and Tooting. / **Details:** midnight; no Amex;
no smoking, SW17.

Mitsukoshi SW1 £53 ★
Dorland Hs, 14-20 Lower Regent St 7930 0317 2–3D
"A corner of Tokyo, not far from Piccadilly Circus"; this "best-kept
secret" store-basement has zero ambience, but its dishes include
arguably "the best traditional sushi in town"; tip from a Japanese
reporter – "eat only at the counter". /
Details: www.mitsukoshi-restaurant.co.uk; 10 pm; closed Sun D; no smoking area.

Miyabi
Great Eastern Hotel EC2 £38 ★

Liverpool St 7618 7100 5–2D

The call of "quality" sushi makes "booking essential" at this small and "stylish" Conran outfit, by Liverpool Street station; even fans, though, often note that it's "expensive", and can get "smokey". / **Details:** www.great-eastern-hotel.co.uk; 10.30 pm; closed Sat & Sun; booking: max 6.

Mju
Millennium Knightsbridge SW1 £64 ★

16-17 Sloane St 7201 6330 4–1D

Shame it feels like an "airport-lounge"; this Knightsbridge dining room offers "innovative" oriental cuisine that's "exquisite" and "divinely presented" – "if the place had better ambience, it would be one of the hottest destinations in town". / **Sample dishes:** lobster mousse with wasabi jelly; rack of lamb with miso & water chestnuts; orange, honey & black pepper sorbet. **Details:** 10.30pm; closed Sun.

Momo W1 £44 𝔸

25 Heddon St 7434 4040 2–2C

"Fabulous, buzzing and atmospheric", this "trendy" West End Moroccan remains a key party and romantic destination; even those in love with its "magic décor", though, can find the food "average and incredibly overpriced", and service "verging on rude". / **Sample dishes:** cod carpaccio with alfalfa & caviar; seared tuna with chickpea polenta; quince & clementines with rose water. **Details:** www.momoresto.com; 11.30 pm; closed Sun L.

Mon Plaisir WC2 £43 𝔸

19-21 Monmouth St 7836 7243 3–2B

This "thoroughly characterful" Covent Garden "old-timer" is renowned as a "little bit of Paris", with "unpretentious" cooking and "friendly" staff; the pre-theatre deal remains "great value", but sliding ratings support those who complain of "slipping standards". / **Sample dishes:** onion, black olive & anchovy tart; confit duck in red wine sauce; cocobut mousse with pineapple gratinée. **Details:** www.monplaisir.co.uk; 11.15 pm; closed Sat L & Sun.

Monkeys SW3 £55 𝔸★

1 Cale St 7352 4711 4–2C

"The best game in England" and "wonderful wine" are highlights at this "eccentric" Chelsea Green fixture; the "fairly simple" Anglo-French fare finds much favour at any time of year, though, as does the "charming", "old-school" ambience. / **Sample dishes:** lobster & leek terrine; roast partridge with traditional trimmings; sorbet. **Details:** 10 pm; closed Sat & Sun; no Amex; booking: max 8.

Monsieur Max TW12 £54 𝔸★★

133 High St 8979 5546

"As close to being in France as possible" (and not just by Hampton Hill standards), this "surprising" suburban "gem" is "worth a large detour" – it was once again hailed in practically every report as "outstanding in all respects"; prices "edge ever upwards", but few seem to begrudge the cost. / **Sample dishes:** foie gras & duck terrine with Sauternes jelly; John Dory with champagne & sorrel risotto; liqorice meringue. **Details:** 9.30pm; closed Sat L.

Moro EC1 £39 𝔸★★

34-36 Exmouth Mkt 7833 8336 5–1A

"Still maintaining incredibly high standards", this "innovative" and fashionable Clerkenwell establishment offers "very interesting" – sometimes "transcendent" – Moorish dishes in a "vibrant" (and "loud") contemporary setting. / **Sample dishes:** Russian salad with smoked anchovies; lamb with roast beetroot & parsley sauce; chocolate & apricot tart. **Details:** www.moro.co.uk; 10.30 pm; closed Sat L & Sun.

Mr Kong WC2   £ 23   ★
21 Lisle St   7437 7341   3–3A
Some consider it "Chinatown's best Cantonese", and this "basic" old-timer wins consistent praise for its "unusual" range of "delicious" dishes (chef's specials in particular); "don't sit in the basement if you can help it". | Details: 2.45 am.

Mr Wing SW5   £ 43   A ★
242-244 Old Brompton Rd   7370 4450   4–2A
*"A fabulous 'jungle' setting, and the food's not bad either" – this "crazy" but "reliably good" Earl's Court Chinese remains "one of the classiest orientals in town"; jazz some nights. |
Details: www.mrwing.com; midnight.*

Naked Turtle SW14   £ 38   A
505 Upper Richmond Rd   8878 1995   6–2A
*"Singing waitresses" feature in many reports on this "relaxed" Sheen wine bar – a perennial local "favourite", where most (but not all) reporters are pleased with their scoff. | Sample dishes: sweet chicory tart; wild boar with sweet potato mash & four-berry sauce; peach & vanilla trifle.
Details: www.naked-turtle.com; 11 pm; D only, ex Sun open L & D; no smoking area.*

Nam Long SW5   £ 33   A
159 Old Brompton Rd   7373 1926   4–2B
The service can be "comically rude" and the food (Vietnamese) is "average", but "excellent cocktails" and "great people-watching" help make this "expensive" bar/restaurant a "fun" South Kensington destination. | Details: 11.30 pm; closed Sat L & Sun; no trainers.

Nautilus NW6   £ 26   ★
27-29 Fortune Green Rd   7435 2532
"Fresh fish, well cooked, both deep-fried and grilled" maintains a solid reputation for this (Kosher) West Hampstead chippy. | Details: 10 pm; closed Sun; no Amex; no booking.

New Mayflower W1   £ 26   ★
68-70 Shaftesbury Ave   7734 9207   3–3A
"If you don't mind rough-and-ready décor", this Chinatown fixture can be an "outstanding" choice (especially in the early hours); "it's always worth asking the staff for a recommendation". | Details: 3.45 am; D only.

New Tayyab E1   £ 15   A ★
83 Fieldgate St   7247 9543   5–2D
This East End pub-conversion offers a "cramped and loud, eating experience", but for "authentic Indian cuisine it cannot be beaten" (and the "spiced lamb chops are to die for"); beware "big queues"; (unlicensed, but you can BYO – no corkage). | Details: www.tayyabs.co.uk; 11.30 pm; no booking at L.

Nicolas Bar à Vins SW10   £ 22   ★
442 King's Rd   7352 9706   4–3B
For a truly Gallic experience, seek out the new World's End wine bar outpost of France's leading chain of wine merchants, which offers simple, well-realised food at reasonable prices; the setting is "naff", but wine at retail prices offers much compensation. | Sample dishes: snails on fennel sauce with garlic bread; smoked salmon with salad, lemon & kippers; nougat ice cream. Details: www.nicolas.com; 11 pm.

Nobu
Metropolitan Hotel W1   **£ 65**   ★
Old Park Lane   7447 4747   2–4A
*"Mind-blowing" Japanese/South American fusion cuisine has won
a legendary reputation for this Mayfair celebrity haunt; the growing
feeling, however, that "it's not all it's cracked up to be" is evidenced by a
surge of complaints about "absurd" prices, "arrogant" service and
"drab" décor. / Sample dishes: 'new-style' sashimi; black cod with miso;
chocolate Bento box. Details: www.noburestaurants.com; 10.15 pm, Fri & Sat
11 pm; closed Sat L & Sun L; no smoking area.*

North Sea Fish WC1   **£ 27**   ★
7-8 Leigh St   7387 5892
*Its Bloomsbury premises – oddly reminiscent of a seaside tea shop –
are "in need of a makeover", but this simple chippy still serves some
of "the best fish and chips". / Sample dishes: smoked cods roe salad; battered
cod & chips; sherry trifle. Details: www.northseafishrestaurant.co.uk; 10.30 pm;
closed Sun.*

Noto EC2   **£ 26**   ★
2-3 Bassishaw Highwalk   7256 9433   5–2B
*"Queues go quickly" at this "clinical" City canteen, which is always
"packed with Japanese ex-pats"; a "huge turnover" ensures
"the freshest food" – in particular "good fast noodles", sushi, sashimi
and tempura, all at "unbeatable" prices. / Details: www.noto.co.uk;
9.45 pm; closed Sat & Sun; no Amex; no smoking at L.*

Noura SW1   **£ 38**   ★
16 Hobart Pl   7235 9444   1–4B
*"Delicious Lebanese food in great variety" and "very attentive" service
are winning a loyal following for this "upmarket", "spacious" and
"relaxed" modern restaurant, near Victoria station; the "great-value
lunch" is a particular plus. / Details: www.noura-brasseries.co.uk; 11.30 pm.*

The Oak W2   **£ 34**   Ⓐ ★
137 Westbourne Park Rd
7221 3599
*"A magical revamp of a grotty boozer" – this "buzzing" Notting Hill
hangout is "more restaurant than pub" these days, offering a simple
menu, on which "great" (if "not cheap") pizza is a highlight; the re-
opening of the more ambitious upstairs dining room is planned for late-
2003. / Sample dishes: spiced aubergine salad; char-grilled longhorn beef; apple
tart. Details: 10.30 pm; closed Mon L; no booking.*

Odette's NW1   **£ 42**
130 Regent's Park Rd   7586 5486
*Long-time owner Simone Green sold this "truly lovely" Primrose Hill
institution (known for its "low lighting, with mirrors everywhere") in the
summer of 2003; let's hope the new régime can maintain its
"impressive" all-round performance. / Sample dishes: sea scallop risotto;
roast lamb with tempura courgettes; chocolate mousse. Details: 11 pm; closed
Sat L & Sun D.*

Odin's W1   **£ 41**   Ⓐ
27 Devonshire St   7935 7296   1–1A
*This "calm", "old world" Marylebone fixture has a "lovely" feel
(to which "faultless service" and the late Peter Langan's art collection
make no small contribution), and "is suited to both business and
pleasure"; in comparison, the food is "not terribly exciting". / Sample
dishes: smoked eel mousse with horseradish; Cumberland sausages with mash &
onion sauce; date & ginger pudding. Details: www.langansrestaurants.co.uk; 11 pm;
closed Sat & Sun; no smoking area.*

Ye Olde Cheshire Cheese EC4 £29 A X

145 Fleet St 7353 6170 5–2A

For "great character", it's hard to beat this famous City inn, rebuilt after the Great Fire; some do like its "traditional" fare, but there were more reporters this year who thought the place "best left to tourists".
/ **Sample dishes:** duck & port pâté with Cumberland sauce; roast pork with apple & cranberry stuffing; treacle sponge & custard.
Details: www.yeoldecheshirecheese.com; 9 pm; closed Sun D; no smoking area at L.

Oliveto SW1 £37 ★

49 Elizabeth St 7730 0074 1–4A

"Lovely fresh, thin pizzas", "great pasta" and other "simple" dishes are winning an ever more following for this "relaxed" and "buzzy" – but "hard-edged" – Belgravia Sardinian. / **Details:** 11.30 pm; booking: max 7 at D.

Olivo SW1 £40 ★

21 Eccleston St 7730 2505 1–4B

"Good, simple rustic food" wins wide-ranging support for this "reliable", "friendly" only "Sardinian; it offers "good value", by Belgravia standards. / **Sample dishes:** Mozzarella with marinated aubergines; seafood risotto; lemon tart. **Details:** 11 pm; closed Sat L & Sun L.

1 Lombard Street EC3 £50

1 Lombard St 7929 6611 5–3C

"Solid cooking, well served" and a "perfect position" by Bank maintain this "airy" former banking hall – with its "bustling" brasserie and its "quiet", and pricier, dining room – as the City's most popular business venue; even many expense-accounters know that prices are "ridiculous", though, and think service "should be improved". / **Sample dishes:** smoked haddock with quail's eggs & mustard sauce; veal with caramelised artichokes & truffles; liquorice crème brûlée with blackcurrant coulis.
Details: www.1lombardstreet.com; 10 pm; closed Sat & Sun.

Opium W1 £50 A

1a Dean St 7287 9608 2–1D

"Good-looking" service, "great" décor and a "very cool" atmosphere make this lavish Soho basement Vietnamese a popular destination, especially at weekends; the "average and overpriced" cooking is rather beside the point. / **Sample dishes:** chicken satay; Vietnamese noodles with monkfish; banana spring rolls. **Details:** 9.30 pm; D only, closed Sun.

Orrery W1 £61 A ★

55 Marylebone High St 7616 8000 1–1A

"Conran's culinary champion" is an "airy" first-floor Marylebone dining room (with "good views" over a churchyard), that boasts "superb" Gallic cuisine and "assured" service; it is "very expensive", though, and just a touch "soulless". / **Sample dishes:** Bayonne ham with celeriac; seared tuna with coco beans; peach soufflé. **Details:** www.orrery.co.uk; 10.30 pm.

Oslo Court NW8 £47 A ★

Prince Albert Rd 7722 8795

"A nostalgic glimpse of what a first-class restaurant used to be like"; "gargantuan" portions from a "'70s-comfort" menu – served by "the friendliest staff around" – maintain the unique appeal of this north London institution; but "can there really be that many birthdays on one night?" / **Sample dishes:** scallop & bacon salad; sea bass; raspberry tart with apple pancakes. **Details:** 11 pm; closed Sun.

Osteria Basilico W11 £35 A ★

29 Kensington Park Rd 7727 9957

If only there were more places like this "brilliant" Notting Hill linchpin, where "generous", "rustic" dishes (with pizza a top tip) are served by "friendly" staff in "intimate" (if "occasionally chaotic") surroundings. / **Sample dishes:** beef carpaccio with pesto & Parmesan; pan-fried swordfish with sun-dried tomatoes; chocolate cake with hot chocolate sauce. **Details:** 11 pm; no booking, Sat L.

(Brasserie)
Oxo Tower SE1 £41 A✗
Barge House St   7803 3888   5–3A
"Impressive" views ("I'm a Londoner and I'm still always amazed")
make Harvey Nichols's eighth-floor South Bank eyrie a popular venue
for business (especially with out-of-towners) and romance; "without its
location it would be empty", though – the staff "aren't really
interested", and the "bland" cooking comes at "extortionate" prices.
/ Sample dishes: snails with mushrooms and smoked bacon; roast pheasant with
caramelised endive; lemon parfait with rhubarb. Details: www.harveynichols.com;
11.30 pm.

The Painted Heron SW10 £39 ★
112 Cheyne Walk
7351 5232   4–3B
"Original" and "subtle" cuisine at "reasonable prices" is drawing
a growing following to this rather "serene" year-old Indian in a Chelsea
backstreet; albeit slowly, it seems to be winning the reputation
it deserves. / Details: www.thepaintedheron.com; 11 pm; no Amex.

Pampa £39 ★
4 Northcote Rd, SW11   7924 1167   6–2C
60 Battersea Rise, SW11   7924 4774   6–2C
Brave the "disinterested" service and the "uncomfortable"
surroundings, and you usually get a "brilliant" steak at these Battersea
Argentineans; standards generally, though, seem to be slipping. /
Details: 11 pm, Fri & Sat 11.30 pm; D only.

Pan-Asian Canteen
Paxton's Head SW1 £25 ★
153 Knightsbridge   7589 6627   4–1D
For "Knightsbridge value", it's difficult to beat the "great, innovative
noodle and rice dishes" on offer at this stylish, first-floor dining room
of a palatial Victorian boozer; service, at communal tables,
is "very quick".
/ Details: 10.30 pm; no smoking area.

Paolo W1 £41 ★
16 Percy St   7637 9900   1–1C
"Very good pasta" and "attentive" service win particular praise for this
rather barely furnished Italian yearling off Charlotte Street; (it also has
a nearby sibling, confusingly called Da Paolo, which fans similarly hail
as "a little gem"). / Sample dishes: artichoke, rocket & pecorino salad;
tagliatelle with wild mushrooms, Parma ham & peas; pear poached in red wine &
cinnamon mousse with chocolate ice cream . Details: www.paolorestaurants.com;
11pm; closed Sun.

Pasha SW7 £40 A
1 Gloucester Rd   7589 7969   4–1B
"Still a 'Casablanca' experience", say fans of this "sumptuous, evocative
and romantic" South Kensington Moroccan; service is so-so, though,
and the cooking can be a "mystery mush". / Sample dishes: mezze;
chicken with preserved lemons; Turkish delight crème brûlée.
Details: www.pasha-restaurant.co.uk; 11pm; closed Sun L; booking: max 10
at weekends.

Passione W1 £44 ★
10 Charlotte St   7636 2833   1–1C
"Genarro is a genius", say fans of the "creative, light and delicious"
Italian fare at this "stark" and "cramped" Fitzrovia hotspot;
some reporters do find it "overpriced". / Sample dishes: grilled vegetables
with buffalo mozzarella; grilled wild boar with mushrooms & grilled polenta; hazelnut
cake with mixed berry sauce. Details: www.passione.co.uk; 10.15 pm; closed
Sat L & Sun.

Patara £39 ★

3&7 Maddox St, W1   7499 6008   2–2C
181 Fulham Rd, SW3   7351 5692   4–2C
9 Beauchamp Pl, SW3   7581 8820   4–1C
"Good"-to-"fantastic" food – with some "different" dishes – is the
theme of almost all reports on these unassuming Thai restaurants;
for Mayfair and Chelsea, prices are "very reasonable", too. /
Details: 10.30 pm; no smoking area.

Pâtisserie Valerie £21

17 Motcomb St, SW1   7245 6161   4–1D
105 Marylebone High St, W1   7935 6240   1–1A
44 Old Compton St, W1   7437 3466   3–2A
27 Kensington Church St, W8   7937 9574   4–1A
"Great croissants" (and a "fab fry-up" too, at some branches) help
make these Gallic pâtiseries key destinations at which to start the day;
at other times, they're "ideal for a quick snack... or a slow cake";
service, though, can be "stroppy". / **Details:** www.patisserie-valerie.co.uk;
7 pm, Sun 6 pm (Soho 7 pm); no smoking area; no booking.

The Pen SW6 £35 A★

51 Parsons Green Ln   7371 8517   6–1B
Above a busy bar, this first-floor dining room, near Parsons's Green tube,
has long made a "cool and relaxed" destination, where "friendly" staff
serve dishes that are "well-cooked" and "interesting".
/ **Details:** www.thepenrestaurant.co.uk; 11 pm; closed Sun D; no Amex.

Pétrus
Berkeley Hotel SW1 £80

Wilton Pl   7235 1200   4–1D
Over four years, Ramsay-associate Marcus Wareing built up a "first-
class" (if "rather stuffy") culinary temple in St James's which re-opened
in Knightsbridge in September 2003 (as we go to press) – let's hope
the move works better it did for Tante Claire (RIP), which was London's
top restaurant... till it moved here! / **Sample dishes:** frogs legs with lemon
and cumin; monkfish with sea urchin sauce; pineapple panna cotta.
Details: 10.45 pm; booking: max 6.

Philpotts Mezzaluna NW2 £33 ★

424 Finchley Rd   7794 0455
"A different set menu every night" adds interest to a visit to this "nice",
"consistent" and "good-value" Italian, on the way to Golders Green.
/ **Sample dishes:** rocket salad with pine nuts & balsamic vinegar; roast plaice with
aubergine & pesto; strawberry tiramisu. **Details:** www.philpotts-mezzaluna.com;
11 pm; closed Mon & Sat L.

Phoenix Palace NW1 £31 ★★

3-5 Glentworth St   7486 3515   1–1A
"Excellent dim sum" helps maintain a high level of enthusiasm for this
comfortable and "authentic" Chinese, near Baker Street tube.
/ **Details:** 11.15 pm.

Pied à Terre W1 £68 ★

34 Charlotte St   7636 1178   1–1C
Shane Osborne's "elegant" and "imaginative" Gallic cooking is helping
to maintain the lofty reputation of this Fitzrovia "gastro-temple";
beware the 'curse of Michelin', though – now the place has regained its
second star, reports of a "stiff" or "sterile" ambience are notably
on the up! / **Sample dishes:** celeriac, chive & salt cod soup; braised lamb with
deep-fried tongue & olives; mandarin parfait with lemon curd.
Details: www.pied.a.terre.co.uk; 10.30 pm; closed Sat L & Sun; no smoking area;
booking: max 8.

Pizza Metro SW11   £ 29   A★★

64 Battersea Rise   7228 3812   6–2C

This Battersea pizzeria – "every ex-pat Italian's favourite" –
may present a picture of "complete mayhem", but it has a huge
following, thanks to its pizza "right from Naples" ("sold by the metre"),
its "incredible" antipasti and its "truly Italian" service. | Sample
dishes: *antipasti; pizza with salami & olives; tiramisu.* **Details:** *11 pm; closed Mon,*
Tue-Fri D only, Sat & Sun open L & D.

Pizzeria Castello SE1   £ 21   ★

20 Walworth Rd   7703 2556

"The best pizzas in London" maintain the "garlic-tastic" appeal of this
"friendly" Elephant & Castle destination; its current site – "iffy" décor
and all – is scheduled for demolition some time in 2004. | Sample
dishes: *prawns in garlic; four cheese pizza; cheesecake.* **Details:** *11 pm, Fri & Sat*
11.30 pm; closed Sat L & Sun.

Pizzeria Oregano N1   £ 27   ★

19 St Albans Pl   7288 1123

"Tucked away off Upper Street", this small and "friendly" café is hailed
by local fans for its "handmade, true Italian pizzas"; doubters find the
whole place pretty "ordinary", though. | Details: 10.45 pm; closed Mon;
no Amex; no smoking area.

PJ's SW3   £ 39   ✗

52 Fulham Rd   7581 0025   4–2C

For "a good buzzy brunch" – or for "watching South Kensington's
beautiful people" – this "fun" American bar/diner has many fans;
"great burgers" aside, though, the fare is "expensively average",
and service "slow". | Sample dishes: crispy duck; fillet steak; warm chocolate
brownie. **Details:** *11.45 pm; no smoking area.*

The Place Below EC2   £ 19   A★

St Mary-le-Bow, Cheapside   7329 0789   5–2C

Veggie food that's "often very good" and an "unusual" church-crypt
setting make this self-service cafeteria a popular City troughing spot;
it can seem a bit "expensive" for what it is, though.
| Details: www.theplacebelow.co.uk; L only, closed Sat & Sun; no Amex; no smoking;
need 15+ to book.

Poissonnerie de l'Avenue SW3   £ 53   ★

82 Sloane Ave   7589 2457   4–2C

This "elegant" Gallic fish restaurant of long standing remains
a "consistently reliable" option near Brompton Cross; even a
septuagenarian reporter, though, found the atmosphere on the "stuffy"
side. | Sample dishes: lobster & salmon ravioli in cream sauce; seared tuna with
salsa; lemon tart. **Details:** *11.30 pm; closed Sun.*

(Ognisko Polskie)
The Polish Club SW7   £ 34   A

55 Prince's Gate, Exhibition Rd   7589 4635   4–1C

For "faded grandeur", few places match this "quiet" and "institutional"
– but "charming" and "intriguing" – émigrés club, near the Science
Museum, which offers solid (if rather "hit-and-miss") Polish fare;
"the rear terrace is unbeatable on a summer night". | Sample
dishes: *beetroot soup with rye bread; pork with red & white cabbage; chocolate &*
almond cheesecake. **Details:** *11 pm; jacket & tie.*

Le Pont de la Tour SE1   £ 63   A

36d Shad Thames   7403 8403   5–4D

With its "wonderful" riverside position, "stunning views", "convenience
for the City" and a "wine list like War & Peace", Conran's grand Gallic
restaurant near Tower Bridge has much going for it; prices are
"way OTT", though, and standards strike many reporters
as "consistently unimpressive". | Sample dishes: Dorset crab & avocado with
gazpacho dressing; pot-roasted lamb with cumin & carrots; vanilla & gingerbread
parfait. **Details:** *www.conran.com; 11 pm; closed Sat L.*

Popeseye £ 35 ★

108 Blythe Rd, W14 7610 4578
277 Upper Richmond Rd, SW15 8788 7733
These Olympia and Putney bistros may be "small, no-frills" joints, but many reporters tip them as home to "simply the best steak and chips in town"; the wine list includes "some serious clarets at reasonable prices". / Sample dishes: fillet steak with fat chips; apple crumble. Details: 10.30 pm; D only, closed Sun; no credit cards.

Porchetta Pizzeria £ 20 ★

33 Boswell St, WC1 7242 2434 1–1D
141-142 Upper St, N1 7288 2488
147 Stroud Green Rd, N4 7281 2892
"Come early, or queue", for these "frenetic" and "brightly-lit" Italians, which have won a huge fan club (the Finsbury Park original in particular) thanks to "pizzas as big as Wales" and "pastas large enough to feed the Vatican" – and all at "bargain basement prices"! / Details: midnight, WC1 10.30 pm; WC1 closed Sat L & Sun, N1 & N4 D only Mon-Thurs; no Amex; need 5+ to book.

La Porte des Indes W1 £ 48 A★

32 Bryanston St 7224 0055 1–2A
*"Sumptuous décor" creates a "memorable" ambience at this "hidden underground palace," near Marble Arch, and its "interesting" Franco-Indian cuisine is hailed by fans as "deserving more recognition"; 'rapport prix/qualité', however, has yet to match its sibling, the Blue Elephant.
/ Details: www.la-porte-des-indes.com; 11.30pm; closed Sat L.*

La Poule au Pot SW1 £ 43 A

231 Ebury St 7730 7763 4–2D
Stay on the right side of the "idiosyncratic, and very French" service, and the "cosy" charms of this "old Pimlico haunt" – yet again voted London's Most Romantic Restaurant – are hard to beat; it serves up "gutsy" bourgeois fare in "dingy" – but "fabulous and intimate" – candlelit surroundings. / Sample dishes: pork & foie gras terrine; roast lamb with green beans; chocolate mousse. Details: 11 pm.

(Tapa Room)
The Providores W1 £ 30 A★

109 Marylebone High St 7935 6175 1–1A
An "imaginative" menu of "light and interesting" dishes (from breakfast onwards) – plus "good wines" and "great juices and coffee" – has made this "fun" and "friendly" bar/café something of a Marylebone linchpin. / Sample dishes: tamarind laksa with prawn dumplings; crispy pork with chorizo mash & lotus root; chocolate mousse cake with wattleseed cream. Details: www.theprovidores.co.uk; 10.30 pm.

Putney Bridge SW15 £ 55 A★

Embankment 8780 1811 6–1B
"At last, the promise is being realised" – a combination of "great" views, "fabulous" (and "beautifully presented") Gallic cooking and "unpretentious" service are making this "swanky", '90s landmark building a true 'destination'; expect a "heavy bill", though. / Sample dishes: roast quail wrapped in vine leaves; sea bass with Jabugo ham & truffles; black fig tart with almond milk sorbet. Details: www.putneybridgerestaurant.com; 10.30pm; closed Sun D.

QC
Chancery Court Hotel WC1 £ 53 ★

252 High Holborn 7829 7000 1–1D
"Very creative" contemporary cooking is the highlight at this "impressive" but "cavernous" former banking hall between the West End and the City; arguably the setting is "too big to have any real ambience", but it makes "an excellent location for a business lunch". / Sample dishes: rabbit ravioli with caramelised king prawns; butternut squash & truffle lasagne; orange cake with candied fennel. Details: www.renaissancehotels.com/loncc; 10.15 pm; closed Sun; no smoking area.

Quaglino's SW1   **£ 49**   ✗
16 Bury St   7930 6767   2–3D
It's still hailed for its "glamour and glitz" in some quarters, but this "incredibly noisy" Conran brasserie in St James's is, for many reporters, just "a huge restaurant that always disappoints". / **Sample dishes:** foie gras terrine with fig jam; roast guinea fowl with buttered spinach; pineapple with ginger & basil. **Details:** www.conran.com; midnight, Fri & Sat 1 am.

Racine SW3   **£ 35**   ★
239 Brompton Rd
7584 4477   4–2C
"French cooking as it should be" and "outstanding service" have – in one short year – won a tremendous following for this refreshingly "untheatrical" Knightsbridge brasserie; in a "generally overpriced part of town", it offers "surprisingly good value". / **Sample dishes:** garlic & saffron mousse; rabbit with mustard & smoked bacon; Mont Blanc dessert. **Details:** 10.30 pm.

Ragam W1   **£ 21**   ★
57 Cleveland St   7636 9098   1–1B
"Why oh why don't they sort out the shabby premises?"; this "friendly" but cramped fixture (in the shadow of the Telecom Tower) delivers "splendid and tasty" South Indian cooking. / **Details:** 10.30 pm.

Rani N3   **£ 23**   ★
7 Long Ln   8349 4386
"Fantastic" veggie South Indian cooking ensures that this North Finchley veteran is still well worth seeking out. / **Details:** www.raniuk.com; 10 pm; D only; no smoking.

Ranoush   **£ 19**   ★
338 Kings Rd, SW3   7352 0044   4–3C
131-135 Earls Court Rd, SW5   7352 0044   4–2A
43 Edgware Rd, W2   7723 5929
"Delicious" cheap kebabs (and juices) "transport you to the Lebanon", at this "wonderful" "late-night diner" in Bayswater; new branches are set to open in Chelsea and Earl's Court.

Rasa   **£ 32**   ★★
6 Dering St, W1   7629 1346   2–2B
55 Stoke Newington Church St, N16   7249 0344
"Stupendous" Keralan vegetarian dishes that "surprise and defy description" (even by the "informative" staff) inspire many positive reports on this exemplary duo; Mayfair is good, but Stokie (formula price £21) is both better and cheaper. / **Details:** 10.30 pm; N16 closed Mon L-Thu L, W1 closed Sun L; no smoking.

Rasa Samudra W1   **£ 37**   ★
5 Charlotte St   7637 0222   1–1C
"Delicious and authentic" cooking wins high praise for this "superb Keralan (SW Indian) seafood and vegetarian restaurant" in Fitzrovia, notwithstanding décor that's "like a badly-furnished front room". / **Details:** www.rasarestaurants.com; 10.30 pm; closed Sun L; no smoking area.

Rasa Travancore N16   **£ 26**   ★
56 Stoke Newington Church St   7249 1340
"Inventive and well-cooked dishes" (here, unusually for the chain, including meat) win very strong support for this Stoke Newington south Indian; "it could use more windows", though. / **Details:** www.rasarestaurants.com; 10.45 pm; D only; no smoking.

sign up for the survey at www.hardens.com

La Rascasse
Café Grand Prix W1   £ 36   ★

50a Berkeley St   7629 0808   2–3C

*It's a shame this "OTT" Belle Epoque-style Mayfair restaurant, now a
year in business, can still seem "quiet"; reporters say its "authentic"
Gallic fare is "under-rated", and that its service is "very good" –
the lunch deal is "great" too. / **Sample dishes:** red snapper, tiger prawns &
scallop parcel with new potatoes; caramelised sea-scallop, lettuce veloute & Serrano
ham; pear tart with red wine syrup. **Details:** www.cafegrandprix.com; 10.30 pm;
closed Sat L & Sun.*

The Real Greek N1   £ 42

15 Hoxton Market   7739 8212   5–1D

*"Marvellously un-Greek, Greek food" (and a "beguiling Greek wine list")
has carved a big name for Theodore Kyriakou's stylish Hoxton venture;
sometimes, though, it can seem "long on hype, and short on delivery"
nowadays. / **Sample dishes:** pork, leek & prune terrine; pork stuffed with spiced
peaches & feta; baklava with peaches & ouzo sorbet.*
Details: *www.therealgreek.co.uk; 10.30 pm; closed Sun; no Amex.*

The Real Greek
Souvlaki & Bar EC1      £ 24   𝔸★★

140-142 St John St
7253 7234   5–1A

*Bound to be "a winner" – this "lively" new Smithfield sibling to the Real
Greek offers a stripped-down menu of "smart Greek street food",
alongside a "very reasonable and good" list of Hellenic wines and
spirits; the "charming" staff, though, can seem "over-stretched".
/ **Details:** www.therealgreek.co.uk; 10.45 pm; no Amex.*

Rebato's SW8   £ 26   𝔸

169 South Lambeth Rd   7735 6388   6–1D

*This "authentic" Spaniard draws loyal supporters to sunny Vauxhall;
the "classic" tapas bar at the front is more popular than the rear
restaurant (which is "like the dining room of a '70s package hotel").
/ **Sample dishes:** stuffed roast piquillo peppers; kidneys in sherry with
mushrooms & bacon; crema Catalan. **Details:** www.rebatos.com; 10.45 pm; closed
Sat L & Sun.*

Red Fort W1   £ 52   ★

77 Dean St   7437 2525   3–2A

*"The cost is high, but the experience is worth it" – a typical reaction
to this "up-to-date" Soho Indian, that's "much improved since its
revamp last year"; service, though, can be "rather pompous".
/ **Details:** www.redfort.co.uk; 11.30 pm; closed Sat L & Sun L.*

The Red Pepper W9   £ 32   ★

8 Formosa St   7266 2708

*"Still the best pizzas in London, if you don't mind having someone's
elbow in your face"; the 'appeal' of this, "appallingly crowded" and
"insanely busy" Maida Vale spot – with its "almost rude" service –
is just the same as ever. / **Sample dishes:** sautéed squid with chilli, spinach &
red pepper; pizza with olives, anchovies, capers & Mozzarella; chocolate mousse.
Details: www.theredpeppergroup.com; 11 pm; closed weekday L; no Amex.*

Red Veg W1   £ 9   ★

95 Dean St   7437 3109   2–1D

*It's a no-meat – sorry, no mean – feat to produce a "decent veggie
burger", but that's a trick that's been mastered by this "cramped,
but excellent" café/take-away, in Soho. / **Sample dishes:** breaded
mushrooms.veggie burger with cheese; **Details:** www.redveg.com; 10 pm; closed
Sun; no credit cards; no smoking; no booking.*

Redmond's SW14 £ 43 ★

170 Upper R'mond Rd West   8878 1922   6–1A
The Redmond family's very "professional" – and not just by East Sheen
standards – venture offers an "imaginative and well-executed" menu,
"a good wine list" and "friendly" service. / **Sample dishes:** leek & ginger
soup with scallops; roast pigeon with thyme polenta & seared foie gras; berry trifle
with blood orange sorbet. **Details:** 10.30 pm; closed Sat L & Sun D.

Restaurant One-O-One
Sheraton Park Tower SW1 £ 70 ★★

William St, 101 Knightsbridge
7290 7101   4–1D
"London's only true gourmet fish and seafood restaurant" serves some
absolutely "phenomenal" dishes; the "airport lobby" style of its
Knightsbridge quarters, however, holds Pascal Proyart's cooking back
from the recognition it deserves. / **Sample dishes:** salmon carpaccio;
peppered fillet steak; strawberry cheesecake. **Details:** 10.30 pm; no smoking area.

The Ritz W1 £ 86 𝔸

150 Piccadilly   7493 8181   2–4C
"Straight from a fairy tale", this "glamorous" Louis XVI-style dining
room offers a "fabulous and unique" venue, tailor-made for romance;
sadly, its perennially "undistinguished" cuisine comes at "Monopoly
money" prices. / **Sample dishes:** spiced potted lobster; monkfish with potato
cakes & pancetta; prune & armagnac parfait. **Details:** www.theritzlondon.com;
11 pm; no jeans or trainers.

Riva SW13 £ 44 ★

169 Church Rd   8748 0434   6–1A
Andreas Riva's "excellent" north Italian cooking has long held foodies
in thrall to this "cramped" Barnes fixture; many reporters still feel it has
"no atmosphere", though. / **Sample dishes:** antipasto; grilled tuna steak with
green beans & sundried tomatoes; sweet milk gnocchi with apple & honey.
Details: 11 pm, Fri & Sat 11.30 pm; closed Sat L.

The River Café W6 £ 56

Thames Whf, Rainville Rd   7386 4200
"Brilliant, simple Italian food" – using "exquisite ingredients" –
has made this obscurely-sited Hammersmith riverside "canteen" into
a legend; a huge proportion of reporters, though – including many fans
– find its "ludicrous" prices increasingly "hard to justify". / **Sample
dishes:** asparagus risotto; crispy Bresse pigeon; chocolate nemesis.
Details: 9.30 pm; closed Sun D.

Rocket £ 28 𝔸

4-6 Lancashire Ct, W1   7629 2889
Brewhouse St, SW15   8789 7875
"Always buzzing", these "young" and "cool" venues offer "tasty" grub
(especially pizza); they are "good-value", too, especially considering the
locations – the hidden-away Mayfair-mews original now has a "superbly
situated" Putney riverside sibling. / **Details:** www.freedombrewery.com;
SW15 10.30 pm, W1 11.30 pm; W1 closed Sun.

Roussillon SW1 £ 56 ★★

16 St Barnabas St   7730 5550   4–2D
Monsieur Gauthier's "consistent and creative" Gallic cooking is at last
winning this Pimlico backstreet spot the following it deserves; a "quiet"
atmosphere that some reporters find "romantic" still strikes others
as rather "hotel-like", though, but "thoughtful and cheerful" service
provides compensation. / **Sample dishes:** millefeuille of asparagus & morels;
crunchy-skin sea bass with salsify in ham; blood orange tart.
Details: www.roussillon.co.uk; 10.30 pm; closed Mon L, Tue L, Sat L & Sun;
no smoking area.

Royal China £31 ★★

40 Baker St, W1 7487 4688 1–1A
13 Queensway, W2 7221 2535
68 Queen's Grove, NW8 7586 4280
30 Westferry Circus, E14 7719 0888

*"Fantastic dim sum" is the special highlight at this "busy" and "loud" oriental chain, decked out in "'70s roller disco-style"; at any time of day, though, legions of fans insist that the food is "just as good as Hong Kong" (especially at the Bayswater original). / **Details:** 10.45 pm, Fri & Sat 11.15 pm; E14 no bookings Sat & Sun L.*

The Royal Exchange Grand Café
The Royal Exchange EC3 £34 𝔸★

Cornhill 7618 2480 5–3C

*Conran's new seafood bar (with other light, mainly cold fare) benefits from a superb setting in the glazed courtyard of the City's Royal Exchange; the food is good, too, though service was still unfocussed on our early (July 2003) visit. / **Sample dishes:** rock oysters; baguette with Serrano ham, quince jelly & manchego cheese; peach Melba.*
***Details:** www.conran.com; 10.30 pm; closed Sat & Sun; no booking.*

Rules WC2 £50 𝔸

35 Maiden Ln 7836 5314 3–3D

*London's oldest restaurant (est 1798) boasts "splendid" décor, helping to make it a big hit with traditionalist businessmen and foreign visitors; the usually commendable realisation of its "hearty British fare" has seemed rather "tired" of late, though, and some reporters fear a "bums on seats" mentality is taking hold. / **Sample dishes:** Stilton & celeriac soup; rabbit casserole with broad beans & mustard mash; champagne sabayon. **Details:** www.rules.co.uk; 11.30 pm; no smoking.*

S & M Café £19 ★

268 Portobello Rd, W10 8968 8898
4-6 Essex Rd, N1 7359 5361
48 Brushfield St, E1 7247 2252 5–1D

*"Consistently good", "no-nonsense" bangers served in "'50s-retro-British-diner" surroundings are making this jolly new chain quite a success, despite "highly erratic" service; the Islington branch is the best to date – coming soon, Soho and Acton. / **Sample dishes:** pork & leek sausages with onion gravy; chocolate torte. **Details:** www.sandm-cafe.co.uk; 10.30 pm; no Amex.*

Saagar W6 £21 ★★

157 King St 8741 8563

*Nothing from the street hints at the quality of this new south Indian veggie on Hammersmith's grungy main drag; incidentals (such as poppadoms and chutneys) can disappoint, but the main dishes are sensational – and super-cheap too – and service really seems to care. / **Details:** 10.45 pm; no smoking area.*

Sabras NW10 £24 ★★

263 High Rd 8459 0340

*"Fabulous" South Indian veggie cooking at "exceptional prices" is the gist of all reports on this simple Willesden Green café of over 25 years' standing; "the ambience is rather cold and bare, but the pleasant service makes up for it". / **Details:** 10.30 pm; D only, closed Mon; no Amex; no smoking area.*

St John EC1 £37 ★

26 St John St 7251 0848 5–1B

*"Animal bits you never knew were edible" top the bill at this former Smithfield smokehouse, renowned for Fergus Henderson's "challenging" traditional British menus; the setting is "stark" and "echoey", but the "welcoming" and "knowledgeable" staff help it to develop "a nice buzz". / **Sample dishes:** duck broth; roast quail with lentils & broad beans; blood orange jelly & shortbread. **Details:** www.stjohnrestaurant.co.uk; 11 pm; closed Sat L & Sun.*

St John Bread & Wine E1 £ 33 ★
94-96 Commercial St 7247 8724 5–1D
Those who relish the 'nose to tail' (offal-rich) menu which has made St John a place of foodie pilgrimage will probably like its all-day Shoreditch sibling, which manages to cram many of the aspects of the original operation into a relatively small space. / **Sample dishes:** smoked eel, potatoes & horseradish; roast pork belly & red cabbage; apple sorbet & vodka. **Details:** www.stjohnbreadandwine.com; 10.30 pm.

St Johns N19 £ 33 𝔸★
91 Junction Rd 7272 1587
"Setting the standards for other gastropubs", this "brilliant" Archway boozer dining room offers an "ever-changing menu" of "hearty and well-cooked" dishes; its also boasts a "thoughtful" wine list, and has a "wonderful" atmosphere – "you need to book". / **Sample dishes:** chicken liver terrine with chutney; grilled black bream; apple crumble. **Details:** 11 pm; closed Mon L; booking: max 10.

Sakonis HA0 £ 18 ★★
129 Ealing Rd 8903 9601
"The food is all vegetarian and wonderfully fresh", at this popular, no-frills Wembley Indian – a top recommendation for "a cheap and cheerful snack". / **Details:** 9.30 pm; no Amex; no smoking.

Salloos SW1 £ 42 ★
62-64 Kinnerton St 7235 4444 4–1D
"Fantastic Pakistani food" has long put this Knightsbridge mews fixture on quite a pedestal; prices can seem "outrageous", though, especially when even some fans admit you get "dreadful 'everything else'". / **Details:** 11.15 pm; closed Sun.

Samphire NW5 £ 34 ★
135 Fortess Rd 7482 4855
This "cramped" and "tastefully Spartan" Tufnell Park newcomer has developed an immediate local name for "delicious" food that's "ambitious, for this part of town", and "good value"; it's safest to book. / **Sample dishes:** asparagus & Bayonne ham parcel; braised lamb shank with colcannon; chocolate tart. **Details:** www.samphire-nw5.co.uk; 10.30 pm; D only, ex Sun open L & D; no Amex; no smoking area; booking: max 8.

Sarastro WC2 £ 33 𝔸✗
126 Drury Ln 7836 0101 1–2D
"You have to see it to believe it"; this Covent Garden madhouse has a "high camp" opera theme which makes it a "fantastic" party spot ("especially if you can get a booth"); "rude" staff and "appalling" food, however, can "blight" its appeal. / **Sample dishes:** grilled sardines; kofte lamb meatballs with rice; cassata ice cream. **Details:** www.sarastro-restaurant.com; 11.30 pm.

Sardo W1 £ 42 𝔸★
45 Grafton Way 7387 2521 1–1B
"A little bit of Sardinia, tucked away in Fitzrovia" – this "friendly" and "unpretentious" establishment is winning quite a following with its "delicious", "different" and "filling" dishes. / **Sample dishes:** sun-dried tuna on a bed of French beans & sun-dried tomatoes; grilled swordfish with rucola & tomatoes; lemon tart with ice cream. **Details:** www.sardo-restaurant.com; 11 pm; closed Sat L & Sun; no smoking area.

Sarkhel's SW18 £ 28 ★★
199 Replingham Rd 8870 1483 6–2B
Udit Sarkhel's "fantastically tasty and original" cooking, from "interesting regional menus", has made his slightly "stark" Southfields subcontinental a culinary destination of great note; service is "happy" and "rapid". / **Details:** www.sarkhels.com; 10.30 pm, Fri & Sat 11 pm; closed Mon; no Amex; no smoking area.

(Savoy Grill)
Savoy Hotel WC2   **£61**
Strand   7592 1600   3–3D
*Marcus Wareing's shake up of this hallowed power scene has made
it less stuffy – but also less dignified – than it was of old; the new
régime has similarities to its predecessor, though – service is still the
strong point (if from rather fresher faces), and the food (though
modernised) is still not particularly memorable. / **Sample dishes:** seared
tuna with coriander couscous; roast chicken with truffles & port sauce; apple &
rhubarb crumble. **Details:** www.savoygroup.com; 11 pm; closed Sat L & Sun;
jacket & tie required.*

(River Restaurant)
Savoy Hotel WC2   **£75**   𝔸✗
Strand   7420 2698   3–3D
*Perhaps the August 2003 arrival of a new chef heralds a long-overdue
shake-up at this "imposing" riverside dining room – the year which has
seen Anton Edelmann's departure has been lacklustre even by the
"geriatric" standards which have recently been the norm here. / **Sample
dishes:** butternut squash soup with tortellini; chicken breast on lyonnaise mash with
garlic carrots; frozen mint chocolate parfait. **Details:** www.savoygroup.com;
11.15 pm; no jeans.*

Seashell NW1   **£26**   ★
49 Lisson Grove   7224 9000
*"Still the best fish and chips in London", say fans of this famous and
touristy Marylebone institution; the dining room feels "like a
disorganised cafeteria", though – "take-away is better".
/ **Details:** www.seashellrestaurant.co.uk; 10.30 pm; closed Sun; no smoking area.*

Segafredo Zanetti W1   **£15**   ★
72 Baker St   7486 2229   1–1A
*In the early days at least (August 2003), this new Marylebone café-
outpost of the Italian coffee brand was a lot less slick than you might
expect; the quality of antipasti and cakes – and the coffee itself –
was high, however.*

Serafino W1   **£41**   ★
8 Mount St   7629 0544   2–3B
*This "great local" is well worth knowing about in the heart of Mayfair;
all reporters attest to its "high-quality" Italian fare
(with "good breakfasts", too) and "friendly" service. / **Sample
dishes:** grilled Italian cheeses with radiccio; veal with Parma ham & sage; tiramisu.
Details: 10.45 pm; closed Sat L & Sun.*

J Sheekey WC2   **£53**   𝔸★★
28-32 St Martin's Ct   7240 2565   3–3B
*"Elegant yet exciting", this West End classic – where "cracking" fish
and seafood dishes are delivered by "consummately professional" staff
in an "intimate" series of parlours – has now ousted its famed sibling,
the Ivy, as the survey's most-mentioned restaurant; "star-spotting
is thrown in for free". / **Sample dishes:** seared tuna; Dover sole with asparagus;
spotted dick. **Details:** midnight.*

Shogun W1   **£50**   ★★
Adam's Row   7493 1255   2–3A
*"One of the best sushi chefs in town" makes it well worth seeking out
this "friendly" and "authentic" Japanese basement of a Mayfair hotel;
as ever, an ambience which some find "enjoyable" strikes others
as "not very charming". / **Details:** 11 pm; D only, closed Mon; no Switch.*

Simpson's Tavern EC3   **£23**   𝔸
38 1/2 Cornhill   7626 9985   5–2C
*"Great fun" – "in a beery, hearty sort of way" – is had by all at this
ancient chophouse, a City "staple" whose "school food" is "always
consistent". / **Details:** 3 pm; L only, closed Sat & Sun.*

Simpsons-in-the-Strand WC2 £56 ✗
100 Strand 7836 9112 3–3D

For its "incomparable" breakfast fry-ups, this grand Covent Garden shrine to traditional British fare has many fans; otherwise, though – "very good" roast beef aside – it strikes many reporters as "a big no-no", thanks to its "musty" feel, and to cooking that's both "unbelievably poor" and "extortionately priced". / Sample dishes: haddock with poached egg & cheese sauce; steak & salad; spotted dick.
Details: www.simpsons-in-the-strand.com; 10.45 pm, Sun 8.30 pm; closed Sat L; no jeans or trainers.

Singapore Garden NW6 £32 ★
83-83a Fairfax Rd 7328 5314

"A super-wide range of authentic south east Asian dishes" maintains a steady following for this tacky but rather "charming" Swiss Cottage Singaporean. / Details: 10.45 pm, Fri & Sat 11.15 pm.

(Gallery)
Sketch W1 £45 ✗
9 Conduit St 0870 777 4488 2–2C

"Love it or hate it", everyone agrees that prices at the "Barbarella"-style downstairs brasserie of this "surreal" and "extraordinary" Mayfair newcomer are "for mugs"; the food is "innovative" or "pretentious tosh", to taste, but "it's the loos people really seem to talk about!" / Details: 10.30 pm; D only, closed Sun.

(Top Floor)
Smiths of Smithfield EC1 £49 Ⓐ★
67-77 Charterhouse St 7251 7950 5–1A

"Clients enjoy the views, and the food" in the "slick" and "trendy" top-floor dining room of this Smithfield warehouse-conversion; some say it's "too pricey", but it has an "amazing" setting (complete with open-air terrace), and offers "the best steaks in the City, bar none". / Sample dishes: lobster omelette with star anise; roast Old Spot pork with crackling & apple sauce; Sauternes custard with armagnac prunes.
Details: www.smithsofsmithfield.co.uk; 11 pm; closed Sat L (café open all day).

(Dining Room)
Smiths of Smithfield EC1 £33 Ⓐ
67-77 Charterhouse St 7251 7997 5–1A

"Very noisy" and "bustling", the "happening" second-floor brasserie of this large Manhattan-style warehouse-conversion in Smithfield serves a "good-value" menu, with "cracking burgers" a highlight; the place makes a handy all-rounder, especially "for groups". / Sample dishes: Thai-style omelette with tiger prawns; roast Welsh black beef with ratatouille; chocolate fondant with strawberry ice cream. Details: www.smithsofsmithfield.co.uk; 10.45 pm; closed Sat L & Sun.

Snows on the Green W6 £31 ★
166 Shepherd's Bush Rd 7603 2142

This long-standing Mediterranean fixture, by Brook Green, is winning ever more consistent praise for its often-"excellent" service, and for its "straightforward" and "reasonably-priced" cooking. / Sample dishes: plum tomato, rocket & parmesan salad; baked cod with truffled leeks; peach Melba.
Details: www.snowsonthegreen.co.uk; 11 pm; closed Sat L & Sun; no smoking area.

So.uk £32 Ⓐ
93-107 Shaftesbury Ave, W1 7494 3040 3–3A
165 Clapham High St, SW4 7622 4004 6–2D

"The food is fine, if the bar isn't too crowded", say fans of these vibey and "expensive" Moroccan hang-outs; the Clapham original now has a sibling on the former West End site of Teatro (RIP).

Sonny's SW13 £38 A★
94 Church Rd 8748 0393 6–1A
"The perfect neighbourhood restaurant" – this *"West End-quality"* place in Barnes wins praise, year in year out, for its *"excellent cuisine"*, *"impeccable"* service and *"wonderful"* atmosphere. / **Sample dishes:** duck liver parfait with sweet pickle; salmon with red lentils & samphire; apple & sultana tart. **Details:** 11 pm; closed Sun D.

Sotheby's Café W1 £38 A★
34 New Bond St 7293 5077 2–2C
"Amusingly rich" customers can add interest to a visit to the *"discreet"* café in the foyer of the famous Mayfair auctioneers; service is *"excellent"*, though (even for poor people), and the menu offers *"good"*, *"simple"* fare. / **Sample dishes:** roast smoked salmon with horseradish cream; pan-fried scallop & lentil salad with salas verde; dark chocolate filo pastry with white chocolate sauce. **Details:** L only, closed Sat & Sun; no smoking.

Le Soufflé
Inter-Continental Hotel W1 £55 ★
1 Hamilton Pl 7409 3131 2–4A
Michael Coaker produces some *"outstanding"* modern French cooking at this Mayfair dining room, and the service is *"excellent"* too; the setting, though, is *"dull"* and *"dated"* – but *"as a quiet venue for an important meeting"*, it can be perfect! / **Sample dishes:** truffle risotto; fillet of sea bass; Grand Marnier soufflé. **Details:** www.london.intercontinental.com; 10.30 pm, Sat 11.15 pm; closed Mon D, Tue D, Sat L & Sun D; no smoking area; booking: max 12.

Souk WC2 £26 A✗
27 Litchfield St 7240 1796 3–3B
"Carry on up the Casbah" – *"wonderful dim lights"* and *"intimate nooks"* make this *"younger-scene"* Moroccan *"cave"* a *"fun"* party or romantic venue (and one with *"great prices"*, for the West End); the food is decidedly *"average"*, though, and service can sometimes be *"really bad"*. / **Details:** www.souk.net; 11.30 pm; no smoking area.

Soulard N1 £31 A★
113 Mortimer Rd 7254 1314
This is the *"definitive"* bistro, claim fans of this *"cosy and very French"* outpost, *"remotely located"* on the fringes of Islington; owner Philippe is *"hilarious"*, too. / **Sample dishes:** grilled goats cheese with honey; smoed haddock with saffron sauce; crème brûlée. **Details:** 10 pm; D only, closed Mon & Sun; no Amex.

Southeast W9 W9 £27 ★
239 Elgin Ave 7328 8883
As its Thai/Vietnamese/Laotian dishes are *"always good"*, this canteen by Maida Vale tube can be *"surprisingly uncrowded"*; perhaps it has something to do with the *"clinical"* surroundings. / **Details:** 11 pm; no smoking area.

The Square W1 £83
6-10 Bruton St 7495 7100 2–2C
With its *"professional"* service, *"endless"* wine list and *"top-notch"* cuisine, this *"smart"* Mayfair dining room is a *"perfect rendezvous for business"* (for which it is now the survey's no 1 choice); its overall ratings are notably sagging, though, perhaps because non-suits can find it just *"so boring"*. / **Sample dishes:** pea & ham soup with morels; sea bass with risotto; blood orange soufflé with chocolate ice cream. **Details:** www.squarerestaurant.com; 10.45 pm; closed Sat L & Sun L.

Sree Krishna SW17 £17 ★
192-194 Tooting High St 8672 4250 6–2C
"Fabulous south Indian food" has long established this *"dreary"*-looking fixture as one of Tooting's few destinations of note, and it's *"always busy"*; standards this year, though, seemed rather under pressure. **Details:** 10.45 pm, Fri & Sat midnight.

Sri Thai Soho W1 £31 ★
16 Old Compton St 7434 3544 3–2A
"Authentic" and *"delicious"* food helps make this long-established Soho
Thai (long known as Sri Siam) one of the more reliable West End
orientals. / **Details:** www.orientalrestaurantgroup.co.uk; 11.15 pm; closed Sun L.

Star of India SW5 £39 ★★
154 Old Brompton Rd 7373 2901 4–2B
"Inventive and delicious" cooking – in a pretty *"nouvelle"* style for one
of London's oldest curry houses – keeps this *"unique"* South Kensington
destination (complete with Italianate frescoes) as busy as ever.
/ **Details:** www.starofindia.co.uk; 11.45 pm.

The Station W10 £27 ★
41 Bramley Rd 7229 1111
A gritty urban view of the Latimer Road tube viaduct adds to the
ambience at this above-average gastropub (whose attractions,
surprisingly, include a vast and attractive rear garden); portions make
up in generosity anything they may lack in finesse. / **Sample
dishes:** Mediterranean mezze platter; beef, Guinness & mushroom pie; pear &
almond cake. **Details:** www.priorybars.com; 10 pm.

The Stepping Stone SW8 £38 𝔸★★
123 Queenstown Rd 7622 0555 6–1C
"Excellent quality for the price" (with some *"unusual dishes"*) once
again puts this *"stylish"* (if *"unpromisingly located"*) Battersea
"favourite" right at the top of the *"neighbourhood restaurant"* league.
/ **Sample dishes:** smoked salmon & balsamic grapes; roast duck with chorizo &
chickpeas; orange & bay leaf panna cotta. **Details:** www.thesteppingstone.com;
11 pm, Mon 10.30 pm; closed Sat L & Sun; no Amex; no smoking area.

Stick & Bowl W8 £15 ★
31 Kensington High St 7937 2778 4–1A
"Good and authentic" Chinese food make this lightning-quick
Kensington canteen a *"cheap"* and handy standby. / **Details:** 10.45 pm;
no credit cards; no booking.

Stratford's W8 £37 ★
7 Stratford Rd 7937 6388 4–2A
"Many evident regulars" make a *"home-from-home"* of this *"little gem
of a fish restaurant"*, in a Kensington *"backwater"*; some find the
interior a touch *"lacklustre"*, but the cooking is *"very simple and always
good"*. / **Sample dishes:** grilled calamari; swordfish with roasted garlic; chocolate
mousse. **Details:** 11.30 pm.

The Sugar Club W1 £50
21 Warwick St 7437 7776 2–2D
Diehard fans applaud this stark and *"expensive"* Soho venture for
"the best innovative fusion food in London", but overall satisfaction
nose-dived this year, with complaints of *"ordinary"* cooking and
"snooty" service much more in evidence. / **Sample dishes:** Indian prawn
fishcakes with mango; venison with apple & pistachio pancakes; banoffi pie with
galangal sorbet. **Details:** www.thesugarclub.co.uk; 11 pm; closed Mon L, Sat L &
Sun L; no smoking area.

Sugar Hut SW6 £41 𝔸
374 North End Rd 7386 8950 4–3A
An *"awesome"* atmosphere helps make this *"intimate"* and *"beautifully
decorated"* Fulham Thai a great destination for romance; it's *"pricey"*,
though, and *"the food doesn't really live up to the promising vibe"*.
/ **Details:** www.sugarhutfulham.com; 11.30 pm; D only.

Sumosan W1 **£ 43** ★★

26b Albemarle St
7495 5999   2–3C

*"Better than Nobu or Zuma, but still much less busy"; it may not be nearly as famous, but this somberly stylish Mayfair spot serves "memorable" dishes (including "fantastic" sushi) and is often favourably compared to its trendier rivals. / **Sample dishes:** beef tataki; lobster teppan-yaki; chocolate parfait. **Details:** 11.30 pm; closed Sat L & Sun L; no smoking area.*

Le Suquet SW3 **£ 47** ★

104 Draycott Ave   7581 1785   4–2C

*"In every way like being on the Côte d'Azur", this "tightly-packed" Brompton Cross veteran still often wins praise for "the best seafood in town"; long-term fans, however, lament the "loss of much of the former buzz". / **Sample dishes:** foie gras; fillet of beef; crème brûlée. **Details:** 11.30 pm.*

Sushi-Say NW2 **£ 31** ★

33b Walm Ln   8459 7512

*"Fabulous sushi" ("so good we rarely try anything else") and other "special" Japanese fare make this family-run Willesden Green café that suburb's greatest claim to culinary fame. / **Sample dishes:** clear soup with picked vegetables; salmon, tuna & eel sushi; ice cream. **Details:** 10.30 pm; closed Mon, Tue-Fri D only, Sat & Sun open L & D; no smoking.*

The Swan W4 **£ 25** A★

119 Acton Ln
8994 8262

*"Truly welcome in North Chiswick", this newly-revamped boozer wins high praise for its "laid-back" style, and its "simple" and "generous" cooking – "just how gastropub food should be"; good garden. / **Sample dishes:** antipasti of the day; Spanish pork & bean stew; chocolate & almond cake. **Details:** 10.30 pm; closed weekday L; no Amex; no booking, Fri & Sat.*

Sweetings EC4 **£ 39** A★

39 Queen Victoria St   7248 3062   5–3B

*"New owners have redecorated (not before time), but standards remain unmatched", at this "fabulous" City Victorian "time warp", where "really fresh, unmucked-about-with fish and shellfish" (and "boys' puds") are served in a "fantastic old-school setting". / **Sample dishes:** crab cocktail; deep-fried halibut & chips; baked jam sponge. **Details:** L only, closed Sat & Sun; no booking.*

Tajine W1 **£ 30** ★

7a Dorset St   7935 1545   1–1A

*"Good food" ("especially starters)" is the highlight at this "nice" Marylebone Moroccan – "a good local place, but not a destination". / **Details:** www.originaltajines.com; 10.30 pm; closed Sat L & Sun; no Amex.*

Talad Thai SW15 **£ 18** ★★

320 Upper Richmond Rd   8789 8084   6–2A

*"Cheap but brilliant" food – "akin to what you find in Thailand" – has won many fans for this "quick", "no-frills" Putney canteen. / **Details:** 10 pm; no Amex; no smoking.*

Tamarind W1 **£ 44** ★

20 Queen St   7629 3561   2–3B

*The "subtle" and "sumptuous" cuisine of this "businessy" Mayfair basement – in recent years, one of the capital's top subcontinentals – is still very good; the departure of the former head chef, however, has seen a slight decline in overall satisfaction. / **Sample dishes:** prawn & scallop tandoori with sour grapes; curried lamb shank with paratha bread; mango kulfi. **Details:** www.tamarindrestaurant.com; 11.15 pm; closed Sat L.*

sign up for the survey at www.hardens.com

Tandoori of Chelsea SW3   £ 39   ★
153 Fulham Rd   7589 7749   4–2C
"It's often empty, which is strange because the food's good", say fans
of this "gracious and friendly" Brompton Cross subcontinental of long
*standing; we share their puzzlement. / **Details:** midnight.*

Tartuf N1   £ 20   ★
88 Upper St   7288 0954
"What could be more romantic than sharing a tarte flambée? ...and
another, and another?" – reporters speak only well of this "intimate"
*and "lively" Alsatian-'pizza' joint, in Islington. / **Details:** midnight; no Amex.*

Tas   £ 23
33 The Cut, SE1   7928 2111   5–4A
72 Borough High St, SE1   7403 7200   5–4C
The "light, modern and noisy" branches of this "buzzy" Turkish chain
have taken the South Bank by storm in recent years, and their mezze,
in particular, offer a "tasty, cheap and plentiful" meal; slipping ratings
betray a "hit-and-miss" element to this year's reports, though,
*and some feel "the menu could use updating". / **Details:** 11.30 pm.*

(Café 7)
Tate Modern SE1   £ 33   𝔸 ✗
Bankside   7401 5020   5–3B
With its "outstanding" views and its "captive audience", it's a shame
the Tate doesn't make more of its "cool" (if "uncomfortable") top-floor
café – "it takes talent to ruin food like this", and service can
be "awful"; let's hope recent 'tweaks' (a change of layout and
acceptance of reservations) signal an effort at general improvements.
*/ **Sample dishes:** beetroot-cured salmon with soda bread; lamb steak with soft*
*Parmesan polenta; Indian mango & lime ice cream. **Details:** www.tate.org.uk;*
5.30 pm, Fri & Sat 9.30 pm; L only, except Fri & Sat open L & D; no smoking.

Tatsuso EC2   £ 75   ★
32 Broadgate Circle   7638 5863   5–2D
"Fantastic for business", this City Japanese is as famous for its "superb
quality" as it is for its "mad prices"; there is both a ground floor
teppan-yaki (the jollier option) and a rather "sterile" but more
"authentic" basement (where "fantastically fresh sushi" is the star
feature).
*/ **Details:** 9.45 pm; closed Sat & Sun; no smoking area.*

Tawana W2   £ 27   ★
3 Westbourne Grove   7229 3785
"Reliably high-quality cooking" makes this "unatmospheric" but handily-
*situated Bayswater Thai a useful stand-by. / **Details:** 11 pm.*

Teca W1   £ 48   ★★
54 Brooks Mews   7495 4774   2–2B
"Superb" cuisine ("with a twist on traditional Italian recipes") and
a "large and fairly-priced wine list" (presented by an "excellent
sommelier") win plaudits for this "comfortable" Mayfair venue;
the setting is undoubtedly "appropriate for business", but it can seem
*a touch "anodyne". / **Sample dishes:** foie gras terrine with cherry bread; bream*
*with red pepper sauce & fried basil; tiramisu. **Details:** 10.30 pm; closed Sun.*

Tendido Cero SW5   £ 23   ★
174 Old Brompton Rd   7370 3685   4–2B
"The BYO policy keeps down the costs" at this "good" – but, on the
food front, sometimes "pricey" – South Kensington tapas bar; reports
are generally favourable, but slightly less so than for its parent
*establishment, Cambio de Tercio. / **Details:** 11 pm; closed Sun D; no credit*
cards.

Tentazioni SE1   £ 47   ★

2 Mill St   7237 1100

After a recent refurbishment, this "out-of-the-way" Italian, near Butler's Wharf seems a more "cosy" destination nowadays; its "corking" modern cooking has made it something of a "foodie beacon" in these parts, but some reporters have found results "more hit-and-miss of late". / **Sample dishes:** *gnocchi with tomatoes & smoked ricotta; pan-fried calves liver with aubergine purée; Gorgonzola with figs & walnuts.* **Details:** *www.tentazioni.co.uk; 10.45 pm; closed Mon L, Sat L & Sun.*

Thai Bistro W4   £ 24   ★

99 Chiswick High Rd   8995 5774

"It smells like Bangkok" at this "Spartan" Chiswick local – a "reliable" modern place where "good Thai food" is served "canteen-style". / **Details:** *11 pm; closed Tue L & Thu L; no Amex; no smoking.*

Thai Corner Café SE22   £ 21   ★

44 North Cross Rd   8299 4041

"BYO makes it very cheap, and while the menu is limited, the food is always good", at this East Dulwich Thai; even its local fanclub, though, thinks service can be so "slow" it's "laughable". / **Details:** *10.30 pm; no credit cards.*

Thai on the River SW10   £ 38   𝔸★

15 Lots Rd   7351 1151   4–4B

"Expensive", by Thai standards, but "worth it", this "sophisticated" Chelsea river-sider found greater favour with reporters this year, and some "outstanding" cooking was noted; there are also "great views" from some tables. / **Details:** *www.thaiontheriver.co.uk; 11 pm, Fri & Sat 11.30 pm; closed Mon L & Sat L.*

Thailand SE14   £ 28   ★★

15 Lewisham Way   8691 4040

"Exceptional" Laotian/Thai food – "worth crossing town for" – gives this "unpromisingly located" and "somewhat dingy" Lewisham fixture a stature belying its location and appearance. / **Details:** *11.30 pm; closed Mon, Sat L & Sun L; no Amex; no smoking.*

3 Monkeys SE24   £ 36   𝔸★

136-140 Herne Hill   7738 5500

"Fantastic food in the nouvelle-Indian mould" can make this "bright and airy" Herne Hill spot "a real treat"; "snail's pace service", though, can take the edge off the experience. / **Details:** *www.3monkeysrestaurant.com; 11 pm; D only; smoking in bar only.*

Thyme SW4   £ 39   ★★

14 Clapham Park Rd

7627 2468   6–2D

"Sublime" cooking that's "effortlessly eclectic without pretension" – not to mention "keen" and "helpful" service – again wins adulatory reviews for this "quirky" (and slightly "stark") Clapham yearling, where dishes are served tapas-style. / **Sample dishes:** *cauliflower soup with truffle butter; peppered beef fillet with red onion confit; honeycomb nougat glacé.* **Details:** *www.thymeandspace.com; 10.30 pm; closed Mon & Sun; smoking in bar only; booking: max 6.*

Timo W8   £ 40   ★

343 Kensington High St   7603 3888

"Excellent food, without prices to match" and "attentive" service win an enthusiastic thumbs-up for this year-old Italian, in the "no man's land" between Kensington and Olympia; its setting manges to be both quite stylish and utterly forgettable. / **Sample dishes:** *ham, celeriac & rocket salad; tomato-crusted monkfish with Sardinian couscous; saffron panna cotta with honey & apple sauce.* **Details:** *www.atozrestaurants.com; 11 pm; no smoking area; booking: max 8.*

Toff's N10   **£ 24**   ★

38 Muswell Hill Broadway   8883 8656
"Traditionally, London's best chippy" – this celebrated Muswell Hill
destination may (after a variable period) once again regain its crown;
all reporters rejoice in its *"huge portions of great and ungreasy fish and
chips"*. / **Details:** 10 pm; closed Sun; no smoking area; no booking, Sat.

Tom Aikens SW3   **£ 55**   ★★

43 Elystan St
7584 2003   4–2C
One-time Pied-à-Terre chef, Tom Aikens's *"exquisite"* and *"intensely
flavoured"* cooking looks set to establish this understated new Chelsea
dining room as one of the few truly top-flight Gallic restaurants in town.
/ **Sample dishes:** roast langoustine with coco bean, jabugo ham & braised chicken;
lamb with aubergine purée, aubergine confit & basil salad; palm sugar & jasmine
crème caffonade with jasmine ice cream. **Details:** www.tomaikens.co.uk; 10.30pm;
closed Sat & Sun; booking: max 6.

Tootsies   **£ 28**

35 James St, W1   7486 1611   2–1A
177 New King's Rd, SW6   7736 4023   6–1B
107 Old Brompton Rd, SW7   7581 8942   4–2B
120 Holland Park Ave, W11   7229 8567
148 Chiswick High Rd, W4   8747 1869
198 Haverstock Hill, NW3   7431 3812
147 Church Rd, SW13   8748 3630   6–1A
48 High St, SW19   8946 4135   6–2B
36-38 Abbeville Rd, SW4   8772 6646   6–2D
"Great all-day breakfasts" (*"the perfect hangover cure"*) and
"good beefy burgers" are key attractions of this *"solid"*, *"no-fuss"* chain;
parents love their *"very family-oriented"* approach. /
Details: 11 pm-11.30 pm, Fri & Sat midnight; some branches have no smoking
areas; some booking restrictions apply.

Toto's SW1   **£ 52**   𝔸★

Lennox Gardens Mews   7589 0075   4–2C
"A marvellous all-round performance" – in particular the *"beautiful"*,
airy setting and *"charming and thoughtful"* service – makes this
"hidden-away" Italian *"classic"*, behind Harrods, *"a favourite, special-
occasion destination"*. / **Sample dishes:** lamb carpaccio; monkfish with
artichokes & pesto; mango mousse. **Details:** 11 pm.

The Trafalgar Tavern SE10   **£ 33**   𝔸

Park Row   8858 2437
You get *"great views over the Thames"* from this *"lovely historic tavern"*
in Greenwich; the traditional pub grub is *"good"*, of its type, but rather
"overpriced". / **Details:** www.trafalgartavern.co.uk; 9 pm; closed Mon D & Sun D;
no Amex; no booking at weekends.

Les Trois Garçons E1   **£ 55**   𝔸

1 Club Row   7613 1924
"It's worth going once", just to see the *"weird and wonderful"* décor
of this former East End boozer; sadly, though, it's *"in decline"* –
the Gallic food is *"lax"*, service can be *"poor"*, and prices are getting
just *"ridiculous"*. / **Sample dishes:** snails in garlic butter; steak with red wine jus
and greens; French cheese platter. **Details:** www.lestroisgarcons.com; 10.30 pm;
D only, closed Sun.

La Trompette W4   **£ 46**   𝔸★★

5-7 Devonshire Rd
8747 1836
"Half the price of Gordon Ramsay, and 95% as good" – *"outstanding"*
food and *"impeccable"* service have won a huge reputation for this
"very good, West End-style restaurant", located in the depths
of Chiswick. / **Sample dishes:** grilled sardine tart with gremolata; duck with foie
gras & madeira sauce; chocolate profiteroles. **Details:** 11 pm; smoking discouraged;
booking: max 6.

Troubadour SW5 £27 𝔸

265 Old Brompton Rd   7370 1434   4–3A

*Despite its expansion, this long-established Earl's Court coffee house remains "one of the best Bohemian cafés in London"; the "staple cheap food" is "nothing special" (except for breakfast, for which this is "the perfect place"). / **Sample dishes:** crab & melon salad; bangers & mash; crème brûlée. **Details:** www.troubadour.co.uk; 11 pm; no Amex.*

Truc Vert W1 £38 ★

42 North Audley St   7491 9988   2–2A

*"How do they manage to produce such tasty food in such confined surroundings?"; this "delight" of a deli/diner has won a dedicated Mayfair following – it's "just like Paris (including the appalling service)". / **Sample dishes:** seared sacllops with egg noodles; wild boar fillet; orange almond torte. **Details:** 9 pm; closed Sat D & Sun D; no smoking.*

Tsunami SW4   £33 ★★

Unit 3, 5-7 Voltaire Rd

7978 1610   6–1D

*"The new Nobu, but at a fraction of the price" – this "funky" find in a "dreary" quarter of Clapham is winning waves of approval as an "unbelievable all-round" destination; the "extraordinarily good sushi" is most roundly praised, but it's just one part of a Japanese menu that's both "innovative" and "subtle". / **Sample dishes:** sautéed foie gras with sautéed Asian pear and truffle sauce; cod in sweet miso; chocolate harumaki with sesame seed ice cream. **Details:** 10.45 pm, Fri & Sat 11.15 pm; no Amex; no smoking area.*

Two Brothers N3 £26 ★★

297-303 Regent's Park Rd   8346 0469

*"If it's good enough for Madonna, it's good enough for me" – when it comes to fish 'n' chips the Material Girl seems to have taste, as the Manzi brothers' "bustling" Finchley institution has a realistic claim to being the best in town. / **Sample dishes:** fish soup.cod & chips; **Details:** www.twobrothers.co.uk; 10.15 pm; closed Mon & Sun; no smoking area; no booking at D.*

Ubon E14 £70

34 Westferry Circus   7719 7800

*"Smashing river views" ("best at night") add life to Nobu's Canary Wharf offshoot; its "less pretentious" ambience is preferred by reporters, but the food slightly lags the standard found in Mayfair. / **Sample dishes:** toro tartare with caviar; rock shrimp donburi (one-pot rice dish); fresh fruit Bento box. **Details:** 10.15 pm; closed Sat L & Sun; no smoking area.*

Uli W11 £25 𝔸★★

16 All Saints Rd   7727 7511

*It's a bit of a local secret, but this tiny and "intimate", family-run café in North Kensington has "the best host in London", and offers some "tremendous value" pan-Asian cooking – no wonder it's "always busy"; "nice garden", too. / **Details:** www.uli-oriental.co.uk; 11 pm; D only, ex Sun open L & D; no Amex.*

Vama SW10 £42 ★★

438 King's Rd   7351 4118   4–3B

*"Fine and complex curries" and other "refined" dishes help win this "chi-chi" World's End subcontinental many nominations as London best "posh" Indian; "they're trying to squeeze too many people in", though, and service can be "slow". / **Details:** www.vama.co.uk; 11 pm.*

Veeraswamy W1 £41 ★

Victory Hs, 99 Regent St   7734 1401   2–3D

*London's oldest Indian restaurant "reinvented itself" a few years ago, and its premises near Piccadilly Circus are now in contemporary style; the "high-quality" menu includes some "delicious" dishes. / **Details:** www.realindianfood.com; 11.30 pm.*

Vegia Zena NW1   £ 34   ★

17 Princess Rd   7483 0192

"Interesting menu choices" distinguish this Genoese restaurant
in Primrose Hill; its *"cramped"* and *"homely"* setting is no particular
attraction, though – *"sit in the garden if you can"*. / **Sample dishes:** *black
tagliatelle with scallops & broccoli; grilled Argentinean beef with sautéed leeks;
ice cream with hot espresso.* **Details:** *www.vegiazena.com; 11 pm.*

El Vergel SE1   £ 15   ★★

8 Lant St   7357 0057   5–4B

*With its "great-tasting, great-value" Hispanic dishes and breezy staff,
this bright and cheery refectory, in the backstreets near Borough tube,
is home to some of the best cheap food in town.*
/ **Details:** *www.elvergel.co.uk; breakfast & L only, closed Sat & Sun; no credit cards;
no smoking; no booking after 12.45 pm.*

Vertigo
Tower 42 EC2   £ 40   Ⓐ

Old Broad St   7877 7842   5–2C

"Go for the champagne, and the great views of London", and you're
unlikely to be disappointed by the former NatWest Tower's 42nd-floor
bar – the *"limited"* menu is *"OK"* but rather incidental; see also
Rhodes24. / **Sample dishes:** *scallop & pancetta brochettes; Cajun beef fajitas;
panna cotta with passionfruit & mango.* **Details:** *www.vertigo42.co.uk; 9.15 pm;
closed Sat & Sun; booking essential.*

Vijay NW6   £ 22   ★★

49 Willesden Ln   7328 1087

"Consistently excellent food" at prices that are just *"a steal"* makes this
long-established Kilburn south Indian as popular as ever; service
is *"extremely friendly"*, too. / **Details:** *www.vijayindia.com; 10.45 pm, Fri & Sat
11.45 pm.*

Vrisaki N22   £ 26   ★

73 Myddleton Rd   8889 8760

"The biggest mezze ever seen" – and at *"reasonable prices"* –
maintain the cult status of this *"noisy but fun"* Bounds Green taverna
(which hides behind a *"misleading kebab shop exterior"*); book ahead,
especially at weekends. / **Sample dishes:** *smoked trout & pitta bread;
moussaka; Greek yoghurt with honey.* **Details:** *midnight; closed Sun; no Amex.*

Wakaba NW3   £ 44   ★

122a Finchley Rd   7586 7960

"The food is the only reason" to go to this austere Japanese opposite
Finchley Road tube (which looks like *"all the atmosphere has been
sucked out of it"*); fans say its sushi is simply *"the best"*. / **Details:** *11 pm;
D only, closed Sun.*

Wapping Food E1   £ 37   Ⓐ

Wapping Pumping Hs, Wapping Wall   7680 2080

"An amazing space, with decent food" – a pretty fair summary of this
"cavernous" venue, in a converted East End pumping station (which
doubles up as an arts centre); it also offers *"a brilliant range of Aussie
wines"*. / **Sample dishes:** *pork with Manchego cheese & sherry vinegar; fillet
steak with leeks & pancetta; lavender panna cotta.* **Details:** *10.30 pm; closed
Sun D.*

The Wells NW3   £ 34   Ⓐ ★

30 Well Walk   7794 3785

'Gastropub' is really too humble a word for this enchantingly-located
Hampstead newcomer; its first-floor dining rooms offers interesting,
light dishes charmingly served in thoroughly 'restaurant' style. / **Sample
dishes:** *crab ravioli with shellfish bisque; linguini with sautéed wild mushrooms &
Jerusalem artichoke; pear & almond tart with vanilla ice cream.*
Details: *www.thewellshampstead.co.uk; 10.15 pm; booking: max 8.*

The Westbourne W2 £32 A

101 Westbourne Park Villas 7221 1332

"Indefatigably trendy", this "chilled" Notting Hill boozer is still "great fun" and, especially when the sun is out, "a great place to hang out"; the "variable" cooking and "complacent" service are rather beside the point. / **Sample dishes:** roast cauliflower soup with Parmesan; confit duck with sage mash & bacon; chocolate tart. **Details:** 10 pm; closed Mon L; need 4+ to book.

Wheeler's of St James's SW1 £39 ★

12a Duke of York St 7930 2460 2–3D

This pint-sized St James's corner site, with its many "nooks and crannies", is undergoing "a renaissance" under the stewardship of Marco Pierre White; most reporters now find it a "quirky but nice" destination for "great" fish and seafood. / **Sample dishes:** quails eggs; Dover sole; chocolate mousse. **Details:** 10.30 pm; closed Sun.

The White House SW4 £35 A

65 Clapham Park Rd 7498 3388 6–2D

A Clapham bar/restaurant "that becomes a nightclub for twentysomethings later on"; as you would expect, the food is not the main point, but it's "pleasant enough". / **Sample dishes:** straw mushroom spring rolls with chilli sauce; roast lamb with leek & potato cakes; blueberry ice cream crumble. **Details:** www.thewhitehouselondon.co.uk; midnight; D only; booking: max 14.

William IV NW10 £30 A★

786 Harrow Rd 8969 5944

"An amazing pub in the most surprising area" – this large Kensal Green gastropub is particularly liked for its "bijou outdoor area" and its "great" Sunday lunches. / **Sample dishes:** smoked duck & Asian vegetable salad; steamed trout with salsa verde; Greek yoghurt with fruit & honey. **Details:** www.william-iv.co.uk; 10.30 pm, Fri & Sat 11 pm.

Willie Gunn SW18 £35 A

422 Garratt Ln 8946 7773 6–2B

"An excellent bistro/pub in an unlikely bit of Earlsfield" – this "chilled" local is fêted by locals for its "fresh and seasonally-changing menu", its "very friendly" service and its "great" ambience. / **Sample dishes:** duck spring rolls with spiced pulm sauce; Lincolnshire sausages with mash & onion gravy; banoffi glacé with baked bananas. **Details:** 11 pm.

Windows on the World
Park Lane Hilton Hotel W1 £89 A

22 Park Ln 7208 4021 2–4A

"Magic views" – from the 28th-floor – make this Mayfair dining room an "ideal romantic destination" (and also an impressive setting for brunch on a bright day); the cooking has "improved" of late, but it's still "too expensive for what it is". / **Sample dishes:** chicken soup with curry glaze; roast lamb with coconut rice & citrus sauce; cherry clafoutis. **Details:** 10.30 pm, Fri & Sat 11.30 pm; closed Sat L & Sun D; jacket & tie required at D; no smoking at breakfast.

The Windsor Castle W8 £26 A

114 Campden Hill Rd 7243 9551

Just off Notting Hill Gate, London's "best year-round pub" has "the top beer-garden in town", and a "totally atmospheric" interior; the food is "nothing earth-shattering". / **Sample dishes:** oysters; steak & ale pie; chocolate sponge pudding. **Details:** www.windsor-castle-pub.co.uk; 9.30 pm; no smoking area at L; no booking.

The Wine Library EC3 £19 A

43 Trinity Sq 7481 0415 5–3D

A "winning formula" of retail-priced wines (choose your own, from over 200 bins) plus "a good simple cheese and pâté buffet" makes these ancient cellars "a great place for a boozy City lunch"; space is "limited", so book ahead. / **Sample dishes:** liver pâté & toast; quiche lorraine & salad; fresh fruit. **Details:** 8 pm; L & early evening only, closed Sat & Sun.

Woodlands   £ 26   ★

37 Panton St, SW1   7839 7258   3–4A
77 Marylebone Ln, W1   7486 3862   2–1A
12-14 Chiswick High Rd, W4   8994 9333
"Good-quality veggie Indian food" is reported by all who comment
on these *"handy"*, *"plainly decorated"* stand-bys; a Hammersmith
branch was added this year. / **Details:** www.woodlandsrestaurant.co.uk;
10.45 pm.

Yming W1   £ 30   ★★

35-36 Greek St   7734 2721   3–2A
*With its "carefully crafted" Chinese dishes, "uncharacteristically helpful"
service and a setting that's "remarkably serene, for Soho", Christine
Yau's low-key fixture is a West End destination of rare appeal.
/ **Details:** www.yming.com; 11.45 pm; closed Sun; no smoking area.*

Yoshino W1   £ 30   ★★

3 Piccadilly Pl   7287 6622   2–3D
"London's best sushi and sashimi", say fans, can be found at this *"great
little hide-away"*, located (paradoxically) about 100 yards from Piccadilly
Circus; the staff are *"very polite"* too, and *"some of them now even
speak English!"* / **Details:** www.yoshino.net; 10 pm; closed Sun; no smoking.

Yum Yum N16   £ 25   𝔸★

30 Stoke Newington Church St   7254 6751
"Must be a contender for one of the best Thais in London"; when you
look at its all-round appeal, few places match this always-busy Stoke
Newington fixture, which complements *"good value"* cooking with
"fantastic" service and an *"atmospheric"* setting.
/ **Details:** www.yumyum.co.uk; 10.45 pm, Fri & Sat 11.15 pm.

Zafferano SW1   £ 48   ★★

15 Lowndes St   7235 5800   4–1D
"Still simply the best Italian"; thanks to its *"fabulously fresh"* and
"sophisticated" cooking, its *"comprehensive Italian list"* and its
"impeccable" service, this *"intimate"* Belgravian goes from strength
to strength; indeed, *"it can be a little noisy and cramped at peak
times"*. / **Sample dishes:** saffon risotto; monkfish with walnuts & caper sauce;
figs with mint sorbet. **Details:** 11 pm.

Zaika W8   £ 49   ★★

1 Kensington High St   7795 6533   4–1A
*Vineet Bhatia's "fragrant" and "wonderfully subtle" cooking has
established this "classy" Kensington subcontinental as arguably the
capital's top 'nouvelle Indian'; the ambience at this converted banking
hall, however, can still seem rather "impersonal".* / **Sample
dishes:** tamarind chicken with milk fritters; crab & spiced scallops with Indian
risotto; deep-fried stuffed dates. **Details:** www.cuisine-collection.co.uk; 10.45 pm;
closed Sat L.

Zuma SW7   £ 60   𝔸★

5 Raphael St   7584 1010   4–1C
"Look out Nobu!" – this year-old Knightsbridge Japanese (already
almost as highly rated in the survey) is widely fêted as an *"exciting"*
haunt whose *"electric"* atmosphere comes *"studded with stars"*;
the food – including *"great sushi"*, and other *"moderately authentic"*
dishes – is *"fabulous"* too. / **Details:** www.zumarestaurant.com; 11 pm.

sign up for the survey at www.hardens.com   86

LONDON
AREA OVERVIEWS

CENTRAL

Soho, Covent Garden & Bloomsbury
(Parts of W1, all WC2 and WC1)

£70+	Savoy Hotel (River Rest.)	*International*	𝔸
£60+	Lindsay House	*British, Modern*	𝔸
	Savoy Grill	*British, Traditional*	-
£50+	QC	*British, Modern*	★
	Axis	*"*	-
	Rules	*British, Traditional*	𝔸
	Simpsons-in-the-Strand	*"*	-
	J Sheekey	*Fish & seafood*	𝔸★★
	The Sugar Club	*Fusion*	-
	Red Fort	*Indian*	★
	Matsuri	*Japanese*	★
	Opium	*Vietnamese*	𝔸
£40+	Indigo	*British, Modern*	𝔸★
	The Ivy	*"*	𝔸★
	Alastair Little	*"*	★
	Mezzo	*"*	-
	L'Escargot	*French*	★
	Mon Plaisir	*"*	𝔸
£35+	French House	*British, Modern*	𝔸★
	British Museum	*"*	𝔸
	The Criterion Grill	*French*	𝔸
	Incognico	*"*	-
	Bohème Kitchen	*International*	𝔸
£30+	Aurora	*British, Modern*	𝔸★
	The Langley	*"*	𝔸
	Café Bohème	*French*	𝔸
	Sarastro	*International*	𝔸
	Balans	*"*	-
	So.uk	*North African*	𝔸
	Yming	*Chinese*	★★
	Fung Shing	*"*	★
	Mela	*Indian*	★
	Chiang Mai	*Thai*	★
	Sri Thai Soho	*"*	★
£25+	Andrew Edmunds	*British, Modern*	𝔸★
	The Endurance	*British, Traditional*	★
	Gordon's Wine Bar	*International*	𝔸
	Mildred's	*Vegetarian*	★
	North Sea Fish	*Fish & chips*	★
	Souk	*North African*	𝔸
	New Mayflower	*Chinese*	★
	Hazuki	*Japanese*	★
	Itsu	*"*	★
£20+	La Porchetta Pizzeria	*Italian*	★
	Pâtisserie Valerie	*Sandwiches, cakes, etc*	-
	Joy King Lau	*Chinese*	★
	Mr Kong	*"*	★
	Chowki	*Indian*	★

	Busaba Eathai	*Thai*	𝔸
£15+	Food for Thought	*Vegetarian*	★
	Kulu Kulu	*Japanese*	★★
£5+	Red Veg	*Vegetarian*	★
	Maison Bertaux	*Sandwiches, cakes, etc*	𝔸★
	Benugo	*"*	★
£1+	Bank Aldwych	*British, Modern*	-

Mayfair & St James's (Parts of W1 and SW1)

£90+	Le Gavroche	*French*	𝔸★★
£80+	The Ritz	*"*	𝔸
	Windows on the World	*"*	𝔸
	The Square	*"*	-
£70+	G Ramsay at Claridges	*"*	-
	Connaught (Angela Hartnett)	*Mediterranean*	-
£60+	Dorchester Grill	*British, Traditional*	𝔸★
	Mirabelle	*French*	𝔸★
	1837	*"*	★
	Nobu	*Fusion*	★
	Hakkasan	*Chinese*	𝔸★
£50+	Le Soufflé	*French*	★
	Deca	*"*	-
	Kai	*Chinese*	★
	Shogun	*Japanese*	★★
	Matsuri	*"*	★
	Mitsukoshi	*"*	★
£40+	Le Caprice	*British, Modern*	𝔸★
	Brian Turner	*"*	★
	Quaglino's	*"*	-
	Fleur	*French*	★
	Sketch (Gallery)	*"*	-
	Teca	*Italian*	★★
	Alloro	*"*	★
	Serafino	*"*	★
	Momo	*Moroccan*	𝔸
	Levant	*Middle Eastern*	𝔸
	Tamarind	*Indian*	★
	Veeraswamy	*"*	★
	Sumosan	*Japanese*	★★
£35+	Wheeler's of St James's	*Fish & seafood*	★
	Sotheby's Café	*Mediterranean*	𝔸★
	La Rascasse	*"*	★
	Truc Vert	*"*	★
	Al Sultan	*Lebanese*	★
	Patara	*Thai*	★
£30+	Rasa	*Indian*	★★
	Yoshino	*Japanese*	★★

£25+	Rocket	Mediterranean	Ⓐ
	Woodlands	Indian	★
£5+	Benugo	Sandwiches, cakes, etc	★

Fitzrovia & Marylebone (Part of W1)

£60+	Orrery	French	Ⓐ★
	Pied à Terre	"	★
£50+	Archipelago	Fusion	Ⓐ
	Garanger Restaurant Bar	Mediterranean	★
£40+	Odin's	British, Traditional	Ⓐ
	Back to Basics	Fish & seafood	★★
	Locanda Locatelli	Italian	Ⓐ★★
	Sardo	"	Ⓐ★
	Eddalino	"	★
	Paolo	"	★
	Passione	"	★
	Fino	Spanish	Ⓐ★★
	La Porte des Indes	Indian	Ⓐ★
£35+	Bam-Bou	French-Vietnamese	Ⓐ★
	Rasa Samudra	Indian	★
£30+	Tapa Room (Providores)	Fusion	Ⓐ★
	Cristini	Italian	★
	Tajine	Moroccan	★
	Royal China	Chinese	★★
	Malabar Junction	Indian	Ⓐ★
£25+	Giraffe	International	-
	Tootsies	Burgers, etc	-
	Woodlands	Indian	★
	Ikkyu	Japanese	★
£20+	Pâtisserie Valerie	Sandwiches, cakes, etc	-
	Ragam	Indian, Southern	★
£15+	Segafredo Zanetti	Sandwiches, cakes, etc	★
£5+	Govinda's	International	★
	Benugo	Sandwiches, cakes, etc	★

Belgravia, Pimlico, Victoria & Westminster (SW1, except St James's)

£80+	Pétrus	French	-
£70+	Restaurant One-O-One	Fish & seafood	★★
£60+	Foliage	French	Ⓐ★
	Mju	Fusion	★
£50+	Goring Hotel	British, Traditional	Ⓐ
	Roussillon	French	★★
	Toto's	Italian	Ⓐ★
	The Cinnamon Club	Indian	★

£40+	La Poule au Pot	French	Ⓐ
	Boxwood Café	International	★
	Zafferano	Italian	★★
	Olivo	"	★
	Ken Lo's Memories	Chinese	★
	Salloos	Pakistani	★
	Mango Tree	Thai	★
£35+	Grenadier	British, Traditional	Ⓐ
	Caraffini	Italian	Ⓐ★
	Oliveto	Pizza	★
	Beiteddine	Lebanese	★
	Noura	"	★
	Hunan	Chinese	★★
£25+	Pan-Asian Canteen	Pan-Asian	★
£20+	Pâtisserie Valerie	Sandwiches, cakes, etc	-
	Jenny Lo's	Chinese	★

WEST

Chelsea, South Kensington, Kensington, Earl's Court & Fulham (SW3, SW5, SW6, SW7, SW10 & W8)

£90+	Gordon Ramsay	*French*	A★★
	Blakes Hotel	*International*	A
£70+	Capital Hotel	*French*	★★
£60+	Clarke's	*British, Modern*	A★★
	Aubergine	*French*	★
	Bibendum	*"*	A
	Zuma	*Japanese*	A★
£50+	Poissonnerie de l'Avenue	*Fish & seafood*	★
	Tom Aikens	*French*	★★
	Monkeys	*"*	A★
	Chutney Mary	*Indian*	A★
£40+	Launceston Place	*British, Modern*	A★
	English Garden	*"*	★
	Admiral Codrington	*"*	-
	Bluebird	*"*	-
	Maggie Jones's	*British, Traditional*	A
	Lundum's	*Danish*	A★
	Le Suquet	*Fish & seafood*	★
	Belvedere	*French*	A
	Timo	*Italian*	★
	Cambio de Tercio	*Spanish*	A★
	Pasha	*Moroccan*	A
	Mr Wing	*Chinese*	A★
	Mao Tai	*"*	★
	Vama	*Indian*	★★
	Zaika	*"*	★★
	Bombay Brasserie	*"*	A★
	Blue Elephant	*Thai*	A★
	Sugar Hut	*"*	A
£35+	PJ's	*American*	-
	The Pen	*British, Modern*	A★
	Bibendum Oyster Bar	*Fish & seafood*	A★
	Lou Pescadou	*"*	★
	Stratford's	*"*	★
	Racine	*French*	★
	Brasserie St Quentin	*"*	-
	The Enterprise	*International*	A
	Black & Blue	*Steaks & grills*	★
	Good Earth	*Chinese*	★
	Star of India	*Indian*	★★
	The Painted Heron	*"*	★
	Tandoori of Chelsea	*"*	★
	Thai on the River	*Thai*	A★
	Patara	*"*	★
£30+	Goolies	*British, Modern*	★
	The Mall Tavern	*"*	★
	Chez Max	*French*	A★

	Balans West	*International*	-
	Balans	*"*	-
	Made in Italy	*Italian*	★
	Ognisko Polskie	*Polish*	A
	El Gaucho	*Steaks & grills*	★
	Aziz	*Middle Eastern*	★
	Bangkok	*Thai*	★
	Nam Long	*Vietnamese*	A
£25+	The Ifield	*British, Modern*	A ★
	The Builder's Arms	*"*	A
	The Windsor Castle	*International*	A
	Giraffe	*"*	-
	Aglio e Olio	*Italian*	★
	The Atlas	*Mediterranean*	A ★
	Tootsies	*Burgers, etc*	-
	Basilico	*Pizza*	★★
	Troubadour	*Sandwiches, cakes, etc*	A
	Khan's of Kensington	*Indian*	★
	Malabar	*"*	★
	Memories of India	*"*	★
	Itsu	*Japanese*	★
£20+	Nicolas Bar à Vins	*French*	★
	Chelsea Bun Diner	*International*	-
	Tendido Cero	*Spanish*	★
	Gourmet Burger Kitchen	*Burgers, etc*	★
	La Delizia	*Pizza*	★
	Pâtisserie Valerie	*Sandwiches, cakes, etc*	-
£15+	Ranoush	*Lebanese*	★
	Stick & Bowl	*Chinese*	★
	Kulu Kulu	*Japanese*	★★
	Churchill Arms	*Thai*	A ★

Notting Hill, Holland Park, Bayswater, North Kensington & Maida Vale (W2, W9, W10, W11)

£40+	Julie's	*British, Modern*	A
	Assaggi	*Italian*	★★
£35+	Osteria Basilico	*"*	A ★
	Mediterraneo	*Mediterranean*	A ★
	Bombay Palace	*Indian*	★★
£30+	Lucky Seven	*American*	★
	The Ladbroke Arms	*British, Modern*	A
	The Westbourne	*"*	A
	The Cow	*Fish & seafood*	A ★
	Edera	*"*	★
	Café Laville	*International*	A
	The Oak	*Italian*	A ★
	The Red Pepper	*"*	★
	Mandarin Kitchen	*Chinese*	★★
	Royal China	*"*	★★
	Ginger	*Indian*	★
	E&O	*Pan-Asian*	A ★★
£25+	The Station	*British, Modern*	★
	Tootsies	*Burgers, etc*	-

	Inaho	Japanese	★★
	Uli	Pan-Asian	Ⓐ ★★
	Southeast W9	"	★
	Tawana	Thai	★
£20+	The Four Seasons	Chinese	★
£15+	S & M Café	British, Traditional	★
	Beirut Express	Lebanese	★★
	Ranoush	"	★
	Mandalay	Burmese	★★
£10+	Khan's	Indian	★
£5+	Lisboa Patisserie	Sandwiches, cakes, etc	★★

Hammersmith, Shepherd's Bush, Olympia, Chiswick & Ealing (W4, W5, W6, W12, W14)

£50+	The River Café	Italian	-
£40+	La Trompette	French	Ⓐ ★★
	Fish Hoek	South African	★★
£35+	Popeseye	Steaks & grills	★
£30+	Snows on the Green	British, Modern	★
	The Gate	Vegetarian	★★
£25+	The Havelock Tavern	British, Modern	Ⓐ ★★
	The Anglesea Arms	"	★
	Ealing Park Tavern	"	★
	Giraffe	International	-
	The Swan	Mediterranean	Ⓐ ★
	Blah! Blah! Blah!	Vegetarian	★★
	Tootsies	Burgers, etc	-
	Madhu's	Indian	★★
	Brilliant	"	★
	Woodlands	"	★
£20+	Saagar	Indian, Southern	★★
	Latymers	Thai	★
	Thai Bistro	"	★
£15+	Abu Zaad	Middle Eastern	★

NORTH

Hampstead, West Hampstead, St John's Wood, Regent's Park, Kilburn & Camden Town (NW postcodes)

£40+	Odette's	British, Modern	-
	L'Aventure	French	🅐★★
	Oslo Court	"	🅐★
	Wakaba	Japanese	★
£35+	The Hill	British, Modern	★
	The Engineer	"	🅐
	Black & Blue	Steaks & grills	★
£30+	The Wells	British, Modern	🅐★
	William IV	"	🅐★
	The Highgate	"	★
	Samphire	"	★
	Philpotts Mezzaluna	Italian	★
	Vegia Zena	"	★
	The Gate	Vegetarian	★★
	Mango Room	Afro-Caribbean	🅐★
	Phoenix Palace	Chinese	★★
	Royal China	"	★★
	Sushi-Say	Japanese	★
	Singapore Garden	Malaysian	★
£25+	The Lord Palmerston	British, Modern	🅐★
	Lemonia	Greek	🅐
	Giraffe	International	-
	Tootsies	Burgers, etc	-
	Nautilus	Fish & chips	★
	Seashell	"	★
	Basilico	Pizza	★★
£20+	Gourmet Burger Kitchen	Burgers, etc	★
	Vijay	Indian	★★
	Chutneys	"	★
	Sabras	Indian, Southern	★★
£15+	Ali Baba	Egyptian	★
	Geeta	Indian	★★
	Diwana B-P House	"	★
£1+	Sakonis	"	-

Hoxton, Islington, Highgate, Crouch End, Stoke Newington, Finsbury Park, Muswell Hill & Finchley (N postcodes)

£40+	Frederick's	British, Modern	🅐★
	The Almeida	French	-
	The Real Greek	Greek	-
	Metrogusto	Italian	★
£35+	The House	British, Modern	🅐★
	Cru	Mediterranean	★
£30+	The Drapers Arms	British, Modern	🅐★

	St Johns	*British, Traditional*	𝔸★
	Chez Liline	*Fish & seafood*	★★
	Soulard	*French*	𝔸★
	Fez	*Moroccan*	★
	Rasa	*Indian*	★★
£25+	Vrisaki	*Greek*	★
	Giraffe	*International*	-
	Pizzeria Oregano	*Italian*	★
	Two Brothers	*Fish & chips*	★★
	Furnace	*Pizza*	★
	Rasa Travancore	*Indian, Southern*	★
	Yum Yum	*Thai*	𝔸★
£20+	Tartuf	*Alsatian*	★
	La Porchetta Pizzeria	*Italian*	★
	Toff's	*Fish & chips*	★
	Gallipoli	*Turkish*	𝔸★
	Iznik	*"*	𝔸
	Rani	*Indian*	★
	Huong-Viet	*Vietnamese*	★★
£15+	S & M Café	*British, Traditional*	★

SOUTH

South Bank (SE1)

£60+	Le Pont de la Tour	British, Modern	🄰
£40+	Brasserie	International	🄰
	Tentazioni	Italian	★
£35+	Champor-Champor	Fusion	🄰★★
£30+	Delfina Studio Café	International	🄰★★
	Tate Modern (Café 7)	"	🄰
	Bermondsey Kitchen	Mediterranean	🄰★
	Baltic	Polish	🄰★
	Bengal Clipper	Indian	🄰★
£20+	Konditor & Cook	British, Modern	★★
	Pizzeria Castello	Pizza	★
	Tas	Turkish	-
£15+	El Vergel	South American	★★

Greenwich, Lewisham & Blackheath
(All SE postcodes, except SE1)

£35+	3 Monkeys	Indian	🄰★
£30+	The Trafalgar Tavern	British, Traditional	🄰
£25+	Chapter Two	British, Modern	🄰★
	Babur Brasserie	Indian	★
	Thailand	Thai	★★
£20+	Thai Corner Café	"	★

Battersea, Brixton, Clapham, Wandsworth
Barnes, Putney & Wimbledon
(All SW postcodes south of the river)

£50+	Putney Bridge	French	🄰★
£40+	Chez Bruce	British, Modern	🄰★★
	Redmond's	"	★
	The Light House	International	★
	Enoteca Turi	Italian	★
	Riva	"	★
	Lan Na Thai	Thai	★
£35+	The Stepping Stone	British, Modern	🄰★★
	Thyme	"	★★
	Sonny's	"	🄰★
	Willie Gunn	"	🄰
	Naked Turtle	International	🄰
	The White House	"	🄰
	Popeseye	Steaks & grills	★
	La Pampa	Argentinian	★
	Bombay Bicycle Club	Indian	🄰★

£30+	Balham Kitchen & Bar	*British, Modern*	Ⓐ ★
	The Depot	*"*	Ⓐ
	So.uk	*North African*	Ⓐ
	Just India	*Indian*	★
	Tsunami	*Japanese*	★★
£25+	Earl Spencer	*British, Modern*	★
	Giraffe	*International*	-
	Antipasto e Pasta	*Italian*	★
	Rocket Riverside	*Mediterranean*	Ⓐ
	El Rincón Latino	*Spanish*	Ⓐ
	Rebato's	*"*	Ⓐ
	Tootsies	*Burgers, etc*	-
	Pizza Metro	*Pizza*	Ⓐ ★★
	Basilico	*"*	★★
	Eco	*"*	★
	Eco Brixton	*"*	★
	Sarkhel's	*Indian*	★★
	Ma Goa	*"*	★
	Coromandel	*Indian, Southern*	★
£20+	Chelsea Bun Diner	*International*	-
	Bar Estrela	*Portuguese*	★
	Gourmet Burger Kitchen	*Burgers, etc*	★
	Brady's	*Fish & chips*	★
	Kastoori	*Indian*	★★
	Indian Ocean	*"*	★
£15+	Boiled Egg & Soldiers	*Sandwiches, cakes, etc*	Ⓐ
	Mirch Masala SW16	*Indian*	★★
	Sree Krishna	*"*	★
	Talad Thai	*Thai*	★★

Outer western suburbs
Kew, Richmond, Twickenham, Teddington

£50+	Monsieur Max	*French*	Ⓐ ★★
	McClements	*"*	★
£40+	The Glasshouse	*British, Modern*	Ⓐ ★★
£30+	Chez Lindsay	*French*	★
£25+	Ma Cuisine	*"*	★★

EAST

Smithfield & Farringdon (EC1)

£40+	Smiths (Top Floor)	British, Modern	A ★
	Club Gascon	French	A ★★
	Bleeding Heart	"	A ★
	Café du Marché	"	A ★
	Gaudi	Spanish	★
£35+	St John	British, Modern	★
	Moro	North African	A ★★
	Cicada	Pan-Asian	★
£30+	Alba	Italian	★
	Smiths (Dining Rm)	Steaks & grills	A
£25+	Carnevale	Vegetarian	★
£20+	The Real Greek Souvlaki	Greek	A ★★
	The Eagle	Mediterranean	A ★
£5+	Benugo	Sandwiches, cakes, etc	★

The City (EC2, EC3, EC4)

£70+	Tatsuso	Japanese	★
£50+	I Lombard Street	British, Modern	-
	Coq d'Argent	French	-
£40+	The Don	British, Modern	A ★
	Chamberlain's	Fish & seafood	★
	Vertigo	"	A
£35+	Sweetings	"	A ★
	Imperial City	Chinese	★
	City Miyama	Japanese	★★
	Miyabi	"	★
£30+	The Royal Exchange	French	A ★
£25+	The Fox	British, Modern	A ★
	Ye Olde Cheshire Cheese	British, Traditional	A
	Bar Capitale	Pizza	★
	K10	Japanese	★★
	Noto	"	★
£20+	Simpson's Tavern	British, Traditional	A
£15+	The Wine Library	"	A
	The Place Below	Vegetarian	A ★

East End & Docklands (All E postcodes)

| £70+ | Ubon | Fusion | - |
| £50+ | Les Trois Garçons | French | A |

£35+	Wapping Food	British, Modern	Ⓐ
	Il Bordello	Italian	Ⓐ★
	Lightship	Scandinavian	Ⓐ
£30+	St John Bread & Wine	British, Traditional	★
	Armadillo	South American	Ⓐ★★
	Royal China	Chinese	★★
	Café Spice Namaste	Indian	★★
	Bar Spice	"	★
£25+	LMNT	British, Modern	Ⓐ
	Haz	Turkish	★
	Itsu	Japanese	★
£20+	Faulkner's	Fish & chips	★★
£15+	S & M Café	British, Traditional	★
	Mangal	Turkish	★★
	Lahore Kebab House	Indian	★★
	New Tayyab	Pakistani	Ⓐ★
£1+	Brick Lane Beigel Bake	Sandwiches, cakes, etc	★★

LONDON INDEXES

BREAKFAST
(WITH OPENING TIMES)

Central
Balans: *all branches (8)*
Bank Aldwych *(7 Mon-Fri, Sat 8)*
Boxwood Café *(6.30)*
Café Bohème *(8)*
The Cinnamon Club *(7.30 Mon-Fri)*
Connaught (Angela Hartnett) *(Mon-Fri 7-10.30 am, Sat-Sun 7-11 am)*
Dorchester Grill *(7, Sun 7.30)*
1837 *(7, Sun 7.30)*
Food for Thought *(9.30)*
Giraffe: *W1 (8, Sat & Sun 9)*
Gordon Ramsay at Claridge's *(7 Mon-Sun)*
Goring Hotel *(7)*
Indigo *(6.30)*
Maison Bertaux *(8.30)*
Pâtisserie Valerie: *Old Compton St W1 (7.30, Sun 9); Marylebone High St W1 (8, Sun 9)*
Tapa Room (Providores) *(9, Sat & Sun 10)*
QC *(7)*
Restaurant One-O-One *(7)*
The Ritz *(7, Sun 8am)*
Savoy Hotel (River Rest.) *(7, Sun 8)*
Serafino *(7)*
Simpsons-in-the-Strand *(7.30 Mon-Fri, 10.30 Sun)*
Sotheby's Café *(9.30)*
Truc Vert *(7.30)*
Windows on the World *(7)*

West
Balans West: *all branches (8)*
Beirut Express *(7.30)*
Blakes Hotel *(7.30)*
Café Laville *(10)*
Capital Hotel *(7, Sun 7.30)*
Chelsea Bun Diner: *all branches (7)*
Clarke's *(cafe Mon-Sat)*
La Delizia *(10)*
Lisboa Patisserie *(7.45)*
Lucky Seven *(7)*
Pâtisserie Valerie: *W8 (7.30, Sun 9)*
Ranoush: *W2 (9)*
The Station *(Sat & Sun 11 am)*
Tootsies: *SW7, W4 (10, Sat & Sun); SW6 (11, Sat & Sun); W11 (8, Sat & Sun 9)*
Troubadour *(9)*

North
The Almeida *(9)*
The Engineer *(9)*
Gallipoli: *all branches (10.30)*
Giraffe: *all north branches (8, Sat & Sun 9)*
Iznik *(10.30)*
S & M Café: *N1 (8)*
Tootsies: *NW3 (11, Sat & Sun 9)*

South
Balham Kitchen & Bar *(8)*
Bar Estrela *(9 am)*
Boiled Egg *(9, Sun 10)*
Chelsea Bun Diner: *all branches (7)*
Chez Lindsay *(daily before 12:30 pm)*
Delfina Studio Café *(10)*
Eco Brixton: *SW9 (8.30)*
Giraffe: *SW11 (8, Sat & Sun 9)*
Konditor & Cook *(8.30)*
Tate Modern (Café 7) *(10)*
Tootsies: *SW19 (10, Sat & Sun); SW13 (11, Sat & Sun)*
El Vergel *(8.30)*

East
Bar Capitale: *EC4 (6 (coffee only))*
Benugo: *St John St EC1 (7.30)*
Brick Lane Beigel Bake *(24 hrs)*
Coq d'Argent *(7.30 Mon-Fri)*
1 Lombard Street *(7.30)*
The Place Below *(7.30)*
The Real Greek Souvlaki *(10)*
The Royal Exchange *(8)*
St John Bread & Wine *(8)*
Wapping Food *(10)*

BRUNCH MENUS

Central
Aurora
Balans: *W1*
Bank Aldwych
Le Caprice
1837
Giraffe: *W1*
Indigo
The Ivy
Mirabelle
Momo
Pâtisserie Valerie: *both W1*
Quaglino's
Restaurant One-O-One
Serafino
The Sugar Club
Tootsies: *W1*
Windows on the World

West
Admiral Codrington
Balans West: *SW5*
Bluebird
Café Laville
Capital Hotel
Chelsea Bun Diner: *SW10*
Clarke's
The Enterprise
Lucky Seven
Lundum's
The Oak
PJ's
Tootsies: *all west branches*
Zuma

North
The Drapers Arms
The Engineer
Giraffe: *all north branches*
Iznik
Tootsies: *NW3*

South
Boiled Egg

Chez Lindsay
El Rincón Latino
Le Pont de la Tour
The Stepping Stone
Tootsies: *SW13, SW19*
Willie Gunn

East
Armadillo
Carnevale
Smiths (Top Floor)
Wapping Food

BUSINESS

Central
Axis
Bank Aldwych
Le Caprice
The Criterion Grill
Deca
Dorchester Grill
Eddalino
1837
L'Escargot
Foliage
Le Gavroche
Goring Hotel
Indigo
The Ivy
Ken Lo's Memories
Lindsay House
Locanda Locatelli
Mango Tree
Mirabelle
Mon Plaisir
Odin's
Orrery
Pied à Terre
QC
Quaglino's
La Rascasse
Restaurant One-O-One
The Ritz
Rules
Savoy Grill
Savoy Hotel (River Rest.)
J Sheekey
Simpsons-in-the-Strand
Le Soufflé
The Square
Tamarind
Teca
Veeraswamy
Windows on the World
Zafferano

West
Aubergine
Bibendum
Bluebird
Capital Hotel
Clarke's
Gordon Ramsay
Launceston Place
Poissonnerie
    de l'Avenue

North
Frederick's
Odette's

South
Delfina Studio Café
Oxo Tower (Brasserie)
Le Pont de la Tour
Putney Bridge

East
Bleeding Heart
Café du Marché
City Miyama
Coq d'Argent
The Don
Imperial City
Moro
1 Lombard Street
Sweetings
Tatsuso

BYO
(BRING YOUR OWN WINE AT MINIMAL CORKAGE. NOTE FOR £5-£15, YOU CAN NORMALLY NEGOTIATE TO TAKE YOUR OWN BOTTLE TO MANY IF NOT MOST PLACES.)

Central
Food for Thought
Ragam

West
Blah! Blah! Blah!
Chelsea Bun Diner: *SW10*
El Gaucho: *SW3*
Tendido Cero

North
Ali Baba
Diwana B-P House
Geeta
Huong-Viet
Seashell

South
Eco Brixton: *SW9*
Mirch Masala: *all branches*
Thai Corner Café

East
Lahore Kebab House
Mangal
New Tayyab
The Place Below

CHILDREN
*(H – HIGH OR SPECIAL CHAIRS
M – CHILDREN'S MENU
P – CHILDREN'S PORTIONS
E – WEEKEND ENTERTAINMENTS
O – OTHER FACILITIES)*

Central
Al Sultan *(hp)*
Alastair Little *(h)*

The Fox *(p)*
Gaudi *(p)*
Haz *(h)*
Lahore Kebab House *(h)*
LMNT *(p)*
Miyabi *(h)*
Moro *(hp)*
The Real Greek Souvlaki *(h)*
Royal China: all branches *(h)*
The Royal Exchange *(p)*
S & M Café: all branches *(m)*
St John *(h)*
Simpson's Tavern *(p)*
Smiths (Top Floor) *(h)*
Smiths (Dining Rm) *(hp)*
Ubon *(hp)*
Wapping Food *(h)*

ENTERTAINMENT
(CHECK TIMES BEFORE YOU GO)

Central
Axis
(jazz, Tue & Wed)
Bank Aldwych
(jazz, Sun)
Bohème Kitchen
(DJ, Sun)
Café Bohème
(jazz, Thu-Sun)
Le Caprice
(pianist, nightly)
The Criterion Grill
(magician, Wed-Thu)
Foliage
(jazz, Mon-Sat)
Garanger Restaurant Bar
(DJ, Thu-Sat)
Goring Hotel
(pianist, nightly)
Hakkasan
(DJ, nightly)
Indigo
(film brunches, Sat & Sun)
Kai
(harpist, Thu & Sat)
The Langley
(DJ, Thu-Sat)
Levant
(live music, Mon-Wed; DJ & bellydancer Thu-Sun)
Mezzo
(live music, nightly)
Mirabelle
(pianist Tue-Sat & Sun L)
Momo
(live world music, Mon-Wed)
Opium
(DJ, Thu-Sat; cabaret, Tue & Wed)
La Porte des Indes
(jazz, Sun brunch)
Quaglino's
(jazz, nightly; pianist, Sat & Sun brunch)
The Ritz
(band, Fri & Sat (nightly in Dec))
Sarastro
(opera, Sun & Mon)
Savoy Hotel (River Rest.)
(dinner dance, Fri & Sat)
Simpsons-in-the-Strand
(pianist, nightly)
Le Soufflé
(string trio, Sun L; pianist nightly)
Souk
(belly dancer, live music & DJ, Thu-Sat)

Sumosan
(DJ, Thu-Sat)
Windows on the World
(dinner dance, Fri & Sat; jazz, Sun brunch)

West
Bluebird
(DJ , Fri & Sat)
Bombay Brasserie
(pianist & singer, nightly; jazz Sat & Sun L)
Chutney Mary
(jazz, Sun)
Mr Wing
(jazz, Fri & Sat)
The Station
(DJ, Thu-Sat; jazz, Sun)
Sugar Hut
(band)
Vama
(jazz, Sun)
William IV
(DJ, Fri & Sat)

North
Fez
(bellydancer, Fri & Sat; DJ, Tue-Sat)
The Highgate
(DJ, Sat & Sun)
The House
(DJ, Sun L)

South
Baltic
(jazz, Sun & Mon)
Bengal Clipper
(pianist, nightly)
Naked Turtle
(live music, nightly)
So.uk: SW4
(DJ, Wed-Sun)
Talad Thai
(karaoke)
Tas: Borough High St SE1
(guitarist, nightly); The Cut SE1
(live music, nightly)
3 Monkeys
(jazz, Sun)
The Trafalgar Tavern
(band, Sat & Sun)
The White House
(DJ, Wed-Sun)

East
Café du Marché
(pianist & bass, nightly)
Coq d'Argent
(pianist Sat; jazz Fri & Sun L)
LMNT
(opera, Sun)

LATE
(OPEN TILL MIDNIGHT OR LATER AS SHOWN; MAY BE EARLIER SUNDAY)

Central
Balans: W1 *(5 am, Sun 1 am)*
Beiteddine *(1)*
Café Bohème *(2.45 am, Thu-Sat open 24 hours)*
Le Caprice *(1)*
Incognico *(1)*
Itsu: W1 *(midnight, Fri & Sat)*
The Ivy *(1)*
Mezzo *(midnight, Thu-Sat 1 am (crustacea till 3 am))*
Mr Kong *(2.45 am)*

NO-SMOKING AREAS
(* COMPLETELY NO SMOKING)

Samphire
Seashell
Sushi-Say*
Toff's
Two Brothers

South
Babur Brasserie
Bermondsey Kitchen
Chapter Two*
Chez Bruce
Coromandel
The Depot
Eco: SW4
Giraffe: all branches*
Gourmet Burger Kitchen: all branches*
Indian Ocean
Konditor & Cook
The Light House
McClements
Mirch Masala: SW17*
Naked Turtle
Sarkhel's
The Stepping Stone
Talad Thai*
Tate Modern (Café 7)*
Thailand*
3 Monkeys*
Thyme*
Tsunami
El Vergel*

East
Bar Spice
Brick Lane Beigel Bake*
Chamberlain's
Cicada
Faulkner's
Haz
Itsu: all branches*
K10*
Noto*
Ye Olde
   Cheshire Cheese
The Place Below*
Tatsuso
Ubon

OUTSIDE TABLES
(PARTICULARLY RECOMMENDED)*

Central
Al Sultan
Aurora*
Back to Basics
Balans: all branches
Brian Turner
Café Bohème
Caraffini
The Endurance
Giraffe: W1
Gordon's Wine Bar*
Mela
Mirabelle*
Momo
Orrery

La Poule au Pot*
Tapa Room (Providores)
The Ritz*
Rocket: all branches
Sarastro
Serafino
Tajine
Tootsies: all branches
Toto's*
Truc Vert

West
Admiral Codrington*
The Anglesea Arms
The Atlas*
Balans West: all branches
Belvedere*
Bibendum Oyster Bar
Black & Blue: W8
Bombay Brasserie
Bombay Palace
The Builder's Arms
Café Laville*
La Delizia
E&O
Ealing Park Tavern
The Gate: W6*
El Gaucho: SW3*
Giraffe: all west branches
The Havelock Tavern
Julie's
The Ladbroke Arms*
Latymers
Lisboa Patisserie
Lou Pescadou
Lundum's
Made in Italy
The Mall Tavern
Mao Tai: SW3
Mediterraneo
Nicolas Bar à Vins
The Oak
Osteria Basilico
The Painted Heron
PJ's
Poissonnerie
   de l'Avenue
Ognisko Polskie*
The Red Pepper
The River Café*
The Station*
The Swan*
Thai on the River*
Tootsies: all branches
La Trompette
Troubadour
Uli*
Vama
The Westbourne*
William IV*
The Windsor Castle*

North
L'Aventure*
Black & Blue: NW3
The Drapers Arms
The Engineer*

INDEXES

North
L'Aventure
The Engineer
Frederick's
Iznik
Odette's
Oslo Court
The Real Greek
Soulard

South
Champor-Champor
Chez Bruce
The Glasshouse
Monsieur Max
Oxo Tower (Brasserie)
Le Pont de la Tour
Putney Bridge
Sonny's
The Stepping Stone

East
Bleeding Heart
Café du Marché
Club Gascon
Lightship
LMNT
Moro
Les Trois Garçons

Teca

West
Bibendum
Clarke's
Monkeys
Nicolas Bar à Vins

North
Cru
Odette's
The Real Greek

South
Chez Bruce
Enoteca Turi
McClements
Le Pont de la Tour
Redmond's
Tentazioni

East
Alba
Bleeding Heart
Club Gascon
The Real Greek Souvlaki
Wapping Food
The Wine Library

ROOMS WITH A VIEW

Central
Foliage
Orrery
The Ritz
Savoy Hotel (River Rest.)
Windows on the World

West
Belvedere
Café Laville
Thai on the River

South
The Depot
Oxo Tower (Brasserie)
Le Pont de la Tour
Putney Bridge
Tate Modern (Café 7)
The Trafalgar Tavern

East
Coq d'Argent
Smiths (Top Floor)
Ubon
Vertigo

NOTABLE WINE LISTS

Central
Andrew Edmunds
1837
Le Gavroche
Mirabelle
Sotheby's Café
Le Soufflé
The Square

LONDON MAPS

MAP 1 — WEST END OVERVIEW

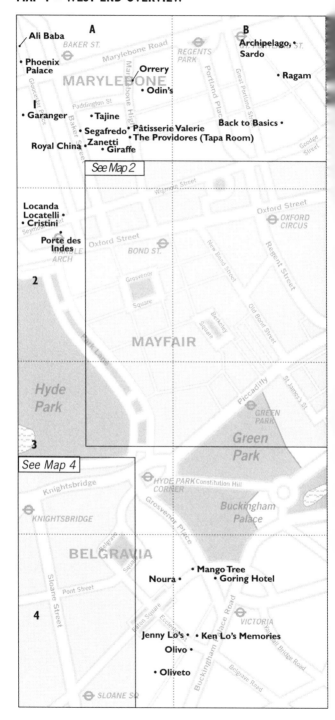

MAP I – WEST END OVERVIEW

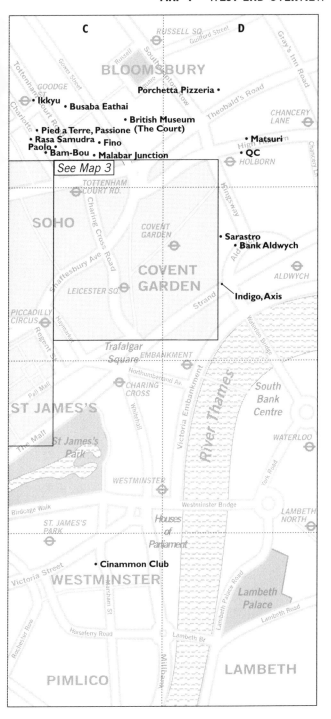

MAP 2 – MAYFAIR, ST JAMES'S & WEST SOHO

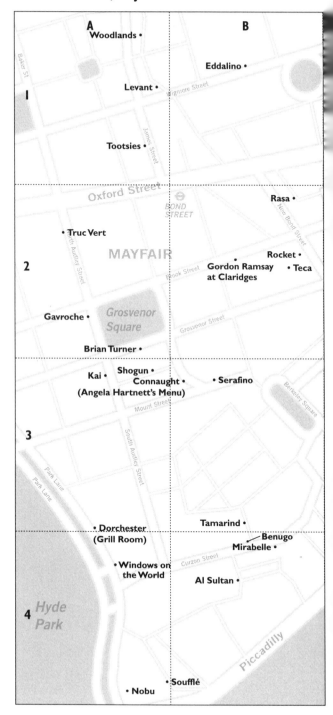

MAP 2 – MAYFAIR, ST JAMES'S & WEST SOHO

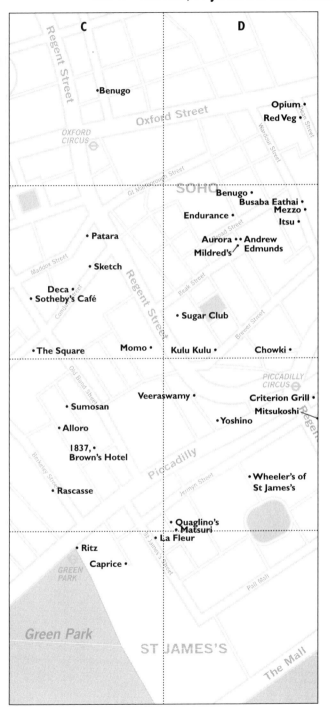

MAP 3 – EAST SOHO, CHINATOWN & COVENT GARDEN

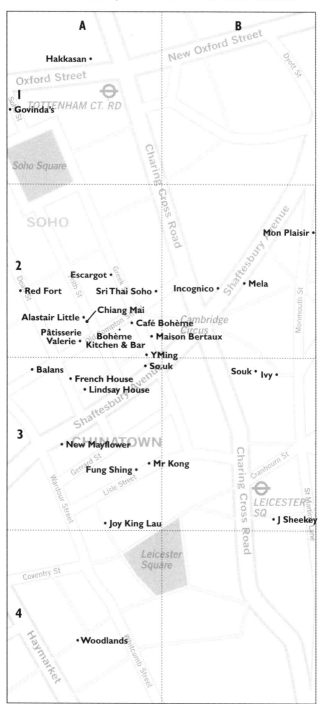

MAP 3 – EAST SOHO, CHINATOWN & COVENT GARDEN

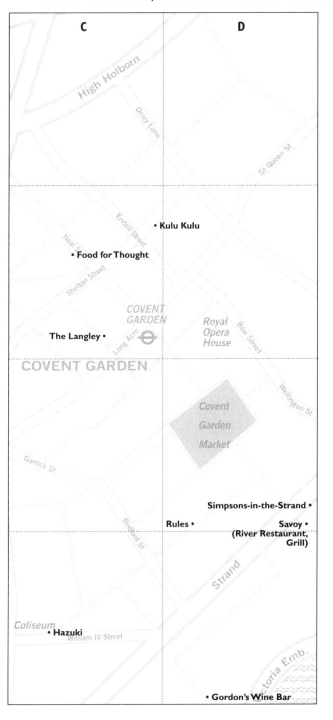

MAP 4 – KNIGHTSBRIDGE, CHELSEA & SOUTH KENSINGTON

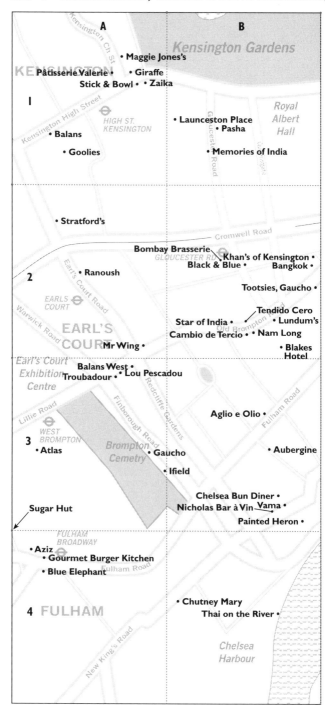

MAP 4 – KNIGHTSBRIDGE, CHELSEA & SOUTH KENSINGTON

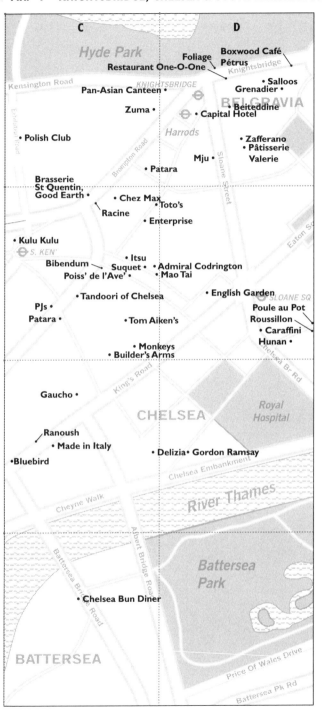

Hyde Park

Boxwood Café
Foliage **Pétrus**
Restaurant One-O-One Knightsbridge
Kensington Road • **Salloos**
KNIGHTSBRIDGE **Grenadier** •
Pan-Asian Canteen • **BELGRAVIA**
• **Beiteddine**
Zuma • • **Capital Hotel**

Harrods

• **Polish Club** • **Zafferano**
• **Pâtisserie**
Mju • **Valerie**

Brasserie • **Patara**
St Quentin;
Good Earth •
• **Chez Max**
Racine • **Toto's**
• **Enterprise**

• **Kulu Kulu**
S. KEN
• **Itsu**
Bibendum **Suquet** • • **Admiral Codrington**
Poiss' de l'Ave' • • **Mao Tai**

• **Tandoori of Chelsea** • **English Garden**
SLOANE SQ
PJs • **Poule au Pot**
Patara • **Roussillon** —
• **Caraffini**
• **Tom Aiken's** **Hunan** •

• **Monkeys**
• **Builder's Arms**

Gaucho •
CHELSEA *Royal*
Hospital

Ranoush
• **Made in Italy**
• **Delizia** • **Gordon Ramsay**
•**Bluebird**
Chelsea Embankment

River Thames

Cheyne Walk

Battersea
Park

• **Chelsea Bun Diner**

BATTERSEA
Price Of Wales Drive
Battersea Pk Rd

MAP 5 – THE CITY

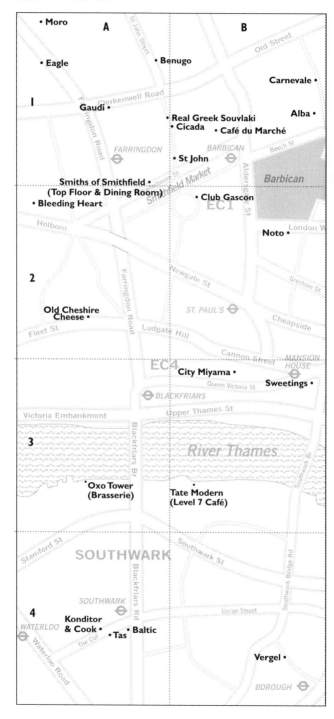

MAP 5 – THE CITY

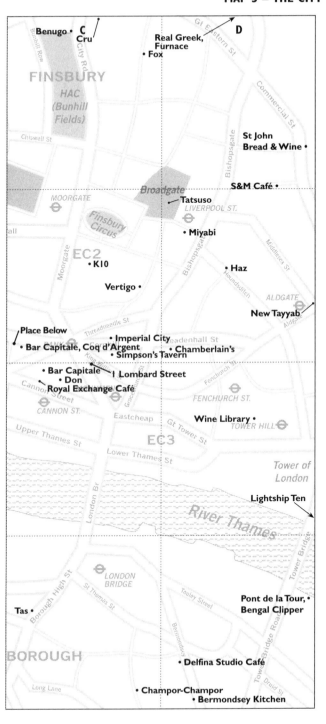

Benugo • **C**
Cru

Real Greek,
Furnace
• **Fox**

FINSBURY

HAC
(Bunhill
Fields)

Chiswell St

Bunhill Row

City Road

Gt Eastern St

D

Commercial St

Bishopsgate

St John
Bread & Wine •

S&M Café •

Broadgate

MOORGATE

Finsbury
Circus

EC2

• **K10**

Vertigo •

—**Tatsuso**

LIVERPOOL ST.

• **Miyabi**

Bishopsgate

Middlesex St

• **Haz**

Houndsditch

ALDGATE

New Tayyab

Aldgate

Moorgate

all

Place Below

• **Bar Capitale, Coq d'Argent**

• **Bar Capitale**
• **Don**
Royal Exchange Café

Cannon Street

CANNON ST.

Upper Thames St

Threadneedle St

• **Imperial City**
• **Simpson's Tavern**

I **Lombard Street**

King William

Eastcheap

EC3

Leadenhall St

• **Chamberlain's**

Gracechurch St

Fenchurch St

FENCHURCH ST.

Gt Tower St

Wine Library •

TOWER HILL

Lower Thames St

Tower of
London

London Br

Lightship Ten

River Thames

Tower Bridge

Tas •

Borough High St

St Thomas St

LONDON
BRIDGE

Tooley Street

Pont de la Tour, •
Bengal Clipper

Bermondsey

Tower Bridge Road

BOROUGH

Long Lane

• **Delfina Studio Café**

Druid St

• **Champor-Champor**
• **Bermondsey Kitchen**

MAP 6 – SOUTH LONDON (& FULHAM)

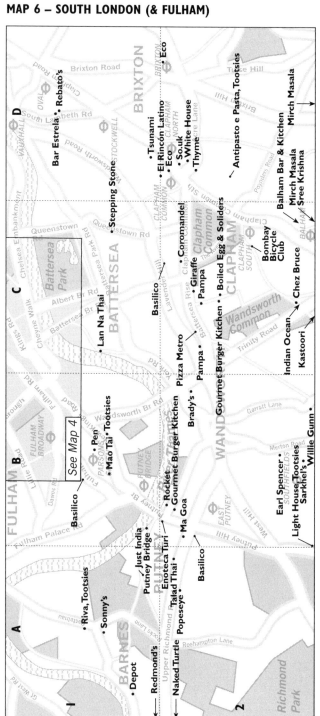

UK SURVEY RESULTS
& TOP SCORERS

PLACES PEOPLE TALK ABOUT

These are the restaurants outside London that were mentioned most frequently by reporters (last year's position is shown in brackets). For the list of London's most mentioned restaurants, see page 19.

1	Manoir aux Quat' Saisons *(1)*	*Great Milton, Oxon*
2	Seafood Restaurant *(2)*	*Padstow, Cornwall*
3	Waterside Inn *(3)*	*Bray, Berks*
4	Fat Duck *(5)*	*Bray*
5	Yang Sing *(4)*	*Manchester*
6	Magpie *(6)*	*Whitby*
7	Winteringham Fields *(–)*	*Winteringham*
8	The Angel *(11)*	*Hetton, N Yorks*
9	Star Inn *(–)*	*Harome*
10	Terre à Terre *(8)*	*Brighton*
11=	The Witchery *(16)*	*Edinburgh*
11=	Whitstable Oyster *(15)*	*Whitstable, Kent*
13=	Croma *(17)*	*Manchester*
13=	Merchant House *(20)*	*Ludlow*
15=	Drum & Monkey *(19)*	*Harrogate*
15=	Vineyard at Stockcross *(–)*	*Stockcross*
15=	Harts *(12=)*	*Nottingham*
15=	Nobody Inn *(–)*	*Doddiscombsleigh*
19	Sharrow Bay *(12=)*	*Ullswater*
20	Restaurant Bar & Grill *(–)*	*Manchester*

TOP SCORERS

All restaurants whose food rating is ★★; plus restaurants whose price is £50+ with a food rating of ★.

(Dublin restaurant prices have been converted to £.)

£110+	Le Manoir aux Quat' Saisons *(Great Milton)*	★Ⓐ
	Waterside Inn *(Bray)*	★
£90+	Gidleigh Park *(Chagford)*	★Ⓐ
£80+	Andrew Fairlie *(Auchterarder)*	★Ⓐ
£70+	Winteringham Fields *(Winteringham)*	★★Ⓐ
	Lords of the Manor *(Upper Slaughter)*	★Ⓐ
	Restaurant Patrick Guilbaud *(Dublin)*	★
£60+	L'Enclume *(Cartmel)*	★★Ⓐ
	Northcote Manor *(Langho)*	★★Ⓐ
	Ynyshir Hall *(Eglwysfach)*	★★Ⓐ
	Bath Priory Hotel *(Bath)*	★Ⓐ
	Chewton Glen *(New Milton)*	★Ⓐ
	Fischers at Baslow Hall *(Baslow)*	★Ⓐ
	Hambleton Hall *(Hambleton)*	★Ⓐ
	Holbeck Ghyll *(Windermere)*	★Ⓐ
	Longueville Manor *(Jersey)*	★Ⓐ
	Mallory Court *(Bishops Tachbrook)*	★Ⓐ
	Midsummer House *(Cambridge)*	★Ⓐ
	Harry's Place *(Great Gonerby)*	★
£50+	Morston Hall *(Morston)*	★★Ⓐ
	Three Chimneys *(Dunvegan)*	★★Ⓐ
	Underscar Manor *(Applethwaite)*	★★Ⓐ
	Champignon Sauvage *(Cheltenham)*	★★
	Drakes On The Pond *(Abinger Hammer)*	★★
	Hotel des Clos *(Nottingham)*	★★
	Old Chesil Rectory *(Winchester)*	★★
	Restaurant Martin Wishart *(Edinburgh)*	★★
	Shanks *(Bangor)*	★★
	The Vanilla Pod *(Marlow)*	★★
	Alexander House *(Turners Hill)*	★Ⓐ
	Auberge du Lac *(Lemsford)*	★Ⓐ
	Eastwell Manor *(Boughton Lees)*	★Ⓐ
	Kinnaird House *(Dunkeld)*	★Ⓐ
	Manor House *(Chippenham)*	★Ⓐ
	The Mirabelle *(Eastbourne)*	★Ⓐ
	Seaham Hall *(Seaham)*	★Ⓐ
	Sharrow Bay *(Ullswater)*	★Ⓐ
	Ston Easton Park *(Ston Easton)*	★Ⓐ
	Tylney Hall *(Hook)*	★Ⓐ
	Vermilion *(Edinburgh)*	★Ⓐ
	36 on the Quay *(Emsworth)*	★
	Adlards *(Norwich)*	★
	Amaryllis *(Glasgow)*	★
	L'Ecrivain *(Dublin)*	★
	Fisherman's Lodge *(Newcastle upon Tyne)*	★
	Horn of Plenty *(Gulworthy)*	★
	Juniper *(Manchester)*	★
	Kaifeng *(Harrow)*	★

TOP SCORERS

	Le Poussin at Parkhill *(Lyndhurst)*	★
	Moss Nook *(Manchester)*	★
	One Paston Place *(Brighton)*	★
	Overton Grange *(Ludlow)*	★
	Pool Court at 42 *(Leeds)*	★
	Sundial *(Herstmonceux)*	★
£40+	22 Mill Street *(Chagford)*	★★𝐴
	Café du Moulin *(St Peters)*	★★𝐴
	Cellar *(Anstruther)*	★★𝐴
	Little Barwick House *(Barwick Village)*	★★𝐴
	Monachyle Mhor *(Balquhidder)*	★★𝐴
	Star Inn *(Harome)*	★★𝐴
	Summer Isles *(Achiltibuie)*	★★𝐴
	5 North Street *(Winchcombe)*	★★
	Hibiscus *(Ludlow)*	★★
	JSW *(Petersfield)*	★★
	Merchant House *(Ludlow)*	★★
£30+	Endeavour *(Staithes)*	★★𝐴
	Fox And Goose *(Armscote)*	★★𝐴
	Gingerhill *(Glasgow)*	★★𝐴
	Great House *(Lavenham)*	★★𝐴
	Jeremys at Borde Hill *(Haywards Heath)*	★★𝐴
	Les Mirabelles *(Nomansland)*	★★𝐴
	Let's Eat *(Perth)*	★★𝐴
	Quince & Medlar *(Cockermouth)*	★★𝐴
	Rowan Tree *(Askrigg)*	★★𝐴
	Terre à Terre *(Brighton)*	★★𝐴
	The Angel *(Hetton)*	★★𝐴
	Three Acres *(Shelley)*	★★𝐴
	Black Chapati *(Brighton)*	★★
	Crannog *(Fort William)*	★★
	Crooked Billet *(Newton Longville)*	★★
	Ee-Usk (Fish Café) *(Oban)*	★★
	Nutter's *(Cheesden)*	★★
	Riverside *(Bridport)*	★★
	Yang Sing *(Manchester)*	★★
£20+	Chiang Mai *(Oxford)*	★★𝐴
	Drum & Monkey *(Harrogate)*	★★𝐴
	Oyster Shack *(Bigbury)*	★★𝐴
	Pier House Hotel *(Port Appin)*	★★𝐴
	Tomlins *(Cardiff)*	★★𝐴
	Koh Samui *(Manchester)*	★★
	Little Yang Sing *(Manchester)*	★★
	Magpie Café *(Whitby)*	★★
	Rumwong *(Guildford)*	★★
	Saagar *(Nottingham)*	★★
	Wheeler's Oyster Bar *(Whitstable)*	★★
£15+	Chez Fred *(Bournemouth)*	★★
	Punjab Tandoori *(Manchester)*	★★
	The Mermaid Café *(Hastings)*	★★
	Trenchers *(Whitby)*	★★
£10+	Mumtaz Paan House *(Bradford)*	★★
	The Company Shed *(West Mersea)*	★★

OPENINGS & CLOSURES

The following lists contain restaurants which have opened or closed since the publication of *Harden's UK Restaurants 2003*.

OPENINGS

Barnsley House	Barnsley
Café Paradiso	Manchester
Darcys	St Albans
Eden	Coventry
Ego	Liverpool
Five North Street	Winchcombe
Francs at The Lowry	Manchester
Graffiti	Cambridge
Ickworth Hotel	Bury St Edmunds
Inn on the Green	Cookham Dean
Kro2	Manchester
Marlow Bar & Grill	Marlow
Michael Caines	Bristol
Le Mont	Manchester
Morgan's	Swansea
New French Partridge	Horton
Red Lion	Stathern
Tavistock at the Grotto	South Shields
Thai Edge	Leeds
Willow Tree	Taunton

CLOSURES

Blinis	Bath
Cassoulet	Cardiff
Chez Gérard	Manchester
Clarks	Bournemouth
Darbar	Manchester
Dermotts	Swansea
Elizabeth's	Oxford
fish!	Birmingham, Guildford
(fitz) Henry	Edinburgh
Fusion	Glasgow
Harbour Lights	Porthgain
Harvey's	Bristol
Hooked	Dartmouth
Josephs	St Ives
Kooky @ Whytes	Brighton
Lemon Tree	Worcester
Markwick's	Bristol
Nairns	Glasgow
Number 7 Café	Liverpool
Old Manor House	Romsey
Old Mill	Shipston-on-Stour
Puppet Theatre	Glasgow
Red Onion Bistro	Sudbury
Reform	Manchester
Rhodes & Co	Manchester
Tandoori Kitchen	Manchester
Yes!	Glasgow

UK DIRECTORY

Comments in "double quotation-marks" were made
by reporters.

ABERDEEN, ABERDEEN 9–2D

Foyer
Trinity Church £29 𝔸★
82a Crown Street AB11 6ET (01224) 582277
You get "good bistro-style food, and support a good cause, too" at this converted church (which is run by a charity for the homeless); "the cooking is great and the changing artwork in the gallery adds to the ambience". / **Sample dishes:** gnocchi with Gorgonzola & spinach; pan-fried chicken with smoked bacon & sage risotto; pecan pie with banana ice cream. **Details:** www.aberdeenfoyer.com; 10 pm; closed Mon & Sun; no Amex; no smoking area; children: 14+ after 8 pm.

Silver Darling £45 𝔸
Pocra Quay, North Pier AB11 5DQ (01224) 576229
"Good-quality seafood in a superb location overlooking the North Sea, but overpriced" – one account neatly summarises reporters' views on this former lighthouse. / **Sample dishes:** prawn ravioli with Parma ham & lobster oil; sea bass with tapenade & aniseed butter; tarte Tatin with green apple sorbet. **Details:** beside lighthouse; 9.30 pm; closed Sat L & Sun; no smoking in dining room.

Simpsons £34
59 Queens Rd AB15 4YP (01224) 327799
There's "good and simple", "Italianate" food to be had at this modern hotel brasserie, convenient for the AECC. / **Sample dishes:** black pudding with apple croquettes; pork with haggis & spring onion frittata; chocolate orange tart. **Details:** www.simpsonshotel.co.uk; 9.45 pm; no smoking area. **Accommodation:** 50 rooms, from £85.

ABERDYFI, 4–3C

Penhelig Arms £31 𝔸★
LL35 0LT (01654) 767215
"A charming setting overlooking the sea" adds to the attractions of this "civilised", "estuary-side" hotel, which offers "a good menu, especially the fish", and a "comprehensive wine list". / **Sample dishes:** spinach & cream cheese lasagne; char-grilled lamb with roast aubergines; raspberry frangipane tart. **Details:** www.penheligarms.com; 9.30 pm; no Amex; no smoking in dining room. **Accommodation:** 14 rooms, from £118.

ABERFORD, WEST YORKSHIRE 5–1C

Swan Hotel £21 𝔸★
Great North Rd LS25 3AA (0113) 281 3205
"You need to get there early", if you're going to enjoy the "high-quality" fare on offer at this attractive 16th-century coaching inn. / **Sample dishes:** seafood salad; chicken with sweet chili; cheesecake. **Details:** www.swanaberford.co.uk; 9.30 pm; closed Mon & Tue, Wed-Sat closed L; book only for restaurant.

ABERGAVENNY, MONMOUTHSHIRE 2–1A

Clytha Arms £32
NP7 9BW (01873) 840206
"Not glam, but very friendly" – this well-established, family-run inn offers "hearty", "better-than-pub" food, and "a good wine list". / **Sample dishes:** melon & avocado salad; roast hake with herb salsa; Sauternes cream with spiced prunes. **Details:** www.clytha-arms.com; on Old Abergavenny to Raglan Road; 9.30 pm; closed Mon & Sun D; no smoking. **Accommodation:** 4 rooms, from £70.

Walnut Tree £41
Llandewi Skirrid NP7 8AW (01873) 852797

"We miss Franco Taruschio" – the glory days of this once-famed converted pub left when Signor T did, and the place now risks falling into obscurity; with subsequent chef Steven Terry's departure (in early 2003), unknown Stefano Lodi-Rizzini has taken the menu back to its Italian roots – one early reporter was impressed.

/ **Sample dishes:** endive, pancetta & Dolcelatte salad; corned beef hash with spinach & fried egg; steamed treacle sponge pudding.
Details: www.thewalnuttreeinn.com; 3m NE of Abergavenny on B4521; 9.45 pm; closed Mon & Sun D; no Amex; no smoking in dining room.

ABINGER HAMMER, SURREY 3–3A

Drakes On The Pond £52 ★★
Docking Rd RH5 6SA (01306) 731174

Steven Drake's *"careful"* cooking is *"highly recommended"* by all who report on his *"outstanding"* venture; some find its style *"lovely"* and *"intimate"*, but others liken it to *"a Travelodge"*.

/ **Sample dishes:** warm salad of asparagus with rocket & pea purée; roast duck breast with potatoes & elderberry sauce; orange & almond savarin with almond ice cream. **Details:** www.drakesonthepond.com; 9.30 pm; closed Mon & Sun; no smoking.

ACHILTIBUIE, HIGHLAND 9–1B

Summer Isles £48 𝔸★★
IV26 2YG (01854) 622282

With its *"great seafood, wonderful cheeses, cracking wine list, and views to die for"*, this remote but celebrated hotel (looking out onto the islands after which it is named) really is a gastronomic *"haven"*, right down to the *"impeccable"* service.

/ **Sample dishes:** grilled mushrooms with Parmesan croutons; grilled turbot with lime & capers; lemon soufflé crêpes. **Details:** www.summerisleshotel.co.uk; 25m N of Ullapool on A835; 8 pm; no Amex; no smoking; children: 6+.
Accommodation: 13 rooms, from £98.

ALDEBURGH, SUFFOLK 3–1D

Lighthouse £27 ★
77 High St IP15 5AU (01728) 453377

Consistency seems to have been much improved at this *"wonderful"* fish bistro; it is very *"well known in the locality"*, so *"safest to book"* if you want to enjoy the *"consistent and delicious"* cooking – *"make sure you order anything that says 'local catch'"*.

/ **Sample dishes:** celery & blue cheese soup; sole with lime butter; boozy banana pancakes. **Details:** 10 pm; open L & D all week; closed for 2 weeks in Jan & 1 week in Oct; no smoking area.

152 £32
152 High St IP15 5AX (01728) 454594

"Interesting seafood" in a *"down-to-earth"* environment is the deal at this *"lovely"* seashore bistro; its wines are *"reasonably priced"*, too. / **Sample dishes:** carrot, tomato & ginger soup; lamb with pea purée & red pepper relish; cappucino crème brûlée. **Details:** www.152aldeburgh.co.uk; 10 pm (9 pm in winter); closed Tue (& Mon in winter); no smoking area.

Regatta   £ 27   ★
171 High St IP15 5AN   (01728) 452011
"Great family atmosphere, good home-style cooking and charming local service" – reporters can see very little to fault with this *"wonderful"* seafood restaurant, which, over the past year, seems to have 'raised its game'. / **Sample dishes:** smoked prawns; duck with French beans; crème brûlée. **Details:** www.regattaaldeburgh.com; 10 pm; closed Mon-Wed in Nov-Mar; no smoking area.

Wentworth Hotel   £ 24
Wentworth Rd IP15 5BD   (01728) 452312
The *"loyal client base"* speaks volumes for the steady charms of this seaside hotel, long in the ownership of the same family; it attracts uniform praise for its *"good food and wine at very sensible prices"*. / **Sample dishes:** platter of smoked salmon; oven baked sea bream topped with roast vegetables; raspberry mousse cake with raspberry sauce & cream. **Details:** www.wentworth-aldeburgh.co.uk; 9 pm; no smoking.

ALDFORD, CHESHIRE   5–3A
The Grosvenor Arms   £ 31   Ⓐ
Chester Rd CH3 6HJ   (01244) 620228
"It is always best to book" for this *"busy gastropub"* in a *"charming ducal village"*; *"excellent real ales and good single malts"* complement the *"good-value"* (but not at all ambitious) cooking, served in *"spacious"* surroundings. / **Sample dishes:** corned beef & black pudding hash cake; pork chops with Stilton rarebit topping; chocolate bread & butter pudding. **Details:** 6m S of Chester on B5130; 10 pm, Sun 9 pm; no smoking area; children: 14+ after 6 pm.

AMBERLEY, WEST SUSSEX   3–4A
Amberley Castle   £ 63   Ⓐ
BN18 9ND   (01798) 831992
"We met and were married here (not on the same day)" – the story-book charms of this *"beautiful"* 12th-century castle make it a 'natural' as a romantic venue; perhaps unsurprisingly, the food can seem rather *"ordinary"* by comparison. / **Sample dishes:** game terrine with plum chutney; salmon pavé with celeriac cream; roast pears with champagne sorbet. **Details:** www.amberleycastle.co.uk; N of Arundel on B2139; 9.30 pm; jacket and/or tie; no smoking; booking: max 8; children: 12+. **Accommodation:** 19 rooms, from £145.

AMBLESIDE, CUMBRIA   7–3D
Drunken Duck   £ 34   Ⓐ
Barngates LA22 0NG   (01539) 436347
An *"idyllic"* setting has been the making, but is also perhaps in some ways the curse, of this *"ever-popular"* (beware queues) pub-cum-brewery – even those who say the food is *"superb"* may also find it *"badly overpriced"*. / **Sample dishes:** chicken with sugar snap peas; quail stuffed with prune risotto; lemon torte with spiced oranges. **Details:** www.drunkenduckinn.co.uk; 3m from Ambleside, towards Hawkshead; 9 pm; no smoking; booking: max 6. **Accommodation:** 16 rooms, from £85.

The Glass House   £ 40   Ⓐ★
Rydal Rd LA22 9AN   (01539) 432137
"Innovative" cooking in a *"gorgeous"* setting makes this *"very trendy"* (*"by Lakes standards"*) mill-conversion all the more worth knowing about; the wine list is also of note. / **Sample dishes:** tomato & Parmesan tart; roast monkfish with Parma ham & vegetable crêpes; mint chocolate chip soufflé. **Details:** www.theglasshouserestaurant.co.uk; behind Little Bridge House; 10 pm; closed Tue (& all of Jan); no Amex; no smoking; children: 5+ at D.

Lucy's on a Plate £32 ★
Church St LA22 0BU (01539) 431191
This "homely" venture "attached to a deli" is "worth going to at any time of day"; it serves "first-class breakfasts", coffee and simple but "inventive" full meals (and its puddings are "the comfort food of the gods"). / *Sample dishes:* scallops with cream & dill; roast lamb with minted bacon jus; Belgian chocolate bread & butter pudding.
Details: www.lucys-on-a-plate.co.uk; 9 pm; no Amex; no smoking.

Rothay Manor £35 🅐★
Rothay Bridge LA22 0EH (01539) 433605
This Regency country house hotel is a good all-rounder with a "beautiful setting", and it's especially popular with families; the "generous" portions served in the "spacious" dining room contribute to an overall "good-value" impression.
/ *Sample dishes:* grilled sardines with rosemary; roast duck with red cabbage & juniper sauce; pavlova with summer fruits. *Details:* www.rothaymanor.co.uk; 9 pm; no smoking in dining room; children: 7+ at D. *Accommodation:* 17 rooms, from £130.

Sheila's Cottage £30
The Slack LA22 9DQ (01539) 433079
Some "mourn the days when it was run by Sheila and her husband", but this cutely-located tea shop (which moonlights as a restaurant) mostly wins praise for its "tasty" food and its "relaxing" atmosphere.
/ *Sample dishes:* salmon mousse with roast tomatoes; roast pheasant with walnut & spinach risotto; treacle tart with custard.
Details: www.amblesideonline.co.uk; next to Queen's Hotel; 9 pm; closed Tue D & Wed D in winter; no Amex; no smoking; children: 8+ after 6 pm.

Zeffirelli's £27 🅐★
Compston Rd LA22 9AD (01539) 433845
"There's a long wait at times, but it's worth it" – this "excellent-all-round" venture (a funky mix of café and cinema) delivers "excellent veggie food" (majoring in pizza) which most reporters judge just "amazing value". / *Sample dishes:* pesto & cherry tomato bruschetta; red chilli bean & Cheddar pizza; tiramisu. *Details:* www.zeffirellis.co.uk; 10 pm; no Amex; no smoking.

AMERSHAM, BUCKINGHAMSHIRE 3–2A
Famous Fish £33
11 Market Sq HP7 0DF (01494) 728665
"Good fish with a South African twist" wins a steady following for this "tightly squeezed" venture, in old Amersham.
/ *Sample dishes:* grilled prawn tails with avocado; Cajun cod with tomato concasse; crème brûlée. *Details:* in Old Amersham; 10 pm; closed Sun; no smoking.

Kings Arms £32
30 High St HP7 0DJ (01494) 726333
The upstairs dining room of this ancient town-centre tavern can make quite a romantic choice, and the comparatively "good" cooking on offer can come as "a nice surprise".
/ *Sample dishes:* pheasant terrine; salmon & monkfish brochettes with ginger dressing; chocolate & hazelnut galettes. *Details:* www.kingsarmsamersham.co.uk; in Old Amersham; 9.30 pm; closed Mon & Sun D.

Santhi £28
16 Hill Ave HP6 5BW (01494) 432621
Some can find the unusual décor "a bit overbearing", but this Indian, near the terminus of the Metropolitan line wins praise from locals for its "great" curries. / *Details:* www.santhirestaurant.co.uk; 10.45 pm; no smoking area.

ANSTRUTHER, FIFE   9–4D

Anstruther Fish Bar   £13   ★

42-44 Shore St KY10 3EA   (01333) 310518
"The best fish and chips in Scotland!", say fans of this "very busy"
chippie; "it's worth a detour, but don't dress up!". / **Details:** 10 pm;
no Amex; no smoking.

Cellar   £44   A★★

24 East Grn KY10 3AA   (01333) 310378
"My favourite Scottish restaurant for over 20 years" – Peter
& Susan Jukes's "very atmospheric" basement (in an historic
building behind the Scottish Fisheries Museum) has long been
known for its "simple, first-class" fish (complemented by a
"well thought-out" wine list). / **Sample dishes:** asparagus & leek soup; roast
pesto-crusted cod; hazelnut praline parfait. **Details:** 9.30 pm; closed Mon L &
Tue L; no smoking pre 9.30 pm; children: 8+.

APPLECROSS, HIGHLAND   9–2B

Applecross Inn   £29   ★

Shore St IV54 8LR   (01520) 744262
"Sit outside and enjoy the view" – the sunsets are "to die for" at this
waterside tavern; its food has "no pretensions", but is notably good –
"seafood fresh from the fishermen, beautifully cooked and
presented". / **Sample dishes:** hot-smoked salmon; venison sausages with
mash & onion gravy; chocolate brûlée. **Details:** www.applecross.co.uk; off A896,
S of Shieldaig; 9 pm; no Amex; no smoking in dining room. **Accommodation:** 7
rooms, from £60.

APPLETHWAITE, CUMBRIA   7–3C

Underscar Manor   £53   A★★

CA12 4PH   (01768) 775000
Robert Thornton's cooking is "always excellent", and this small
country house hotel overlooking Derwent Water has "breathtaking"
views ("watch red squirrels while you eat"!) and a "wonderful"
ambience. / **Sample dishes:** Swiss cheese soufflé with buttered spinach; roast
lamb with moussaka gâteau; mini citrus desserts. **Details:** on A66, 17m W of M6,
J40; 8.30 pm; jacket at D; no smoking; children: 12+. **Accommodation:** 11 rooms,
from £180.

ARDEN, ARGYLL & BUTE   9–4B

Duck Bay Hotel & Marina   £33   A

Duck Bay G83 8QZ   (01389) 751234
"Large helpings" contribute to the "great-value" impression of dining
at this lochside dining room (which has great views).
/ **Sample dishes:** kromesky (deep-fried meat parcels); roast lamb; mocha chocolate
mousse. **Details:** www.duckbayhotel.com; off A82; 10 pm; no trainers.
Accommodation: 18 rooms, from £85.

ARMSCOTE, WARWICKSHIRE   2–1C

Fox And Goose   £33   A★★

Armscote CV37 8DD   (01608) 682293
This pub "in a quiet village" can surprise first-time visitors with its
"fantastic cosy atmosphere", but that's not the only unexpected
feature – food, wine and service are all simply "excellent".
/ **Sample dishes:** warm goats cheese with red onion marmalade; tagliatelle; panna
cotta. **Details:** www.aboveaverage.co.uk; 10m S of Stratford-upon-Avon on the
A4300; 9.30 pm; booking: max 10.

ASCOT, BERKSHIRE   3–3A

Ascot Oriental   £34   A★

London Rd SL5 0PU (01344) 621877
"A delicious mix of Asian cuisines" (and "surprisingly good" wines, too) puts this attractive restaurant "head and shoulders above" most country orientals; in the evenings, it's quite an "intimate" place, too, so it's no great surprise that it's "very popular".
/ **Details:** www.ascotoriental.com; 2m E of Ascot on A329; 10.15 pm.

The Thatched Tavern   £35

Cheapside Rd SL5 7QG (01344) 620874
"New owners are doing a great job" with this local favourite, say fans of this part-thatched 17th-century boozer, praised for its "good food of restaurant quality". / **Sample dishes:** crispy oriental duck salad; steak & kidney pie; lemon & ginger crunch.
Details: www.thethatchedtavern.co.uk; 2m from Ascot, signed to Cheapside village; 10 pm.

ASENBY, NORTH YORKSHIRE   8–4C

The Crab & Lobster   £41   A

Dishforth Rd YO7 3QL (01845) 577286
"Not quite as good as it used to be, but still great fun"; under new ownership, this renowned, quirky thatched boozer – "decorated like the Old Curiosity Shop" – still offers "a varied menu with a focus on fish", and maintains its status as a local dining 'destination'.
/ **Sample dishes:** Irish oysters on ice; crab-crusted salmon with saffron mash; chocolate torte. **Details:** www.crabandlobster.co.uk; at junction of Asenby Rd & Topcliffe Rd; 9 pm; no smoking in dining room. **Accommodation:** 12 rooms, from £150.

ASHBURTON, DEVON   1–3D

Agaric   £39   ★

30 North St TQ13 7QD (01364) 654478
An ex-Carved Angel chef "does wonders with local ingredients" ("particularly fish and game") at these "café-like" premises; the wine list, however, "could benefit from further attention".
/ **Sample dishes:** fresh soup with garlic croutons; steamed lemon sole fillets with prawn mousseline & sauce; sticky toffee pudding.
Details: www.agaricrestaurant.co.uk; 9.30 pm; closed Mon, Tue & Sun D; no smoking.

Holne Chase Hotel   £40

TQ13 7NS (01364) 631471
This well-reputed country house hotel – a converted Dartmoor hunting lodge, in its current use for over half a century – may not set pulses racing, but those of a mellow disposition find it a "lovely" place, with "good food, and a good wine list". / **Sample dishes:** creamy sweetcorn soup with chive oil; calves liver & bacon with sage butter; steamed chocolate sponge. **Details:** www.holne-chase.co.uk; 8.45 pm; no Amex; no smoking; children: 12+ at D. **Accommodation:** 17 rooms, from £140.

ASKRIGG, NORTH YORKSHIRE   8–4B

The King's Arms   £32

Market Pl DL8 3HQ (01969) 650817
This "old-fashioned" coaching inn is of most interest for its rôle as 'The Drovers Arms' in 'All Creatures Great and Small'; objectively speaking, it's "OK". / **Sample dishes:** spicy salmon fishcakes; chicken & cheese wrapped in smoked bacon; sticky toffee pudding. **Details:** 9 pm; no Amex; no smoking area.

Rowan Tree £ 33 A ★★
Market Pl DL8 3HT (01969) 650536

"How can two people serve such consistently great food to a packed restaurant night after night" – Derek Wylie's 22-seater in the Dales is acclaimed as an *"intimate"* place where *"staff go out of their way to make you feel welcome"*, and whose cooking is *"fantastic"*.
/ **Sample dishes:** *Louisiana prawn & okra gumbo; lamb cutlets with colcannon & Shiraz jus; coffee, chocolate & cardamom truffle torte.* **Details:** *4m from Aysgarth falls; 8.30 pm; D only Wed-Sat, L only Sun; closed Mon & Tue; no credit cards; no smoking at D; children: 12+.*

ASTBURY, CHESHIRE 5–3B

Pecks £ 32
Newcastle Rd CW12 4SB (01260) 275161

Views can differ on the one-sitting-at-eight dinner at this attractive modern outfit – what is *"a faultless and well-priced seven-course meal"* to fans can be *"too much food, and too much fuss"* to doubters; lunch is a more standard affair. / **Sample dishes:** *broad bean & goats cheese risotto; braised lamb with black olive mash; rum & raisin cheesecake.* **Details:** *www.pecksrest.co.uk; off A34; 8 pm (one sitting only); closed Mon & Sun D; no smoking at D; booking essential.*

AUCHTERARDER, PERTH & KINROSS 9–3C

Andrew Fairlie
Gleneagles Hotel £ 80 A ★
PH3 1NF (01764) 662231

"A sublime place to eat and feel special", where the *"relaxed but excellent"* service *"treats you like royalty"* (but *"without stuffiness"*); there is the very occasional let-down, but for the most part Andrew Fairlie's modern French cuisine is proclaimed simply *"excellent"*.
/ **Sample dishes:** *foie gras terrine with caramelised apple; roast venison with wild mushrooms; chocolate orange pudding.* **Details:** *www.gleneagles.com; 10 pm; L only, closed Sun; smoking in bar only; children: 12+.* **Accommodation:** *273 rooms, from £320.*

AYLESBURY, BUCKINGHAMSHIRE 3–2A

Hartwell House £ 59 A
Oxford Rd HP17 8NL (01296) 747444

Fans (typically retirees) of this grand part-Jacobean country house hotel laud its "historic" interior and "exceptional" cuisine; given its location, it attracts surprisingly little feedback, though, and there's a definite feeling that it's "expensive" for what it is.
/ **Sample dishes:** *smoked chicken & spring onion sausage; sea bass with spinach & port wine sauce; mango mousse with pineapple crisps.*
Details: *www.hartwell-house.com; 2m W of Aylesbury on A418; 9.45 pm; jacket & tie required; no smoking in dining room; children: 8+.* **Accommodation:** *49 rooms, from £145.*

BABINGTON, SOMERSET 2–3B

Babington House £ 42 A
BA11 3RW (01373) 812266

The team from the funky London club, Soho House, has established this trendified country house as a Mecca for urban trendies, and it certainly offers "good people-watching"; the cooking is "ordinary", though, and the wine list "disappointing"; (note: you have to be a member or hotel resident to eat here). / **Sample dishes:** *smoked duck, dandelion & hazelnut salad; monkfish with clams & bacon; trio of chocolate puddings.* **Details:** *www.babingtonhouse.co.uk; 11 pm; open to residents & members only for L & D all week; booking essential.* **Accommodation:** *28 rooms, from £215.*

BAKEWELL, DERBYSHIRE   5–2C

Aitch's Wine Bar   £ 36   ★
4 Buxton Rd DE45 1DA   (01629) 813895
*Occasional jazz spices up the atmosphere at this always-"lively"
market-town fixture, which offers "imaginative" and "varied" cuisine,
as well as "a good selection of wines". / Sample dishes: spicy Thai
fishcakes; crispy duck with stir-fried vegetables; champagne cheesecake with cassis
ice cream. Details: www.aitchswinebar.co.uk; 9.30 pm; closed Sun (open Sun D
in summer); no Amex; smoking in bar only.*

Monsal Head   £ 24   ★
DE45 1NL   (01629) 640250
*"Beautiful views and food" is the gist of most (if not quite all)
commentary on this 'private hotel in the centre of the Peak District
National Park', which, for most reporters, offers "quality
throughout". / Details: www.monsalhead.com; just outside the town; 9.30 pm;
restaurant closed Mon-Wed in winter; no Amex; no smoking in dining room.
Accommodation: 7 rooms, from £100.*

Renaissance   £ 31   ★
Bath St DE45 1BX   (01629) 812687
*This "intimate" (in a rather middle-aged way) and comfortable Gallic
restaurant maintains its consistently high standards.
/ Sample dishes: French onion soup; chicken stuffed with crab mousse; chocolate &
pear terrine with claret sauce. Details: www.renaissance-restaurant.com; 9.30 pm;
closed Mon & Sun D; no smoking; booking essential at L.*

BALLATER, ABERDEEN   9–3C

Darroch Learg   £ 44   𝔸 ★
Braemar Rd AB35 5UX   (01339) 755443
*With its "superb views over the Dee valley towards Lochnagar",
this late Victorian mansion (run by the Franks family for four
decades) has been "a favourite for many years", due in no small
part to its "memorable" modern Scottish cooking.
/ Sample dishes: Loch Fyne scallops; loin of venison; lemon tart.
Details: www.darrochlearg.demon.co.uk; 9 pm; D only, except Sun open L &
D. Accommodation: 12 rooms, from £65.*

BALQUHIDDER, PERTHSHIRE   9–3C

Monachyle Mhor   £ 42   𝔸 ★★
FK19 8PQ   (01877) 384622
*"Inventive cooking, local ingredients, superb countryside and lovely
hosts" – one reporter neatly summarises the tenor of the uniformly
ecstatic reports on this hotel in a former farmhouse; "it's well worth
the seven miles of single-track to get there!" / Sample dishes: creamed
spinich & quail tart; fillet of John Dory with garden vegetables; creamed sago
pudding on carmelized banana with brown bread ice cream
. Details: www.monachylemhor.com; 8.45pm.*

BANBURY, OXFORDSHIRE   2–1D

Thai Orchid   £ 29
56 Northbar St OX16 0TL   (01295) 270833
*A greenhouse-like oriental that continues to offer a solid
performance across the board. / Details: 10 pm; closed Sat L; no smoking
area.*

sign up for the survey at www.hardens.com

BANGOR, COUNTY DOWN   10–1D

Shanks   £53   ★★

150 Crawfordsburn Rd BT19 1GB   (028) 9185 3313
Cooking which is "always of the highest quality" makes this oddly
located (golf-club) dining room almost certainly the best in Northern
Ireland; its "unassuming" style (it was designed by Conran) creates
a "relaxed" ambience. / **Sample dishes:** smoked salmon blinis; peppered pork
with Parmesan mash; chocolate mousse with raspberries.
Details: www.shanksrestaurant.com; A2 to Bangor, follow signs for Blackwood golf
centre; 10 pm; closed Mon, Sat L & Sun.

BANGOR, GWYNEDD   4–1C

The Fat Cat Café Bar   £23

161 High St LL57 1NU   (01248) 370445
"A good range of food, pleasant service, a nice outside area
in summer, reasonable prices…" – this "very busy" cafe/bar
epitomises the virtues of the northerly chain of which it was the
original branch; even those who find its approach "a little
uninspiring" concede that "everything is of a reasonable standard".
/ **Sample dishes:** chicken quesadillas; tuna with stir-fried vegetables in oyster sauce;
Caribbean banana charlotte. **Details:** www.fatcat.to; 10 pm; no smoking area;
children: 18+ only.

BARNARD CASTLE, COUNTY DURHAM   8–3B

Blagraves House   £32   A★

30 The Bank DL12 8PN   (01833) 637668
This "atmospheric" 16th-century townhouse – said to have played
host to Cromwell in his day – generates only limited feedback;
such as there is says the modern British menu is realised
to "excellent" effect. / **Sample dishes:** smoked salmon mousse; roast loin
of venison with wild mushrooms; orange parfait with fresh raspberry sauce.
Details: 9.30 pm; D only, closed Mon & Sun; no Amex; no smoking in dining room;
children: 8+.

BARNSLEY, GLOUCESTERSHIRE   2–2C

Barnsley House   £50

GL7 5EE   (01285) 740000
Opened in 2003, reports were scarce on this trendy, new boutique
hotel, occupying a 17th century house in grounds laid out by a famed
garden writer; the appointment of Italian legend, Franco Taruschio
as consultant chef has helped it with much PR – let's hope it injects
more culinary excitement than some of his other consultancies.
/ **Details:** www.barnsleyhouse.com.

The Village Pub   £33   ★

GL7 5EF   (01285) 740421
"It's does what it says on the sign" – this "great" gastropub "in an
old Cotswold village" wins praise for its "mellow" (some say
"gloomy") ambience and its "unpretentious, consistently high-quality
food"; (over summer 2003 the former chef went to Barnsley House,
see also, run by the same owners in the village – Michael Carr
is now at the stoves). / **Sample dishes:** sausages with beans, potato, tomato &
olives; pan-fried sea bass with salad; baked pear puff pastry with toffee sauce.
Details: www.thevillagepub.co.uk; 9.30 pm; no Amex; no smoking area.
Accommodation: 6 rooms, from £80.

BARTON UPON HUMBER, NORTH LINCOLNSHIRE   6–2A

Elio's   £36   ★
11 Market Pl DN18 5DA   (01652) 635147
"A newly-covered-in courtyard has increased the number of tables and improved the ambience", at this well-established and "friendly" Italian in the Market Place; it's notably "upmarket" by local standards, and all reports attest to its "very good standards".
/ **Sample dishes:** *cannelloni alla romana; seafood risotto; amaretto cheesecake* . **Details:** *A15 towards Humber Bridge, first exit into Barton upon Humber; 9.45 pm; D only, closed Sun; no smoking area.*

Rafters   £32   ★
24 High St DN18 5PD   (01652) 660669
"A jewel in the desert"; this "easy-going" market-town restaurant is unanimously hailed for its "well-cooked, honest and very tasty" dishes; "good-value set lunches" are especially approved.
/ **Sample dishes:** *antipasti with avocado; curried pork with dried fruits; chocolate Scotch pancakes.* **Details:** *www.rafters.co.uk; just S of Humber Bridge off A15; 10 pm; closed Mon & Sun D; smoking in bar only.*

BARWICK VILLAGE, SOMERSET   2–3B

Little Barwick House   £46   Ⓐ★★
BA22 9TD (01935) 423902
"Just fabulous" – almost all reporters extol the "outstanding food and location" of Tim & Emma Ford's "ravishing" but "relaxed" country house hotel, which offers a "truly wonderful eating experience". / **Sample dishes:** *pink-roast quail with mushroom risotto; brill with baby leeks & girolles; hot plum soufflé.* **Details:** *www.littlebarwick.co.uk; 9 pm; closed Mon, Tue L & Sun D; no smoking in dining room.* **Accommodation:** *6 rooms, from £94.*

BASLOW, DERBYSHIRE   5–2C

Cavendish   £48   ★
Church Ln DE45 1SP (01246) 582311
"Magnificent views of the Chatsworth Estate" set the scene at this ducally-owned hotel; a local reporter rails at its "cold" décor, but for the most part this "outstanding" establishment draws praise for its "superb" service and its "quality" cooking. / **Sample dishes:** *timbale of black pudding with quails egg in hollandaise sauce; roast squab breast with potato rosti buttered cabbage & port jus; lemon curd bread & butter pudding with lemon meringue ice cream.* **Details:** *www.cavendish-hotel.net; 10 pm; no smoking.* **Accommodation:** *24 rooms, from £130.*

Fischers at Baslow Hall   £65   Ⓐ★
Calver Rd DE45 1RR (01246) 583259
"Classic" cooking which "plays on the strengths of the establishment's location and the seasons" helps make Max & Susan Fischer's "delightful", "old-fashioned" country house hotel a simply "brilliant" choice for almost all of the many reporters who comment on it. / **Sample dishes:** *sea bream with butternut squash ratatouille; pigs trotter with morels & truffle mash; passion fruit soufflé.*
Details: *www.fischers-baslowhall.co.uk; 9.30 pm; closed Mon L & Sun D; no jeans; no smoking; children: 12+ after 7 pm.* **Accommodation:** *11 rooms, from £120.*

BASSENTHWAITE, CUMBRIA   7–3C

Pheasant Hotel   £41   Ⓐ
CA13 9YE   (01768) 716234
"Foreign friends will envy us our culture" after a visit to this "super atmospheric inn" – that's at least one reporter's view on this "good old-fashioned, calm and relaxing" spot, which serves "decent" food. / Sample dishes: smoked breast of duck with dressing; pan-fried fillet of red bream; pistachio parfait with white chocolate wafers.
Details: *www.the-pheasant.co.uk; 8.30 pm; no Amex; no smoking in dining room.*

BATH, BATH & NE SOMERSET   2–2B

Given that many would regard this as England's most civilised city, it's a shame that in culinary terms Bath is currently – in spite of its plethora of places to eat – something of an 'also-ran' destination.

As we go to press, though, it is reported that early in 2004, the city is to regain the services of star local chef Martin Blunos (who made a big name when he created the now-defunct Lettonie): see under *Pimpernel's* below. His recent track record has had its ups and downs, but – potentially at least – this could become a really major destination.

As things stand, there are a couple of notable, if rather pricey, places to eat – *Bath Priory* and *Moody Goose*. There is also an extremely popular veggie in the shape of *Demuths*; and as a 'practical' mid-price destination, the handily-located *Moon & Sixpence* stands out.

Though in no sense a foodie destination, the town's raison d'être – the Roman Baths – has, in the Pump Rooms, one of the most atmopsheric period eating halls in the country.

Bath Priory Hotel   £65   Ⓐ★
Weston Rd BA1 2XT   (01225) 331922
"Now Martin Blunos has gone, this is Bath's premier eatery", say fans of this "plush" small hotel, "in beautiful gardens on the outskirts"; even those who "can't fault the first-class cuisine", though, think prices "a bit excessive". / Sample dishes: crab & ginger ravioli with langoustine sauce; roast guinea fowl with lemon & sage; caramelised lemon tart. **Details:** *www.thebathpriory.co.uk; 1m W of city centre, past Victoria Park; 9.30 pm; no jeans or trainers; no smoking; children: 7+ at D.* **Accommodation:** *28 rooms, from £245.*

Beaujolais   £35
5 Chapel Rw, Queen Sq BA1 1HN   (01225) 423417
"Ooh-la-la" – this "always lively" Gallic wine bar scores well for its "fun" ambience, and "good-quality" Gallic cooking; there is the occasional gripe, though, about service seemingly "oblivious to non-regulars". / management declined to provide further information

Browns   £28   ✗
Old Police Station, Orange Grove BA1 1LP
(01225) 461199
"With its wonderful building, this place should be fantastic" – reporters were unanimously unimpressed, though, with this outpost of the national brasserie chain, with its lackadaisical service and its "terrible", "boring" food. / Sample dishes: buffalo Mozzarella & plum tomato salad; steak, mushroom & Guinness pie; sticky toffee pudding.
Details: *www.browns-restaurants.com; 11 pm; no smoking area; need 5+ to book.*

Café Fromage   £15   ★
1 John St BA1 2JL   (01225) 313525
Thanks to the "good simple food" – and, perhaps, the "friendly buzz" – there's "often a queue" for this "tiny café above a cheese shop", where the "quiches, soups and salads are all excellent".
/ **Sample dishes:** *grilled goats cheese salad with olives; cheesecake.* **Details:** *L & afternoon tea only; closed Sun; no credit cards; no smoking.*

Demuths   £31   ★
2 North Parade Passage BA1 1NX   (01225) 446059
"A great variety of excellent veggie fare" generally earns rave reviews for this superior city-centre veggie; enthusiasm was tempered this year, though, by incidents of "appalling" service.
/ **Sample dishes:** *feta, mint & pea pâté with walnut bread; goats cheese soufflé with tomato salsa; Indonesian black rice pudding.* **Details:** *www.demuths.co.uk; 10 pm; no smoking; booking: max 4 at D, Fri & Sat; children: 6+ after 7 pm.*

The Eastern Eye   £24   🄰
8a Quiet St BA1 2JS   (01225) 422323
"An incongruous Georgian setting" provides the grand location for this "large" central Indian, which serves "good but rather pricey" scoff. / **Details:** *www.easterneye.co.uk; 11 pm; no smoking area.*

Firehouse Rotisserie   £35
2 John St BA1 2JL   (01225) 482070
"Good albeit strange pizza" and other "great" Californian fare maintains the popularity of this "busy" and "relaxed" venture; even fans, though, note that it's totally "not cheap".
/ **Sample dishes:** *Brie & grape quesadillas; Pacific crab & smoked salmon fishcakes; chocolate pecan pie.* **Details:** *www.firehouserotisserie.co.uk; 10.30 pm; closed Sun D; no smoking area.*

FishWorks   £42
6 Green St BA1 2JY   (01225) 448707
The original, recently expanded branch of this growing chain of fishmongers (with fish cafés attached) induced oddly little feedback this year; such as there was lauded its "very good, very fresh fish in cafeteria surroundings". / **Sample dishes:** *crab salad with tarragon mayonnaise; cod with mash & parsley sauce; Sicilian lemon tart.* **Details:** *www.fishworks.co.uk; 10.30 pm; closed Mon & Sun D; no smoking.*

Hole in the Wall   £37   🄰
16 George St BA1 2EN   (01225) 425242
"Unpretentious" and "intimate", this basement restaurant – famous among foodies as one of the seminal post-war English restaurants – is a "romantic" place that's "great for a winter evening"; some reporters say the cooking is "consistently of a high standard", but it can also seem "bland" and "heavy-handed".
/ **Sample dishes:** *warm scallop & bacon salad; guinea fowl with beetroot & garlic sauce; caramelised pears with coffee ice cream.* **Details:** *10 pm; closed Sun; no smoking area.*

Loch Fyne   £33
24 Milsom St BA1 1DG   (01225) 750120
"An old NatWest" provides the setting for this "relaxed" branch of the "predictable" national seafood chain. / **Sample dishes:** *lobster bisque with garlic rouille; rosemary-infused bream with tomatoes & black olives; lemon sorbet.* **Details:** *www.loch-fyne.com; 10 pm; no smoking area.*
Accommodation: *9 rooms, from £75.*

sign up for the survey at www.hardens.com

Mai Thai £ 24 ★
6 Pierrepont St BA2 4AA   (01225) 445557
*"Easily the best Thai in Bath", this "cosy" central spot
is unanimously hailed by reporters for its "fabulous" dishes –
"beautifully presented from an extensive menu" – and its
"good value". / Details: 10.30 pm, Fri & Sat 10.45 pm; no smoking area;
children: 9+.*

Moody Goose £ 45 ★
74 Kingsmead Sq BA1 2AB   (01225) 466688
*Stephen Shore's "beautifully crafted" cooking and "attentive" service
have won a dedicated following for his "discreet" central
establishment; not everyone is impressed by the "subterranean"
setting, although there are those who find it "romantic".
/ Sample dishes: smoked haddock ravioli with goats cheese; chicken with
crayfish & artichoke mousse; passion fruit soufflé. Details: www.moody-goose.com;
9.30 pm; closed Sun; no smoking in dining room; children: 7 +.*

Moon & Sixpence £ 36 🄰★
6a Broad St BA1 5LJ   (01225) 460962
*In its "secluded" city-centre location – down a cobbled alley,
and with "a courtyard for warm evenings" – this "buzzy" haunt
is one of the most popular places in town; "excellent steak" is a
highlight of the "good, modern bistro fare". / Sample dishes: guinea
fowl & pistachio ballotine; sea bass with pak choy & sweet chilli; white, milk & dark
chocolate mousses. Details: www.moonandsixpence.co.uk; 10.15 pm; no smoking
area.*

No 5 Bistro £ 37
5 Argyle St BA2 4BA   (01225) 444499
*It's nothing remarkable, but it's worth knowing about this long-
established bistro, just off the Pulteney Bridge, which makes
a generally "OK" choice. / Sample dishes: goats cheese mousse with
grapefruit salad; pan-fried sea bass with aubergine caviar; chocolate truffle &
pineapple cake. Details: www.no5restaurant.uk.com; 10 pm, Fri 10.30 pm,
Sat 11 pm; closed Mon L & Sun; no smoking.*

Olive Tree
Queensberry Hotel £ 43
Russel St BA1 2QF   (01225) 447928
*Post-survey, new owners have taken over the hotel in which this
popular Mediterranean basement dining room resides (and we've
accordingly left it unrated); opinions have divided in recent years
between those who found it "complacent" and those who found it a
"classic" – here's hoping the latter view will now prevail.
/ Sample dishes: red mullet & roast aubergine salad; braised pork with morels &
savoy cabbage; roast peach tart. Details: www.thequeensberry.co.uk; 10 pm; closed
Mon L; no Amex; no smoking. Accommodation: 29 rooms, from £120.*

Pimpernel's
Royal Crescent Hotel £ 62
16 Royal Cr BA1 2LS   (01225) 823333
*Most reporters basically like this "elegant" basement, and praise its
"superb" cooking (though it drew some flak for its "hotel-y" feel,
"OTT" presentation and "London prices"); NB. as we go to print
there is news that legendary local chef Martin Blunos is to open
a venture at the hotel (details as yet unclear) in early-2004.
/ Sample dishes: smoked salmon with capers & horseradish; rump of lamb
Lyonnaise with white bean purée; Cointreau & pecan nougat parfait.
Details: www.royalcrescent.co.uk; in centre of Royal Crescent; 10 pm; no smoking;
booking: max 8. Accommodation: 45 rooms, from £170.*

sign up for the survey at www.hardens.com   142

Pump Rooms £ 27 🄰
The Pump Room, Stall St BA1 1LZ (01225) 444477
"The nicest heritage catering we know"; for "a sandwich, coffee or cake, with a string quartet playing", this "splendid" Georgian rendezvous offers "a lovely experience". / **Sample dishes:** *warm chilli garlic mushrooms; smoked haddock with spinach & ricotta tortellini.* **Details:** *by the Abbey; L only, open until 10pm in Aug; no smoking; no booking, Sat & Sun.*

Rajpoot £ 28
4 Argyle St BA2 2BA (01225) 466833
It has been a rocky year for this "amazing basement hideaway", in impressive cellars near the Pulteney Bridge; it struck most reporters as being "too pricey for its quality", but a local assures us it's "getting better again". / **Details:** *www.rajpoot.com; 11 pm, Fri & Sat 11.30 pm; mainly non-smoking.*

Richmond Arms £ 26 ★
7 Richmond Pl BA1 5PZ (01225) 316725
"Carnivores do well" (veggies less so) at this popular Lansdown boozer – a "great-value" spot where "new ideas" are often on the menu; it has a nice little garden, too. / **Sample dishes:** *Indonesian-spiced prawns with coconut milk rice; duck with plum & tamarind sauce; moist orange cake with mango coulis.* **Details:** *8.30 pm, Fri & Sat 9 pm; closed Mon & Sun D; no credit cards; children: 14+.*

Sukhothai £ 23
90a Walcot St BA1 5BG (01225) 462463
To some reporters this Thai restaurant is "the best in town", but to others its "somewhat anglicised" – "nice but not worth a detour". / **Details:** *10.30 pm; closed Sun L; no Amex; no smoking in dining room.*

Tilley's Bistro £ 29 🄰
3 North Parade Pas BA1 1NX (01225) 484200
A "cosy" and "friendly" Anglo/French bistro, in a pretty central pedestrianised lane; its menu includes "lots for veggies". / **Sample dishes:** *Caesar salad; pork Dijonnaise; warm banana pancake with toffee sauce.* **Details:** *www.tilleysbistro.co.uk; 11 pm; closed Sun; no Amex; no smoking area.*

Vellore, Bath Spa £ 55 ✗
Sydney Rd BA2 6JF (01225) 444424
"The grand setting is not matched by the cooking", at this luxury hotel dining room, which too many reporters dismiss as "overbearing, pretentious and poor". / **Sample dishes:** *minestrone soup; roast halibut served with crispy noodles; fresh chocolate soufflé.* **Details:** *9.45 pm; D only, except Sun open L & D; no smoking.* **Accommodation:** *98 rooms, from £169.*

Woods £ 34
9-13 Alfred St BA1 2QX (01225) 314812
"Basic", but "comfortable" and "congenial" – this "old faithful" Gallic brasserie of over two decades' standing remains a "popular" haunt (but, even so, "they never seem to hurry you"). / **Sample dishes:** *roast tomato & basil soup; lamb & roast garlic casserole; chocolate torte.* **Details:** *www.bathshopping.co.uk; 10.30 pm; closed Sun D; no Amex.*

BAWTRY, SOUTH YORKSHIRE 5–2D
China Rose £ 34 ★
16 South Parade DN10 6JH (01302) 710461
Despite it's "vast" size, by local standards, this popular Chinese is still acclaimed for its "consistent quality". / **Details:** *10 pm; D only; no jeans or trainers; no smoking in dining room.*

sign up for the survey at www.hardens.com

BEACONSFIELD, BUCKINGHAMSHIRE 3–3A

Leigh House £31
53 Wycombe End HP9 1LX (01494) 676348
For most (if not quite all) reporters, this "comfortable" and
"consistent" Chinese remains a key local ("especially in a group").
/ Details: 10 pm; no smoking area.

Loch Fyne £33
70 London End HP9 2JD (01494) 679960
Though fans say you get "an excellent selection of fresh fish and
seafood" at this "pleasantly warehousy" branch of the national
chain, others say it's too "canteen-like", or complain of its "ordinary"
cooking; it's certainly convenient for the A40! / Sample dishes: Loch
Fyne oysters; breaded roast mussels; toffee pudding. **Details:** www.loch-fyne.com;
10 pm; no smoking area.

BEAUMARIS, ISLE OF ANGLESEY 4–1C

Ye Olde Bull's Head £41 Ⓐ★
Castle St LL58 8AP (01248) 810329
"A surprising brasserie-type restaurant behind the façade of an old
pub" – "imaginative" cooking and an "impressive" wine list help the
"formal" and "opulent" dining room of this famous old coaching inn
to move with the times. / Sample dishes: lettuce soup with smoked goose
ravioli; beef with horseradish crust; clementine sponge with Grand Marnier ice cream.
Details: www.bullsheadinn.co.uk; 9.30 pm; D only, closed Sun; no smoking; children:
7+ at D. **Accommodation:** 13 rooms, from £92.

BEDFORD, BEDFORDSHIRE 3–1A

St Helena's £45 Ⓐ
High St MK42 9XP (01234) 344848
"More expensive that other restaurants in the area, but still
excellent value for money", this "fun" and "well-run" establishment
attracts consistent local praise. / Sample dishes: marinated, smoked
Scottish salmon with dressing; fillet of beef stuffed with Stilton wrapped in bacon;
apple bread & butter pudding with custard. **Details:** 9 pm; closed Mon, Sat L &
Sun; jacket & tie required; no smoking; children: 12+.

BELFAST, COUNTY ANTRIM 10–1D

Paul Rankin's *Cayenne* has long dominated visitors impressions
of Belfast's dining scene, mainly thanks to his prominence as a
TV chef. In classic celeb-chef mould, his restaurant has often
disappointed reporters in the past, but reporters judged
it notably more favourably this year.

For the most ambitious cooking, *Aldens* remains probably the
best destination. The alternative is a trip out of town to *Shanks*
in Bangor.

In the city centre, *Nick's Warehouse* – the 'grand-daddy'
of Belfast's contemporary restaurant scene – remains a key
destination.

Aldens £38 A★
229 Upper Newtownards Rd BT4 3JF (028) 9065 0079
"*Imaginatively cooked and impeccably presented*" *modern cooking has won this* "*understated suburban restaurant*" *(in a converted supermarket) a reputation in some quarters for* "*the best food in Northern Ireland*"; *reporters continue to file unanimously positive (if sometimes slightly qualified) reports.* / **Sample dishes:** *beetroot & herring salad; roast cod with Parma ham butter; rhubarb granita with apple brandy.* **Details:** *www.aldensrestaurant.com; 2m from Stormont Buildings; 10 pm, Fri & Sat 11 pm; closed Sat L & Sun; no smoking area.*

Cayenne £35 ★
7 Ascot Hs, Shaftesbury Sq BT2 7DB (028) 9033 1532
"*Spearheading Belfast's emerging dining scene*", *Paul Rankin's long-established restaurant hit an unexpectedly impressive stride this year;* "*very good food (including vegetarian options)*", *a* "*diverse and reasonably-priced wine list*" *and* "*superb*" *service were all singled out for praise.* / **Sample dishes:** *Caesar salad; salmon with coconut rice & black bean vinaigrette; spiced ginger pudding.* **Details:** *www.cayennerestaurant.com; near Botanic Railway Station; 10.15 pm, Sun 8.45 pm; closed Sat L; no smoking area.*

Deanes £40
34-40 Howard St BT1 6PF (028) 9056 0000
"*Thinks it's better than it is, and acts it*" – *a constant refrain about Michael Deane's famed central venture, although the upstairs fine-dining restaurant gets a somewhat better press than the large, rather brash street-level brasserie (price shown).* / **Sample dishes:** *goats cheese with salami & asparagus; ground beef with onion mash & spiced ketchup; steamed pineapple pudding.* **Details:** *www.deanesbelfast.com; near Grand Opera House; 9.30 pm; closed Sun.*

Nick's Warehouse £37 ★
• 35 Hill St BT1 2LB (028) 9043 9690
"*Lots of buzz*" – *or* "*too much noise*", *if you prefer* – *is something of a defining feature at this long-established, city-centre wine bar-cum-restaurant, whose* "*reasonably-priced*" *lunches are something of an institution for Belfast businessmen.* / **Sample dishes:** *lemon & chilli chicken tempura; salmon & roast tomatoes with rocket mayonnaise; white peach cheesecake.* **Details:** *www.nickswarehouse.co.uk; behind St Anne's Cathedral; 10 pm; closed Mon D, Sat L & Sun; children: before 9 pm only.*

BEVERLEY, EAST RIDING OF YORKSHIRE 6–1A
Wednesdays £30
8 Wednesday Mkt HU17 0DG (01482) 869727
"*Consistently good food*" *maintains the popularity of this well-established local (to which, on the eponymous weekday, you can BYO).* / **Sample dishes:** *Thai fishcakes with sweet & sour cucumber sauce; lamb shank in pearl barley broth; spicy date & ginger pudding.* **Details:** *www.wednesdaysathome.co.uk; near Beverley Minster; 9.30 pm; closed Sun.*

BIDDENDEN, KENT 3–4C
Three Chimneys £36 A★
Hareplain Rd TN27 8LW (01580) 291472
An "*idyllic*" *beamed inn praised by all for its* "*brilliant atmosphere and great food*"; *in summer, when you can eat outside, it gets* "*packed*". / **Sample dishes:** *baked mushrooms with goats cheese; sea bass with sweet potato & coconut chowder; lemon tart with plum compote.* **Details:** *A262 between Biddenden and Sissinghurst; 9.45 pm; no Amex; no booking, Sun L.*

BIGBURY, DEVON   1–4D
Oyster Shack   £29   A★★
Millburn Orchard Farm, Stakes Hills TQ7 4BE
(01548) 810876
"Pack a cool box with dry white" and head off to this *"casual"* BYO
seafood spot, overlooking Burgh Island, which serves *"a huge
choice"* of *"excellent"* fish and seafood; *"finding the place is a
challenge"*, but *"booking is essential"*. / **Sample dishes:** grilled oysters with
cream; smoked fish medley with salad; raspberry pavlova.
Details: www.oystershack.co.uk; 2.30 pm; L only, closed Mon; no Amex;
no smoking; booking essential; children: only at L.

BIRCHOVER, DERBYSHIRE   5–3C
Druid Inn   £30
Main St DE4 2BL   (01629) 650302
With its *"warm"* atmosphere and *"extensive"* menu, this busy
Victorian pub has won quite a following; on the quality front, though,
some reporters feel the food *"still needs spicing up"*.
/ **Sample dishes:** port & Stilton pâté; rack of lamb with redcurrant & gooseberry
sauce; date & ginger pudding with butterscotch sauce.
Details: www.druidinnbirchover.co.uk; Sw of Bakewell off B5056; 9 pm; closed Mon;
no smoking area.

BIRKENHEAD, MERSEYSIDE   5–2A
Capitol   £29   ★
24 Argyle St CH41 6AE   (0151) 647 9212
"Consistently excellent", say fans of this Chinese fixture overlooking
Hamilton Square Gardens. / **Details:** www.capitol-restaurant.co.uk; 2m from
Liverpool city centre; 11 pm; L only, closed Sat & Sun.

BIRMINGHAM, WEST MIDLANDS   5–4C

The reinvention of Birmingham continues apace, but England's
self-proclaimed second city has a little way to go before it can
really claim much interest to visiting foodies.

That isn't to seek in any way to denigrate the huge strides
which are being made, but the problem is that the style and
scale of many of the new sites in the revitalised city-centre
is such that they only really suit major (and, by definition,
rather boring) operators, often national groups.

The places which are emerging as of greatest distinction are
by and large not those run by 'big players' – *Metro*, the city's
leading modern non-ethnic restaurant, and *Thai Edge* are cases
in point. *La Toque d'Or* has also emerged with credit.

Apart from balti houses (which are mostly concentrated
in Moseley and Sparkbrook), the city is weak in ethnic appeal.
The giant Chineses – *Chung Ying* and *Chung Ying Garden* –
as ever offer a solid performance, if not one with great
personality.

Adils   £13   ★
148-150 Stoney Ln B12 8AJ   (0121) 449 0335
"Brum's first-ever balti house" remains a *"Mecca"* for curry-lovers,
serving *"consistently good cheap food"* in *"very basic surroundings"*.
/ **Details:** 3m from city centre on A41; 12.30 am; no smoking area.

Bank   £ 42
4 Brindleyplace B1 2JB   (0121) 633 4466
*The food can be "bland and formulaic", but "efficient" service and
stylish "minimalist" surroundings help make this large brasserie
by the canal an "efficient and well-located" choice for business
(and "there's a good-value menu for theatre-goers").*
/ ***Sample dishes:*** *five-onion soup with cheese croutons; calves liver & bacon with
red onion confit; rum & raisin cheesecake.* ***Details:*** *www.bankrestaurants.com;
10.30 pm, Sun 9.30 pm; no smoking area.*

Café Ikon   £ 21
Ikon Gallery B1 2HS   (0121) 248 3226
*"A good variety of dishes" – with some "tremendous" tapas,
and "surprisingly generous" raciones – makes this "smart" and
"buzzing" central bar, attached to an art gallery, a very popular
rendezvous; the odd report, though, is a mite mixed (dragging down
its overall ratings).* / ***Sample dishes:*** *cured Spanish meats; seared tuna with
roast vegetables; baked custard flan.* ***Details:*** *www.ikon-gallery.co.uk; 10.30 pm;
closed Mon & Sun D; no smoking area; children: before 9 pm only.*

Chez Jules   £ 25
5a Ethel St, off New St B2 4BG   (0121) 633 4664
*"Very good prices" help win many "cheap 'n' cheerful" nominations
for this "good basic French bistro" – complete with wooden benches
and red check tablecloths – in the city-centre; "excellent cheap set
lunches" win particular praise.* / ***Sample dishes:*** *chicken liver & mushroom
pâté; pork in honey & grain mustard sauce; crème brûlée.*
Details: *www.chezjules.co.uk; 11 pm; closed Sun D; no smoking area; no booking,
Sat L.*

Chung Ying Garden   £ 29   ★
17 Thorp St B5 4AT   (0121) 666 6622
*There's a "huge range of dishes", "dependably" realised, at this vast
"classic" Chinatown Cantonese, where the "excellent dim sum"
receives a particular thumbs-up; some say the older Chung Ying
(nearby at 16-18 Wrottesley St, tel 622 5669) is "better".*
/ ***Details:*** *www.chungying.co.uk; 11.30 pm.*

Denial   £ 35
120-122 Wharfside St B1 1RQ   (0121) 632 1232
*"Becoming very popular", this high-class shopping mall venue is a
key brunch spot (offering "the best eggs Benedict ever"), and can
even be "romantic" – "after dark, get a canalside window table
if you can".* / ***Sample dishes:*** *seared scallops with rocket & chorizo; semi-dried
beef with pink peppercorn béarnaise; cheesecake with blackcurrant & lime compote.*
Details: *www.denial.ltd.uk; 10 pm.*

The Green Room   £ 27
Arcadian Centre, Hurst St B5 4TD   (0121) 605 4343
*"Excellent before the Hippodrome"; this relaxed bar/restaurant is "a
great place" attracting a diverse crowd, and is uniformly praised for
its "good value and service".* / ***Sample dishes:*** *deep-fried broccoli; spicy
chicken with curly fries & coleslaw; poached pears.* ***Details:*** *10.30 pm,
Thu midnight, Fri & Sat 1.30 am; no smoking area.*

Hotel du Vin et Bistro £ 43 𝔸
25 Church St B3 2NR (0121) 200 0600

"Brum's best"? – certainly on the atmosphere front, this year-old boutique-hotel dining room has established itself as an "utterly delightful" destination that's "ideal for romance", and offers the "good" wine list you'd expect, too; the menu, though, can sometimes seem "beyond the kitchen's abilities". / **Sample dishes:** *Mozzarella & avocado salad; duck with apple & foie gras; butterscotch cheesecake with chocolate sauce.* **Details:** *www.hotelduvin.co.uk; 9.45 pm; booking: max 12.* **Accommodation:** *66 rooms, from £110.*

Jyoti £ 16 ★
569-571 Stratford Rd B11 4LS (0121) 766 7199

"A wide-ranging Gujerati (vegetarian) menu of a high standard, and at really cheap prices" wins universal support for this "very small and low-key" Sparkhill venture. / **Details:** *9.15 pm; closed Mon & Tue L-Thu L; no Amex; no smoking.*

Kababish £ 23 ★
29 Woodbridge Rd B13 8EH (0121) 449 5556

It's still as "busy" as ever, and fans extol this Moseley balti house as a "reliably excellent" spot. / **Details:** *11.15 pm; D only.*

Living Room £ 30 𝔸
Regency Whf, 2 Broad St B1 2JZ (0870) 4422 539

"You get good food, for a chain" at this "busy city-centre location" – part of an expanding group of loungey piano bar/restaurants. / **Sample dishes:** *salt & pepper squid; cheese & bacon burger; hot chocolate fudge cake.* **Details:** *www.thelivingroom.co.uk; 11 pm, Wed & Thu 11.30 pm, Fri & Sat midnight .*

Maharaja £ 24 ★
23-25 Hurst St B5 4SA (0121) 622 2641

"Reliability, year in year out" wins a loyal fanclub for this early-'70s, city-centre Indian. / **Details:** *www.maharaja-indiancuisine.co.uk; 11 pm; closed Sun.*

Malt Shovel £ 17 𝔸
1 Newton Rd B43 6HN (0121) 357 1148

"Excellent service and atmosphere" are highlights of this busy boozer (in Great Barr, just north of the city); it offers "tasty" and "imaginative" cooking, both in the bar and in the more formal restaurant. / **Sample dishes:** *melon; roast pork & traditional trimmings; ice cream.* **Details:** *8.30 pm, Fri & Sat 9 pm; no smoking; need 10+ to book.*

Metro £ 35 ★
73 Cornwall St B3 2DF (0121) 200 1911

"Where it's at in the centre of Brum"; this "slick", "light" modern brasserie is tipped – especially if you're on business – for its "straightforward" and "consistent" modern cooking. / **Sample dishes:** *deep-fried squid with peanut butter & mango salsa; minted lamb with summer vegetables; apricot & nectarine crumble.* **Details:** *www.themetrobar.co.uk; 9.30 pm; closed Sun.*

Le Petit Blanc £ 30
9 Brindleyplace B1 2HS (0121) 633 7333

The Brummie branch of Raymond Blanc's brasserie chain has always been one of its weaker members – perhaps its new managers from mid-2003 (the group which owns Loch Fyne) can drag its standards up to where they ought to be? / **Sample dishes:** *smoked chicken & chilli linguine; Thai-baked sea bass with coriander rice; sticky toffee pudding.* **Details:** *www.lepetitblanc.co.uk; 11 pm; no smoking area.*

Rajdoot £25

78-79 George St B3 1PY   (0121) 236 1116

It may have moved from its old Albert Street premises, but this is still, according to its fans a "calm", "confident" and "professional" Indian. / Details: www.rajdoot.co.uk; 11.15 pm; closed Sat L & Sun L.

San Carlo £38

4 Temple St B2 5BN   (0121) 633 0251

It's difficult to dispute the conclusion that this "busy" and "bustling" city-centre Italian – which used to be our top tip in Brum – has "deteriorated greatly in recent years"; the food sometimes seems "totally boring", nowadays, and service can be "slow" and "rude". / **Sample dishes:** barbecue spare ribs; veal in wine & mushroom sauce; coffee bean ice cream. Details: near St Philips Cathedral; 10.45 pm.

Shimla Pinks £31 ✕

214 Broad St B15 1AY   (0121) 633 0366

"All décor and no substance… they're risking the good name of a whole nation!" – an authoritative pronouncement (from a reporter of Indian origins) on this once-trendy designer curry house; some do still praise its "creative" food, but it's hard to avoid the conclusion that the place is "resting on its laurels". / Details: www.shimlapinks.com; 11 pm; closed Sat L & Sun L.

Thai Edge £34 ★

7 Brindleyplace B1 2HS   (0121) 643 3994

This "large and modern" city-centre oriental enjoys "an attractive canalside setting" and delivers "better-than-average" Thai fare; unsurprisingly, it can get rather "crowded". / Details: 11 pm, Fri & Sat 11.30 pm.

La Toque d'Or £37 ★

27 Warstone Ln B18 6JQ   (0121) 233 3655

"Serious and delicious" Gallic cooking makes this "interestingly housed" Jewellery Quarter restaurant a veritable local gem; most reporters seem disposed to forgive the fact that it's rather "quiet" and "lacking in atmosphere". / **Sample dishes:** rainbow trout with lemon dressing; marinated lamb with vegetables; vanilla crème brûlée. **Details:** www.latoquedor.co.uk; 9.30 pm; closed Mon, Sat L & Sun (& 2 weeks in Aug).

Zinc £38 ✕

Regency Whf, Gas Basin St B1 2DS   (0121) 200 0620

"Why do we put up with this?" – the most striking feature of commentary on this "stark" and "overpriced" Conran brasserie is just how much of it is negative, some stridently so. / **Sample dishes:** chilli squid; wild mushroom & spinach linguine; lemon tart. **Details:** www.conran-restaurants.co.uk; 10.30 pm; closed Sun.

BISHOPS STORTFORD, HERTFORDSHIRE 3–2B

The Lemon Tree £32 Ⓐ

14-16 Water Ln CM23 2LB   (01279) 757788

Located in a converted Georgian terrace, Sue & Luke Fishpool's venture wins praise for its "lovely" ambience and its "good" contemporary cooking. / **Sample dishes:** cured salmon with avocado salsa; roast salmon with asparagus; rhubarb & apple sponge. **Details:** www.lemontree.co.uk; 9.30 pm; closed Mon & Sun D; no Amex; no smoking in dining room.

BISHOPS TACHBROOK, WARWICKSHIRE   5–4C

Mallory Court   £61   A★
Harbury Ln CV33 9QB   (01926) 330214
"It was always good, but now it's exceptional" – Simon Haigh's *"ambitious"* modern cuisine seems to be scaling new heights at this *"elegant"*, *"comfortable"* and *"unfussy"* hotel (occupying a Lutyens-style house), which benefits from *"beautiful"* gardens.
/ **Sample dishes:** goats cheese ravioli with caramelised walnuts; sea bass with tarragon mousse; raspberry soufflé. **Details:** www.mallory.co.uk; 2m S of Leamington Spa, off B4087; 10 pm, Sat 10.30 pm; no smoking in dining room; children: 9+. **Accommodation:** 18 rooms, from £185.

BISPHAM GREEN, LANCASHIRE   5–1A

Eagle & Child   £28   ★
Maltkiln Ln L40 3SG   (01257) 462297
"One of the few rural pubs that's managed to stay a pub as well as serving great food", this *"lively"* boozer (run by a team formerly at Liverpool's Ziba) makes quite an *"interesting"* culinary destination – *"at weekends it can get too busy"*. / **Sample dishes:** deep-fried goats cheese; toasted chicken & red pepper panini; sticky toffee pudding. **Details:** M6, J27; 8.30 pm; no Amex; no smoking area.

BLACKPOOL, LANCASHIRE   5–1A

Kwizeen   £26   ★
47-49 King St FY1 3EJ   (01253) 290045
"Worthy of an entry in any food guide" – this ambitious *"modern"* bistro of three years' standing still only generates limited feedback, but fans say that its trendy menu really delivers. / **Sample dishes:** wild mushroom soup with rosemary shortbread; glazed duck breast with plum & blackberry sauce; vanilla panna cotta with strawberries.
Details: www.kwizeen.co.uk; 9 pm; closed Sat L & Sun; no Amex.

September Brasserie   £32
15-17 Queen St FY1 1PU   (01253) 623282
Some still hail this once-well-reputed first-floor brasserie as *"an attractive place with beautifully-presented food"*; others, though, speak in terms of *"tatty"* décor, *"slapdash"* cooking and *"fading"* standards. / **Sample dishes:** pumpkin & goats cheese soufflé; braised pork knuckle; sticky date pudding. **Details:** www.septemberbrasserie.co.uk; just past North Pier, opp Cenotaph; 9.30 pm; closed Mon & Sun.

BLAIRGOWRIE, PERTH & KINROSS   9–3C

Kinloch House   £45
PH10 6SG   (01250) 884237
On the basis of the Allan family's last venture (Airds in Argyll), hopes are high for their new régime at this country house hotel (a grand 19th century mansion); feedback, to-date, has been scarce (hence no rating), but a report from one fan of their former 'gaff' felt there was room for improvement to meet their old standards.
/ **Sample dishes:** wild mushroom, chicken & sweetbread terrine; fillet steak with Lanark Blue cheese; chocolate truffle cake with mint cream.
Details: www.kinlochhouse.com; 9 pm; no jeans or trainers; no smoking area; children: 7+ at D. **Accommodation:** 18 rooms, from £220.

BLAKENEY, NORFOLK   6–3C

The White Horse Hotel   £36

4 High St NR25 7AL   (01263) 740574

"A great location overlooking the sea" is a special draw to this "friendly" and "relaxed" inn; the food "varies from good to poor", so it's worth knowing that "it's just the same in the bar as it is in the (pricier) restaurant". / **Sample dishes:** smoked cod, leek & Parmesan tartlet; roast black bream with chilli & fennel dressing; chocolate mousse. **Details:** www.blakeneywhitehorse.co.uk; 9 pm; D only, closed Mon & Sun; no smoking in dining room; children: 6+. **Accommodation:** 10 rooms, from £60.

BOLTON ABBEY, NORTH YORKSHIRE   8–4B

Devonshire Arms   £62   Ⓐ

BD23 6AJ   (01756) 710441

The "fabulous location" helps make a visit to this "refined" (ducally-owned) inn a special event, and the food (under new chef Steve Williams) can sometimes be "brilliant", too; many also find it "very expensive", though, so the cheaper brasserie (£33) is still perhaps the 'safer' choice. / **Sample dishes:** goose, mango & smoked foie gras salad; roast cod with fennel & olive sauce; chocolate & Turkish Delight soufflé. **Details:** www.devonshirehotels.co.uk; on A59, 5m NE of Skipton; 9.30 pm; D only, except Sun open L & D; no jeans; no smoking. **Accommodation:** 41 rooms, from £210.

BOLTON, LANCASHIRE   5–2B

Strawbury Duck   £21   Ⓐ

Overshores Rd, Entwistle BL7 0LU   (01204) 852013

This "large pub on the edge of the Moors" has quite a reputation locally, and is always "lively and bustling"; there was the odd gripe this year about "overcooked" food. / **Sample dishes:** black pudding tower; lamb Devonshire; Italian trifle. **Details:** 100 yds from Entwistle railway station; 9.15 pm, Sat 10 pm; no Amex. **Accommodation:** 4 rooms, from £39.50.

BOSTON SPA, WEST YORKSHIRE   5–1C

Spice Box   £31   ★

152 High St LS23 6BW   (01937) 842558

A "cosy", "intimate" and "consistently good" modern brasserie that fans tip for "the best food in the area". / **Sample dishes:** fishcakes with Thai sauce; duck with bacon & thyme potatoes; chocolate truffle. **Details:** www.spicebox.com; 2m E of A1, on A659; 9.30 pm; closed Mon & Sun; no smoking.

BOUGHTON LEES, KENT   3–3C

Eastwell Manor   £57   Ⓐ★

Eastwell Pk TN25 4HR   (01233) 213000

"First-class food in fabulous surroundings" – that's the verdict on this "classy country house hotel and spa" (where a new chef was installed a year ago), a Victorian pile set in "wonderful grounds". / **Sample dishes:** white bean soup with langoustine & truffles; chicken supreme with mustard cream sauce; apple & rhubarb crumble. **Details:** www.eastwellmanor.co.uk; 3m N of Ashford on A251; 9.30 pm; no jeans; no smoking; booking: max 8. **Accommodation:** 69 rooms, from £200.

BOURNEMOUTH, DORSET   2–4C

Bistro on the Beach   £33   🅰★

Solent Promenade BH6 4BE   (01202) 431473

"By day a beach café (which serves excellent breakfasts)"…
at night, this "marvellously located" venture become a candlelit
"delight", offering "first-rate food, and a welcome to match".
/ Sample dishes: smoked salmon & prawn terrine; braised lamb with mint mash;
bread & butter pudding. Details: 9.30 pm; D only, closed Sun-Tue, in summer open
Tue; no smoking.

Chez Fred   £16   ★★

10 Seamoor Rd BH4 9AN   (01202) 761023

"No starters, few puds, just great fresh fish" – this "smart" and
"welcoming" chippy is hailed as simply "superb" by all who
comment on it. / Sample dishes: cod & chips with mushy peas; treacle
sponge & custard. Details: www.chezfred.co.uk; 1m W of town centre; 9.45 pm;
closed Sun L; no Amex; no smoking; no booking.

Mandarin   £26   ★

194-198 Old Christchurch Rd BH1 1PD   (01202) 290681

Fans proclaim as "excellent" the cooking at this more than usually
"elegant" Chinese, in the centre of the town.
/ Details: www.themandarin.net; 11 pm; no smoking area.

Ocean Palace   £31   ★

8 Priory Rd BH2 5DG   (01202) 559127

Beside the Bournemouth International Centre, this "plain" Chinese
is a "friendly" place, where the cooking "never disappoints".
/ Details: www.oceanpalace.co.uk; 11 pm.

BOWNESS, CUMBRIA   7–3D

Miller Howe   £53   🅰

Rayrigg Rd LA23 1EY   (01539) 442536

"Memories are made looking out over the lake", at this Lakeland
hotel made famous under the previous, John Tovey regime;
Paul Webster's cooking is "pricey, but not outrageously so for what
you get". / Sample dishes: warm chicken liver salad; roast halibut with sage
mash; sticky toffee pudding & toffee sauce. Details: www.millerhowe.com; on A592
between Windermere & Bowness; 8 pm; closed for 2 weeks in Jan; no smoking
in dining room; children: 8+. Accommodation: 15 rooms, from £160.

Porthole   £40   🅰★

3 Ash St LA23 3EB   (01539) 442793

"The Berton's really know how to make an occasion special",
say fans of this Italian veteran (of 30 years standing) in a 17th-
century house at the heart of the village; it boasts "one of the best
wine cellars in the county". / Sample dishes: antipasto; veal with
mushrooms; sticky toffee pudding. Details: www.porthole.fsworld.co.uk; near Old
England Hotel; 10 pm; closed Mon L, Tue, Wed L & Sat L.

BRADFORD ON AVON, WILTSHIRE   3–3B

Thai Barn   £35   ★

24 Bridge St BA15 1BY   (01225) 866443

Fans vaunt both the "authentic" food and the "historic" and
"beautiful" setting of this self-explanatory operation; some find the
setting "cramped" though, and service wanting to "get you in and
get you out". / Sample dishes: royal platter; sauté pork, pineapple, onion,
cucumber & tomato in sweet & sour sauce; pineapple ice cream. Details: opp
Bridge St car park; 10.30 pm; closed Mon & Tue L; no Amex; no smoking area.

BRADFORD, WEST YORKSHIRE   5–1C

Aagrah   £ 22
483 Bradford Rd LS28 8ED   (01274) 668818
Part of a small Yorkshire chain, this modern Indian once again wins praise for its "tasty" and "authentic" cooking.
/ **Details:** www.aagrah.com; on A647, 3m from city centre; 11.30 pm, Fri & Sat midnight; D only; no smoking area.

Akbars Balti   £ 18   Ⓐ★
1276 Leeds Rd BD3 3LF   (01274) 773311
"Superb Indian food in an atmospheric setting" helps make this a "tremendous-value" balti house; don't miss the "amazing" naans.
/ **Details:** www.akbars.co.uk; midnight; D only; no credit cards; no smoking area.

Clarks   £ 26
46-50 Highgate BD9 4BE   (01274) 499890
"Value for money" helps endear this useful decade-old brasserie to local reporters. / **Sample dishes:** pea & mint soup; bacon chop with Cheddar mash & parsley sauce; treacle tart. **Details:** www.clarksrestaurant.co.uk; 5 mins from city centre on A650 to Shipley; 9.30 pm; closed Sat L & Sun L; no smoking area.

Karachi   £ 9   ★
15-17 Neal St BD5 0BX   (01274) 732015
A visit by Rick Stein seems to have prompted redecoration at this "authentic and basic curry house"; it's still "not fancy", though, but it does offer "freshly cooked food at amazingly cheap prices".
/ **Details:** 1 am, Fri & Sat 2 am; no credit cards.

Kashmir   £ 12   ★
27 Morley St BD7 1AG   (01274) 726513
"Truly wonderful flavours and cheap to boot" – that's the deal at this "basic", "canteen-style" Indian (the oldest in town), which is praised for its "well-cooked food at down-to-earth prices".
/ **Details:** 3 am; no Amex; no smoking area.

Love Apple Cafe   £ 15   Ⓐ
34 Great Horton Rd BD7 1AL   (01274) 744075
This "friendly cafe/bar" offers "a wide range of daytime and evening menus", all of which find favour with reporters – "great veggie breakfasts", "excellent sandwiches", "great nachos" (a house speciality) and "fantastic fish dishes" are all singled out for praise.
/ **Sample dishes:** nachos; chana massala with fresh tomatoes & coriander; chocolate truffle cheesecake served with cream & ice cream. **Details:** 9 pm; no smoking area.

Mumtaz Paan House   £ 14   ★★
Great Horton Rd BD7 3HS   (01274) 571861
The home of "Britain's best curry"? – "thronged and authentic", this "vast" and "cosmopolitan" subcontinental has about as good a claim as most; no booze, though. / **Details:** www.mumtaz.co.uk; midnight, weekends 1 am; no smoking.

Nawaab   £ 24   ★
32 Manor Rw BD1 4QE   (01274) 720371
"Some unusual dishes" add interest to a visit to this legendary subcontinental, where the cooking is always "well cooked, and nicely presented" and can be "excellent". / **Details:** www.nawaab.com; 11 pm; closed Sat L & Sun L; no smoking area.

BRANCASTER, NORFOLK   6–3B

White Horse   £31   Ⓐ
Main Rd PE31 8BY   (01485) 210262
*The occasional nomination as "meal of the year" is still received
by this "friendly" inn, which enjoys "wonderful views over the
Marches" (if you want a window table, "book ahead"); the food can
be no more than "OK", though, and some sense a place "resting
on its laurels". /* **Sample dishes:** *salmon & crab fishcakes, roast beetroot salad,
lime créme fraiche; pan-fried skate wing with capers; strawberry shortbread.*
Details: *www.whitehorsebrancaster.co.uk; 9 pm; no Amex; no smoking in dining
room.* **Accommodation:** *15 rooms, from £68.*

BRANSCOMBE, DEVON   2–4A

Masons Arms   £33
Main St EX12 3DJ   (01297) 680300
*The "romantic", "traditional pub ambiente" is key to the appeal
of this ancient boozer; fans hail its "simple but tasty" fare, but other
recent reports have been of a very up-and-down experience.
/* **Sample dishes:** *smoked duck with pineapple pickle; grilled plaice with garlic &
prawns; chocolate truffle torte.* **Details:** *www.masonsarms.co.uk; 9 pm; D only,
closed Mon & Sun; no Amex; no smoking; children: 14.* **Accommodation:** *25
rooms, from £50.*

BRAY, WINDSOR & MAIDENHEAD   3–3A

The Fat Duck   £78
1 High St SL6 2AQ   (01628) 580333
*"Crazy" but "truly astonishing", Heston Blumenthal's creations are
acclaimed by many fans as "the most original cooking in the UK";
they are not for everyone, though – doubters can find the whole
performance "deadly, uninspiring and overblown", and neither the
"cramped" setting nor the sometimes "unwelcoming" service offer
much compensation. /* **Sample dishes:** *cuttlefish cannelloni with duck & maple
syrup; slow-cooked lamb with lambs tongue & onion purée; tarte Tatin with bay
leaf & almond foam.* **Details:** *www.fatduck.co.uk; 9.30 pm, Fri & Sat 10 pm; closed
Mon & Sun D; closed 2 weeks at New Year; no smoking.*

Fish   £31
Old Mill Ln SL6 2BG   (01628) 781111
*After a difficult patch – and the occasional reporter still dismisses
the place as a "bland wannabe" – this "stylish" modern venture and
its "incredibly fresh fish" are again winning more consistent support.
/* **Sample dishes:** *oysters; char-grilled tuna with black olive mash; chocolate truffle
cake.* **Details:** *www.thefishatbray.com; 9.15 pm; closed Sun D; no smoking area.*

Riverside Brasserie   £42   ★
Monkey Island Ln, Bray Marina
SL6 2EB   (01628) 780553
*Heston Blumenthal's often "fantastic" cooking (here,
"less experimental than at the Fat Duck") helps win huge popularity
for his second establishment; its "hard to find" location (a "shed"
in Bray Marina) can seem "Spartan" and "cold", so visit on a sunny
day when you can enjoy the "idyllic" setting with "views over the
water". /* **Sample dishes:** *sardine tart; rib-eye steak & chips with marrowbone
sauce; strawberry soup with butter biscuits.* **Details:** *follow signs for Bray Marina off
A308; 10 pm; closed Mon & Sun D; no Amex.*

Waterside Inn £116 ★

Ferry Rd SL6 2AT (01628) 620691

"A delightful setting", *"classic French cuisine served in the grand manner"* and a *"draw-dropping"* wine list come together to make Michel Roux's (and son Alain's) famous Thames-side fixture a *"blissfully romantic"* destination for many reporters; its style can seem rather *"dated"*, though, and a number find prices *"OTT"*.
/ **Sample dishes:** *spiced foie gras terrine with poached figs; grilled rabbit with glazed chestnuts; golden plum soufflé.* **Details:** *www.waterside-inn.co.uk; off A308 between Windsor & Maidenhead; 10 pm; closed Mon & Tue (open Tue D Jun-Aug); booking: max 10; children: 12+.* **Accommodation:** *9 rooms, from £150.*

BREARTON, NORTH YORKSHIRE 8–4B

The Malt Shovel £21 ★

HG3 3BX (01423) 862929

This *"popular small pub"* (a converted barn) *"in a rather remote village"* is highly rated for its *"good basic grub"* (*"excellent fish and chips"*, for instance), its *"efficient"* service and its *"real"* atmosphere.
/ **Sample dishes:** *goats cheese & leek tart; steak & ale pie; treacle tart.* **Details:** *off A61, 6m N of Harrogate; 9 pm; closed Mon & Sun D; no credit cards; no smoking area; no booking.*

BRECON, POWYS 2–1A

Felin Fach Griffin £33 ★

Felin Fach LD3 0UB (01874) 620111

"The best news for Mid-Wales in a long time" – this renovated inn, outside Brecon, has established quite a reputation in the last two years; it offers *"terrific contemporary cooking"*, featuring *"excellent local ingredients"*. / **Sample dishes:** *wild mushroom tagliatelli; rib of welsh black beef with chips; lemon tart.* **Details:** *www.eatdrinksleep.ltd.uk; 20 mins NW of Abergavenny on A470; 9.30 pm; closed Mon L; no Amex; no smoking at D.* **Accommodation:** *7 rooms, from £82.50.*

BRIDPORT, DORSET 2–4B

Riverside £35 ★★

West Bay DT6 4EZ (01308) 422011

"Excellent local fish, served with imagination" has secured a vast and widespread fanclub for this sometimes rather *"crowded"* local favourite; it has a *"wonderful"* location, too, *"amongst the reeds overlooking West Bay"*. / **Sample dishes:** *warm oysters with laver bread; halibut with rarebit topping; Limoncello panna cotta.* **Details:** *9 pm; closed Mon & Sun D; no Amex; smoking discouraged.*

BRIGHTON, EAST SUSSEX 3–4B

Brighton has always had lots of restaurants, but until recently they were generally rather more notable for their variety than their quality. But this is beginning to change.

At the top end of the market, the position is pretty much as ever – *One Paston Place* has for a number of years been regarded by many as one of the South Coast's best restaurants, and remains so. For more day-to-day restaurant-going, though, a proper second tier of quality restaurants is finally emerging, such as *Gingerman*, *The Saint*, *Seven Dials* and *Strand*. The quirky but very interesting *Black Chapati* continues to offer some highly original cooking.

Vegetarians are especially well catered for, with *Terre à Terre* – probably the best place of its type in the country – being the most commented-on establishment in town. For quintessential seaside seafood, the *Regency* is hard to beat. In *English's*, Brighton boasts one of England's few true period restaurants.

Those looking for the more obvious ethnic cuisines will find an unusually wide choice of relatively inexpensive establishments of good quality. The Lanes and the trendier 'hang-out' districts of North Laine and Kemptown continue to boast a host of decent-enough mid-range places.

Al Duomo £24

7 Pavilion Building BN1 1EE (01273) 326741
Given its tourist trap location by the Royal Pavilion, this vast fixture is surprisingly "real" – "a bustling Italian, with something for everyone" (and, in particular, "good pizzas"); 2003 saw expansion and a complete revamp in striking modern style.
/ **Sample dishes:** *calamari; fusilli with tomatoes & anchovies; tiramisu.*
Details: *www.alduomo.co.uk; near the Royal Pavilion; 11 pm; no smoking area.*

Aumthong Thai £27 ★

60 Western Rd BN3 1JD (01273) 773922
"Spicy, high-quality Thai cooking", "smiley" staff and "agreeable" surroundings generate all-round satisfaction with this long-established oriental, near the seafront. / **Details:** *www.aumthong.com; 10.45 pm; closed Mon L.*

Black Chapati £34 ★★

12 Circus Pde, New England Rd BN1 4GW
(01273) 699011
"Surprises are guaranteed" at this unimpressive-looking and hard-to-find destination, which is "always worth a trip" for its "unusual" and "intelligent" Asian-fusion cuisine; the usual diatribes against the service were not in evidence this year. / **Details:** *10 pm; D only, closed Mon, Tue & Sun.*

Blanch House £48

17 Atlingworth St BN2 1PL (01273) 645755
"Beautifully-executed food in a stunning environment" is hailed by fans of this trendy design-hotel dining room on the edge of Kemptown; portions can be "stingy", though, and some find the place "way too far up its own derrière". / **Sample dishes:** *celeriac ravioli with goats cheese; juniper-crusted lamb with ratatouille & rosemary polenta; pink peppercorn meringue with strawberries.* **Details:** *www.blanchhouse.co.uk; 10.30 pm; closed Mon & Sun.* **Accommodation:** *12 rooms, from £100.*

Bombay Aloo £14 ★

39 Ship St BN1 1AB (01273) 771089
"We vote it top every year, and nothing has changed", says one of the fans of this "really good vegetarian buffet". / **Details:** *near the Lanes; 11 pm; no Amex; no smoking area; need 6+ to book; children: under 5s eat free.*

Browns £29 ✕

3-4 Duke St BN1 1AH (01273) 323501
"Seems like they've stopped trying" at this (the original) outlet of the well-known British brasserie chain – a "seedy" place, where the menu is "dull" and "overpriced". / **Sample dishes:** *smoked salmon with soda bread; chicken & leek pie; sticky toffee pudding.*
Details: *www.browns-restaurants.com; 11.30 pm; no smoking area; no booking at weekends.*

China Garden   £ 29   ★
88-91 Preston St BN1 2HG   (01273) 325124
"Great dim sum" is the highlight at this large but *"consistent"* café-style oriental, but its cooking is *"very good"* at any time, and served by *"attentive"* staff. / **Details:** *opp West Pier; 11 pm; no Amex; no smoking area.*

Donatello   £ 30   ✗
1-3 Brighton Pl BN1 1HJ   (01273) 775477
"Why do people rave about this place?" was a question much-asked about this *"packed"* and *"touristy"* Italian in the Lanes, which reporters repeatedly judged *"dire"*. / **Sample dishes:** *grilled sardines; tagliatelle with smoked salmon & cream; cherries in liqueur with ice cream.* **Details:** *www.donatello.co.uk; 11.30 pm; no smoking area.*

The Dorset Street Bar   £ 25   𝔸
28 North Rd BN1 1YB   (01273) 605423
"Good for coffee, Sunday lunch with the family, or just a drink at any time" – this *"atmospheric"* café in a converted North Laine pub makes a pleasant all-day rendezvous. / **Sample dishes:** *salmon fishcakes; grilled chicken with salami & Camembert; chocolate brioche.* **Details:** *10 pm; no smoking area; booking: max 8.*

English's   £ 38   𝔸
29-31 East St BN1 1HL   (01273) 327980
This Victorian Lanes survivor (150 years old, and owned by the same family since 1945) is perennially knocked for being too touristy; there were indeed gripes about *"slow"* service, *"high prices"* and *"lacking"* ambience this year, but most reporters found it *"lovely and old-fashioned"* with *"very good local fish"*.
/ **Sample dishes:** *avocado, feta & nectarine salad; Dover sole & prawns with sorrel & lobster sauce; apple Bakewell tart.* **Details:** *www.englishs.co.uk; 10 pm; no smoking area.*

Food for Friends   £ 18   ★
17-18 Prince Albert St BN1 1HF   (01273) 202310
"A bit slow, but the food is good when it arrives" – this long-established veggie remains a popular Lanes rendezvous, despite its rather *"rough and ready"* style. / **Sample dishes:** *Jerusalem artichoke soup; Cheddar & mushroom risotto with spicy tomato sauce; Bramley & blackberry crumble.* **Details:** *www.foodforfriends.com; 10 pm; no smoking area.*

La Fourchette   £ 32
101 Western Rd BN1 2AA   (01273) 722556
This cramped French venture is moving to new premises as we go to press, two doors down from the old; hopefully the new space will be a better showcase for its *"great choice"* of fish and seafood, which has developed quite a following. / **Sample dishes:** *spinach, asparagus & Mozzarella lasagne; confit duck with mash & veal sauce; citron tart.* **Details:** *10.30 pm; closed Mon L & Sun.* **Accommodation:** *8 rooms, from £70.*

The George   £ 20   ★
5 Trafalgar St BN1 4EQ   (01273) 681055
"Fun, funky and central", this boozer, near the railway station, has many advocates of its *"cheap"* but *"high-quality"* veggie pub grub (*"with a twist"*); unsurprisingly, it can get *"too crowded"*.
/ **Sample dishes:** *tomato & Mozzarella bruschetta; smoked Applewood rarebit with leeks & salsa; tarte Tatin.* **Details:** *9.30 pm, Fri & Sun 8.30 pm; no smoking area; children: before 7 pm only.*

Gingerman £36 ★

21a Norfolk Square BN1 2PD (01273) 326688

"Still amongst Brighton's best"; Ben McKellar's "simply decorated" five-year-old in the Lanes may be "cramped", but it again wins consistent praise for its "marvellous" modern cooking and its "very good" service. / **Sample dishes:** beetroot & anchovy salad; swordfish with plum tomato tart; passion fruit soufflé. **Details:** off Norfolk Square; 10 pm; closed Mon & Sun.

Harry's £25

41 Church Rd BN3 2BE (01273) 727410

This "posh" (well this is Hove) but "friendly" diner has quite a reputation for "proper fry-ups", and, later in the day, its "great club sandwiches"; it's less of a dinner place, though. / **Sample dishes:** prawn cocktail; cheese & chilli burger; banoffi pie. **Details:** www.harrysrestaurant.co.uk; 10.30 pm.

Havana £49 Ⓐ

32 Duke St BN1 1AG (01273) 773388

The approach can still seem a bit "pretentious", but this very spacious, "contemporary" and "romantic" venue in the Lanes at last seems to be beginning to live up to its potential; presumably it's down to new chef Michael Benjamin, who comes with quite a respectable pedigree. / **Sample dishes:** haddock & poached egg tartlet; roast venison; Baileys parfait with biscuits. **Details:** www.havana.uk.com; 10.30 pm; no trainers; no smoking area; booking: max 10, Sat pm; children: 6+ a D.

Hotel du Vin et Bistro £41

Ship St BN1 1AD (01273) 718588

"It's great to have one of these in Brighton", say fans, but (at first, at least) this new, fifth outpost of the boutique hotel chain is rated notably lower than its peers – "teething problems with service" and "underwhelming" cooking too often made it an "average and predictable" experience. / **Sample dishes:** moules marinière; duck with apple & foie gras; chocolate tart. **Details:** www.hotelduvin.com; 9.45 pm; booking: max 10. **Accommodation:** 37 rooms, from £115.

The Latin in the Lane £34

10-11 Kings Rd BN1 1NE (01273) 328672

"Simple and juicy fish dishes" are a highlight for fans of this "old-fashioned" Italian near the seafront; it takes different reporters very different ways, though, and critics find it "ridiculously overpriced". / **Sample dishes:** linguine with clams; profiteroles. **Details:** 11 pm.

One Paston Place £53 ★

1 Paston Pl BN2 1HA (01273) 606933

"Sublime" cooking with "meticulous attention to detail" makes this "friendly" and "welcoming" Kemptown townhouse quite possibly "the best restaurant on the South Coast"; its "refined" ambience, however, often fails to excite. / **Sample dishes:** skate stuffed with potted shrimps & fennel; duck with balsamic jus & butternut squash; caramel soufflé. **Details:** www.onepastonplace.co.uk; between the pier & marina; 9.45 pm; closed Mon & Sun; booking: max 10; children: no babies.

Regency £20 ★

131 Kings Rd BN1 2HH (01273) 325014

"Recently expanded, but the food and service are as good as ever" – this "excellent cheap and cheerful seafront fish restaurant" ("everything from simple fish and chips, upwards") remains an ever-"boisterous" Brighton institution; staff are "notably family-friendly", too. / **Sample dishes:** oysters; dressed crab salad; peach Melba. **Details:** www.theregencyrestaurant.co.uk; opp West Pier; 11 pm; no smoking area. **Accommodation:** 30 rooms, from £65.

The Saint   £33   ★
22 St James's St BN2 1RF   (01273) 607835
*"High-quality" fare from a tasty ("if not very ambitious") menu
makes this "buzzy" Kemptown two-year-old unanimously popular
with reporters; "excellent cocktails", too.* / **Sample dishes:** *antipasti; roast
duck with courgette cakes & liquorice sauce; trio of brûlées.* **Details:** *10 pm; closed
Mon.*

Sanctuary Café   £21   Ⓐ
51-55 Brunswick Street East BN3 1AU   (01273) 770002
*"A chilled vibe" adds to the appeal of this "stylish", "hippy"
Brunswick café; it serves a veggie selection that's "tasty, good-value
and healthy", as well as "the best coffee".* / **Sample dishes:** *vegetarian
pâté with pitta bread; aubergine lasagne; carrot cake.*
Details: *www.sanctuarycafe.co.uk; 10 pm; no Amex; no smoking area.*

Saucy   £30
8 Church Rd BN3 2FL   (01273) 324080
*"Interesting, good-quality food" served at "reasonable prices" helps
make this "fun" brasserie a popular Hove destination; as ever,
though, there a minority which says it's "OK, but not quite up to its
reputation".* / **Sample dishes:** *crayfish tails with linguine; beef with smoked
anchovy tapenade; banana & butterscotch steamed pudding.*
Details: *www.saucyrestaurant.com; 10.30 pm; closed Sun D; no smoking area;
booking: max 6, Fri & Sat.*

Seven Dials   £37   ★
1-3 Buckingham Pl BN1 3TD   (01273) 885555
*"Reliable" contemporary cooking "with a twist" at "sound prices"
wins high ratings for this year-old "classy" bistro, whose "cosy but
modern" look creates a "buzz" that suits business or romance;
service, however, could do with some attention.*
/ **Sample dishes:** *herb-crusted goats cheese salad; stuffed quail with pancetta &
truffle jus; lavender panna cotta.* **Details:** *www.sevendialsrestaurant.co.uk;
10.30 pm, Sun 9 pm; closed Mon, Tue L & Wed L; no smoking area.*

Strand   £28   Ⓐ★
6 Little East St BN1 1HT   (01273) 747096
*"Seemingly psychic" staff, "creative" cooking and a "cosy"
atmosphere continue to win praise for this small restaurant near the
Royal Pavilion; seafood and veggie dishes predominate.*
/ **Sample dishes:** *Dolcelatte gnocchi; Thai fish wrapped in leeks; banana cream pie
with honeycomb ice cream.* **Details:** *10 pm, Fri & Sat 10.30 pm; closed Mon L;
booking: max 8, Fri & Sat.*

Terre à Terre   £37   Ⓐ★★
71 East St BN1 1NQ   (01273) 729051
*"Really exciting" and "imaginative" vegetarian fare justifies this
"stylish" and "bustling" Lanes café's reputation as the UK's top no-
meat destination; even so, it can seem "pricey" for what it is.*
/ **Sample dishes:** *fried corn cakes with salsa; asparagus pasta parcel with sun-dried
tomato pesto; rhubarb & rosehip sorbet.* **Details:** *www.terreaterre.co.uk; 10.30 pm;
closed Mon L; mainly non-smoking; booking: max 8 at weekends.*

BRIMFIELD, SHROPSHIRE   5–4A
The Roebuck Inn   £ 34
SY8 4NE   (01584) 711230
*"Above-average" food helps make this handsome gastropub (not far
from Ludlow) "well worth a journey", and it's "very popular";
it changed hands just as our survey for this year was drawing to a
close (so we've removed ratings). / Sample dishes: gin-soused salmon with
dill crème fraiche; steak & mushroom suet pudding with ale gravy; pear, rhubarb &
ginger charlotte. Details: www.roebuckinn.demon.co.uk; 9.30 pm; no Amex;
no smoking. Accommodation: 3 rooms, from £70.*

BRINKWORTH, WILTSHIRE   2–2C
The Three Crowns   £ 29
The Street SN15 5AF   (01666) 510366
*"Still No. 1 locally"; "rich" dishes from an extensive menu –
"crocodile to chicken pie" – come in "very generous" portions at this
large and popular gastro-boozer; "you can't book", so arrive early.
/ Sample dishes: grilled kangaroo, venison & ostrich with vegetables; sticky toffee
pudding. Details: www.threecrowns.co.uk; 9.30 pm; no smoking area; no booking.*

BRISTOL, CITY OF BRISTOL   2–2B

Lady Bracknell would not have approved – to lose one
destination restaurant in a season is a misfortune, but to have
lost two (the long-celebrated Harvey's and the most impressive
Markwick's) smacks of carelessness. At a stroke, Bristol's (rare)
duo of central fixtures of high ambition have been obliterated.

On the plus side, the opening of the year has been *Michael
Caines's* spin-off outlet at the old Royal Hotel – sadly too
recently for our survey to rate. If he can make a success of it,
it may be a case of out with the old, in with the new.

Reliable continuing destinations of some note include *A
Cozinha, Fishworks, Red Snapper* and *San Carlo*, but otherwise
the city's European restaurants seem to be more about
atmosphere than food. A couple of long-established Indians
aside, the city is – oddly for a port! – notably weak on ethnics.

Anthem   £ 30   Ⓐ
27-29 St Michaels Hl BS2 8DZ   (0117) 929 2834
*The menu is certainly eclectic ("from falafel to venison"),
but reporters speak only well of this "very good" city-centre
establishment; a "cosy" setting in a selection of small and "intimate"
rooms is not the least of its attractions. / Sample dishes: smoked duck
with gin & orange dressing; chicken with pine nut stuffing in Sauternes sauce;
chocolate truffle terrine. Details: 10.30 pm; D only, closed Mon & Sun; no Amex;
no smoking area.*

Bell's Diner   £ 32   Ⓐ
1 York Rd BS6 5QB   (0117) 924 0357
*A "mellow" atmosphere helps underpin the enduring appeal of this
"cosy" Bristol "old-timer", in the backstreets of Montpelier; most –
if not quite all – locals are also very impressed by its "consistently
good" and "innovative" cooking. / Sample dishes: braised octopus with
black pudding; monkfish, saffron & broad bean risotto; Muscat jelly with Granny
Smith sorbet. Details: www.bellsdiner.co.uk; 10 pm; closed Mon L, Sat L & Sun D;
no smoking.*

Blue Goose £ 28
344 Gloucester Rd BS7 8TP   (0117) 942 0940
"Interesting" menus – combining classic and adventurous dishes – help make this Horfield bistro a pleasant option in an area without a huge number of competing attractions; it's "good value", too. / **Details:** *9 pm; D only, except Sun open L & D.*

Bocanova £ 38 Ⓐ
90 Colston St BS1 5BB   (0117) 929 1538
A "noisy", "busy" and "fun" atmosphere and "colourful" cooking have made this year-old city-centre Brazilian a big hit with a youthful crowd. / **Sample dishes:** *goats cheese salad with raspberry dressing; salmon with prawn & lime leaf sauce; panna cotta with plums & whisky syrup.* **Details:** *10.30 pm, Fri & Sat 11 pm; closed Sun; no Amex; no smoking.*

Boston Tea Party £ 16 Ⓐ
75 Park St BS1 5PF   (0117) 929 8601
"A lovely terraced garden" adds much charm to this "relaxed" and "Bohemian" café – a destination celebrated locally for "superb coffee, as well as tasty cakes and sandwiches". / **Sample dishes:** *carrot & coriander soup; Spanish chicken; rum & raisin cheesecake.* **Details:** *10 pm, Sun 7 pm; closed Mon D & Sun D; no smoking in dining room; no booking.*

Brazz £ 28
85 Park St BS1 5PJ   (0117) 925 2000
"Lots of (very flash) style – little substance"; the new outpost of Kit Chapman's ambitious West Country chain of brasseries has supporters who proclaim its "quality and value", but, as at its other outlets, results seem very mixed. / **Sample dishes:** *mushrooms & spinach on toast; fishcakes with tartare sauce; chocolate Cathedral pudding.* **Details:** *www.brazz.co.uk; 10.30 pm, Thu-Sat 11 pm; closed Mon & Sun; smoking in bar only.*

Browns £ 27
38 Queens Rd BS8 1RE   (0117) 930 4777
Some say it's "best avoided", but this vast branch of the national brasserie chain mostly escapes the drubbing meted out to others in the group, even if it is the "stylish" ambience which is the chief attraction. / **Sample dishes:** *scallops; english lamb rump; sticky toffee pudding.* **Details:** *www.browns-restaurants.com; 11.30 pm; no smoking area; need 10+ to book.*

Brunel Raj £ 23
Waterloo St BS8 4BT   (0117) 973 2641
A "favourite", "cosy" Indian, in the heart of Clifton. / **Details:** *11.30 pm.*

Budokan £ 19
Clifton Down, Whiteladies Rd BS8 2PH   (0117) 949 3030
"The Rapid Refuel is a particularly good-value option", at these "excellent", "cheap 'n' cheerful" Clifton and city-centre orientals (also at 31 Colston Street, tel 08708 377300) – "Bristols first and best noodle bars". / **Details:** *www.budokan.co.uk; 10.30 pm.*

Byzantium £ 39 Ⓐ
2 Portwall Ln BS1 6NB   (0117) 922 1883
The lavish Moroccan-style décor is extremely "appealing", but even those who say this impressive-looking venue is "a great place to eat" may concede that the food is a "let-down". / **Sample dishes:** *crab, chilli & coriander tart; smoked lamb with Swiss chard gratin; chocolate & Grand Marnier mousse.* **Details:** *www.byzantium-restaurant.co.uk; near Temple Meads, opp St Mary's Redcliffe church; 11 pm; D only, closed Sun (open for L in Dec); no smoking area.*

A Cozinha £32 ★
40 Alfred Pl BS2 8HD   (0117) 944 3060

"Authentic" cooking and *"delightful"* service distinguish the city's only Portuguese restaurant in town, which is handily located for the city-centre. / **Sample dishes:** salt cod & chick pea salad; Catalan pork, fish & seafood stew; honey & cinnamon cake. **Details:** 9.30 pm; L only Tue- Fri, open Sat D; no Amex; children: 14+ at D.

Fishers £31
35 Princess Victoria St BS8 4BX   (0117) 974 7044

"While the menu is not striking, the cooking sets quality standards" at this reliable bistro (an offshoot of the popular establishment of the same name in Oxford). / **Sample dishes:** grilled sardines with parsley & lemon; beer-battered fish & chips; banana fritters with Amaretto ice cream. **Details:** www.fishers-restaurant.com; 10.30 pm; closed Mon L; no Amex; no smoking.

FishWorks £40 ★
128 Whiteladies Rd BS8 2RS   (0117) 974 4433

"Wonderful fresh fish, plainly cooked" is the forte of this *"easy-going"*, *"café-style"* operation (with fishmongers attached); it can seem *"pricey"*, though, and the ratings do hint that a degree of complacency may be setting in. / **Sample dishes:** spaghetti with crab & chilli; grilled plaice with black butter; lemon tart. **Details:** www.fishworks.co.uk; 10.30 pm; closed Mon & Sun; no smoking.

Glasnost £27
I William St BS3 4TU   (0117) 972 0938

Despite its location *"away from the bustle of the city"*, this sometimes *"imaginative"* restaurant has a relatively widespread following; some former fans, though, note that *"standards have slipped steadily over the past couple of years"*. / **Sample dishes:** mushrooms stuffed with Stilton; pork in Parma ham with peach compote; chocolate & praline soufflé. **Details:** www.glasnostrestaurant.co.uk; 10 pm; D only, closed Mon & Sun; no Amex; no smoking.

The Glass Boat £39
Welsh Back BS1 4SB   (0117) 929 0704

"A lovely setting in the docks" endears this moored barge to some locals (and it is especially tipped for its *"cheap and cheerful"* lunchtime specials); as ever, though, critics see it as an *"overpriced"* place with *"only its location to recommend it"*. / **Sample dishes:** goats cheese with radish & chive salad; roast duck with duck spring rolls & mango; Szechuan-peppered crème brûlée. **Details:** www.glassboat.co.uk; below Bristol Bridge; 9.30 pm; closed Sat L & Sun; no smoking area.

Hope & Anchor £21 Ⓐ
38 Jacobs Wells Rd BS8 1DR   (0117) 929 2987

"Huge portions of good scoff", *"interesting well-kept ales"* and a *"lovely garden"* ensure that this *"trendy"* city-centre pub, which attracts a wide-ranging crowd, is *"always busy"*. / **Sample dishes:** crayfish tail & anchovy salad; lamb & rosemary pie; sticky toffee pudding & custard. **Details:** 10 pm; no booking.

Hotel du Vin Et Bistro £43 Ⓐ
The Sugar House, Narrow Lewins Mead BS1 2NU
(0117) 925 5577

"A lovely setting in a converted sugar warehouse" helps make this *"buzzy"* outpost of the design-hotel chain the most commented-on member of the group; its *"robust"* Gallic cooking accompanied by a *"very extensive"* list of wines (*"without excessive mark-ups"*) wins consistent approval too. / **Sample dishes:** gravadlax with citrus oil; braised lamb shank with olive jus; banana tarte Tatin. **Details:** www.hotelduvin.com; 10 pm; booking: max 10. **Accommodation:** 40 rooms, from £125.

Howards £33

1a-2a, Avon Cr BS1 6XQ   (0117) 926 2921

"Always friendly and helpful", this Hotwells stalwart has been around since the '70s and remains a useful option in a thin area, attracting only upbeat reports. / **Sample dishes:** *chicken, asparagus & leek terrine; seafood tagliatelle; lemon meringue pie.* **Details:** *11 pm; closed Sat L & Sun; no smoking area.*

Michael Caines
The Royal Marriott Bristol £48

College Grn BS1 5TA   (0117) 910 5309

Summer 2003 saw Gidleigh Park chef Michael Caines, together with head chef Shane Goodway launch a brand new restaurant at this landmark hotel in the city centre; his spin off in Exeter has had its ups and downs, but this newcomer might just become the gastronomic champion Bristol now signally lacks. / **Sample dishes:** *salad of cornish lobster with Parmesan; turbot with cannelloni of scallops; raspberry parfait with vanilla mousse.* **Details:** *10 pm; closed Sun; no smoking.* **Accommodation:** *242 rooms, from £150.*

Mud Dock £28

40 The Grove BS1 4RB   (0117) 934 9734

The "relaxed location overlooking the waterfront" is the special attraction of this café above a cycle shop; the food is "average", though, and "slow" service brings new meaning to the term "lazy brunch". / **Sample dishes:** *spinach, yoghurt & mint soup; grilled tuna with olive oil mash; banoffi pie.* **Details:** *www.mud-dock.com; close to the Industrial Museum & Arnolfini Gallery; 10.30 pm; no smoking area; no booking.*

Muset £32

16 Clifton Rd BS8 1AS   (0117) 973 2920

It serves "fairly good" food, "but the best bit is the BYO policy" at this "fun" bistro (which changed hands and took on a new chef this year). / **Sample dishes:** *sun dried tomato & tarragon; braised lamb shank with mashed potaoes & rosemary jus; chocolate crème brûlée.* **Details:** *www.muset.co.uk; 10.15 pm; closed weekday L; no Amex.*

Olive Shed £37

Floating Harbour, Princes Whf BS1 4RN   (0117) 929 1960

"One of the few harbourside places doing decent food" – though not as well-known as the others, this small joint (hidden away near the Industrial Museum) wins consistent support for its "fantastic selection" of "interesting and good-value tapas dishes". / **Details:** *www.therealolivecompany.co.uk; 10 pm; closed Mon & Sun D; no Amex; no smoking.*

One Stop Thali Cafe £18 ★

12 York Rd BS6 5QE   (0117) 942 6687

This "lively", "Bollywood-style" Montpelier diner – "a veggie Indian, where a fiver buys you a feast" – is unanimously hailed by local reporters as a "good-value" spot which "never disappoints". / **Sample dishes:** *veggi pakora; three-curry plate with rice & raita.* **Details:** *www.onestopthali.co.uk; 11.30 pm; D only, closed Mon; no credit cards; no smoking.*

Primrose Café £28 𝔸★

1 Boyces Ave BS8 4AA   (0117) 946 6577

"Breakfast is an institution" at this "great neighbourhood café/restaurant" in Clifton Village; in the evenings, "delicious" dinners – featuring "brilliant fish dishes" from a "daily menu" – are served by candlelight; "BYO keeps costs in check". / **Sample dishes:** *crab risotto with avocado ice cream; curried Welsh mutton with black pepper rice; brown sugar meringues with grilled bananas.* **Details:** *9.30 pm; closed Mon D & Sun D; no Amex; no smoking area; no booking at L.*

Quartier Vert £37
85 Whiteladies Rd BS8 2NT   (0117) 973 4482
"Superbly cooked and presented organic food, served with cheerful panache" makes this Mediterranean restaurant in Clifton a destination of some note locally; even fans, though, can find it *"overpriced"* for what it is. / **Sample dishes:** *pan-fried scallops with pea purée; pork chops with smoked pimento mash; lemon & almond polenta cake.* **Details:** *www.quartiervert.co.uk; 10.30 pm; closed Sun D; no Amex.*

Rajdoot £25 ★
83 Park St BS1 5PJ   (0117) 926 8033
"For more than 20 years, the region's best Indian", say fans of this smart central subcontinental. / **Details:** *www.rajdoot.co.uk; 11.30 pm; closed Sun L.*

Rajpoot £33 ★
52 Upper Belgrave Rd BS8 2XP   (0117) 973 3515
It's *"a bit expensive"*, but standards are *"above-average"* at this superior Indian. / **Details:** *11 pm; D only, closed Sun; no smoking.*

Red Snapper £36 ★
1 Chandos Rd BS6 6PG   (0117) 973 7999
The exterior *"doesn't look special"*, and the interior is *"cramped"* and a bit *"sterile"*, but this converted shop in the backstreets near Clifton is well known locally for its *"fresh and well-cooked fish"*. / **Sample dishes:** *Stilton & bacon salad; skate with sprouting broccoli & anchovy butter; mango & muscat crème brûlée.* **Details:** *10 pm; closed Mon L & Sun; no smoking before 9.30 pm.*

riverstation £34
The Grove BS1 4RB   (0117) 914 4434
"Beautiful views of the Avon" and an *"airy"* and *"attractive"* setting are among the features which commend this *"sophisticated"* conversion of a river police station to reporters; it's *"expensive"*, though, the quality of the food *"fluctuates"*, and service can be poor. / **Sample dishes:** *sautéed morels & asparagus; sea trout with summer vegetables & aioli; gooseberry & elderflower fool.* **Details:** *www.riverstation.co.uk; 10.30 pm, Fri & Sat 11 pm; no Amex; no smoking area; no booking in deli bar.*

San Carlo £36 𝔸★
44 Corn St BS1 1HQ   (0117) 922 6586
Universally hailed by reporters as *"a good all-rounder"*, this popular Italian has moved much ahead of its Brum sibling in reporter esteem; *"fantastic"* pizzas are a highlight. / **Sample dishes:** *oysters & calamari; rack of lamb.* **Details:** *11 pm.*

Sands £26 𝔸
95 Queens Rd BS8 1LW   (0117) 973 9734
"Great mezze" are the star turn at this cellar Lebanese; it's *"better midweek"* – the last Thursday of every month (generally speaking) sees a banquet, with music and dancing. / **Sample dishes:** *fried aubergine with chick peas; Lebanese mixed grill; lemon sorbet.* **Details:** *11 pm; no smoking area.*

Severnshed £30
The Grove, Harbourside BS1 4RB   (0117) 925 1212
The prices *"reflect the location"* of this strikingly-designed venture on the waterfront, but there's a strong feeling among reporters that its Middle Eastern cooking *"fails to deliver"*. / **Sample dishes:** *fish mezze platter; hot chicken & rosemary salad; lemon curd tart.* **Details:** *www.severnshed.co.uk; 10.30 pm; no smoking area.*

Teohs £ 23
26-34 Lower Ashley Rd BS2 9NP (0117) 907 1191
*"It gets very busy, and very noisy", at these "bustling" pan-Asian joints (whose original St Agnes branch now has a sibling in The Tobacco Factory, Raleigh Road, tel 902 1122); a good few locals praise the places' "efficient and friendly" style, and say that "for the price, they're brilliant". / **Details:** 100 yds from M32, J3; 10.30 pm; closed Sun; no Amex; no smoking.*

BROAD HAVEN, PEMBROKESHIRE 4–4B

Druidstone Hotel £ 31 A
Druid Haven SA62 3NE (01437) 781221
*"Homely, friendly, dogs, kids – I love it"; "magnificent sea views" set the scene at this small hotel – a converted, Victorian house, where the dining room serves a wide-ranging menu prepared from "fresh ingredients". / **Sample dishes:** Polish meat soup; sea bass & mullet with watercress cream; chocolate orange cheesecake. **Details:** www.druidstone.co.uk; from B4341 at Broad Haven turn right, then left after 1.5m; 9.30 pm; closed Sun D; no smoking in dining room. **Accommodation:** 11 rooms, from £52.*

BROADHEMBURY, DEVON 2–4A

Drewe Arms £ 40 A★
EX14 3NF (01404) 841267
*"Fish still tasting of the sea" is the highlight of the "splendid" cooking at this celebrated and "lovely" pub, "in the heart of a beautiful village". / **Sample dishes:** mixed seafood selection; grilled turbot with hollandaise; bread pudding with whisky butter. **Details:** 5m from M5, J28, on A373 to Honiton; 9.30 pm (9 pm in winter); closed Sun D; no Amex; no smoking; children: 14+.*

BROADWAY, WORCESTERSHIRE 2–1C

Lygon Arms £ 61
High St WR12 7DU (01386) 852255
*We include for completeness only this famous Elizabethan coaching inn – sold by the Savoy Group in the summer of 2003; its potentially wonderful barrel-vaulted dining room has, in recent years, been trading so hideously "on former glories" that surely the only way is up? / **Sample dishes:** leek & mushroom lasagne with truffle oil; sea bass with creamed leeks & chorizo; plum crumble soufflé with liquorice ice-cream. **Details:** www.the-lygon-arms.co.uk; just off A44; 9.15 pm, Fri & Sat 10 pm; closed weekday L; no smoking; children: 6+, 12+ in Great Hall at D. **Accommodation:** 69 rooms, from £179.*

BROCKENHURST, HAMPSHIRE 2–4C

Simply Poussin £ 31 A★
The Courtyard, Brookley Rd SO42 7RB (01590) 623063
*Some feel "it's still looking for its niche" (since the main operation shifted to Le Poussin at Parkhill a few years back), but most reporters are full of admiration for this "intimate" bistro, lauding its "very high all round standards". / **Sample dishes:** ham hock & foie gras terrine; chicken provençale; chocolate truffle cake. **Details:** www.simplypoussin.co.uk; behind Bestsellers Bookshop; 10 pm; closed Mon & Sun; no smoking; children: 8+.*

BRODICK, ISLE OF ARRAN 7–1A

Creelers Seafood Restaurant £33 ✗
Home Farm KA27 8DD (01770) 302810
*This quirky old hut has now spawned a growing national chain;
perhaps the strain is proving too much, as – though some reporters
do note "seafood cooked to perfection" – feedback has soured
noticeably, and there are now far too many damning reports.*
/ **Sample dishes:** *smoked fish pâté with Arran oatcakes; sea bass with caper &
lemon butter; strawberry cheesecake.* **Details:** *www.creelers.co.uk; 9.30 pm; closed
Mon; no Amex or Switch.*

BUCKLAND, GLOUCESTERSHIRE 2–1C

Buckland Manor £72
WR12 7LY (01386) 852626
*"A pricey but satisfying gastronomic experience" is the theme
of most commentary on this "beautiful", but perhaps slightly
"stuffy", dining room, in a country house whose origins date back
to Domesday; it boasts an "encyclopaedic" wine list.*
/ **Sample dishes:** *smoked duck, fennel & orange salad; Angus beef with truffled
lentils; pear & apple crumble with Calvados sauce.*
Details: *www.bucklandmanor.com; 2rn SW of Broadway on B4632; 9 pm; jacket &
tie required at D; no smoking in dining room; booking: max 8; children: 12+.*
Accommodation: *14 rooms, from £225.*

BUCKLAND, OXFORDSHIRE 2–2C

Lamb at Buckland £34
Lamb Ln SN7 8QN (01367) 870484
*"Good" and "consistent" pub food that's "not cheap but worth the
money" – that's the pretty much invariable tenor of reports on this
"atmospheric" village inn.* / **Sample dishes:** *lemon sole with chive butter;
pan-fried skate wing; peach & almond flan.* **Details:** *on A420 between Oxford &
Swindon; 9.30 pm; closed Mon & Sun D; no Amex; no smoking.*
Accommodation: *1 room, at about £90.00.*

BURFORD, OXFORDSHIRE 2–2C

The Lamb £42 Ⓐ
Sheep St OX18 4LR (01993) 823155
*"New owners seem to be trying hard" at this "comfortable"
Cotswold inn, but its ambience remains "as timelessly beauteous
as ever"; even those who warn "it's on the tourist trail" say it's
"well worth a visit", though the consensus is that the food is "good,
rather than anything more".* / **Sample dishes:** *Parma ham & Brie fritters;
steak & Guinness pie; coffee profiteroles.* **Details:** *www.lambinn-burford.co.uk;
A40 from Oxford toward Cheltenham; 9.30 pm; no Amex; no smoking.*
Accommodation: *15 rooms, from £125.*

BURLEY IN WHARFEDALE, WEST YORKSHIRE 5–1C

Mantra £34
78 Main St LS29 7BT (01943) 864602
*This well-established village restaurant (fka David Woolley's), has –
under D Woolley's continued ownership – 'morphed' into this more
contemporary venture; an early reporter rated the new culinary
approach as "good", and wondered if it's "perhaps now a little too
ambitious".* / **Sample dishes:** *salmon platter; blackened duck with orange &
honey; brown bread parfait with butterscotch sauce.* **Details:** *www.mantra.uk.net;
10 pm; D only, except Sun L only; no Amex; no smoking area.*

BURNHAM MARKET, NORFOLK 6–3B

Fishes £36 ★
Market Pl PE31 8HE (01328) 738588
"The freshest fish, with a minimum of fuss" wins consistent very high praise for this simple, whitewashed establishment; for one reporter at least "it outshone Rick Stein's" – well, the chef/patron did used to work for the great man. / **Sample dishes:** potted brown shrimps; monkfish with fennel & cream sauce; strawberry mousse. **Details:** 9 pm, Sat 9.30 pm; closed Mon & Sun L; no Amex; no smoking; children: 8+ after 8.30 pm.

Hoste Arms £32
The Green PE31 8HD (01328) 738777
Such is its fashionable appeal (especially with visitors from the Smoke) that one reporter describes this "relaxed" boozer as "North Norfolk's answer to The Ivy"; it serves "decent"-enough food – "a relief, in these parts" – but over-popularity seems to cause "variable" standards. / **Sample dishes:** Cullen Skink with poached quails egg; honey-glazed ham hock with minted mash; apple tart with cinnamon ice cream. **Details:** www.hostearms.co.uk; 6m W of Wells-next-the-Sea; 9 pm; no Amex; no smoking area. **Accommodation:** 43 rooms, from £92.

BURNSALL, NORTH YORKSHIRE 8–4B

Red Lion £35
BD23 6BU (01756) 720204
For "a good bar menu in an atmospheric old Dales inn", some reporters would recommend this "bustling and popular riverside pub", on the banks of the Wharfe. / **Sample dishes:** gravadlax & avocado with lemon dressing; chilli-marinated chicken with spiced tomato sauce; treacle tart with candied lemon. **Details:** www.redlion.co.uk; off A59; 9.30 pm; no smoking in dining room. **Accommodation:** 13 rooms, from £100.

BURPHAM, WEST SUSSEX 3–4A

George & Dragon £35 🄰★
BN18 9RR (01903) 883131
A "lovely" South Downs country pub "on the road to nowhere", where the "relaxed" atmosphere and "excellent bar and restaurant food" make for "an all-round good eating experience". / **Sample dishes:** terrine of duck studded with pistachio; pork tenderloin with spinach, fennel & Pernod sauce; hot chocolate fondant, hazelnut & white chocolate ice cream. **Details:** 3m from Arundel station, off A27; 9.30 pm; D only, except Sun when L only; smoking discouraged; children: 8+.

BURY ST EDMUNDS, SUFFOLK 3–1C

Ickworth Hotel £47
Horringer IP29 5QE (01284) 735350
"Fine surroundings" are the highlight you would hope for at this grandly housed new member of the Luxury Family Hotels empire; it inspired a good amount of survey commentary, but standards – especially of service – are very up-and-down. / **Sample dishes:** pan-fried scallops with black pudding on celeriac; roast duck breast or pan fried red snapper; pina colada sorbe. **Details:** www.ickworthhotel.com; 9.30 pm; D only, except Sun open L & D; no smoking; booking: max 8. **Accommodation:** 27 rooms, from £155.

Maison Bleue £33 A★
30-31 Churchgate St IP33 1RG (01284) 760623
"An intimate French fish restaurant in a country town" –
this "reliable" offshoot of the Great House at Lavenham is widely
hailed for its "wonderful" cooking (with "good meat, too") and its
notably "friendly" and "helpful" service. / **Sample dishes:** fish soup with
garlic croutons; Dover sole with pink peppercorn butter; white chocolate & lime
mousse. **Details:** www.maisonbleue.co.uk; 9.30 pm; closed Mon & Sun; no smoking.

BUSHEY, HERTFORDSHIRE 3–2A

St James £35
30 High St WD23 3HL (020) 8950 2480
This "reliable" but "noisy" Italian – with "a brasserie feel" –
has long been "the only decent restaurant near Watford", and is
well-known in the area as a result. / **Sample dishes:** grilled vegetable
antipasti; roast lamb with creamed leeks & basil jus; Toblerone cheesecake.
Details: opp St James Church; 9.45 pm; closed Sun; no smoking area.

CAMBRIDGE, CAMBRIDGESHIRE 3–1B

Cambridge remains by and large a fairly dismal place to eat,
with the continued popularity of the city's unremarkable
branch of Loch Fyne (ditto Browns) speaking volumes about the
dearth of good or atmospheric places locally.

For the most part, the selection below is of interest as the best
of a bad bunch. Two developments bring some cheer to the
picture, though – one, the arrival of Graffiti, which seems
promising; and two, the continued emergence of Midsummer
House (where ongoing niggles are being outshone by ever-
greater culinary excellence).

Browns £28 X
23 Trumpington St CB2 1QA (01223) 461655
"Formulaic and impersonal", this large branch of the English
brasserie chain maintains the dismal standards that are now its
trademark; with kids or for brunch, though, it has its uses.
/ **Sample dishes:** Caesar salad; steak, mushroom & Guinness pie; hot fudge
brownie. **Details:** www.browns-restaurants.com; opp Fitzwilliam Museum; 11 pm;
no smoking area; need 5+ to book.

Cafe Adriatic £28
12 Norfolk St CB1 2LF (01223) 355227
This "small, bistro-type place" is quite an "authentic" Italian, which
some reporters find "excellent"; "lots of fish and good veggie dishes"
are among the highlights. / **Sample dishes:** rocket, pear & Parmesan salad;
char-grilled squid & spinach risotto; Amaretti biscuits with Mascarpone.
Details: 10 pm; closed Sun; no Amex.

Cazimir £14
13 King St CB1 1LH (01223) 355156
"Consistently good sandwiches and homemade soup" are the sort
of fare that make it worth seeking out this small Polish-run café;
"the home-baked sweets are also worth a try". / **Sample dishes:** roast
vegetable bruschetta; Polish sausage & Mozzarella salad; chocolate cake.
Details: L & afternoon tea only; no credit cards; no smoking area.

Curry Queen £ 19
106 Mill Rd CB1 2BD (01223) 351027
*This "bog-standard" tandoori is "insalubriously located",
and wouldn't rate a mention in most cities; in this benighted city,
though, some say it's arguably "the best of a bad lot".*
/ **Details:** *midnight.*

Dojo £ 18
1-2 Millers Yd, Mill Ln CB2 1RQ (01223) 363471
*"Great grub + a real buzz = student heaven" at this "cramped",
"bustling" and "noisy" noodle bar "in the heart of the city"; "eating
at shared tables is perfect for a quick bite".*
/ **Details:** *www.dojonoodlebar.co.uk; off Trumpington St; 11 pm; no Amex;
no smoking; no booking.*

Fitzbillies £ 37
52 Trumpington St CB2 1RG (01223) 352500
*"Excellent value at lunchtime" is one of the attractions of the
"attractive" restaurant, adjacent to the famous cake shop of the
same name; service is "attentive", but can get "stretched" at busy
times.* / **Sample dishes:** *shrimp & leek tart; pink bream on crab cake with
asparagus & lemon vinaigrette; fresh fruit tart with chantilly cream.*
Details: *www.fitzbillies.com; 9.30 pm; closed Sun D; no smoking in dining room.*

Graffiti
Hotel Felix £ 42
Whitehouse Ln CB3 0LX (01223) 277977
*"A good cosy atmosphere, for an hotel", characterises the dining
room of this ambitious new venture, in a Victorian mansion on the
fringes of the city; we've had little feedback, to-date (hence
no rating), but some early fans say the Mediterranean cooking
is "outstanding".* / **Sample dishes:** *venison carpaccio with baby artichokes &
baked tomatoes; tournedos of beef with gorgonzala mousse potatoes; honey &
bourbon mousse with candied filo pastry & strawberry salsa.*
Details: *www.hotelfelix.co.uk; 10 pm; no smoking in dining room.*
Accommodation: *52 rooms, from £155.*

Kingston Arms £ 24 𝔸
33 Kingston St CB1 2NU (01223) 319414
*"The best pub food in Cambridge" is claimed by fans of this
revamped boozer (owned by Lidstone the brewers) not too far from
the station; it serves "hearty" and "upmarket" fare in a "lovely"
simple setting.* / **Details:** *9 pm; closed Mon L; no credit cards.*

Loch Fyne £ 33
37 Trumpington St CB2 1QY (01223) 362433
*"One of the best restaurants in Cambridge, which doesn't say
much" – an outlet of the national seafood chain.*
/ **Sample dishes:** *smoked salmon; lobster platter; ice cream.*
Details: *www.loch-fyne.com; opp Fitzwilliam Museum; 10 pm; no smoking area.*

Maharajah £ 22
9-13 Castle St CB3 0AH (01223) 358399
*"An above-average Cambridge curry" is on offer at this veteran
subcontinental; neither service nor ambience are selling points,
though.* / **Details:** *midnight.*

Michels Brasserie £37
21-24 Northampton St CB3 0AD   (01223) 353110
"Inexplicably popular"; even those saying "it's useful for lunches with parents", consider the food to be "dull" at this cosy — some would say hackneyed — brasserie, by St John's back gate. / **Sample dishes:** *charcuterie with rustic pickles; fish kebabs with samphire; chocolate bread & butter pudding.* **Details:** *10 pm; no smoking.*

Midsummer House £68 🄰★
Midsummer Common CB4 1HA   (01223) 369299
Even fans say Cambridge's top place "takes itself rather seriously" and can find it "wholly overpriced"; however, it has a "fine location" (a Victorian Villa by the Cam, overlooking a common), and Daniel Clifford's "exquisite, mouth-tingling" cuisine — "with hints of Blumenthal's Fat Duck" — is beginning to find considerable acclaim. / **Sample dishes:** *deep-fried snails with bacon risotto; slow-roast beef with mushroom gnocchi; prune & armagnac soufflé.*
Details: *www.midsummerhouse.co.uk; facing University Boathouse; 10 pm; closed Mon & Sun; no smoking.*

Peking Restaurant £34
21 Burleigh St CB1 1DG   (01223) 354755
"Consistent if expensive", a long-established Chinese, near the Grafton Centre. / **Details:** *10.30 pm; no credit cards; no smoking area.*

Sala Thong £24
35 Newnham Rd CB3 9EY   (01223) 323178
Not all are convinced, but most reporters say this "cramped" Thai is "a little gem", with "decent" food and "a really nice atmosphere". / **Details:** *9.45 pm; closed Mon; no Amex; no smoking.*

22 Chesterton Road £35
22 Chesterton Rd CB4 3AX   (01223) 351880
Can you be "too cosy"? – this year's commentary on this domestically-scaled fixture in an Edwardian house near the Cam suggests you can, but the "well thought-out menu" offers compensation, and it is complemented by "a good range of wines, to suit all budgets". / **Sample dishes:** *pork & rabbit terrine with plum sauce; crab cakes with spring onion risotto; steamed marmalade pudding.*
Details: *www.restaurant22.co.uk; 9.45 pm; D only, closed Mon & Sun; no smoking; children: 12+.*

Venue £32
Third Floor, 6 St Edward's Pas CB2 3BJ   (01223) 367333
This restaurant-cum-jazz venue has moved not once but twice in the last couple of years, most recently in the summer of 2003 into an impressive space in the Arts Theatre building; we've left it unrated — historically it's been an 'atmosphere' place with OK food. / **Sample dishes:** *Thai-style mussels; butternut squash gnocchi; dark chocolate truffle cake.* **Details:** *www.venuerestaurant.com; 10.30 pm; closed Sun; no Amex; no smoking area.*

Wrestlers Pub £18 ★
337 Newmarket Rd CB5 8JE   (01223) 566553
"Cambridge's best Thai fare" is served at this basic boozer, near the Cambridge United ground; "it even has the authentic plastic plates!" / **Details:** *www.wrestlers.co.uk; 9 pm; closed Sun (for food); need 10+ to book.*

CANTERBURY, KENT   3–3D

Augustines   £ 34   𝔸★
1-2 Longport CT1 1PE   (01227) 453063
This "small but beautifully formed" venture (occupying part of a
Georgian house) is establishing itself as "the best place in town";
it wins all-round praise for its "pleasant and efficient service" and its
"imaginative" and "satisfying" cooking. / **Sample dishes:** provençale fish
soup; marsh lamb with parsley mash; lemon tart with raspberry sauce.
Details: near the Cathedral; 9.30 pm; closed Mon & Sun D; no smoking; booking:
max 7; children: no babies.

Cafe des Amis   £ 29   𝔸
95 St Dunstan's St CT2 8AA   (01227) 464390
For a "cheap and cheerful" occasion (buoyed by "lovely strawberry
daiquiris"), this "atmospheric" Mexican has a strong local following.
/ **Sample dishes:** prawn & Serrano ham cakes; lamb with Merguez sausages;
pineapple tarte Tatin. **Details:** by Westgate Towers; 10 pm; no smoking area;
booking: max 6 at D, Fri & Sat.

CARDIFF, CARDIFF   2–2A

The Welsh capital still has yet really to join the 21st century
as far as eating out is concerned.

In other cities, its top places would be middle-rankers.
The suburban Le Gallois y Cymro and Cardiff Bay's Tides are –
by some margin – the most talked-about places in town.
The former is OK, the latter poor.

The centre of town is lamentably poorly provided for, with the
complex incorporating Le Monde, Champers and La Brasserie
really the only choice of any quality.

The Cardiff Bay development has attracted one or two fair
options in the shapes of Woods Brasserie and the quirky Izakaya.

The best-rated cooking in the area is to be had a few miles
from the city-centre in Penarth, where the veggie Tomlins
generates outstanding reports.

Armless Dragon   £ 30
97 Wyeverne Rd CF2 4BG   (029) 2038 2357
"The chef/owner is a stickler for first-rate ingredients", at this long-
established backstreet bistro, which achieves "good" overall
standards. / **Sample dishes:** liver parfait with date chutney; roast chicken with
leeks & truffle oil; crème brûlée. **Details:** www.thearmlessdragon.co.uk; 10 min
outside city centre; 9.30 pm, Sat 10.30 pm; closed Mon & Sun; no Amex;
no smoking in dining room.

La Brasserie   £ 30
60 St Mary St CF10 1FE   (029) 2023 4134
A "quaint", "sawdust on the floor" theme is quite successfully
applied to this rambling joint – for many year's the sole decent place
to eat in central Cardiff; you select your meat or seafood for them
to prepare – "the food is fresh, and can be excellent".
/ **Sample dishes:** frogs legs with garlic mayonnaise; lemon sole with new potatoes;
apple tart. **Details:** www.le-monde.co.uk/brasserie.html; midnight; closed Sun D;
need 8+ to book.

Champers £ 28

61 St Mary St CF10 1FE (029) 2037 3363

This "busy city-centre brasserie" is part of the La Brasserie complex, and its choose-your-own steaks and fish dishes are "reliably good"; the set lunch menu is "great value", too. / **Sample dishes:** garlic prawns; stuffed chicken breast; chocolate truffle. **Details:** www.le-monde.co.uk; nr Castle; midnight; closed Sun L.

Cibo £ 27   𝔸

83 Pontcanna St CF11 9HS (029) 2023 2226

"Little Italy in Pontcanna!" – this "groovy little bistro" wins praise for "Cardiff's best pizza and pasta". / **Sample dishes:** vegetable antipasti; salami & Mozzarella ciabatta; lemon cheesecake. **Details:** 9 pm; no Amex; no smoking; booking: max 10.

The Cinnamon Tree £ 23

173 Kings Rd CF11 9BZ (029) 2037 4433

"An oasis in a desert", say fans of this Canton curry house; others, though, say "it's the best in Cardiff, but not special compared to others in the UK". / **Sample dishes:** lamb curry; duck cooked with dry chili; sponge pudding. **Details:** www.thecinnamontree.co.uk; 10.45 pm; closed Sun; no smoking area.

Da Vendittos £ 52

7-8 Park Pl CF10 3DP (029) 2023 0781

"The best Italian in Cardiff"; this stylish modern eatery wins unanimous approval from reporters (and is particularly tipped for it's "superb value business lunch"); even some who say "the food's very good and everything" think "it doesn't merit its prices", though (and as we go to press, its future is uncertain as the receivers have been called in). / **Sample dishes:** risotto with Parma ham & peas; roast pigeon; basil ice cream. **Details:** 10.45 pm; no smoking area.

Le Gallois Y Cymro £ 46   ★

6-10 Romilly Cr CF11 9NR (029) 2034 1264

"Imaginative and beautifully-presented" modern dishes (from a "frequently changing" menu) win many fans for what's generally regarded as "Cardiff's most reliably excellent restaurant" (in Canton); a voluble minority, however, still finds the place "overpriced and over-rated". / **Sample dishes:** Roquefort soufflé with poached pears; roast pork with truffle mash & clove sauce; spiced pineapple with pepper ice cream. **Details:** www.legallois-ycymro.com; 1.5m W of Cardiff Castle; 10.30 pm; closed Mon & Sun; no smoking area.

The Greenhouse Café £ 25   ★

38 Woodville Rd CF24 4EB (029) 2023 5731

"Original seafood and vegetarian fare" win praise for this "basic" but "ever-popular" café, near the university. / **Sample dishes:** potato, leek & celeriac soup; parsley-crusted salmon with saffron mayonnaise; banoffi pie. **Details:** near Cardiff University; 10.30 pm; closed Mon; no Amex; no smoking in dining room.

Happy Gathering £ 26

233 Cowbridge Road East CF11 9AL (029) 2039 7531

"Watch what the Chinese families order" – the best advice on this, suitably-named ("large", "loud" and "noisy") oriental. / **Details:** 11 pm, Sun 9; no smoking area.

Divertimenti Retail Ltd

33-34 Marylebone High St
London
W1U 4PT

Tel: 020 7935 0689

Vat   62b 6469 14
Till   7
Sale   7098/103
FEB 20 04 11:42

05186
HARDEN'S BRITISH   12.50
RESTAURANT GUIDE 2004

Total goods   12.50
Total VAT   0.00

Cash   12.50
Change   0.00
Total goods   12.50

Izakaya £26 Ⓐ
Mermaid Quay CF10 5BW   (029) 2049 2939
*This Japanese tavern can seem a bit incongruous in Cardiff Bay
(it always makes one reporter "want to laugh out loud"); it's a
"friendly" outfit, though, with "great views", and serving "cheap"
(especially at lunch) and "interesting" fare.*
/ **Details:** *www.izakaya-japanese-tavern.com; 10.30 pm; no smoking area.*

Le Monde £31 Ⓐ
62 St Mary St CF10 1FE   (029) 2038 7376
*"Simple cooking of excellent ingredients" ("first-class fish"
in particular) and "a great atmosphere" win fans for this elegant but
"busy" first-floor "stalwart" – part of La Brasserie, and offering
similar you-pick-it-they-cook-it formula.* / **Sample dishes:** *marinated
seafood salad; venison with port wine sauce; Welsh cheeses.*
Details: *www.le-monde.co.uk; midnight; closed Sun; no jeans; no booking.*

Noble House £24
9-11 St Davids Hs, Wood St CF10 4ER   (029) 2038 8430
*"Flavoursome" cooking is the theme of all commentary on this city-
centre oriental.* / **Details:** *next to Millennium stadium; 11 pm; no smoking area.*

El Puerto £33
Penarth Marina CF64 1TT   (029) 2070 5551
*"Martinez needs to wave his magic wand" – this expensively
refurbished customs house (from the creator of La Brasserie, etc) –
"overlooking the Bay" in outlying Penarth – "is taking some time
to hit its stride"; its "glorified steak & chips" formula is not much
liked by reporters, and fans the flames of those who say "his empire
of chill-cabinet restaurants has ruined Cardiff's culinary scene –
they really think this is fine dining round here!"*
/ **Sample dishes:** *scallops; Dover sole; sorbet.* **Details:** *opposite Cardiff barrage;
11 pm; closed Sun D.*

Scallops £35
Unit 2 Mermaid Quay CF10 5BZ   (029) 2049 7495
*"Yes, it has an iffy name, awful logo and stark interior, but it's the
only specialist fish restaurant in Cardiff and makes a bold stab
at what it does", and most reporters commend the "reasonable
prices" of this waterfront Cardiff Bay café.* / **Sample dishes:** *king scallops
with roast tomatoes; monkfish wrapped in bacon with curried mussels; Eton Mess.*
Details: *www.scallopsrestaurant.com; 9.30 pm.*

Tides
St David's Hotel & Spa £44 ✕
Havannah St CF10 5SD   (029) 2031 3018
*"Nice location, shame about the food"; it may offer "unbeatable"
(and "constantly-changing") views of Cardiff Bay, but reports on the
restaurant of this swanky modern hotel dining room – "supposedly
in collaboration with Marco Pierre White" – are overwhelmingly dire.*
/ **Sample dishes:** *kipper pâté with whisky; smoked haddock colcannon; sherry trifle.*
Details: *www.thestdavidshotel.com; in Cardiff Bay; 10.30 pm; no smoking.*
Accommodation: *132 rooms, from £165.*

Tomlins £ 28 A★★
46 Plassey St CF64 1EL (029) 2070 6644
"An organic orgasm", "a veggie delight" and "equally enjoyable for
carnivores"! – David and Lorraine Tomlinson's cheerfully-decorated
establishment offers "seriously good" and "imaginative" cooking
to those prepared to travel a few miles from this city-centre; all this,
plus "dedicated" and "friendly" staff. / **Sample dishes:** won-tons with
black bean sauce; black olive polenta with grilled vegetables; steamed syrup pudding.
Details: www.tomlinsvegetarianrestaurant.co.uk; 10 pm; closed Mon, Tue L-Thu L &
Sun D; no smoking.

Woods Brasserie £ 37
Pilotage Building, Stuart St CF10 5BW (029) 2049 2400
This "lively" modern brasserie has a "good location" in an interesting
building on the Bay, and its "great steaks" and other "consistently
good" dishes are praised by most reporters; many reports have
some sense of reservation, though, and the "crowded" and
"corridor-like" setting comes in for particular flak.
/ **Sample dishes:** crispy beef salad with Thai dressing; pan-fried John Dory with
parsnip pureé; Bakewell tart & custard. **Details:** in the Inner Harbour; 10 pm;
closed Sun D.

CARTERWAY HEADS, NORTHUMBERLAND 8–3B

Manor House £ 28
DH8 9LX (01207) 255268
"Imaginative pub grub" helps make this "welcoming" boozer,
near the Derwent Reservoir, consistently popular; by local standards,
it can seem a touch "pricey". / **Sample dishes:** ham & lentil soup; chicken
stuffed with crayfish & chives; plum & almond upside-down cake. **Details:** A68 just
past turn-off for Shotley Bridge; 9.30 pm; no smoking area. **Accommodation:** 4
rooms, from £60.

CARTMEL, CUMBRIA 7–4D

L'Enclume £ 60 A★★
Cavendish St LA11 6PZ
(01539) 536362

Set in a "beautiful" Lakeland location, Simon Rogan's "converted
smithy-with-rooms" is undeniably "expensive", but it is probably the
most ambitious provincial opening of the year; the cuisine is "bold"
(if "occasionally batty"), but is "mostly highly successful", and neither
the "expert" service nor the copious wine list (300 bins) does
anything to let it down. / **Details:** www.lenclume.co.uk; 9.30 pm; closed
Mon & Sun D; children: 12+ at D. **Accommodation:** 7 rooms, from £125.

Uplands £ 42 A★
Haggs Ln LA11 6HD (01539) 536248
"Reliable cooking of a high standard" is the most common
evaluation of the grub at this prettily-located country house hotel,
but fans say its straightforward fare is plain "wonderful".
/ **Sample dishes:** hot salmon soufflé; honey-roast duck; chocolate Grand Marnier
mousse. **Details:** www.uplands.uk.com; 8 pm; closed Mon, Tue-Thu L; no smoking;
no booking, Sat; children: 8+ at D. **Accommodation:** 5 rooms, from £81.

CASTLE DOUGLAS, DUMFRIES & GALLOWAY 7–2B

The Plumed Horse £ 43 ★
Crossmicheal DG7 3AU (01556) 670333
For most reporters, Tony Borthwick is "a chef who really knows and cares about his work", and this village restaurant is a "wonderful find"; doubters, though, complain of a "grim" locality, "naff" décor and iffy service. / **Sample dishes:** *smoked salmon & scallop soup; pork loin & kidneys with candied turnips; chocolate tart with apricot sorbet.* **Details:** *9 pm; closed Mon, Sat L & Sun D; no Amex; no smoking.*

CAUNTON, NOTTINGHAMSHIRE 5–3D

Caunton Beck £ 27
Main St NG23 6AB (01636) 636793
This "younger sibling of Lincoln's Wig and Mitre" – "not far from the A1" – offers a similar all-day-opening formula, that's "ideal for dropping in"; "it's only in a small village, but never far from full". / **Sample dishes:** *chicken laksa with pork wontons; duck with bean & chorizo cassoulet; passion fruit & ginger cheesecake.* **Details:** *6m NW of Newark past British Sugar factory on A616; midnight; no smoking in dining room.*

CHADDESLEY CORBETT, WORCESTERSHIRE 5–4B

Brockencote Hall £ 45 🅐★
DY10 4PY (01562) 777876
"A little bit of France, in the heart of the Midlands"; Monsieur Petitjean's "beautiful" and "luxurious" country house offers a "cocooning" environment – tipped by many for romance – where "attentive" Gallic staff serve cooking of high quality, using "the best local ingredients". / **Sample dishes:** *scallops with juniper berry sauce; rabbit wrapped in Parma ham with marjoram sausages; lemon tart with Earl Grey sorbet.* **Details:** *www.brockencotehall.com; on A448, just outside village; 9.30 pm; closed Sat L; no smoking area.* **Accommodation:** *17 rooms, from £116.*

CHAGFORD, DEVON 1–3D

Gidleigh Park £ 96 🅐★
TQ13 8HH (01647) 432367
Michael Caine's "inspirational" cooking won particularly high praise this year for the dining room of Paul and Kay Henderson's "remote" but renowned '30s country house hotel, which is set in "beautiful" gardens near Dartmoor; an "incredible cellar" is not the least of its attractions. / **Sample dishes:** *langoustines & frogs legs with pasta in truffle cream; roast duckling with honey & spices; hot apple tart.* **Details:** *www.gidleigh.com; from village, right at Lloyds TSB, take right fork to end of lane; 9 pm; no smoking; children: 7+ at D.* **Accommodation:** *14 rooms, from £420.*

22 Mill Street £ 40 🅐★★
22 Mill St TQ13 8AW (01647) 432244
"The chef came from Gidleigh Park, and waits tables too!" – Duncan Walker is completely 'hands-on' at this "tiny" restaurant-with-rooms in the village near his old employers; the style is "very welcoming", and the "outstanding" cooking is "great-value" too. / **Sample dishes:** *saffron lasagne of crab & red pepper; roast pigeon with pea purée; hot raspberry soufflé.* **Details:** *www.22millstreet.co.uk; 9 pm; closed Mon L, Tue L & Sun; no Amex; no smoking area; children: 14+.* **Accommodation:** *2 rooms, from £55.*

CHAPELTOWN, SOUTH YORKSHIRE   5–2C

Greenhead House   £44   A★

84 Burncross Rd S35 1SF   (0114) 246 9004

"Everything is first-class", say supporters of the Allen family's restaurant in a *"beautiful"* and *"intimate"* 17th-century house, set in pleasant gardens. / **Sample dishes:** *rabbit rillettes with honey-pickled grapes; venison with apple & Calvados sauce; raspberry meringues.* **Details:** *1m from M1, J35; 9 pm; closed Mon, Tue, Wed L, Sat L & Sun; no smoking in dining room; children: 5+.*

CHEADLE, STAFFORDSHIRE   5–3B

Thornbury Hall Rasoi   £28   A★

Lockwood Rd ST10 2DH   (01538) 750831

Mr & Mrs Siddique's one-off subcontinental inspired only a small volume of survey feedback, but such as there was affirmed that the Pakistani cooking at this former manor house remains of a high standard. / **Details:** *www.thornburyhall.co.uk; 10 pm; Mon-Thu D only, Fri-Sun open L & D; no Amex; no smoking area.*

CHEESDEN, LANCASHIRE   5–1B

Nutter's   £38   ★★

Edenfield Rd OL12 7TY   (01706) 650167

"How does he do it at the price?"; TV-chef Andrew Nutter's *"brilliant"* cooking – full of *"imagination and flair"* – helps make his family's *"remote"* but *"homely"* venture (*"high on the moors outside Rochdale"*) a *"roaringly popular"* local destination. / **Sample dishes:** *black pudding wontons; pork with bubble 'n' squeak & tomato jus; cappuccino panna cotta.* **Details:** *between Edenfield & Norden on A680; 9.30 pm; closed Tue; closed 2 weeks in Aug; smoking in bar only.*

CHELMSFORD, ESSEX   3–2C

Waterfront Place   £33

Wharf Rd CM2 6LU   (01245) 252000

With over 200 covers, this restaurant (which forms part of a canalside conference centre) is 'a bit different', and provides a "great" (if "noisy") setting; even some fans find it "pricey" for what it is, though. / **Sample dishes:** *goats cheese, prosciutto & fig bruschetta; char-grilled salmon with mango & lime salsa; banoffi brûlée in chocolate.* **Details:** *www.waterfront-place.co.uk; 10 pm; closed Sun D; no smoking area.*

CHELTENHAM, GLOUCESTERSHIRE   2–1C

Champignon Sauvage   £52   ★★

24-26 Suffolk Rd GL50 2AQ   (01242) 573449

"Trailblazing" cooking – with *"unmissable combinations"* – has won a huge foodie reputation for David & Helen Everitt Matthais's humble-looking but *"charming"* fixture, just outside the town centre; veggies must pre-notify. / **Sample dishes:** *eel tortellini with watercress cream; lamb with cauliflower dumplings; lemon mousse with milk sorbet.* **Details:** *www.lechampignonsauvage.com; near Cheltenham Boys College; 9 pm; closed Mon & Sun; no smoking before 10.30 pm.*

Daffodil   £ 39   Ⓐ
18-20 Suffolk Parade GL50 2AE   (01242) 700055
*"You're purely paying for the location", say critics of this venture in a
"stunning" Art Deco former cinema; it's best enjoyed for its "cheap
and interesting" lunches – the food can otherwise
be "disappointing".* / **Sample dishes:** *rabbit confit with leek risotto; swordfish
with Toulouse sausage & tomato cassoulet; lemon crème brûlée with chocolate
shortbread.* **Details:** *www.thedaffodil.co.uk; just off Suffolk Square; 10.30 pm;
closed Sun; no smoking in dining room.*

Lumiere   £ 47   Ⓐ ★
Clarence Pde GL50 3PA   (01242) 222200
*"Go now before the stars arrive, and it gets too full" – reporters are
unanimous that Lin & Geoff Chapman's "small but perfectly
formed" town-centre restaurant should be "in contention for big
awards".* / **Sample dishes:** *lime baked monkfish on wilted spinach with saffron
jus; roast guinea fowl breast with sweet chilli potato puree; Stilton cheesecake with
port syrup & pear.* **Details:** *www.lumiere.co.uk; 8.30 pm; D only, closed Mon &
Sun; no smoking.*

Mayflower   £ 31   ★
32-34 Clarence St GL50 3NX   (01242) 522426
*A slightly "busy" atmosphere aside, reporters can see little to gripe
about at this long-established Chinese, where menu highlights
include "great scallops" and "plenty of choice for veggies"
("including mock-duck pancakes").*
/ **Details:** *www.themayflowerrestaurant.co.uk; 10 pm; appreciated if guests try
to refrain from smoking.*

Le Petit Blanc   £ 31
Promenade GL50 1NN   (01242) 266800
*"With this name and at these prices one expects more than very
average food, served indifferently, sometimes shambolically" –
one reporter says it all about this Raymond Blanc-branded brasserie
in a converted ballroom; let's hope new managers Loch Fyne can get
the grip the place desperately needs.* / **Sample dishes:** *twice-baked
Roquefort soufflé; tuna with pine kernel crust & red pepper relish; chocolate fondant
with pistachio ice cream.* **Details:** *www.lepetitblanc.co.uk; 10.30 pm; no smoking
in dining room.*

Ruby   £ 28
52 Suffolk Rd GL50 2AQ   (01242) 250909
*"Lots of little rooms" add privacy to dining experience at this "nice"
Chinese, which remains some reporters' top tip in town.*
/ **Details:** *near Cheltenham Boys College; 11.30 pm; no smoking area.*

Storyteller   £ 28   Ⓐ ★
11 North Pl GL50 4DW   (01242) 250343
*You browse a "helpfully annotated" wine room – not a list – at this
"unpretentious but effective" outfit, and its moderately exotic menu
often displays "real thought".* / **Sample dishes:** *Mauritian beef skewers;
roast lamb with new potatoes; chocolate mud pie.* **Details:** *www.storyteller.co.uk;
10 pm; no smoking area.*

CHESTER, CHESHIRE 5–2A

Arkle
The Chester Grosvenor £71
Eastgate CH1 1LT (01244) 324024
"A high-class venue that always impresses", say fans of the "old-fashioned" dining room of this (very) grand hotel, picturesquely-located in the city centre; as ever, though, a number of reporters leave disenchanted, largely because it's "so overpriced" – consequently the "bustling brasserie", with access from the street, is tipped by some in preference. / **Sample dishes:** *oxtail ravioli with langoustine tails; duck with black fig sauce; basil blancmange with iced gingerbread.* **Details:** *www.chestergrosvenor.co.uk; 9.30 pm; closed Mon & Sun D; jacket at D; no smoking in dining room.* **Accommodation:** *80 rooms, from £150.*

Blue Bell £34 ★
Northgate St CH1 2HQ (01244) 317758
This "compact bistro" near the cathedral is well worth seeking out, especially for its "great-value" (pre-7pm) menu; it's an "efficient" place at any time, however, offering cooking that makes "good use of local ingredients". / **Sample dishes:** *beignets with tomato fondue & avocado salsa; fillet of beef with blue cheese & tarragon; warm chocolate mousse with praline ice cream.* **Details:** *www.blue-bell-restaurant.co.uk; 9.45 pm; no Amex; no smoking.*

Francs £25
14 Cuppin St CH1 2BN (01244) 317952
"Cheap and cheerful, and with definite French style", the city's long-established bistro remains a "reliable" destination; even those who say it's "lost its edge" under new ownership, say it's "still a good bet". / **Sample dishes:** *smoked salmon, melon & avocado salad; lambs liver & bacon with mash; lemon tart.* **Details:** *www.francs.co.uk; 11 pm; no smoking area.*

CHICHESTER, WEST SUSSEX 3–4A

Comme Ça £38 Ⓐ
67 Broyle Rd PO19 6BD (01243) 788724
"It's difficult to fault the service" at this "very French" establishment, which fans find "ideal for pre-Festival Theatre" (and which "has a leafy garden in summer"); some say the Gallic food is "excellent", but the consensus is that it's "good, but nothing special". / **Sample dishes:** *asparagus hollandaise; cured Scottish salmon; summer pudding.* **Details:** *www.commeca.co.uk; 0.5m N of city centre; 10.30 pm; closed Mon & Sun D; no smoking area.*

CHILGROVE, WEST SUSSEX 3–4A

White Horse £39
High St PO18 9HX (01243) 535219
"The wine list is legendary" – running to hundreds of bins – at this well-known South Downs boozer; fans say the vino is complemented by "solid and quite reliable" food, but critics say it's "wasted" on what's "little more than pub grub". / **Sample dishes:** *chicken liver salad with raspberry dressing; braised oxtail with potato pureé; warm chocolate gâteau.* **Details:** *8m NW of Chichester on B2141; 9.30 pm; closed Mon & Sun D; no smoking.* **Accommodation:** *8 rooms, from £85.*

CHINNOR, OXFORDSHIRE   2–2D

Sir Charles Napier   £41   A★
Spriggs Alley OX9 4BX   (01494) 483011
An "idyllic" Chilterns location and "a pretty drive to get there" have
long made this "comfy" fixture – a smartly converted pub, with an
artified garden – a "nice outing" from the Smoke; the "updated
traditional" cooking seems currently to be on a high, but service can
be "stressed" and "very slow" (especially on Sundays).
/ **Sample dishes:** butternut squash soup; skate wing with capers, saffron
potatoes & spinach; date cake with toffee sauce. **Details:** M40, J6 into Chinnor,
turn right at roundabout; 10 pm; closed Mon & Sun D; no smoking area; children:
6+ at D.

CHIPPENHAM, WILTSHIRE   2–2C

Manor House
Bybrook Restaurant   £55   A★
Castle Combe SN14 7HR   (01249) 782206
"It feels as if you've journeyed back in time" when you visit this
"superb medieval manor house" (now an hotel and golf club), set in
"beautiful" grounds; it offers "sophisticated" cooking, using
"the finest local produce". / **Sample dishes:** chicken, artichoke & wild
mushroom terrine; smoked salmon & crayfish with horseradish potatoes; glazed
lemon tart. **Details:** www.exclusivehotels.co.uk; 9 pm; no Amex; no smoking.
Accommodation: 48 rooms, from £145.

CHIPPING CAMPDEN, GLOUCESTERSHIRE   2–1C

Cotswold House   £42   A★
Chipping Campden GL55 6AN   (01386) 840330
"The brasserie is a lot cheaper than the restaurant, and of excellent
quality", say some supporters of this brace of commendable eateries
– both overseen by the same chef, Simon Hulstone – at this
Georgian townhouse hotel. / **Sample dishes:** roast scallops with cauliflower
purée & smoked bacon; rump of lamb with buttered spinach & tomatoes;
ice strawberry parfait with hot banana spring rolls.
Details: www.cotswoldhouse.com; 9.30 pm; D only, except Sun open L &
D; no smoking. **Accommodation:** 22 rooms, from £175.

Eight Bells   £30
Church St GL55 6JG   (01386) 840371
The oldest surviving pub in this charming Cotswold town offers
"a very pleasant all-round experience", with "better than usual" pub
fare. / **Sample dishes:** twice-baked cheese soufflé; braised lamb with julienne
vegetables; dark chocolate cheesecake. **Details:** www.eightbellsinn.co.uk; 10m S
of Stratford upon Avon; 9.30 pm, Fri & Sat 10 pm; no Amex; no smoking area.
Accommodation: 5 rooms, from £70.

Seymour House   £37   ★
High St GL55 6AH   (01386) 840429
At this "good" town-centre hotel (which is of Georgian origin),
the dining room is lauded for its good – and sometimes "great" –
cooking. / **Sample dishes:** scallops wrapped in bacon; fillet el piato.
Details: www.seymourhousehotel.com; 10 pm; no smoking. **Accommodation:** 16
rooms, from £110-180.

CHOBHAM, SURREY · 3–3A

Quails · £38 · ★

1 Bagshot Rd GU24 8BP   (01276) 858491
"Classic, reliable and improving all the time", Chris Wale's
"pleasant" town-centre fixture – of over a decade's standing –
continues to win very positive reviews from all who comment on it.
/ **Sample dishes:** chilli-glazed salt & pepper squid; BBQ chicken & smoked Gouda
pizza; raisin pancakes with butterscotch bananas. **Details:** 2m SE of M3,
J3; 9.30 pm; D only, closed Mon & Sun.

CHRISTCHURCH, DORSET · 2–4C

FishWorks · £39

10 Church St BH23 1BW   (01202) 487000
"Superb fish, perfectly cooked" wins praise for this branch of the
expanding West Country (and now also London) chain
of café/fishmongers; it's *"Spartan"* and *"pricey"*, though – especially
as *"portions are not over-generous, and sides are extra"* –
and service could be much improved. / **Sample dishes:** spaghetti with
crab & chilli; grilled plaice with black butter; lemon tart.
Details: www.fishworks.co.uk; 9 pm; closed Mon & Sun; no smoking.

Splinters · £46 · 𝔸★

12 Church St BH23 1BW   (01202) 483454
"Romantic booths" and *"excellent service"* are star attractions
at these *"small and intimate"* dining rooms near the Priory; it was
recently sold to the chef, and the high quality of his *"original"*
cooking remains *"the same"*. / **Sample dishes:** Gorgonzola & spinach tart;
sea bream with roast vegetables; cappuccino brûlée. **Details:** www.splinters.uk.com;
10 pm; closed Mon & Sun; no Amex; no smoking in dining room.

CIRENCESTER, GLOUCESTERSHIRE · 2–2C

Tatyan's · £28

27 Castle St GL7 1QD   (01285) 653529
"Good Chinese food" is the theme of all reports on this
"very friendly" family-run, town-centre restaurant; even so, *"it can
be quiet, even at weekends"*. / **Details:** www.tatyans.com; near junction
of A417 & A345; 10.30 pm; closed Sun.

CLACHAN, ARGYLL & BUTE · 9–3B

Loch Fyne Oyster Bar · £29 · ★

PA26 8BL   (01499) 600236
"The management buyout seems to have been a success", says one
reporter satisfied with recent developments at *"the original"* Loch
Fyne (which gave its name to, but is not connected with, the group
which bears its name); most reports do indeed applaud *"the most
wonderful and freshest oysters ever"* (plus other good fishy fare),
but some feel the food's *"not brilliant, not bad"*.
/ **Sample dishes:** smoked haddock chowder; king scallops; ice cream.
Details: www.loch-fyne.com; 10m E of Inveraray on A83; 10 pm; no smoking area.

CLAVERING, ESSEX   3–2B

The Cricketers   **£ 32**

Wicken Rd CB11 4QT   (01799) 550442

*Some feel "Jamie Oliver's folks are trading on their son's fame"
at the "lovely", "traditional" village inn owned and run by his father;
it's hardly their fault if "too many people try to pack in", but the
food, on most accounts, is "not very exciting". / Sample dishes: turmeric
tempura monkfish; veal with Savoy cabbage & blue cheese sauce; chocolate
cheesecake. Details: www.thecricketers.co.uk; on B1038 between Newport &
Buntingford; 10 pm; no smoking in dining room. Accommodation: 14 rooms,
from £100.*

CLAYGATE, SURREY   3–3A

Le Petit Pierrot   **£ 40**   ★

4 The Parade KT10 0NU   (01372) 465105

*"Deservedly popular locally" ("book well in advance"),
this "friendly", small and "discreet" shop-conversion is universally
popular with reporters for its "very Gallic" approach, and its
"unvarying" standards. / Sample dishes: pan-fried foie gras with sweetcorn
galette; guinea fowl with morel risotto; sweet chestnut & prune pudding.
Details: 9.30 pm; closed Sat L & Sun; children: 8+.*

CLENT, WORCESTERSHIRE   5–4B

The Fountain Inn   **£ 31**   ★

Adams HI DY9 9PU   (01562) 883286

*The fare may be "traditional", but it's "cooked to perfection",
say supporters of this "pleasantly located" beamed boozer,
and beers are served "in exceptional condition".
/ Sample dishes: deep-fried goats cheese with raspberry coulis; chicken Wellington;
summer fruit cheesecake. Details: 2m from Hagley by Clent Hills; 9.30 pm;
no Amex; no smoking area.*

CLEOBURY MORTIMER, SHROPSHIRE   5–4B

Spice Empire   **£ 21**   ★

17 High St DY14 8DG   (01299) 270419

*It's no wonder this "fab" Indian in "a small country town"
is "very popular with the locals" – it offers "high-quality food,
well presented, and served by friendly staff". / Details: 11 pm; closed
Mon.*

CLEVEDON, BATH & NE SOMERSET   2–2A

Junior Poon   **£ 29**   ★

16 Hill Rd BS21 7NZ   (01275) 341900

*"The freshness of the food is superb", say fans of this "rather
formal" Chinese, located in a Georgian house; even doubters
concede that it's a "reasonably priced" destination.
/ Details: www.juniorpoon.com; near Clevedon Pier; 10 pm; D only.*

The Olive Garden   **£ 33**   ★

91 Hill Rd BS21 7PN   (01275) 341555

*Doubters find it "rather expensive for what's really an upmarket
pizza 'n' pasta place", but the Murray family's restaurant – adjacent
to their deli – wows most reporters with its "interesting" menu and
its "relaxed" style. / Sample dishes: poached salt cod with butter beans;
braised Orkney beef with bubble 'n' squeak; crème brûlée. Details: 10 pm; closed
Mon & Sun; smoking in bar only; booking: max 8.*

CLIPSHAM, RUTLAND 6–4A

Olive Branch £29 A★
Main St LE15 7SH (01780) 410355
This "friendly and unpretentious" gastropub, with its "wonderful", "unusual" cooking, has become a beacon of "enterprising" standards; it's still "unspoilt", too, despite its Michelin star! / **Sample dishes:** honey-roast parsnip soup; roast sea bream with olive mash & tomato relish; coconut rice pudding. **Details:** 2m E from A1 on B664; 9.30 pm; closed Sun D; no Amex; no smoking area.

CLITHEROE, LANCASHIRE 5–1B

Inn at Whitewell £35 A★
Forest of Bowland BD7 3AT (01200) 448222
"Simple seasonal fare, served amidst crackling fires and superb scenery" – that's the formula which puts this "relaxed" and "very friendly" inn, "beautifully located" by a river in the Trough of Bowland, simply in a class of its own (and booking ahead is an absolute 'must'); service this year, however, has not been quite up to usual standards. / **Sample dishes:** goats cheese cannelloni with sweet pepper sauce; grilled black pudding with lambs kidneys; British & Irish cheeses. **Details:** 9.30 pm; D only (bar meals only at L); no Amex. **Accommodation:** 17 rooms, from £89.

COBHAM, SURREY 3–3A

La Capanna £42
48 High St KT11 3EF (01932) 862121
It's been in business for a quarter of a century, but this popular, barn-like Italian can still be "variable"; fans insist that "the ambience makes up for any other disappointments". / **Sample dishes:** fresh crab salad; veal & scallops with mushroom sauce; profiteroles. **Details:** 10.45 pm; closed Sat L.

Cricketers £29
Downside KT11 3NX (01932) 862105
If you're looking for a "traditional pub, overlooking the village green", they don't come much more picture postcard perfect than this "thriving" establishment, whose conservatory restaurant offers a "good" and (moderately) "interesting" menu. / **Sample dishes:** smoked haddock & salmon with poached egg; roast lamb with garlic & rosemary; cheesecake. **Details:** 2m from Cobham High St; 9.30 pm; closed Mon & Sun D; no booking in bar.

COCKERMOUTH, CUMBRIA 7–3C

Quince & Medlar £31 A★★
13 Castlegate CA13 9EU (01900) 823579
"An intimate, distinctive and utterly relaxing vegetarian restaurant in a beautiful market town" – one reporter speaks for all about Colin & Louisa Le Voi's "highly original" cuisine, served in the dining room of their Georgian home. / **Sample dishes:** French onion tart; lentil & apricot strudel with wilted spinach; spiced quince cheesecake. **Details:** next to Cockermouth Castle; 9.30 pm; D only, closed Mon & Sun; no Amex; no smoking; children: 5+.

COGGESHALL, ESSEX   3–2C
Baumann's Brasserie   £33
4-6 Stoneham St CO6 1TT   (01376) 561453
*Views continue to diverge on this suburban brasserie, once linked
to the late Peter Langan; fans say it serves "consistently good" fare,
but others find it plain "dire". / **Sample dishes:** watercress soup with crispy
spring onions; blackened beef with Worcestershire sauce butter; maple syrup custard
with apple cookies. **Details:** www.baumannsbrasserie.co.uk; 9.30 pm; closed Mon &
Tue; no smoking area.*

COLCHESTER, ESSEX   3–2C
Lemon Tree   £26   𝔸★
48 St Johns St CO2 7AD   (01206) 767337
*"A great location" – set into the town's Roman walls – helps win all-
round praise for Patrick & Joanna Minder's five-year-old modern
bistro; "excellent set meals" offer particular value.
/ **Sample dishes:** pan-fried scallops & spicy chorizo salad; roast lamb with garlic &
rosemary with salsa; baked black cherry cheesecake.
Details: www.the-lemon-tree.com; 9 pm, weekends 10 pm; closed Sun; no smoking.*

COLERNE, WILTSHIRE   2–2B
Lucknam Park   £78   𝔸
SN14 8AZ   (01225) 742777
*"Elegant" surroundings and an "excellent" wine list are among the
chief assets of this attractive Georgian country house; some people
find the cooking "very good", too, but it can also seem "ordinary".
/ **Sample dishes:** spinach cappuccino with truffled quails eggs; roast venison with
game chips & spiced pears; citrus sorbets with citrus jelly.
Details: www.lucknampark.co.uk; 6m NE of Bath; 9.30 pm; D only, except Sun
open L & D; jacket & tie required; no smoking; children: 12+ at D.
Accommodation: 42 rooms, from £215.*

COLN ST ALDWYNS, GLOUCESTERSHIRE   2–2C
New Inn at Coln   £42   𝔸
GL7 5AN   (01285) 750651
*It does strike some as a touch "pricey" for what is, but most
reporters praise this "unspoilt" Cotswold inn for its "superior"
contemporary cooking. / **Sample dishes:** wild mushroom & baby vegetable
consommé; pan-fried cod with tomato fondue; rich chocolate tart.
Details: www.new-inn.co.uk; off B4425, 2m SW of Bibury; 9 pm, Fri & Sat
9.30 pm; no smoking in dining room; children: 10+ at D. **Accommodation:** 14
rooms, from £115.*

COLSTON BASSETT, NOTTINGHAMSHIRE   5–3D
Martins Arms Inn   £51
School Ln NG12 3FD   (01949) 81361
*This "prettily located" pub (and restaurant) is an "above-average"
destination of some repute; it's "on the dear side", though,
and some reporters are beginning to query whether it's worth it.
/ **Details:** 1.5 miles off A46; 9.30 pm; closed Sun D; smoking in bar only.*

COLWYN BAY, CONWY   4–1D
Pen Y Bryn   £26   𝔸
Pen Y Bryn Rd LL29 6DD   (01492) 533360
*"A modern New England-style pub in a new housing estate on hills
above Conwy", boasting "panoramic views" and "above-average"
cooking. / **Sample dishes:** smoked salmon & haddock fish cake; braised half
shoulder of lamb; steamed syrup sponge on custard.
Details: www.brunningandprice.co.uk; 9.30 pm; no Amex; no smoking area.*

COMPTON, SURREY   3–3A

The Withies Inn   £ 40   Ⓐ

Withies Ln GU3 1JA   (01483) 421158

This "genuinely quaint" country pub ("with beams and open fires")
is "set in the incredibly pretty Surrey Hills"; "it can be expensive",
but "very freshly prepared" meals, "friendly service" and "lovely
gardens" make most reporters feel it justifies the premium.
/ **Sample dishes:** pan-fried sardines with lemon; roast lamb with rosemary; treacle
tart & custard. **Details:** off A3 near Guildford, signposted on B3000; 10 pm; closed
Sun D; booking essential.

CONSTANTINE, CORNWALL   1–4B

Trengilly Wartha Inn   £ 37   Ⓐ

Nancenoy TR11 5RP   (01326) 340332

"Tucked away near the Helford estuary", this large rural pub has
a "lovely" garden and "lively" ambience; the top culinary feature
is the "very good wine list" (also sold retail), but there's also
an extensive range of eating options. / **Sample dishes:** scallops with
creamed cabbage; duck with sherry & puy lentils; nougat parfait.
Details: www.trengilly.co.uk; 1m outside village; 9.30 pm; D only; no smoking area.
Accommodation: 8 rooms, from £78.

COOKHAM, BERKSHIRE   3–3A

Bel & The Dragon   £ 38

High St SL6 9SQ   (01628) 521263

This "jumping" gastro-boozer (part of a small chain) is an
"upmarket" venture with an "interesting" menu and "great" outdoor
dining facilities; doubters find it "very noisy", though,
and "expensive, for somewhere that's really just a pub".
/ **Sample dishes:** goats cheese & spinach strudel; roast lamb with herb mash &
raspberry jus; banoffi cheesecake. **Details:** www.belandthedragon.co.uk; opp Stanley
Spencer Gallery; 10 pm.

Inn on the Green   £ 39   Ⓐ

The Old Cricket Common SL6 9NZ   (01628) 482638

Given the fact that "they've spent a lot of money" on this new
boutique-hotel, and the involvement of well-known chef Garry
Hollihead, the place inspired oddly little commentary – such as
there is vaunts "welcoming" service, "amazing" bedrooms and
"good" cooking. / **Details:** www.theinnonthegreen.com; 9.30 pm; closed Mon L;
no smoking area. **Accommodation:** 9 rooms, from £130.

Maliks   £ 34   Ⓐ★

High St SL6 9SF   (01628) 520085

"Set in a Tudor beamed old-pub" (complete with "open fires and
antiques"), this "romantic" joint is hardly your typical cuzza;
it's "certainly not the cheapest", either, but most reporters seem
to think the "well prepared" food is worth it. / **Details:** www.maliks.co.uk;
11 pm.

CORBRIDGE, NORTHUMBERLAND   8–2B

The Angel of Corbridge   £ 32

Main St NE45 5LA   (01434) 632119

Revamped in slightly "clinical" style, this "large" coaching inn has
been "much improved", with most reporters rating its cooking
at least "good". / **Sample dishes:** smoked salmon soufflé; roast guinea fowl;
chocolate tart. **Details:** 9.30 pm; D only, except Sun open L & D; no smoking
in dining room. **Accommodation:** 5 rooms, from £74.

The Valley   **£ 28**
Old Station Hs NE45 5AY   (01434) 633434
*The novel 'Package to India' (you order on the train and dinner
awaits you here on arrival) runs nightly from Newcastle to this well-
known rural cuzza (sibling to the Valley Junction); reports were
scarce but upbeat this year. / **Details:** 11 pm; D only, closed Sun;
no smoking.*

CORSCOMBE, DORSET   2–4B

Fox Inn   **£ 33**   Ⓐ
DT2 0NS   (01935) 891330
*"Worth every mile of the trip", say fans of this "surprise find in a
tiny village" – an "excellent" thatched country inn serving "good if
pricey pub food"; let's hope new owner Clive Webb keeps up the
good work! / **Sample dishes:** roast aubergines with tomato & Mozzarella;
chicken with celery, red pepper & cream sauce; plum crumble.
Details: www.fox-inn.co.uk; 5m off A37; 9 pm, Fri & Sat 9.30 pm; no smoking area.
Accommodation: 4 rooms, from £80.*

CORSE LAWN, GLOUCESTERSHIRE   2–1B

Corse Lawn Hotel   **£ 41**   ★
GL19 4LZ   (01452) 780771
*"Very well run by the Hine family" – this "cosy and immaculate
country hotel" (occupying a Queen Anne building overlooking the
village green) is consistently praised for its "all-round-good" cooking.
/ **Sample dishes:** char-grilled squid with rocket & chilli oil; pigeon with lentils &
black sausage; poached fruits with vanilla cream.
Details: www.corselawnhousehotel.co.uk; 5m SW of Tewkesbury on B4211;
9.30 pm; no jeans or trainers; no smoking; children: 6+ at D. **Accommodation:** 19
rooms, from £105.*

COTEBROOK, CHESHIRE   5–2B

Fox & Barrel   **£ 25**
Forest Rd CW6 9DZ   (01829) 760529
*"An old-fashioned but well-run country restaurant" that forms part
of a pub and is generally lauded for its "interesting menu
at reasonable prices". / **Sample dishes:** warm salad of shredded duck with
bacon & toasted pine kernels; char-grilled pork loin with pan-fried pear &
parmentier potatoes; sticky toffee pudding. **Details:** www.thefoxandbarrel.co.uk;
on A49 NE of Tarporley; 9.30 pm; closed Mon D; no smoking.*

COVENTRY, WEST MIDLANDS   5–4C

Eden   **£ 32**
1-3 Ryley St CV1 4AJ   (024) 7655 1234
*On most accounts, an (ex-Savoy) chef offers "well-prepared" and
"delicious" cooking at this newcomer near the Belgrade Theatre;
there is the odd gripe, but the opening of a place of any ambition
here is definitely a step forward! / **Sample dishes:** fan of melon, cassis
sorbet & Parma ham; smoked salmon with lobster coleslaw, king prawns,
crabmeat & chive oil; lemon tart with fresh cream. **Details:** www.discovereden.com;
behind the Belgrade theatre; 10.30 pm; closed Sun D; no smoking.*

Thai Dusit   **£ 24**
39 London Rd CV1 2JP   (024) 7622 7788
*A rare half-decent Coventry oriental, praised for its "lovely people
and great food". / **Details:** 10.45 pm; no Amex.*

COWBRIDGE, VALE OF GLAMORGAN 2–2A

Farthings £28
54 High St CF71 7AH (01446) 772990
"Great desserts" are something of a refrain in commentary
on Natalie & Nick Dobson's pleasant brasserie.
/ **Sample dishes:** French onion soup; wild boar & pheasant sausages with grain
mustard mash; hazelnut & raspberry meringue. **Details:** 10 pm; closed Mon D &
Sun D; no Amex; no smoking area.

COWLEY, GLOUCESTERSHIRE 2–1C

Cowley Manor £45   𝔸★
GL53 9NL (01242) 870900
*"The only other country house hotel that's nearly as hip
as Babington House"* – this converted 19th-century mansion wins
all-round praise for its *"fantastically positive"* staff,
its *"very comfortable"* décor and its *"competent"* cooking
at *"realistic"* prices. / **Sample dishes:** seared Scotish scallops; fillet of wild
trout; chocolate pudding. **Details:** www.cowleymanor.com; 10 pm; closed Fri D &
Sat D; no smoking in dining room. **Accommodation:** 30 rooms, from £220.

COWLING, WEST YORKSHIRE 5–1B

Harlequin £32
139 Keighley Rd BD22 0AH (01535) 633277
An *"imaginative menu of excellent quality"* is hailed by local fans
of this *"reliable"* wine bar cum restaurant. / **Sample dishes:** calamari &
chorizo salad; roast duckling with rhubarb compote; Yorkshire ginger sponge.
Details: on A6068 towards Colne; 9.30 pm; closed Mon & Tue; no smoking;
children: 7+ at D.

CRASTER, NORTHUMBERLAND 8–1B

Jolly Fisherman £12   ★
NE66 3TR (01665) 576461
"Excellent crab sandwiches" are the star attraction at this *"homely"*
and *"friendly"* boozer, which enjoys quite a following among
reporters, and *"what a sea view!"* / **Sample dishes:** crab soup with whisky;
kipper pâté with melba toast; blackcurrant crumble with custard. **Details:** near
Dunstanburgh Castle; 7.45 pm; L only; no Amex; no booking.

CREIGIAU, CARDIFF 2–2A

Caesars Arms £32   ★
Cardiff Rd CF15 9NN (029) 2089 0486
"Always busy and buzzing"; thanks to its *"consistently good"* cooking
and its *"prompt"* service, this rural *"choose-your-fish"* restaurant
(whose formula is similar to Cardiff's La Brasserie) remains
a *"very popular"* destination. / **Sample dishes:** smoked salmon with eggs &
capers; honey-roast duckling; raspberry pavlova. **Details:** beyond Creigiau, past golf
club; 10.30 pm; closed Sun D.

CRICKHOWELL, POWYS　　　　　　　　　2–1A

The Bear　　　　　　　　　　　　　　£36
High St NP8 1BW　(01873) 810408

This ancient and "atmospheric" coaching inn on the market place has quite a reputation, not least for its "hearty" dishes ("ideal after a long walk in the hills") from "local produce"; the "excellent bar meals" attract reports at least as good as those served in the main restaurant. / Sample dishes: seared king scallops with noodles; swordfish with wild rice; summer fruit pudding. **Details:** 9.30 pm; closed Mon, Tue-Sat D only, closed Sun D; no smoking area; children: 7+. **Accommodation:** 34 rooms, from £72.

Nantyffin Cider Mill　　　　　　　　£32　　　Ⓐ★
Brecon Rd NP8 1SG　(01873) 810775

"Well-cooked, imaginative, no-frills food" still figures in most reports on this "intriguing" building, "in the heart of the countryside"; let's hope that the small minority of reports which hint at "a recent decline in standards" is just a 'blip'. / Sample dishes: chicken liver parfait with red onion confit; red mullet with saffron linguine & crab; Drambuie panna cotta with figs. **Details:** www.cidermill.co.uk; on A40 between Brecon & Crickhowell; 9.30 pm; closed Tue (& Sun D in winter); no smoking.

CROSTHWAITE, CUMBRIA　　　　　　　7–4D

The Punch Bowl　　　　　　　　　　£34　　　★
LA8 8HR　(01539) 568237

"The true meaning of 'gastropub'"; Roux-trained chef Steven Doherty's "fabulous food at sensible prices" wins praise from reporters nationwide for this "out-of-the-way" Lakeland inn. / Sample dishes: beetroot & goats cheese tart; slow-cooked lamb with leek & white bean stew; chocolate & ginger tart with honey ice cream. **Details:** www.punchbowl.fsnet.co.uk; off A5074 towards Bowness, turn right after Lyth Hotel; 9 pm; closed Mon & Sun L; no Amex; no smoking. **Accommodation:** 3 rooms, from £60.

CROYDON, SURREY　　　　　　　　　　3–3B

Banana Leaf　　　　　　　　　　　£19　　　★
7 Lower Addiscombe Rd CR0 6BQ　(020) 8688 0297

"Consistent high quality" earns fans for this popular south Indian canteen – a "good-value" spot (but with "variable" service). / Details: near East Croydon station; 11 pm; no smoking area.

CUCKFIELD, WEST SUSSEX　　　　　　　3–4B

Ockenden Manor　　　　　　　　　£46　　　Ⓐ
Ockenden Ln RH17 5LD　(01444) 416111

All reporters praise the "elegant" and "intimate" atmosphere of the dining room at this Elizabethan country house hotel, where the cooking is generally "good" and "reasonably priced". / Sample dishes: truffle risotto; grilled beef with mustard sauce; warm apple fritters. **Details:** www.hshotels.co.uk; 9.30 pm; no jeans; no smoking. **Accommodation:** 22 rooms, from £155.

CUPAR, FIFE　　　　　　　　　　　　9–3D

Ostlers Close　　　　　　　　　　£43　　　★
25 Bonnygate KY15 4BU　(01334) 655574

Over two decades in business, this family-run outfit, just off the high street, is a local "long-term favourite". / Sample dishes: monkfish with red pepper salsa; oxtail & pigs trotter roly poly with oxtail gravy; pineapple syrup sponge. **Details:** www.ostlersclose.co.uk; 9.30 pm; closed Sun & Mon, D only Tue-Fri, Sat L & D; no smoking; children: 6+ at D.

The Peat Inn £ 42 Ａ★
KY15 5LH (01334) 840206
A "superb wine list" and "perfectly-blended" cooking maintain the
reputation of this former coaching inn as a "refined" but
"expensive" restaurant, which has long been a well-known
"destination". / **Sample dishes:** roast scallops with leeks & smoked bacon;
roe deer fillet with cocoa bean purée; trio of caramel desserts.
Details: www.thepeatinn.co.uk; at junction of B940 & B941, SW of St Andrews;
9.30 pm; closed Mon & Sun; no smoking. **Accommodation:** 8 rooms, from £155.

DALRY, AYRSHIRE 9–4B

Braidwoods £ 38 ★
Drumastle Mill Cottage KA24 4LN (01294) 833544
"Hard to find, but worth the trouble"; Keith & Nicola Braidwood's
small and "friendly" restaurant offers very "assured" modern
cooking and "charming" service, in a converted cottage setting.
/ **Sample dishes:** curried prawn & coriander soup; honey-glazed duck with spiced
beetroot; raspberry crème brûlée. **Details:** www.braidwoods.co.uk; 9 pm; closed
Mon, Tue L & Sun D; closed 2 weeks in Jan & Sep; no smoking; children: 12+.

DARTMOUTH, DEVON 1–4D

Carved Angel £ 55 ✗
2 South Embankment TQ6 9BH (01803) 832465
This famous fish restaurant, by the waterside seems to have badly
lost its way; but while fans say "new owners are getting the cooking
back to its glory days", others think it "dire" nowadays, and damn
service as "crass" or "fumbling". / **Sample dishes:** Dartmouth crab with
smoked pepper relish; lamb with root vegetable strudel & cherry jus; rhubarb soufflé.
Details: www.thecarvedangel.com; opp passenger ferry pontoon; 9.30 pm; closed
Mon L & Sun D; no smoking; children: 10+ at D.

DAVENTRY, NORTHANTS 2–1D

Fawsley Hall £ 52 Ａ
NN11 3BA (01327) 892000
"A glorious Elizabethan house", recently given a modern revamp
and turned into an attractive hotel; the food, though, is "rather
expensive for what it is". / **Sample dishes:** foie gras terrine with pickled
cherries; herbed lamb with creamed shallots; raspberry soufflé with chocolate sorbet.
Details: www.fawsleyhall.com; on A361 between Daventry & Banbury; 9.30 pm;
no smoking in dining room. **Accommodation:** 43 rooms, from £130.

DEAL, KENT 3–3D

Dunkerley's £ 36
19 Beach St CT14 7AH (01304) 375016
"Consistently high standards" and "superb presentation" are themes
of most commentary on this hotel dining room, which is known for
its seafood (but also does good meat dishes); service can be "slow",
though, and the occasional "let-down" is not unknown.
/ **Sample dishes:** caramelized scallops served with smoked bacon & velouté;
barbary duck breast with thyme roast vegetables; dark chocolate tart with lemon
grass ice cream & kumquat syrup. **Details:** www.dunkerleys.co.uk; 9.30 pm; mainly
non-smoking.

DEDHAM, ESSEX   3–2C

Milsoms   £ 32   A★
Stratford Rd CO7 6HW   (01206) 322795
With its "chic, bubbling ambience", this offshoot of the famous
Talbooth strikes some reporters as "like a city-centre bar and bistro
in the middle of the countryside"; thanks to its "simple", "generous"
and "well priced" cooking, it's "always packed", so you'd better get
there early. / *Sample dishes:* glass noodle & tiger prawn salad; braised lamb
with mustard mash & sage fritters; raspberry ripple cheescake.
Details: www.talbooth.com; 9.30 pm; no smoking area; no booking.
Accommodation: 14 rooms, from £90.

Le Talbooth   £ 46   ✗
Gun Hill CO7 6HP   (01206) 323150
The Milsom family's famous "timbered" veteran in Constable
Country seems to trade increasingly shamelessly on its "lovely"
riverside setting – the cooking is "average and overpriced",
and service can be "snooty" and "slow". / *Sample dishes:* foie gras
terrine; seabass with braised fennel & cucumber; hot chocolate & orange fondant.
Details: www.talbooth.com; 5m N of Colchester on A12, take B1029; 9.30 pm;
closed Sun D. *Accommodation:* 10 rooms, from £160.

DERBY, DERBYSHIRE   5–3C

Darleys   £ 45
Darley Abbey Mill DE22 1DZ   (01332) 364987
"The fine river and weir-side setting is as much of an attraction
as the interesting and enjoyable cooking" at this "out-of-the-way"
venture on the Derwent; some feel "it doesn't justify the price tag",
though, and there's a feeling that "the place needs a bit more effort
to make it really good". / *Sample dishes:* scallops with crispy crab risotto
cakes; roast pork belly with black pudding & mustard mash; spiced poached pears
with cinnamon shortbread. *Details:* www.darleys.com; 2m N of city centre by River
Derwent; 10 pm; closed Sun D; no smoking.

DODDISCOMBSLEIGH, DEVON   1–3D

Nobody Inn   £ 28   A
EX6 7PS   (01647) 252394
"The only thing better than the wine list is the cheese list!" –
this "captivating" inn may be lost "in the long, winding Devon
lanes", but it's one of the best-known pubs in the UK due to its
"mammoth" vino selection (500+ bins, plus malts) and its cheeses
(especially local ones). / *Sample dishes:* pork meatballs with sweet & sour
sauce; quail stuffed with rice & apricots; sticky toffee pudding.
Details: www.nobodyinn.co.uk; off A38 at Haldon Hill (signed Dunchidrock); 9 pm;
D only, closed Mon & Sun; no smoking area; max: 8; children: 14+.
Accommodation: 7 rooms, from £70.

DOGMERSFIELD, HAMPSHIRE   3–3A

Queen's Head   £ 28   ★
Pilcot Ln RG27 8SY   (01252) 613531
"Surprisingly good combinations and a well thought-out menu"
make this rural boozer a popular destination, to the extent that
it can get "overcrowded at weekends". / *Sample dishes:* potato skins with
cheese & bacon; steak & ale pie; treacle sponge & custard. *Details:* off A287
between Farnham & Odiham; 9 pm; closed Mon.

DOLGARROG, CONWY   4–1D

Lord Newborough   £ 26   ★
Conway Rd LL32 8JX   (01492) 660549
*"Reasonable" pricing and a "varied" selection of dishes continue the
all-positive report profile of this pleasant rural gastropub.*
/ **Sample dishes:** *bacon & cheese salad; pan-fried chicken with leek & mushroom
sauce; summer pudding.* **Details:** *9.15 pm; closed Mon & Sun D; no smoking area.*

DUBLIN, COUNTY DUBLIN, *ROI*   10–3D

*Though clearly not geographically within the ambit of a
guide called* **UK Restaurants***, we have included a small
range of the best-known names in the Irish capital. These
tend to be 'destination' establishments. Visitors looking for
less expensive dining may like to bear in mind that,
like London's Covent Garden, the popular touristy area
of Temple Bar is best avoided by those in search of good
value.*

Bang Café   € 52   𝔸★
11 Merrion Row D2   (01) 676 0898
*"A great buzz" adds to an "outstanding all-round experience" say
fans of this fashionable, multi-level haunt, near St Stephen's Green
(whose menu puts some emphasis on fish). / **Sample dishes:** pan roast
scallops with muslin potato & grilled pancetta; baked sea bass with fragrant rice &
snake beans; warm chocolate brownie with vanilla ice cream.*
Details: *www.bangrestaurant.com; 10.30 pm, Thu-Sat 11 pm; closed Sun;
no Switch; no smoking area.*

Clarence Hotel (Tea Rooms)   € 82
6-8 Wellington Quay D2   (01) 407 0800
*Ownership by U2 raises the media profile of the dining room of this
boutique hotel, but reports are few (one of which noted that the
place seemed "almost empty"); it remains most tipped as a brunch
spot. / **Sample dishes:** deep-fried potato & bacon cakes; chicken with spinach &
black pudding jus; chocolate clafoutis with tiramisu ice cream.*
Details: *www.theclarence.ie; opp New Millennium Bridge; 10.45 pm; closed Sat L;
no Switch; no smoking area.* **Accommodation:** *50 rooms, from £200.*

L'Ecrivain   € 95   ★
109a, Lower Baggot St D2   (01) 661 1919
*"One of the best venues for lunch, and just as good in the evening";
Derry & Sally Anne Clarke's "friendly" but ambitious Gallic fixture
maintains its reputation for "top-quality produce prepared with
imagination and skill"; it has a "great wine list", too.*
/ **Sample dishes:** *baked rock oysters with cabbage & bacon; seared blue fin tuna;
summer berry truffle cake.* **Details:** *www.lecrivain.com; opp Bank of Ireland;
10.30 pm; closed Sat L & Sun; no Switch; no smoking area; booking essential.*

Eden   € 60
Meeting House Sq D2   (01) 670 5372
*If you're looking for a "fun" place "in the heart of Temple Bar",
this sleek bar/restaurant – with its "very passable" food – remains
a popular, if obvious, choice. / **Sample dishes:** smoked eel salad; organic
pork & apricot stew; crème brûlée.* **Details:** *www.edenrestaurant.ie; near Olympia
Theatre; 10.30 pm; no Switch; no smoking area.*

Jacob's Ladder   € 60   ★
4-5 Nassau St D2   (01) 670 3865
*Some discern a tendency to "over-complication" in some dishes,
but Adrian Roche's "bright" first-floor establishment is an "efficient"
place, and the set menus offer "excellent value"; "ask for a window
seat", to ensure a view over Trinity College. / Sample dishes: roast quail
with quails eggs & celeriac cream; roast pigeon with lentils; rum & raisin brûlée.
Details: www.jacobsladder.ie; beside Trinity College; 10 pm; closed Mon & Sun;
no Switch; no smoking area.*

King Sitric   € 76
East Pier, Howth   (01) 832 5235
*Most reporters find the MacManuses' long-established seafood
restaurant-with-rooms (in a pretty harbour suburb at the end of the
DART) a "solid and reliable" venue, where "top-quality" fish
is prepared "in fairly traditional style"; others, though, arrived with
high expectations… and left disappointed. / Sample dishes: grilled
scallops with black & white pudding; poached fillet of turbot, gigas oysters & caviar
cream sauce; iced hazelnut parfait with passion fruit coulis.
Details: www.kingsitric.ie; 10.30 pm; closed Sat L & Sun; no Switch; no smoking
area. Accommodation: 8 rooms, from £126.*

Mermaid Café   € 63   ★
69-70 Dame Street D2   (01) 670 8236
*"Imaginative", 'mid-Atlantic' cooking "at moderate prices", a "buzzy
atmosphere" and good wine underpin the appeal of this "unfussy
and unpretentious" haunt, on the fringe of Temple Bar.
/ Sample dishes: smoked fish chowder with celery biscuits; rabbit fricassée with
oyster mushrooms & pancetta; pecan pie with maple ice cream.
Details: www.mermaid.ie; near Olympia Theatre; 11 pm, Sun 9 pm; no Amex
or Switch; no smoking area.*

Restaurant Patrick Guilbaud   €128   ★
21 Upper Merrion St D2   (01) 676 4192
*"This has been the best restaurant in Dublin for many years, and it
just keeps getting better and better"; all reports confirm this very
grand French veteran continues to offer "a superb dining
experience… at a price"; a biblical wine list and "fantastic terrace"
are further draws. / Sample dishes: lobster ravioli in coconut cream; venison
with pumpkin cream & black radishes; black fig confit with fennel.
Details: www.merrionhotel.com; 10.15 pm; closed Mon & Sun; no Switch;
no smoking.*

Roly's Bistro   € 56   𝔸★
7 Ballsbridge Ter D4   (01) 668 2611
*A legendarily "buzzy" Ballsbridge brasserie, which attracts "a good
mix of customers", and which – for a perennially fashionable
experience – offers "good value". / Sample dishes: spiced crab with angel
hair pasta; Dublin Bay prawns with tarragon rice; Jaffa Cake torte.
Details: www.rolysbistro.ie; near American Embassy; 9.45 pm; no Switch;
no smoking area.*

La Stampa   € 60   𝔸
35 Dawson St D2   (01) 677 8611
*"You're just blown away" by this large and "sumptuous" dining room
(which was originally built as a ballroom); "menu/food/wine etc are
all good", but "prices are high" and "it's the atmosphere that makes
it so special". / Sample dishes: pan-fried foie gras brioche; roast fillet of beef;
chocolate fondant. Details: www.lastampa.ie; off St Stephen's Green; midnight,
Sat 12.30 am; D only; no Switch; no smoking area. Accommodation: 24 rooms,
from £165.*

Thorntons
Fitzwilliam Hotel €140
119 St Stephen's Grn D2 (003531) 478 7008

These days, Kevin Thornton has an HQ much more in keeping with his Michelin hungry aspirations – the very central, modern hotel dining room that once housed Peacock Alley – than his old, hard-to-find location; it provoked suprisingly little feedback this year, though (hence we've left it unrated). / **Sample dishes:** *sautéed foie gras & scallops; roast suckling pig; apple tarte Tatin with butterscotch ice cream.* **Details:** *www.fitzwilliam-hotel.com; 10 pm; D only, except Fri when L & D; closed Mon & Sun; no Switch; no shorts; no smoking area.* **Accommodation:** *130 rooms, from £225.*

DUNDRUM, COUNTY DOWN   10–2D

Bucks Head £35   Ⓐ
77-79 Main St BT33 0LU (028) 4375 1868

It has recently been revamped, but Alison Crothers's charming country inn "maintains its usual high standards". / **Sample dishes:** *garlic soda bread with Parmesan; rib-eye beef with burnt onion mash; marshmallow meringue with pistachio ice cream.* **Details:** *www.thebucksheadinn.co.uk; 3m N of Newcastle; 9.30 pm; closed Mon (in winter only); no smoking area.*

DUNKELD, PERTH & KINROSS   9–3C

Kinnaird House £59   Ⓐ★
Kinnaird Estate PH8 0LB (01796) 482440

This "fabulous" Edwardian country house hotel is not just of note for its "luxurious" furnishings and its beautiful location on the River Tay – Trevor Brooks's "inventive" but "precise" cooking is "really good", too, and there's a "superb" wine list. / **Sample dishes:** *squab pigeon salad; pan-fried John Dory with peas; hot pear soufflé.* **Details:** *www.kinnairdestate.com; 8m NW of Dunkeld, off A9 onto B898; 9.30 pm; closed Mon-Wed in Jan & Feb; jacket & tie at D; no smoking; booking essential; children: 12+.* **Accommodation:** *9 rooms, from £275.*

DUNVEGAN, ISLE OF SKYE   9–2A

Three Chimneys £57   Ⓐ★★
Colbost IV55 8ZT (01470) 511258

"A candlelit old stone croft house in the middle of a very beautiful nowhere" provides the setting for this famed foodie destination, where the cooking of "locally-sourced" ingredients (fish in particular) is "sublime"; "deplorable" service, though, caused a few "let-downs" this year. / **Sample dishes:** *carrot, orange & ginger soup; black pudding with leek & potato mash; warm apple & almond tart.* **Details:** *www.threechimneys.co.uk; 5m from Dunvegan Castle on B884 to Glendale; 9.30 pm; closed Sun L; closed part of Jan & Feb; no smoking; children: 6+ at D.* **Accommodation:** *6 rooms, from £190.*

DURHAM, COUNTY DURHAM   8–3B

Almshouses £19
Palace Grn DH1 3RL (0191) 386 1054

"One of the best places for tea or light meals in town" – this veggie establishment near the Cathedral offers a "good variety" of simple dishes. / **Sample dishes:** *tomato, olive & peanut butter soup; fishcakes with lemon & chive mayonnaise; orange & lemon treacle tart.* **Details:** *5 pm, 8pm in summer; L only; no Amex; no smoking; no booking.*

sign up for the survey at www.hardens.com   -

Bistro 21 £35

Aykley Heads Hs DH1 5TS (0191) 384 4354

*In a converted riverside warehouse, this spin-off from Newcastle's Café 21 has long had a name as "the only decent place in town"; its ratings drifted a bit this year, though – "Terry Laybourne should check up on this one". / **Sample dishes:** Cheddar & spinach soufflé; slow-cooked beef with polenta & Parmesan crisps; profiteroles with pistachio ice cream. **Details:** near Durham Trinity School; 10.30 pm; closed Sun; no smoking; booking: max 10.*

Hide Café Bar & Grill £31

39 Saddler St DH1 3NU (0191) 384 1999

*"Delicious, fresh and authentic" pizza is the culinary highlight at this "pleasant" – and, by local standards, quite "exciting" – modern spot, near the Cathedral; it's "THE place for morning coffee or lunch". / **Sample dishes:** duck spring rolls with wasabi mayo; pizza with anchovies & roast peppers; sticky toffee pudding. **Details:** www.hidebar.com; 10 pm; closed Sun D; no Amex; no smoking area.*

Shaheens Indian Bistro £22 ★

Old Post Office, 48 North Bailey DH1 3ET
(0191) 386 0960

*"A good Indian", especially worth knowing about in a city with so few competing attractions. / **Details:** 11 pm; D only, closed Mon; no Amex or Switch; no smoking area.*

EAST CHILTINGTON, EAST SUSSEX 3–4B

Jolly Sportsman £35

BN7 3BA (01273) 890400

*"Metropolitan smartness" comes as a bit of a surprise at this "cosy" and "relaxed" boozer, "lost in a maze of country lanes"; its "good and interesting" fare has won it quite a large fanclub, but there have been some reports of "chaotic" meals of late. / **Sample dishes:** ham, asparagus & Manchego salad; grilled halibut with crab mash & capers; apricot, walnut & ginger toffee pudding. **Details:** NW of Lewes; 9 pm, Fri & Sat 10 pm; closed Mon & Sun D; no Amex; no smoking.*

EAST GRINSTEAD, WEST SUSSEX 3–4B

Gravetye Manor £72 Ⓐ

Vowels Ln RH19 4LJ (01342) 810567

*"A perfect country setting" in "beautiful gardens" amid "idyllic" countryside helps create a memorable experience at this renowned, family-run Elizabethan manor house hotel; the "modernish European food" is of a "high standard", but then "so it should be at these prices". / **Sample dishes:** quail, black pudding & lardon salad; roast John Dory; panna cotta with rhubarb. **Details:** www.gravetyemanor.co.uk; 2m outside Turner's Hill; 9.30 pm; no Amex; jacket & tie required; no smoking; children: 7+. **Accommodation:** 18 rooms, from £190.*

EAST LINTON, EAST LOTHIAN 9–4D

Drovers Inn £30 ★

5 Bridge St EH40 3AG (01620) 860298

*New ownership seems to have reinvigorated this "busy" coaching inn, just off the A1 – its "well-balanced menu", "real ales" and "roaring fires" all get the thumbs-up. / **Sample dishes:** chicken liver pâté with oatcakes; beef stew with herb dumplings; raspberry trifle. **Details:** 9.30 pm; no smoking area.*

---

sign up for the survey at www.hardens.com

EAST LOOE, CORNWALL   1–4C

Trawlers   £38   A★

On The Quay   PL13 1AH   (01503) 263593

"The chef is from Louisiana and cooks the freshest of fish dishes with a Creole slant", at this *"well-kept secret"* on the quayside; it's not hugely commented on, but those who do so say it offers a *"wow"* experience. / **Sample dishes:** steamed mussels; fillet of John Dory with rocket, capers & olives; fresh raspberry shortbread with cream & ice cream. **Details:** www.trawlersrestaurant.co.uk; 9.30 pm; D only, closed Mon & Sun; no Amex; no smoking; booking: max 6; children: 7+.

EAST WITTON, NORTH YORKSHIRE   8–4B

Blue Lion   £33   A★

DL8 4SN   (01969) 624273

"Excellent food in a lovely country setting" remains the strong majority view on this *"cosy"* and renowned village inn; there were a few *"disasters"* also reported this year, though. / **Sample dishes:** onion & blue Wensleydale tart; chicken with smoked foie gras sauce; lemon mousse with lemon shortbread. **Details:** www.thebluelion.co.uk; between Masham & Leyburn on A6108; 9.30 pm; D only, except Sun open L & D; no Amex. **Accommodation:** 12 rooms, from £69.

EASTBOURNE, EAST SUSSEX   3–4B

The Mirabelle
The Grand Hotel   £55   A★

King Edwards Parade   BN21 4EQ   (01323) 412345

Gerald Roser – who closed his eponymous Hastings restaurant in mid-2002 – is *"as brilliant as ever"* in the *"smart"*, if *"conventional"*, dining room of Eastbourne's large luxury hotel; this has always been a commendable venue, but his *"memorable"* cuisine now helps make it *"outstanding in every respect"*. / **Sample dishes:** salmon terrine with sweet pepper coulis; pork with Cumberland stuffing & Bramley apple sauce; warm toffee & date pudding. **Details:** www.grandeastbourne.com; 10 pm; closed Mon & Sun; jacket & tie required at D; no smoking; children: 14+ at D. **Accommodation:** 152 rooms, from £165.

EDENBRIDGE, KENT   3–3B

Haxted Mill   £45

Haxted Rd   TN8 6PU   (01732) 862914

"Beautiful views" – and, for the winter, a cosy interior – add charm to a visit to this *"fully restored mill"*, in the leafy Edenbridge valley; the food is often *"beautifully cooked"*, too, but – given the not inconsiderable prices – is arguably on the *"simple"* side. / **Sample dishes:** grilled oysters with spinach; roast rack of lamb with rosemary jus; fig tarte Tatin. **Details:** www.haxtedmill.co.uk; between Edenbridge & Lingfield; 9 pm; closed Mon & Sun D; no Amex; no smoking.

EDINBURGH, CITY OF EDINBURGH   9–4C

The options for eating out in Auld Reekie have improved considerably in recent times.

Gastronomically speaking, *Restaurant Martin Wishart* – the modern destination restaurant of a type the city so obviously lacked until a few years ago – goes from strength to strength.

This is a city in which fish-lovers do particularly well – and, in the land of the Aberdeen Angus, arguably better than carnivores! The two *Fishers* bistros, *Mussel Inn* and, in particular, *The Shore* are cases in point. More general establishments of note include *Martins*, *Off the Wall*, *Vermillion* and the funkier *Outsider*.

For sheer charm of location, the city has two remarkable venues – the *Vintners' Rooms* and the *Witchery by the Castle* (the best-known place in town). As a room with a view, *The Tower* (under the same ownership as The Witchery) is a relative newcomer that has become one of the most commented-upon places in town (and which seems to be overcoming its more serious initial teething troubles).

Edinburgh is not especially strong in ethnic restaurants, though those in search of a budget curry are quite well catered-for (*Kalpna*, *Khushi's*, *Suruchi*). The long-established Italian deli and wine merchant *Valvona & Crolla* retains a cult following.

Ann Purna £19
44-45 St Patrick's Sq EH8 9ET (0131) 662 1807
"Solid" Gujerati fare (with plenty for vegetarians) and "very friendly" service win continuing plaudits for this family-run institution.
/ **Details:** 10.30 pm; closed Sat L & Sun L; no Amex or Switch; no smoking.

Apartment £24
7-13 Barclay Pl EH10 4HW (0131) 228 6456
"Everyone in Edinburgh eats here!" – this "lively" and "intriguing" venture (on the fringe of the Old Town) continues to make quite a splash locally with its "casual", "modern" and "imaginative" approach; (it's arguably being upstaged somewhat by its trendy younger sibling The Outsider, though). / **Sample dishes:** wild mushrooms with aubergine & sweet potato; peppered rib-eye steak & fries; profiteroles with Cointreau sauce. **Details:** between Tollcross & Bruntsfield; 11 pm; D only Mon-Fri; no Amex; no smoking area.

The Atrium £42
10 Cambridge St EH1 2ED (0131) 228 8882
Year in year out, reports on this (seminal, for Auld Reekie) modern restaurant are irreconcilably mixed – for fans, it's "excellent" and "engaging", but for doubters just "bleak" and "pretentious".
/ **Sample dishes:** courgette & Parmesan soup; roast duck with cabbage & bacon; marjoram crème brûlée. **Details:** www.atriumrestaurant.co.uk; by the Usher Hall; 10 pm; closed Sat L & Sun (except during Festival); no smoking in dining room.

Bann UK £30
5 Hunter Sq EH1 1QW (0131) 226 1112
New owners have if anything boosted the appeal of this "stylish" and "innovative" vegetarian, just off the Royal Mile, which is hailed by most reporters for its "fine food at reasonable prices".
/ **Sample dishes:** aubergine cannelloni; veggie bangers & mash; coconut & lime brûlée. **Details:** www.urbann.co.uk; 11 pm; no smoking area.

blue bar café £33
10 Cambridge St EH1 2ED (0131) 221 1222
The Atrium's "bright" and "cheerful" sibling (in the same building) makes a useful stand-by which suits most informal occasions; the staff are "surprisingly good with young children".
/ **Sample dishes:** char-grilled tuna niçoise; sea bream with tomato & courgette galette; apple tart with Calvados parfait. **Details:** www.bluebarcafe.com; by the Usher Hall; 11 pm; closed Sun (except during Festival); no smoking area.

Le Café St-Honoré   £37   A

34 NW Thistle Street Ln EH2 IEA   (0131) 226 2211
"Business meals can be relaxed and productive" – while the
"fantastic atmosphere" is also "perfect for romance" – at this
"real French" brasserie in the Old Town; it's not cheap, but its style
is "simple and professional". / **Sample dishes:** carrot & ginger soup; sirloin
steak with caramelised shallots; chocolate & fig steamed pudding.
Details: www.cafesthonore.com; between George St and Queen St; 10 pm;
no smoking area.

Daniel's   £28

88 Commercial St EH6 6LX   (0131) 553 5933
This "welcoming" modern bistro offers "the cooking of Alsace,
by the North Sea"; for its fans, it's "one of Leith's best", but not all
reporters are convinced. / **Sample dishes:** tarte flambé; duck confit with
spring greens; spicy ice cream terrine.
Details: www.edinburghrestaurants.co.uk/daniels.html; 10 pm; no smoking area.

Duck's at Le Marché Noir   £39

2-4 Eyre Pl EH3 5EP   (0131) 558 1608
Most (if not quite all) reporters find Malcolm Duck's New Town
restaurant a "romantic" place, and praise its "good" food.
/ **Sample dishes:** seared wasabi tuna with pickled cucumber; monkfish wrapped
in prosciutto with chilli sauce; flourless chocolate cake with white chocolate ice cream.
Details: www.ducks.co.uk; 10 pm, Fri & Sat 10.30 pm; closed Mon L, Sat L &
Sun L; no smoking area.

Fisher's Bistro   £35   A ★

I The Shore EH6 6QW   (0131) 554 5666
There are "always the same high standards" at this seafood bistro
near the Leith waterfront, where "excellent" fish is served in a "fun"
setting. / **Sample dishes:** red snapper with sweet potato & Parmesan rosti;
monkfish & swordfish brochette with spinach tagliatelle; Turkish delight in brandy
snaps. **Details:** www.fishersbistros.co.uk; 10.30 pm.

Fishers in the City   £33   A ★

58 Thistle St EH2 IEN   (0131) 225 5109
An "amazing range of fish and seafood" and "fantastic friendly
staff" are among the features which make it "always a pleasure"
to visit this New Town warehouse-conversion; its ratings are even
higher than that of its elder sibling in Leith. / **Sample dishes:** squid &
octopus salad; whole Dover sole topped with roast hazelnut; orange sorbet.
Details: www.fishersbistros.co.uk; 10.30 pm; no smoking area.

Forth Floor
Harvey Nichols   £38

30-34 St Andrew Sq EH2 3AD   (0131) 524 8388
Harvey Nichols has never really lived up to its initial promise as a
restaurant operator, but, even so, there's a surprising dearth
of commentary on this smart new restaurant and brasserie –
the group's first operation north of the border; the place is "busy",
apparently, but – apart from an impressive view – doesn't seem
in any way remarkable. / **Sample dishes:** cured salmon with buckwheat blinis;
grilled sea bass; strawberry & Mascarpone tart. **Details:** www.harveynichols.com;
10.30 pm; closed Mon D & Sun D; no smoking area; booking: max 8.

Glass & Thompson   £21   ★

2 Dundas St EH3 6SU   (0131) 557 0909
"A very good café", this "elegant" New Town establishment (which
also houses a deli) is praised for its "beautiful ingredients" and
makes "a perfect lunch rendezvous". / **Sample dishes:** spinach & walnut
pâté with rye bread; passion cake. **Details:** L & afternoon tea only; no Amex;
no smoking.

Hadrian's
Balmoral Hotel   £28
1 Princes St EH2 2EQ   (0131) 557 5000
*The Balmoral's number two restaurant is light and bright
(and perhaps a touch lacking in character), but reporters find it a
refreshingly "unpretentious" venue, and its "bistro-style" cooking
is consistently approved. / **Sample dishes:** saffron risotto Milanese; sirloin
steak with fries & green beans; orange & grapefruit in Sauternes jelly.
Details: www.thebalmoralhotel.com; 10.30 pm; no smoking area.
Accommodation: 185 rooms, from £210.*

Henderson's   £19
94 Hanover St EH2 1DR   (0131) 225 2131
*"Good veggie fare" is the theme of all commentary on this self-
service buffet, which has inhabited a grungy but characterful
basement, just off Princes Street, for nearly four decades.
/ **Sample dishes:** vegetable soup; baked aubergine & tomato with Mozzarella;
banoffi pie. **Details:** www.hendersonsofedinburgh.co.uk; 10 pm; closed Sun; mainly
non-smoking.*

Indian Cavalry Club   £26
3 Atholl Pl EH3 8HP   (0131) 228 3282
*There is the odd gripe of "bland" cooking at this smartish, slightly
'80s, colonial-style subcontinental but it can still be a "good all
round" option. / **Details:** between Caledonian Hotel & Haymarket Station;
11.30 pm; no smoking area.*

Jacksons   £37
209 High St EH1 1PZ   (0131) 225 1793
*"Gloomy" or "perfect", to taste – this basement just off the Royal
Mile, offers the full Olde Edinburgh experience; it's particularly good
"for an inexpensive lunch". / **Sample dishes:** potato soup with pea ravioli;
lamb with spring greens & pearl barley; pear & almond tart.
Details: www.jacksons-restaurant.com; 10.30 pm, Fri & Sat 11 pm.*

Kalpna   £20   ★
2-3 St Patrick Sq EH8 9EZ   (0131) 667 9890
*"Subtle and brilliantly put-together veggie curries" – "wonderful",
"fragrant" and "delicate" – ensure continuing popularity for this
legendary Gujerati of long standing, near the University.
/ **Details:** 10.30 pm; closed Sun L; no Amex or Switch; no smoking.*

Khushi's   £18   ★
16 Drummond St EH8 9TX   (0131) 556 8996
*"Perfect" Indian "home-cooking" that's "cheap" and great "value-
for-money" is the invariable theme of commentary on this studenty
"Edinburgh institution" of over 50 years standing. / **Details:** next
to New Festival Theatre; 9 pm; closed Sun; no credit cards.*

Malmaison   £33   Ⓐ
1 Tower Pl EH6 7DB   (0131) 468 5000
*Even those who find its "discreet" design a mite "gloomy" say this
"classy" waterfront design-hotel eatery offers "good bistro food".
/ **Sample dishes:** black pudding & potato pancake with apple; roast lamb with
minted peas & beans; crème brûlée. **Details:** www.malmaison.com; 11 pm.
Accommodation: 100 rooms, from £125.*

sign up for the survey at www.hardens.com   197

Marque Central £ 32

Grindlay St EH3 9AX (0131) 229 9859

"In the centre of the theatre district", this two-level modern establishment has quite an *"imaginative"* approach (and, as you'd hope it offers an *"excellent pre-show menu"*); doubters, though, can find it *"pretentious"*; (there's also the original branch, Marque, at 19-21 Causewayside, tel 466 6660). / **Sample dishes:** smoked haddock fish cake with bacon & egg salad; corn-fed chicken with Parma ham & roast potatoes; warm chocolate pudding. **Details:** 10 pm, 11 pm weekends; closed Mon & Sun; no smoking.

Martins £ 41 ★

70 Rose St, North Ln EH2 3DX (0131) 225 3106

"The charm of finding the place" plus notably personal service makes up for the bland décor at this long-established New Town fixture, *"tucked away in a back alley"*; it serves an *"interesting short menu"*, which fans say is *"exceptional"*, plus an *"outstanding cheese board"*. / **Sample dishes:** sea trout cannelloni with artichoke confit; guinea fowl with morel mousse; basil-marinated strawberries. **Details:** between Frederick & Castle St; 10 pm; closed Mon, Sat L & Sun; no smoking; children: 7+.

Mussel Inn £ 29 ★

61-65 Rose St EH2 2HN (0131) 225 5979

"The quality of the fish makes up for the 'school dining room' atmosphere" – at this *"lively"*, inexpensive and hugely popular seafood bistro, handily located not far from Princes Street. / **Sample dishes:** hot-smoked salmon Caesar salad; mussels with leeks & horseradish; sticky date pudding. **Details:** www.mussel-inn.com; 10 pm; booking: max 12.

North Bridge Brasserie
The Scotsman £ 35

20 North Bridge EH1 1YT (0131) 556 5565

This *"smart"* new brasserie, (housed in the impressive foyer of the *"central"* landmark that was the former offices of the eponymous newspaper), has got off to a reasonable start; menu choice is *"limited"*, though, and *"sloppy"* service can let the place down. / **Sample dishes:** crabcakes with sweet chilli salsa; beef fillet with pepper sauce; mango delice & melon sorbet. **Details:** www.thescotsmanhotel.co.uk; 10 pm. **Accommodation:** 68 rooms, from £180.

Number One
Balmoral Hotel £ 61

1 Princes St EH2 2EQ (0131) 557 6727

One of the grandest spots in town, this *"spacious"* basement is praised by fans as an *"elegant"* venue (where discussions have *"no chance of being overheard"*); critics, though, say it suffers from zero ambience, and for such a 'key' venue the cooking inspires surprisingly little commentary (such as there is being rather mixed). / **Sample dishes:** crab & avocado salad with caviar; Dover sole roulade with langoustines; rice pudding with basil sorbet. **Details:** www.thebalmoralhotel.com; 10 pm, Fri & Sat 10.30 pm; closed Sat L & Sun L; no smoking area. **Accommodation:** 188 rooms, from £215.

Off The Wall £ 46 ★

105 High St EH1 1SG (0131) 558 1497

"Not what you'd expect from its entrance on the Royal Mile" – this is a *"lovely"*, if low-key, venture where David Anderson's modern Scottish cooking can be *"top-class"*. / **Sample dishes:** slow roast belly of pork with caramelised turnip; saddle of venison & chicory with date sauce; coconut parfait with Scottish strawberries. **Details:** www.off-the-wall.co.uk; 10 pm; closed Sun.

Oloroso £ 43 ✗
33 Castle St EH2 3DN   (0131) 226 7614
*"Great views over Edinburgh add a touch of class to this swish,
if rather pricey, eatery", says one fan of this grand, year-old venture;
doubters, however — who are many — just find it "decidedly
mediocre" and "way overpriced". / **Sample dishes:** tandoori quail with
pickled cucumber salad; halibut with linguine & champagne sauce; deep-fried jam
sandwich with custard. **Details:** www.oloroso.co.uk; 10.30 pm; closed Sun (in winter
only); no smoking in dining room.*

Outsider £ 23 A ★
15-16 George 4th Bridge
EH1 1EE (0131) 226 3131
*"Interesting menus" — with dishes designed for sharing —
have helped make an immediate trendy hit of Malcolm Innes's
"beautiful" and "sumptuous" Old Town spot (he also owns The
Apartment); the prices are notably "reasonable", too.
/ **Sample dishes:** steamed mussels; king prawns with pinapple & coriander
dressing; warm apple tarte Tatin with cinnamon & vanilla pod ice cream.
Details: 11 pm; no Amex; no smoking area; booking: max 10.*

Le Petit Paris £ 28 A
38-40 Grassmarket EH1 2JU   (0131) 226 2442
*It may be "cramped", but there's a "super atmosphere" at this
"tiny French place", near the Castle, which is praised for its
"friendly" staff and its "classic" cooking. **Sample dishes:** smoked
chicken & wild mushroom pancake; broccoli-crusted salmon with lemon butter;
chocolate truffle with cherries. **Details:** www.petitparis-restaurant.co.uk; near the
Castle; 11 pm; no Amex.*

Point Hotel £ 24
34 Bread St EH3 9AF   (0131) 221 5555
*With its "interesting" fixed-price menus, the minimalist (noisy) dining
room of this trying-hard-to-be-stylish budget hotel (formerly an office-
block) is praised by some as an "exceptional-value" location.
/ **Sample dishes:** smoked chicken salad with pineapple salsa; courgette & broccoli
frittata; champagne sorbet with raspberries. **Details:** www.point-hotel.co.uk;
10.30 pm; closed Sat L & Sun. **Accommodation:** 140 rooms, from £95.*

The Restaurant at the Bonham £ 39
35 Drumsheugh Gdns EH3 7RN   (0131) 623 9319
*"Enough space for business discussions" would, perhaps, be the
main reason to seek out the "impressive" dining room of this trendy
townhouse hotel (which does "a very reasonable set-price lunch");
considering bills in the evening, though, both food and service can
fall "below expectations". / **Sample dishes:** timbale of crab & avocado with
mango salsa; pan fried fillet of beef, spinach & roast potato. **Details:** off west end
of Princes St; 9.30 pm; no smoking area. **Accommodation:** 48 rooms, from £165.*

Restaurant Martin Wishart £ 50 ★ ★
54 The Shore EH6 6RA   (0131) 553 3557
*"Excellence throughout" is the theme of almost all commentary
on this Leith water-sider, which has improved on all fronts since its
recent expansion; M Wishart's "divinely imaginative" Gallic cooking
is undoubtedly the "best in Scotland" — at this rate, it will soon
be challenging for the best in Britain! / **Sample dishes:** tortellini
of asparagus, leek cream & white wine velouté; roast saddle of lamb, ratatouille,
sage beignet, pomme croustillante & tapenade; Armagnac parfait, poached pear,
praline biscuit. **Details:** www.martin-wishart.co.uk; near Royal Yacht Britannia;
9.30 pm; closed Mon, Sat L & Sun; no smoking before 10 pm; booking: max 10.*

sign up for the survey at www.hardens.com

Rogue £35
67 Morrison St EH3 8BU (0131) 228 2700
This (impressive) "style-led bar/restaurant" has suffered "too few customers" in recent times (though a well-publicised threat to close earlier in the year led to a surge of renewed interest); fans hail an "outstanding kitchen" and "interesting" decor – critics find the culinary style "confused". / Sample dishes: potato, rocket & goats cheese soup; roast monkfish with black pudding & mushy peas; pineapple soup with citrus sorbet. Details: www.rogues-uk.com; 11 pm; closed Sun.

The Shore £33 A★
3-4 The Shore EH6 6QW (0131) 553 5080
*"Candles and picture windows" help create a "good atmosphere" at this bar/restaurant, near the Leith waterfront, where "a simple and reliable fish-based menu" is agreeably served.
/ Sample dishes: grilled sardines with smoked paprika sauce; grilled fish with couscous; plum & orange crumble.
Details: www.edinburghrestaurants.co.uk/shore.html; 10 pm; no smoking in dining room.*

Skippers £33 A
1a Dock Pl EH6 6LU (0131) 554 1018
*"A happy place to linger over lunch" – this cosy bistro is a "relaxed" haunt on the Leith waterfront, serving an "interesting" menu, specialising in "zingy" fish; service, though, can be "slothful".
/ Sample dishes: chicken liver parfait; seared salmon with Prosciutto-wrapped asparagus; treacle tart. Details: www.skippers.co.uk; 10 pm.*

Stac Polly £42
29-33 Dublin St EH3 6NL (0131) 556 2231
"Good and reliable", this Scottish duo offer "tasty" fare ("the haggis starter in particular") and maintain a loyal following; the branch listed is in New Town cellars, and the other is at 8-10 Grindlay Street (tel 229 5405). / Sample dishes: baked filo pastry parcels of haggis; pan-fried fillet of Aberdeen angus beef; chocolate tart with Mascarpone ice cream. Details: www.stacpolly.co.uk; 10 pm; closed Sat L & Sun L; no smoking area.

Suruchi £25 ★
14a Nicolson St EH8 9DH (0131) 556 6583
"No other Indian will do", say fans of the "large and varied" menu (translated 'Scottish-style') offered by this classy curry house, opposite the Festival Theatre; service is "patient and friendly", too; there is also a Leith branch at 121 Constitution St (tel 554 3268). / Details: www.suruchirestaurant.com; opp Festival Theatre; 11.30 pm; closed Sun L.

Susies £15
51-53 West Nicolson St EH8 9DB (0131) 667 8729
*"Good veggie food" is the attraction of this long-standing self-service café, by the University; it's licensed, but you can BYO.
/ Sample dishes: falafel with houmous; chilli bean enchiladas; pear frangipane flan. Details: 9 pm; closed Sun (except Festival time); no credit cards; no smoking area; no booking.*

Thai Orchid £28 ★
44 Grindlay St EH3 9AP (0131) 228 4438
This "cheerful" Thai, off Lothian Road, has quite a following, thanks to its "delicious" cooking and its "friendly" staff; "book early if you want to choose when to dine". / Details: 10.45 pm; closed Sat L & Sun L; no smoking.

Tinelli's £ 29
139 Easter Rd EH7 5QA   (0131) 652 1932
"A top simple Italian" – Signor Tinelli's fixture of more than two
decades' standing, near Leith Links remains a consistently popular
fixture for those in the know. / *Sample dishes: snails with bacon &
mushrooms; baked rabbit with cream & rosemary sauce; strawberry gelati.*
Details: 11 pm; closed Mon & Sun.

The Tower
Museum of Scotland £ 44
Chambers St EH1 1JF   (0131) 225 3003
*Some still find it "overpriced and over-confident", but this elevated
dining room – which has "tremendous views of the Castle" –
is finding more favour with reporters, most of whom now report
"very good" results. / *Sample dishes: lobster claw & pickled vegetable salad;
chicken with cep mash & Madeira jus; chocolate truffle torte.*
*Details: www.tower-restaurant.com; at top of Museum of Scotland; 11 pm;
no smoking.*

Valvona & Crolla £ 30 ★
19 Elm Row EH7 4AA   (0131) 556 6066
"A haven of Italiana" – the café at this famous deli and wine
merchants has long been known as "one of the best places
to breakfast or lunch in town", offering a "limited menu of high-
quality snacks", "excellent coffee" and "delicious" cakes;
it's "pricey", though, and "you may have to queue".
/ *Sample dishes: pumpkin tortellini; Italian spicy sausage pizza; lemon tart.*
*Details: www.valvonacrolla.com; at top of Leith Walk, near Playhouse Theatre;
L only; no smoking.*

Vermilion
The Scotsman £ 53 A★
North Bridge EH1 1YT   (0131) 556 5565
*Geoff Balharrie delivers some outstanding Scottish cooking according
to the (relatively few) reporters who commented on this "wonderful
and intimate" newcomer* – the swankiest of the dining rooms at this
landmark-building boutique-hotel. / *Sample dishes: foie gras ballottine with
white peach soup; venison with celeriac croquettes & chocolate sauce;
dark chocolate tart with orange Mascarpone. **Details:** www.thescotsmanhotel.com;
9.45 pm; D only, closed Mon & Sun; no shorts; smoking in bar only; children: 12+.*
Accommodation: 68 rooms, from £120.

Vintners Rooms £ 42 A
87a, Giles St EH6 6BZ   (0131) 554 6767
"A wonderfully atmospheric favourite" – this "delightful dining room
and bar" occupies hugely characterful 16th-century wine vaults
in Leith (but set back from the waterfront); we've 'unrated' the –
good, in the past – food on a change of ownership, but let's hope
the new (French) owners do full justice to the Auld Alliance!
/ *Sample dishes: smoked salmon with sweet cucumber pickle; chicken supreme
with lime & Madeira; chocolate pecan pie with coffee sauce.*
*Details: www.thevintnersrooms.com; 9.45 pm; closed Sun; no smoking in dining
room.*

The Waterfront £ 31 A
1c Dock Pl EH6 6LU   (0131) 554 7427
"The newly refurbished conservatory has improved the ambience",
say fans of this ever-popular Leith seafood restaurant; while it's
never going to set the world on fire, it's "a lovely place in which
to while away an afternoon". / *Sample dishes: grilled sardines with feta &
chick peas; swordfish with hot & sour sauce; white chocolate & Bailey's cheesecake.*
*Details: www.sjf.co.uk; near Royal Yacht Britannia; 10 pm, Fri & Sat 10.30 pm;
no smoking area.*

The Witchery by the Castle £45 👪
Castlehill, The Royal Mile EH1 2NF (0131) 225 5613
"For romance", it's "hard to beat" the "Gothic charm" of this "amazing" and "enchanting", candlelit venue near the Castle; there's a "telephone directory" of a wine list, too, which it's no real criticism to say rather overshadows the cooking.
/ **Sample dishes:** home-smoked salmon with sautéed green beans; seared scallops with lobster risotto; lemon meringue pie with rhubarb sauce.
Details: www.thewitchery.com; 11.30 pm. **Accommodation:** 7 rooms, from £225.

EGLINGHAM, NORTHUMBERLAND 8–1B
Tankerville Arms £27
15 The Village NE66 2TX (01665) 578444
"The food's always good" at this cosy coaching inn; they're "excellent with children", too. / **Sample dishes:** smoked trout salad with lime dill sauce; rump steak with creamed green peppercorn sauce; fruits of the forest cheesecake.
Details: 9 pm; no smoking in dining room.

EGLWYSFACH, POWYS 4–3D
Ynyshir Hall £60 👪★★
SY20 8TA (01654) 781209
"You feel utterly spoilt", at this "blissful" establishment, in a Georgian manor house, near the Dyfi estuary (decorated with the owner's works of art); with its "fabulous" service and "excellent" cooking, it's tipped by some as "the best place in Wales".
/ **Sample dishes:** prawn cannelloni with caviar; seared turbot with lemon potatoes; hot mango & apricot soufflé. **Details:** www.ynyshir-hall.co.uk; signposted from A487; 8.45 pm; no jeans or trainers; no smoking; booking essential at L; children: 9+.
Accommodation: 10 rooms, from £160.

ELSTEAD, SURREY 3–3A
Woolpack £28
The Green GU8 6HD (01252) 703106
A "cosy and reliable" town-centre pub, worth knowing of for its "large and varied" menu. / **Sample dishes:** deep-fried calamari; steak & kidney pie; fruit pavlova. **Details:** 7m SW of Guildford, on village green; 9.45 pm; no Amex; no smoking in dining room; no booking.

ELTERWATER, CUMBRIA 7–3D
Britannia Inn £24 ★
LA22 9HP (01539) 437210
"A great location, especially for lunch on a sunny day" is not the only feature which keeps this "no-nonsense" old inn very "busy" – its "traditional pub food" maintains "a high standard".
/ **Sample dishes:** potted shrimps; roast lamb with minted gravy & braised leeks; lemon cheesecake. **Details:** www.britinn.co.uk; 9.30 pm; no smoking in dining room; booking: max 6; children: before 9 pm only. **Accommodation:** 9 rooms, from £72.

ELY, CAMBRIDGESHIRE 3–1B
Old Fire Engine House £33 👪
25 St Mary's St CB7 4ER (01353) 662582
"Reliably-cooked traditional fare" has been the aim of this "welcoming" English fixture near the Cathedral for over three decades – it generally succeeds, and it's "quirky" wine list is "reasonably priced", too. / **Sample dishes:** lovage soup; lemon sole with prawn & dill sauce; old-fashioned sherry trifle.
Details: www.theoldfireenginehouse.co.uk; 9 pm; closed Sun D; no Amex; no smoking area.

EMSWORTH, HAMPSHIRE   2–4D
36 on the Quay   £ 53   ★
47 South St PO10 7EG   (01243) 375592
"Inspired and inspiring cooking" with *"simply astonishing attention
to detail"* makes Ramon Farthing's beautifully-located restaurant,
overlooking Emsworth harbour, *"a real find"* (*"especially in this part
of the world"*). / **Sample dishes:** pan-fried mullet with pesto; scallops with
chicken & goose liver sausage; quartet of lemon desserts. **Details:** www.36onthe
quay.co.uk; off A27 between Portsmouth & Chichester; 10 pm; closed Mon L,
Sat L & Sun; no smoking in dining room. **Accommodation:** 4 rooms, from £80.

ENGLEFIELD GREEN, SURREY   3–3A
Edwinns   £ 38   𝔸
Wick Rd TW20 0HN   (01784) 477877
"In an area with few restaurants", this comfortable establishment
(one of a small group) provides *"competent and reliable"* cooking
in an agreeable location (on the fringe of Windsor Great Park).
/ **Sample dishes:** warm duck salad; lamb steak; sticky pudding.
Details: www.edwinns.co.uk; 10 pm; closed Sat L & Sun D; no smoking.

EPSOM DOWN, SURREY   3–3B
Le Raj   £ 30   ★
211 Fir Tree Rd KT17 3LB   (01737) 371371
"Service can leave a lot to be desired", but this *"airy"* subcontinental
is world-famous in Surrey on account of its *"excellent, modern
menu"*. / **Details:** www.leraj.co.uk; next to Derby race course; 11 pm; strict smart
dress code; no smoking area.

EPWORTH, NORTH LINCOLNSHIRE   5–2D
Epworth Tap   £ 35
DN9 1EU   (01427) 873333
The food is *"fine"* (*"if expensive by Lincolnshire standards"*) but the
"real attraction" of this remote but eminent bistro is its *"amazing-
value wine list"*. / **Sample dishes:** duck spring rolls; pork with bacon & spiced
red cabbage; apple, apricot & pecan strudel. **Details:** 3m from M180, J2; 9.30 pm;
D only, closed Sun-Tue; no Amex; no smoking.

ESHER, SURREY   3–3A
Good Earth   £ 39
14-18 High St KT10 9RT   (01372) 462489
*"A pricey, suburban Chinese, where you always get a first-class
meal"* – a *"consistently reliable"* and well-known establishment
of many years' standing. / **Details:** www.goodearthgroup.co.uk; 11 pm;
booking: max 12, Fri & Sat.

Il Corallo   £ 24
104-106 High St KT10 4DU   (01372) 469555
"Crowded and bustling", this *"real trattoria"* is unanimously hailed
by reporters as a *"bright"*, *"cheerful"* and *"good-value"* spot
(and one that's *"great for kids"*). / **Details:** 10.45 pm; closed Sun.

Siam Food Gallery   £ 32
95-97 High St KT10 9QE   (01372) 477139
Some consider it *"overpriced"*, but this local Thai generally wins
praise for its *"beautifully presented"* cooking, *"charming"* service
and *"nice"* setting. / **Details:** 11 pm.

---

sign up for the survey at www.hardens.com

ETON, WINDSOR & MAIDENHEAD   3–3A
Gilbey's   £33
82-83 High St SL4 6AF (01753) 854921
"Good-quality wine at very reasonable prices" are the key draw
to this *"pleasantly situated"* fixture (once known as The Eton Wine
Bar), though the food is *"rather hit and miss"*; views diverge as to
which is more atmospheric – the front bar or rear conservatory.
/ **Sample dishes:** pork chilli pistachio galantine; grilled fillet of black bream with
new potato & watercress salad; toffee apple with brown bread ice cream.
Details: www.gilbeygroup.com; 10 min walk from Windsor Castle; 10.30 pm.

EVERSHOT, DORSET   2–4B
Summer Lodge
Country House Hotel & Restaurant   £47   Ⓐ
DT2 0JR (01935) 83424
For a *"cosseting"* country house dining experience, this attractive
18th-century building (with *"beautiful"* walled gardens) attracted
more consistent support this year; notably *"unhurried"* (in the
positive sense) service is a highlight. / **Sample dishes:** assorted melons &
ham with raspberry & mint coulis; seared cod with orange butter sauce; iced honey
parfait with seasonal berries. **Details:** www.summerlodgehotel.co.uk; 12m NW
of Dorchester on A37; 9.30 pm; jacket at D; no smoking in dining room; children:
7+ at D. **Accommodation:** 17 rooms, from £145.

EVESHAM, WORCESTERSHIRE   2–1C
Evesham Hotel   £35
Coopers Ln WR11 1DA (01386) 765566
*"A fantastically amusing landlord with a sense of humour akin
to that of Basil Fawlty"* sets the tone at this *"special and individual"*
hotel; some reporters find it *"outstanding in every way"*, but it's the
"biggest-ever wine list" (from which France and Germany are
excluded) which is the special attraction. / **Sample dishes:** smoked
chicken, cherry & watercress salad; baked cod with red wine risotto & mushrooms;
lemon meringue ice cream. **Details:** www.eveshamhotel.com; 9.30 pm; no smoking.
Accommodation: 40 rooms, from £118.

EXETER, DEVON   1–3D
Brazz   £31
10-12 Palace Gate EX1 1JA (01392) 252525
"The best bit is the cylindrical, floor-to-ceiling fish tanks" –
the cooking at this determinedly *"modern"* and *"upbeat"* outpost
of a West Country brasserie chain is only *"fair-to-middling"*.
/ **Sample dishes:** mushroom brioche; chicken with lemon, leeks & wild mushroom
sauce; chocolate brownie with white chocolate sauce. **Details:** www.brazz.co.uk;
10.30 pm, Fri & Sat 11 pm; no smoking.

Double Locks   £22   Ⓐ
Canal Banks, Alphington EX2 6LT (01392) 256947
"Great fun and fab pub-food" – that's the deal at this ever-popular
canalside boozer; *"especially on Sundays"*, though, *"service can
be slow"*. / **Sample dishes:** garlic bread with Cheddar; turkey & mushroom pie;
sticky toffee pudding. **Details:** through Marsh Barton industrial estate, follow
dead-end track over bridges to end of towpath; 10.30 pm; no Amex; no booking.

Herbies   £19
15 North St EX4 3QS (01392) 258473
"Jolly and friendly", this *"good old-fashioned"* veggie makes a very
useful *"cheap and cheerful"* choice in this under-served town.
/ **Sample dishes:** houmous with garlic bread; mushroom sundried tomato; apple
pie. **Details:** 9.30 pm; closed Mon D & Sun; no Amex; no smoking area.

Hotel Barcelona £ 36
Magdalen St EX2 4HY (01392) 281000
*"Especially nice in summer, with doors open to the garden",
the dining room of this "original" and funky boutique hotel is a
"lively" (and "noisy") hang out; its Italian (and pizza) menu is "tasty
enough, but not cheap". / **Sample dishes:** beef carpaccio with rocket &
Parmesan; magret of duck with couscous; chocolate fondant pudding.
Details: www.hotelbarcelona-uk.com; 9.45 pm; no smoking; booking: max 8.
Accommodation: 46 rooms, from £80.*

Michael Caines
Royal Clarence Hotel £ 51
Cathedral Yd EX1 1HD (01392) 310031
*"Last year we had an excellent meal, so we were very surprised
by the decline in value" – one reporter sums up feedback on this
ambitious venture near the cathedral (a 'spin-off', overseen from
afar by the head chef of Gidleigh Park), which produced rather too
many "forgettable" meals this year. / **Sample dishes:** red mullet with
saffron risotto; duck with roast garlic & spiced jus; chocolate nougatine with cherries.
Details: www.michaelcaines.com; 10 pm; closed Sun; no smoking.
Accommodation: 56 rooms, from £85.*

St Olave's Court Hotel £ 35
Mary Arches St EX4 3AZ (01392) 217736
*New owners have "much improved" this slightly old-fashioned hotel
"in the heart of the city"; even now, no one suggests that its dining
room is a gastronomic 'destination', but "professional all-round"
standards make it a "welcoming" and "pleasant" location.
/ **Sample dishes:** creamy sweet potato soup; braised duck with creamed
potatoes & green peppercorn sauce; honey cheesecake with lemon curd ice cream.
Details: www.olaves.co.uk; 8.45 pm; no smoking; children: 10+.
Accommodation: 15 rooms, from £105.*

Thai Orchid £ 27
5 Cathedral Yd EX1 1HJ (01392) 214215
*"A small Thai next to Cathedral"; it's "quite authentic", and its set
menus offer "very good value". / **Details:** next to Exeter Cathedral;
10.30 pm; closed Sun.*

FARNHAM, SURREY 3–3A

Vienna £ 42
112 West St GU9 7HH (01252) 722978
*"Pretty good in an area bereft of culinary excellence",
this "comfortable, store-front place" – more than two decades
in business – wins special praise for "the best fish and seafood
dishes for miles around". / **Sample dishes:** deep-fried Brie; seafood risotto
with sun-dried tomato jus; cappuccino brûlée. **Details:** 10.30 pm; closed Sun;
no Amex or Switch; mainly non-smoking; children: 5+.*

FAVERSHAM, KENT 3–3C

The Dove £ 36 ★
Plum Pudding Ln ME13 9HB (01227) 751360
*With its "gorgeous" setting and "blissful" food, reporters speak only
well of Nigel Morris's "friendly" gastropub, which offers a "fresh,
if limited, menu" and a "good pub atmosphere".
/ **Sample dishes:** spring onion & crab risotto; duck with lentils & foie gras; baked
chocolate pudding. **Details:** 9 pm; closed Mon, Tue D & Sun D; no Amex; booking
essential.*

Read's £58

Macknade Manor, Canterbury Rd ME13 8XE
(01795) 535344

"The improved ambience of the new premises", in a country house
– the former location was a converted supermarket! – helps win
good (if not ecstatic) reports for this long-established, family-run
venture; there's "nothing comparable hereabouts".
/ **Sample dishes:** smoked eel with beetroot; calves liver with chive mash & melted
onions; lemon & white chocolate mousse. **Details:** www.reads.com; 9.30 pm; closed
Mon & Sun. **Accommodation:** 6 rooms, from £150.

FERRENSBY, NORTH YORKSHIRE 8–4B

General Tarleton £39

Boroughbridge Rd HG5 0PZ (01423) 340284

An "extensive bar menu at reasonable prices" is the lead attraction
at this upmarket pub/restaurant; some reporters say "it's as good
as its sibling, the Angel at Hetton", but – given such illustrious
heritage – there are also people surprised by how "bog-standard"
it can be. / **Sample dishes:** Jerusalem artichoke soup; tuna with butter bean
mash & Parmesan crisps; lemon & ginger cheesecake.
Details: www.generaltarleton.co.uk; 2m from A1, J48 towards Knaresborough;
9.30 pm; D only, except Sun when L only; no smoking. **Accommodation:** 14
rooms, from £85.

FISHGUARD, PEMBROKESHIRE 4–4B

Three Main Street £42 ★

3 Main St SA65 9HG (01348) 874275

"Excellent fish" is a highlight at Inez Ford and Marian Evans's well-
established harbourside restaurant-with-rooms, which occupies
a "lovely" Georgian house. / **Sample dishes:** goats cheese with char-grilled
vegetables; pan-fried beef & mushrooms with pepper sauce; warm pear frangipane
flan. **Details:** off town square; 9 pm; closed Mon & Sun; no credit cards; no smoking
in dining room; booking: max 12. **Accommodation:** 3 rooms, from £70.

FLEET, DORSET 2–4B

Moonfleet Manor £37

DT3 4ED (01305) 786948

A Georgian manor house hotel (in a "lovely" location overlooking
Lime Bay), which specialises in being a "relaxed" and family-friendly
destination; the food doesn't set the world on fire, but is "of a good
standard". / **Sample dishes:** duck liver & foie gras parfait; confit duck with olive
mash & cherry sauce; caramelised rice pudding.
Details: www.moonfleetmanor.com; from Weymouth, B3157 then follow signs;
9.30 pm; no smoking; children: before 7.30 pm only. **Accommodation:** 39 rooms,
from £175.

FLETCHING, EAST SUSSEX 3–4B

The Griffin Inn £38 🅰 ★

TN22 3SS (01825) 722890

"One of the best pub eateries around", this "atmospheric" boozer
(with a "great garden") in a "pretty village" is "family-run,
very hospitable and has a bit of class" – "many rich game dishes"
are a menu highlight. / **Sample dishes:** grilled sardines with chilli & wild garlic;
roast lamb with Mediterranean vegetables; rhubarb, honey & saffron tart.
Details: www.thegriffininn.co.uk; off A272; 9.30 pm; closed Sun D (in winter only);
appreciated if guests try to refrain from smoking. **Accommodation:** 8 rooms,
from £85.

FORT WILLIAM, HIGHLAND   9–3B

Crannog   £34   ★★
Town Pier PH33 7NG (01397) 705589

"The seafood's so fresh it almost swims out of the kitchen" at this *"pleasant"* establishment *"on the pier"*, with its *"hard-to-beat"* views of Loch Linnhe; some reporters find it a mite *"touristy"* or *"lacking atmosphere"*, though. / **Sample dishes:** surf clams & mussels with lemon mayonnaise; pistachio-crusted halibut with risotto; treacle toffee pudding. **Details:** www.crannog.net; 10 pm (9 pm Dec-Mar); no Amex; no smoking area.

Inverlochy Castle   £65   𝔸
Torlundy PH33 6SN (01397) 702177

"Fresh local ingredients are beautifully prepared and imaginatively presented" in the *"formal"* and *"expensive"* dining room of this Baronial pile, which has an *"outstanding"* location in the foothills of Ben Nevis. / **Sample dishes:** wild mushroom tart with veal kidneys; roast duck with vanilla mash & pickled cherries; orange crème brûlée with lemon & lime sorbet. **Details:** www.inverlochycastlehotel.com; off A82, 4 m N of Ft. William; 9.15 pm; closed Jan & part of Feb; no Amex; jacket & tie required; no smoking; children: 12+. **Accommodation:** 17 rooms, from £395.00.

Old Pines   £44   𝔸★
Old Pines Spean Bridge PH34 4EG (01397) 712324

"Book early", to secure your place for dinner at this *"beautifully-located"* restaurant-with-rooms; its slightly unusual formula – the menu offers no choice, and much of the seating is communal – may appear *"slightly chaotic"*, but all reports confirm this *"friendly"* establishment is *"first-class"*. / **Sample dishes:** scallops with lobsters, mussels & spinach; loin of venison with spiced red cabbage, wild fungi & thyme sauce; brown sugar meringue with pink gooseberries & elderflower ice cream. **Details:** www.oldpines.co.uk; 8pm; closed Mon; no Amex; no smoking; children: 6+. **Accommodation:** 8 rooms, from £117 w/d.

FOWEY, CORNWALL   1–4B

Food For Thought   £37   𝔸★
4 Town Quay PL23 1AT (01726) 832221

"A quayside restaurant with bags of character", whose *"wonderful"*, *"professional"* standards are attested to by all reporters; *"lovely"* fish is, of course, the highlight. / **Sample dishes:** pan-fried scallops; roast shellfish with garlic olive oil; chocolate marquise. **Details:** 9.30 pm; D only, closed Sun; no Amex; no smoking; children: 10+.

Fowey Hall   £47   𝔸★
Hanson Drive PL23 1ET (01726) 833866

That it's *"perfect for families"* is much of the attraction of this comfortable Italianate member of the Luxury Family Hotels group, overlooking the estuary; reporters are impressed by the cooking too, though, and say the dining room here can be *"excellent"*. / **Sample dishes:** foie gras; sea bass; raspberry & basil soufflé. **Details:** www.luxury-family-hotels.co.uk; on the main road next to the car park; 9.30 pm; no smoking; booking: max 10; children: 12+. **Accommodation:** 24 rooms, from £155.

FOWLMERE, CAMBRIDGESHIRE   3–1B

Chequers   £30   ★
SG8 7SR (01763) 208369

A *"vibrant"* kitchen and *"superb"* beer again win applause for this *"little country pub"*, near Cambridge. / **Sample dishes:** Spinach & walnut risotto; calves liver with horseradish mash & spinach; rhubarb & almond crumble. **Details:** on B1368 between Royston & Cambridge; 10 pm; no smoking area.

FRIDAY STREET, SURREY   3–1D

Stephan Langton   **£30**   ★

RH5 6JR   (01306) 730775

"Greatly improved over the last couple of years" – the arrival of John
& Alison Coombe has really bucked up this remote country pub, in a
"beautiful" Surrey Hills location; its *"superb"* food is praised
by pretty much all reporters. / **Sample dishes:** terrine of chicken livers;
duck confit; chocolate brownies. **Details:** 10 pm; closed Mon & Sun D; no Amex;
no smoking in dining room.

FRITHSDEN, HERTFORDSHIRE   3–2A

Alford Arms   **£33**

HP1 3DD   (01442) 864480

"Book, for this really good country inn!"; it has a *"jolly"* and
"relaxed" ambience, and serves an *"interesting"* modern gastropub
menu – there's a *"dearth of local alternatives"*, too.
/ **Sample dishes:** Dolcelatte & fig tart; roast cod & chorizo with spinach; lemon
crème brûlée. **Details:** near Ashridge College, by vineyard; 10 pm; booking: max 12.

GANTS HILL, ESSEX   3–2B

Elephant Royale   **£36**

579-581 Cranbrook Rd IG2 6JZ   (020) 8551 7015

Beware the *"loud"* live entertainment (Fri & Sat), but this suburban
Thai on the A12 – which has a newer sibling on the Isle of Dogs –
is a useful place in a thin area, and its dishes are sometimes
"superb". / **Details:** www.elephantroyale.com; 11.15 pm; children: no babies.

GLASGOW, CITY OF GLASGOW   9–4C

As in London, the city's 'Gastronomic Champion' is presided
over by (native son) Gordon Ramsay. *Amaryllis* at One
Devonshire Gardens is the most commented-upon place
in town, although as Ramsay's empire (south of the border)
continues its dash for growth, standards continue to come
under pressure.

Two of Glasgow's other great culinary institutions of long
standing – *Rogano* and the *Ubiquitous Chip* – are both mired
in complacency. (Indeed, complacency seems to be something
of an occupational hazard among Glasgow's restaurateurs.) The
same used to be true of *The Buttery*, although our (scarce)
feedback on its resurrected form is positive.

Real contemporary highlights are thin on the ground. *Gamba* –
a notable destination for fish-lovers – is an honourable
exception, and another is the quirky *Gingerhill*.

Glasgow scores highly for well-established atmospheric
institutions. In addition to the Chip and Rogano (above),
examples include *Sarti's*, *Babbity Bowster* and *Café Gandolfi*.

The city boasts a good range of Indian restaurants (*Ashoka* and
Mother India). The oriental options tend to be solid, but rather
unremarkable.

Air Organic £29
36 Kelvingrove G3 7SA   (0141) 564 5200
"Excellent bread" and *"brilliant brunches"* are the sort of things
done particularly well at this organic specialist in Kelvingrove;
the vaguely sci-fi setting, though, can be *"something of a let-down"*.
/ **Sample dishes:** roast tomato & Mozzarella crostini; beef fillet bento box; white
chocolate & lemon cheesecake. **Details:** www.airorganic.co.uk; near Kelvingrove art
galleries; 10 pm, Fri & Sat 10.30 pm; no smoking area; booking: max 10
at weekends.

Amaryllis
One Devonshire Gardens £50 ★
1 Devonshire Gardens G12 0UX   (0141) 337 3434
"Gordon Ramsay's Scottish division" – the grandest hotel dining
room in the star-chef's home town – is praised by almost all
reporters for *"first-class ingredients, carefully prepared and
presented"*; service is *"a little inconsistent"*, though, and an early
report on recent *'improvements'* (including the availability of a
cheaper 'brasserie' menu) found them to be a backwards step.
/ **Sample dishes:** lobster & langoustine ravioli in lobster bisque; venison with red
cabbage & bitter chocolate sauce; chocolate fondant tart.
Details: www.gordonramsay.com; 1.5m from M8, J17; 9.30 pm; closed Mon, Tue &
Sat L; no smoking in dining room; booking: max 8. **Accommodation:** 38 rooms,
from £125.

Amber Regent £38
50 West Regent St G2 2RA   (0141) 331 1655
"Still the best Chinese in town"; this *"expensive"* and *"unchanging"*
city-centre fixture remains a *"reliable"* oriental (though there are
those who find it *"overhyped"*). / **Details:** www.amberregent.com; 10.45 pm;
closed Sun.

Ashoka £24 ★
19 Ashton Ln G12 8SJ   (0800) 454817
'Ashoka' might as well be the Glaswegian for curry, so common are
the outlets of this local brand's; it's all very confusing, though, as the
best-known bearer of the name at 108 Elderslie Street (tel 221
1761) is run separately from the rest – fortunately, all the Ashokas
seem to be pretty reliable, if sometimes rather *"crowded"*.
/ **Details:** www.harlequin-leisure.co.uk; behind Hillhead station; 11.30 pm; closed
Sun L.

Babbity Bowster £30 Ⓐ
16-18 Blackfriar's St G1 1PE   (0141) 552 5055
"A great mein host" adds much to the charms of this famed
Merchant City pub (occupying a James Adam building), where the
Scottish fare is often *"very good"* (*"especially oysters"*); the ground-
floor bar is preferred by some to the 'Schottische' restaurant
upstairs. / **Sample dishes:** poached Scottish oysters; beef with port & foie gras
sauce; chocolate terrine. **Details:** 11 pm; D only, closed Mon & Sun.
Accommodation: 6 rooms, from £50.

Brian Maule at Chardon D'Or £38
176 West Regent St G2 4RL   (0141) 248 3801
"The chef trained at Le Gavroche and it shows" is the most common
reaction to this city-centre two-year-old near Blythswood Square;
overall, though, middling ratings give some credence to criticisms
that the place is *"coasting"* or *"ambience-free"*.
/ **Sample dishes:** salmon with cucumber & dill dressing; coley with warm celery &
lentil salad; roast pears with caramel sauce. **Details:** www.lechardondor.com;
10 pm; closed Sat L & Sun; no smoking in dining room.

Buttery £55
652 Argyle St G3 8UF   (0141) 221 8188
*This historic, clubby restaurant site (oddly located, cut off from the
city-centre by the M2) has seen mixed fortunes in recent years
(it closed then re-opened in 2002); we received too few reports for
a rating, this year, but one reporter's encouraging take was that
"its tired image has gone". / Sample dishes: apple & beetroot pasta pave
on a confit of venison; lamb with a minted sausage hotpot; tiramisú with white
chocolate & vanilla ice cream. Details: 10 pm; closed Mon L, Sat L & Sun L;
no smoking.*

Café Gandolfi £31
64 Albion St G1 1NY   (0141) 552 6813
*"Distinctive", woody furnishings help create a "wonderful", "laid-
back" atmosphere at this "busy" Merchant City veteran;
many reporters also cite the "eclectic" cooking as an attraction,
but not all are impressed, and some find the place "better for
a snack than a full meal". / Sample dishes: warm potato & chorizo salad;
polenta with wild mushrooms & Gorgonzola; rhubarb summer pudding.
Details: near Tron Theatre; 11.30 pm; no smoking area; no booking, Sat.*

Café India £26
171 North St G3 7DA   (0141) 248 4074
*A cavernous city-centre curry house that has had its ups and downs
over the years; fans, though, still insist that it's a "quality"
establishment, with "outstanding" food.
/ Details: www.cafeindia-glasgow.com; next to Mitchell Library; midnight;
no smoking area.*

Café Mao £27
84 Brunswick St G1 1ZZ   (0141) 564 5161
*It's "sometimes too busy", but this bright oriental fusion outfit
is consistently popular with reporters, not least for its "very tasty"
fare. / Details: www.cafemao.com; 11 pm; L only; no smoking area.*

City Merchant £37
97-99 Candleriggs G1 1NP (0141) 553 1577
*For "Scotland with a touch of France", this Merchant City institution,
with its "old-fashioned" service provides much "traditional" appeal;
as ever, though, not all reporters are 100% convinced by its
standards. / Sample dishes: smoked duck & bacon salad; venison with black
pudding mousse & apple jus; meringue nest with berry compote.
Details: www.citymerchant.co.uk; 10.30 pm; closed Sun; no smoking area; children:
5.*

Crème de la Crème £28
1071 Argyle St G3 8LZ   (0141) 221 3222
*A building which was formerly a "very large cinema" manages
to provide a surprisingly "unexciting" setting for this mega-scale
subcontinental; most, but not all, reporters find it a "good-value"
option nonetheless. / Details: near Scottish Exhibition Centre; 11.45 pm; closed
Sun L; no smoking area.*

Elliott's Bar & Restaurant £28
203-204 Bath St G2 4HZ   (0141) 248 2060
*"An exciting range of flavours at sensible prices in interesting
surroundings" – that's how fans see this "Italian-leaning" city-centre
spot, which is of particular note for its "good-value lunch and pre-
theatre menus". / Sample dishes: steamed mussels; duck supreme with
stir-fried tagliatelle with cherry, port & orange sauce; chocolate fudge cake.
Details: www.elliottsbathst.com; 10 pm; closed Sun.*

Gamba £ 43 ★

225a West George St G2 2ND (0141) 572 0899

"The freshest possible fish", "precisely cooked and served", is the stock-in-trade of this "innovative" and "delightful" central basement; the staff are "very clued-up", too. / Sample dishes: mackerel with potato & horseradish salad; roast cod with mussel & thyme stew; panna cotta with strawberries & mint syrup. Details: www.gamba.co.uk; 10.30 pm; closed Sun; children: 14+.

Gingerhill £ 36 𝔸★★

1 Hillhead St G62 8AF (0141) 956 6515

This "little gem of place" may have an unpromising location (above a suburban chemists) but all reporters sing the praises of its "exciting" menu – chef Alan Burns has "a real dedication to top quality", and costs are kept low the by the fact that you BYO. / Sample dishes: boudin of halibut, monk fish & lentils; confit of beef shin with veal loin & sweetbreads; strawberry consommé with basil ice cream. Details: www.gingerhill.co.uk; 9.30 pm; closed Mon & Tue, Wed-Sun D only; no Amex; no smoking; booking: max 12; children: 14+ at D.

Gordon Yuill & Company £ 34

257 West Campbell St G2 4SQ (0141) 572 4052

A "businesslike" mini-chain run by the ex-Maître D' of Roganos – feedback such as "OK, but I probably wouldn't go back" typifies the low levels of excitement it incites across the board. / Sample dishes: crispy duck & watercress salad; sea bass with braised fennel; triple chocolate marquise. Details: www.gordonyuillandcompany.co.uk; 10 pm.

Ichiban £ 17 ★

50 Queen St G1 3DS (0141) 204 4200

"Just how noodle bars should be" – this "fast" and "friendly" oriental duo (there's another branch at 184 Dumbarton Road, tel 334 9222) serve "fresh-tasting" and "good-value" ramen, soups, sushi and other main meals. / Details: www.ichiban.co.uk; 9.45 pm, Thu-Sat 10.45 pm; no smoking; no booking at weekends.

Kama Sutra £ 26 𝔸

331 Sauchiehall St G2 3HW (0141) 332 0055

"The best of the Harlequins" (a local subcontinental group), this "cool" OTT Indian in the city centre offers "adventurous dishes at sensible prices"; service is "friendly", too. / Details: www.kama-sutra-restaurant.com; midnight; closed Sun L.

Killermont Polo Club £ 25 𝔸

2022 Maryhill Rd G20 0AB (0141) 946 5412

A colonial-themed Maryhill subcontinental which, over the years, has carved out a fair reputation for dishes, "which include the unusual as well as the familiar". / Details: www.killermont-polo-club.co.uk; near Maryhill station; 10.30 pm; no smoking area.

Lux £ 36 ★

1051 Great Western Rd G12 0XT (0141) 576 7576

"In the leafy West End, a treat which is worth seeking out"; it doesn't attract a huge degree of commentary, but this "well-run" bar/restaurant is consistently praised for its "fine food, served in relaxing and stylish surroundings" (a converted railway station). / Sample dishes: roast pear & Stilton cheese puffs with port compote; baked supreme of chicken with black pudding & apple risotto; crème brûlée with homemade short bread. Details: 2m W of city centre; 10.30 pm; D only, closed Sun; no smoking area; children: 12+.

Mitchell's £34
157 North St G3 7DA   (0141) 204 4312
"Angus Boyd still knows his stuff" say loyal fans of his West End-fringe bistro – which has a Carmunnock branch at 107 Waterside Rd (tel 644 2255) – who laud its "imaginative" Mediterranean/Scottish cuisine and "courteous" service.
/ **Sample dishes:** grilled squid with chorizo; beef with crispy potatoes & mustard lentils; coconut tart with orange sorbet. **Details:** 10.30 pm; closed Mon & Sun; smoking discouraged.

Mother India £28   *A* ★
28 Westminster Ter G3 7RU   (0141) 221 1663
Some reporters say that this "cramped" and "busy" Indian, south of Kelvingrove Park, "used to be better", but even they concede that it's a "pretty decent" place where the curries "are always good and sometimes exceptional". / **Details:** beside Kelvingrove Hotel; 10.30 pm, Fri & Sat 11 pm; closed Mon L, Tue L & Sun L.

Mr Singh's India £25
149 Elderslie St G3 7JR   (0141) 204 0186
"Indian waiters with Scottish accents" (and a "great sense of humour") are part of the "winning" formula which ensures that this "stylish" and "friendly" Kelvingrove Park subcontinental is "always busy". / **Sample dishes:** pan-fried prawns with lime; south Indian garlic spiced chicken; toffee pudding. **Details:** 11.30 pm.

Number 16 £31   ★
16 Byres Rd G11 5JY   (0141) 339 2544
"Top-class" cooking and "charming" service come together to make a simple-but-good formula at this tiny and relaxed bistro, near the Dumbarton Road. / **Sample dishes:** hot cheese fritters with apple & port sauce; roast venison with spiced red cabbage; sticky toffee pudding. **Details:** 10 pm; no Amex; no smoking at D.

Parmigiana £38
447 Great Western Rd G12 8HH   (0141) 334 0686
This family-run Kelvinbridge Italian is an "intimate" place, long known as one of the city's better destinations – "good and efficient and not overpriced"; this year, though, support was a little less unanimous than usual. / **Sample dishes:** lobster ravioli; fish & shellfish soup with bruschetta; lemon tart with cherries. **Details:** www.laparmigiana.co.uk; near Kelvinbridge station; 10.45 pm; closed Sun.

Rogano £50   *A*
11 Exchange Pl G1 3AN   (0141) 248 4055
Sheer "Art Deco opulence" makes this famous '30s seafood restaurant (whose interior was supposedly modelled on one from the Queen Mary) a rarity among British restaurants; prices (especially of wines) are "heroic", though, and the food is no more than "good enough". / **Sample dishes:** smoked salmon with quails eggs & caperberries; sea bream with cabbage & bacon; chocolate & ginger snap cheesecake. **Details:** www.rogano.co.uk; 10.30 pm; no smoking before 10 pm.

Saint Judes £37   *A*
190 Bath St G2 4HG   (0141) 352 8800
This spin-off from the famous Soho media club (once known as Groucho St Judes) attracts a mixed bag of comments; fans say it's a "fun" all-rounder for "trendy Glasgow", but even some who concede it serves "decent food" can find it "pricey" or "overstyled". / **Sample dishes:** duck liver mousse in Madeira aspic; John Dory with asparagus & lime mayonnaise; dark chocolate & cherry fudge cake. **Details:** www.saintjudes.com; 10.30 pm; closed Sat L & Sun L. **Accommodation:** 6 rooms, from £90.

Sarti's   £ 27   Ⓐ
121 Bath St   G2 2SZ   (0141) 204 0440
"An effortless Italian atmosphere" and *"top-notch"*, *"easy-going"*
staff help maintain this small chain (also at 42 Renfield Street,
tel 572 7000) as a "perennial Glasgow favourite"; foodwise, "it may
not be the best", but it "never disappoints". / Sample dishes: minestrone
soup; four cheese pizza; tiramisu. Details: 11 pm; no smoking area; no booking
at L.

78 St Vincent   £ 38   Ⓐ
78 St Vincent's St   G2 5UB   (0141) 248 7878
The "elegant surroundings" of a former banking hall house this
"attractive" modern brasserie in the city-centre; fans say its "good"
modern British cooking makes it a "super all-rounder", but the odd
misfire is not unknown. / Sample dishes: rainbow trout with sweet pepper
butter; halibut with braised fennel & rocket; white chocolate praline tart.
Details: www.78stvincent.com; 2 mins from George Sq; 10 pm, Fri & Sat
10.30 pm; no smoking area.

Shish Mahal   £ 24   ★
66-68 Park Rd   G4 9JF   (0141) 334 7899
"A legend in Glasgow's curry scene" – this "quality" Indian "has not
dropped in quality since the '70s" and offers "a warm welcome"
and "tasty cooking". / Details: 11 pm; closed Sun L; no smoking area.

Stravaigin   £ 39
28 Gibson St   G12 8NX   (0141) 334 2665
"It's reputation in Glasgow is high", and Colin Clydesdale's quirky bar
and basement dining room near the University wins much praise for
its "friendly" and "unstuffy" commitment to "very innovative food
and wines"; there is something of a feeling, however, that it's
"resting on its laurels". / Sample dishes: roast artichoke & garlic broth;
chicken stuffed with red pepper & pesto; Belgian chocolate & ginger truffle tart.
Details: www.stravaigin.com; 11 pm; closed Mon, Tue L, Wed L & Thu L;
no smoking before 10 pm.

Stravaigin 2   £ 31
8 Ruthven Ln   G12 9BG   (0141) 334 7165
Colin Clydesdale's spin off venture, has a "delightful location in a
converted mews building behind Byres Road"; even those praising its
"interesting and excellent cooking" can find "service repeatedly
lacklustre", though and – as at No 1. – there are general
accusations of "laurel resting". / Sample dishes: mackerel on tapenade
toast with balsamic bacon relish; spiced coconut crusted bream with yoghurt-dressed
leaves; Sherry soaked lemon & poppy seed trifle with vanilla anglaise.
Details: www.stravaigin.com; 11 pm; no smoking area at L, no smoking at D.

Thai Fountain   £ 37
2 Woodside Cr   G3 7UL   (0141) 332 1599
Some fear "slipping standards" at this long-established Thai, citing
"uncaring staff" and "inauthentic" food; others, though, still see
it as a smart and "dependable" venue, with "high-quality" cooking.
/ Details: www.thai-fountain.com; 11 pm, Fri & Sat midnight; closed Sun; children:
7+.

Two Fat Ladies   £ 37
88 Dumbarton Rd   G11 6NX   (0141) 339 1944
Although this quirky, long-established fixture (majoring in fish) has
generated very limited feedback under its new ownership, we're
reluctant to drop this "unpretentious" outfit, still praised for its
"good food and good wine". / Sample dishes: asparagus spears with
hollandaise; lemon sole & salmon roulade with spinach; strawberry pavlova.
Details: www.twofatladies.5pm.co.uk; 10.30 pm; closed Mon & Sun L.

Ubiquitous Chip £ 49
12 Ashton Ln G12 8SJ (0141) 334 5007
The "rich and original" Scottish cuisine at this famous celebratory venue in the West End still pleases some reporters; to critics, though, the place suffers increasing "delusions of adequacy", drawing flak for a formula they find expensive, "outdated" and "pretentious"; the "quite remarkable wine list", is not in doubt.
/ *Sample dishes:* vegetarian haggis & neeps; Loch Fyne herrings with tapenade mash & aubergine caviar; Caledonian oatmeal ice cream.
Details: www.ubiquitouschip.co.uk; behind Hillhead station; 11 pm.

GODALMING, SURREY 3–3A

Bel & The Dragon £ 35 Ⓐ
Bridge St GU7 3DU (01483) 527333
A "beautifully converted church" provides the "marvellous setting" for this outpost of a chain of foodie pubs, which numbers "impeccable" service among its attractions; the food pleases most reporters, too, but doubters find portions "too big, too average or too expensive". / *Sample dishes:* Thai crab & spring onion dumplings; Cumberland sausages with cabbage & bacon mash; apricot & honeycomb cheesecake. *Details:* www.belandthedragon.co.uk; 10 pm.

GOLCAR, WEST YORKSHIRE 5–1C

The Weavers Shed £ 39 ★
Knowl Rd HD7 4AN (01484) 654284
"Superb food with home-grown produce" wins very consistent praise for this "hospitable" restaurant-with-rooms – a mill conversion with a "low-key" but "relaxing" first-floor dining room.
/ *Sample dishes:* potted crab & avocado with egg mayonnaise dressing; rib-eye steak with potato wedges; sticky toffee pudding. *Details:* www.weaversshed.co.uk; 9 pm, Sat 10 pm; closed Mon & Sat L; no smoking in dining room.
Accommodation: 5 rooms, from £55.

GORING, BERKSHIRE 2–2D

Leatherne Bottel £ 45 Ⓐ
Bridleway RG8 0HS (01491) 872667
"Your lover will approve", say fans of this "secluded" fixture, which "oozes charm" (especially in sunny weather, "when you sit outside, overlooking a stunning stretch of the Thames"); it's "expensive", but fans insist it's "worth it". / *Sample dishes:* flat mushrooms on black olive toast; steak with chilli onions & deep-fried cabbage; sticky toffee pudding.
Details: www.leathernebottel.co.uk; 0.5m outside Goring on B4009; 9 pm; closed Sun D; children: 10+.

GRANGE MOOR, WEST YORKSHIRE 5–1C

Kaye Arms £ 34 ★
29 Wakefield Rd WF4 4BG (01924) 848385
"A dining pub that's maintained high standards over many years", where "cheerful" staff offer "imaginative" food and "a really extensive wine list". / *Sample dishes:* smoked duck with sweetcorn & walnuts; Cheddar cheese soufflé with stuffed peppers; coconut tart. *Details:* 7m W of Wakefield on A642; 9.30 pm; no Amex; no smoking area; no booking on Sat; children: 14+ at D.

GREAT BARROW, CHESHIRE 5–2A

The Foxcote £ 34 ★
Station Ln CH3 7JN (01244) 301343
"It's in the heart of the country, but its standards would go down well in any city", say fans of this former pub, where "the freshest of fish" is cooked "with flair". / **Sample dishes:** battered haggis with mustard; Thai red snapper with sticky rice; sticky toffee pudding. **Details:** www.thefoxcote.com; 10 pm; closed Mon & Sun D; no Amex; mainly non-smoking.

GREAT DUNMOW, ESSEX 3–2C

Starr £ 46 Ⓐ
Market Pl CM6 1AX (01371) 874321
This 500-year-old inn in the market square wins consistent praise with its "high standard of cooking" and its "lovely" ambience. / **Sample dishes:** smoked salmon with marinated vegetables; roast guinea fowl & celery with grapes; aniseed parfait. **Details:** www.the-star.co.uk; 8m E of M11, J8 on A120; 9.30 pm; closed Sun D; no jeans or trainers; smoking in bar only. **Accommodation:** 8 rooms, from £110.

GREAT GONERBY, LINCOLNSHIRE 5–3D

Harry's Place £ 66 ★
17 High St NG31 8JS (01476) 561780
"It's excellent in every way", say fans of Harry Hallam's tiny and idiosyncratic venture, in his family's front room, which has long been known for his highly accomplished cooking; there was some feeling this year, though, that standards are "not outstanding at the prices", though, and that atmosphere was "lacking". / **Sample dishes:** mushroom soup with truffle oil; roe deer fillet with black pudding & Madeira sauce; cherry brandy jelly. **Details:** on B1174 1m N of Grantham; 9.30 pm; closed Mon & Sun; no Amex; no smoking; booking essential; children: 5+.

GREAT MILTON, OXFORDSHIRE 2–2D

Le Manoir aux Quat' Saisons £110 Ⓐ★
Church Rd OX44 7PD (01844) 278881
"Sublime" modern French cooking and an "idyllic" setting help Raymond Blanc's manor house near Oxford – with its "stunning" gardens (and bedrooms "to die for") – to maintain its position as England's prime destination restaurant; for quite a large dissident element, though, prices verge on "criminal". / **Sample dishes:** quail egg ravioli with Parmesan & truffles; roast Trelough duck with vinegar & tamarind sauce; pistachio soufflé with bitter cocoa sorbet. **Details:** www.manoir.com; from M40, J7 take A329; 9.30 pm; no smoking. **Accommodation:** 32 rooms, from £295.

GREAT TEY, ESSEX 3–2C

The Barn Brasserie £ 30
Dicken Barn, Brook Rd CO6 1JE (01206) 212345
A "beautifully-converted" 500-year-old barn is the venue for this informal brasserie; the experience is dented for some, though, by "hit-and-miss" food and "careless" service. / **Sample dishes:** grilled garlic mushrooms; crispy duck on sea-spiced aubergine; deep-fried chocolate ravioli with raspberries. **Details:** www.barnbrasserie.co.uk; 10 pm; no smoking in dining room.

GREAT YELDHAM, ESSEX
3–2C

White Hart
£38   Ⓐ

Poole St CO9 4HJ   (01787) 237250

"Low oak beams belie the modern cooking", at this large half-timbered inn; fans say it's *"everything I want in a pub"*, with *"a good mix of food"* (as well as interesting ales, wines, fruit beers and traditional barleys). / **Sample dishes:** wild mushroom & pigeon salad; steamed venison & onion pudding; raspberry & Amaretto trifle.
Details: www.whitehartyeldham.co.uk; between Haverhill & Halstead on A1017; 9.30 pm; no smoking.

GUERNSEY, CHANNEL ISLANDS

La Frégate
£40   Ⓐ★

Les Cotils, St Peter Port GY1 1UT   (01481) 724624

Fans say you get *"the best fish and seafood in the UK"*, at the dining room (with terrace) of this manor house hotel, which enjoys striking views over St Peter Port; service can be *"superb"*, too.
/ **Sample dishes:** lobster bisque; stir-fried beef with ginger, garlic & black beans; chocolate terrine with caramel sauce. **Details:** www.lafregatehotel.com; 9.30 pm; no smoking area. **Accommodation:** 13 rooms, from £165.

GUILDFORD, SURREY
3–3A

Café de Paris
£38

35 Castle St GU1 3UQ   (01483) 534896

The *"good-value"* brasserie attracts more support than the pricier restaurant at this long-established city-centre fixture; some, though, dismiss the cooking as *"quasi-French"*. / **Sample dishes:** onion & anchovy tartlet; guinea fowl casserole with tarragon sauce; lemon tart.
Details: www.cafedeparisguildford.co.uk; 10.30 pm, Fri & Sat 11 pm; closed Sun.

Cambio
£41   Ⓐ★

2-4 South Hill GU1 3SY   (01483) 577702

"An old Guildford favourite now moved to better premises"; this now much-modernised Italian offers *"bistro fare at its best"*.
/ **Sample dishes:** black lasagne with crab; veal with Parma ham & sage; Amaretto mousse. **Details:** www.cambiorestaurant.co.uk; by Guildford Castle; 10.30 pm, Fri & Sat 11 pm; closed Sun D; no smoking in dining room.

Rumwong
£27   ★★

16-18 London Rd GU1 2AF   (01483) 536092

"Stunning" food – *"the best starter I've had outside Thailand"* – which offers *"amazing value for money"* is the gist of almost all commentary on this Thai, adjacent to an oriental market (under the same ownership); service is *"attentive"*, too.
/ **Details:** www.rumwong.com; 10.30 pm; closed Mon; no Amex or Switch; no smoking area.

GULWORTHY, DEVON
1–3C

Horn of Plenty
£55   ★

PL19 8JD   (01822) 832528

"Magnificent views over the Tamar valley" add lustre to this *"distinguished"* but *"relaxed"* restaurant-with-rooms; there is the odd gripe about *"tired"* décor and *"slipping standards"*, but most reporters still praise *"pampering"* service and *"very good quality"* cuisine. / **Sample dishes:** millefeuille of smoked salmon & crab; roast lamb with mint & pesto tagliatelle; cappuccino parfait & coffee meringue.
Details: www.thehornofplenty.co.uk; 3m W of Tavistock on A390; 9 pm; closed Mon L; no smoking; children: 13+ at D. **Accommodation:** 10 rooms, from £115.

HALE, CHESHIRE   5–2B

Amba   £ 29
106-108 Ashley Rd WA14 2UN   (0161) 928 2343
*"Lovely" but "noisy", this fashionable year-old offshoot of the White
House at Prestbury offers tapas and snacks all day, as well as more
substantial fare.* / **Sample dishes:** *sweet & sour stir-fried prawns; Mexican
char-grilled chicken; lemon & lime brûlée tart.* **Details:** *www.amba.uk.com; 0.5m SE
of Altrincham; 10.30 pm.*

HALIFAX, WEST YORKSHIRE   5–1C

Design House   £ 32
Dean Clough HX3 5AX   (01422) 383242
*This "interesting" mill-conversion attracted only a small number
of reports under its new ownership, but all were upbeat, especially
regarding the "good range" of dishes.* / **Sample dishes:** *smoked salmon &
saffron risotto; pork belly with noodles & tempura vegetables; pear & cinnamon
fritters.* **Details:** *www.designhouserestaurant.co.uk; from Halifax follow signs
to Dean Clough Mills; 9.30 pm; closed Sat L & Sun; no Amex; no smoking; booking
essential.*

HAMBLETON, RUTLAND   5–4D

Finch's Arms   £ 28
Oakham Rd LE15 8TL   (01572) 756575
*"Freshly prepared food from good ingredients" awaits visitors to this
characterful "gastropub", which has a "lovely outlook" over Rutland
Water (and whose large outside area is "great on a sunny day");
service is "friendly" but can sometimes be "a bit rushed".*
/ **Sample dishes:** *artichoke tagliatelle; steamed beef with marrow & thyme
dumplings; panna cotta with glazed kumquats.* **Details:** *www.finchsarms.co.uk;
9.30 pm; no Amex; no smoking in dining room.* **Accommodation:** *6 rooms,
from £65.*

Hambleton Hall   £ 68   A ★
LE15 8TH   (01572) 756991
*"A lovely experience all round" is the gist of most commentary
on this "formal" country house hotel, overlooking Rutland Water;
"first-class" ingredients are used, and usually "cooked to perfection"
– some reporters, though, do feel that "the lack of much local
competition" leads to "excessive" prices.* / **Sample dishes:** *langoustine
cannelloni; roast pigeon with foie gras ravioli & truffle sauce; pavé of white & dark
chocolate.* **Details:** *www.hambletonhall.com; 9.30 pm; no smoking; children: 7+.*
Accommodation: *17 rooms, from £186.*

HAMPTON COURT, SURREY   3–3A

Caffe La Fiamma   £ 30   A
Hampton Court Rd KT8 8BY   (020) 8943 2050
*"A vibrant Italian with a good choice of food and a decent wine list";
its other attractions include "a wonderful site overlooking Bushy
Park" and notably "child-friendly" service.* / **Sample dishes:** *prawns with
white wine sauce & mango salsa; pasta with seafood & white wine tomato sauce;
zabaglione.* **Details:** *www.clfuk.com; 11 pm.*

HARLECH, GWYNEDD   4–2C

Maes y Neuadd   £ 43   𝔸 ★
LL47 6YA   (01766) 780200
*Distant views of Snowdonia are just part of the formula which
makes this "above-average country house hotel and restaurant"
an "absolutely fabulous" destination, for most reporters; the kitchen
uses "very good produce", sometimes to "exciting" effect.*
/ **Sample dishes:** soused mackerel with Waldorf salad; chicken with bacon & garlic
risotto; strawberry & mint delice. **Details:** www.neuadd.com; 3m N of Harlech off
B4573; 8.45 pm; no smoking area in dining room; children:
8. **Accommodation:** 16 rooms, from £150.

HAROME, NORTH YORKSHIRE   8–4C

Star Inn   £ 40   𝔸 ★★
YO62 5JE   (01439) 770397
*"Perfection in a pub"; Andrew and Jacquie Pern's "quintessential"
14th-century inn – a thatched building in a "peaceful village" – is a
"truly outstanding" destination, where "always-welcoming" staff
serve up "English homely food with a modern twist" in thoroughly
"cosy" surroundings.* / **Sample dishes:** gammon terrine with fried quails eggs;
braised rabbit with pea & mint risotto; lemon tart with blueberry sauce.
Details: www.thestaratharome.co.uk; 3m SE of Helmsley off A170; 9.30 pm; closed
Mon & Sun D; no Amex; no smoking in dining room. **Accommodation:** 11 rooms,
from £90.

HARPENDEN, HERTFORDSHIRE   3–2A

Chef Peking   £ 29
5-6 Church Grn AL5 2TP   (01582) 769358
*"A good local Chinese in a bit of a gastronomic desert"; "it's a little
more pricey than its rivals, but worth it".* / **Details:** just off the High Rd;
10.45 pm; no smoking area.

HARROGATE, NORTH YORKSHIRE   5–1C

Attic   £ 35
62a, Union St HG1 1BS   (01423) 524400
*This "bright" modern restaurant makes a "cheerful" option
(and one that's "convenient for the conference centre", too) –
even those not entirely convinced by the "youthful" cooking concede
that the overall experience can be "worthwhile".*
/ **Sample dishes:** pigeon salad with beetroot & sour cream; roast duck with
caramelised bananas & pak choy; passion fruit tart with Mascarpone ice cream.
Details: www.attic-harrogate.co.uk; 10 pm; closed Sun; appreciated if guests try
to refrain from smoking.

Bettys   £ 29   𝔸 ★
1 Parliament St HG1 2QU   (01423) 877300
*"The only place in Harrogate that's always busy", these "pricey-but-
worth-it", "classic" tea-rooms – with their "excellent" cakes and
their "lovely light bites" – are "still going strong".*
/ **Sample dishes:** Yorkshire rarebit; sausages & mash; fresh fruit tart.
Details: www.bettysandtaylors.co.uk; 9 pm; no Mastercard or Amex; no smoking;
no booking.

The Boar's Head   £ 33   𝔸 ★
Ripley Castle Estate HG3 3AY   (01423) 771888
This grand coaching inn a few miles outside the town is a
"welcoming" (if sometimes "mildly snooty") establishment, with a
"beautiful" setting; its "very well-presented" dishes are favourably
commented on by almost all reporters – "the bistro and the
*restaurant are equally good". / **Sample dishes:** rabbit with caramelised*
apples; duck with summer vegetable risotto; hot strawberry soufflé.
Details: *www.boarsheadripley.co.uk; off A61 between Ripon & Harrogate; 9 pm;*
no smoking; booking essential. ***Accommodation:*** *25 rooms, from £120.*

Cutlers on the Stray   £ 32
19 West Pk HG1 1BL   (01423) 524471
Most (but by no means all) reporters are basically satisfied by this
"smart bistro" in an old coaching inn near the town centre, where
*"all types of food are served, in a lively setting". / **Sample dishes:** warm*
crispy bacon salad with pine kernels; salmon & crab sushi with avocado wasabi;
sticky toffee pudding. ***Details:*** *www.cutlersonthestray.activehotels.com/TUK;*
9.30 pm. ***Accommodation:*** *19 rooms, from £85.*

Drum & Monkey   £ 29   𝔸 ★★
5 Montpellier Gardens HG1 2TF   (01423) 502650
"Outstanding value" ensures that this "buzzing", "traditional"
Victorian "favourite" – with its "superb" but "unfancy" fish and
seafood and "unique" setting – is "constantly packed"; you can
"book well in advance" for the upstairs restaurant, but some feel the
*downstairs bar has a "better atmosphere". / **Sample dishes:** lobster*
delice; smoked haddock florentine; crème brûlée. ***Details:*** *10.15 pm; closed Sun;*
no Amex; appreciated if guests try to refrain from smoking; booking: max 10.

Rajput   £ 21   ★
11 Cheltenham Pde HG1 1DD   (01423) 562113
"Original Indian dishes at extraordinarily modest prices" and
"friendly" service makes Mrs Perveen Khan (and son)'s "basic"
subcontinental an "excellent" choice for most (if not quite all)
*reporters. / **Details:** midnight; D only, closed Mon; no Amex.*

Villu Toots
Balmoral Hotel   £ 34
Franklin Mount HG1 5EJ   (01423) 705805
"Brilliant for a restaurant in an hotel" – though feedback is quite
limited, those who comment on this "newish and stylish" dining
room again proclaim its "interesting and different nouvelle cuisine".
*/ **Sample dishes:** game terrine with chicory & apple salad; tuna teriyaki with*
mango, lychee & red chard salad; apple & cinnamon crumble tart.
Details: *www.villutoots.co.uk; 9.45 pm; closed Sat L; no smoking area.*
Accommodation: *20 rooms, from £110.*

HARROW, MIDDLESEX   3–3A
Golden Palace   £ 29   ★
146-150 Station Rd HA1 2RH   (020) 8863 2333
"Dim sum comparable to most in Chinatown" are the special
strength of this above-average Chinese; it's "very busy", but service
*is "quick" and "helpful". / **Details:** 11.30 pm; no booking, Sat & Sun.*

Kaifeng   £ 50   ★
51 Church Road NW4 4DU   (020) 8203 7888
"The bill is almost as much as a ticket to Beijing", but most
reporters say the quality (and "novelty value") of this suburban
*Kosher Chinese is "worth it". / **Details:** www.kaifeng.co.uk; 10.30 pm.*

Old Etonian £31 ★

38 High St, Harrow On The Hill HA1 3LL (020) 8422 8482
"Great food at fantastic prices" is on offer at this quirkily-named,
"traditional" Gallic bistro of very long standing; it has *"a great
location for a stroll before your meal"*, too. / **Sample dishes:** *crêpe aux
fruits de mer; fillet Dijon.* **Details:** *11 pm; closed Sat L & Sun D.*
Accommodation: *5 rooms, from £75.*

HARWICH, ESSEX 3–2D

The Pier at Harwich £38

The Quay CO12 3HH (01255) 241212
"Wonderful views over the harbour" and *"good seafood"* are the key
features at this traditional hotel, run by the Milsom Family (owners
of the famed Talbooth). / **Sample dishes:** *roast pigeon breast salad with fresh
figs; Dover sole with nut brown butter & lemon; basket of chocolate & hazelnut
parfait with white chocolate sauce.* **Details:** *www.pieratharwich.com; 9.30 pm;
no smoking.* **Accommodation:** *14 rooms, from £90.*

HASCOMBE, SURREY 3–3A

White Horse £42 ★

The Street GU8 4JA (01483) 208258
*Fans find the food "outstanding" at this cosy 16th-century inn, which
comes complete with a pretty garden.* / **Sample dishes:** *Thai fishcakes;
roast rack of lamb; sticky toffee pudding.* **Details:** *10 pm.*

HASSOP, DERBYSHIRE 5–2C

Hassop Hall £38 🅐★

DE45 1NS (01629) 640488
"Elegant but not OTT", this *"welcoming"* country house hotel
is unanimously hailed by reporters for its *"excellent"* cuisine and its
"romantic" setting. / **Sample dishes:** *smoked chicken & avcocado salad with
bacon, orange & honey dressing; grilled fillet steak Rossini; vanilla & dark chocolate
mousse.* **Details:** *9 pm; closed Mon L & Sun D; no smoking.*

HASTINGS, EAST SUSSEX 3–4C

The Mermaid Café £15 ★★

2 Rock-a-Nore Rd TN34 3DW (01424) 438100
"Sublime" fish and chips are vouched for by all who report on this
celebrated seaside café; it's a pretty classy joint, too – the wine list
"extends all the way from box-white to box-red!"
/ **Sample dishes:** *prawn salad; skate & chips; spotted dick & custard.*
Details: *7.30 pm; no credit cards; no booking, except D in winter.*

HATCH END, GREATER LONDON 3–3A

Rotisserie £32

316 Uxbridge Rd HA5 4HR (020) 8421 2878
*"I used to be a fan of the Shepherd's Bush branch, and I'm really
chuffed to find one in Hatch End"* – this outpost of the small, no-
fuss rôtisserie chain brings good-value grills to the burbs.
/ **Sample dishes:** *char-grilled spare ribs; ostrich with red wine & garlic sauce;
maple & pecan bread pudding.* **Details:** *www.therotisserie.co.uk; 10.30 pm;
Mon-Thu D only, Fri-Sun open L & D.*

Sea Pebbles £24 ★
348-352 Uxbridge Rd HA5 4HR (020) 8428 0203
*"Just like authentic chippies up North" – this "nice and clean"
establishment serves "excellent fish and chips", and "good side
dishes" too. / Sample dishes: calamari rings; deep-fried scampi & chips;
bread & butter pudding. Details: 9.45 pm; closed Mon L & Sun; only Switch;
need 10+ to book.*

HATFIELD PEVEREL, ESSEX 3–2C

Blue Strawberry £35
The Street CM3 2DW (01245) 381333
*Hailed as a "wonderful venue" in the locality, this busy modern
bistro makes an unusual find in a rural cottage in the middle
of nowhere; all reporters praise its "good-value" cooking, but it
doesn't scale the heights it once did. / Sample dishes: Colchester oysters;
duck with prune & pistachio stuffing; dark chocolate & raisin pudding. Details: 3m
E of Chelmsford; 10 pm; closed Sat L & Sun D.*

HATHERSAGE, DERBYSHIRE 5–2C

The Plough Inn £31
Leadmill Bridge S32 1BA (01433) 650319
*This well-known inn on the banks of the Derwent, inside the Peak
District National Park, serves a "large" menu that fans find
"exceptional for a pub"; there are those, however, who say it's
"pretentious, and not brilliantly executed". / Sample dishes: wild
mushroom & leek tart; Hungarian pork hot pot with leeks & saffron rice; bread &
butter pudding. Details: www.theploughinn-hathersage.com; 9.30 pm; no Amex;
no smoking in dining room; booking: max 10; children: 5+. Accommodation: 5
rooms, from £69.50.*

HAWORTH, WEST YORKSHIRE 5–1C

Weavers £35 🅐★
15 West Ln BD22 8DU (01535) 643822
*"What a gem!" – Colin & Jane Rushworth's "no-nonsense" venture
(a converted row of cottages near the Brontë Museum) wins warm
all-round praise for the "friendly folk" who serve, the "romantic"
setting and the "remarkably consistent" modern cooking.
/ Sample dishes: monkfish, scallops & prawns; seared pork with wilted greens;
sticky toffee pudding. Details: www.weaverssmallhotel.co.uk; 1.5m W on B6142
from A629, near Parsonage; 9.15 pm; closed Mon, Tue L, Sat L & Sun D;
no smoking in dining room. Accommodation: 3 rooms, from £80.*

HAYWARDS HEATH, WEST SUSSEX 3–4B

Jeremys at Borde Hill £37 🅐★★
Balcombe Rd RH16 1XP (01444) 441102
*Most reporters "can't wait to go back" to Jereremy Ashpool's "lovely"
small establishment, set in extensive gardens; "friendly", "unrushed"
service delivers "fabulous" dishes, that just "melt in the mouth".
/ Sample dishes: prawn bisque with prawn & coriander dumplings; rabbit with
bubble 'n' squeak; apple & rhubarb tart. Details: www.homeofgoodfood.co.uk;
15m S of M23, J10a; 10 pm; closed Mon & Sun D; no smoking.*

HAZLEWOOD, NORTH YORKSHIRE   5–3C

1086
Hazlewood Castle Hotel   £ 44
Paradise Ln LS24 9NJ (01937) 535354
*Mixed feedback again characterised reports on the dining room
at this "beautiful castle set in acres of grounds"; even those who
thought it "pompous and stuffy", though, praised the "gorgeous"
setting, and the cooking, if "overpriced", is generally "interesting".
/ **Sample dishes:** hot smoked salmon with dried fruit chutney; salmon with oriental
greens; 'predictable' cheese & biscuits. **Details:** www.hazlewood-castle.co.uk;
signposted off A64; 9.30 pm; closed Mon, Tue-Sat D only, Sun open L &
D; no smoking; children: before 7 pm only. **Accommodation:** 21 rooms,
from £140.*

HELMSLEY, NORTH YORKSHIRE   8–4C

Black Swan   £ 38
Market Pl YO62 5BJ (01439) 770466
*This "comfortable" town-centre hotel (in the Macdonald Hotels
stable) makes a satisfactory spot of a fairly "traditional" variety;
note that lunchtime fare tends to "snacky". / **Sample dishes:** poached
egg & smoked salmon with caviar hollandaise; duck breast & confit leg with
raspberry jus; vodka & lime parfait. **Details:** www.macdonaldhotels.co.uk; 9 pm;
no smoking. **Accommodation:** 45 rooms, from £77.*

HENLEY IN ARDEN, WEST MIDLANDS   5–4C

Edmunds   £ 35   ★
64 High St B95 5BX
(01564) 795666
*Chef Andy Waters (ex Simpson's in Kenilworth) has made
a "storming start" at his year-old venture in a brightly revamped
half-timbered house – "good-quality ingredients are locally sourced
and cooked with care"; it's already "always packed", and can
be "difficult to book". / **Sample dishes:** pan-fried sea scallops; fillet of lamb
with hotpot; poached pear with hazelnut cream & caramel sauce.
Details: 9.45 pm; closed Mon, Sat L & Sun; no Amex; no smoking; booking: max 6.*

HEREFORD, HEREFORDSHIRE   2–1B

Floodgates
Left Bank   £ 38   𝔸★
20-22 Bridge St HR4 9DF (01432) 349009
*"In the heart of the city" – and with "a lovely riverside setting,
complete with terrace" – this "very impressive" brasserie, part of
a modern development, has made quite a stir, not least for its "fine"
and "imaginative" cooking. / **Details:** www.leftbank.co.uk; 10 pm.*

La Rive at Castle House
Castle House Hotel   £ 53
Castle St HR1 2NW (01432) 356321
*The dining room at this townhouse hotel (in a listed Georgian
building) wins praise for its "pleasant" style and its dependable
cooking; being by the river, it makes a "great location on a sunny
day". / **Sample dishes:** Thai risotto with tempura frogs legs; salmon & crab
brandade with lobster won tons; Pimm's jelly with cucumber ice.
Details: www.castlehse.co.uk; 10 pm; no jeans or trainers; no smoking in dining
room. **Accommodation:** 15 rooms, from £165.*

HERSHAM, SURREY   3–3A

Dining Room   **£34**   𝔸★
10 Queens Rd KT12 5LS (01932) 231686
"Traditional English tucker at its best" wins consistent praise for this
"friendly and cosy" fixture – *"a must for lovers of old-style home
cooking"*. / **Sample dishes:** *Double Gloucester, ale & mustard pot; lamb & mint
pie; spotted dick.* **Details:** *www.the-dining-room.co.uk; just off A3, by village green;
10.30 pm; closed Sat L & Sun D; no smoking area.*

HERSTMONCEUX, EAST SUSSEX   3–4B

Sundial   **£50**   ★
Gardner St BN27 4LA (01323) 832217
*Fans praise "excellent" Gallic cuisine and "attentive" service at this
"comfortable" fixture, run by the Mary & Vincent Rongier; doubters
can find it "pricey", though, for what it is.* / **Sample dishes:** *langoustine
tails with vegetable tempura; sea bass with stuffed courgette flowers; Breton
shortbread with lime & basil sorbet.* **Details:** *9.30 pm; closed Mon & Sun D;
no Amex; no smoking in dining room.* **Accommodation:** *1 room, at about £85.*

HETTON, NORTH YORKSHIRE   5–1B

The Angel   **£37**   𝔸★★
BD23 6LT (01756) 730263
"Amazingly good food, for the price" (with fish a highlight) and
a *"comprehensive and sensibly-priced wine list"* have helped make
this *"splendid"* Dales *"institution"* one of the country's best-loved
pubs; it may be *"remote"*, but it still gets *"crowded"*.
/ **Sample dishes:** *black pudding with lentils & pancetta; rack of lamb with thyme
mash; sticky toffee pudding.* **Details:** *www.angelhetton.co.uk; 5m N of Skipton off
B6265 at Rylstone; 9 pm; D only, except Sun when L only; no smoking area.*
Accommodation: *5 rooms, from £120.*

HINTLESHAM, SUFFOLK   3–1C

Hintlesham Hall   **£48**   𝔸
Dodge St IP8 3NS (01473) 652334
"The epitome of grandeur" – the fine country house hotel first made
famous by Robert Carrier maintains *"a very impressive,
and traditionally romantic ambience"; most reporters are also
impressed by the food, but there is also a minority that finds
it "disappointing".* / **Sample dishes:** *smoked haddock, mussel & roast
vegetable salad; lamb chump with harissa mash; iced raspberry parfait.*
Details: *www.hintleshamhall.com; 4m W of Ipswich on A1071; 9.30 pm; closed
Sat L; jacket & tie required; no smoking; children: 12+.* **Accommodation:** *33
rooms, from £110.*

HISTON, CAMBRIDGESHIRE   3–1B

Phoenix   **£26**
20 The Green CB4 4JA (01223) 233766
*Fans rate this "very popular" Chinese, near the village green,
as "well above average"; others though claim the place is "over-
rated", in particular citing poor service.* / **Details:** *10.30 pm; no Amex
or Switch; no smoking area.*

HOCKLEY HEATH, WARWICKSHIRE   5–4C

Nuthurst Grange   £ 65
Nuthurst Grange Ln B94 5NL   (01564) 783972
*Off the M40 – about half-way between Birmingham and Stratford –
this "accommodating" country house hotel is a useful place in an
area without a huge number of rival attractions; gripes this year
included that it can be "expensive", or that its dishes "offer too
many competing flavours".* / **Sample dishes:** tomato, red pepper & olive oil
soup; smoked sirloin steak with artichokes & wild mushrooms; Victoria plum & ginger
soufflé. **Details:** www.nuthurst-grange.com; J4 off M42, A3400; 9.30 pm; closed
Sat L; no jeans or trainers; no smoking area. **Accommodation:** 15 rooms,
from £165.

HOGNASTON, DERBYSHIRE   5–3C

Red Lion   £ 28   ★
Main St DE6 1PR   (01335) 370396
*The "extensive" menu here is "surprisingly exotic, for a pub" –
not least once located on the fringe of the Peak District – and all
reporters spoke favourably of the place's "friendly" atmosphere,
and "superb value for money".* / **Sample dishes:** New Zealand green-lipped
mussels; warm smoked chicken salad; whisky bread & butter pudding.
Details: www.lionrouge.com; 8.45 pm; closed Mon & Sun D; no smoking area;
no booking Sun L; children: 5+. **Accommodation:** 3 rooms, from £80.

HOLKHAM, NORFOLK   6–3C

Victoria Hotel   £ 43
Park Rd NR23 1RG   (01328) 711008
*"The Raj meets the coast" at this trendified former pub (with rooms)
opposite one of Norfolk's best beaches; supporters say "it tries hard
and almost gets there", but, for critics, it just serves "ordinary food
at London prices".* / **Sample dishes:** smoked eel with apple & horseradish
vinaigrette; venison with creamed cabbage & chocolate sauce; tarte Tatin with green
apple sorbet. **Details:** www.victoriaatholkham.co.uk; 9.30 pm; no Amex; no smoking
area; children: 7+ at D. **Accommodation:** 11 rooms, from £110.

HOLT, NORFOLK   6–3C

Yetman's   £ 48   ★
37 Norwich Rd NR25 6SA   (01263) 713320
*"Quirky, friendly and very fairly-priced"; Alison and Peter Yetman
"really know their stuff", and their (perhaps slightly "twee") cottage-
restaurant makes a "reliably very good" destination.*
/ **Sample dishes:** Louisiana crabcakes with red pepper mayonnaise; char-grilled
duck with spiced figs; passion fruit & mango bombe. **Details:** www.yetmans.net;
on A148, 20m N of Norwich; 9.30 pm; D only, except Sun when L only (open Sun D
Jul & Aug); no smoking in dining room.

HONLEY, WEST YORKSHIRE   5–2C

Mustard & Punch   £ 30
6 Westgate HD9 6AA   (01484) 662066
*Reporters say only good things about this "homely" and "down-to-
earth" village bistro – even those who find the cooking
"unadventurous" note that it's "sound".* / **Sample dishes:** veal sweetbread
ravioli with langoustine consommé; venison with oxtail macaroni & chanterelles; white
chocolate tart. **Details:** www.mustardandpunch.com; 10 pm; closed Mon, Sat L &
Sun; booking: max 6, Sat.

HOOK, HAMPSHIRE   2–3D

Tylney Hall   £55   A★
Rotherwick RG27 9AZ   (01256) 764881
The formal dining room at the heart of this "beautiful" 18th-century
building can deliver some "very very good" contemporary cooking;
even some fans feel "it's declined of late", though, and one reporter
who stayed for a week found standards "inconsistent".
/ **Sample dishes:** goats cheese & sweet pepper terrine; lamb with roast
Mediterranean vegetables; chocolate & Grand Marnier soufflé.
Details: www.tylneyhall.com; 9.45 pm; jacket and/or tie required; no smoking
in dining room. **Accommodation:** 112 rooms, from £165.

HORNDON ON THE HILL, ESSEX   3–3C

The Bell Inn   £33   A★
High Rd SS17 8LD   (01375) 642463
"A lovely old pub, with an excellent restaurant serving top-quality
food in pleasant surroundings" – one reporter speaks for all on the
qualities of this "small and historic" boozer. / **Sample dishes:** sweet
potato & garlic soup; roast duck with stuffed squid & parsnips; apple crumble with
praline ice cream. **Details:** www.bell-inn.co.uk; signposted off B1007, off A13;
9.45 pm; no smoking in dining room. **Accommodation:** 15 rooms, from £50.

HORTON, NORTHANTS   3–1A

The New French Partridge   £36   ★
Newport Pagnell Rd NN7 2AP   (01604) 870033
"The New French Partridge is spot on" – that's the universal verdict
on this village restaurant (relaunched by a husband-and-wife team
in December 2002 after a closure of almost two years);
the "atmosphere is easier", nowadays, and the cuisine
is "promising", too. / **Sample dishes:** galatine of chicken, boudin noir, guinea
fowl, sauce gribiche; rack of lamb, three-peppercorn crust with vegetable gâteau &
redcurrant jus; raspberry brulée with blackcurrant sorbet.
Details: www.newfrenchpartridge.co.uk; on B526 between Newport Pagnell &
Northampton; 9.30 pm; closed Mon & Sun; no credit cards; no jeans; mainly
non-smoking.

HOUGHTON CONQUEST, BEDFORDSHIRE   3–2A

Knife & Cleaver   £35
The Grove MK45 3LA   (01234) 740387
"A bright conservatory" provides the setting for dining at this former
17th-century inn (now a restaurant-with-rooms); most reporters
applauded its "rich", "well-presented" fare, but it can also seem
"a bit pricey" or "dull". / **Sample dishes:** salt cod tortilla with black olive
sauce; beef with wild mushrooms, Stilton & crispy onions; chocolate marquise with
raspberry coulis. **Details:** www.knifeandcleaver.com; off A6, 5m S of Bedford;
9.30 pm; closed Sat L & Sun D; no smoking. **Accommodation:** 9 rooms,
from £53.

HOYLAKE, MERSEYSIDE   5–2A

Linos   £32   ★
122 Market St CH47 3BH   (0151) 632 1408
"First class" ("rich") Anglo/French cooking and "impeccable" service
make the Galantini family's restaurant "a well-established favourite".
/ **Sample dishes:** three cheese & onion tartlet; roast duck with bitter sweet orange
sauce; nut, rum & raisin chocolates. **Details:** 3m from M53, J2; 10 pm; closed
Mon & Sun; closed Aug; no Amex.

HUDDERSFIELD, WEST YORKSHIRE 5–1C

Bradley's £26 ★
84 Fitzwilliam St HD1 5BB (01484) 516773
"Friendly service and reliable food" – that's the combination at this town-centre spot, which is often quite *"lively"*, too; there's an *"excellent-value"* set lunch. / **Sample dishes:** chicken fritters with peanut & lime dip; roast lamb with cherry tomato couscous; mango tart with caramel ice cream. **Details:** www.bradleysrestaurant.co.uk; 10 pm; closed Sat L & Sun L; no Amex; no smoking area.

Nawaab £26 ★
35 Westgate HD1 1NY (01484) 422775
The presence of "many regulars" attests to the "excellent" general standards at this popular curry house, which is "always busy". / **Details:** www.nawaab.com; between bus & railway stations; 11 pm, Fri & Sat midnight; D only.

HULL, KINGSTON UPON HULL 6–2A

Cerutti's £38 ★
10 Nelson St HU1 1XE (01482) 328501
"Lots of nooks and crannies" add character to this locally famous fish place – in the old Georgian Station Master's House, overlooking the Humber – whose ambience is *"lovely"* or *"sombre"*, to taste; there's general agreement, though, that it serves *"consistently good food"*, if at prices some find a bit *"silly"*. / **Sample dishes:** seared scallops served with black pudding; roast fillet of turbot with a crayfish sauce; double chocolate mousse. **Details:** www.ceruttis.co.uk; follow signs to the fruit market; 9.30 pm; closed Sat L & Sun; smoking in bar only.

Hitchcocks £16 Ⓐ★
1 Bishop Ln HU1 1PA (01482) 320233
A *"unique atmosphere"* created by an old warehouse location adds to the appeal of this *"top-class veggie"*; *"the first person to book for any particular evening gets to choose the culinary theme!"* (indeed, they only open if they have at least one booking). / **Sample dishes:** guacamole & bean dip; veggie satay with fried noodles; pecan pie. **Details:** follow signs to Old Town or Museums Quarter; 8.30 pm; D only, closed Mon & Sun; no credit cards; booking essential.

HUNTINGDON, CAMBRIDGESHIRE 3–1B

Old Bridge Hotel £43 Ⓐ
1 High St PE29 3TQ (01480) 424300
"Good food served with style" (and accompanied by an *"excellent wine list"*) wins mainly positive reports for the dining room of this hotel in an 18th-century building by the River Ouse; it *"can have its off-days"*, though. / **Sample dishes:** garlic & mushroom risotto with parsley; roast salmon with Swiss chard & mussels; lemon tart.
Details: www.huntsbridge.com; off A1, off A14; 10 pm; no smoking in dining room. **Accommodation:** 24 rooms, from £105.

Pheasant Inn £36
Loop Rd PE28 0RE (01832) 710241
"Superior food, for a pub" still wins praise for this quite *"formal"* thatched inn – part of the Huntsbridge group which also own Madingley's Three Horseshoes. / **Sample dishes:** deep-fried Brie de meaux; lamb fillet with vegetables & bread; vanilla & lavender panna cotta with red fruits. **Details:** www.huntsbridge.com; 1m S of A14 between Huntingdon & Kettering, J15; 9.30 pm; no smoking area.

ILKLEY, WEST YORKSHIRE   5–1C

Bettys   £29
32-34 The Grove LS29 9EE   (01943) 608029
"As good as ever despite the queues" – these "very bustling
tearooms" provide a comforting venue for a light bite or bun;
"you pay for tradition, though". / **Sample dishes:** Swiss potato rosti;
Yorkshire rarebit with apple chutney; fresh fruit tart.
Details: www.bettysandtaylors.com; L & afternoon tea only; no Amex; no smoking;
no booking.

The Box Tree   £45   ✗
35-37 Church St LS29 9DR   (01943) 608484
"What a let-down!"; this "stuffy and old-fashioned" (but still-famous)
restaurant is "vastly, vastly over-rated" in some circles, and a high
proportion of reporters find a visit here simply a "cold",
"disappointing" or "depressing" experience. / **Sample dishes:** roast
quail & hazelnut salad; sea bass with lobster & fennel; honey & lime crème brûlée.
Details: www.theboxtree.co.uk; on A65 near town centre; 9.30 pm; closed Mon &
Sun D; closed 2 weeks in Jan; no smoking in dining room.

Far Syde   £31   ★
1-3 Brook St LS29 8DQ   (01943) 602030
This "troughing spot for Ilkley yuppies" is "always full" and can
be "a bit noisy", but it offers an "interesting" daily-changing menu
that's served by "cheerful" staff. / **Sample dishes:** chicken & prawn risotto;
lamb wrapped in Mozzarella & aubergine; cappuccino cup. **Details:** 10 pm; closed
Mon & Sun; no Amex; no smoking area.

ILMINGTON, WARWICKSHIRE   2–1C

The Howard Arms   £31   𝔸
Lower Grn CV36 4LT   (01608) 682226
"There's every ingredient for a good evening out", say fans of this
"airy" pub on the village green, which offers "good-value" cooking
in a "lovely" atmosphere. / **Sample dishes:** avocado, French bean & bacon
salad; beef, ale & mustard pie; pear, plum & apple flapjack crumble.
Details: www.howardarms.com; 8m SW of Stratford-upon-Avon off A4300; 9 pm;
no Amex; no smoking area; children: 8+ after 7 pm. **Accommodation:** 3 rooms,
from £84.

IPSWICH, SUFFOLK   3–1D

Baipo   £23
63 Upper Orwell St IP4 1HP   (01473) 218402
"Very consistent and authentic", this town-centre Thai attracts only
positive reports; it's all the more worth knowing about in an area
without a huge number of competing attractions.
/ **Details:** www.baipo.co.uk; 10.45 pm; closed Mon L & Sun.

The Galley   £38   ★
25 St Nicholas St IP1 1TW   (01473) 281131
"Wonderful Mediterranean food with a nod to Turkey" (betraying
the origins of the chef) again wins praise for this trendy, town-centre
bistro. / **Sample dishes:** crispy Feta & parsley filo pastry; Norfolk smoked trout;
Belgian chocolate delice. **Details:** www.galley.uk.com; 10 pm (11 pm in summer);
closed Sun; no smoking area.

Mortimer's Seafood Restaurant   £31   ★
1 Duke St IP3 0AE   (01473) 230225
*Some find the new non-waterside location of this long-established restaurant "strange" and "less atmospheric" than of old, but the "great selection of fresh fish" is "just as good, if not better, than before". / **Sample dishes:** Brittany sardines with garlic butter; swordfish & tuna kebab with smoked paprika; baked apple & almond pudding.* **Details:** *www.mortimersrestaurant.com; 9.15 pm, Mon 8.30 pm; closed Sun; no smoking in dining room.*

IRONBRIDGE, SHROPSHIRE   5–4B

Malt House Inn   £28
The Wharfage TF8 7NH   (01952) 433712
*"Lively crowds and great atmosphere", or "a bit noisy and impersonal"? – either way, this "reliable" and "nicely-located" boozer (which occasionally features "live music") serves "good burgers" and the like. / **Sample dishes:** white crab salad beetroot tartare; roast chump of lamb; lemon pudding with ginger fudge sauce.* **Details:** *www.malthousepubs.co.uk; 500 metres from the Iron Bridge; 9.45 pm; no Amex; smoking in bar only.* **Accommodation:** *9 rooms, from £65.*

IVINGHOE, BEDFORDSHIRE   3–2A

Kings Head   £55
Station Rd LU7 9EB   (01296) 668388
*This '70s survivor, in an old beamed building, is known particularly for its Aylesbury Duck; it can seem "very expensive, for the quality of cooking". / **Sample dishes:** tomato, Mozzarella & chorizo tartlet; pink bream with lobster risotto & fennel; lemon tart with berry compote.* **Details:** *www.kingsheadivinghoe.co.uk; 3m N of Tring on B489 to Dunstable; 9.45 pm; closed Sun D; jacket & tie required at D; no smoking in dining room.*

JERSEY, CHANNEL ISLANDS

Longueville Manor   £63   A★
Longueville Rd, St Saviour JE2 7WF   (01534) 725501
*"One of the best", say fans of this grand (Relais & Châteaux) manor house hotel; it provides a "wonderful" setting for some "first-rate cuisine". / **Sample dishes:** foie gras terrine with orange salad & brioche; brill & calamari with aromatic noodles; mint & white chocolate soufflé.* **Details:** *www.longuevillemanor.com; 9.30 pm; no smoking area.* **Accommodation:** *31 rooms, from £230.*

JEVINGTON, EAST SUSSEX   3–4B

Hungry Monk   £42   A
BN26 5QF   (01323) 482178
*"You can cosy up in a tiny inglenook" at this "picture postcard" '60s survivor – "lots of tiny cottages knocked into one" – to which a visit is certainly "an experience"; as ever, though, critics find it "complacent" – "even the famous Banoffi pie was disappointing". / **Sample dishes:** crab & avocado tian; lamb with Moroccan spiced crust & butternut squash; baked chocolate & raspberry Alaska.* **Details:** *www.hungrymonk.co.uk; 5m W of Eastbourne; 9.30 pm; D only, except Sun open L & D; no smoking in dining room; children: 5+.*

KELSALE, SUFFOLK   3–1D
Harrisons   £33
Main Rd IP17 2RF   (01728) 604444
"Peter Harrison uses fresh local ingredients and cooks them superbly", say fans of this thatched cottage-restaurant, whose proud possession of a Michelin bib gourmand has put it modestly on the map; it inspires notably up-and-down commentary, though, and there are those who say *"the whole formula needs tweaking"*. / **Sample dishes:** spiced aubergine with yoghurt & mint; rack of lamb with haricot beans. **Details:** off the A12; 9.45 pm; closed Mon & Sun; no Amex; no smoking; children: no babies at D.

KENILWORTH, WARWICKSHIRE   5–4C
Bosquet   £44   ★
97a Warwick Rd CV8 1HP   (01926) 852463
"There's no atmosphere, but the food is lovely" at Jane & Bernard Lignier's *"relaxed"* and *"unpretentious"* Gallic fixture, where the *"best ingredients are deftly treated"*. / **Sample dishes:** watercress soup with caviar; roast veal with chive & cream sauce; blueberry & almond tart. **Details:** 9.30 pm; closed Mon, Sat L & Sun; closed Aug.

Simpsons   £47   ★
101-103 Warwick Rd CV8 1HL   (01926) 864567
"Locally, you just can't beat it" – the Antona family's town-centre veteran has quite a name for its *"top-notch"* modern cooking, but it drew some flak from reporters this year, in particular for its *"poor"* atmosphere. / **Sample dishes:** crab tart with smoked salmon; roast brill with spring vegetables; turrón parfait with marinated pineapple. **Details:** www.simpsons-restaurant.co.uk; 10 pm; closed Mon & Sun; no smoking area.

KINCLAVAN, PERTH & KINROSS   9–3C
Ballathie House   £50   Ⓐ
PH1 4QN   (01250) 883268
This grand country house hotel, overlooking the River Tay, attracted only modest commentary this year, but such as there was praised its *"delicious"* and *"good-value"* fare. / **Sample dishes:** game sausage with lentils & bacon; seared scallops with chilli polenta & pesto; citrus tart. **Details:** www.ballathiehousehotel.com; off B9099, take right from 1m N of Stanley; 8.45 pm; jacket & tie; no smoking. **Accommodation:** 42 rooms, from £170.

KINGSTON UPON THAMES, GREATER LONDON   3–3B
Ayudhya   £30   ★
14 Kingston Hill KT2 7NH   (020) 8549 5984
"For many years, a most reliable Thai" – this *"cramped"*, *"neighbourhood"* Kingston Hill oriental wins consistent praise from locals for its *"simple"* and *"fresh-tasting"* fare. / **Sample dishes:** chicken sauté; spicy seafood; butternut toffee pudding. **Details:** 10.30 pm; no smoking area.

Frère Jacques   £30   Ⓐ
10-12 Riverside Walk KT1 1QN   (020) 8546 1332
"A great location on the river" is the prime asset of this *"jolly and friendly"* 'restaurant-bar-cafe', near Kingston Bridge, which is praised for its *"honest French bistro food"*. / **Sample dishes:** smoked salmon; liver; crème brûlée. **Details:** www.frerejacques.co.uk; next to Kingston Bridge and the market place; 11 pm; no smoking area.

KINGUSSIE, HIGHLAND
9–2C

The Cross
£ 48
𝔸★

Tweed Mill Brae, Ardbroilach Rd PH21 ITC
(01540) 661166

It's still early days for the new régime at this eminent restaurant-with-rooms in a former mill; an early reporter, however, speaks in the most positive terms of the "straightforward" cooking, from seasonal produce. / **Sample dishes:** *scallop & prawn sausage with fennel; saddle of lamb with rosemary & red wine sauce; lime cheesecake.* **Details:** *www.thecross.co.uk; head uphill on Ardbroilach Rd, turn left into private drive after traffic lights; 8.30 pm; D only, closed Mon & Sun; no smoking area.* **Accommodation:** *8 rooms, from £95.*

KIRKBY LONSDALE, CUMBRIA
7–4D

Snooty Fox Hotel
£ 29

Main St LA6 2AH (01524) 271308

Standards seem to be on the mend at this once-celebrated town-centre hostelry, now in group ownership; it's "nothing fancy", mind, but most reports are of "good basics, served with a welcoming smile". / **Sample dishes:** *duck & pistachio parfait; smoked haddock risotto; sticky toffee pudding.* **Details:** *www.mortal-man-inns.co.uk; off A65, 6m from M6, J36; 10 pm; no smoking area.* **Accommodation:** *9 rooms, from £56.*

KNIGHTWICK, WORCESTERSHIRE
2–1B

The Talbot
£ 34

WR6 5PH (01886) 821235

"Fine locally-grown food" makes this riverside coaching inn and brewery a popular local destination; even those who say it's "usually reliable", however, may concede that "disappointments are not unknown". / **Sample dishes:** *warm game liver salad; roast sea bass with pesto; sticky toffee pudding.* **Details:** *www.the-talbot.co.uk; 9m from Worcester on A44; 9 pm; no smoking area.* **Accommodation:** *11 rooms, from £69.50.*

KNUTSFORD, CHESHIRE
5–2B

Belle Époque
£ 37
𝔸

King St WA16 6DT (01565) 633060

A "more inviting" new menu seems to be winning more approval for this "sophisticated" Art Nouveau landmark (which some think of as "the grande dame of Cheshire eateries") – the "amazing setting", however, is still a greater attraction (especially for those with romance in mind). / **Sample dishes:** *Tuscan spring salad; sea bass with red onion salsa; apricot fritters with Cointreau mousse.* **Details:** *1.5m from M6, J19; 10 pm; closed Sat D & Sun D; no smoking area.* **Accommodation:** *6 rooms, from £80.*

LACOCK, WILTSHIRE
2–2C

At the Sign of the Angel
£ 37
𝔸

6 Church St SN15 2LB (01249) 730230

"A location in a beautiful 14th century building in the middle of a quaint village owned by the National Trust" makes this a destination of some interest; otherwise, "more could be made of the place". / **Sample dishes:** *Stilton & walnut pâté; steak & kidney pudding; crème brûlée.* **Details:** *www.lacock.co.uk; close to M4, J17; 9 pm; closed Mon L.* **Accommodation:** *10 rooms, from £99.*

LALESTON, VALE OF GLAMORGAN   1–1D
Great House   £36
CF32 0HP   (01656) 657644
*"Excellent lunch menus" are a top tip at this comfortable dining
room, part of a "lovely" small country house hotel.*
*/ **Details:** www.great-house-laleston.co.uk; 9.30 pm; closed Sun D; no smoking.*

LANCASTER, LANCASHIRE   5–1A
Bay Horse   £31   ★
Bay Horse Ln LA2 0HR   (01524) 791204
*An "up and coming" pub, just off the M6, praised by locals for its
contemporary menu of surprising quality; seafood is "particularly
good". / **Sample dishes:** potted Morecambe Bay shrimps; braised lamb with ale &
thyme sauce; lemon tart & lemon fruit ice. **Details:** www.bayhorseinn.com; 0.75m
S of A6, J33 M6; 9.30 pm; closed Mon & Sun D; no Amex; no smoking in dining
room.*

Pizza Margherita   £20   ★
2 Moor Ln LA1 1QD   (01524) 36333
*"Top-notch pizza" is the draw to this "long-established Lancaster
institution" (founded by the sister of the founder of PizzaExpress),
universally hailed by reporters for its "reliable" standards.
/ **Sample dishes:** garlic bread with cheese; pizza; dime bar crunch pie.
Details: www.pizza-margherita.co.uk; 10.30 pm.*

Simply French   £24   𝔸
27a St Georges Quay LA1 1RD   (01524) 843199
*With its "varied, well-presented food", "cheerful" staff and "lively"
ambience, this riverside bistro ticks all the boxes to be considered
a "reliable" local destination. / **Sample dishes:** baked courgette stuffed with
spinach & salmon mousse; chicken marinated in lemon & olive oil; apricot tart.
Details: 9.30 pm; Mon-Thu D only, Fri-Sun open L & D; no Amex.*

Sultan of Lancaster   £17   𝔸★
Old Church, Brock St LA1 1UU   (01524) 61188
*"A fantastic restoration of a Methodist church, in Asian style" has
created a "wonderful" setting for this "well above average curry
house"; its "genuine Pakistani food" is even "good enough
to compensate for the lack of alcohol"!
/ **Details:** www.sultanoflancaster.com; 11 pm; D only; no Amex; no smoking area.*

Sun Café   £33   ★
Sun Street Studios, 25 Sun St LA1 1EW   (01524) 845599
*"Stylish" and "friendly", this café adjoining an art gallery remains
generally popular for its "generous portions of home-cooked fare".
/ **Sample dishes:** asparagus & poached egg with Parmesan; scallops & shrimps
with teryaki dressing; cheesecake with pistachios & honey. **Details:** 9.30 pm; closed
Sun D; closed Mon-Tue D unless booked.*

LANGAR, NOTTINGHAMSHIRE   5–3D
Langar Hall   £44   𝔸
NG13 9HG   (01949) 860559
*A "lovely" setting helps boost feedback on this "nice country house
hotel"; most reporters find the cooking "interesting", too, but there
are also those for whom it's "over-rated". / **Sample dishes:** asparagus &
pea soup; roast duck with citrus sauce; banana parfait with caramel ice.
Details: www.langarhall.com; off A52 between Nottingham & Grantham; 9.30 pm,
Sat 10 pm; no Amex; no smoking area. **Accommodation:** 12 rooms, from £90.*

---

sign up for the survey at www.hardens.com   *231*

LANGHO, LANCASHIRE   5–1B
Northcote Manor   £61   Ⓐ★★
Northcote Rd BB6 8BE (01254) 240555
*"Nigel Haworth gets better and better", say fans of his "refined and
excellent" cooking – probably the best in the North West – which
is known for its use of local ingredients; his restaurant-with-rooms –
a "comfortable" Victorian villa in the Ribble Valley – also wins praise
for its "professional, but unstuffy" approach.* / **Sample dishes:** *black
pudding & pink trout with nettle sauce; Pendle lamb with lemon marmalade & chive
mash; apple crumble soufflé with Lancashire cheese ice cream.*
Details: *www.northcotemanor.com; M6, J31 then A59; 9.30 pm; closed Sat L;
no smoking.* **Accommodation:** *14 rooms, from £130.*

LANGTON GREEN, KENT   3–4B
The Hare   £27
Langton Rd TN3 0JA (01892) 862419
*A "big", "attractive" and "busy" gastropub, "overlooking the village
green"; many reporters note its "generous portions", but some find
prices "over-generous", too.* / **Sample dishes:** *bacon, lentil & goats cheese
tart; seared salmon with sweetcorn fritters; Malibu roulade with pineapple.*
Details: *www.hare-tunbridgewells.co.uk; on A264 to East Grinstead; 9.30 pm;
no Amex; no smoking area.*

LAPWORTH, WARWICKSHIRE   5–4C
The Boot   £35
Old Warwick Rd B94 6JU (01564) 782464
*This well-known (in these parts) boozer strikes some as a "showy
and pricey" sort of place; most, if not all, reporters find the food
"above-average" nonetheless.* / **Sample dishes:** *rustic bread with olive oil;
chicken with goats cheese & saffron; Bailey's cheesecake.*
Details: *www.thebootatlapworth.co.uk; off A34; 10 pm.*

LAVENHAM, SUFFOLK   3–1C
Angel   £30
Market Pl CO10 9QZ (01787) 247 388
*This 14th-century inn on the market place is "always full"
(and sometimes "too crowded") due to its "good food and wine".*
/ **Sample dishes:** *smoked salmon trout; ducks breast with juniper & mushroom
sauce; sticky pudding.* **Details:** *www.lavenham.co.uk/angel; on A1141 6m NE
of Sudbury; 9.15 pm; no smoking area; booking: max 14.* **Accommodation:** *8
rooms, from £75.*

Great House   £36   Ⓐ★★
Market Pl CO10 9QZ (01787) 247431
*"Excellent and authentic French cooking", served by "friendly and
attentive Gallic staff", wins consistent rave reviews for the Crépy
family's half-timbered restaurant-with-rooms, which overlooks the
market square.* / **Sample dishes:** *moules marinière; venison in red wine with
duck foie gras sauce; saffron crème brûlée.* **Details:** *www.greathouse.co.uk; follow
directions to Guildhall; 9.30 pm; closed Mon & Sun D; closed Jan; no smoking
in dining room.* **Accommodation:** *5 rooms, from £76.*

Swan Hotel   £38
High St CO10 9QA (01787) 247477
*All agree this "historic" inn has a "lovely" interior, complete with
"romantic" and "intimate" corners; a new chef seems to be pepping
the cooking up, but too many reporters still find it "boring" and
"overpriced".* / **Sample dishes:** *scallops & Parma ham with green bean salad;
sea bass with salt crust & lemon sauce; peach & thyme ice cream.*
Details: *www.macdonaldhotels.com; 9 pm; D only, except Sun open L &
D; no smoking.* **Accommodation:** *51 rooms, from £160.*

LEEDS, WEST YORKSHIRE   5–1C

Though the Leeds restaurant scene continues to develop along broadly positive lines, recent years have been short on the kind of exciting new openings that stir up particular interest. The town's top place remains – as it has been for some time – *Pool Court at 42.*

The city does boast a fair number of good mid-range restaurants. *No 3 York Place* rates mention for having maintained the standard set by its previous incumbent (well-known local chef, Simon Gueller), and other examples include *Brio*, *Casa Mia Grande*, and *Millrace*. On the basis of limited feedback, *Quantro* also seems to hold promise. In contrast, the well-established *Leodis* and *Sous le Nez* both generate many reports – on the basis of which they achieve middling ratings.

Italians continue to provide many of the best options. Aside from those mentioned above, the two best-known places – *Bibis* and *Salvos* – are arguably better known for their buzz than for their cooking.

There are also some good Indians, among which *Aagrah*, *Darbar* and *Hansa's* stand out.

Aagrah   £21   A ★
Aberford Rd LS25 1BA   (0113) 287 6606
With its "high standard of cooking" and "super-efficient service", this "bright and spacious" Indian is the best known of the Yorkshire chain; it may be huge, but it's "always busy".
/ **Details:** www.aagrah.co.uk; from A1 take A642 Aberford Rd to Garforth; 11.30 pm; D only; no smoking area.

Amigos   £18
70 Abbey Rd LS5 3JG   (0113) 228 3737
Near Kirkstall Abbey, this "scruffy" but "fun" tapas bar makes an "authentic" and "very cheap" rendezvous.
/ **Sample dishes:** meatballs in chilli & tomato sauce; paella; Manchego cheese with apple. **Details:** on A65 in Kirkstall; 11 pm; no Amex.

Art's Bar (Café)   £25   A
42 Call Ln LS1 6DT   (0113) 243 8243
Even those who say the food is "sometimes hit-and-miss" still find this "chilled" and "quirky" café/bar of long standing a "great" hang out; its "great-value lunch plates" are particularly praised.
/ **Sample dishes:** roast garlic & thyme risotto; crispy duck with halloumi & herb salad; Belgian chocolate cake. **Details:** www.artscafebar.co.uk; near Corn Exchange; 10.00 pm, Fri & Sat 10.30 pm; no booking, Sat L.

Bibis   £38   A
Minerva Hs, 16 Greek St LS1 5RU   (0113) 243 0905
"Rowdy and perennially packed", this vast city-centre Italian remains quite a destination – "it can't be the food, so it must be something to do with the fact it's been about so long". / **Sample dishes:** beef tomatoes with basil oil dressing; pigeon & foie gras terrine; chocolate & Amaretto cake. **Details:** www.bibisrestaurant.com; off Park Row; 11.15 pm, 10 pm Sun; no booking, Sat.

Brasserie Forty Four £38
44 The Calls LS2 7EW   (0113) 234 3232
*Even some fans say it's "pricey", but for the most part this "solid"
'90s brasserie wins consistent praise as a local "benchmark",
with "reliable" cooking and a "buzzy" ambience.*
*/ **Sample dishes:** home-made corned beef with beetroot relish; smoked cod with
leeks & Gorgonzola; Toblerone & Amaretto fondue. **Details:** www.brasserie44.com;
10.30 pm, Fri & Sat 11 pm; closed Sat L & Sun.*

Brio £36 ★
40 Great George St LS1 3DL   (0113) 246 5225
*"Fresh and interesting food in stylish surroundings" earns consistent
popularity for this "buzzy" city-centre Italian; ditto its new offshoot,
Brio Pizza (28 The Headrow, tel 243 5533). / **Sample dishes:** haricot
beans in chilli & wine sauce; seared tuna niçoise; panna cotta.
Details: www.brios.co.uk; 10.30 pm; closed Sun.*

Browns £29 Ⓐ
The Light, The Headrow LS1 8EQ   (0113) 243 9353
*"The location and décor are superb", say fans of this "enormous"
ex-banking hall branch of the national brasserie chain; the food,
though, is typically "disappointing". / **Sample dishes:** smoked salmon &
watercress salad; pan-fried bream with wilted spinach; hot fudge brownie with vanilla
ice cream. **Details:** www.browns-restaurants.com; 11 pm; no smoking area; need 6+
to book.*

Bryan's £25
9 Weetwood Ln LS16 5LT   (0113) 278 5679
*Oh dear!; some still tip it as "Leeds's best", but this celebrated
Headingley chippy "used to be much better", and some reporters
find it plain "disappointing" nowadays. / **Sample dishes:** chicken goujons
with spicy BBQ dip; Jumbo deep-fried haddock & chips; treacle sponge & custard.
Details: off Otterley Rd.; 9 pm; no Amex; no smoking; need 8+ to book.*

The Calls Grill £31
Calls Landing, 38 The Calls LS2 7EW   (0113) 245 3870
*"Grills with flair" and a "sophisticated modern atmosphere" are
hailed by fans of this canalside fixture; doubter, though, say it's
"mediocre, apart from the location". / **Sample dishes:** smoked tuna with
Spanish omelette; Dover sole with citrus butter; rice pudding bavarois.
Details: www.callsgrill.co.uk; opp Tetleys brewery on waterfront; 10.30 pm; D only,
closed Sun; booking: max 6, Sat.*

Casa Mia Grande £31 ★
33-35 Harrogate Rd LS7 3PD   (0113) 239 2555
*Though there are gripes that it's "over-rated", this "lively",
"crowded" and "noisy" Chapel Allerton Italian is hailed as a top
"cheap and cheerful" destination, which numbers "excellent fish"
and "lovely pizzas" among its gastronomic highlights; it has a sibling,
Casa Mia, at 10-12 Steinbeck Lane (tel 239 2555).
/ **Sample dishes:** smoked chicken salad with mango vinaigrette; honey-roast salmon
with spinach & lemon sauce; tiramisu. **Details:** www.casa-mia.co.uk; 10.30 pm;
no Amex; no smoking area.*

Darbar £29 Ⓐ★
16-17 Kirkgate LS1 6BY   (0113) 246 0381
*"Hidden away upstairs", this "fantastic" Indian provides "cracking"
curries in a "surprising" setting that wouldn't be out of place in a
"Maharajah's palace". / **Details:** www.darbar.co.uk; midnight; closed Sun.*

Dare Café £19
49 Otley Rd LS6 3AB (0113) 230 2828
A proprietor who's "always checking and eager to please" helps make this "friendly bistro-style café" a useful Headingley stand-by; the Mexican fare, though, can sometimes verge on "mediocre". / *Sample dishes:* tomato & Mozzarella salad; chicken fajitas; chocolate fudge cake. *Details:* 10 pm; no Amex; no smoking area.

Flying Pizza £29   Ⓐ
60 Street Ln LS8 2DQ (0113) 266 6501
"Wear lots of jewellery and a fake tan", if you don't want to stand out at this "beautiful people" pizzeria, which critics say is the 'San Lorenzo' of West Yorkshire – "only worth visiting to see who else is there". / *Sample dishes:* rolled Italian ham with Mozzarella; chicken with farfalle in spicy tomato sauce; tiramisu. *Details:* www.theflyingpizza.co.uk; just off A61, 3m N of city centre; 11 pm, Thu-Sat 11.30 pm; no smoking area; no booking at weekends.

Fourth Floor Café
Harvey Nichols £34
107-111 Briggate LS1 6AZ (0113) 204 8000
"Better for a drink than to eat" – though some see this outpost of AbFab chic as a "classy" venue, too many reporters just find it "depressing", "indifferent" and "overpriced"; even critics, though, concede that service is "solicitous". / *Sample dishes:* smoked chicken with pears & Roquefort; rib-eye steak with sweet potato mash; passion fruit mousse. *Details:* www.harveynichols.com; 10 pm; L only, except Thu-Sat when L & D; no smoking area; no booking, Sat L.

Fuji Hiro £16   ★
45 Wade Ln LS2 8NJ (0113) 243 9184
"Lovely fresh soup and noodles" are the mainstays of the "top-quality", "cheap 'n' cheerful" menu at this "basic" oriental café. / *Details:* 9.45 pm, Fri & Sat 10.45 pm; no credit cards; no smoking; need 5+ to book.

La Grillade £29
Wellington St LS1 4HJ (0113) 245 9707
"Still the place for a business lunch in Leeds, if steak and red wine are your thing" – this "little bit of France in the centre of town" is solidly supported for its "lively" ambience and its "authentic" cooking. / *Sample dishes:* French onion soup; char-grilled rib-eye steak; bread & butter pudding. *Details:* 10.30 pm; closed Sat L & Sun.

Hansa's £20   ★
72-74 North St LS2 7PN (0113) 244 4408
"Creative and very tasty Gujerati (veggie) food" has long been the draw to Mrs Hansa-Dabhi's "simple and cheap" fixture; it was back on more consistent form this year. / *Details:* www.hansas.co.uk; 10.30 pm; D only, closed Sun; no Amex; no smoking area; children: under 5s eat free.

Leodis £40
Victoria Mill, Sovereign St LS1 4BJ (0113) 242 1010
Opinions on this large canalside brasserie of over ten years standing remain divided; fans say it's a "professional" and "reliable" haunt with "lovely" food and a "perpetual buzz about it" – to critics it's just "pretentious", "bland" and "snooty". / *Sample dishes:* warm bacon & poached egg salad; steak & kidney sausages with mash; chocolate nut brownie. *Details:* www.leodis.co.uk; 10 pm; closed Sat L & Sun.

Lucky Dragon £24

Templar Ln LS2 7LP (0113) 245 0520

"It's the best in Leeds… but then there's not much opposition"; "lots of oriental customers" speak for the merits of this "cavernous" city-centre basement, but some think it "too cocky", given its iffy standards – "it takes a special talent to make Chinese food tasteless". / Details: 11.30 pm.

Maxi's £29

6 Bingley St LS3 1LX (0113) 244 0552

A "huge and busy Chinese" on the fringe of the city-centre, which has put in a rather "lazy" performance in recent times, with "uninspiring" food and "slow" service; some reporters claim it has "improved of late". / Details: www.maxi-s.co.uk; 11.30 pm; no smoking area.

Millrace £35 ★

2-4 Commercial Rd LS5 3AQ (0113) 275 7555

"Organic food which is usually delicious" is what this stylish shop-conversion is all about; even fans say "it can be hit-and-miss", though, and some jibe at "too much going on the plate" (but it must be doing something right as November 2003 is to see a major extension, longer opening and a new bar menu).
/ Sample dishes: seared scallops; roast ham with smoked Cheddar hash; triple chocolate cheesecake. Details: www.themillrace-organic.com; near Kirkstall Abbey; 10 pm; D only, except Sun open L & D; no Amex; no smoking in dining room.

No 3 York Place £38 ★

3 York Pl LS1 2DR (0113) 245 9922

"Standards haven't slipped since Simon Gueller left" – successor Martel Smith is making quite a go of this townhouse-restaurant in the business district, which is praised for its "friendly and informal" style and its "first-class" modern cooking.
/ Sample dishes: lobster, mango & avocado salad with basil oil; pigs trotter stuffed with ham hock & morels; blood orange mousse. Details: www.no3yorkplace.co.uk; 10 pm; closed Sat L & Sun; no smoking in dining room; children: 5+.

Pool Court at 42 £54 ★

44 The Calls LS2 7EW (0113) 244 4242

"Imaginative" cooking won solid praise this year for "Leeds's best place by far" – a "small", "smart" and "tucked-away" (but perhaps slightly "cold") boutique hotel dining room, with "a small terrace overlooking the canal". / Sample dishes: beef tartare with quail eggs; roast sea bass with anchovy-stuffed squid; chilled pineapple & lemongrass soup. Details: www.poolcourt.com; 10 pm; closed Sat L & Sun; no smoking; children: no babies.

Quantro £32 ★

62 Street Ln LS8 2DQ (0113) 288 8063

This "friendly", modern brasserie ("two doors down from Flying Pizza, but in a different century stylewise and foodwise") attracts a small number of very enthusiastic reports. / Sample dishes: Parma ham celeriac remoulade; lamb with black olive mousse; green apple & grapefruit bavarois. Details: www.quantro.co.uk; 10pm Mon-Fri, 10.30 pm Sat; closed Sun; no smoking; children: 8+.

The Reliance £23   Ⓐ
76-78 North St LS2 7PN (0113) 295 6060
*"A good, varied menu" and "really nice staff" are part of the
winning formula which has earned instant popularity for this
"very friendly" and "relaxed" bar/restaurant, near the Grand
Theatre. / **Sample dishes:** pan-fried smoked haddock fish cakes with fresh herb
salad & chutney; roast chicken breast with Parma ham, stuffed with spinich &
Parmasan; banoffi pie. **Details:** 10.30 pm; no booking.*

Sala Thai £26
13-17 Shaw Ln LS6 4DH (0113) 278 8400
*This Headingley oriental has quite a local following, but is beginning
to attract very variable reports – fans insist that it's an "authentic"
place, with "calm" service and "thoughtful" presentation, whereas
doubters just find it "disappointing" and "down-at-heel".
/ **Details:** www.salathaileeds.com; just off Otley Rd, near Arndale Centre; 10.30 pm;
closed Sat L & Sun; no smoking.*

Salvo's £29   Ⓐ
115 Otley Rd LS6 3PX (0113) 275 5017
*A "trendy" and "studenty" Italian local in Headingley, that gets
"very busy and lively" (and you may have to queue); its "great pizza
and pasta" offers pretty "good value". / **Sample dishes:** deep-fried Brie
with raspberry vinaigrette; veal with field mushrooms & Parma ham crisps; Malteser
mousse. **Details:** www.salvos.co.uk; 2m N of University on A660; 10.45 pm, Fri &
Sat 11 pm; closed Sun; no smoking area; no booking at D.*

Sheesh Mahal £19   ★
346-348 Kirkstall Rd LS4 2DS (0113) 230 4161
*"A charismatic and personable owner" adds life to this "fun and
lively" Indian (near the Warner Village), praised by locals for its
"excellent curries". / **Details:** www.sheeshmahal.co.uk; next to Yorkshire
TV centre; midnight; D only; no smoking area.*

Simply Heathcote's £32
Canal Whf, Water Ln LS11 5PS (0113) 244 6611
*Paul Heathcote's relaunch of the canalside premises once known
as Rascasse as part of his (otherwise trans-Pennine) brasserie chain
seems pretty much in line with his standards elsewhere, inspiring
feedback all the way from "modern, stylish and pleasant" to "never
again". / **Sample dishes:** warm black pudding & poached egg salad; herb-roast
chicken with oyster mushrooms; bread & butter pudding.
Details: www.heathcotes.co.uk; off M621, J3, behind Granary Wharf; 10pm,
Sat 11 pm; no smoking.*

Sous le Nez en Ville £30
Quebec House, Quebec St LS1 2HA (0113) 244 0108
*An "absolute bargain" pre-7.30pm menu and "interesting and fairly
priced wines" again feature in many reports on this "enjoyable" –
but "too busy" – city-centre basement wine bar; the "solid,
bourgeois Gallic cooking" plays something of a supporting rôle.
/ **Sample dishes:** deep-fried Brie with pepper & mango sauce; rib of beef with
béarnaise sauce; white chocolate pâté. **Details:** 10 pm, Fri & Sat 10.30 pm; closed
Sun.*

Tampopo £25
15 South Pde LS1 5QS (0113) 245 1816
*"A pleasant surprise" – this city-centre noodle joint is "clean" and
"good-value". / **Sample dishes:** vegetable gyoza; prawns with coconut & Asian
basil sauce; mango sorbet. **Details:** 11 pm, Sun 10 pm; no smoking; need 7+
to book.*

Thai Edge   £30
7 Calverly St LS1 3DY   (0113) 243 6333
*"Leading the pack for Thai in Leeds", this "very modern-looking"
central newcomer is hailed by most reporters for its "well-spiced"
food, its "superb", "traditional" service and its "calm" ambience;
it has critics, though, who find it "overpriced" and "full of poseurs".*
/ **Details:** *no smoking.*

Whitelocks Luncheonette   £20   Ⓐ
Turk's Head Yd, off Briggate LS2 6HB   (0113) 245 3950
*"Ornate", "venerable" and thoroughly "Victorian", this "historic city-
centre pub" is a destination no one should miss; even a critic who
says "the food never fails to disappoint" thinks "the rest of the
experience makes up for it!"* / **Sample dishes:** *crispy haddock fingers;
steak & Stilton pie; jam roly-poly with custard.* **Details:** *7 pm; children: 18+ only.*

LEICESTER, LEICESTER CITY   5–4D

Bobby's   £18   ★
154-156 Belgrave Rd LE4 5AT   (0116) 266 0106
*"Wonderful, proper Indian food, especially for veggies" ensures
continuing popularity for this great (but basic) Curry Mile canteen;
its array of "lovely Indian sweeties" (which you can take away from
the counter) are an attraction in themselves.*
/ **Details:** *www.eatatbobbys.com; 9.30 pm; closed Mon; no Amex; no smoking.*

Case   £35   Ⓐ
4-6 Hotel St LE1 5AW   (0116) 251 7675
*A "brilliant setting" in an interesting, "light, airy and relaxed" space
near St Martins (complete with a "good champagne bar") helps
make this stylish restaurant very popular; the cooking is "enjoyable
and slightly different, but a bit variable".* / **Sample dishes:** *red onion &
goats cheese tart; turkey escalope with roast polenta; brioche pudding.*
Details: *www.thecase.co.uk; near the Cathedral; 10.30 pm; closed Sun; no smoking
area.*

Friends Tandoori   £26   ★
41-43 Belgrave Rd LE4 6AR   (0116) 266 8809
*"Fresh herbs are used liberally to create mouth-watering dishes"
at this comfortable curry house, where "helpful staff" are
a particular highlight; for some reporters, this is "the best" choice
on the Golden Mile.* / **Details:** *11.30 pm; closed Sat L & Sun; no smoking
in dining room.*

Jones Cafe   £29
93 Queens Rd LE2 1TT   (0116) 270 8830
*This Clarendon Park café is "as good as many restaurants", say its
fans, and comes recommended as "a great brunch or lunch venue".*
/ **Sample dishes:** *warm duck salad with Thai dressing; coriander-crusted chicken
with red onion confit; Malteser tiramisu.* **Details:** *9.30 pm; closed Mon; no Amex;
no smoking area; booking: max 10, Sat pm.*

Opera House   £40
10 Guildhall Lane LE1 5FQ   (0116) 223 6666
*"If only the food and service matched up to the room" –
some reporters feel that "little effort" is made at this town-centre
restaurant, which seems to rely for its (considerable) custom on the
charms of its "intimate" setting in an historic building.*
/ **Sample dishes:** *twice-baked Cheddar soufflé; plaice with herb risotto & lobster
sauce; chocolate tart with praline ice cream.* **Details:** *10 pm; closed Sun; no Amex;
no smoking.*

Shimla Pinks £24

65-69 London Rd LE2 0PE (0116) 247 1471

*"Tasty" and "well-prepared" dishes figure in pretty much all reports on this "clean" and "bright" subcontinental, part of a (very variable) national chain. / **Details:** opp railway station; 11 pm; closed Sat L & Sun; no smoking area.*

Stones £33 Ⓐ

29 Millstone Ln LE1 5JN (0116) 291 0004

*"Very lively and full of a smart young set", this stylish city-centre mill-conversion provides an "excellent overall night out"; it offers "a variety of food-types, the tapas selection being the best". / **Sample dishes:** antipasto platter; harissa-glazed salmon with saffron fettuccine; chocolate pudding. **Details:** www.stonesrestaurant.co.uk; 10.30 pm, weekends 11.30 pm; closed Sun; smoking discouraged.*

The Tiffin £26

1 De Montfort St LE1 7GE (0116) 247 0420

*"Fast" and professional service and smart décor underpin the local popularity of this Indian restaurant, near the railway station; even some fans concede the cooking is "nothing remarkable", though, and critics find it far too "bland". / **Details:** www.the-tiffin.co.uk; near railway station; 10.45 pm; closed Sat L & Sun; no smoking area.*

Watsons £27

5-9 Upper Brown St LE1 5TE (0116) 222 7770

*This "modern" warehouse-conversion is the best-known place in town, and wins praise for its "cool" and "spacious" design and its "interesting" menu; some find it "soulless", though, and food quality "can vary". / **Sample dishes:** fish soup with rouille; salmon with wok-fried greens; strawberry millefeuille. **Details:** next to Phoenix Art Theatre; 10.30 pm; closed Sun; no smoking in dining room.*

LEINTWARDINE, SHROPSHIRE 5–4A

Jolly Frog £34 ★

SY7 0LX (01547) 5402498

*You "must book", if you want to enjoy the "superb" fish (and other) dishes for which this "fun" and "quirky" pub has quite a local name. / **Sample dishes:** seared king scallops with beetroot reduction; grilled Torbay sole with butter; white chocolate lasagne with lemon ice cream. **Details:** www.jolly-frog.com; 10.30 pm; no Amex; no smoking area.*

LEMSFORD, HERTFORDSHIRE 3–2B

**Auberge du Lac
Brocket Hall** £55 Ⓐ★

AL8 7XG
(01707) 368888

*JC Novelli is widely credited with "turning around" this "previously frumpy" place – a "beautifully situated" lodge "overlooking the lake at Brocket Hall"; fans praise his "very personal approach" (with the maestro "much in evidence"), and "mouthwatering" modern French cuisine. / **Sample dishes:** foie gras terrine with Szechuan pepper; brill with endives & red wine sauce; frozen vanilla soufflé with rhubarb compote. **Details:** www.brockethall.co.uk; on B653 towards Harpenden; 10 pm; closed Mon & Sun D. **Accommodation:** 16 rooms, from £185.*

sign up for the survey at www.hardens.com 239

LEWDOWN, DEVON   1–3C

Lewtrenchard Manor   £ 45
EX20 4PN   (01566) 783256

"Original everything" adds to the *"agreeably eccentric"* charm
of this *"Elizabethan house, deep in the countryside"*; we've removed
ratings given its recent acquisition by the voracious luxury hotel
chain, Von Essen. / **Sample dishes:** *langoustine cappuccino with truffled leeks;
sautéed liver with garlic mash & crispy bacon; apricot bread & butter pudding.*
Details: *www.lewtrenchard.co.uk; off A30 between Okehampton & Launceston;
9 pm; closed Mon; no jeans or trainers; no smoking in dining room; children: 8+.*
Accommodation: *9 rooms, from £130.*

LEWES, EAST SUSSEX   3–4B

Circa   £ 38   Ａ★
145 High St BN7 1XT   (01273) 471777

"Extraordinary: fusion food which actually works every time!" –
this Asian/Italian *"oddball"* does what it does with *"utter
professionalism"*, and is ever more widely hailed for its *"imaginative"*
culinary creations. / **Sample dishes:** *Thai buttnernut squash soup; tandoori
trout with potatoes & tzatziki; red gooseberry crème brûlée.*
Details: *www.circacirca.com; 10 pm; closed Mon & Sun D; no smoking area.*

LICKFOLD, WEST SUSSEX   3–4A

Lickfold Inn   £ 33   Ａ
GU28 9EY   (01798) 861285

*"On a hot summer night, you can eat in the gardens, or in the
depths of winter you can warm yourself beside the roaring log fire"*,
at this *"beautiful"* South Downs pub/restaurant, praised for its
"friendly" service and *"enjoyable"* cooking. / **Sample dishes:** *grilled goats
cheese with red pepper relish; pan-fried sea bass with black olive mash; white
chocolate crème brûlée.* **Details:** *3m N of A272 between Midhurst & Petworth;
9.30 pm.*

LIDGATE, SUFFOLK   3–1C

Star Inn   £ 33   Ａ
The Street CB8 9PP   (01638) 500275

*"It seems odd when you first arrive, but you soon get caught up in
the great atmosphere"*; this *"beautiful"* and *"friendly"* pub offers
"interesting", *"well-prepared"*… and mainly Spanish cooking –
Sunday lunches, for example, may include *"a proper paella, as well
as a roast"*! / **Sample dishes:** *Catalan salad; paella Valenciana; treacle tart.*
Details: *on B1063 6m SE of Newmarket; 10 pm; closed Sun D; no smoking
in dining room.*

LIFTON, DEVON   1–3C

Arundell Arms   £ 42
Fore St PL16 0AA   (01566) 784666

This old-fashioned hotel has long been justly reputed as a *"tweedy"*
destination for fishin' types, with often- *"wonderful"* traditional
cooking; even fans speak of *"occasional lapses"*, though, and there
were a couple of shocking reports this year of *"careless"* cooking
and *"inattentive"* service. / **Sample dishes:** *spiced potted chicken with apricot
chutney; roast monkfish with scallop & lentil fricassée; passion fruit delice.*
Details: *0.5m off A30, Lifton Down exit; 9.30 pm; no smoking.*
Accommodation: *27 rooms, from £130.00.*

LINCOLN, LINCOLNSHIRE   6–3A

Browns Pie Shop   £ 25   ★
33 Steep Hill LN2 1LU   (01522) 527330
"Superb food, from starters to puddings" – particularly, of course,
"spectacular pies with interesting fillings" – has created a deserved
reputation for this *"cramped"* but *"friendly"* spot, near the
Cathedral. / **Sample dishes:** Yorkshire pudding with spiced onion gravy; fish pie;
Bailey's cheesecake. **Details:** near the Cathedral; 10 pm; no smoking area.

Jew's House   £ 39
15 The Strait LN2 1JD   (01522) 524851
*"You're paying for the admittedly attractive surroundings of probably
the oldest building in Lincoln"* – that's the clear verdict on this
comfortable establishment, where this year's cooking was rather
"patchy". / **Sample dishes:** wild mushroom vol-au-vents; braised monkfish with
spinach; white chocolate cheesecake. **Details:** www.thejewshouse.co.uk; halfway
down Steep Hill from Cathedral; 9.30 pm; closed Mon & Sun; no smoking in dining
room.

The Wig & Mitre   £ 37
30-32 Steep Hill LN2 1TL   (01522) 535190
*Old-timers at this large and rambling "favourite" by the cathedral
say "it misses the spark of its old location", but, even so,
many reporters would support the notion that "every town should
have a pub like this"* – open every day of the year from early
morning, and offering a wide-ranging menu of *"decent scoff".*
/ **Sample dishes:** wild mushroon & Madeira soup; chicken in Parma ham with
pistachio & lemon stuffing; baked vanilla cheesecake.
Details: www.wigandmitre.com; between Cathedral & Castle; 11 pm; no smoking
in dining room.

LINLITHGOW, WEST LOTHIAN   9–4C

Champany Inn   £ 53
EH49 7LU   (01506) 834532
"A quite exceptional wine list" and *"truly friendly and knowledgeable
staff"* – not to mention *"pretty mean steaks"* – make this famous
inn a destination of considerable note; it can seem *"cruelly
overpriced"*, though – the adjacent Chop & Ale house is a less
expensive alternative. / **Sample dishes:** quail with bacon & tarragon stuffing;
steak with chips & asparagus; hazelnut meringues. **Details:** www.champany.com;
2m NE of Linlithgow on junction of A904 & A803; 10 pm; closed Sat L & Sun;
no jeans or trainers; children: 8+. **Accommodation:** 16 rooms, from £125.

LITTLE SHELFORD, CAMBRIDGESHIRE   3–1B

Sycamore House   £ 35   ★
1 Church St CB2 5HG   (01223) 843396
"Feel your stresses dissolve away" – reporters are very upbeat about
the Sharpes' *"beautifully housed"* and *"romantic"* restaurant, where
a *"thoughtful"* (if *"limited"*) menu is served. / **Sample dishes:** Stilton &
celery soup; steamed prawns with sour cream & sweet chilli; Campari & orange
sorbet. **Details:** 1.5m from M11, J11 on A10 to Royston; 9 pm; D only, closed
Sun-Tue; no Amex; no smoking; children: 12+.

LIVERPOOL, MERSEYSIDE 5–2A

A little behind most of the other major conurbations, Liverpool is beginning to develop a quality restaurant scene.

The best place in town remains the appropriately-named *60 Hope Street*, while – somewhat bizarrely for a Manchester-based business – *Simply Heathcote's* remains the best member of that North Western group. Promising recent openings include the relaunch of *Ziba*, and as the city gears up to be 'European City of Culture' in 2008, it seems reasonable to hope for an increase in momentum.

Those looking for atmosphere on a budget – or at least at relatively reasonable cost – are also well catered for. The *Everyman Bistro*, *The Other Place*, *L'Alouette*, *The Left Bank* and *Keith's Wine Bar* are the best-known of a good selection.

L'Alouette £36   A

2 Lark Ln L17 8US (0151) 727 2142
"You feel like you're in a traditional restaurant in France", at this *"intimate"*, *"longtime favourite"* in Sefton Park; the cooking is solidly rated, but inspires much less feedback than the *"sexy"* surroundings.
/ **Sample dishes:** snails & frogs legs in garlic; steak with Roquefort; lemon tart. **Details:** 10 pm; closed Mon.

Casa Italia £23   A

40 Stanley St L1 6AL (0151) 227 5774
"Ever-busy", this *"traditional Italian ristorante"* – in a former warehouse – has a lively style which can make it quite *"an experience"*; pizza is the top culinary attraction.
/ **Sample dishes:** smoked & cured meat platter; Ventresca bacon & olive pizza; cassata. **Details:** off Victoria St; 10 pm; closed Sun; no Amex; need 8+ to book.

Chung Ku £26   A★

Riverside Drive, Columbus Quay L3 4DB (0151) 726 8191
"Purpose-built and with magnificent river views" – fans say this striking, circular three-year-old is *"fast becoming THE place for oriental food in the area"*; Sunday dim sum and *"a great choice of fish and seafood"* are amongst the top attractions.
/ **Details:** www.chungkurestaurant.co.uk; 10 pm, Fri & Sat midnight.

Ego £30

Federation Hs, Hope St L1 9BS (0151) 706 0707
Hailed as a *"very good newcomer"* by some reporters, this Mediterranean café next to the Philharmonic Hall (the newest in a small local chain) wins praise for its *"wide and interesting menu"*; *"slow"* service, though, is a repeated complaint.
/ **Sample dishes:** Andalucian chicken salad; roast salmon fillet served with a langoustine & spinach sauce; summer berries in wine jelly, served with greek yoghurt. **Details:** www.egorestaurants.com; 10.30 pm; no Amex.

Everyman Bistro £20   A

5-9 Hope St L1 9BH (0151) 708 9545
"Great for a night out, or pre-theatre", this self-service bistro beneath the eponymous theatre has won a huge following with its *"healthy, home-made and always-interesting"* fare (with *"amazing"* puddings a highlight); it has been in business over 30 years, though, and a few former fans are beginning to feel it's *"past its best"*.
/ **Sample dishes:** nutty parsnip soup; red chilli chicken with yellow rice; apricot & almond cobbler. **Details:** www.everyman.co.uk; midnight, Fri & Sat 2 am; closed Sun; no Amex; no smoking area.

Far East £22

27-35 Berry St L1 9DF   (0151) 709 3141

This "busy", "cavern of a restaurant" in Chinatown (above an oriental cash & carry) may be a bit "tacky", but it attracts consistent praise for its "fresh" and "reliable" fare. / **Details:** by church on Berry St; 11 pm; no smoking area.

Gulshan £24 ★

544-548 Aigburth Rd L19 3QG   (0151) 427 2273

Devotees come "from far and wide" to appreciate the "wide range of dishes" ("from the mundane to the adventurous") at this suburban subcontinental, located "in a nondescript parade of shops". / **Details:** www.gulshan-liverpool.com; 10.45 pm; D only; no smoking area.

Keiths Wine Bar £16 Ⓐ

107 Lark Ln L17 8UR   (0151) 728 7688

"Good food and wine, at cheap prices" maintains the "wide-ranging" appeal of this "student-district" wine bar, near Sefton Park; service can be "slow", but the cooking "maintains good standards, despite the high turnover". / **Sample dishes:** grilled halloumi with pitta bread; Spanish-style chicken with rice; sticky toffee pudding. **Details:** 10.30 pm; no smoking area.

Left Bank £35

1 Church Rd L15 9EA   (0151) 734 5040

"Good food at good-value prices" continues to win favour from most (if not quite all) reporters for this "friendly" bistro; "the only drawback is the lack of space between tables". / **Sample dishes:** tomato & Mozzarella tart; roast duck with honey & thyme glaze; crème brûlée. **Details:** www.leftbankrestaurant.co.uk; off Penny Lane; 10 pm; closed Sat L.

The Living Room £32 Ⓐ

Victoria St, Victoria Buildings 15 L2 5QS   (0870) 442 2535

A trendy city-centre outpost of a cool, national piano-bar chain, which – considering that it's clearly not a foodie destination – inspires feedback of the "excellent all-round" variety. / **Sample dishes:** duck spring rolls with shitake salsa; Cumberland bangers & mash; Belgian waffles. **Details:** www.thelivingroom.co.uk; 11 pm; no jeans or trainers; no smoking area at L.

The Other Place £28 Ⓐ★

141-143 Allerton Rd L18 2DD   (0151) 724 1234

"Interesting" food and "stylish" design win consistent praise for this "fun" Mossley Hill hang out; "great-breakfasts" are a highlight, and "outside eating in summer is a bonus". / **Sample dishes:** goats cheese & red pepper spring rolls; grilled cod with hazelnut & herb potato cake; passion fruit & coconut tart. **Details:** 10 pm; closed Mon & Sun D; no Amex; appreciated if guests try to refrain from smoking.

Pod £21 Ⓐ

137-139 Allerton Rd L18 2DD   (0151) 724 2255

A "great buzz" features in many reports on this "eclectic" Allerton snackery, which offers "tapas from around the world"; "it can get too busy at weekends", and some feel it's becoming "a victim of its own success". / **Sample dishes:** prawn & squid tempura with wasabi mayonnaise; chicken stuffed with chorizo & coriander; sticky toffee pudding. **Details:** 9.30 pm; booking: max 6 at weekends.

Siam Garden £25
607 Smithdown Rd L15 5AG (0151) 734 1471
An "extensive" and "authentic" menu contributes to the charms
of this unpretentious Sefton Park oriental, which locals hail as a
"lovely" Thai. / **Details:** 11.45 pm; closed Sun L.

Simply Heathcote's £30   Ⓐ
Beetham Plaza 25, The Strand L2 0XL (0151) 236 3536
"For a business lunch", this year-old restaurant "in the main
business district" (by the Liver Building) wins much praise with its
"smart" and "spacious" décor and its "first-class service"; the food –
notably better than in Manchester – is "generally good".
/ **Sample dishes:** pan-fried sardines with tomato salsa; char-grilled chicken Caesar
salad; bread & butter pudding. **Details:** www.heathcotes.co.uk; 10 pm; no smoking
in dining room.

60 Hope Street £40   Ⓐ★
60 Hope St L1 9BZ
(0151) 707 6060
"Liverpool is crying out for more places like this" – an "elegant"
converted Georgian townhouse near the University where
"professional" staff deliver "sophisticated and well-executed food";
"upstairs is smart, downstairs there's a cheaper, casual café/bar",
but "you get the same attention to detail in both".
/ **Sample dishes:** fishcakes with smoked pepper aioli; lamb with crispy spinach
risotto; peanut butter brûlée. **Details:** www.60hopestreet.com; between the
Cathedrals; 10.30 pm; closed Sat L & Sun; no Amex; no smoking area.

Tabac £21   Ⓐ
126 Bold St L1 4JA (0151) 709 9502
"Freshly-baked bread, great soups and plenty of veggie options" –
such are the attractions of this city-centre café, which is especially
popular as a place to start the day. / **Sample dishes:** roast aubergine &
red pepper pâté; shepherds pie; chocolate espresso mousse. **Details:** 10 pm;
no Amex; no smoking area.

Tai Pan £21
WH Lung Building, Gt Howard St L5 9TZ (0151) 207 3888
It's a bit of a "barn", but "it must be a good sign" that "most of the
city's large oriental community" seems to descend on this restaurant
above a Chinese supermarket; the food, though, is "good value"
rather than anything more remarkable. / **Details:** 11.30 pm,
Sun 9.30 pm.

Yuet Ben £21   ★
1 Upper Duke St L1 9DU (0151) 709 5772
"It feels a bit like a cafeteria", but this "long-standing Liverpudlian
favourite" – "just outside the Chinatown arch" – still wins general
praise with its "friendly" service and "good-standard" cooking.
/ **Details:** www.yuetben.co.uk; 11 pm; D only, closed Mon.

Ziba £35
Hargreaves Building, 5 Chapel St L3 9AG (0151) 236 6676
"The food is just as good as before", opines an early-days reporter
on this very popular and stylish venture, which (after a break) re-
opened in the former Racquet Club in 2003; in the absence
of greater feedback, though, we've left awarding a rating till the next
edition. / **Sample dishes:** tian of crab, mango & avocado with shellfish dressing;
roast veal with crushed potato & shallot jus; soft-centered chocolate cake, with greek
yoghurt sorbet. **Details:** www.racquetclub.org.uk; 10 pm; closed Sun; no smoking
area. **Accommodation:** 8 rooms, from £95.

LLANDDEINIOLEN, GWYNEDD 4–1C
Ty'n Rhos £ 32 ★
LL55 3AE (01248) 670489
This small hotel in a converted farmhouse (with beautiful views of the Menai Strait) makes "a very handy base for Snowdonia", and one "with good food and service" too. / Sample dishes: crab tart with crab bisque dressing; lamb with bean & rosemary casserole; gooseberry & elderflower tart. Details: www.tynrhos.co.uk; 8.30 pm; closed Mon L; no smoking; children: 6+. Accommodation: 14 rooms, from £80.

LLANDEGLA, WREXHAM 5–3A
Bodidris Hall Hotel £ 42 🄰★
LL11 3AL (0870) 729 2292
A "romantic" manor house, which – most reports suggest – delivers "delicious" food in a "wonderful" location. / Sample dishes: confit duck terrine with Cumberland sauce; lamb with leek & mint mousse; roast pear & almond tart. Details: www.bodidrishall.com; on A5104 from Wrexham; 9.15 pm; no smoking in dining room; children: 14+. Accommodation: 9 rooms, from £99.

LLANDRILLO, DENBIGHSHIRE 4–2D
Tyddyn Llan £ 44 🄰
LL21 0ST (01490) 440264
The Webb family (who used to run the eminent Gallic fixture, Hilaire in South Kensington) now run this quite stately, rural restaurant-with-rooms; it has won instant accolades in other guides, but the few initial reports we have divide between those who say it's now "excellent", and others who say it's "good", but "not up to its previous standards". / Details: www.tyddynllan.co.uk; on B4401 between Corwen and Bala; 9 pm; closed Mon, (L Tue-Thu only by prior arrangement); no smoking; booking essential Tue L-Thu L. Accommodation: 12 rooms, from £130.

LLANDUDNO, CONWY 4–1D
Bodysgallen Hall £ 53 🄰
LL30 1RS (01492) 584466
This grand country house hotel has a "stunning" position on a hill outside the town (best enjoyed "from a window table on a sunny day"); the food plays something of a supporting rôle, but fans say it's "fine" stuff. / Sample dishes: roast tomato soup with pesto tortellini; lamb with bacon potato cake & mint jus; grape & grenadine jelly. Details: www.bodysgallen.com; 2m off A55 on A470; 9.30 pm; no Amex or Switch; jacket & tie required at D; no smoking in dining room; children: 8+. Accommodation: 19 rooms, from £165.

Richards £ 35 🄰★
7 Church Walks LL30 2HD (01492) 877924
"After a day's walking by the sea, this is the perfect spot for a quiet tête-à-tête", and you get "accomplished food" at Richard Hendey's "intimate" and "cosy" bistro in this atmospheric seaside town. / Sample dishes: chicken, venison & pistachio terrine; pork with Bramley apple sauce; Caribbean rum, raisin & coffee ice cream. Details: 11 pm; D only, closed Mon & Sun.

St Tudno Hotel £ 47 ★
Promenade LL30 2LP (01492) 874411
Fans find "exceptional food and service" at this "quiet" family-owned hotel, near the pier – for a seaside resort dining room, it is of rare quality. / Sample dishes: crab risotto with parmesan; lamb with cabbage & oatmeal; warm chocolate fondant with coconut ice cream. Details: www.st-tudno.co.uk; 9.30 pm; no smoking area; children: no babies or toddlers at D. Accommodation: 19 rooms, from £100.

LLANGAMMARCH WELLS, POWYS 4–4D

Lake Country House £53

LD4 4BS (01591) 620202

If you're looking for an "old-style" country house hotel this grand Edwardian establishment fits the bill (and offers "wonderful grounds in which to walk off your meal"); the standard of cooking is arguably no better than par-for-the-course, but the list of (mainly French) wines is "formidable". / **Sample dishes:** roast Mediterranean vegetable soup; confit duck & foie gras terrine; rum & mango crème brûlée. **Details:** www.lakecountryhouse.co.uk; off A483 at Garth, follow signs; 9 pm; jacket & tie required; no smoking; children: 7+ at D. **Accommodation:** 19 rooms, from £160.

LLANGOLLEN, DENBIGHSHIRE 5–3A

Corn Mill £25 🅰

Dee Ln LL20 8PN (01978) 869555

"Glorious views" over the River Dee add atmosphere to this impressively restored watermill near the town's ancient bridge; attractions include an "interesting" menu and some "well-kept real ales". / **Sample dishes:** melon, feta & pine kernel salad; aubergine & goats cheese with red pepper dressing; bread & butter pudding. **Details:** www.brunningandprice.co.uk; 9.30 pm; no smoking area.

LLANWDDYN, POWYS 4–2D

Lake Vyrnwy Hotel £42 🅰★

Lake Vyrnwy SY10 0LY (01691) 870692

"Views to die for" are not the only appeal of this grand Victorian hotel dining room (originally constructed to house the engineers building the reservoir it now overlooks); the cooking – much of it using meat and game from the estate – is often "amazing", too. / **Sample dishes:** tuna carpaccio with smoked quails eggs; pot-roast pork with sage mash; lime panna cotta with peppered strawberries. **Details:** www.lakevyrnwy.com; on B4393 at SE end of Lake Vyrnwy; 9.15 pm; no smoking. **Accommodation:** 35 rooms, from £120.

LLANWRTYD WELLS, POWYS 4–4D

Carlton House Hotel £47 ★

Dolecoed Rd LD5 4RA (01591) 610248

"Simple and perfectly-executed" dishes make this family-run venture quite a gourmet destination, not least by local standards; service, though, can be "overwhelming" when the place is quiet, and "slow" when it is busy. / **Sample dishes:** seared king scallops; warm peppered beef salad; apple & Calvados sorbet. **Details:** www.carltonrestaurant.com; 8.30 pm; D only, closed Sun; no Amex; no smoking in dining room. **Accommodation:** 5 rooms, from £65.

LLYSWEN, POWYS 2–1A

Griffin Inn £29 🅰★

LD3 0UR (01874) 754241

"Good" and "fresh" – and sometimes "original" – cooking commends the dining room of this cosy, creeper-clad, ancient inn to reporters. / **Sample dishes:** hot smoked salmon salad; braised lamb shank with roast garlic; treacle tart. **Details:** on A470; 8.45 pm; closed Sun D; no smoking area; children: not at D. **Accommodation:** 7 rooms, from £70.

LOCH LOMOND, DUNBARTONSHIRE 9–4B

Cameron House £61
G83 8QZ   (01389) 755565
"It's the location which really makes the place", at this dining room on the banks of Loch Lomond, which offers "quality cooking, attractively presented"; even those who say it's "delightful", though, concede that it's "expensive" for what it is. / **Sample dishes:** asparagus, leek & mushroom terrine; lobster & langoustine with black olive pasta; banana tarte Tatin with pineapple sorbet. **Details:** www.cameronhouse.co.uk; over Erskine Bridge to A82, follow signs to Loch Lomond; 9.45 pm; D only, closed Mon; jacket & tie required; no smoking; booking essential; children: 14+. **Accommodation:** 96 rooms, from £124.

LOCKSBOTTOM, KENT 3–3B

Chapter One £40 ★
Farnborough Common BR6 8NF   (01689) 854848
"Much better than you'd expect in the area", this suburban favourite is "an excellent find", offering a "beautifully prepared" menu that's almost unanimously hailed by reporters for its "very good value". / **Sample dishes:** smoked goose, walnut & raspberry salad; provençale salmon, clam & mussel confit; apple tart & thyme ice cream. **Details:** www.chaptersrestaurants.co.uk; 2m E of Bromley on A21; 10.30 pm; booking: max 12.

LONG CRENDON, BUCKINGHAMSHIRE 2–2D

Angel £41 ★
Bicester Rd HP18 9EE   (01844) 208268
"It continues to get better", say fans of this popular restaurant occupying "peacefully situated" pub premises in the Chilterns; its speciality is "a good and extensive fish menu". / **Sample dishes:** feta, tomato & olive gateau; duck & smoked bacon with blueberry sauce; cranberry toffee tart. **Details:** 2m NW of Thame, off B4011; 9.30 pm; closed Sun D; no Amex; no smoking area; booking: max 12, Fri & Sat. **Accommodation:** 3 rooms, from £75.

LONG MELFORD, SUFFOLK 3–1C

Scutchers Bistro £37
Westgate St CO10 9DP   (01787) 310200
"Seasonal produce" is cooked "with flair" at this "smart" and "lively" bistro. / **Sample dishes:** seared scallops; roast lamb with stuffed tomatoes; crêpes Suzette. **Details:** www.scutchers.com; 9.30 pm; closed Mon & Sun; no smoking in dining room.

LONGFRAMLINGTON, NORTHUMBERLAND 8–2B

Anglers Arms £26 Ⓐ
Weldon Bridge NE65 8AX   (01665) 570271
The "daily specials" win praise at this rural riverside coaching inn, where you can eat either in the bar or restaurant (located in a Pullman railway carriage). / **Sample dishes:** soup of the day; fillet of beef stuffed with Stilton wrapped in bacon; apple pie. **Details:** www.anglersarms.com; 9.30 pm; no Amex; no smoking in dining room.

LONGRIDGE, LANCASHIRE   5–1B

The Longridge Restaurant   £42
104-106 Higher Rd PR3 3SY   (01772) 784969
*Though fans of Paul Heathcote's original, rural cottage HQ (which last year adopted a new name and a "more relaxed" style) say it's "keeping up high standards", the overall verdict remains pretty much the same – "he can and should do better". / **Sample dishes:** herb polenta with char-grilled vegetables; crispy pork belly with spinach & red wine; iced apricot & gingerbread parfait. **Details:** www.heathcotes.co.uk; follow signs for Jeffrey Hill; 9.30 pm; closed Mon & Sat L; no smoking area.*

LOUGHBOROUGH, LEICESTERSHIRE   5–3D

Thai House   £26
5a High St LE11 2PY   (01509) 260030
*"Great-value lunchtime menus" are an added bonus at this well-liked high street oriental, praised for its "attentive" staff and "authentic" cuisine. / **Details:** 11 pm.*

LOW FELL, TYNE & WEAR   8–2B

Eslington Villa Hotel   £33   A ★
8 Station Rd NE9 6DR   (0191) 487 6017
*"Great food in a relaxed setting" is the gist of all reports on the dining room of this Victorian country house hotel (where a new chef took over in 2002); service is "friendly", too. / **Sample dishes:** smoked haddock & chive risotto; pork & pancetta with sage & onion mash; British cheeses with quince jelly. **Details:** A1 exit for Team Valley Retail World, then left off Eastern Avenue; 9.30 pm; closed Sat L & Sun D; no smoking. **Accommodation:** 18 rooms, from £59.50.*

LOWER ODDINGTON, GLOUCESTERSHIRE   2–1C

The Fox Inn   £29   A
GL56 0UR   (01451) 870555
*"More a restaurant than a pub" (and with very good rooms, too), this ancient Cotswolds inn is unanimously hailed by reporters as a "relaxed" place, with "consistently good" food. / **Sample dishes:** smoked haddock & watercress tart; braised lamb shank with lemon zest; steamed treacle sponge. **Details:** www.foxinn.net; on A436 near Stow on the Wold; 10 pm; no Amex. **Accommodation:** 3 rooms, from £58.*

LOWER WIELD, HAMPSHIRE   2–3D

Yew Tree   £41   ★
Alresford SO24 9RX
(01256) 389224
*It may be "difficult to find" but it's "well worth the trek" to Christopher & Donna Richard's small and "unpretentious" converted pub "out in the countryside"; "fantastic" use of "excellent ingredients" is winning it ever-greater recognition. / **Sample dishes:** home made soup; pan fried fillet of venison; fresh raspberry soufflé. **Details:** 9.30 pm; no smoking area.*

LOWER WOLVERCOTE, OXFORDSHIRE   2–2D

Trout Inn   £ 26   Ⓐ
195 Godstow Rd OX2 8PN   (01865) 302071
*The food is only "OKish", and service can be "appallingly
unreliable", but most reporters think that – thanks to its "perfect
setting on the Thames" – it's "worth the long wait" to eat at the
olde worlde pub made famous by Inspector Morse.*
/ *Sample dishes: salmon & broccoli fishcakes; Mediterranean chicken with new
potatoes; toffee apple bread & butter pudding.* **Details:** *2m from junction of A40 &
A44; 9 pm; mainly non-smoking; no booking; children: no children.*

LUDLOW, SHROPSHIRE   5–4A

The Cookhouse   £ 32
Bromfield SY8 2JR   (01584) 856565
*In a town full of places trying very hard on the food front, reporters
unanimously applaud the "good portions" of food that's
"well cooked and presented" – but not aiming for any fireworks –
at this "nice", "quiet" and "dependable" spot.* / **Sample dishes:** *Cornish
crab with saffron lemon & crème fraîche; noisette of lamb with herb crust, scented
with lavender honey; vanilla & lime panacotta.* **Details:** *2m N of Ludlow on A49
to Shrewsbury; 9.30 pm; no Amex; no smoking area.* **Accommodation:** *15 rooms,
from £60.*

Ego Café Bar   £ 30
Quality Square SY8 1AR   (01584) 878000
*This "good casual eatery" is "stylish" for the locale, and provides
some relief from all the haute cuisine hereabouts; portions can
be "tiny", though, and service "thoughtless".* / **Sample dishes:** *pork
kebabs with satay sauce; baked trout with rhubarb mayonnaise; pan-fried bananas
in rum.* **Details:** *off Castle Square, through timber arches; 9.30 pm; no Amex;
no smoking area.*

Hibiscus   £ 45   ★★
17 Corve St SY8 1DA   (01584) 872325
*"Big competition for the Merchant House"; "imaginative",
"interesting" and "beautifully balanced" Gallic cooking – "the very
definition of modern haute cuisine" – is making a big name for the
Bosis' "comfortable" manor house dining room; notably "friendly"
service adds to the experience.* / **Sample dishes:** *white onion & lime ravioli
with broad beans; roast turbot with tarragon & orange; chocolate tart with star anise.*
Details: *9.30 pm; closed Mon & Sun; no Amex; no smoking; booking: max 14.*

Koo   £ 25
127 Old St SY8 1NU   (01584) 878462
*"An imaginative Japanese/Thai fusion menu" (with "full explanations
of dishes") makes this small oriental a 'different' but worthwhile
venture.* / **Details:** *www.koo-ook.com; 9.45 pm; closed Mon & Sun; no Amex.*

Merchant House   £ 45   ★★
Lower Corve St SY8 1DU   (01584) 875438
*"Wonderful, unfussy cooking, perfectly executed" has won
a legendary reputation for Shaun Hill's "one-of-a-kind" townhouse
restaurant (and, in his wake, for the whole town); most reporters
find the small-scale setting "charming", too, although service strikes
some as "dour".* / **Sample dishes:** *grilled sea bass with allspice; roast pigeon
with morels; Hungarian apricot trifle.* **Details:** *9 pm; closed Mon, Tue-Thu L & Sun;
no Amex or Switch; no smoking in dining room; booking: max 8.*

Mr Underhill's £ 44 A ★
Dinham Wier SY8 1EH (01584) 874431
*No menu choice comes as a "shock" to some reporters, but you get
"exciting food from first-class ingredients" at Chris & Judy Bradley's
"personal" restaurant-with-rooms, which has a "lovely setting" by a
weir. / **Sample dishes:** smoked haddock with confit tomatoes; Perigord duck with
olives & honey; Italian bread & butter pudding. **Details:** www.mr-underhills.co.uk;
8.30 pm; closed Tue; no Amex; no smoking. **Accommodation:** 7 rooms, from £85.*

Overton Grange £ 53 ★
Hereford Rd SY8 4AD (01584) 873500
*"Tastefully refurbished" by new owners, this Edwardian house seems
to have found more consistent form, and all reports support the
view that is now offers "a good formal dining experience"; the odd
reporter, though, still discerns "a lack of atmosphere".
/ **Sample dishes:** roast scallops & langoustines with truffles; seared turbot with
salsify & roast shallots; chocolate cup with pistachio ice cream.
Details: www.overtongrangehotel.com; off A49, 1.5m S of Ludlow; 9.30 pm; D only;
no Amex; no smoking area. **Accommodation:** 14 rooms, from £95.*

The Dartmoor Inn £ 35 ★
EX20 4AY (01822) 820221
*"Philip Burgess excels at producing memorable meals using local
ingredients", says one of the many admirers of this "charming"
place, which "calls itself a pub, but it really a very reasonable
restaurant", on the fringe of the Dartmoor National Park.
/ **Sample dishes:** artichoke purée tart with baby onions; grilled mixed fish with
courgette flower fritters; Bramley apple ice cream with roasted cob nuts.
Details: 9.30 pm; closed Mon & Sun D; no Amex; no smoking in dining room;
children: 5+ at weekends.*

White Hart £ 35 ★
51 Stockport Rd OL4 4JJ (01457) 872566
*Most reporters express all-round satisfaction with this "traditional"
moors pub, with its "beautiful" cooking (home-made sausages
a speciality); one or two, though, were less impressed.
/ **Sample dishes:** grilled tandoori chicken with cucumber yoghurt; calves liver with
pickled cabbage & thyme; lime & raspberry cheesecake. **Details:** 2m E of Oldham
on A669, then A6050; 9.30 pm; no smoking pre 11 pm. **Accommodation:** 12
rooms, from £98.50.*

Egan's £ 37 ★
Gosport St SO41 9BE (01590) 676165
*"Excellent-value" cooking (especially fish) underpins support for John
Egan's "lovely" bistro. / **Sample dishes:** seafood tempura; rack of lamb with
leeks; strawberries & ice cream. **Details:** 10 pm; closed Mon & Sun; no smoking
in dining room; booking: max 6, Sat.*

LYNDHURST, HAMPSHIRE 2–4C
Le Poussin at Parkhill £51 ★

Beaulieu Rd SO43 7FZ (023) 8028 2944

Alex Aitken's "adventurous" and "eclectic" menu is realised to "brilliant" effect at this Georgian country house hotel (relocated from Brockenhurst a few years ago); the "smart" setting is "beautiful" or "slightly lacking in atmosphere", to taste. / **Sample dishes:** salmon with cucumber salad & caviar; rare beef with red wine sauce; hot chocolate fondant. **Details:** www.lepoussin.co.uk; 9.30 pm; no smoking in dining room; children: 8+ at D. **Accommodation:** 19 rooms, from £110.

MADINGLEY, CAMBRIDGESHIRE 3–1B
Three Horseshoes £37

CB3 8AB (01954) 210221

This smart dining pub ("in a quaint village just north of Cambridge") has long been known as one of the best places in the area, though, the feeling that it's "variable" and "trading on its reputation" risks becoming overwhelming. / **Sample dishes:** leek & morel tortellini with leek mousse; venison with star anise noodles & pak choy; lemon tart with cherry vodka sorbet. **Details:** www.huntsbridge.com; 2m W of Cambridge, off A14 or M11; 9.30 pm; closed Sun D; no smoking in dining room.

MAIDENSGROVE, OXFORDSHIRE 2–2D
Five Horseshoes £30 𝔸

RG9 6EX (01491) 641282

"A real gem, with great views over rolling hills"; new owners "have continued a super tradition" at this Chilterns favourite, where "tasty BBQs" are the star attraction, but which offers "well-executed" bar and restaurant menus all year; service can be "slow". / **Sample dishes:** wok-fried strips of aromatic duck in a soft pancake; Thai spiced braised shank of lamb with corriander steamed rice; mars bar cheesecake. **Details:** on B481 between Nettlebed & Watlington; 9.30 pm; closed Sun D; no smoking in dining room.

MALMESBURY, WILTSHIRE 2–2C
Old Bell £35 𝔸

Abbey Rw SN16 0AG (01666) 822344

The 'oldest hotel in England' is a "super, relaxing place" (and one that welcomes minors, too), and its cooking – though not especially ambitious – offers "a great selection of local produce"; afternoon tea also comes recommended. / **Sample dishes:** chicken liver crostini; shepherds pie; chocolate fondant with pistachio ice cream. **Details:** www.oldbellhotel.com; next to Abbey; 9.15 pm; no smoking; children: 12+ at D. **Accommodation:** 31 rooms, from £110.

MANCHESTER, GREATER MANCHESTER 5–2B

In *Mont*, Manchester at last potentially has the quality, European, city-centre linchpin it has so signally lacked in recent years. Perhaps it symbolises the fact that the city is, at last, beginning to turn the broadest restaurant culture outside London into one of quality.

That isn't to say that there's yet a huge field of top-end, but the city does now boast three interesting European places. The other two – the long-established *Moss Nook* and Altrincham's *Juniper* (now back on better form) – are admittedly some way from the city-centre.

The middle ranges have also seen some notable additions over the past few years: the *Restaurant Bar & Grill*, *Lounge 10*, and the improving *Stock* join the long-running, idiosyncratic *Market*. *Croma* may be just a fancy pizza-parlour, but it's established quite a position as a popular city-centre stand-by. Many Mancunians in search of a good-quality, atmospheric venue, though, still journey out of the city-centre to West Didsbury's impressive *Lime Tree*. In Whalley Grange, *Palmiro* – after a rocky phase – looks set to re-emerge as that rare beast: an interesting, provincial modern Italian.

The city boasts the most impressive range of oriental restaurants outside the capital. The legendary *Yang Sing* – by far the best known place in Manchester – is also the country's most famous Chinese restaurant, and justifiably so. It is ably supported by *East*, *Koh Samui*, *Koreana*, *Little Yang Sing*, *New Emperor*, *Pacific*, *Pearl City*, *Tai Pan* and *Wong Chu*. Fans of the Indian subcontinent are well catered for – but only at the cheaper end of the market – not just with Rusholme's curry strip (*Lal Haweli*, *Punjab Tandoori*), but also with the likes of West Didsbury's *Great Kathmandu*.

Western Europe's largest student population helps to support a growing number of fun and/or affordable places (*Cachumba*, *Cafe Pop* and *The Mark Addy*). The institutionalised alternative lifestyle of the Gay Village sustains what is perhaps the UK's best gay bar/restaurant, *Velvet*.

The Bridgewater Hall   £30
Lower Mosley St M2 3WS   (0161) 950 0000
With its "imaginative food (including excellent soups and sandwiches)", this concert hall café is, by cultural-centre standards, a place of some note – not least because "the menu is often related to the style of the music"! / **Sample dishes:** shredded chicken salad; roast cod with pesto gnocchi; chocolate marquise with poached apricots.
Details: www.bridgewater-hall.co.uk; 10.30 pm; openings affected by concert times; no smoking.

Cachumba   £15   ★
220 Burton Rd M20 2LW   (0161) 445 2479
"You're guaranteed a different food experience" at Seema Gupta's "cheap and cheerful" BYO café in West Didsbury, where "flavoursome", "African/Asian fusion" dishes are "lovingly prepared". / **Details:** 9.30 pm; closed Sun D; no credit cards.

Cafe Paradiso
Hotel Rosetti   £30   𝐴★
107 Piccadilly M1 2DB   (0161) 247 7744
"Good simple food" is still not that easy to find in downtown Manchester, so this "funky bistro-style space in a new hotel" (sibling to Cheltenham's Kandinsky), with its "good attention to detail", is well worth knowing about. / **Sample dishes:** blue cheese tart; halibut fillet seared with couscous & oil dressing; oriental spiced rice pudding.
Details: www.aliasrossetti.com; 10 pm; no smoking.

Café Pop   £ 9   Ⓐ★
34-36 Oldham St M1 1JN   (0161) 237 9688
*"Good veggie breakfast in a Pop Art frenzy" captures the essence
of this "trendy" café in the gritty Northern Quarter; its "great" no-
meat cooking wins consistent praise, but it's as a place to start the
day that the place wins most nominations. /* **Sample dishes:** *tomato &
Mozzarella salad; triple-decker veggie breakfast sandwich; chocolate fudge cake.*
Details: *off Piccadilly Gardens; L & afternoon tea only; no credit cards; no smoking
area.*

Croma   £ 22   Ⓐ
1 Clarence St M2 4DE   (0161) 237 9799
*"Stylish surroundings, a good central location, prompt service and
good value" make this "busy and buzzing" joint just
"like PizzaExpress but better" – no great surprise as the owners
used to be franchisees of the city's (fantastically successful) branch
of that chain. /* **Sample dishes:** *goats cheese bruschetta; chicken Caesar salad
pizza; crème brûlée cheesecake.* **Details:** *www.cromamanchester.co.uk; off Albert
Square; 11 pm; no smoking area; need 6+ to book.*

Dimitri's   £ 29
Campfield Arc M3 4FN   (0161) 839 3319
*"Cheap and cheerful" – and "child-friendly", too – this well-known,
semi-al fresco Greek taverna makes a handy rendezvous, in a
Victorian arcade just off Deansgate (and its "amazing" platters help
make it "good for groups"); it's "not especially authentic", though,
and some reporters fear its standards are getting "shoddy".
/* **Sample dishes:** *chorizo salad; ribs with vegetable couscous; baklava.*
Details: *www.dimitris.co.uk; near Museum of Science & Industry; 11.30 pm.*

Dukes 92   £ 22   Ⓐ
19-25 Castle St M3 4LZ   (0161) 839 8646
*"Amazing cheese platters" (featuring "massive" portions) help make
this lively pub in Castlefield "good for a cheap and cheerful 'light'
meal". /* **Sample dishes:** *roast tomato soup; ciabatta with bacon & pesto;
hot fudge cake.* **Details:** *off Deansgate; 8 pm; no Amex.*

East   £ 22   ★
52-54 Faulkner St M1 4SH   (0161) 236 1188
*"Not quite up with the Yang Sing, but close" – reporters speak only
well of the Pacific's conventionally-styled Chinatown sibling.
/* **Details:** *www.theeastrestaurant.co.uk; 11 pm; no Amex.*

Eighth Day Café   £ 10
111 Oxford St M1 7DU   (0161) 273 4878
*"A super vegetarian option in studentland", which retained its
popularity as a "good-value" destination while in temporary digs;
post-survey, it has returned to new premises on its original site.
/* **Sample dishes:** *Armenian lentil soup; vegan pâté with pitta bread & salad; vegan
chocolate cake.* **Details:** *www.eighth-day.co.uk; 7 pm; closed Sun; no smoking;
no booking.*

Francs   £ 31
2 Goose Grn WA14 1DW   (0161) 941 3954
*No one makes exaggerated claims for the "solid", "reasonably
priced" French fare at this local "favourite"; practically all reporters,
though, say it's "consistently reliable". /* **Sample dishes:** *salmon
dauphinoise; chicken in coconut & lime; chocolate praline tartlet.*
Details: *www.francs-altrincham.com; 10.30 pm, Fri & Sat 11 pm; no smoking area.*

sign up for the survey at www.hardens.com

Francs
The Lowry   £31   ✗
Pier 8, Salford Quays M50 3AZ (0161) 876 2121
It's "convenient pre-theatre" and has "excellent views", but this
cultural centre eatery is widely panned by reporters as a "soulless"
place, with "mediocre" cooking, "poor" service and "vastly inflated"
prices. / *Sample dishes:* sauteed chicken livers, wholegrain mustard sauce,
warm onion tart; pork & caramelized apple sausages, rosemary and red onion
marmalade, champ, calvados jus; chocolate orange torte with chocolate Creme
Anglaise. *Details:* www.thelowry.com; 7.45 pm, 9.45 pm Fri-Sat; L only, D on
performance nights only; no smoking.

French Restaurant
Midland Hotel   £34
Peter St M60 2DS (0161) 236 3333
It's something of a Mancunian institution, but this venerable grand
hotel dining room doesn't inspire much attention these days;
even diehard fans admit it's a touch "pricey", but they applaud the
"classic cuisine" and the "high standard of service".
/ *Details:* 10.30 pm; closed Mon D, Tue D & Sat L; no jeans; no smoking.
Accommodation: 303 rooms, from £165.

Great Kathmandu   £20   ★
140 Burton Rd M20 1JQ (0161) 434 6413
"Restoring faith in the subcontinent for those jaded by greasy Brit-
curries", this West Didsbury Nepalese serves "fresh food that's full
of flavour"; beware, though, this is a "cramped" place that's usually
"heaving". / *Details:* near Withington hospital; midnight.

Green's   £27
43 Lapwing Ln M20 2NT (0161) 434 4259
A few reporters say it's "not quite as good as it used to be", but this
café-like West Didsbury veggie remains a "fun" (and "noisy") joint,
whose "tasty" fare still has many fans; BYO. / *Sample dishes:* feta,
watermelon & cucumber salad; aubergine & potato Massaman curry; chocolate &
honeycomb mocha pot. *Details:* 4m S of city centre; 10.30 pm; closed Mon L &
Sat L; no Amex.

The Greenhouse   £17
331 Great Western St M14 4AN (0161) 224 0730
A decade in business – "honest" vegetarian and vegan cooking still
wins praise for this cosy Rusholme fixture, in an end-of-terrace
house. / *Sample dishes:* houmous & pitta bread; peppers stuffed with cashews &
pilau rice; Knickerbocker glory. *Details:* www.dineveggie.com; 9.30 pm; closed Aug;
no Amex; no smoking.

The Grinch   £24   𝔸
5-7 Chapel Walks, off Cross St M2 1HN (0161) 907 3210
Its the "great buzz" which endears this "bijou" café/bar to people –
a great rendezvous just off St Anne's Square, with a "limited" menu.
/ *Sample dishes:* crispy duck & Japanese cucumber salad; grilled chilli chicken
Caesar salad; marshmallow ice cream & chocolate fudge sauce.
Details: www.grinch.co.uk; 10 pm.

Gurkha Grill   £18   ★
198 Burton Rd M20 1LH (0161) 445 3461
"Forget Rusholme" – this small and "interestingly scruffy" Nepalese
"knocks the curry mile into a cocked hat", at least according to its
ardent fanclub; its ratings, though, declined a little this year.
/ *Details:* 11.30 pm, Fri & Sat 12.30 am; D only.

Jamfish £ 30
28-32 Greenwood St WA14 1RZ (0161) 928 6677
That it's "great with children" is a key selling point of this trendy Altrincham bar/restaurant, which majors in weekend brunches.
/ **Sample dishes:** tomato risotto cakes; deep-fried cod with pesto butter; rhubarb crumble. **Details:** www.jamfish.co.uk; 10 pm; closed Mon.

Juniper £ 50 ★
21 The Downs WA14 2QD (0161) 929 4008
"The bizarre-sounding dishes worked perfectly" – Paul Kitching's "adventurous" cuisine won much more consistent acclaim from reporters this year for this otherwise low-key Altrincham spot – Greater Manchester's "foodiest" destination by far; "prices are high", though, especially "given the size of the portions".
/ **Sample dishes:** scallops with curried pea sauce; lamb with raisins & sweetbreads in espresso sauce; lemon tart with Florida fruit cocktail. **Details:** 10 pm; closed Mon, Sat L & Sun; no smoking.

Koh Samui £ 27 ★★
16 Princess St M1 4NB (0161) 237 9511
"Manchester's finest Thai restaurant" – "no surprises, just great, well-presented food and in good portions" – makes this "authentic" Didsbury spot a worthy successor to the eminent Chiang Rai (which formerly stood on the site); seafood dishes are a highlight.
/ **Details:** www.kohsamuirestaurant.co.uk; opp City Art Gallery; 11.30 pm; closed Sat L & Sun L.

Koreana £ 23 ★
40a King St W M3 2WY (0161) 832 4330
"A must-visit, why isn't it in your guide?" – we're happy to rectify the omission of this "fantastic Korean", in a basement hidden off Deansgate, which is noted for its "interesting and different" food at "good prices". / **Details:** www.koreana.co.uk; 10.30 pm; closed Sat L & Sun.

Kro Bar £ 21
325 Oxford Rd M1 7ED (0161) 274 3100
"Excellent UK and Continental beers", "super coffee", "good cocktails" and "great-value snacks" (notably, "awesome full English breakfasts") again win the thumbs-up for this "lively" café/bar, in a large, 19th-century terrace house; for the summer "there's a nice garden at the back". / **Sample dishes:** smoked fish chowder; African-spiced chicken with coconut rice; hot chocolate fudge cake. **Details:** www.kro.co.uk; 11 pm; no Amex; no smoking area; children: 18+ only.

Kro2 £ 24
Oxford Hs, Oxford Rd M1 7ES (0161) 236 1048
A "nice", "bright" and "busy" atmosphere makes this new offshoot of the growing Kro empire a pleasant rendezvous; the Danish fare is "interesting", too. / **Sample dishes:** gravadlax plate with sweet mustard sauce & rye bread; haddock cooked in soy, ginger, garlic & sake. **Details:** www.kro.co.uk/two/; 10 pm; no smoking area; children: not allowed in bar.

Lal Haweli £ 19 ★
68-72 Wilmslow Rd M14 (0161) 248 9700
A cramped, lesser-known Rusholme Indian which "maintains good standards on the food front". / **Details:** 1.15 am; no smoking area.

sign up for the survey at www.hardens.com 255

Lead Station £24
99 Beech Rd M21 9EQ (0161) 881 5559
*"A great place to chill, read papers and chat" – this "friendly and bustling café/bar" (in an "airy ex-municipal building") serves "a good variety of light meals" and specialises in "superb" breakfasts and brunches. / **Sample dishes:** baked goats cheese with honey; Spanish lamb casserole with chorizo & mash; Belgian chocolate cheesecake. **Details:** 9.30 pm, Thu-Sat 10 pm; no booking.*

The Lime Tree £33 Ⓐ★
8 Lapwing Ln M20 2WS (0161) 445 1217
*"You leave wanting to return" to this "first-class" Didsbury brasserie whose "wonderful", "buzzy" atmosphere, "helpful" and "knowledgeable" service and "skillful" cooking maintain its position as one of the best places of its type in the country.
/ **Sample dishes:** peppered tuna carpaccio; fillet steak with black pepper & cream sauce; Baileys cheesecake with honeycomb ice cream.
Details: www.thelimetreerestaurant.com; toward Manchester airport; 10.30 pm; closed Mon L & Sat L; no smoking area; booking essential.*

The Lincoln £38
1 Lincoln Sq M2 5LN (0161) 834 9000
*This "smart city-centre restaurant" is a "lively" spot that's especially popular as a venue for business; mostly it was found to be an "efficient and good" operation, but there are also reports of meals that were simply "dreadful". / **Sample dishes:** Moroccan beef salad; tandoori monkfish with spinach & raita; spotted dick with custard ice cream. **Details:** www.lincolnrestaurant.com; opp Manchester Evening News building; 10.30 pm, Fri & Sat 11 pm; closed Sat L & Sun D.*

Little Yang Sing £25 ★★
17 George St M1 4HE (0161) 228 7722
*"Since the make-over, it's just got better"; in terms of reporters' ratings, this "great Chinese restaurant" – on the Yang Sing's original site – is now only narrowly pipped to the post by its mega-famous Chinatown sibling. / **Details:** www.littleyangsing.co.uk; 11.30 pm.*

Livebait £32
22 Lloyd St M2 5WA (0161) 817 4110
*Though critics deride "pedestrian cooking" in a setting "like a glorified WC", this city-centre fish and seafood specialist still has quite a number of fans – they admit it "sometimes feels overpriced", but find it "surprisingly good, for a chain".
/ **Sample dishes:** Mediterranean fish soup; lobster with new potato salad; panna cotta & strawberries. **Details:** www.santeonline.co.uk; 10.30 pm; closed Sun; no smoking area.*

Lounge 10 £32 Ⓐ★
10 Tib Ln M2 4JB
(0161) 834 1331
*"Very decadent", "very trendy", "very romantic" – the "sumptuous" look is the highlight at this candlelit yearling, but the "friendly" service and "interesting" menu are far from incidental attractions.
/ **Sample dishes:** goats cheese with seaweed & chilli dressing; salt & pepper duck with onion bhaji & plum sauce; white chocolate mousse.
Details: www.lounge10manchester.com; 11 pm.*

sign up for the survey at www.hardens.com

Love Saves The Day £21 𝔸★
Smithfield Buildings, Tib St M4 1LA (0161) 832 0777
This "ultra-cool" and "relaxed" NYC-style deli/diner has a "unique" appeal in downtown Manchester; "simple but excellent" breakfasts are a highlight, and the place also makes a "great lunch stop".
/ **Sample dishes:** Cheshire ham & cheeses with picalilli; sausages with bacon bubble 'n' squeak; sticky toffee pudding. **Details:** www.lovesavestheday.co.uk; 7 pm; closed Sun; no smoking.

The Lowry Hotel £39
50 Dearmans Pl M3 5LH (0161) 827 4000
"The ambience is awful and nothing lives up to the hype" – symptomatic feedback on the "rather soulless" dining room in Rocco Forte's new (and otherwise quite commendable) design-hotel, a few minutes' walk from Deansgate; let's hope new (from July 2003) chef Steve McLaughlin can pep things up. / **Sample dishes:** pistou soup with scallops; roast duck breast with juniper jus; praline crème brûlée.
Details: www.theloweryhotel.com; 10.30 pm; booking: max 8.
Accommodation: 165 rooms, from £234.

Malmaison £33
Piccadilly M1 3AQ (0161) 278 1000
"Dull cooking, despite constant menu changes" has deadened reporters' enthusiasm for the once-very-fashionable brasserie of this city-centre design-hotel. / **Sample dishes:** eggs benedict; sea bream with asparagus; champagne & strawberry jelly. **Details:** www.malmaison.com; near Piccadilly Station; 10.45 pm; no smoking area. **Accommodation:** 167 rooms, from £125.

The Mark Addy £18 ★
Stanley St M5 5EJ (0161) 832 4080
Those who appreciate a "no-nonsense" formula continue to praise the cheese (mainly) and pâté menu at these river-view cellars.
/ **Sample dishes:** chive & onion cheese with bread; duck pâté & salad; no puddings. **Details:** 9 pm, hot food 6.50 pm; no Amex.

The Market £33 𝔸★
104 High St M4 1HQ (0161) 834 3743
The décor ("like stepping back to the '40s") and the cooking ("best of British") make this long-established city-centre restaurant a truly "unique" Mancunian "institution"; indeed, the very worst complaint – and from a good number of reports – was the "limited opening times". / **Sample dishes:** potato ravioli with mint; Parmesan turkey with red pepper confit; banana & passion fruit pavlova.
Details: www.market-restaurant.com; 10 pm; closed Mon, Tue, Sat L & Sun.

Metropolitan £25 𝔸
2 Lapwing Ln M20 2WS (0161) 374 9559
"A trendy pub in a trendy area" – a "great" atmosphere helps make this "very popular" Withington gastropub one of Manchester's most commented-on hang-outs; the food plays a bit of a supporting rôle, but it's "freshly cooked" (and "very good" burgers are a top tip).
/ **Sample dishes:** Stilton fritters with lemongrass dressing; pork & leek sausages with apple mash; sticky toffee pudding. **Details:** near Withington hospital; 9.30 pm; no smoking area.

Le Mont
Urbis Science Museum

£48 Ａ★

Cathedral Gdns M4 3BG
(0161) 605 8282

"Panoramic views over the city" are just one of the features which have added "wow"-factor to this "sleek" and "exciting" dining room above a trendy new museum; the cooking is "better than you'd expect", too, with some reporters already hailing it as "the best in Manchester". / *Sample dishes:* creamy white onion & cider soup with cheese croutons; grilled & roast lamb with vegetables; cinnamon poached pear with ice cream. *Details:* www.urbis.org.uk; 10.30 pm; closed Sat L & Sun; no smoking area.

Moss Nook   £53   ★

Ringway Rd M22 5WD   (0161) 437 4778

Opinions differ on this plush, bordello-style Gallic veteran, near the airport; to critics it's just "dated and over-rated", but those who take to its "old-fashioned" style say it offers "unwavering quality". / *Sample dishes:* twice-baked cheese & chive soufflé; beef with foie gras pâté & rosti; crème brûlée. *Details:* on B5166, 1m from Manchester airport; 9.30 pm; closed Mon, Sat L & Sun; children: 11+.

Mr Thomas's Chop House   £32   Ａ

52 Cross St M2 7AR   (0161) 832 2245

"Like stepping back in time, but with better food" – this unspoilt Victorian chophouse is "that all-too-rare beast, a pub with real character"; it makes "an excellent lunch spot" (especially for business), with "better-than-average" grub, "well-looked-after beer" and "excellent wines". / *Sample dishes:* black pudding, egg & smoked bacon salad; roast cod with bubble 'n' squeak; jam sponge with custard. *Details:* L only.

New Bouchon   £26

63 Bridge St M3 3BQ   (0161) 832 9393

"Intimate" and "very French", this bistro near Kendal's is worth knowing about for its "good" Gallic cooking. / *Sample dishes:* Burgundy snails with garlic confit; beef with dauphinoise potatoes; profiteroles. *Details:* 9.30 pm; phone ahead for open hours; no smoking.

New Emperor   £25   ★

52-56 George St M1 4HF   (0161) 228 2883

"Excellent food and service" at "reasonable" prices (and including "good-value banquets") maintain the appeal of this gaudy Chinatown spot. / *Details:* www.newemperor.co.uk; 11.45 pm, Sat 12.45 am; no smoking.

The Nose   £20

6 Lapwing Ln M20 8WS   (0161) 445 3653

Whether you're just looking for "a cup of tea and a chat", "a bowl of soup with a crusty roll" or some "interesting" more substantial fare, this West Didsbury bar/restaurant is a "really relaxed" choice that's consistently popular with reporters. / *Sample dishes:* Welsh rarebit; mixed fish kebabs; sticky toffee pudding. *Details:* between Palatine Road & Withington hospital; 9.30 pm; no smoking area; need 10+ to book.

The Ox   £26

71 Liverpool Rd M3 4NQ   (0161) 839 7740

"Cosy" and "professionally-run", this large Castlefield gastropub offers provides an "original" menu of modern pub grub. / *Sample dishes:* teriyaki beef; roast rack of lamb; toffee & pecan cheesecake. *Details:* www.theox.co.uk; Mon-Wed 10 pm, Thu-Sat 11 pm, Sun 9.30 pm; no Amex; no smoking area. *Accommodation:* 9 rooms, from £44.95.

Pacific £33 ★
58-60 George St M1 4HF (0161) 228 6668
*Decked out in (slightly "clinical") "feng shui-style" minimalism,
this two-tier "Chinatown gem" (upstairs Thai, downstairs Chinese)
again wins rave reviews for its "great range" of "impressive" food;
the buffet Thai lunch, in particular, is "renowned for its value".*
/ **Details:** www.pacific-restaurant-manchester.co.uk; 10.45 pm; no smoking area;
children: 3+.

Palmiro £28 ★
197 Upper Chorlton Rd M16 OBH (0161) 860 7330
*After a couple of years of variable reports feedback on this
"unexpected" shop-conversion "gem" in Whalley Grange is back
almost to the hymn of praise it was of old; the Italian cooking
is "gutsy", "eclectic" and "authentic", and there's a "fascinating" all-
Italian wine list.* / **Sample dishes:** slow-roast tomato risotto; char-grilled sea
bass; poached pears & caramel with polenta. **Details:** www.palmiro.net; 10.30 pm;
D only, except Sun open L & D.

Pearl City £21 ★
33 George St M1 4PH (0161) 228 7683
*Vast and long-established, this Chinatown stand-by still offers
"fine food".* / **Details:** 1.15 am, Fri & Sat 3 am.

Le Petit Blanc £31
55 King St M2 4LQ (0161) 832 1000
*"I hope the place gets through liquidation in one piece!"; before
financial problems set in, Raymond Blanc's bright modern brasserie
established itself as the best in the group (and one of the best
modern eateries in downtown Manchester) – since summer 2003,
the chain has been managed by Loch Fyne.* / **Sample dishes:** snail &
spinach fricassée; roast chicken with braised leeks & morels; lemon tart with
raspberry sorbet. **Details:** www.lepetitblanc.co.uk; 11 pm; no smoking area.

Punjab Tandoori £17 ★★
177 Wilmslow Rd M14 5AP (0161) 225 2960
*"The best food on Manchester's Curry Mile" is again hailed by the
numerous fans of this friendly Rusholme Indian; its "more interesting
menu than most" includes a "vast veggie selection".*
/ **Details:** 11.45 pm; no Amex.

The Restaurant Bar & Grill £30 Ⓐ
14 John Dalton St M2 5JR
(0161) 839 1999
*The "big comfy booths" are "excellent for talking business", at this
"stylish" and "bustling" two-year-old "in the heart of the city-centre";
even fans concede the food's "not innovative", but "what they do,
they do well".* / **Sample dishes:** spicy shrimp risotto; crispy duck with pear &
watercress salad; bread & butter pudding. **Details:** www.individualrestaurants.co.uk;
10.45 pm; booking: max 8 at weekends.

El Rincon £26 Ⓐ
Longworth St, off St John's St M3 4BQ (0161) 839 8819
*"There's a terrific Spanish feel" to this "busy" but "very friendly"
basement bar, tucked away behind Deansgate; it attracts "a nice
mix of locals and Spaniards", and offers a "wide selection" of tapas
which are "authentic" and "good value".* / **Sample dishes:** prawns 'pil-pil';
grilled sea bass with lemon; cheesecake. **Details:** off Deansgate; 11.30 pm; booking
essential.

Sam's Chop House £24

Black Pool Fold, Chapel Walks M2 1HN (0161) 834 3210

"Good English food in a traditional atmosphere" is the gist of most commentary on this tucked-away, "old-fashioned" local "institution"; it "doesn't come cheap", though, and some reporters find it "too tightly packed". / **Sample dishes:** soup of the day; home-made corn beef hash; steamed pudding. **Details:** www.samschophouse.com; 9.30 pm; closed Sun.

Sangam £15 ★

9-19 Wilmslow Rd M14 5TB (0161) 257 3922

A "wide variety" of dishes – with an accommodating approach to those wishing to go 'off-menu' – helps make this Rusholme subcontinental a "better-than-average" choice, on the street of a thousand curries. / **Details:** www.sangam.co.uk; midnight; no smoking area.

Shere Khan £18

52 Wilmslow Rd M14 5TQ (0161) 256 2624

It's a "reliable" culinary option rather than a remarkable one, but this bright fixture on the curry mile is popular locally, notwithstanding the sometimes "poor service and attitude". / **Details:** www.skrestaurant.com; midnight, Fri & Sat 3 am; no smoking area.

Siam Orchid £25

54 Portland St M1 4QU (0161) 236 1388

"Good, reasonably-priced Thai food" makes this restaurant behind Piccadilly station an ever-handy stand-by. / **Details:** 11.30 pm; closed Sat L & Sun L.

Simply Heathcote's £30 ✕

Jackson Row, Deansgate M2 5WD (0161) 835 3536

Paul Heathcote's "pretentious" brasserie off Deansgate is often censured by reporters for its "high" prices, its "condescending" service and its "cold" and "featureless" setting – indeed, the overwhelming impression is that it's just "too big for its boots"! / **Sample dishes:** ham hock terrine; roast lamb with couscous; rice pudding with vanilla ice cream. **Details:** www.heathcotes.co.uk; near Opera House; 10 pm, Sat 11 pm; no smoking in dining room.

Stock £43 Ⓐ

4 Norfolk St M2 1DW (0161) 839 6644

Impressively housed in the "fantastic surroundings" of the old Stock Exchange, this Italian restaurant is for some reporters "the best of the openings of recent years", offering cooking that's "pretty good", if arguably "expensive" for what it is. / **Sample dishes:** linguine with crayfish tails; calves liver in balsamic vinegar sauce; caramelised peach tartlet. **Details:** www.stockrestaurant.co.uk; 10.30 pm; closed Sun.

Tai Pan £24 ★

81-97 Upper Brook St M13 9TX (0161) 273 2798

"Superb Hong Kong-style Sunday dim sum" is a highlight of the "good-quality" Chinese menu on offer at this warehouse-like place, a little way from the city-centre; it's all a bit "chaotic", though (and recent reports are slightly up-and-down). / **Details:** 11 pm, Sun 9.30 pm.

Tampopo £24 ★

16 Albert Sq M2 5PF (0161) 819 1966

"Fresh, tasty noodle and rice dishes" are served by "brisk", "efficient" and "friendly" staff at this popular and very consistent noodle canteen, which has become something of a city-centre "staple". / **Details:** 11 pm; no smoking; need 7+ to book.

That Café £35 ★
1031-1033 Stockport Rd M19 2TB (0161) 432 4672
*"A unique restaurant with a quirky and intimate atmosphere";
reporters speak in glowing terms of the "splendid" cooking at this
"impressive" little place – all the more of a surprise in its "run-
down" Levenshulme location. / **Sample dishes:** pan-fried squid & king prawn
salad; beef fillet with celeriac rosti; passion fruit tart. **Details:** www.thatcafe.co.uk;
on A6 between Manchester & Stockport; 10.30 pm; closed Mon, Tue-Sat D only,
closed Sun D; no Amex; no smoking area.*

This & That £5 ★
3 Soap St M4 1EW (0161) 832 4971
*The "cheapest quality meal around" is to be had at this "transport
caff"-style Indian, where "you queue up to be served" for the
"excellent" 'rice-and-three' (rice and your choice from a "wide daily
selection of curries"). / **Details:** 5 pm; closed Sat; no credit cards.*

Velvet £27 Ⓐ
2 Canal St M1 3HE (0161) 236 9003
*"Always fun", this Gay Village stalwart is a "buzzy" and "attitude-
free" hang out which remains very popular; the food, if hardly the
main attraction, is "good-value". / **Sample dishes:** soup of the day; steak
with pepper sauce & chips; chocolate fudge cake. **Details:** 10 pm, Fri & Sat
midnight; children: not permitted.*

Wong Chu £21 ★
63 Faulkner St M1 4FF (0161) 236 2346
*"Good, reasonably-priced, authentic and friendly" – this "café-style"
Chinatown spot "may not be the place for a romantic evening",
but fans say it offers "the best value". / **Details:** midnight; no Amex.*

Woodstock Tavern £23
139 Barlow Moor Rd M20 2DY (0161) 448 7951
*"Excellent specials" – sometimes using exotic ingredients –
contribute to the attractions of this lively Chorlton-cum-Hardy
boozer, which attracts "a nicely mixed clientèle".
/ **Sample dishes:** salt & pepper chicken wings; kangaroo steak with port &
mushroom sauce; strawberry Daiquiri cheesecake. **Details:** 8.30 pm; no Amex;
no smoking area; no booking; children: before 8.30 pm.*

Yang Sing £30 ★★
34 Princess St M1 4JY (0161) 236 2200
*"I've eaten Cantonese around the world – none as good as here";
thanks to Harry Yeung's "continually evolving" cuisine and the
"sparky" service, this celebrated Chinatown veteran remains quite
probably "the best Chinese restaurant in Europe"; it's not just
novices who say "let them choose a banquet for you".
/ **Details:** www.yang-sing.com; 11.45 pm, Fri & Sat 12.15 am; smoking discouraged.*

Zinc Bar & Grill £35 ✗
The Triangle, Hanging Ditch M4 3ES (0161) 827 4200
*An outlet of Conran's dire and "overpriced" nationwide brasserie
chain; when things (not infrequently) go wrong, they can go horribly
wrong, and too many reporters note experiences that offered
"zero value for money". / **Sample dishes:** fried squid with chilli; lamb kebabs
with bulgar wheat salad; lemon tart. **Details:** www.conran.com; 10 pm.*

MANNINGTREE, ESSEX 3–2C

Stour Bay Café £30
39-43 High St CO11 1AH (01206) 396687
"They try very hard to please", at this *"friendly"* bistro *"near the seafront"*, where *"good seafood"* is the highlight of a *"reliable, if not outstanding"* selection. / **Sample dishes:** *crab bisque with whisky; seared tuna with bean & tomato salad; pecan pie.* **Details:** *www.stourbaycafe.com; 9.30 pm; closed Mon, Tue & Sun D; no Amex; no smoking.*

MARKET HARBOROUGH, LEICESTERSHIRE 5–4D

Han's £24 ★
29 St Mary's Rd LE16 7DS (01858) 462288
Fans find "reliably excellent" Chinese cooking at this "comfortable" town-centre spot. / **Details:** *11 pm; closed Sat L & Sun.*

MARLOW, BUCKINGHAMSHIRE 3–3A

Compleat Angler £57 ✗
Marlow Bridge SL7 1RG (0870) 400 8100
Thanks to the "wonderful waterside location", "love can blossom" at this famous Thames-side hotel (these days a Macdonald Hotels property); the prices can be "unbelievable", though, given standards that too many just find "terrible, terrible, terrible".
/ **Sample dishes:** *smoked haddock & potato terrine; roast duck with marinated white cabbage; Baileys & honey parfait.* **Details:** *www.macdonald-hotels.co.uk; 10 pm; no smoking area.* **Accommodation:** *64 rooms, from £225.*

Danesfield House Hotel £65 Ⓐ
Henley Rd SL7 2EY (01628) 891010
A "beautiful setting" has always been the undoubted strength of this wedding cake-style Victorian country house hotel; the food is perhaps not the main point of a visit, but those who go for "a romantic treat" are rarely disappointed. / **Sample dishes:** *cauliflower pannacotta with oysters; venison with artichoke & shallot fricassée; apricot & ginger crème brûlée.* **Details:** *www.danesfieldhouse.co.uk; 3m outside Marlow on the A4155; 9.30 pm; no smoking.* **Accommodation:** *87 rooms, from £225.*

Marlow Bar & Grill £34 Ⓐ
92-94 High St SL7 1AQ (01628) 488544
"A fun place, especially at weekends" – this smart modern newcomer is off to a good start, with a *"great atmosphere"* (*"don't go if you want quiet"*) and some *"consistently good"* food.
/ **Sample dishes:** *fried chilli squid with thai noodle salad; grilled fillet steak; warm chocolate pudding with Malteser ice cream.* **Details:** *10.30 pm; no smoking area.*

The Vanilla Pod £50 ★★
31 West St SL7 2LS
(01628) 898101
After only a year or so in business, it's "almost impossible to get a table" at Michael Macdonald's "creative" and "excellent" Gallic restaurant; the setting is "intimate" or "claustrophobic", to taste.
/ **Sample dishes:** *scallops with vanilla-poached pears; sea bass with Szechuan sauce; bitter chocolate fondant.* **Details:** *www.thevanillapod.co.uk; 9 pm; closed Mon & Sun; smoking in bar only.*

MASHAM, NORTH YORKSHIRE   8–4B

Black Sheep Brewery Bistro   £ 29

Wellgarth HG4 4EN   (01765) 680101

"Basic food, that's good and plentiful" is on offer at this *"enjoyable"* destination, which enjoys a *"great view"*; as it's *"part of a brewery visitor centre"*, much of its appeal is in liquid form.
/ **Sample dishes:** *beaujolais paté with sweet green pickles; lamb shank marinated in ale served with mash & rosemary jus; treacle tart with ice cream.*
Details: *www.blacksheep.co.uk; 9.30 pm; closed Mon D, Tue D & Sun D; no Amex; no smoking area.*

Floodlite   £ 28   ★

7 Silver St HG4 4DX   (01765) 689000

"Local game and the best of other local produce" are prepared to a *"very acceptable"* standard at Charles Flood's *"consistent"* small-town restaurant in the Dales. / **Sample dishes:** *Arbroath Smokie soufflé; chicken stuffed with banana & curry sauce; strawberry shortbread.* **Details:** *9 pm; closed Mon, Tue L, Wed L, Thu L & Sun D; no Switch; no smoking area.*

MELBOURN, CAMBRIDGESHIRE   3–1B

The Pink Geranium   £ 52

25 Station Rd SG8 6DX   (01763) 260215

Reports on this pretty, thatched restaurant remain mixed – fans laud "beautiful presentation" of a "superb" modern menu, but doubters just find the whole performance "disinterested".
/ **Sample dishes:** *niçoise vegetable terrine with tapenade dressing; boudin of lobster with new potatoes; crème brûlée with raspberry coulis.*
Details: *www.pinkgeranium.co.uk; off A10, 2nd exit (opp church); 9.30 pm; closed Mon; no smoking in dining room.*

Sheene Mill   £ 45   Ⓐ

Station Rd SG8 6DX   (01763) 261393

"A 17th-century mill with a sensational garden" provides the *"wonderful"* setting for TV-chef Steven Saunders HQ; many praise his *"creative"* cooking and *"friendly"* staff, but a few mixed reports undercut the ratings. / **Sample dishes:** *crispy duck spring rolls with sweet chilli sauce; wild venison with mushroom risotto; banana tarte Tatin.*
Details: *www.sheenemill.co.uk; off A10, 10m S of Cambridge; 10 pm; closed Sun D; no smoking before 9.30 pm.* **Accommodation:** *9 rooms, from £90.*

MELBOURNE, DERBYSHIRE   5–3C

Bay Tree   £ 39   ★

4 Potter St DE73 1DW   (01332) 863358

"The food gets better and better", say fans of this *"old-favourite"* former coaching inn, where chef Rex Howell's dishes can be *"unusual"* and *"interesting"*. / **Sample dishes:** *minted melon with lemongrass granita; pork tenderloin with goats cheese gnocchi; Canadian pancakes with maple syrup.* **Details:** *www.baytreerestaurant.co.uk; 10 pm; closed Mon & Sun D; no smoking area.*

MELLOR, CHESHIRE   5–2B

Oddfellows Arms   £ 27   Ⓐ

73 Moor End Rd SK6 5PT   (0161) 449 7826

"Hard to find, but a nice surprise when you do"; this *"casual"* pub – complete with *"slate floors, beams, open fires, etc"* – *"gets very busy"*, thanks in good measure to the quality of its affordable scoff.
/ **Sample dishes:** *soused herrings with mustard sour cream; Catalan pork tenderloin with basil ragu; frosted peach schnapps cheesecake.* **Details:** *7m S of Stockport; 9.30 pm; closed Mon & Sun D; no Amex; no smoking in dining room; book for D & Sun L only.*

sign up for the survey at www.hardens.com

MELMERBY, CUMBRIA   8–3A
Shepherd's Inn   £23   𝔸★
CA10 1HF   (0870) 745 3383
*Martin Baucutt's "welcoming" boozer is a "consistent" venture,
praised by most (if not quite all) reporters for its "good restaurant
food at pub prices". / Sample dishes: dill-marinated herrings; breaded
wholetail scampi; lemon cheesecake. **Details:** 9.45 pm weekends 9pm weekdays;
no Amex; no smoking area; no booking.*

Village Bakery   £23   ★
CA10 1HE   (01768) 881811
*For breakfast or lunch, this "excellent" café (part of the well-known
Lakeland firm of specialist bakers) is "always worth a detour";
"organic food is well presented in a pleasant setting, overlooking the
village green". / Sample dishes: vegetable soup; grilled trout with herb butter;
upside down pear & ginger pudding. **Details:** www.village-bakery.com; 10m NE
of Penrith on A686; 5 pm; L only; no Amex; no smoking; need 6+ to book.*

MERTHYR TYDFIL, MERTHYR TYDFIL   4–4D
Nant Ddu Lodge   £30   ★
Brecon Rd   CF48 2HY   (01685) 379111
*"An oasis in a desert"; this hotel "nestling in the Brecon Beacons"
boasts an "excellent bar and restaurant". / Sample dishes: duck mousse
with caramelised oranges; ham hock with mustard mash & parsley sauce;
plum crumble. **Details:** www.nant-ddu-lodge.co.uk; 6m N of Merthyr on A470;
9.30 pm; no smoking; booking: max 8. **Accommodation:** 28 rooms, from £79.50.*

MICKLEHAM, SURREY   3–3A
King William IV   £27   ★
Byttom Hl   RH5 6EL   (01372) 372590
*The "good honest" food "sets the standards" hereabouts, at this
well-known, hillside free house, praised for its "well-kept beers, wide-
ranging menu and lovely gardens". / Sample dishes: garlic bread with
Mozzarella; steak & kidney pie; treacle tart. **Details:** www.king-williamiv.com;
off A24; 9.30 pm; closed Sun D; no Amex; no booking in summer; children: 12+
inside.*

MILTON KEYNES, MILTON KEYNES   3–2A
Jaipur   £26
599 Grafton Gate East   MK9 1AT   (01908) 669796
*"Worth it for the novelty, if nothing else" – Europe's largest purpose-
built Indian occupies "ranch-sized" premises which some reporters
find surprisingly "elegant"; you get a "warm" reception, too, and
reports on the cooking are mainly positive. / **Details:** www.jaipur.co.uk;
11 pm; no smoking in dining room.*

MORSTON, NORFOLK   6–3C
Morston Hall   £51   𝔸★★
Main Coast Rd   NR25 7AA   (01263) 741041
*The "unparalleled north Norfolk coast nearby" is not the only
advantage enjoyed by this "consistently exceptional" country house
hotel – set in "beautiful gardens", it offers a "superlative menu"
delivered by "friendly" and "very professional" staff (who "treat
small children like human beings"). / Sample dishes: Milanese risotto with
deep-fried leeks; roast lamb with buttery mash; sticky toffee pudding with
butterscotch sauce. **Details:** www.morstonhall.com; between Blakeney & Wells
on A149; 8 pm; D only, except Sun open L & D; no smoking; booking essential.
Accommodation: 7 rooms, from £100.*

MOULSFORD, OXFORDSHIRE   2–2D

Beetle & Wedge   £ 48   Ⓐ
Ferry Ln   OX10 9JF   (01491) 651381
A "glorious" Thames-side location helps create a "memorable and relaxing" experience at this picturesque hotel; the more informal 'Boathouse' – with its "good grill menu" – is often preferred to the more formal dining possibilities of the main hotel dining room.
/ *Sample dishes:* onion tart with foie gras & truffle sauce; monkfish & surf clams in champagne & saffron sauce; Cointreau soufflé with raspberry coulis.
Details: www.beetleandwedge.co.uk; on A329 between Streatley & Wallingford, take Ferry Lane at crossroads; 9.45 pm; D only Thurs-Sat & Sun L only, Boathouse open daily; no smoking in dining room. **Accommodation:** 11 rooms, from £160.

MOULTON, NORTH YORKSHIRE   8–3B

Black Bull   £ 38   Ⓐ★
DL10 6QJ   (01325) 377289
"How do they keep it up after 40 years?"; this celebrated, quirky dining pub – where you can eat either in a Pullman railway carriage or dining conservatory – offers some "lovely" cooking (including "the best seafood"). / *Sample dishes:* shellfish bisque; lemon sole in prawn, leek & cheese sauce; pancakes with lemon sauce. **Details:** 1m S of Scotch Corner; 10.15 pm; closed Sun; children: 7+.

MOUSEHOLE, CORNWALL   1–4A

Cornish Range   £ 36   Ⓐ
6 Chapel St   TR19 6SB   (01736) 731488
This smallish venture near the harbour is "very popular locally", thanks to its "cosy" ambience and its "fresh" and generally "reliable" food – this year's reports, however, were not without the odd disappointment. / *Sample dishes:* steamed mussels & clams with creamy saffron broth; roast monkfish tail with chorizo, razor clams & herbs; trio of mini brûlées . **Details:** www.cornishrange.com; on coast road between Penzance & Lands End; 9.30 pm (9 pm in winter); D only; no Amex; mainly nonsmoking.
Accommodation: 3 rooms, from £65.

MYLOR BRIDGE, CORNWALL   1–4B

Pandora Inn   £ 32   Ⓐ
Restronguet Creek   TR11 5ST   (01326) 372678
"Honest" and "enjoyable" are the sort of words used by most (if not quite all) reporters to describe the fare at this ancient, thatched smugglers' inn; it's the "idyllic" location, however – with a pontoon out on the water – which is its special attraction.
/ *Sample dishes:* avocado, mango & smoked salmon salad; turbot with fresh greens; lemon ricotta cheesecake. **Details:** signposted off A390, between Truro & Falmouth; 9 pm; no Amex; no smoking.

NAILSWORTH, GLOUCESTERSHIRE   2–2B

Calcot Manor   £ 41   ★
GL8 8YJ   (01666) 890391
With its "beautiful location", "simple well-done" food, "interesting" wine and "excellent" service, the dining room at this "charming" small hotel delivers an excellent, "chilled out" (and child-friendly) experience. / *Sample dishes:* scallops with spiced couscous; roast pork confit with lardons & red onion; bread & butter pudding. **Details:** www.calcotmanor.co.uk; junction of A46 & A4135; 9.30 pm; no smoking area; booking essential; children: not at D. **Accommodation:** 28 rooms, from £165.

NAYLAND, SUFFOLK 3–2C

White Hart £ 35

11 High St C06 4JF (01206) 263382

Ownership by Michel Roux creates high expectations in visitors to this "popular" rural pub; consistency, however, is most conspicuous by its absence in this year's reports – views on the cooking run the gamut from "very good" to "appalling". / **Sample dishes:** rock fish soup; roast suckling pig with sweet potato pureé; ginger & lemon gâteau. **Details:** www.whitehart-nayland.co.uk; off A12, between Colchester & Sudbury; 9.30 pm. **Accommodation:** 6 rooms, from £190.

NETHER ALDERLEY, CHESHIRE 5–2B

Wizard £ 34 A★

Macclesfield Rd SK10 4UB (01625) 584000

A "charming-converted country pub", which wins all-round praise as a "comfortable and relaxed" establishment, offering "well-prepared traditional and more innovative dishes", and "attentive" service. / **Sample dishes:** baby spinach, avocado & Gorgonzola salad; herb-crusted cod with pea pureé; rice pudding with stem ginger & maple syrup. **Details:** from A34, take B5087; 9.30 pm; closed Mon & Sun D; no smoking area.

NETTLEBED, OXFORDSHIRE 2–2D

White Hart £ 46 ★

High St RG9 5DD (01491) 641245

This "old pub, now 'modernised'" offers both a bistro and a restaurant of some ambition; the latter, in particular, can seem a touch "overpriced", but most reports tend to the view that the food is "fabulous". / **Sample dishes:** pan-fried scallops with roast fennel & orange salad; duck with white bean cassoulet; iced chestnut parfait with rum sauce. **Details:** www.whitehartnettlebed.com; Between Wallingford & Henley-on-Thames on the A430; 9 pm; closed Mon & Sun (bistro open every day for L & D); no Amex; no smoking in dining room; booking essential; children: 14+ in dining room. **Accommodation:** 12 rooms, from £105.

NEW MILTON, HAMPSHIRE 2–4C

Chewton Glen £ 63 A★

Christchurch Rd BH25 6QS (01425) 275341

"Superb in all respects"… "the best hotel in the World!"…; this "ultra-luxurious" country house on the fringe of the New Forest earns ever more superlatives for its "totally spoiling" service, "super" setting and "first class cooking"; and the recent arrival of chef Alan Murchison from L'Ortolan may even improve matters! / **Sample dishes:** tiger prawn ravioli with white truffle sauce; Angus beef with green pepper hollandaise; caramelised apples with cinnamon ice cream. **Details:** www.chewtonglen.com; on A337 between New Milton & Highcliffe; 9.30 pm; jacket required at D; no smoking; children: 6+. **Accommodation:** 59 rooms, from £290.

NEWARK, NOTTINGHAMSHIRE 5–3D

Café Bleu £ 29 A★

14 Castle Gate NG24 1BG (01636) 610141

"Definitely the best in town" – the food is "always good and imaginative" at this modern and "well-spaced" riverside brasserie, which attracts only very positive reviews. / **Sample dishes:** sardines with saffron couscous; braised Aberdeen beef with baby carrots; lemon posset with champagne sorbet. **Details:** www.cafebleu.co.uk; 9.30 pm; closed Sun D; no Amex; no smoking area.

NEWCASTLE UPON TYNE, TYNE & WEAR

8–2B

Newcastle is famously a going-out sort of place, and the city sustains a fair number of interesting eateries. Most of the action is around the Quayside – an area utterly transformed over the past decade where *Café 21* and a couple of notable upmarket Indians (*Leela's*, *Vujon*) lead the pack. Across the river, in Gateshead, *McCoys at the Baltic* has been more of an 'atmosphere' success than a culinary one. It is sadly too early to report in detail on the attractions of the new incarnation of the popular Barn Again Bistro, now *Barn @ the Biscuit Factory*.

A short taxi-ride from the centre, the city's grandest restaurant, *Fisherman's Lodge* is improving under new ownership. It enjoys a particularly picturesque situation in the leafy Jesmond Dene.

For diners on a budget, such Italians as *Francesca's* and *Pani's* offer a number of options with character; also the Indian *Valley Junction*, housed in an old railway carriage.

Barn @ the Biscuit Factory   £35
18 Stoddard St NE2 1AN   (0191) 230 3338
It did use to occupy a barn (when it was called Barn Again Bistro), but this popular brasserie moved to a former biscuit factory as our survey for the year was drawing to a close; an early reporter praises the continuation of "good food and good prices", but insufficient general feedback means we've left the place unrated.
/ *Sample dishes:* wild garlic leaf risotto with Parmesan; spiced lamb with aubergine & Mozzarella; fallen chocolate soufflé. *Details:* follow Biscuit factory signs; 9.45 pm; closed Sun D; no smoking in dining room.

Blake's   £10
53 Grey St NE1 6QH   (0191) 261 5463
"A wide range of interesting sandwiches" helps make this studenty café a top, local, light-bite rendezvous. / *Details:* 5 pm, Sun 10-4.30 pm; L only; no credit cards; no smoking area; no booking.

Café 21   £37   ★
21 Queen St, Princes Whf NE1 3UG   (0191) 222 0755
"Still Newcastle's premier restaurant"; Terry Laybourne's HQ went café-style a couple of years ago and is "busier" nowadays (if "not that atmospheric"); it still offers "imaginative" cuisine – "little changed in quality since the days of 21 Queen Street" – and at "great prices". / *Sample dishes:* duck & green peppercorn pâté; sirloin with parsley butter & chips; crème brûlée. *Details:* 10.30 pm; closed Sun; no smoking area.

Café Royal   £21
8 Nelson St NE1 5AW   (0191) 231 3000
"A vibrant place, that's excellent for coffee or lunch" – this airy all-day grand café and brasserie also makes "a great place to chill on lazy Sundays". / *Sample dishes:* crispy duck & watercress salad; beefburger; Irish chocolate cake. *Details:* www.sjf.co.uk; 7 pm; L only except Thu open L & D; no smoking.

Fisherman's Lodge £59 ★
Jesmond Dene NE7 7BQ (0191) 281 3281
After a recent change of ownership, standards are drifting gently upwards at this "highly professional" fish-specialist of long standing; though it has a "lovely location in Jesmond Dene", the restaurant itself is "not hugely atmospheric (and so ideal for business!)".
/ **Sample dishes:** assiette of crab; trio of salmon with langoustine sauce; chocolate ganache tart. **Details:** www.fishermanslodge.co.uk; 2m from city centre on A1058, follow signposts to Jesmond Dene; 10.30 pm; closed Sun; no smoking in dining room; children: 8+.

Francesca's £18 🄰
Manor House Rd NE2 2NE (0191) 281 6586
"Queues around the block" advertise the presence of this "humorous", "happy" and "noisy" family-run pizzeria – "for atmosphere and calories, it just can't be beaten!"
/ **Sample dishes:** garlic king prawns; mixed fish grill; tiramisu. **Details:** 9.30 pm; closed Sun; no Amex; no booking.

Heartbreak Soup £31
77 The Quayside NE1 3DE (0191) 222 1701
"Small but perfectly-formed", this "quirky" joint on the Quayside is a "favourite" destination for some reporters. / management declined to provide further information

King Neptune £33 ★
34-36 Stowell St NE1 4XQ (0191) 261 6657
"Beats the local competition hands down" – that's the verdict on this well-established Chinese, which, despite its high prices, remains reporters' Chinatown favourite. / **Details:** 10.30 pm.

Leela's £29 ★
20 Dean St NE1 1PG (0191) 230 1261
"Get in quick, as Leela talked to me of quitting" – that would be a shame as this "basic" but "authentic" family-run Indian in the city-centre has a great reputation for its "interesting" (and sometimes "amazing") south Indian cooking. / **Details:** 11.30 pm; closed Sun; no Switch; no smoking area at L.

Malmaison £33
Quayside NE1 3DX (0191) 245 5000
This boutique hotel brasserie seems to rely rather too much on its "great" Quayside location – the food is "oh-so-ordinary", and the "poor" service often comes "with attitude".
/ **Sample dishes:** artichokes & asparagus with walnut oil; steamed sea bass with radish & aubergine salad; English cheese platter. **Details:** www.malmaison.com; 10.30 pm. **Accommodation:** 116 rooms, from £125.

McCoys at the Baltic
Baltic £38 🄰
South Shore Rd NE8 3BA (0191) 440 4949
The "fantastic" setting has helped win quite a following for this high-profile (in every sense) Gateshead arts-centre restaurant; the food "ranges from exceptional to average", though, and "half-hearted" service figures in most reports. / **Sample dishes:** langoustine ravioli with shellfish reduction; braised pork wrapped in Parma ham with potato rosti; chocolate bread pudding. **Details:** www.balticmill.com; 10 pm; closed Sun D; no Amex; no smoking in dining room.

Pani's £21 A★
61-65 High Bridge NE1 6BX (0191) 232 4366
*"Real Italian food, just like Mama makes, served by real Italians"
is the deal at this "amazing-value" café; it remains "exceptionally
popular".* / **Sample dishes:** *bruschetta; chicken stuffed with Dolcelatte; tiramisu.*
Details: *www.paniscafe.com; off Gray Street; 10 pm; closed Sun; no Amex;
no booking at L.*

Paradiso £28
1 Market Ln NE1 6QQ (0191) 221 1240
*A "lively" café/bar/restaurant, where Italian staff serve quite
an "interesting" menu of Mediterranean and north African dishes.*
/ **Sample dishes:** *goats cheese & courgette lasagne; Indian-spiced cod with
couscous & roast vegetables; egg custard tart.* **Details:** *www.paradiso.co.uk; opp fire
station; 10.45 pm; closed Sun D; no Amex; no smoking area.*

Sachins £26
Forth Banks NE1 3SG (0191) 261 9035
*Fans say it offers "great value", and this long-established
Bangladeshi behind Central Station maintains a good following,
especially for business.* / **Details:** *www.sachins.co.uk; behind Central Station;
11.15 pm; closed Sun.*

Valley Junction 397 £28 A★
Old Jesmond Station, Archbold Ter NE2 1DB
(0191) 281 6397
*"Beats its older sibling, the Valley at Corbridge, hands down for
quality and atmosphere" – in spite of its 'novelty' location ("in an old
signal box and railway carriage"), almost all reports on this
"superior" Indian are very positive.* / **Details:** *near Civic Centre,
off Sandyford Rd; 11.15 pm; closed Mon; no smoking area.*

Vujon £32
29 Queen St NE1 3UG (0191) 221 0601
*This popular quaysider remains, on most reports, "a very good
modern-style Indian"; this year, however, there were a disgruntled
minority who found it "no better than a standard tandoori".*
/ **Details:** *11 pm; closed Sun L.*

Three Choirs Vineyards £38
GL18 1LS (01531) 890223
*"You get a truly local wine list" at this simple eatery (at the heart
of one of England's best-known vineyards); for most reporters, it's a
"favourite", with "very good" contemporary cooking, but it can also
provoke the odd "disappointment".* / **Sample dishes:** *seared scallops with
pine nut dressing; seared duck breast with confit of butternut squash; sticky pear &
ginger pudding with clotted cream & butterscotch.*
Details: *www.three-choirs-vineyards.co.uk; 9 pm; closed Mon & Sun D; no Amex;
no smoking.* **Accommodation:** *8 rooms, from £95.*

Celtic Manor £45 ★
NP18 1HQ (01633) 413000
*Reports on the "surprisingly innovatively-designed" dining room
at this grand resort-hotel are not especially copious, but such as they
are praise its "Celtic-fusion" (!) cuisine, and its use of "fine Welsh
produce".* / **Sample dishes:** *red mullet; roast fillet of beef; vanilla & raspberry
brûlée.* **Details:** *www.celtic-manor.com; 10.30 pm; no smoking.*

The Chandlery £ 34 ★
77-78 Lower Dock St NP20 1EH (01633) 256622
This "wonderful town-centre restaurant" doesn't have a huge
following among reporters, but all sing the praises of its "short and
interesting" menu. / **Sample dishes:** tian of Pembrooke crab & mango with red
pepper salsa; roast loin of venison with garlic mash, mushy peas & wild mushrooms;
hot chocolate fondant with pistachio ice cream.
Details: www.chandleryrestaurant.co.uk; 10 pm; closed Mon, Sat L & Sun;
no Switch; no smoking area.

Station Approach NP10 8LD (01633) 891891
"Busy, noisy and rushed" it may be, but this venture in a converted
railway station is rather better than its name might suggest, and it
serves up some "good-value" modern cooking.
/ **Sample dishes:** mushroom & pancetta risotto; Thai red monkfish & prawn curry;
chilled melon soup with mint sorbet. **Details:** off M4, J28 towards Caerphilly;
9.30 pm; closed Sun D; smoking discouraged.

NEWTON LONGVILLE, BUCKINGHAMSHIRE 3–2A

Crooked Billet £ 35 ★★
2 Westbrook End MK17 0DF (01908) 373936
"A dazzling selection of wines by the glass" boosts the much above-
average culinary tone of this candlelit, thatched gastropub, where
"excellent food is served at good prices". / **Sample dishes:** watercress
soup with goats cheese crostini; rack of lamb with coriander couscous & tapenade
jus; roasted peaches with thyme ice cream. **Details:** www.thebillet.co.uk; 10 pm;
closed Mon, Tue-Sat D only, closed Sun D; no smoking.

NEWTON, CAMBRIDGESHIRE 3–1B

Queens Head £ 12 𝔸★
Fowlmere Rd CB2 5PG (01223) 870436
"Basic and unchanged for at least two centuries", the Shorts'
"atmospheric" rural boozer – which serves "amazing cold meat
platters", and "soups described only by their colour" – is hard
to beat. / **Sample dishes:** pâté; beef sandwiches; chocolate. **Details:** off A10;
9.30 pm; no credit cards; no booking.

NEWTON-ON-THE-MOOR,
NORTHUMBERLAND 8–2B

Cook & Barker £ 28
NE65 9JY (01665) 575234
"Very well cooked pub meals" win continuing praise for this
"welcoming" inn; "it gets very busy". / **Sample dishes:** avocado, tandoori
chicken & rocket salad; pot-roast lamb with bubble 'n' squeak; Belgian chocolate
truffle cake. **Details:** 12m N of Morpeth, just off A1; 9 pm. **Accommodation:** 19
rooms, from £65.

NOMANSLAND, WILTSHIRE 2–3C

Les Mirabelles £ 31 𝔸★★
Forest Edge Rd SP5 2BN (01794) 390205
A happy union of "France and the New Forest" leads to only the
most glowing reviews for Eric Nicholas's (chef) and Claude Laage's
"small village" restaurant; it doesn't generate a huge volume
of feedback, but fans say its cooking is simply "excellent".
/ **Sample dishes:** smoked salmon mousse; lamb fillet; crème brûlée. **Details:** off
A36 between Southampton & Salisbury; 9.30 pm; closed Mon & Sun D; no smoking
at D.

NORTHALLERTON, NORTH YORKSHIRE 8–4B
Arden Arms £ 29 𝔸 ★
Atley Hill, South Cowton DL7 0JB (01325) 378678
The former owner of That Café, in Manchester, has now set up at this "sympathetically restored" boozer, offering "restaurant food at pub prices"; the place offers "modernity without pretension", and is consistently praised by all who report on it.
/ **Sample dishes:** Scottish salmon with avocado ice cream; fillet of halibut with artichokes, mushrooms & saffron sauce; cherry clafoutis. **Details:** 9 pm; closed Mon & Sun D; no smoking area.

NORTON, SHROPSHIRE 5–4B
Hundred House £ 45
Bridgnorth Rd TF11 9EE (01952) 730353
"The very attractive building and garden justify at least one visit" to this "lovely" half-timbered inn; fans say it's "great" all round, but others find the food "variable" and service "patchy".
/ **Sample dishes:** shallot, fennel & goats cheese tartlet; wild boar with white bean casserole & chorizo; raspberry & meringue ice cream.
Details: www.hundredhouse.co.uk; on A442 between Bridgnorth & Telford; 9.30 pm; no smoking area. **Accommodation:** 10 rooms, from £99.

NORWICH, NORFOLK 6–4C
Adlards £ 50 ★
79 Upper Giles St NR2 1AB (01603) 633522
"Probably the best in Norfolk" – David Adlard's townhouse fixture is unanimously hailed by reporters for its "warm welcome", "lovely" cooking and a wine list that's "surprisingly good", too; let's hope his new chef, Tom Kerridge will only improve things. / **Sample dishes:** foie gras in cumin with toasted brioche; veal with mash & roast parsnips; banana tarte Tatin. **Details:** www.adlards.co.uk; near the Roman Catholic Cathedral; 10.30 pm; closed Mon L & Sun; no smoking.

Brummells £ 43 𝔸 ★
7 Magdalen St NR3 1LE (01603) 625555
"Always very fresh fish and seafood" is the key feature of this good-all-rounder, which occupies an interesting 17th-century building.
/ **Sample dishes:** seafood pancakes with aniseed sauce; sea bass & leeks with prawn butter; apple & wild mushroom crumble with cider sorbet.
Details: www.brummells.co.uk; 10.30 pm.

By Appointment £ 40 𝔸 ★
25-29 St George's St NR3 1AB (01603) 630730
For a more "theatrical" dining experience than usual, this "wonderful" and "relaxing" city-centre restaurant-with-rooms comes highly recommended, and its "quiet" and "intimate" setting is "a real winner for romance and fun". / **Sample dishes:** tuna carpaccio with capers; guinea fowl, chorizo & mushrooms with basil sauce; pineapple tarte Tatin with cardamom ice cream. **Details:** in a courtyard off Colegate; 9 pm; D only, closed Mon & Sun; no Amex; no smoking in dining room; children: 12+.
Accommodation: 4 rooms, from £95.

Delia's City Brasserie £ 36
Norwich City Football Ground, Carrow Rd NR1 1JE (01603) 218705
All of the limited feedback we receive on the football-themed dining room at the home of the Canaries suggests it's "a bit disappointing" – let's hope director Delia Smith is more demanding of performance on the pitch than she is in 'her' kitchen here. / **Sample dishes:** Thai fishcakes with sesame & lime sauce; roast salmon with Pecorino & pesto topping; chocolate crème brûlée. **Details:** www.deliascanarycatering.co.uk; 9.30 pm; open Sat D only; no Amex; no smoking during dinner.

Tatlers £ 36 ★
21 Tombland NR3 1RF   (01603) 766670
"A great venue, without pretensions" – this *"airy"*, *"trendy"* and *"relaxed"* city-centre bistro is praised by almost all reporters for its *"consistent"* quality. / **Sample dishes:** *salad Lyonnaise; rib-eye steak with red wine & mushroom sauce; lemon tart.* **Details:** *www.tatlers.com; near Cathedral, next to Erpingham Gate; 10 pm; closed Sun; no smoking area.*

The Tree House £ 19 ★
14-16 Dove St NR2 1DE   (01603) 763258
"Cooking with conscience and passion" is hailed by fans of this *"inventive veggie"*, run as a workers' co-op. / **Sample dishes:** *spicy tomato & lentil soup; potato & cauliflower curry with rice; blueberry tofu cheesecake.* **Details:** *9 pm; L only Mon-Wed, closed Sun; no credit cards; no smoking; no booking at L.*

Waffle House £ 20
39 St Giles St NR2 1JN   (01603) 612 790
"A menu entirely of waffles" goes down well with local fans of this '80s survivor, who say it's a *"fast"* and *"good-value"* spot. / **Sample dishes:** *garlic mushrooms; ham, cheese & mushroom waffle; banana & butterscotch waffle.* **Details:** *50 yds from city hall and main market square; 10 pm; no Amex; no smoking area; need 6+ to book.*

NOTTINGHAM, CITY OF NOTTINGHAM 5–3D

Nottingham has a number of quality dining establishments – especially at the mid-price level – reflecting its growing reputation as a business, leisure (and student) centre.

In *Hart's*, the city has a modern brasserie of rare quality (having now totally eclipsed its chief rival, the longer-established *Sonny's*). Eye-catching design has helped *World Service* become the place locally to see and be seen, even if it has no claims to being a foodie hot spot. A little way from the centre, *La Toque* is starting to make quite a name for itself.

At the top level, there's really only one choice: the relatively new *Hotel des Clos*. It's a good choice, though, giving Nottingham a culinary standard-bearer of the first rank.

The city also boasts a number of very acceptable ethnic restaurants, with good examples of both Thai (*Royal Thai*) and Indian (*Saagar*) establishments.

Atlas £ 8 ★
9 Pelham St NG1 2EH   (0115) 950 1295
"Great tea and coffee" are not the only attractions of this central Mediterranean café; it also offers *"sandwiches like no others"* (with *"delicious bread"*) and *"cheery"* service; there's a *"useful deli"*, too. / **Sample dishes:** *ciabatta with tuna, basil & plum tomatoes; Danish pastry.* **Details:** *L only; no Amex; no smoking.*

Bees Make Honey £ 29
12 Alfreton Rd NG7 3NG   (0115) 978 0109
Michael Walton's *"relaxed"* BYO café continues to exert its *"intimate"* and *"home-spun charms"*, and it's a spot which some find quite romantic. / **Sample dishes:** *cuttlefish tagliatelle; sea bass with ackee & okra; white chocolate cheesecake.* **Details:** *5 mins from Playhouse & Theatre Royal; 10.15 pm; D only, closed Mon & Sun; no credit cards.*

French Living £ 23 ★
27 King St NG1 2AY (0115) 958 5885
*"Proper" French cooking (from a "seasonally-changing menu"), "charming and good-natured" service and a "country Gallic atmosphere" win high praise for this "packed" basement bistro. / **Sample dishes:** Burgundy snails with garlic & parsley butter; venison with peppered blueberry sauce; white chocolate bavarois. **Details:** www.frenchliving.co.uk; near Market Square; 10 pm; closed Mon & Sun; booking: max 8.*

Hart's £ 42 Ⓐ★
Standard Ct, Park Row NG1 6GN (0115) 911 0666
*Tim Hart's "innovative" brasserie near the Castle continues to win high praise for "expert and simple" cooking that's just "spot on"; its "light" and "stylish" interior also finds general approval (though there are those to whom the place seems "noisy" or "unsympathetic"). / **Sample dishes:** courgette tart with goats cheese; veal with spinach & Parmesan risotto; tarte Tatin with caramel ice cream. **Details:** www.hartsnottingham.co.uk; near Castle; 10.30 pm; no smoking in dining room. **Accommodation:** 32 rooms, from £112.*

Hotel des Clos £ 51 ★★
Old Lenton Ln NG7 2SA
(0115) 986 6566
*Sat Bains's "innovative and imaginative" cuisine is carving out a lofty reputation for this "intimate" restaurant-with-rooms (in a former farmhouse, a little way from the city-centre); there is the odd concern about "patchy" service or "restricted" menus, but even those who say the place is "not cheap" agree the food is "stunning". / **Sample dishes:** roast scallops with Indian-spiced cauliflower; duck with apple & foie gras; apple tart with Granny Smith sorbet. **Details:** www.hoteldesclos.com; 9.30 pm; closed Mon, Sat L & Sun; no smoking; children: 8+. **Accommodation:** 9 rooms, from £99.50.*

Mem Saab £ 28
12-14 Maid Marian Way NG1 6HS (0115) 957 0009
*This "posh curry house, favoured by the younger set" is a "modern", "relaxed" and "professional" venture which seems to be finding a more consistent rhythm – it generated much more positive commentary this year, for its "varied and well-priced" dishes. / **Details:** near Castle; 10.30 pm, Fri & Sat 11 pm; D only, closed Sun; no smoking area; children: 5+.*

Merchants
Lace Market Hotel £ 33 ✗
29-31 High Pavement NG1 1HE (0115) 852 3232
*"Still trying, but hit-and-miss" – this city-centre brasserie (part of a design-hotel) remains most notable for the "inconsistency" of its food and service. / **Sample dishes:** aubergine, smoked Mozzarella & chorizo tart; tuna steak with cherry tomato salad; vanilla & blackcurrant bavarois. **Details:** www.lacemarkethotel.co.uk; 10.30 pm; closed Sat L & Sun D; smoking discouraged; children: 18. **Accommodation:** 42 rooms, from £109.*

Mr Man's £ 26 ★
Wollaton Park NG8 2AD (0115) 928 7788
*"Ideally situated, with the best seats having views of Wollaton Park", this flashily decked-out Cantonese has quite a local reputation; its "light and lovely" food continues to find general (if not universal) support – "large parties" seem to be an ever-present risk. / **Details:** 11 pm.*

sign up for the survey at www.hardens.com 273

Petit Paris £27
2 Kings Walk NG1 2AE (0115) 947 3767
The names says its all about this "happy and lively" city-centre "favourite", which offers "good-value, if slightly ersatz, Gallic bistro cooking". / Sample dishes: smoked chicken & mushroom pancake; veal with mushroom & brandy flambé; profiteroles with hot chocolate sauce. Details: near Theatre Royal; 10.30 pm; closed Sun; no smoking area.

Pretty Orchid £29
12 Pepper Street NG1 2GH (0115) 958 8344
A well-established city-centre Thai, universally hailed by local reporters as a "friendly", "reliable" and "good-value" oriental. / Details: 11 pm; no Amex; no smoking area.

Royal Thai £23 ★
189 Mansfield Rd NG1 3FS (0115) 948 3001
This year's commentary on this "courteous" Thai adhered to its usual themes of "good service and good value"; lunches are especially recommended. / Details: 11 pm; closed Sun L; no Amex; no smoking.

Saagar £25 ★★
473 Mansfield Rd NG5 2DR (0115) 962 2014
"Who cares about the décor and service?" – "reliably excellent food at all times" (and "in huge portions") is the pretty much invariable theme of feedback on this Sherwood Indian. / Details: 1.5m from city centre; midnight; closed Sun L; no smoking area; children: 5+.

Siam Thani £25
16-20 Carlton St NG1 1NN (0115) 958 2222
"Polite" and "attentive" service features in most of the good number of reports on this large Thai in the Lace Market, where "tasty" food is served in a "relaxed" modern setting. / Details: www.siamthani.co.uk; 10.30 pm; closed Sun L; no Amex; no smoking area.

Sonny's £34
3 Carlton St NG1 1NL (0115) 947 3041
Most reporters continue to give the thumbs-up to this "light" and "stylish" modern brasserie in the city-centre; the cooking is only "mostly good", though, and strikes some as "overpriced" for what it is. / Sample dishes: tomato linguine with roast peppers; roast lamb; blueberry & almond tart. Details: near Victoria Centre; 10.30 pm, Fri & Sat 11 pm; no smoking area.

La Toque £40 Ⓐ★
61 Wollaton Rd NG9 2NG (0115) 922 2268
The chef (Swedish) creates "outstanding" Gallic cooking, say fans of this "intimate" venture – something of a "find" in "one of Nottingham's less attractive areas"; even so, though, some feel that "prices are too high for Beeston". / Sample dishes: quail consommé & toasted brioche; lemon sole with green bean fricassée; baked prune soufflé. Details: off A52 towards Beeston; 9.30 pm; closed Mon, Sat L & Sun; no smoking area.

Travellers Rest £27
Mapperley Plains, Plains Rd NG3 5RT (0115) 926 4412
"A large and popular pub with an extensive menu and good guest beers" – one reporter says it all about the attractions of this Mapperley boozer. / Sample dishes: black pudding tower; lamb en croûte; chocolate muffin sundae. Details: off B684 between Nottingham & Woodborough; 10 pm; no smoking area; no booking.

Victoria Hotel   £ 20   ★
Dovecote Ln NG9 1JG   (0115) 925 4049
*"Always crowded", this sawdusty pub – a conversion of a railway
hotel by Beeston Station – is lauded by locals for its "classic",
"homely" dishes and its "very good" real ales.*
/ **Sample dishes:** *spinach & apple soup; herb-crusted rack of lamb; Mars bar
cheesecake.* **Details:** *www.tynemill.co.uk/nottm/vic.htm; by Beeston railway station;
8.45 pm, Sun 7.45 pm; no Amex; no smoking; need 6+ to book; children: before
8 pm only.* **Accommodation:** *11 rooms, from £110.*

World Service   £ 38   Ⓐ
Newdigate Hs, Castle Gate NG1 6AF   (0115) 847 5587
*Critics say "more effort has gone into finding funky water glasses
than delivering good food", but "sleek" décor and "welcoming"
service help win this 'designer' haunt a huge local fanclub, who say
its "eclectic" fusion cuisine "can be very good".* / **Sample dishes:** *salt &
pepper squid with orange salad; roast lamb with braised fennel & crispy garlic;
pear & cinnamon tarte Tatin.* **Details:** *www.worldservicerestaurant.com; 10 pm;
no smoking.*

NUTFIELD, SURREY   3–3B

Nutfield Priory (The Cloisters)   £ 54   Ⓐ
RH1 4EL   (01737) 824400
*Even those who note "gloomy" public rooms at this large Victorian
pile of an hotel concede the dining room itself provides a "splendid"
setting, and one where the contemporary cooking is "good value".*
/ **Sample dishes:** *home-cured gravadlax; poached fillet of beef with vegetables;
glazed apple tart with caramel ice cream.* **Details:** *www.nutfield-priory.com;
M25 from E: J6 to Redhill. from W: J8, signs to Reigate and Redhill; 10 pm; closed
Sat L; no smoking.* **Accommodation:** *60 rooms, from £135.*

OAKHAM, RUTLAND   5–4D

Nicks
Lord Nelson's House   £ 38   ★
11 Marketplace LE15 6DT   (01572) 723199
*"Consistently high standards" remains the gist of most (if not quite
all) commentary on this "good, old-fashioned restaurant" on the
corner of the marketplace – even a critic of the service and setting
conceded that "the food is very good".* / **Sample dishes:** *roast goats
cheese with poached pears; steak with rosti & caramelised onions; walnut & ginger
steamed pudding.* **Details:** *www.nelsons-house.com; 9.30 pm; closed Mon & Sun;
no Amex; no smoking.* **Accommodation:** *4 rooms, from £80.*

OBAN, ARGYLL & BUTE   9–3B

Ee-Usk (Fish Café)   £ 34   ★★
104 George St PA34 5NS
(01631) 565666
*"Fantastically fresh fish, and plenty of it" has won renown for Callum
McLeod's seaside venture; post-survey he moved into striking glazed
premises overlooking Mull and Kerrera – our rating assumes he can
maintain standards in this now larger location.* / **Sample dishes:** *mussels
with garlic butter; monkfish with mornay sauce & savory mash; bread & butter
pudding with Irish cream.* **Details:** *10 pm; no Amex; no smoking area.*

OCKLEY, SURREY 3–4A

Bryce's at the Old School House £32
RH5 5TH (01306) 627430
"The best fish in Surrey" is claimed by advocates of this *"friendly"* pub/restaurant of over a decade's standing; there are doubters, though, who think it *"over-rated"*. / **Sample dishes:** coconut crab cakes with sweet & sour scallops; plaice with brioche herb crust; butterscotch & honeycomb cheesecake. **Details:** www.bryces.co.uk; 8m S of Dorking on A29; 9.30 pm; closed Sun D in Nov, Jan & Feb; no Amex; no smoking in dining room.

OLD AMERSHAM, BUCKINGHAMSHIRE 3–2A

Gilbey's £34
1 Market Sq HP7 0DF (01494) 727242
"Price are reasonable and the wine list is superb – they sell at cost price" – at this *"friendly"*, slightly *"olde worlde"* fixture near the clock tower; the food's *"OK but nothing special"*. / **Sample dishes:** crab cakes with lime pickle; braised lamb with mint mash & red wine jus; rhubarb oat crumble. **Details:** www.gilbeygroup.com; in Old Amersham; 9.30 pm; appreciated if guests try to refrain from smoking.

OLD DALBY, LEICESTERSHIRE 5–3D

Crown Inn £32
7 Debdale Hill LE14 3LF (01664) 823134
"London prices in the middle of nowhere" again drew some flak for this rural inn; it's mostly praised, though, for its good, *"traditional"* fare. / **Sample dishes:** asparagus, spinach & poached egg salad; slow-roast rib-eye beef; oranges in Cointreau cream. **Details:** www.old-dalby.org; 5m N of Melton Mowbray; 9.30 pm; closed Sun D; no Amex; no smoking; children: 5+ at L, 10+ at D.

OLDHAM, GREATER MANCHESTER 5–2B

Ho Ho's £30
57-59 High St OL4 3BN (0161) 620 9500
"One of the first modern-style Chinese restaurants in this neck of the woods" – it's still a superior operation of its type.
/ **Details:** follow signs from M62, J20; 11 pm.

OMBERSLEY, WORCESTERSHIRE 2–1B

Kings Arms £27 🄺
Main Rd WR9 0EW (01905) 620142
A *"very nice"* half-timbered country pub (with a *"lovely"* walled garden); it offers *"a wide choice of assured dishes"* – *"from frugal to rib-sticking"*. / **Sample dishes:** black pudding, bacon & quails egg salad; calves liver & bacon with mash; chocolate praline brûlée.
Details: www.kingsarmsombersley.co.uk; 10.15 pm; no Amex; no smoking area.

ONGAR, ESSEX 3–2B

Smiths Brasserie £42
Fyfield Rd CM5 0AL (01277) 365578
As a *"car park full of Jags and Porsches"* hints, this *"London brasserie in deepest Essex"* is at the *"upmarket"* end of local eating options and majors in *"excellent seafood, simply served"* (not least *"posh fish and chips"*); it's *"trendy"* and *"buzzy"*, but can also seem a tad *"pretentious"*. / **Sample dishes:** asparagus hollandaise; salmon fillet cake with parsley; roasted pineapple with butterscotch sauce.
Details: www.smithsbrasserie.co.uk; left off A414 towards Fyfield; 10 pm; closed Mon; no Amex; children: 12+.

ORFORD, SUFFOLK   3–1D
Butley Orford Oysterage   **£30**   ★
Market Hill IP12 2LH   (01394) 450277
"Plastic chairs, paper napkins, basic atmosphere, very fresh fish" –
that's the formula (as it has been for three decades) that keeps this
resolutely *"unpretentious"* café *"very busy"*; the menu includes
*"the catch of the day, plus their own smoked fish and home grown
oysters"*. / **Sample dishes:** smoked salmon pâté; hot smoked mackerel with
mustard sauce; rum baba. **Details:** 9 pm; closed Mon D-Thu D & Sun D in winter;
no Amex; no smoking.

The Crown & Castle   **£38**
IP12 2LJ   (01394) 450205
"A lovely location by the estuary and the castle" adds lustre to this
well-known Victorian hotel; the cooking *"is mostly good but can have
off days"* (though there were fewer gripes about *"erratic"* service
this year). / **Sample dishes:** cockle, bacon & endive salad; crispy pork with spiced
lentils & gingered greens; hot bitter chocolate mousse.
Details: www.crownandcastle.co.uk; 9 pm; closed Sun D in winter; no Amex;
no smoking; booking: max 8; children: under 8s L in Parlour only.
Accommodation: 18 rooms, from £75.

ORKNEY ISLANDS, ORKNEY ISLANDS
The Creel   **£40**   ★
Front Rd, St Margaret's Hope, South Ronaldsay KW17 2SL
(01856) 831311
"Worth a trip to Orkney" – fans don't stint in their praise for Allan
Craigie's *"lovely"* waterside restaurant-with-rooms, where the menu
is *"short"*, but includes some *"superb"* fish; service
is *"accommodating"*, too. / **Sample dishes:** crab bisque; supreme of cod;
Drambuie panna cotta. **Details:** www.thecreel.co.uk; off A961 S of town, across
Churchill barriers; 9 pm; D only; closed Jan-Mar; no Amex; no smoking.
Accommodation: 3 rooms, from £70.

ORPINGTON, KENT   3–3B
Xian   **£25**   ★
324 High St BR6 0NG   (01689) 871881
"Very good for a Chinese outside London" – this suburban oriental,
with its *"very good"* food, is *"always busy"* (and can be rather
"noisy"). / **Details:** 11.15 pm, Fri & Sat 11.45 pm; closed Sun L.

OSMOTHERLEY, NORTH YORKSHIRE   8–4C
Golden Lion   **£28**   Ⓐ
6 West End DL6 3AA   (01609) 883526
"A nice atmosphere and friendly service" are the key attractions
at this rural boozer; the menu strikes some as *"interesting"*,
but others as *"in need of a re-think"*. / **Sample dishes:** spaghetti with
clams; pork & Parma ham with sage mash; lemon & passion fruit pavlova.
Details: 10.30 pm; no Amex; no smoking area.

Three Tuns   **£38**
9 South End DL6 3BN   (01609) 883301
This *"modernised"* brewery inspired rather ambivalent commentary
this year; even fans of its *"beautiful interior"* think the place
"ever more expensive", and others say *"appearances raise false
expectations of food-quality"*. / **Sample dishes:** crab & salmon fishcakes;
Dover sole with lemon & chive butter; mini croque-en-bouche.
Details: www.lifeandstyle.co.uk; 6m NE of Northallerton; 9.30 pm; no smoking
in dining room. **Accommodation:** 7 rooms, from £65.

OSWESTRY, SHROPSHIRE   5–3A

Sebastians   £ 42
45 Willow St SY11 1AQ   (01691) 655444
*Mark Sebastian Fisher's "French-style restaurant-with-rooms"
inspired slightly mixed reports this year – even a reporter who
"expected more adventurous cooking", though, observed that
"its loyal clientèle seemed happy". / Sample dishes: seafood cassoulet with
bacon & cannellini beans; roast duck with caramelised apples & sage sauce;
cinnamon cream with spiced rhubarb. Details: www.sebastians-hotel.co.uk;
near town centre, follow signs towards Selattyn; 9.45 pm; D only, closed Mon & Sun;
no smoking. Accommodation: 8 rooms, from £65.*

OTFORD, KENT   3–3B

Bull   £ 23
High St TN14 5PG   (01959) 523198
*Most reports speak only well of the "great pub food" on offer at this
"cottage"-style country boozer – ditto its "good value" and its "not-
bad" ale; it doesn't please everyone, though. / Sample dishes: spinach &
Roquefort tart; beef & Theakston's pie; banana toffee crumble. Details: 10 pm;
no smoking area; children: before 5 pm only.*

OTLEY, WEST YORKSHIRE   5–1C

Korks   £ 30   Ⓐ
40 Bondgate LS21 1AD   (01943) 462020
*This "nice wine bar" seems to have raised its game somewhat since
the arrival of its new chef in 2002 – it's the "excellent wine list",
though, which wins most plaudits from reporters.
/ Sample dishes: tandoori chicken with coriander noodles; pork with cauliflower &
turmeric jus; summer berry pavlova. Details: 10 pm, Fri & Sat 11 pm; closed
Sat L & Sun.*

OUNDLE, NORTHANTS   3–1A

Falcon Inn   £ 34   ★
Fotheringay PE8 5HZ   (01832) 226254
*"Imaginative" (Mediterranean-style) cooking and a "cramped" but
"friendly" setting combine to make this old stone hostelry, in a
"picturesque" village, a "very popular" destination.
/ Sample dishes: pea & mint soup with Parma ham; curried pork with fruity rice &
poppadums; sticky toffee pudding. Details: www.huntsbridge.co.uk; just off A605;
9.15 pm; no smoking.*

OVINGTON, HAMPSHIRE   2–3D

The Bush Inn   £ 32
SO24 0RE   (01962) 732764
*"Friendly" and old-fashioned, this Wadworth's boozer serves
"good pub food". / Sample dishes: chicken liver pâté with brandy & port;
spinach & wild mushroom lasagne; chocolate & black cherry bread & butter
pudding. Details: www.wadworth.co.uk; just off A31 between Winchester &
Alresford; 9.30 pm; closed Sun D; no smoking area.*

OXFORD, OXFORDSHIRE   2–2D

The fact which says most about the Oxford dining scene is that the two top restaurants are both Thai. Admittedly *Chiang Mai* and *Bangkok House* are two of the country's best Thai all-rounders, but the fact remains that the best food in Oxford is largely ethnic. Indian restaurants, in particular, are well represented at most price-levels (*Aziz*, *Bombay*, *Chutney's* and *Jamals*).

Oxford's best restaurant is in fact in nearby Great Milton, in the shape of the Raymond Blanc's Manoir aux Quat' Saisons – the best-known restaurant in the UK outside London. Those who settle for Monsieur Blanc's much-frequented spin-off brasserie in Jericho, *Le Petit Blanc* may wonder, however, quite what his name is supposed to stand for (though perhaps new owners *Loch Fyne* – who have a branch a few doors down – can buck up standards). Equally, the city's other European restaurants – *Cherwell Boathouse*, *Gees*, *The Old Parsonage* and *Quod* – generally seem to rely on the charm of their location, offering food that is no more than satisfactory. The famous *Browns* is now a dismal shadow of its former self.

Al Shami   £ 22   ★
25 Walton Cr OX1 2JG   (01865) 310066
"The very good-value mezze are the thing" at this *"lively"* and *"unpretentious"* Jericho Lebanese; it's *"cheap"*, too, and *"perfect for a group"*. / **Details:** www.al-shami.co.uk; 11.45 pm; no Amex; no smoking area. **Accommodation:** 12 rooms, from £45.

Aziz   £ 30   ★
228-230 Cowley Rd OX4 1UH   (01865) 794945
"Consistent", *"upmarket"*, *"popular"* – three words say it all about this *"well above-average"* curry house, where *"booking is essential"*. / **Details:** www.aziz.uk.com; 10.45 pm; closed Fri L; no shorts; no smoking area.

Bangkok House   £ 24   Ⓐ★
42a High Bridge St OX1 2EP   (01865) 200705
"Good-quality" Thai fare and *"lovely"*, *"interesting"* surroundings earn consistent popularity for this central oriental; *"booking is essential"*. / **Details:** 10.45 pm; no smoking except D Fri & Sat.

Bombay   £ 18   ★
82 Walton St OX2 6EA   (01865) 511188
"Better-than-average" food and *"very pleasant"* service maintain the appeal of this Jericho Indian; BYO keeps prices low.
/ **Details:** 11.15 pm; closed Fri L; no Amex.

Branca   £ 33
111 Walton St OX2 6AJ   (01865) 556111
A *"very cool and trendy look"* is the chief asset of this *"cheerful and young"* modern brasserie; its mainly Italian menu includes some fancy pizzas, but realisation tends to *"so-so"*. / **Sample dishes:** summer minestrone soup; linguine with tiger prawns & chilli; tiramisu.
Details: www.branca-restaurants.com; 11 pm; no smoking area.

Browns £ 28 ✗
5-11 Woodstock Rd OX2 6HA (01865) 319655
"Alas, how the mighty are fallen"; the *"demise"* of this *"once-excellent"* English brasserie *"institution"* leaves the dwindling number of those who can bother to report on it asking *"what happened"* to their *"former favourite"* – *"it has totally lost the plot"*. / **Sample dishes:** grilled goats cheese salad; confit duck with plum relish; bread & butter pudding. **Details:** www.browns-restaurants.com; 11.30 pm; no smoking area; need 5+ to book.

Café Coco £ 22 Ⓐ
23 Cowley Rd OX4 1HP (01865) 200232
"Fresh thin pizzas" with *"imaginative toppings"* – not least the *"yummy all-day breakfast option"* – help win *"extreme popularity"* for this *"small"*, *"fun"* hang-out. / **Sample dishes:** houmous & garlic bread; Greek wine, sausage & ham pizza; tiramisu. **Details:** 11 pm; no Amex; no booking.

Cherwell Boathouse £ 30 Ⓐ✗
Bardwell Rd OX2 6ST (01865) 552746
"Forget the food" – it's *"pretty ordinary"*, anyway – and *"just enjoy the ambience"* of this *"idyllically-located"* riversider (recently enlarged); the place is owned by a wine merchant and offers the *"fantastic"* list you might hope for. / **Sample dishes:** sweetcorn & spring onion risotto; chicken in bacon with cranberry confit; lime pie. **Details:** www.cherwellboathouse.co.uk; 10 pm; no smoking.

Chiang Mai £ 27 Ⓐ★★
Kemp Hall Passage, 130a High St OX1 4DH
(01865) 202233
The food is *"superb"* and the building *"so atmospheric"* at this *"brilliant"* if *"slightly bizarre"* oriental *"favourite"* – an *"authentic"* Thai in a *"beautiful"* Tudor house, *"tucked down a quiet alley"* (off the High Street). / **Details:** www.chiangmaikitchen.co.uk; 10.30 pm; no smoking area.

Chutney's £ 27 ★
36 St Michaels St OX1 2EB (01865) 724241
"Busy", *"cheap"* and *"reliable"*, this *"good, standard Indian"* remains a very popular city-centre destination; it's *"good for veggies"*, too. / **Details:** www.chutneysoxford.co.uk; 11 pm; closed Sun.

Edamame £ 18 ★
15 Holywell St OX1 3SA (01865) 246916
"There's always a long queue, even in the rain", to gain entry to this *"tiny"* oriental *"pit stop"*, which serves *"good-quality"*, *"home-style"* Japanese food. / **Details:** www.edamame.co.uk; opp New College; 8.30 pm; L only, except Fri & Sat when L & D, closed Mon; no Amex; no cards at L; no smoking; no booking.

Fishers £ 35
36-37 St Clements OX4 1AB (01865) 243003
The food (mainly fish) is *"sometimes excellent, sometimes ordinary"*, but this *"lively"* bistro remains an ever-*"popular"* local destination; service – finally! – seems to have been sharpened up.
/ **Sample dishes:** king prawns with garlic mayonnaise; seared tuna with aubergine salsa & herb oil; sticky toffee pudding. **Details:** www.fishers-restaurant.com; by Magdalen Bridge; 10.30 pm; closed Mon L & Tue L; no Amex; mainly non-smoking.

Gees £40 Ⓐ
61 Banbury Rd OX2 6PE (01865) 553540
*A "very, very pretty" setting in "a huge conservatory" helps create
a "delightful", "buzzy" atmosphere at this "romantic" north Oxford
favourite; the "stylishly served" cooking can be on the "predictable"
side, though, and "incompetent" service is not unknown.*
*/ Sample dishes: king scallops with leeks; roast lamb with borlotti beans &
tapenade; chocolate soufflé with pistachio sauce. Details: 11 pm; no smoking.*

The Gourmet Pizza Co £25
100-101 Gloucester Grn OX1 2BU (01865) 793146
*"Worth the queues" – pizzas topped with "delicious combinations"
and a "great riverside location" make this outpost of the London
chain universally popular with reporters. / Sample dishes: Caesar salad;
Mexican lime chicken pizza; banoffi pie. Details: 11 pm; no smoking area.*

Jamals £21 ★
108 Walton St OX2 6AJ (01865) 310102
*"Consistently decent" cooking, at very reasonable prices, makes
it worth knowing about this curry house near the Phoenix Cinema.
/ Details: www.jamals.co.uk; 11.15 pm; no smoking area.*

Kazbah £21 Ⓐ
25-27 Cowley Rd OX4 1HP (01865) 202920
*"You feel like you're on holiday", at this "lively and eclectic" haunt,
near the city-centre – "done out in Moroccan/Southern Spanish
style"; it serves a "good range" of "tasty tapas".
/ Sample dishes: anchovies cured in vinegar; chicken & olive tajine with preserved
lemon; baklava. Details: 11 pm; no Amex; no booking.*

Loch Fyne £34
55 Walton St OX2 6AE (01865) 292510
*Oxford seems to have embraced the middle-of-the-road formula
offered by this Jericho outpost of the national seafood chain as a
"good all-round option", at least by the unimpressive local standard.
/ Sample dishes: lobster bisque with garlic rouille; rosemary-infused bream with
tomatoes & black olives; lemon sorbet. Details: www.loch-fyne.com; 10 pm;
no smoking area.*

The Old Parsonage £33 Ⓐ
1 Banbury Rd OX2 6NN (01865) 310210
*"Traditional and cosy", this medieval townhouse-hotel offers
a "comfortable" oasis, not far from the city-centre; service
is unimpressive, though, and the "unambitious" cooking is "rather
pricey" for what it is. / Sample dishes: seared smoked salmon; rare marinated
beef & salad; cheesecake. Details: www.oxford-hotels-restaurants.co.uk; 0.5m N
of city centre; 10.30 pm; no smoking. Accommodation: 30 rooms, from £155.*

Le Petit Blanc £31
71-72 Walton St OX2 6AG (01865) 510999
*Many reporters noted a "fall in standards" (and they were never
that hot in the first place) at Raymond Blanc's Jericho brasserie
"spin-off", which – like others in the chain – had to be rescued from
receivership this year; let's hope new managers Loch Fyne can help
Monsieur Blanc cure the perennially "unexciting" cooking and
"graceless" service. / Sample dishes: foie gras & chicken liver pâté; confit
of guinea fowl with wild mushrooms; 'floating island' dessert.
Details: www.lepetitblanc.co.uk; 11 pm; no smoking in dining room.*

Quod
Old Bank Hotel   £31   X
92-94 High Street OX1 4BN (01865) 799599
*This original branch of Brown's-founder Jereremy Mogford's Italianate
chain is a "lively" and "popular" venture; "perhaps it's all down
to the location", speculates one reporter – the "nondescript" food
and too-often "surly" service seem unlikely to be responsible!
/ Sample dishes: crab salad with sweet chilli; confit duck with caramelised
prunes & lardons; chocolate marble brownie. Details: www.oldbank-hotel.co.uk;
opp All Souls College; 11 pm; no smoking area; no booking, Sun L.
Accommodation: 42 rooms, from £160.*

Radcliffe Arms   £13
67 Cranham St OX2 6DE (01865) 514762
*"A firm favourite among those in the know", this studenty pub
in Jericho offers "home-cooked pub food at Happy Eater prices" –
"how do they do it?" / Sample dishes: tomato soup; lasagne & salad;
chocolate fudge cake. Details: 9 pm; no Amex; no booking.*

Randolph   £45   X
Beaumont St OX1 2LN (0870) 400 8200
*This grand city-centre institution, now under the ownership
of Macdonald Hotels, retains something of a reputation as a dining
destination – unjustifiably, given the number of reporters who find
it "disappointing" nowadays. / Sample dishes: clam chowder; spiced duck
with red cabbage; walnut tart with maple syrup ice cream.
Details: www.macdonaldhotels.com; opp Ashmolean Museum; 10 pm; no smoking.
Accommodation: 119 rooms, from £140.*

Saffron   £22
204-206 Banbury Rd OX2 7BY (01865) 512211
*"A strange mixture of dishes – French and Indian, but mainly the
latter" – confronts visitors to this north Oxford spot, which is quite
"glamorous", by Summertown standards, and "not too pricey".
/ Details: 11.30 pm; no smoking area.*

Savannah
Royal Oxford Hotel   £34
17 Park End St OX1 1HU (01865) 793793
*"A massive range of wine, with free tasting prior to ordering" is a
feature of this "upmarket steakhouse" near the station; it doesn't
seem to be generating the enthusiasm it did in its first year, though
– unimpressive service doesn't help. / Sample dishes: beef carpaccio;
sirloin steak with hollandaise; lemon tart. Details: www.savannah.co.uk; 10.30 pm;
no smoking area.*

Thai Orchid   £25   Ⓐ
58a, St Clements St OX4 1AH (01865) 798044
*Even those who say "there are good days and there are boring
days" at this East Oxford Thai admit that the cooking can
be "impressive", and that the place has a "good atmosphere".
/ Details: nr Headington Park; 11 pm; closed Sat L & Sun L; no smoking area.*

White House   £31
2 Botley Rd OX2 0AB (01865) 242823
*The style of this 'lounge bar and restaurant', can seem "dreary"
(particularly the exterior), but the garden is "lovely", and the food
is "good". / Sample dishes: sizzling red mullet & spring onions; beef medallions
with sweet chilli sauce; tarte Tatin. Details: www.thewhitehouseoxford.co.uk;
9.30 pm; no Amex.*

PADSTOW, CORNWALL   1–3B

Margot's   £36   ★
11 Duke St PL28 8AB   (01841) 533441
*"Forget Rick Stein, eat here", say fans of this "small", "friendly" and
notably "reliable" seafood restaurant, which is "really making
a name for itself". / Sample dishes: sardines with watercress & radish salad;
rack of lamb with spring onion crust; saffron poached pears with shortbread.
Details: www.margots.co.uk; 9.30 pm; closed Mon L & Tue; closed Jan; no smoking.*

No 6 Café   £42   ★
6 Middle St PL28 8AP   (01841) 532093
*Reporters speak little but good of this "interesting" bistro
(now under new owners), with its "fabulous" seafood, its "fantastic"
puddings and its "very attentive" service; according to one long-time
visitor in these parts, "it's just like the Seafood Restaurant was
at the start". / Sample dishes: Cornish scallops with sweet chilli sauce; sea bass
with lemongrass risotto; chocolate pot with Tia Maria cream. Details: 10.30 pm
(9.30 pm in winter); D only Fri- Sun, except for residents; no Amex; no smoking;
children: 18+. Accommodation: 3 rooms, from £105.*

Rick Stein's Café   £33   ★
10 Middle St PL28 8AP   (01841) 532700
*"It's excellent if you can't afford the Seafood Restaurant" –
Rick Stein fans have given a warm reception to the "great-value"
fresh fish at this determinedly cheaper spin-off. / Sample dishes: Thai
fishcakes with sweet & sour cucumber dressing; char-grilled steak with tomato & red
onion salad; lime posset with balsamic strawberries. Details: www.rickstein.com;
9.30 pm; closed Sun; no Amex; no smoking; booking essential at D.
Accommodation: 3 rooms, from £60.*

The Seafood Restaurant   £65
Riverside PL28 8BY   (01841) 532700
*"Excellent food, with an emphasis on simplicity" – not to mention
a bit of TV exposure now and again – has made Rick Stein's
harbourside HQ a 'destination' restaurant par excellence; a minority
of reporters have always railed against "shockingly mediocre"
cooking and "heart-stopping" prices – such complaints were again
more vocal this year. / Sample dishes: cuttlefish salad; shark & Dover sole
vindaloo; panna cotta with stewed rhubarb. Details: www.rickstein.com; 10 pm;
no Amex; no smoking in dining room; booking: max 14; children: 3+.
Accommodation: 13 rooms, from £105.*

St Petroc's House Bistro   £43   ★
4 New St PL28 8EA   (01841) 532700
*Curiously, Rick Stein's "relaxed" (and quite child-friendly) number
two dining room – a few paces from the waterfront – seems a safer
bet for "very good" cooking than his headline-grabbing harbour-
sider; the ambience, though, is "rather like the provincial hotel
restaurant this is". / Sample dishes: poached egg, bacon & crouton salad;
lemon sole with sea salt & lemon; Gorgonzola with honey & walnuts.
Details: www.rickstein.com; 9.30 pm; no smoking. Accommodation: 10 rooms,
from £105.*

sign up for the survey at www.hardens.com

PAINSWICK, GLOUCESTERSHIRE 2–2B

Painswick Hotel £51 🄐

Kemps Ln GL6 6YB (01452) 812160

"Good food and service" is the gist of most commentary on this grand (but *"friendly"*) Cotswold country house hotel; the cooking can be quite *"innovative"*, too (*"in a place where you wouldn't necessarily expect it"*). / **Sample dishes:** smoked quail ravioli; monkfish wrapped in Parma ham & basil; rhubarb & custard upside-down crème brûlée. **Details:** www.painswickhotel.com; 9.30 pm; no smoking in dining room. **Accommodation:** 19 rooms, from £125.

PARK GATE, HAMPSHIRE 2–4D

Kam's Palace £32 🄐★

1 Bridge Rd SO31 7GD (01489) 583328

"Not cheap, but very cheerful", this OTT (pagoda-style) Chinese – with its *"lovely clean flavours"* (and *"no MSG hangover"*) – is a *"well-run"* place, where *"attentive"* service is a highlight. / **Details:** 11 pm.

PARKGATE, CHESHIRE 5–2A

Marsh Cat £25

1 Mostyn Sq CH64 6SL (0151) 336 1963

"Fine views across the estuary of the Dee" add lustre to this *"friendly"* bistro – a *"cheap and cheerful"* local favourite whose set deals offer *"wonderful value for early diners"*. / **Sample dishes:** crab claws & monkfish in Thai coconut sauce; Cajun blackened swordfish & catfish; nutty torte with raspberries. **Details:** www.marshcat.com; 10.30 pm; smoking discouraged.

PAXFORD, GLOUCESTERSHIRE 2–1C

Churchill Arms £32

GL55 6XH (01386) 594000

Fans still hail *"restaurant-quality food"* at this *"rustic"* but *"smart"* inn (which has *"lovely rooms"*, too); some reporters feel it's *"lost its way"* of late, however, with cooking that's *"more ordinary than in the past"*. / **Sample dishes:** duck with grapefruit & fennel salad; guinea fowl in Madeira & mushroom cream sauce; sticky toffee pudding. **Details:** www.thechurchillarms.com; off Fosse Way; 9 pm; no Amex; no booking. **Accommodation:** 4 rooms, from £70.

PENSHURST, KENT 3–3B

Spotted Dog £32

Smarts Hill TN11 8EP (01892) 870253

With its *"good views"* and *"interesting nooks and crannies"*, this country pub has long enjoyed something of a culinary reputation; it changed hands this year, and we've removed the ratings in the face of unsettled feedback. / **Sample dishes:** crispy seafood platter; chicken in tarragon & garlic sauce; chocolate Bailey's mousse. **Details:** near Penshurst Place; 9.30 pm, Sun 8 pm; no Amex; no smoking area; children: 10+ after 7 pm.

PERTH, PERTH & KINROSS   9–3C

Let's Eat   £ 34   A★★

77-79 Kinnoull St PH1 5EZ   (01738) 643377

Tony Heath's "wonderful", "relaxed" bistro is "hard to beat"; there's "always a warm welcome and genuine concern to ensure you enjoy the food", which makes "inventive use of local produce".
/ **Sample dishes:** smoked salmon with spiced prawns & avocado; herb-crusted lamb with rosemary jus; steamed ginger pudding with rhubarb.
Details: www.letseatperth.co.uk; opp North Inch Park; 9.45 pm; closed Mon & Sun; no smoking area.

63 Tay Street   £ 37   ★

63 Tay St PH2 8NN   (01738) 441451

"High and consistent standards" of contemporary cooking typifies commentary on Jeremy & Shona Wares' minimally-decorated venture, in the heart of the city. / **Sample dishes:** smoked trout salad with lardons; Angus beef with spring onion mash; date & fig pudding.
Details: www.63taystreet.co.uk; on city side of River Tay, 1m from Dundee Rd; 9 pm; closed Mon & Sun; no smoking; children: 10+ at D.

PETERSFIELD, HAMPSHIRE   2–3D

River Kwai   £ 26

16-18 Dragon St GU31 4JJ   (01730) 267077

Some feel the cooking could "benefit from more attention to detail", but this opulent Thai is still of some note for its rarity-value in these parts. / **Details:** 10.30 pm; closed Mon L & Sun L; mainly non-smoking.

PETERSFIELD, SUSSEX   2–3D

JSW   £ 42   ★★

1 Heath Rd GU31 4JE   (01730) 262030

"Real, innovative gourmet cooking" is winning ever-greater recognition for this "small but sophisticated" family-run restaurant; despite the efforts of the "incredibly friendly and helpful" staff, however, the atmosphere can seem rather flat. / **Sample dishes:** roast foie gras with shallot tarte Tatin; wild salmon with summer vegetables; milk chocolate fondant. **Details:** 9.30 pm; closed Mon & Sun; no Amex; no smoking.

PETWORTH, WEST SUSSEX   3–4A

Well Diggers Arms   £ 35   ★

Pulborough Rd GH28 0HG   (01798) 342287

"There's always good tucker", of a fairly traditional variety, to be had at this "cramped" Georgian inn, which benefits from a "beautiful" location. / **Sample dishes:** French onion soup; roast duck; crème brûlée.
Details: 1m out of town on Pulborough Road; 9.30 pm; closed Mon & Sun D.

PHILLEIGH, CORNWALL   1–4B

Roseland Inn   £ 33   A

TR2 5NB   (01872) 580254

This "lovely old pub" (complete with a "suntrap garden"), attracted mixed reviews this year; fans say you get "plentiful" food in "idyllic" surroundings, while sceptics say it's "over-rated". / **Sample dishes:** duck liver pâté; rump steak with potatoes & salad; chocolate bread & butter pudding.
Details: www.roseland-inn.co.uk; near King Harry ferry; 9 pm; no Amex; no smoking area.

sign up for the survey at www.hardens.com

PICKERING, NORTH YORKSHIRE   8–4C

White Swan   £ 35   ★
Market Pl YO18 7AA   (01751) 472288
The "brilliant" wine list is probably the high point of dining at this
ancient town-centre coaching inn, but its "honest cooking from the
best local ingredients" is also heartily approved.
/ **Sample dishes:** chicken liver & foie gras terrine; rack of lamb with aubergine &
tomato caviar; grilled figs & Amaretto cream. **Details:** www.white-swan.co.uk; 9 pm;
no smoking. **Accommodation:** 12 rooms, from £110.

PINNER, GREATER LONDON   3–3A

Friends   £ 39   ★
11 High St HA5 5PJ   (020) 8866 0286
"Consistently good, and even better with the new chef",
this "friendly" restaurant in a pretty Tudor building is roundly praised
for its "imaginative" Gallic menu and its "excellent" wine list;
it enjoys a "huge local following". / **Sample dishes:** leek & goats cheese
strudel; lamb steak with bubble 'n' squeak; Bramley apple crumble.
Details: www.friendsrestaurant.co.uk; near Pinner Underground station; 10 pm;
closed Mon & Sun D; no smoking area.

La Giralda   £ 18
66-68 Pinner Grn HA5 2AB   (020) 8868 3429
"The menu never seems to change", but this long-established
suburban Spaniard is a "congenial" fixture with a large local fan
club; "excellent" wines are a highlight. / **Sample dishes:** melon with
Serrano ham; pink trout with nut butter; poached pears with syrup. **Details:** A404
to Cuckoo Hill Junction; 10 pm; closed Mon & Sun D.

PLOCKTON, HIGHLAND   9–2B

Plockton Inn   £ 25
Innes St IV52 8TU   (01599) 544222
"The best pub grub for miles around" (with "top kippers" and other
fish and seafood a highlight) draws reporters to "the stone bar,
or small dining room" of this "idyllic" lochside hotel (in the heart
of the territory made famous by PC Hamish MacBeth).
/ **Sample dishes:** smoked seafood platter; salmon with orange vinaigrette; sorbet.
Details: www.plocktoninn.co.uk; 9 pm; no Amex; no smoking. **Accommodation:** 7
rooms, from £32.

PLUMTREE, NOTTINGHAMSHIRE   5–3D

Perkins   £ 31
Old Railway Station NG12 5NA   (0115) 937 3695
This long-running bistro – the kind of place "featured for years
in the Good Food Guide" – retains quite a following, and generates
a fair number of reports; there's a definite sense that its approach
is "tired" nowadays, but some reporters feel they are trying to pull
their socks up. / **Sample dishes:** spicy tomato & oatmeal soup; fillet steak with
pickled walnut sauce; lime torte with dark chocolate pastry.
Details: www.perkinsrestaurant.co.uk; off A606 between Nottingham & Melton
Mowbray; 9.45 pm; closed Mon & Sun D; no smoking area; children: 10+.

PLYMOUTH, DEVON | 1–3C

Chez Nous £ 48 ★
13 Frankfort Gate PL1 1QA (01752) 266793
*The food – "from a short but superb menu" – is "second to none",
says fans of this well-established Gallic traditionalist, unpromisingly
located in the '60s urban hell of downtown Plymouth.*
/ **Sample dishes:** crab & orange salad; fillet steak with wild mushrooms; tarte Tatin.
Details: www.business.thisisplymouth.co.uk/cheznous; near Theatre Royal;
10.30 pm; D only, closed Mon & Sun; children: 12+.

Thai Palace £ 26
3 Elliot St, The Hoe PL1 2PP (01752) 255770
*"An oasis in a desert of mediocrity"; this "charming" oriental is all
the more worth knowing about in this under-served town.*
/ **Details:** www.thaipalace.co.uk; 11 pm; D only, closed Sun.

PONTELAND, NORTHUMBERLAND | 8–2B

The Smithy £ 31
3 Bell Villas NE20 9BD (01661) 820020
*"An excellent range of modern dishes" help win popularity for this
village bistro (attached to a "lovely" inn near the airport); a number
of reports note that it's "a bit pricey", though, nowadays.*
/ **Sample dishes:** seared scallops in leek & ginger broth; duck confit & puy lentils
with blackberry jus; roast peaches with nougatine. **Details:** 10 pm; closed Sat L &
Sun D; no smoking in dining room.

POOLE, DORSET | 2–4C

Mansion House £ 36   Ⓐ
Thames St BH15 1JN (01202) 685666
*An "oak-panelled dining room" and "clubby" ambience (a dining
club is, in fact, part of the set-up) lend a sense of occasion to dinner
at this hotel in a Georgian townhouse; the cooking, though, is often
"unmemorable".* / **Sample dishes:** mackerel terrine; scallops with lentils &
Indian spices; bread & butter pudding. **Details:** www.themansionhouse.co.uk; follow
signs for Ferry, turn left onto quayside; 9.30 pm; closed Sat L & Sun D; no shorts;
smoking in bar only; children: 5+ at D. **Accommodation:** 32 rooms, from £110.

PORT APPIN, ARGYLL & BUTE | 9–3B

Pier House Hotel £ 29   Ⓐ★★
PA38 4DE (01631) 730302
*No wonder this hotel is "extremely popular" – its "wonderful"
restaurant on the shores of Loch Linnhe has an "idyllic" location,
and serves "superb" fish ("caught that day") and "excellent"
seafood; service is "the best", too!* / **Sample dishes:** scallops with rice;
beef Stroganoff; death by chocolate. **Details:** www.pierhousehotel.co.uk; just off
A828 by pier; 9.30 pm; no Amex; no smoking. **Accommodation:** 12 rooms,
from £65.

PORTAFERRY, COUNTY DOWN | 10–2D

The Narrows £ 32   Ⓐ
8 Shore Rd BT22 1JY (028) 4272 8148
*"Glorious views enhance the sturdy and freshly prepared modern
Ulster cuisine" at this restaurant-with-rooms, near Strangford Lough;
as you might expect, "superb" seafood is a strong point.*
/ **Sample dishes:** lobster & marinated tomato salad; grilled turbot with tarragon
cream; strawberries with hazelnut meringue. **Details:** www.narrows.co.uk; opposite
the marina; 9 pm; no smoking area. **Accommodation:** 13 rooms, from £85.

Portaferry Hotel £ 37 A★

10 The Strand BT22 1PE (028) 4272 8231

"The ideal place for a quiet, romantic weekend", this hotel overlooking Strangford Lough attracts only positive reports, not least for its "splendid seafood". / **Sample dishes:** warm goats cheese, Parma ham & fig salad; salmon & champ with prawn cream; double chocolate torte with coconut ice cream. **Details:** www.portaferryhotel.com; on shore front, opposite ferry slipway; 9 pm; D only, except Sun open L & D. **Accommodation:** 14 rooms, from £90.

PORTMEIRION, GWYNEDD 4–2C
Portmeirion Hotel £ 45 A★

LL48 6ET (01766) 770000

"A lovely restaurant in a gorgeous setting"; all reporters sing the praises of the sea-view dining room of the hotel at Sir Clough Williams-Ellis's fantasy Mediterranean village, which is rated as "wonderful in every way"; the set lunch in particular offers "fantastic value". / **Sample dishes:** crab & smoked salmon potato cake; chicken & pancetta with wild mushroom tartlet; bara brith bread & butter pudding. **Details:** www.portmeirion-village.com; off A487 at Minffordd; 9 pm; no jeans or trainers; no smoking. **Accommodation:** 14 rooms, from £150.

PORTPATRICK, DUMFRIES & GALLOWAY 7–2A
Crown Hotel £ 28

North Cr DG9 8SX (01776) 810261

As you might hope, "fantastic seafood" is a highlight of the "pub food" on offer at this comfortable harbourside hotel dining room. / **Sample dishes:** herring & prawn platter; venison in pepper & brandy sauce; strawberry shortcake. **Details:** 10 pm; no smoking area. **Accommodation:** 12 rooms, from £72.

PORTREATH, CORNWALL 1–4A
Tabb's £ 32 ★

Tregea Ter TR16 4LD (01209) 842488

"Always an enjoyable experience"; Nigel Tabb's restaurant in a former granite forge continues to be something of a beacon in these parts. / **Sample dishes:** smoked mackerel & vegetable pâté; baked chicken with shredded leeks; dark chocolate marquise. **Details:** 9 pm; D only (except Sun open L & D), closed Tue; no Amex; no smoking in dining room.

PORTRUSH, COUNTY ANTRIM 10–1C
Ramore £ 25 A★

The Harbour BT56 8D3 (028) 7082 4313

With its "unusual dishes in a vibrant setting", this stylish coastal bar/canteen remains popular for its good-value Mediterranean cooking (including pizza), and its buzzy ambience.
/ **Sample dishes:** tortilla chips with guacamole; pizza with spicy meatballs & peppers; tiramisu. **Details:** 10 pm; no Amex; need 10+ to book; children: before 8 pm only.

PORTSMOUTH, HAMPSHIRE 2–4D
Lemon Sole £ 32 ★

123 High St PO1 2HW (023) 9281 1303

"Select your fish from the slab, and your wine from the rack" at this "trendy little restaurant" – its no-nonsense approach using "very fresh" ingredients commends it to all reporters.
/ **Sample dishes:** pan-fried scallops in garlic; grilled sea bass with home made chips; lemon & lime mousse. **Details:** www.lemonsole.co.uk; 10 pm; closed Sun; no smoking area.

PRESTBURY, CHESHIRE   5–2B

White House   £39   ★
New Rd SK10 4DG   (01625) 829376
"Consistent quality every visit" wins popularity for this village
restaurant-with-rooms, which celebrates two decades under the
Wakehams' ownership this year; perhaps unsurprisingly, considering
its chichi location, the place can seem *"expensive for what it is"*.
/ **Sample dishes:** *Caesar salad with sautéed tiger prawns; Dover sole with sea
salt & lime; strawberry brûlée with roast rhubarb.*
Details: *www.thewhitehouse.uk.com; 2m N of Macclesfield on A538; 10 pm; closed
Mon L & Sun D.* **Accommodation:** *11 rooms, from £110.*

PRESTEIGNE, POWYS   5–4A

Hat Shop   £26
7 High St LD8 2BA   (01544) 260017
"A cosy spot with some decent food" – this small outfit offers
a *"daily-changing menu"*, using local, organic ingredients where
possible. / **Sample dishes:** *aubergine & sweet potato samosas; chicken with
bacon & walnut stuffing; chocolate charlotte.* **Details:** *9 pm; closed Sun; no credit
cards; no smoking area.*

PRESTON, LANCASHIRE   5–1A

Simply Heathcote's   £34
23 Winckley Sq PR1 3JJ   (01772) 252732
Fans applaud this *"modern"* city-centre original of Paul Heathcote's
chain of brasseries as a *"stylish venue"* serving *"consistent"* cooking;
to others, though, it seems a mite *"pretentious"*; (there's also now
a cheaper, £25, basement Italian bar & grill – the Olive Press).
/ **Sample dishes:** *grilled mackerel with sour cream; wild mushroom linguine with
Parmesan & basil; rum & raisin parfait.* **Details:** *www.heathcotes.co.uk; 10 pm,
Sat 11 pm; no smoking in dining room.*

PRESTWOOD, BUCKINGHAMSHIRE   3–2A

Polecat   £26
170 Wycombe Rd HB16 0HJ   (01494) 862253
"Reliable" cooking that's *"good value"* (especially from the *"great
daily board"*) ensures that this agreeable roadside tavern is *"always
crowded"*. / **Sample dishes:** *baked field mushrooms with melted cheese;
walnut-crusted pork with spring onion salsa; coconut meringues with mango syllabub.*
Details: *on A4128 between Great Missenden & High Wycombe; 9 pm; closed
Sun D; no credit cards; no smoking area; need 8+ to book; children: limited in dining
area.*

PRIORS HARDWICK, WARWICKSHIRE   2–1D

Butchers Arms   £40   ★
Church End CV47 7SN   (01327) 260504
A *"Portuguese-English"* menu adds interest to this rural inn, praised
for its *"consistent"* standards and its *"extensive wine list"*.
/ **Sample dishes:** *mushroom & Stilton tart; beef Stroganoff; profiteroles.*
Details: *www.thebutchersarms.com; 9.30 pm; closed Sat L & Sun D; no smoking
in dining room.*

sign up for the survey at www.hardens.com

PURTON, WILTSHIRE   2–2C
Pear Tree at Purton   £ 42   ★
SN5 4ED   (01793) 772100
This *"lovely and friendly"*, rural restaurant-with-rooms (in a former vicarage), continues to win praise for its *"metropolitan quality of food and service"*. / **Sample dishes:** creamed leek & smoked haddock broth; roast lamb with olive mash & pesto gravy; pear & hazelnut tart with fudge ice cream. **Details:** www.peartreepurton.co.uk; 9.15 pm; closed Sat L.
Accommodation: 17 rooms, from £110.

PWLLHELI, GWYNEDD   4–2C
Plas Bodegroes   £ 49   🅐 ★
Nefyn Rd LL53 5TH   (01758) 612363
Chris Chown's *"delightful country restaurant"* (with rooms) remains a *"perfect"* destination, for most reporters, offering *"good local produce, beautifully served"*; this year's feedback, however, was a shade less rapturous than usual. / **Sample dishes:** cod with Carmarthen ham & laver bread; roast spiced lamb with couscous; cardamom crème brûlée. **Details:** www.bodegroes.co.uk; on A497 1m W of Pwllheli; 9.30 pm; closed Mon, Tue, Wed L, Thu L, Fri L, Sat L & Sun D; no Amex; no smoking (except in bar).
Accommodation: 11 rooms, from £80.

RAMSBOTTOM, LANCASHIRE   5–1B
Ramsons   £ 34   🅐 ★
18 Market Pl BL0 9HT   (01706) 825070
"Your guide doesn't include it, but it should!"; an *"Italian-themed"* menu using *"exceptional ingredients"* is *"creatively"* prepared – according to the disciplines of 'Slow Cooking' – at this small village restaurant. / **Sample dishes:** loin of tuna with cucumber spaghetti; loin of lamb & baby potatoes; panna cotta. **Details:** www.ramsons.org.uk; 9.30 pm; closed Mon & Sun D; no smoking; booking: max 10.

RAMSGILL-IN-NIDDERDALE, NORTH YORKSHIRE   8–4B
Yorke Arms   £ 47   ★
HG3 5RL   (01423) 755243
For *"a real gourmet meal in the heart of the Yorkshire countryside"*, it's hard to beat Frances Atkins's *"excellent if expensive"* inn, where *"enthusiastic"* staff serve dishes that are both *"innovative"* and *"beautifully presented"*. / **Sample dishes:** lobster ravioli; lamb in parsley crust; warm pear & butterscotch tart. **Details:** www.yorke-arms.co.uk; 4m W of Pateley Bridge; 9.15 pm; no smoking; booking: max 6; children: 12+. **Accommodation:** 14 rooms, from £190.

READING, BERKSHIRE   2–2D
London Street Brasserie   £ 39
2-4 London St RG1 4SE   (0118) 950 5036
"First stop when in Reading" – this *"lively"* brasserie (in the town-centre, by the river) has quite a reputation; most reporters hail its *"cool"* look and its *"imaginative"* cooking, but there are those who find it *"too costly for what it is"*. / **Sample dishes:** foie gras & duck terrine with raisin toast; sea bass with baby squid & saffron dressing; Bakewell tart & custard. **Details:** www.londonstbrasserie.co.uk; 10.30 pm.

Old Siam   £ 28
Kings Wk, Kings St RG1 2HG   (0118) 951 2600
A slightly offbeat location *"in a small shopping arcade"* does nothing to dent enthusiasm for this *"attractive"*, good-quality Thai.
/ **Details:** www.oldsiam.co.uk; 10 pm; closed Sun; no smoking in dining room.

Standard Nepalese Tandoori   £ 26   ★
142-145 Caversham Rd RG1 8AU   (0118) 959 0093
*This long-established Indian continues to attract solid ratings as one
of the best quality options in a town with a limited range
of alternatives.* / **Details:** *11 pm; no smoking area.*

REIGATE, SURREY   3–3B

La Barbe   £ 41
71 Bell St RH2 7AN   (01737) 241966
*Twenty one years old this year, this "classic", "lively" bistro continues
to please most people most of the time; "it has some cosy crannies",
and "even if the food varies a bit it can be very good".*
/ **Sample dishes:** *Roquefort mousse with poached pears; chicken, apple & cider
casserole; iced coffee mousse with lavender sauce.* **Details:** *www.labarbe.co.uk;
9.30 pm; closed Sat L & Sun; no smoking area.*

Tony Tobin @ The Dining Room   £ 47
59a High St RH2 9AE   (01737) 226650
*Things finally seem to be settling down again at TV-chef Toby Tobin's
"tightly-packed" town-centre dining room; in its "revamped and
extended" form, supporters claim it's now "Surrey's best restaurant",
but the overall consensus amongst reporters is that it's "solid" rather
than spectacular.* / **Sample dishes:** *crispy squid with fried green tomatoes;
crispy duck with melted onions; banana tart with vanilla ice cream.* **Details:** *10 pm;
closed Sat L & Sun D; smoking in bar only; booking: max 8, Fri & Sat.*

REYNOLDSTON, SWANSEA   1–1C

Fairyhill   £ 43   𝔸★
SA3 1BS   (01792) 390139
*With its "superb location in the heart of the Gower peninsula" this
"comfy" – but not grand – country house hotel is known for one
of the best dining rooms in Wales with "locally sourced produce
cooked to perfection"; those who go with "excessively high
expectations", however, may be disappointed.* / **Sample dishes:** *crab
bisque; chicken supreme with mustard risotto cake; banana soufflé pancakes with
fudge sauce.* **Details:** *www.fairyhill.net; 20 mins from M4, J47 off B4295; 9 pm;
no smoking area; children: 8+.* **Accommodation:** *8 rooms, from £140.*

RICHMOND, SURREY   3–3B

Chez Lindsay TW10   £ 30   ★
11 Hill Rise 8948 7473
*"The perfect place for delicious crêpes and cider"; "it feels like you're
in Brittany", at this "friendly" bistro – a "haven" of "real French food",
near Richmond Bridge.* / **Sample dishes:** *mussels; seafood pancake; crepes
Suzette.* **Details:** *11 pm; no Amex.*

Petersham Hotel   £ 48   𝔸
Nightingale Ln TW10 6UZ   (020) 8940 7471
*"Wonderful view over the Thames" (across Richmond's picturesque
Petersham Meadows) are the star attraction at this comfortable
dining room (previously called Nightingales); by night, it makes
a location that's "surprisingly romantic, for an hotel", by day the
"good-value" lunch menu is especially recommended.*
/ **Sample dishes:** *pan-fried baby Dover sole; seared fillet of beef with bone marrow
tart & roast ceps; warm bitter chocolate mousse with pistachios.*
Details: *www.petershamhotel.co.uk; 9.45 pm; closed Sun D.* **Accommodation:** *61
rooms, from £160.*

RIPLEY, SURREY   3–3A

Michels   £ 46
High St GU23 6AQ   (01483) 224777
*Reports remain very unsettled on this grandly-housed restaurant
on a cobbled high street (which changed owner two years ago,
and chef again this year); fans say it's "improved" and serves
"excellent French food", while critics say it "charges extraordinary
prices for dull cooking".* / **Sample dishes:** *potato pancake with smoked
salmon & caviar; roast sea bass with artichoke hearts; rhubarb & strawberry terrine.*
Details: *www.michelsrestaurant.co.uk; 9.15 pm; closed Mon, Tue-Sat D only, closed
Sun D; no smoking.*

ROADE, NORTHANTS   3–1A

Roade House   £ 39   ★
16 High St NN7 2NW   (01604) 863372
*"Consistent quality time and time again" endears Chris & Sue
Kewley's "personally run" hotel and restaurant to all reporters;
"its very relaxed atmosphere belies the seriousness of the food".*
/ **Sample dishes:** *tomato & basil tartlet with prosciutto; sea bass with ginger & lime
sauce; apple & blackcurrant crumble.* **Details:** *www.roadehousehotel.co.uk;
9.30 pm; closed Mon L & Sun D; no smoking in dining room.* **Accommodation:** *10
rooms, from £67.*

ROCKBEARE, DEVON   1–3D

Jack in the Green Inn   £ 30   ★
London Rd EX5 2EE   (01404) 822240
*"Very busy" and "consistently good", this pub just off the old A30
offers "unpretentious cooking at excellent prices"; some feel
"the bar has more ambience than the restaurant".*
/ **Sample dishes:** *smoked seafood mousse; roast pigeon with salsify & pink
peppercorns; rice pudding with pralines.* **Details:** *www.jackinthegreen.uk.com;
9.30 pm; no Amex; no smoking in dining room.*

ROMALDKIRK, COUNTY DURHAM   8–3B

The Rose & Crown   £ 34
DL12 9EB   (01833) 650213
*This "County Durham jewel" – an old coaching inn on a village
green – seems to have won every gong going in 2003; oddly, then,
while there were some reports of "memorable" meals this year,
there were also experiences which were a "let-down".*
/ **Sample dishes:** *Cotherstone cheese fritters with sweet & sour aubergines; roast
lamb with puy lentils & pesto; baked chocolate cheesecake.*
Details: *www.rose-and-crown.co.uk; 6m NW of Barnard Castle on B6277; 9 pm;
D only, except Sun open L & D; no Amex; no smoking; children: 6+.*
Accommodation: *12 rooms, from £96.*

ROTHWELL, NORTHANTS   5–4D

The Thai Garden   £ 30
3 Market Hl NN14 6EP   (01536) 712345
*Locals proclaim as "excellent" this popular oriental – a rare
attraction in these parts.* / **Details:** *off A14 near Kettering; 11 pm;
no smoking area.*

ROWDE, WILTSHIRE   2–2C

George & Dragon   £36   ★
High St SN10 2PN   (01380) 723053
"Very good" fish and seafood are the menu highlights at this *"foodie
pub, which serves cheerful, wholesome food with a local emphasis"*;
some find it *"expensive, though, for the sticks"*.
/ **Sample dishes:** spinach & watercress soup; curried smoked haddock pancakes;
baked orange custard. **Details:** on A342 between Devizes & Chippenham; 10 pm;
closed Mon & Sun; no Amex; no smoking; booking: max 8.

ROYAL LEAMINGTON SPA, WARWICKSHIRE   5–4C

Emperors   £26
Bath Pl CV31 3BP   (01926) 313666
Cooking *"head and shoulders above"* local rivals ensures continuing
popularity for this popular Chinese. / **Details:** 10.45 pm; closed Sun.

Loves   £40   ★
15 Dormer Pl CV32 5AA   (01926) 315522
"Interesting, well-cooked dishes" win high (if not quite universal)
praise for this basement venture, from ex-Mallory Court chef,
Stephen Love; service can be *"slow"*. / **Sample dishes:** meli melo
of salmon caviar & rock oyster; saddle of lamb with garlic purée & red wine jus;
chocolate pudding. **Details:** 9.45 pm; closed Mon & Sun; no smoking; no booking,
Sat.

Thai Elephant   £32
20 Regent St CV32 5HQ   (01926) 886882
"Lovely service" and *"many plants"* help create a welcoming
ambience at this superior Thai; it's *"always packed"*.
/ **Details:** 10.30 pm; closed Sat L.

RYE, EAST SUSSEX   3–4C

Landgate Bistro   £27   ★
5-6 Landgate TN31 7LH   (01797) 222829
"I've been coming for 20 years and nothing changes" – this bistro
on the fringe of the town-centre may be a bit *"unatmospheric"*,
but it provides an *"excellent standard of cooking"*.
/ **Sample dishes:** broad bean & pecorino tart; lambs kidneys with grain mustard
sauce; Jamaican chocolate cream. **Details:** www.landgatebistro.co.uk; 9.30 pm,
Sat 10 pm; D only, closed Mon & Sun; no Amex; no smoking in dining room.

Mermaid   £51   Ⓐ
Mermaid St TN31 7EY   (01797) 223065
Given the *"magnificent"* Tudor dining room of this town-centre inn,
one might fear that its cooking would be incidental; reports, though,
place it somewhere between *"good"* and *"excellent"*.
/ **Sample dishes:** pan-fried scallops & langoustines; lobster thermidor; crème
brûlée. **Details:** www.mermaidinn.com; 9.30 pm; no jeans; no smoking area.
Accommodation: 31 rooms, from £160.

SALISBURY, WILTSHIRE   2–3C

Jade   £28   ★
109a Exeter St SP1 2SF   (01722) 333355
"Not your average Chinese" – *"excellent seafood"* is the highlight
at this superior local oriental, which is praised for its *"enthusiastic
service"*. / **Details:** near the Cathedral; 11.30 pm; closed Sun; no Amex.

LXIX £29

69 New St SP1 2PH (01722) 340000

Now a bar and bistro (the 'restaurant' part of the operation is no more), this "small and central" venture near the Cathedral remains a useful rendezvous; it offers "well-presented" fare, albeit in sometimes "smallish portions". / **Sample dishes:** blue fin tuna with chilli salsa; roast cod with lime oil & noisette butter; chocolate marquise. **Details:** adjacent to Cathedral Close; 9.30 pm; closed Sat L & Sun; children: 12+.

SALTAIRE, WEST YORKSHIRE 5–1C

Salts Diner £23 🄰

Salts Mill, Victoria Rd BD18 3LB (01274) 530533

"An ideal retreat after viewing the Hockneys", this "big old mill-conversion" is a "cheap" and "cheerful" joint that's often "busy"; it's "American-style" menu is "limited", but portions are "generous". / **Sample dishes:** garlic bread; confit duck leg; sticky toffee pudding. **Details:** 2m from Bradford on A650; L only; no Amex; no smoking area.

SAPPERTON, GLOUCESTERSHIRE 2–2C

The Bell At Sapperton £36 🄰★

GL7 6LE (01285) 760298

This "pretty" Cotswolds establishment is "the best kind of gastropub", according to reporters; it won very consistent praise for its "imaginative" and "wide-ranging" menu (on which "fish is a speciality"), its "smiley" service and its "interesting" ambience. / **Details:** www.foodatthebell.co.uk; 9.30 pm; no Amex; no smoking area; no booking at L; children: 10+ at D.

SARK, CHANNEL ISLANDS

La Sablonerie Hotel £30 🄰★

GY9 0SD (01481) 832061

Just "so different", this former 16th-century farmhouse, now a restaurant-with-rooms, has an "astonishing" and remote location on this island with no motor cars; its cuisine – which, of necessity, makes much use of local produce – was consistently praised. / **Sample dishes:** smoked salmon roulard with citrus dressing; fillet steak with casserole of wild mushrooms; rum & chocolate pot with orange syrup. **Details:** 8.45pm; no smoking area. **Accommodation:** 20 rooms, from £120.

SAWLEY, LANCASHIRE 5–1B

Spread Eagle £24 🄰

BB7 4NH (01200) 441202

"A lovely setting", by the River Ribble, has helped win much fame for this "dignified" old inn; most (if not quite all) reports continue to laud its "homely", "generous" and "good-value" cooking. / **Sample dishes:** fish hors d'oeuvres; braised lamb with root vegetable sauce; tarte Tatin. **Details:** www.the-spreadeagle.co.uk; NE of Clitheroe off A59; 9 pm; closed Mon & Sun D; no smoking.

SAWSTON, CAMBRIDGESHIRE 3–1B

Jade Fountain £23

42-46 High St CB2 4BG (01223) 836100

A classic Chinese whose "reasonable pricing" and "good" standards make it one of the best orientals for miles around. / management declined to provide further information

SCAWTON, NORTH YORKSHIRE   8–4C

Hare Inn   £30   A★
YO7 2HG   (01845) 597289
"Good-quality food" is the theme of all commentary on this isolated
but *"welcoming"* pub (and it comes in *"big portions"*, too); booking
is *"a must"*. / **Sample dishes:** warm smoked duck & bacon salad; deep-fried
Whitby haddock; strawberry pavlova. **Details:** www.thehareinn.co.uk; off A170;
9 pm; no Amex; no smoking area.

SEAHAM, COUNTY DURHAM   8–2B

Seaham Hall   £56   A★
Lord Byron's Walk SR7 7AG
(0191) 516 1400
"A great revamp of an old country house" – this *"wonderful"*,
"understated" two-year-old establishment is already the North East's
top destination hotel, and its dining room wins praise for *"fabulous"*
contemporary cuisine; it's *"very expensive"*, though, and service can
be *"lackadaisical"* (and both the original general manager and head
chef moved on this year). / **Sample dishes:** assiette of foie gras; venison with
chocolate & coffee jus; chocolate & orange tart with citrus confit.
Details: www.seaham-hall.com; 9.30 pm; no smoking in dining room.
Accommodation: 19 rooms, from £175.

SEAVIEW, ISLE OF WIGHT   2–4D

Seaview Hotel   £36   A★
High St PO34 5EX   (01983) 612711
"Excellent fresh fish", *"good bar snacks"* and *"delicious breakfasts"*
are highlights of the *"very consistent"* catering at this traditional
family-owned hotel – many reporters' first choice for a good meal
on the Island. / **Sample dishes:** hot crab ramekin; monkfish wrapped in Parma
ham with crab bisque; blackcurrant sorbet with forest fruits.
Details: www.seaviewhotel.co.uk; 9.30 pm; closed Sun D; no smoking area; children:
5+ at D. **Accommodation:** 16 rooms, from £70.

SEDGEFIELD, COUNTY DURHAM   8–3B

Dun Cow   £27   ★
43 Front St TS21 3AT   (01740) 620894
By the village green, this is your archetypal country boozer,
made popular by *"the best pub food"* hereabouts.
/ **Sample dishes:** freshwater prawns with lime dressing; medallions of pork with
apple sauce; cheesecake. **Details:** www.mortal-man-inns.co.uk; 9.30 pm;
no smoking area. **Accommodation:** 6 rooms, from £65.

SELLACK, HEREFORDSHIRE   2–1B

The Lough Pool Inn   £31   ★
HR9 6LX   (01989) 730236
*"The relaxed and basic atmosphere belies the urbane quality of the
cooking"*, at this *"rural"* boozer, which is now the *"strange"* – unless
you happened to grow up in Herefordshire – location in which ex-
London restaurateur Stephen Bull's *"classy"* style of modern cooking
is now to be found. / **Sample dishes:** butternut squash risotto; roast monkfish
with curried red lentil salsa; warm ginger cake with brown bread ice cream.
Details: 9.30 pm; no Amex; no smoking; booking: max 8 at weekends.

SHEFFIELD, SOUTH YORKSHIRE   5–2C

Bahn Nah   £26   ★
19-21 Nile St S10 2PN   (0114) 268 4900
"Food of an unvaryingly high standard, if from an unvarying menu"
makes Mrs Low's "local favourite" Thai a continuing success.
/ **Details:** on A57 from Sheffield to Manchester; 10.30 pm; D only, closed Sun;
no smoking.

Candy Town Chinese   £20   ★
27 London Rd S2 4LA   (0114) 272 5315
This "efficient" family-run Chinese is notable for the "consistency"
it brings to all aspects of its operations; in particular, "brilliant value-
for-money feasts" help make it "a good choice for large groups and
families". / management declined to provide further information

Everest   £22
59-61 Chesterfield Rd S8 0RL   (0114) 258 2975
"Always friendly and welcoming", this above average Indian is worth
knowing about – especially in this under-provided city – for its
"interesting" cuisine, and "good value".
/ **Details:** www.everest-restaurant.co.uk; close to Newbridge; 12.45 am,
Thu 1.45 am, Fri & Sat 2.45 am; D only.

Kashmir Curry Centre   £13   ★
123 Spital Hill S4 7LD   (0114) 272 6253
The setting may be "basic", but the food is "excellent, considering
the prices" at this Formica-tables curry house; drinks are cheap too
– "bring your own in from the real ale pub across the road!"
/ **Details:** midnight; D only, closed Sun; no credit cards; no smoking area.

Marco @ Milano   £33   ★
Archer Rd S8 0LA   (0114) 235 3080
This "stylish modern Italian" has become a local "favourite", thanks
to its "consistently good" cooking and its "personal" service.
/ **Sample dishes:** spicy mussel & cannelloni bean soup; lamb with Gorgonzola
polenta; chocolate fudge cake with raspberry sorbet. **Details:** 11.30 pm; D only,
closed Sun; no Amex; no smoking in dining room.

Nirmals   £24
189-193 Glossop Rd S10 2GW   (0114) 272 4054
How you take to chef/patron Mrs Gupta seems to be key to the
enjoyment of this well-known local "institution"; fans hail her
"authentic" curries and welcome her "personal supervision", while
critics say the food is "only average" and find her style "overbearing"
or even "rude". / **Details:** near West St; midnight, Fri & Sat 1 am; closed Sun L;
no smoking area.

Nonna's   £30   ★
539-541 Eccleshall Rd S11 8PR   (0114) 268 6166
"Famous", at least hereabouts, this "buzzing" deli and espresso bar
serves a wide variety of "good (and occasionally great) food" –
from "unbeatable coffee and soups" to "reasonably priced" main
meals. / **Sample dishes:** chilli tuna carpaccio with rocket; polenta with Italian
sausage & roast tomatoes; vanilla & lemon cream with plums.
Details: www.nonnas.co.uk; M1, J33 towards Bakewell; 9.45 pm; no Amex;
no smoking area.

sign up for the survey at www.hardens.com   296

Rafters   £36   ★
220 Oakbrook Rd, Nether Green S11 7ED
(0114) 230 4819
"Small", "cosy" and brightly decked out modern restaurant, whose
small but dedicated fanclub say chef (and recently also patron)
Marcus Lane's cooking can be "excellent". / **Sample dishes:** twice-baked
Cheddar soufflé; rack of lamb with smoked aubergine caviar; baked apple bread &
butter pudding. **Details:** www.raftersrestaurant.co.uk; 10 pm; D only, closed Tue &
Sun; children: 7+.

Richard Smith at Thyme   £36   ★
32-34 Sandygate Rd S10 5RY   (0114) 266 6096
"It's not all grim up North!"; Richard Smith's "beautifully presented
and tasty" modern cooking makes his "contemporary" café
an "excellent and surprising find in this city"; no-one really raves
about the ambience, but the place is "welcoming" enough.
/ **Sample dishes:** smoked salmon & haddock with cucumber gazpacho; Tuscan veal
casserole with polenta mash; sticky toffee pudding & toffee sauce.
Details: www.thymeforfood.co.uk; 9.30 pm; closed Sun D; smoking in bar only.

Slammers   £33   ★
625a Ecclesall Rd S11 8PT   (0114) 268 0999
"Always packed, even though it's now been extended", this "first-
rate" fish restaurant is unanimously hailed for its "well-prepared,
fresh and interesting dishes"; some reporters complain of a
"restrictive" two-sittings policy, but prices are kept very reasonable
by the BYO option (Mon-Thu). / **Sample dishes:** roast cod spring rolls with
lemongrass; smoked salmon & prawn tagliatelle with truffle oil; apple galette with
vanilla ice cream. **Details:** www.slammersseafood.co.uk; 10 pm; closed Mon L &
Sun; no Amex; no smoking.

Zing Vaa   £16
55 The Moor S1 4PF   (0114) 275 6633
"Great dim sum" and "an authentic atmosphere (helped by an
influx of Chinese customers for Sunday lunch)" maintains the strong
local following for this "friendly" ten-year-old. / **Details:** 11.30 pm;
no smoking area.

SHELLEY, WEST YORKSHIRE   5–2C
Three Acres   £38   𝔸★★
Roydhouse HD8 8LR   (01484) 602606
Belying its "remote location" ("right next to the Emley Moor
TV mast"), this "mega-popular" coaching inn is incredibly well-
known, and it's "always packed", thanks to its "really buzzing" feel
and the "superb quality" of the food in its bar and restaurant;
you can also take-away from a deli-operation. / **Sample dishes:** oxtail &
spring vegetable terrine; chicken with pak choy in sweet & sour sauce; meringue with
muscat poached fruits. **Details:** 3acres.com; near Emley Moor TV tower; 9.45 pm;
closed Sat L. **Accommodation:** 20 rooms, from £75.

SHEPPERTON, SURREY   3–3A
Edwinns   £38
Church Rd TW17 9JT   (01932) 223543
"London style in the suburbs" is hailed by fans of this "modern, light
and airy" bistro – the original member of a small chain; it's a
"friendly" and "good-value" spot, too – you "need to book".
/ **Sample dishes:** char-grilled artichoke with Parmesan crisps; crispy duck with Thai
vegetables; lemon & ginger steamed sponge. **Details:** www.edwinns.co.uk;
opp church & Anchor Hotel; 10.10 pm, Fri & Sat 10.30 pm; closed Sat L & Sun;
no smoking area.

SHEPTON MALLET, SOMERSET   2–3B

Charlton House   £ 62
Charlton Rd BA4 4PR   (01749) 342008
*This "Mulberry flagship" country house hotel – decked out in the
"sumptuous" style of the brand which owns it – is hailed as a
"fabulous" and "romantic" destination by most reporters; its dining
room, however, inspired less favourable commentary this year,
drawing flak for "pretensions beyond its ability to deliver".*
*/ **Sample dishes:** salt beef terrine with cumin seed bread; bream with smoked
salmon & leek tart; raspberry tart with spicy praline mousse.*
Details: *www.charltonhouse.com; on A361 towards Frome; 9.30 pm; no smoking.*
Accommodation: *17 rooms, from £155.*

SHERE, SURREY   3–3A

Kinghams   £ 38   𝐴★
Gomshall Ln GU5 9HB   (01483) 202168
*"Interesting food in an old cottage" is the proposition at "one of
Surrey's top rural restaurants"; reporters' praise for Paul Baker's
cooking is eclipsed only by that for the "exceptional ambience and
service".* */ **Sample dishes:** seared scallops with pea & bacon patties; roast lamb
with sweet potato mash; chocolate pudding with espresso sauce.*
Details: *www.kinghams-restaurant.co.uk; off A25 between Dorking & Guildford;
9.30 pm; closed Mon & Sun D; no smoking.*

SHINFIELD, BERKSHIRE   2–2D

L'Ortolan   £ 84
Church Ln RG2 9BY
(0118) 988 8500
*What is it with this site? – Alan Murchison quickly re-established
a big name for his and Peter Newman's "fantastic" revamp of this
former Georgian rectory (originally made famous by John Burton-
Race), but he's recently upped sticks for Chewton Glen; new chef
Daniel Galmiche has a hard act to follow – we've removed all
ratings, as he arrived post-survey.* */ **Sample dishes:** crab blinis & caviar;
roast sea bass with Thai shellfish; passion fruit tart with mango sorbet.*
Details: *www.lortolan.com; 11 pm; closed Sun D; no smoking.*

SHIPLEY, WEST YORKSHIRE   5–1C

Aagrah   £ 22   𝐴★
4 Saltaire Rd BD18 3HN   (01274) 530880
*All-round satisfaction is the theme of reports on this "relaxed" and
"lively" outlet of the "sophisticated" Yorkshire curry chain; it offers
"an excellent range of Indian food, to suit all tastes".*
*/ **Details:*** *www.aagrah.com; 11 pm; no smoking area.*

SHREWSBURY, SHROPSHIRE   5–3A

Cromwells Hotel   £ 25
11 Dogpole SY1 1EN   (01743) 361440
*A handy town-centre boozer, with a modern and quite varied menu
– solid but unspectacular ratings suggest it makes a useful stand-by.*
*/ **Sample dishes:** baked aubergine & goats cheese; Cajun seafood sausages;
rhubarb tart with ginger custard. **Details:** www.cromwellsinn.com; opp Guildhall;
10 pm; no smoking in dining room. **Accommodation:** 6 rooms, from £60.*

sign up for the survey at www.hardens.com

SIDMOUTH, DEVON   2–4A

Belmont Hotel   **£ 33**   ★

The Esplanade EX10 8RX   (01395) 512555
*"A consistent performer across the board" — you get "good food"
(from a traditional menu) "in a quality hotel facing the sea" at this
large Victorian establishment.* / **Details:** www.brend-hotels.co.uk; 8.45 pm;
jacket & tie; no smoking. **Accommodation:** 50 rooms, from £64.

Swan Inn   **£ 20**   ★

37 York St EX10 8BY   (01395) 512849
*"A pub with very good fresh fish" — that's the gist of all reports
on this "simple" but satisfying establishment.*

SKENFRITH, MONMOUTHSHIRE   2–1B

Bell   **£ 38**   𝔸 ★

NP7 8UH   (01600) 750235
*A "peacefully located" riverside inn — "recently refurbished
in wonderfully understated style" — which is praised for its "local
produce, cooked to perfection".* / **Sample dishes:** whole globe artichoke
with hollandaise; pork tenderloin with shallot mash; cherry & cashew frangipane tart.
Details: www.skenfrith.co.uk; on B4521, 10m NE of Abergavenny; 9.30 pm; closed
Mon (Nov-Mar only); no smoking in dining room. **Accommodation:** 8 rooms,
from £85.

SLEAT, ISLE OF SKYE   9–2A

Kinloch Lodge   **£ 46**   𝔸

IV43 8QY   (01471) 833333
*You really do get a pretty authentic country house dining experience
at Lord Macdonald of Macdonald's former hunting lodge, but it
seems to take different people different ways — fans say Lady M's
cooking is "wonderful", whereas detractors can find it "out of its
depth".* / **Sample dishes:** smoked Skye salmon with lime & cucumber; roast rack
of lamb with oatmeal stuffing; ginger steamed sponge.
Details: www.kinloch-lodge.co.uk; D only (closed weekdays in winter); no smoking;
booking essential. **Accommodation:** 14 rooms, from £50.

SNAPE, SUFFOLK   3–1D

The Crown Inn   **£ 30**   𝔸 ★

Bridge Rd IP17 1SL   (01728) 688324
*"The best cooking in Suffolk, and probably the warmest welcome
in any county" — supporters are not shy in their praise of this pretty
rural boozer; it's "reasonably priced", too.* / **Sample dishes:** coarse game
pâté with chutney; scallops with lemon couscous & spiced sauce; sticky toffee
pudding. **Details:** off A12 towards Aldeburgh; 9 pm; no Amex; no smoking in dining
room; children: 14+. **Accommodation:** 3 rooms, from £70.

SNETTISHAM, NORFOLK   6–4B

Rose & Crown   **£ 38**

Old Church Rd PE31 7LX   (01485) 541382
*"An excellent spot for winter breaks" — this "thatched pub", parts
of which date back to the 13th century, comes complete with
"log fires", and offers "a varied menu with lots of fish".*
/ **Sample dishes:** grilled smoked salmon in vinaigrette; fillet of bream & mussels jus;
almond tart. **Details:** www.roseandcrownsnettisham.co.uk; 9 pm; no Amex;
no smoking area. **Accommodation:** 11 rooms, from £90.

---

sign up for the survey at www.hardens.com

SOLIHULL, WEST MIDLANDS   5–4C

Beau Thai   £ 28   ★
761 Old Lode Ln B92 8JE   (0121) 743 5355
*"What more could you want?", say fans of this family-run Thai,
lauding its "freshly cooked food and friendly staff".*
/ **Details:** www.beauthai.co.uk; 10 pm; closed Mon L & Sat L; no smoking area.

SONNING ON THAMES, WOKINGHAM   2–2D

Bull Inn   £ 29
High St RG4 6UP   (0118) 969 3901
*A "lovely location", by the village church, is not the only attraction
of this "olde worlde" boozer – it offers a "good" and "varied" menu
of "fashionable pub food".* / **Sample dishes:** smoked salmon with Thai
prawns; lambs liver & bacon casserole; blueberry tortellini with coconut ice cream.
Details: www.infotel.co.uk; off A4, J10 between Oxford & Windsor; 9 pm;
no smoking; no booking. **Accommodation:** 7 rooms, from £85.

The French Horn   £ 65   𝔸
RG4 6TN   (0118) 969 2204
*A 'clincher' for a first date or an anniversary" – that's how one
(sexagenarian!) reporter summarises the attractions of this "posh"
Gallic riverside veteran, where everything is done well ("in the old
style"), where the wine list is "extensive" and whose location
is "hard to beat"; prices, of course, can seem "ridiculous".*
/ **Sample dishes:** scallops in bacon with creamed pea soup; rack of lamb with olive
jus; poached pear with chocolate sorbet. **Details:** www.thefrenchhorn.co.uk; M4, J8
or J9, then A4; 9.30 pm. **Accommodation:** 21 rooms, from £130.

SOUTH SHIELDS, TYNE & WEAR   8–2B

Tavistock at the Grotto   £ 36   𝔸
Coast Rd NE34 7BS   (0191) 455 6060
*This "stunning" new pub is literally "built in to the cliff-face",
and even reporters who find the bar food "average" and the
restaurant "overpriced" concede that the views and setting "make a
visit worthwhile".* / **Sample dishes:** pan-fried scallops with lemon, mint &
toasted pine nut salad; wild salmon with samphire fresh pasta & tomato sauce;
toasted brioche with summer berries. **Details:** 10 pm; closed Mon L.

SOUTHALL, GREATER LONDON   3–3A

Giftos Lahore Karahi   £ 15   ★
162-164 The Broadway, UB1 1NN   (020) 8813 8669
*"The best grilled meat in the country" is hailed by aficionados of this
well-known, "basic" but "bustling" Southall kebab fixture, and the
breads are "excellent" too; the place is "invariably full".*
/ **Details:** 11.45 pm.

SOUTHAMPTON, SOUTHAMPTON   2–3D

Kuti's   £ 24
37-39 Oxford St SO14 3DP   (023) 8022 1585
*"Reliable and interesting, if not brilliant" – this "consistently good"
subcontinental is a very popular option in a city without too many
rival attractions; the menu's "huge selection" includes "a good choice
for vegetarians".* / **Details:** www.kutis.co.uk; near Ocean Village; midnight.

sign up for the survey at www.hardens.com   300

SOUTHPORT, MERSEYSIDE   5–1A

Auberge Brasserie   £32
1b Seabank Rd PR9 0EW   (01704) 530671
This "attractive" brasserie is "perhaps less French than it used
to be", but earns praise nonetheless for its "varied and seasonal"
cooking. / *Sample dishes:* hot duck & apple salad; lemon sole with prawn & dill
mousse; chocolate & basil marquise. *Details:* www.auberge-brasserie.com;
10.30 pm; no smoking area.

Hesketh Arms   £20
Botanic Rd PR9 7NA   (01704) 509548
"Proper pub food" ("well cooked and nicely presented") and
"friendly" staff maintain the appeal of this agreeable boozer.
/ *Sample dishes:* potted shrimps; steak & kidney pie; bread & butter pudding.
Details: near Botanical Gardens; 8 pm; closed Mon D & Sun D; no smoking area;
children: before 9 pm.

Warehouse Brasserie   £32   ★
30 West St PR8 1QN   (01704) 544662
This "stylish and comfortable" brasserie is a top find in this part
of the North West, where "friendly staff" serve an "interesting"
menu of "good modern cooking"; it's recently been revamped and
expanded. / *Sample dishes:* Lebanese mezze; grilled chicken with smoked
cheese & leek risotto; chocolate & honeycomb torte.
Details: www.warehouse-brasserie.co.uk; 10.15 pm; closed Sun.

SOUTHWOLD, SUFFOLK   3–1D

The Crown   £36
High Street IP18 6DP   (01502) 722275
According to its fans, the "main problem" at this "perennial
favourite" bar – with its "friendly, busy and noisy" feel, and its
"excellent" Adnams wines and beers – is still the fact that you can't
book; ratings are sliding across the board, though, supporting those
who say the place has been "disappointing, since the old chef left".
/ *Sample dishes:* Norfolk crab with potato salad; cod tempura with sweet potato
chips; apple & cinnamon tart. *Details:* www.adnams.co.uk; 10 pm; no Amex;
smoking in bar only; children: 5+ after 7 pm. *Accommodation:* 14 rooms,
from £75.

Sutherland House   £32   ★
56 High St IP18 6DN   (0152) 722260
"The well-cooked contemporary fare contrasts with the olde-worlde
décor of the dining room", at this "friendly" Elizabethan townhouse;
all reporters, though, say the dishes are "delicious". / *Details:* 9 pm;
no smoking. *Accommodation:* 3 rooms, from £100.

The Swan   £36   🄰
The Market Pl IP18 6EG   (01502) 722186
A "grand setting", a "good wine list" and "delightfully amateurish
service" have long been defining features of the "elegant" dining
room of this "lovely" market square hotel (owned by Adnams the
brewers); the "traditional" cooking, though, has slipped quite
noticeably in recent years. / *Sample dishes:* seared tuna with Niçoise style
salad; roast lemon chicken; caramelised lemon tart. *Details:* www.adnams.co.uk;
9 pm; no Amex; no smoking; children: 5+ at D. *Accommodation:* 42 rooms,
from £130.

SOWERBY BRIDGE, WEST YORKSHIRE   5–1C

Gimbals   £32   A ★
Wharf St HX6 2AF   (01422) 839329
"Surprisingly good, try it!" – reporters speak only in the fondest
terms of this *"small but well-run"* bistro. / **Sample dishes:** *Dolcelatte &
mushroom open lasagne; mustard-glazed pork with parsnip mash; bread & butter
pudding.* **Details:** *9.15 pm; D only, closed Tue; no Amex; no smoking.*

The Millbank   £37   ★
Millbank HX6 3DY   (01422) 825588
"You can eat West End-quality food at Yorkshire prices", at this
refreshing Pennine gastropub, which enjoys a *"lovely hillside setting"*
(with *"good views in summer"*); the *"trendy"* décor can seem *"a bit
uninviting"* on gray days. / **Sample dishes:** *pea soup with potato & ham
dumplings; lamb with artichoke & chestnuts in pastry; Yorkshire parkin with toffee
apple mousse.* **Details:** *www.themillbank.com; 9.30 pm; closed Mon, Tue L &
Sun D; no Amex; no smoking in dining room.*

SPARSHOLT, HAMPSHIRE   2–3D

Plough Inn   £32
SO21 2NW   (01962) 776353
"An amazing range of dishes" and *"pleasant staff"* are among the
plus-points of this village inn; sometimes, though, it can seem
"a victim of its own success", and waits can be *"long"*.
/ **Sample dishes:** *grilled goats cheese with herb croutons; roast pork in smoked
bacon, apricot & ginger sauce; pear Condé with chocolate sauce.* **Details:** *9 pm,
Fri & Sat 9.30 pm; no Amex; no smoking area.*

SPEEN, BUCKINGHAMSHIRE   3–2A

Old Plow   £40
HP27 0PZ   (01494) 488300
"Always reliable" cooking helps win a steady following for this family-
run, converted country pub given over to eating; the style of service
can seem *"a touch OTT"*, though, and some prefer the bistro to the
more *"starchy"* restaurant. / **Sample dishes:** *game terrine with redcurrant &
beetroot preserve; goats cheese, leek & Stilton tart; caramel tart with coffee sauce.*
Details: *20 mins from M40, J4 towards Princes Risborough; 8.45 pm; closed Mon,
Sat L & Sun D; smoking in bar only.*

ST ALBANS, HERTFORDSHIRE   3–2A

La Cosa Nostra   £21
62 Lattimore Rd AL1 3XR   (01727) 832658
"Noisy and busy", this *"small"* Italian pizza and pasta joint is a
popular local fixture, not least thanks to its *"fair prices"*.
/ **Sample dishes:** *grilled aubergine salad; spaghetti with garlic & parsley; tiramisu.*
Details: *near railway station; 11 pm; closed Sat L & Sun.*

Darcy's   £35
2 Hatfield Rd AL1 3RP   (01727) 730777
*"Now the best restaurant in the town-centre and the second-best
of St. Albans's 66 eating establishments!"* – not only this rather
precise reporter sings the praises of this *"pleasant"* newcomer,
which is worth knowing about in an under-served area.
/ **Sample dishes:** *duck spring roll with sweet chilli sauce & cucumber salad; chicken
breast with Mozzarella & pesto wrapped in Prosciutto; Amaretti baked peaches &
vanilla bean ice cream .* **Details:** *www.darcysrestaurant.co.uk; 9.30 pm; no smoking
in bar; booking essential.*

The St Michaels Manor £40 Ⓐ
Fishpool St AL3 4RY (01727) 864444
Not everyone is totally convinced, but this "graceful" hotel down by the river impresses most commentators with its "welcoming" style, "beautiful" setting and "quality" traditional cooking.
/ **Sample dishes:** *marinated saffron noodles with crayfish, asparagus & mango lime coulis; red mullet & ham with cous cous; blackberry & almond tart.*
Details: *www.stmichaelsmanor.com; nr Cathedral; 9 pm; no smoking.*
Accommodation: *22 rooms, from £170.*

Sukiyaki £25
6 Spencer St AL3 5EG (01727) 865009
A decade old, this minimalist oriental is still hailed by locals for its "great service" and its "good-value" selection of Japanese dishes.
/ **Details:** *10 pm; closed Mon & Sun; children: no babies, no children post 7.30 pm.*

The Waffle House
Kingsbury Water Mill £20 Ⓐ
St Michael's St AL3 4SJ (01727) 853502
"You can feed the ducks" – with your lunch, if you don't like it! – at this "olde worlde" waterside spot, which is famous locally for its "excellent sweet and savoury waffles"; it can seem "pricey" for what it is, though, and queues can be "a turn-off". / **Sample dishes:** *chunky vegetable soup; ham, cheese & mushroom waffle; banana & butterscotch waffle.*
Details: *near Roman Museum; L only; no Amex; no smoking in dining room; no booking.*

ST ANDREWS, FIFE 9–3D

Vine Leaf Garden £36 ★
131 South St KY16 9UN (01334) 477497
On the basis of limited feedback, the Hamilton family's "great neighbourhood restaurant" – with its "rich" Scottish fare leavened by "imaginative fish and veggie dishes" – continues to be a "very dependable" choice. / **Sample dishes:** *Indian-spiced prawns with mini poppadoms; venison with mushroom, brandy & peppercorn soup; brown sugar pavlova with strawberries.* **Details:** *9.30 pm; D only, closed Mon & Sun; no smoking.* **Accommodation:** *2 rooms, from £80.*

ST IVES, CORNWALL 1–4A

Alfresco £34 Ⓐ★
Harbourside Wharf Rd TR26 1LF (01736) 793737
"Good views" and "excellent seafood" offer a hard-to-beat combination at this charming harbourside establishment, where new chef Crispin Jones seems to have got off to a good start.
/ **Sample dishes:** *steamed crab dumplings; red mullet tart with basil; strawberry pavlova with raspberry coulis.* **Details:** *www.stivesharbour.com; on harbour front; 9.30 pm; no Amex; no smoking.*

Blue Fish £36 Ⓐ★
Norway Ln TR26 1LZ (01736) 794204
With its "zingy", "simple" food and "buzzy" atmosphere, this "laid-back" venture above an arts centre remains "a lovely place for holiday eating". / **Sample dishes:** *shrimps in garlic; chicken & goats cheese salad; chocolate ganache.* **Details:** *behind the Sloop Inn; 10.30 pm (9 pm in winter); no Amex; no smoking in dining room.*

Porthgwidden Beach Cafe £29 A★
TR26 ISL (01736) 796791
"I actually prefer this to their fancier place, the Porthminster Beach" – this "calming" café is universally praised by reporters for its "perfect and innovative dishes", and its "lovely, sheltered cove location". / Details: www.restaurantsstives.co.uk; 10 pm; closed in Winter; no Amex; no smoking; booking: max 10.

Porthminster Café £34 A★
Porthminster Beach TR26 2EB (01736) 795352
"Stunning views as the sun sets" help create a "special atmosphere" at this terrific café "perched on the beach", which is becoming quite a destination; its staff are "really friendly and helpful", and they serve up some "excellent" and "imaginative" fish and seafood. / Sample dishes: grilled scallops & goats cheese; turbot with braised leeks; chocolate pudding with orange ice cream. Details: www.porthminstercafe.co.uk; near railway station; 10 pm; closed Nov-Mar; no Amex; no smoking in dining room.

The Seafood Café £31 ★
45 Fore St TR26 IHE
(01736) 794004
"A brilliant idea, combining fresh produce with style" – this simple fish restaurant offers "excellent portions and value for money"; the staff are "really helpful" (and "child-friendly"), too. / Sample dishes: Cornish shellfish; catch of the day with seasonal vegetables; sticky toffee pudding. Details: www.seafoodcafe.co.uk; map on website; 10.30 pm; no Amex; no smoking area.

ST KEYNE, CORNWALL 1–3C

The Well House £44 A★
PL14 4RN (01579) 342001
"Beautifully cooked food" and "attentive" staff complete the experience of dining at this "formal but romantic" dining room – part of a charming country house hotel in the peaceful Looe valley. / Sample dishes: ham terrine with pineapple tart; vanilla-seared bream with Swiss chard; pecan tart with coffee bean ice cream. Details: www.wellhouse.co.uk; half way between Liskeard & Looe off the B3254; 8.30 pm; no Amex; no smoking in dining room; booking essential at L; children: 8+ at dinner. Accommodation: 9 rooms, from £115.

ST MARGARETS AT CLIFFE, KENT 3–3D

Walletts Court £49
Westcliffe CT15 6EW (01304) 852424
Overlooking the North Downs, the Oakley family's old-fashioned and long-established country house hotel has fans who proclaim its cooking "still the best"; former concerns about overpricing seem to have abated. / Sample dishes: grilled squid with blackened green peppers; partridge stuffed with game parfait; crème brûlée with raspberries. Details: www.wallettscourt.com; on B2058 towards Deal, 3m NE of Dover; 9 pm; closed Mon L & Sat L; no smoking; children: 8+, no children allowed after 8 pm. Accommodation: 16 rooms, from £90.

ST MAWES, CORNWALL   1–4B

Hotel Tresanton   **£ 45**   🅐
27 Lower Castle Rd TR2 5DR   (01326) 270055
*An "idyllic" location, complete with a "wonderful sea-view terrace"
helps create a "splendid" atmosphere at Olga Polizzi's (née Forte)
"fun" design-hotel; "at the price", though, some reporters feel the
cuisine "lacks excitement". / Sample dishes: Gorgonzola & spinach tart;
roast John Dory with saffron gnocchi; honey fritters with lemon ricotta.
Details: www.tresanton.com; near Castle; 9.30 pm; no smoking at D; children:
8. Accommodation: 29 rooms, from £195.*

Rising Sun   **£ 38**
The Square TR2 5DJ   (01326) 270233
*"Get there early", if you want to enjoy the "good selection
of specials" ("using local produce") included on the menu of this
stylish inn, where you can dine in the bar or, quite formally, in the
restaurant. / Sample dishes: smoked salmon kedgeree & quails egg; ballotine
of duck; raspberry oatmeal meringue. Details: www.innsofcornwall.co.uk; 8.30 pm;
D only, except Sun open L & D; no smoking. Accommodation: 8 rooms,
from £100.*

ST MERRYN, CORNWALL   1–3B

Ripleys   **£ 39**   ★
PL28 8NQ   (01841) 520179
*"Very much on the up"; ex-Stein chef, Paul Ripley's two-year-old
establishment ("handily located for Newquay Airport") offers some
highly ambitious fish dishes, which have no doubt helped it win its
Michelin gong – however, "it's the simple dishes that please most".
/ Sample dishes: twice-baked goat cheese soufflé; roast monkfish with mussels &
clam chowder; hot chocolate fondant with banana ice cream. Details: 9.30 pm;
no Amex; no smoking; booking: max 8.*

ST MONANS, FIFE   9–4D

Seafood Restaurant   **£ 38**   🅐★
16 West End KY10 2BX   (01333) 730508
*"Right by the sea, with the breakers coming at you" – all reporters
extol the "first-class" seafood at this "family-run, small and very
friendly" venture. / Sample dishes: seared sea bass with truffle & herb risotto;
roast cod fillet with bacon mash, spinach, onion ice cream & garlic sauce; pineapple
tarte Tatin with coconut sorbet. Details: www.theseafoodrestaurant.com; 9.30 pm;
closed Mon & Sun D in Winter; no smoking.*

ST PETERS, GUERNSEY

Café du Moulin   **£ 41**   🅐★★
Rue De Quanteraine GY7 9DP   (01481) 265944
*With its "great local ingredients, prepared in the French way",
a "beautiful country setting", "superb" wines and "friendly" service
– this venture in a former granary attracts nothing less than a hymn
of praise. / Sample dishes: lobster salad with mango & ginger dressing; oxtail
cannelloni with truffle shavings & Parmesan; crème brûlée. Details: 9 pm; closed
Mon & Tue L; closed Sun D in winter; no Amex; no smoking in dining room.*

STADDLEBRIDGE, NORTH YORKSHIRE   8–4C
McCoys at the Tontine   £ 40
DL6 3JB   (01609) 882671

Fans of this well-known bistro and restaurant (celebrating its quarter century this year) praise its "great atmosphere" and its "fresh and tasty" cooking; others find it "past its best", though, citing slapdash service as the weakest link. / **Sample dishes:** *grilled black pudding with beetroot sauce; salmon & mussels with langoustine butter; sticky toffee pudding.* **Details:** *www.mccoysatthetontine.co.uk; junction of A19 & A172; 10 pm; bistro L & D all week; restaurant Sat D only.* **Accommodation:** *6 rooms, from £100.*

STADHAMPTON, OXFORDSHIRE   2–2D
Crazy Bear   £ 44   A
Bear Ln OX44 7UR   (01865) 890714

The décor may be "bizarre", but it can make a visit at this "quirkily-converted" pub "a fun surprise"; the place boasts both a dining room with "eclectic upmarket pub food" and a Thai brasserie – it sounds odd, but "it works!". / **Sample dishes:** *Roquefort soufflé with pears & walnuts; roast duck with cider braised potatoes; warm chocolate cake.* **Details:** *www.crazybearhotel.co.uk; 10 pm.* **Accommodation:** *12 rooms, from £120.*

STAITHES, NORTH YORKSHIRE   8–3C

Endeavour   £ 34   A★★
1 High St TS13 5BH
(01947) 840825

"If only they could silence the seagulls!" – that's the worst anyone has to say about this former fisherman's cottage, which – with their "fantastic" seafood dishes – new owners Brian Kay & Charlotte Willoughby are making a "must-visit" destination. / **Sample dishes:** *parsnip & orange soup; fillet steak with foie gras butter; iced Drambuie mousse.* **Details:** *www.endeavour-restaurant.co.uk; 10m N of Whitby, off A174; 9.30 pm; D only, closed Mon & Sun; no smoking in dining room.* **Accommodation:** *3 rooms, from £60.*

STAMFORD, LINCOLNSHIRE   6–4A
The George Hotel   £ 46   A
St Martins PE9 2LB   (01780) 750750

This "wonderful", "unspoilt" and "luxurious" coaching inn sits at the heart of a beautiful Georgian town; critics find it "overpriced" or "mediocre", but most reporters speak in terms of "classic, old-fashioned dishes" served in "imposing, oak-panelled surroundings" (and there's a "super" outside brasserie in summer). / **Sample dishes:** *chicken & wild mushroom sausage with lentils; pork & tarragon mustard in filo pastry; British cheeses.* **Details:** *www.georgehotelofstamford.com; off A1, 14m N of Peterborough, onto B1081; 10.30 pm; jacket & tie required; no smoking before 10 pm; children: 7+ at D.* **Accommodation:** *47 rooms, from £110.*

STANTON, SUFFOLK   3–1C
Leaping Hare Vineyard   £ 38   A
Wyken Vineyards IP31 2DW   (01359) 250287

Sir Kenneth & Lady Carlisle's "old barn conversion" makes a "fantastic setting" to sample "excellent locally-grown wines", complemented by simple modern food from "fine ingredients"; its ratings slipped this year, though. / **Sample dishes:** *tempura courgette flowers stuffed with Thai crab; vine-smoked guinea fowl with bacon mash; apricot sorbet.* **Details:** *9m NE of Bury St Edmunds; follow tourist signs off A143; 9 pm; L only, except Fri & Sat open L & D; no Amex; no smoking.*

STATHERN, LEICESTERSHIRE   5–3D

Red Lion Inn **£28**   A★

2 Red Lion St LE14 4HS
(01949) 860868

"Sister to Clipsham's Olive Branch and promising to reach similar
standards" – this newly jazzed-up pub near Belvoir Castle offers
a winning combination of "quality produce, excellently cooked",
"enthusiastic young staff", an "innovative wine list" and a "relaxed
ambience". / **Sample dishes:** peppered beef salsa with rocket & Stilton;
Lincolnshire sausages with sage mash & onion gravy; apple pie with cream.
Details: 9 pm; closed Sun D; no Amex; no smoking in dining room.

STOCKBRIDGE, HAMPSHIRE   2–3D

Les Copains d'Abord   **£42**   A★

London Rd SO20 6DE (01264) 810738

"Run by two French brothers in a rather incongruous old pub in the
middle of nowhere", this "relaxed" and "comfortable" venture
is hailed by almost all reporters for its "intimate" charm and its
"very good value". / **Sample dishes:** tiger prawns with fresh ginger,
corriander & garlic; turbot & fresh vegetables; pain perdu. **Details:** 9 pm; closed
Mon & Sun D; no Amex; no smoking in dining room.

Greyhound   **£35**   ★

31 High St SO20 6EY (01264) 810833

"A gastropub that puts others to shame"; "inventive" and
"very high-quality" cooking is reported by most who comment
on this revitalised hostelry. / **Details:** 10 pm; closed Sun D; no Amex;
no smoking area; booking: max 10.

STOCKCROSS, BERKSHIRE   2–2D

Vineyard at Stockcross   **£75**

RG20 8JU (01635) 528770

New chef John Campbell is finally pushing Sir Peter Michael's hugely
ambitious restaurant-with-rooms – which looks like a "low-rise, late-
'80s wedding cake" – into the league it has always craved,
and some fans compare his style to that of Heston Blumenthal
(and favourably, too); this is still a rather "stiff" place, though, where
"Europe's greatest list of Californian wines" is the only indubitable
attraction. / **Sample dishes:** pressed chicken & foie gras terrine; roast sea bass
with butter bean purée; warm chocolate fondant. **Details:** www.the-vineyard.co.uk;
from M4, J13 take A34 towards Hungerford; 9 pm; no smoking area.
Accommodation: 31 rooms, from £269.

STOKE BRUERNE, NORTHANTS   2–1D

Bruerne's Lock   **£37**   A

5 The Canalside NN12 7SB (01604) 863654

The canalside location adds a "romantic" air to this "quiet and
contemplative" venture ("near a favourite local spot for
an afternoon out watching the barges"); reports put the food
somewhere between "good-to-average" and "very good".
/ **Sample dishes:** deep-fried quails eggs with pancetta; beef Wellington with port
jus; apple & cinnamon crumble. **Details:** www.bruerneslock.co.uk; 0.5m off A508
between Northampton & Milton Keynes; 9 pm; closed Mon & Sat L; no smoking
in dining room.

STOKE BY NAYLAND, ESSEX   3–2C

Angel Inn   £34
Polstead St   CO6 4SA   (01206) 263245
"The only downside is that you have to arrive early to nab a seat"
at this "lovely inn", which serves a "drool-worthy" selection
of "comfort food". / **Sample dishes:** mushroom & pistachio pâté; roast pork
with apple mousse & red cabbage; raspberry bavarois. **Details:** 5m W of A12,
on B1068; 9 pm; no Amex; no smoking area; children: 14+. **Accommodation:** 6
rooms, from £67.50.

STOKE HOLY CROSS, NORFOLK   6–4C

Wildebeest Arms   £34
Norwich Rd   NR14 8QJ   (01508) 492497
"Surprisingly good food, for the back of beyond";
this "unpretentious" pub conversion continues to offer standards
"a notch or two above the norm". / **Sample dishes:** sautéed calamari with
squid ink risotto; roast lemon & thyme pork fillet; passion fruit tart & rhubarb sorbet.
Details: from A140, turn left at Dunston Hall, left at T-junction; 10 pm; no smoking
area.

STOKE ROW, OXFORDSHIRE   2–2D

The Crooked Billet   £38   𝔸
Newlands Ln   RG9 5PU   (01491) 681048
"A great olde worlde atmosphere" is the highlight at this "low-
beamed old village pub", which has a "secluded" rural location near
Henley; the menu has some "interesting twists" and satisfies most,
if not quite all, reporters. / **Sample dishes:** onion & pepper tartlet with
Roquefort glaze; gammon hock with Polish sausage & sauerkraut; Bakewell tart &
custard. **Details:** www.thecrookedbillet.co.uk; on A4130; 10 pm; no Amex or Switch.

STOKE SUB HAMDON, SOMERSET   2–3B

The Priory House   £44
1 High St   TA14 6PP   (01935) 822826
This exceptional restaurant was sold in the summer of 2003
to Peter & Sonia Brooks; we've therefore left it unrated pending our
next survey. / **Sample dishes:** mushroom risotto with Parmesan; grilled cod with
black olive tapenade & mash; burnt lemon cream with raspberry sorbet.
Details: 9 pm; closed Mon, Wed D & Sun; closed 2 weeks in Aug & Dec; no jeans
or trainers; no smoking; children: 14.

STON EASTON, SOMERSET   2–3B

Ston Easton Park   £54   𝔸★
Ston Easton   BA3 4DF   (01761) 241631
This "glorious house" – a grade I listed Palladian mansion – boasts
a splendid dining room, and wins all-round praise for its "charming"
service, its "excellent and varied" wine list and its first-rate
traditional cooking. / **Sample dishes:** foie gras with apples; quail with goats
cheese; banana soufflé. **Details:** www.stoneaston.co.uk; 11m SW of Bath on A39;
9.30 pm, 10 pm Fri & Sat; jacket & tie; no smoking; children: 7+.
Accommodation: 23 rooms, from £185.

STONEHAVEN, ABERDEEN   9–3D

Lairhillock Inn   £ 27

Netherley AB39 3QS (01569) 730001

This cosy pub (and adjacent dining room, £39) is a popular destination for Aberdonians and is hailed by fans as "a rare oasis in the culinary desert of north east Scotland"; there was the odd disastrous visit this year, though. / **Sample dishes:** chunky seafood chowder; wild boar sausage with mustard mash; sticky toffee pudding.

Details: www.lairhillock.co.uk; 7m S of Aberdeen; 9.30 pm; no smoking area.

Tolbooth   £ 33

Old Pier Rd AB39 2JU (01569) 762287

Known for its "wonderful fresh fish", this attractive seafood restaurant was sold to new chef/patron Robert Cleaver as our survey for the year was drawing to a close – hence we've removed ratings pending the next edition. / **Sample dishes:** smoked salmon with Parma ham & pesto; wolf fish with champagne & watercress sauce; sticky toffee pudding.

Details: www.tolboothrestaurant; 9.30 pm; D only, closed Mon & Sun; no Amex; no smoking; children: 8+.

STONY STRATFORD, MILTON KEYNES   2–1D

Peking   £ 27

117 High St MK11 1AT (01908) 563120

Views differ on this "beautifully decorated" Chinese, but even those who say it's "excellent" can feel it's "getting a bit pricey for what it is". / **Details:** off A5; 11.30 pm; no smoking area.

STORRINGTON, WEST SUSSEX   3–4A

Fleur de Sel   £ 49   ★

Manley's Hill RH20 4BT (01903) 742331

"A bit dear, but still very good value" – that's the clear thread running through the many reports on Michel & Bernadette Perraud's "charming" and "so very French" country restaurant, where the food is "very, very good", and service "efficient and discreet".

/ **Sample dishes:** roast prawns with French bean salad; duck with honey & ginger sauce; mango tarte Tatin. **Details:** W of Storrington on A283; 9.30 pm; closed Mon, Sat L & Sun D; no smoking in dining room; children: 12+.

STOURBRIDGE, WORCESTERSHIRE   5–4B

French Connection   £ 31   ★

3 Coventry St DY8 1EP (01384) 390940

"Classic", "correct", "safe", "cosy", "comfortable" – that's most of what you need to know about this family-run, French restaurant, which is all-the-more worth remembering in this thinly-served area; it's "reasonably priced", too. / **Sample dishes:** chicken liver, brandy & garlic pâté; baked pesto-crusted cod; brioche bread & butter pudding.

Details: www.frenchconnectionbistro.co.uk; 9.30 pm; closed Mon, Tue D & Sun; mainly non-smoking.

sign up for the survey at www.hardens.com

STOW ON THE WOLD, GLOUCESTERSHIRE 2–1C

The Royalist (947AD)
Eagle & Child £35
Digbeth St GL54 1BN (01451) 830670
Guinness Book of Records-approved as the oldest pub in England, this Cotswold inn is quite a "professional" destination, offering some "generous and well-prepared dishes". / **Sample dishes:** *avocado & pine nut salad; crab & cod cakes with tomato & ginger sauce; caramelised orange & pineapple pancake.* **Details:** *www.theroyalisthotel.co.uk; 10 pm; closed Mon & Sun D; no smoking; need 6+ to book; children: 6+.* **Accommodation:** *8 rooms, from £90.*

STRATFORD UPON AVON, WARWICKSHIRE 2–1C

Lambs £30 Ⓐ
12 Sheep St CV37 6EF (01789) 292554
"A good bistro atmosphere, amongst the old oak beams" is the highpoint of a visit to this "very busy" fixture that's "pitched at the pre-theatre set"; "uncaring" and "slow" service, though, can be a problem. / **Sample dishes:** *crispy duck & watercress salad; roast chicken & mango in lime butter; banoffi pie.* **Details:** *www.lambsrestaurant.co.uk; 10 pm; no Amex; booking: max 12.*

Opposition £30
13 Sheep St CV37 6EF (01789) 269980
"A banker" – this "cramped" and "cosy" wine bar of long standing isn't going to set the world on fire, but it is "consistent", "good value" and "dependable pre-theatre". / **Sample dishes:** *Greek salad with deep-fried halloumi; chorizo & red pepper pizza; tiramisu.* **Details:** *www.theopposition.co.uk; 10.30 pm; no Amex; booking: max 12.*

Russons £32
8 Church St CV37 6HB (01789) 268822
"Reliable" and "friendly" are the two words which tend to crop up most in reports on this town-centre restaurant; it's "excellent pre-theatre", but "it can be difficult to get a seat". / **Sample dishes:** *snails in garlic butter with spiced croutons; monkfish, salmon & bacon brochettes; sticky toffee cheesecake.* **Details:** *9.30 pm; closed Mon & Sun; no smoking area; booking: max 8; children: 8+ after 7pm.*

Thai Kingdom £28
11 Warwick Rd CV37 6YW (01789) 261103
Don't let a visit in recent years by the Crown Prince of Thailand induce undue expectations, but this popular oriental offers "quality" food and "charming" service. / **Details:** *10.45 pm; no smoking area.*

STUCKTON, HAMPSHIRE 2–3C

Three Lions £42 ★
Stuckton Rd SP6 2HF (01425) 652489
"A splendid husband-and-wife team" produce "wonderful" food in a "friendly" atmosphere at the Womersley family's former pub near the New Forest; even fans may find it on the pricey side, though, or find the décor "a mite twee". / **Sample dishes:** *crab bisque with shrimps; roast roe buck with ceps; hot chocolate pudding.* **Details:** *www.thethreelionsrestaurant.co.uk; 1m E of Fordingbridge off B3078; 9.30 pm; closed Mon & Sun D; no smoking in dining room.* **Accommodation:** *4 rooms, from £65.*

STUDLAND, DORSET   2–4C

Shell Bay Seafood   **£ 38**   Ⓐ★
Ferry Rd BH19 3BA   (01929) 450363
"Great views" are an undisputed highlight of this *"idyllically located"* café overlooking the harbour, but its *"simply prepared and cooked"* fish and seafood menu is also highly praised. / **Sample dishes:** *seared tuna loin with peppercorn crust; grilled sea bass with garlic & rosemary; raspberry & vanilla panna cotta.* **Details:** *9 pm; no smoking pre 10 pm; children: 12+ at D.*

STURMINSTER NEWTON, DORSET   2–3B

Plumber Manor   **£ 34**
DT10 2AF   (01258) 472507
A *"reliably high standard"* is the theme of all commentary on the dining room of this *"lovely"* country house hotel – after three decades in the same ownership, it *"never changes"*, but *"standards are kept up-to-date"*. / **Sample dishes:** *wild mushroom millefeuille with brandy cream; peppered sirloin steak with mustard sauce; lemon meringue pie.* **Details:** *www.plumbermanor.com; off A357 towards Hazelbury Bryan; 9.30 pm; D only, except Sun open L & D; smoking discouraged; booking essential.* **Accommodation:** *16 rooms, from £100.*

SUNDERLAND, TYNE & WEAR   8–2C

throwingstones
National Glass Centre   **£ 24**   Ⓐ★
Liberty Way SR6 0GL   (0191) 565 3939
It's not just the *"beautiful setting"* (an impressively *"light and airy"* space overlooking the River Wear) which makes this museum café well worth seeking out; it also offers *"good portions"* of *"unusual and delicious"* cooking, at *"reasonable prices"*. / **Sample dishes:** *roast pepper & Mozzarella salad; salmon with rocket & orange salad; brandy snap with toffee ice cream.* **Details:** *A19 to Sunderland, follow signs for National Glass Centre; L only; no Amex; no smoking.*

SURBITON, SURREY   3–3B

The French Table   **£ 36**   ★
85 Maple Rd KT6 4AW   (020) 8399 2365
"A surprisingly good find, hidden away in Surbiton"; locals (and a few visitors) hail this *"increasingly reputed"* modern bistro, where *"distinctly above-average food"* is charmingly served in a *"rather ordinary"* setting. / **Sample dishes:** *mushroom cannelloni with truffle oil; pork stuffed with chorizo mousse & endive; lemon curd ice cream.* **Details:** *10.30 pm; closed Mon, Tue-Sat D only, closed Sun D; no Amex; no smoking area; booking: max 10, Fri & Sat.*

SUTTON GAULT, CAMBRIDGESHIRE   3–1B

Anchor   **£ 36**   Ⓐ★
Bury Ln CB6 2BD   (01353) 778537
"A lovely small ex-pub (no bar) in the wilds about 10 miles from Cambridge"; reporters universally hail its food, service and ambience as *"heavenly"*, so it's no surprise that it's often *"busy"*, too. / **Sample dishes:** *Cornish crab salad with baby leeks; calves liver with Bayonne ham on bacon mushroom mash; warm chocolate mousse.* **Details:** *www.anchor-inn-restaurant.co.uk; 7m W of Ely, signposted off B1381 in Sutton; 9 pm; no smoking area; children: 6+ after 8 pm.* **Accommodation:** *2 rooms, from £62.*

SWANSEA, SWANSEA   1–1D

La Braseria   £32
28 Wind St SA1 1DZ   (01792) 469683
*"Consistent reliability" is the continuing theme of commentary
on this "reasonably-priced", basic Spanish-themed restaurant; as at
its Cardiff cousin (to which it's no longer affiliated), you choose steak
and seafood at the bar for the kitchen to prepare.*
/ Sample dishes: devilled chicken livers; halibut Mornay; crème caramel.
Details: www.labraseria.com; 11.30 pm; closed Sun; need 6+ to book; children: 6+.

Hanson's   £33   ★
Pilot House Whf, Trawler Rd SA1 1UN   (01792) 466200
*"A fabulous waterside setting" (by the marina) isn't the only appeal
of this "small and discreet" first-floor restaurant; it wins consistent
praise for its "good choice" of "very fresh fish".*
/ Sample dishes: cockles & laver bread; roast rack of Welsh lamb with bubble &
squeak; lemon & Cointreau tart with summer berries. **Details:** 9.30 pm; no Amex.

Morgans Hotel   £33   𝔸★
Somerset Pl SA1 1RR   (01792) 484848
*Dermott Slade may have moved on, but all reports speak in glowing
terms of the "imaginative and stylish food" served in the "beautiful"
and "civilised" dining room of the former Associated Ports building,
part of a trendy new luxury hotel.* **/ Sample dishes:** salmon & crab potato
cakes with garlic saffron sauce; roast tenderloin of pork bubble with bubble &
squeak; pot au chocolat with ice cream. **Details:** 9.30 pm; no smoking.
Accommodation: 20 rooms, from £100.

PA's Wine Bar   £29   𝔸
95 Newton Rd SA3 4BN   (01792) 367723
*Though "always full", this small traditional wine bar in the Mumbles
boasts an "intimate" atmosphere; it offers "a good range of fish and
well-cooked dishes, mainly Mediterranean in origin".*
/ Sample dishes: crispy king prawn won tons; fillet of ostrich served with duo
of sauces; banoffi pie. **Details:** www.paswinebar.co.uk; 9.30 pm; closed Sun D.

Patricks   £30   𝔸
638 Mumbles Rd SA3 4EA   (01792) 360199
*"A bold brasserie that's sometimes wide of the mark" –
this "informal" (and rather "cramped"), restaurant (with rooms)
enjoys an "excellent location" on the Mumbles seafront, and can get
"very busy".* **/ Sample dishes:** feta sorbet with char-grilled watermelon;
sesame-crusted pork with satay sauce; cappuccino & chocolate terrine.
Details: www.patricks-restaurant.co.uk; in Mumbles, 1m before pier; 9.50 pm;
closed Sun D; no smoking in dining room. **Accommodation:** 8 rooms, from £95.

SWINTON, SCOTTISH BORDERS   8–1A

Wheatsheaf Inn   £33   ★
Main St TD11 3JJ   (01890) 860257
*A popular and comfortable Borders pub where fans say the cooking
– using "locally-sourced ingredients" – is "excellent".*
/ Sample dishes: chicken, spring vegetable & herb broth; beef in claret & cep oil
sauce; iced Drambuie parfait. **Details:** www.wheatsheaf-swinton.co.uk; between
Kelso & Berwick-upon-Tweed, by village green; 9.15 pm; closed Mon & Sun D
(to non-residents); no Amex; no smoking. **Accommodation:** 7 rooms, from £90.

TADCASTER, NORTH YORKSHIRE 5–1D

Aagrah £22
York Rd LS24 8EG (01937) 530888
This branch of the estimable Yorkshire curry chain can get
"excessively busy", but it serves "good food nonetheless".
/ **Details:** www.aggrah.com; 7m from York on A64; 11.30 pm; D only; no smoking
area.

TAPLOW, BERKSHIRE 3–3A

Terrace
Cliveden House £78 A
Berry HI SL6 0JF (01628) 668561
Cliveden's main restaurant may be a touch cheaper than Waldo's,
but it's still "only for the well-heeled"; it does have a view, though
(no small consideration in such a "glorious" setting), and most
reporters find the food "in keeping with the location".
/ **Sample dishes:** lobster crab salad; fillet of steak; pear & choc soufflé.
Details: www.clivedenhouse.co.uk; no smoking.

Waldo's
Cliveden House £85 A
Berry HI SL6 0JF (01628) 668561
"As a place to impress" and "indulge your fantasies" this imposing
palazzo, in a vast estate, is just a can't-fail proposition;
the "intimate" basement dining room is the grander of the two main
restaurants, and inspires a whole range of views from "indescribably
good" to "hopeless". / **Sample dishes:** sea bass poached in champagne; roast
partridge with blackcurrant vinegar; fig tartlet with honey ice cream.
Details: www.clivedenhouse.co.uk; M4, J7 then follow National Trust signs; 9.30 pm;
D only, closed Mon & Sun; jacket & tie required; no smoking; booking: max 6;
children: 12+. **Accommodation:** 39 rooms, from £190.

TAUNTON, SOMERSET 2–3A

Brazz
Castle Hotel £32
Castle Bow TA1 3NF (01823) 252000
The modern décor is "interesting", at least by Taunton standards,
but this town-centre brasserie (the original branch of what is now
a small West Country chain) can be "terribly noisy", and reports
on all aspects of its operation are very mixed.
/ **Sample dishes:** walnut & blue cheese salad; sirloin steak with sauce béarnaise;
Eton Mess. **Details:** www.brazz.co.uk; 10.30 pm; smoking in bar only.

The Castle Hotel £59
Castle Grn TA1 INF (01823) 272671
This wisteria-clad landmark's dining room came to particular
prominence when, many years ago, Gary Rhodes was at the stoves;
its "all-regions" wine list is still of note, but the cooking can seem
"uninspired" nowadays. / **Sample dishes:** rabbit pie with mustard dressing;
sea bass with truffled macaroni cheese; golden raisin soufflé.
Details: www.the-castle-hotel.com; follow tourist information signs; 9.45 pm; closed
Sun D; no smoking. **Accommodation:** 44 rooms, from £165.

sign up for the survey at www.hardens.com 313

Sanctuary Wine Bar   £ 29   ★
Middle St TA1 1SJ   (01823) 257788
The setting may be "cramped", but standards – especially the "super" food – are "consistently good and professional" at this wine bar, a short walk from Somerset County Cricket Ground.
/ **Sample dishes:** lemon chicken with veggie crisps & rocket salad; Thai crab cakes with chilli salsa; chocolate terrine with honey-roasted oranges.
Details: www.sanctuarywinebar.co.uk; 11.30 pm; closed Sat L & Sun; no Amex; no smoking area.

Willow Tree   £ 35   🄰★
3 Tower Ln TA1 4AR
(01823) 352835
"A total surprise" – "I didn't know you could get this quality of cooking outside the big cities"; this "small and intimate" newcomer is universally praised by reporters for its "consistently excellent" standards, and in particular for the "clean" and "subtle" flavours produced by Roux-trained chef Darren Sherlock.
/ **Sample dishes:** roast pigeon breaded with bacon & chestnut mushrooms in red wine sauce; sauteed medalions of monkfish with spaghetti of celeriac carrot; hot mango soufflé with a pricot sauce. **Details:** 10 pm; closed Mon, Tue L, Sat L & Sun; no Amex; no smoking.

TAYVALLICH, ARGYLL & BUTE   9–4B

Tayvallich Inn   £ 28   ★
PA31 8PL   (01546) 870282
"Excellent fresh fish" makes it "worth a detour" to this small coastal village inn (actually a converted bus garage); "the simplicity of the food makes the dishes all the more enjoyable".
/ **Sample dishes:** pan-fried scallops; seafood platter; crème brûlée.
Details: www.tayvallich.com; signposted off Crinan canal at Bellanoch, 9 miles from Lochgilphead; 9 pm; closed Fri L & Sat L; no Amex; no smoking area; booking: max 12.

TETBURY, GLOUCESTERSHIRE   2–2B

Trouble House Inn   £ 34
Cirencester Rd GL8 8SG   (01666) 502206
Fans hail a "great roadside find" at this "cosily updated country inn", praising its "innovative dishes, served in a clubby, pubby setting"; ratings are held back, though, by the few reporters who find it "unremarkable" and "disappointing". / **Sample dishes:** wild mushroom casserole; lemon sole with braised leeks & mussels; white chocolate cheesecake with lemon ice cream. **Details:** www.troublehouse.co.uk; 1.5m from Tetbury on A433 towards Cirencester; 9.30 pm; closed Mon; closed 2 weeks in Jan; no smoking area; booking: max 8; children: 14+ in bar.

THORNBURY, GLOUCESTERSHIRE   2–2B

Thornbury Castle   £ 57
Castle St BS35 1HH   (01454) 281182
Initial reports suggest that a new chef has pepped up the cooking at this Tudor landmark – part of the very grand Von Essen group – and suggest it's "expensive, but top-quality"; there was insufficient feedback, however, to justify the 'star' the place may well deserve.
/ **Sample dishes:** pan-fried French quail with tomato confit; grilled halibut with tomato fondue & caviar cream; pecan & maple chocolate brownie.
Details: www.thornburycastle.co.uk; near intersection of M4 & M5; 9.30 pm, Sat 10 pm; no smoking in dining room. **Accommodation:** 25 rooms, from £140.

sign up for the survey at www.hardens.com

THORNHAM, NORFOLK   6–3B

Lifeboat Inn   £31
PE36 6LT   (01485) 512236
This "friendly", "olde worlde" inn – with a "great location near the
harbour and beach" – has quite a following for its "well-prepared
seafood" (and "top breakfasts"); standards are "inconsistent",
though, and some reporters continue to think that the place is "a
victim of its own success". / **Sample dishes:** Thai crab cakes with capsicum
chutney; lemon sole with crisp capers & prawns; fruit crumble.
Details: www.lifeboatinn.co.uk; 20m from Kings Lynn on A149 coast road; 9.30 pm;
D only, except Sun L only; no Amex. **Accommodation:** 14 rooms, from £76.

THORPE LANGTON, LEICESTERSHIRE   5–4D

Bakers Arms   £31   Ⓐ
Main St LE16 7TS   (01858) 545201
"Good home-cooked food at reasonable prices" wins continued
popularity for this relaxed village inn (which is more dining pub than
watering hole nowadays). / **Sample dishes:** fresh mussels; sea bass with
sweet potato mash; chocolate tart with caramelised bananas. **Details:** near Market
Harborough off the A6; 9.30 pm; open only Tue-Fri for D, all day Sat & Sun L;
no smoking area; children: 12+.

TITLEY, HEREFORDSHIRE   2–1A

Stagg Inn   £35   ★
HR5 3RL   (01544) 230221
Steven Reynolds's Gavroche-training probably gave Michelin comfort
when it awarded this smart pub the first ever star for such
an establishment, and cooking "of a quality not seen outside the
best restaurants" figures in most reports; there are also doubters,
though, who insist "you shouldn't believe the hype".
/ **Sample dishes:** mussel & saffron risotto; braised lamb with tomato & tarragon
gravy; treacle tart with clotted cream. **Details:** www.thestagg.co.uk; on B4355,
NE of Kington; 9.30 pm; closed Mon & Sun D (& 2 weeks in Nov); no Amex;
no smoking area. **Accommodation:** 2 rooms, from £70.

TODMORDEN, WEST YORKSHIRE   5–1B

The Old Hall Restaurant   £35   Ⓐ
Hall St OL14 7AD   (01706) 815998
"What hospitality is all about" – "brilliant staff" add lustre to the
Hoyles' "grand but relaxed" 17th-century house, which serves
"excellent food at good prices"; ambience may be lacking at quiet
times, though (and "parking can be a problem").
/ **Sample dishes:** grilled mackerel with potato cakes; crispy duck & watercress
salad; winter berry pavlova. **Details:** 15 mins from M62; 9 pm, Sat 9.30 pm; closed
Mon & Sun D; no Amex; no smoking in dining room.

TOPSHAM, DEVON   1–3D

The Galley   £47
41 Fore St EX3 0HU   (01392) 876078
Even some fans of this "quirky" venture, occupying interesting
premises overlooking the estuary, concede that it's rather
"expensive", but they do say the fish is "excellent"; not everyone,
however, is convinced. / **Sample dishes:** deep-fried Thai fishcakes; roast
salmon with blinis & mango; meringues with iced Turkish Delight.
Details: www.galleyrestaurant.co.uk; 11 pm; closed Mon; no smoking; booking
essential; children: 12+. **Accommodation:** 4 rooms, from £50.

sign up for the survey at www.hardens.com

TORCROSS, DEVON   1–4D

Start Bay Inn   £24   ★
TQ7 2TQ   (01548) 580553
"Queues on sunny days show the popularity of this local beach-side pub", where the fish can be "frighteningly fresh" – both "excellent fish and chips" and "interesting specials" win lavish praise.
/ **Sample dishes:** scallops pan-fried in garlic; pan-fried monkfish in garlic; treacle tart. **Details:** www.startbayinn.co.uk; 10 pm; no Amex; no smoking area; no booking.

TORQUAY, DEVON   1–3D

No 7 Fish Bistro   £35   ★
Beacon Ter   TQ1 2BH   (01803) 295055
"A good variety of very fresh fish" is the theme of all commentary on this "buzzy" family-run bistro, at which some meals can be "really memorable". / **Sample dishes:** hot shellfish platter; tempura special; brandy snap basket topped with amaretti. **Details:** www.no7-fish.co.uk; 9.30 pm; closed Sun & Mon in Winter.

TREEN, CORNWALL   1–4A

Gurnards Head   £30   ★
TR26 3DE   (01736) 796928
"Surrounded by spectacular coast", this "cheerful" and "cosy" boozer appropriately has quite a name for its "excellent fish"; "wonderful" soups are among the attractions ensuring it's often "packed". / **Sample dishes:** Cornish seafood broth; seared pigeon with bacon & mushrooms; bread & butter pudding. **Details:** www.gurnardshead.fsnet.co.uk; on coastal road between Land's End & St Ives, near Zennor B3306; 9.15 pm; no smoking area. **Accommodation:** 6 rooms, from £55.

TROON, SOUTH AYRSHIRE   9–4B

Lochgreen House   £40
Lochgreen Hs, Monktonhill Rd   KA10 7EN   (01292) 313343
Prepare for "an overdose of tartan and Scottish Baronial" at this Edwardian golf hotel (recently considerably expanded), which attracts nothing but praise for cooking that makes "good use of local produce"; the brasserie is open for lunch, the grander restaurant only in the evening. / **Sample dishes:** scallops with celeriac & mustard oil; horseradish-crusted lamb with rosemary noodles; hot chocolate & cherry pudding. **Details:** www.lochgreenhouse.co.uk; 9.30 pm; no smoking. **Accommodation:** 40 rooms, from £195, incl D.

The Oyster Bar   £33   𝔸★
The Harbour, Harbour Rd   KA10 6DH   (01292) 319339
The "simply-cooked" fish and seafood can be "wonderful" at this "friendly", family-run mill-conversion, which benefits from a rather "unusual" location, by the harbour. / **Sample dishes:** roast scallops & tomatoes with Prosciutto; baked turbot with mushrooms, leeks & truffles; lemon Mascarpone with blueberry coulis. **Details:** follow signs for Sea Cat Ferry Terminal, past shipyard; 9.30 pm; closed Mon & Sun D; no Amex.

TROUTBECK, CUMBRIA 7–3D

Queen's Head £ 26 𝔸 ★

Townhead LA23 1PW (01539) 432174

"High-quality pub food" and an *"attractive"* location have made quite a name for this 17th-century Lakeland coaching inn; it can get very busy, so early arrival is advised. / **Sample dishes:** wild mushroom, Stilton & black olive terrine; supreme of chicken with mash; bread & butter pudding. **Details:** www.queensheadhotel.com; A592, on Kirkstone Pass; 9 pm; D only; no Amex; no smoking area; booking: max 8, Fri & Sat. **Accommodation:** 14 rooms, from £75.

TRURO, CORNWALL 1–4B

Numberten £ 31 ★

10 Kenwyn St TR1 3DJ (01872) 272363

"A place which deserves to succeed" say fans of this *"unpretentious"* and *"friendly"* Aussie-run, town-centre café/bistro. / **Sample dishes:** prawn & chick pea fritters; chicken with sweet potato mash; lemon tart. **Details:** 9.30 pm; closed Sun L (& Sun D in winter); no Amex; no smoking in dining room; booking: max 8, Fri & Sat.

TUNBRIDGE WELLS, KENT 3–4B

Hotel du Vin et Bistro £ 43 𝔸

Crescent Rd TN1 2LY (01892) 526455

"Much-improved" food and a *"great"* ambience feature in this year's reports on this *"gorgeous"*, stripped-down Victorian hotel (which, until now, has been the poor relation in the boutique hotel chain); as usual, *"the wine list is a delight and education"*, but service can be *"leisurely"*. / **Sample dishes:** salt cod brandade with peppers; chicken with creamed leeks & black pudding; pineapple crème brûlée. **Details:** www.hotelduvin.com; 9.45 pm; booking: max 10. **Accommodation:** 36 rooms, from £89.

Signor Franco £ 40

5a High St TN1 1UL (01892) 549199

"Good, if pricey, food" and *"great"* service have sustained the popularity of this town-centre Italian for over a decade. / **Sample dishes:** smoked sturgeon; pasta filled with white truffles; pancakes with crème pâtissière. **Details:** 11 pm; closed Sun; no Amex.

Thackeray's House £ 46 ★

85 London Rd TN1 1EA (01892) 511921

It may occupy a *"characterful"* historic building, but the style at Richard Phillips's well-reputed venture is decidedly contemporary *"chic"* nowadays (to the extent that some find it a mite hard-edged); his *"stunningly presented"* cuisine is *"very good"*, but some reporters cannot avoid noting that *"at these prices, it should be"*. / **Sample dishes:** roast quail salad; grilled tuna with potatoes; banana tarte Tatin. **Details:** www.thackerays-restaurant.co.uk; 10.30 pm; closed Mon & Sun D; no smoking area in main restaurant.

TUNSTALL, LANCASHIRE 7–4D

Lunesdale Arms £ 25 𝔸

LA6 2QN (01524) 274203

"Stylishly refurbished with a female touch", by chef/patron Emma Gillibrand, this *"friendly"* gastropub serves *"varied and imaginative"* cooking in a *"bright and cheerful"* setting. / **Sample dishes:** tomato bruschetta with pesto; lime & lemongrass chicken with rice; cappuccino mousse. **Details:** www.thelunesdale.com; 15 min from J34 on M6 onto A683; 9 pm; closed Mon; no Amex.

TURNBERRY, SOUTH AYRSHIRE 7–1A
Westin Turnberry Resort £ 63 _A_

KA26 9LT (01655) 331000

The views are "astonishing" and the service "exceptional" at this renowned coastal golf hotel ("with two world-class courses"); some reporters found "every dish a masterpiece", but one or two detractors concluded that the "accountants have taken charge!".
/ **Sample dishes:** oak-smoked Scottish salmon; seared monkfish with basil polenta; raspberries & mango. **Details:** www.turnberry.co.uk; A77, 2m after Kirkswald turn right, then right again after 0.5m; 9.30 pm; closed Sun L; no smoking. **Accommodation:** 221 rooms, from £220.

TURNERS HILL, WEST SUSSEX 3–4B
Alexander House £ 55 _A_★

RH10 4QD (01342) 714914

This "exquisite country house", "beautifully located" in extensive grounds, doesn't produce a huge amount of feedback; such as there is, though, hails the "wonderful" contemporary cuisine.
/ **Sample dishes:** warm goats cheese ballotine with curry lentils; braised shank of lamb with cream potatoes & ratatouille sauce; glazed coconut custard served on warm macaroon with caramel sauce. **Details:** www.alexanderhouse.co.uk; off the M23 J10, follow signs to E. Grinstead and Turner's Hill, on the B2110; 9 pm; shirt, no jeans; no smoking; children: 7+. **Accommodation:** 15 rooms, from £140.

TWICKENHAM, MIDDLESEX 3–3A
Brula £ 31 ★

43 Crown Rd TW1 3EJ (020) 8892 0602

The menu focusses on "what French bistros do best" at this "cosy" venture in St Margarets, rated highly by reporters for its "personal touch" and its "cheap but notably tasty" cooking.
/ **Sample dishes:** pork & veal terrine with onion marmalade; roast duck with courgette & basil cream sauce; baked chocolate pot. **Details:** 50 yards from St Margarets station; 10.30 pm; closed Sun; no Amex; booking: max 8.

Ma Cuisine TW1 £ 27 ★★

6 Whitton Rd
8607 9849

If every town had a tiny, no-frills bistro like John McClement's newcomer (a few doors down from his main gaff), would anyone ever bother going to France?; it offers wonderful, simple dishes, cheerily and efficiently, and all at prices that would have seemed reasonable ten years ago!
/ **Sample dishes:** boudin of foie gras with mango salsa; bouillabaisse; crêpe suzette. **Details:** 11.30 pm; closed Sun.

McClements TW1 £ 56 ★

2 Whitton Road 8744 9610

No one doubts the quality of the "classic, ancien-régime" cooking at this "really surprising" Twickenham fixture (which also boasts a wine list of real note); however, its "formal" style – perhaps intended to catch the eye of Michelin – does the place no favours. / **Sample dishes:** scallops with cep risotto; roast pigeon & foie gras wrapped in spinach; baked lime & rhubarb mousse. **Details:** www.mcclementsrestaurant.com; 10.30 pm; closed Sun D; no smoking area.

Monsieur Max TW12 £ 54 _A_★★

133 High St 8979 5546

"As close to being in France as possible" (and not just by Hampton Hill standards), this "surprising" suburban "gem" is "worth a large detour" – it was once again hailed in practically every report as "outstanding in all respects"; prices "edge ever upwards", but few seem to begrudge the cost. / **Sample dishes:** foie gras & duck terrine with Sauternes jelly; John Dory with champagne & sorrel risotto; liquorice meringue. **Details:** 9.30pm; closed Sat L.

TYN-Y-GROES, CONWY   4–1D

Groes Inn   £32
LL32 8TN   (01492) 650 545
With its "wide choice" of "good, home-cooked fare" and its "friendly" staff, "Wales's oldest licensed inn" wins enthusiastic applause from a silver-haired fan club. / **Sample dishes:** crispy black pudding, bacon & red onion salad; braised knuckle of lamb; bread & butter pudding. **Details:** www.groesinn.com; on B5106 between Conwy & Betws-y-coed, 2m from Conwy; 9 pm; no jeans; no smoking area. **Accommodation:** 14 rooms, from £90.

TYNEMOUTH, TYNE & WEAR   8–2B

Sidney's   £27   Ⓐ★
3-5 Percy Park Rd NE30 4LZ   (0191) 257 8500
"A lovely bistro, with super food"; this "tiny" spot wins continued praise for its "consistent" and "straightforward" cooking – attractions stretch all the way from a "wonderful" cooked breakfast to a "well thought-out" wine list. / **Sample dishes:** honey-roast duck with noodles & plum salad; Moroccan-braised lamb with couscous; chocolate-stuffed prune tart. **Details:** www.sidneys.co.uk; 10 pm; closed Sun; no smoking.

ULLAPOOL, HIGHLAND   9–1B

Ceilidh Place   £33   Ⓐ
14 West Argyle St IV26 2TY   (01854) 612103
It's not a fancy place, but a visit to the arts and music centre in this waterside town can be "memorable"; it provides some "super seafood" and – amazingly for the highlands – lots for veggies, as well as "fantastic beers and a good whisky selection". / **Sample dishes:** Cullen Skink; medallions of venison; chocolate amaretti trifle. **Details:** www.theceilidhplace.com; 55m NW of Inverness on A835; 9 pm; no smoking in dining room. **Accommodation:** 13 rooms, from £45.

ULLINGSWICK, HEREFORDSHIRE   2–1B

The Three Crowns Inn   £32   ★
HR1 3JQ   (01432) 820279
This "relaxed" and "welcoming" half-timbered inn is popular with almost all who comment on it, thanks to its "reliably careful and original cooking, using fresh and tasty local ingredients". / **Sample dishes:** smoked salmon with cucumber & lovage vinaigrette; rack of lamb with shallots & spinach; chocolate tart. **Details:** www.threecrownsinn.com; 1.5m from A417; 9.30 pm; closed Mon; no Amex; no smoking area.

ULLSWATER, CUMBRIA   7–3D

Sharrow Bay   £59   Ⓐ★
CA10 2LZ   (01768) 486301
A "magical" Lakeland setting and "outstanding" service continue to distinguish this "classic country house hotel" (founded in 1948, and usually credited as the original of the breed); the food is often "exceptional", too, but younger bloods can find it "rather traditional" or "repetitive"; (as we go to press, a purchase by Von Essen hotels is mooted). / **Sample dishes:** crab & scallop pancake with crayfish oil; lamb in herb brioche crust & thyme jus; syllabub. **Details:** www.sharrow-bay.com; on Pooley Bridge Rd towards Howtown; 8 pm; jacket & tie required; no smoking; children: 13+. **Accommodation:** 26 rooms, from £320.

ULVERSTON, CUMBRIA 7–4D

Bay Horse £35 ✕

Canal Foot LA12 9EL (01229) 583972

This "small pub-cum-hotel, with views of Morecambe Bay and the Lake District" has quite a reputation; it's "not as good as it used to be", though, with "ridiculous" prices inspiring a number of very unhappy recent reports. / **Sample dishes:** chilled tomato & redcurrant soup; guinea fowl with grape & chestnut stuffing; Irish coffee meringues. **Details:** www.thebayhorsehotel.co.uk; after Canal Foot sign, turn left & pass Glaxo factory; 7.30 pm; closed Mon L; no Amex; no smoking; children: 12+. **Accommodation:** 9 rooms, from £165.

UPPER SLAUGHTER, GLOUCESTERSHIRE 2–1C

Lords of the Manor £74 🅰★

GL54 2JD (01451) 820243

"A successful romantic outcome is guaranteed", says one of the many fans of the "wonderful" dining room at this country house hotel, where former Box Tree chef Toby Hill's cooking is pronounced "amazing" by most reporters; the "superb" wine list is also highly regarded. / **Sample dishes:** quail ravioli with morels; roast John Dory with Parma ham & foie gras; pistachio soufflé. **Details:** www.lordsofthemanor.com; 2m W of Stow on the Wold; 9.30 pm; no jeans or trainers; no smoking; children: 7+. **Accommodation:** 27 rooms, from £155.

UPPINGHAM, RUTLAND 5–4D

The Lake Isle £35

16 High Street East LE15 9PZ (01572) 822951

Opinions continue to vary on the new (two-year-old) régime at this well-reputed local destination (part of a small hotel, near the market square); fans say it's "maintaining good standards" and offers an "excellent wine list" – critics say the place is "living on its past reputation". / **Sample dishes:** asparagus & Parmesan tart; chicken with tarragon & cranberry risotto; bread & butter pudding with cherry custard. **Details:** www.lakeislehotel.com; 9.30 pm; closed Mon L; no smoking. **Accommodation:** 13 rooms, from £70.

WADDESDON, BUCKINGHAMSHIRE 3–2A

Five Arrows £36 ★

High St HP18 0JE (01296) 651727

"Excellent food and setting, but at these prices they should be!" – well, you'd hardly expect a Rothschild to have built any old boozer, and this Waddesdon Manor estate inn is a very "safe" option, offering "interesting" and "enjoyable" fare (and "good wines"). / **Sample dishes:** beetroot & cumin soup; Moroccan lamb stew with cardamom rice; bourbon mousse with mango & raspberry coulis. **Details:** www.waddesdon.org.uk; on A41; 9.30 pm; no Amex; no smoking area; children: special area for under 10s. **Accommodation:** 11 rooms, from £85.

WAKEFIELD, WEST YORKSHIRE 5–1C

Aagrah £21 ★

Barnsley Rd WF1 5NX (01924) 242222

"Excellent flavours of India" are the theme of all reports on this "reasonably-priced" outpost of the commendable Yorkshire chain; it's a "pleasant" place, too, with "attentive" and "polite" service. / **Details:** www.aagrah.com; from M1, J39 follow Denby Dale Rd to A61; 11.30 pm; closed Mon L, Sat L & Sun L; no smoking area. **Accommodation:** 13 rooms, from £40.

WAREHAM, DORSET   2–4C

Priory   £ 43   A

Church Grn BH20 4ND   (01929) 551666

The cooking is "average-to-good", but it's the "peaceful" and "beautiful" surroundings – in gardens next to the River Frome (or in the undercroft when the sun isn't shining) – which can make dining at this well-regarded hotel quite an occasion. / **Sample dishes:** seared scallops with rhubarb butter; lamb with herb polenta & roast garlic jus; ginger crème brûlée. **Details:** www.theprioryhotel.co.uk; 10 pm; no Amex; no smoking; children: 8+. **Accommodation:** 18 rooms, from £140.

WARHAM ALL SAINTS, NORFOLK   6–3C

Three Horseshoes   £ 20   A

Bridge St NR23 1NL   (01328) 710547

"It's a great experience to visit this traditional hostelry", say fans of this old inn who applaud "both the venue and the food" – reports on the latter, however, are not consistent. / **Sample dishes:** shellfish & cheese bake; Norfolk beef pie; ice cream & sorbet. **Details:** 1m off A148; 8.30 pm; no credit cards; no smoking area; no booking. **Accommodation:** 6 rooms, from £24.

WATERMILLOCK, CUMBRIA   7–3D

Leeming House Hotel   £ 46   A

CA11 0JJ   (01768) 486622

"An exceptional garden, lake and hill view" add charm to the dining room at this early-19th century Lakeland house (these days a Macdonald Hotel); the cooking is traditional, but it's the "extensive" list of wines which attracts most commentary. / **Sample dishes:** smoked salmon; guinea fowl; chocolate extreme mousse. **Details:** www.macdonald-hotels.co.uk; near A592; 9 pm; no smoking. **Accommodation:** 40 rooms, from £55.

Rampsbeck Hotel   £ 32   A

CA11 0LP   (01768) 486442

"Wonderful" gardens and "spectacular views of Ullswater" combine to create a "beautiful" setting for this "magnificent" country house hotel; its dining room seems to do the simplest things best. / **Sample dishes:** baked goat cheese with roast beetroot; roast fillet of beef with veal sweetbread; hot blackberry souffle with toffee apple ice cream. **Details:** www.hotel-lakedistrict.com; next to Lake Ullswater, J40 on M6, take A592 to Ullswater; no Amex; no smoking; children: 8+. **Accommodation:** 20 rooms, from £100.

WATH-IN-NIDDERDALE, NORTH YORKSHIRE   8–4B

Sportsman's Arms   £ 34

HG3 5PP   (01423) 711306

As you might perhaps expect of a ("beautifully-located") Dales restaurant that's been in the same ownership for a quarter of a century, the style of Ray Carter's establishment can seem "rather quaint"; it offers a "good range" of "hearty" dishes, though – in the bar or the restaurant. / **Sample dishes:** goats cheese with caramelised red onions; duck with rosti, prunes & oranges; summer pudding. **Details:** take Wath Road from Pateley Bridge; 9 pm; D only, closed Sun; no Amex; no smoking. **Accommodation:** 11 rooms, from £80.

WATTON AT STONE, HERTFORDSHIRE   3–2B

George & Dragon   **£ 28**   A★

82 High St SG14 3TA   (01920) 830285

This "cosy" and "real" old pub again wins praise for "cooking with imagination and consistency", as well as for its "beamed and comfortable setting". / **Sample dishes:** potted crab with ginger; fillet steak stuffed with oysters; lemon & passion fruit tart.
Details: www.georgeanddragon-watton.co.uk; A602 from Stevenage; 10 pm; closed Sun D; no smoking in dining room; children: before 9pm.

WELLS, SOMERSET   2–3B

Ritchers   **£ 33**   ★

5 Sadler St BA5 2RR   (01749) 679085

Entered via a passageway off the town's main drag, this "somewhat cramped" two-floor fixture (café-bar downstairs, restaurant above) wins loud applause for its "utterly consistent" and "inventive" French cooking at "good prices". / **Sample dishes:** Mozzarella & plum tomato tortellini; pan-fried pheasant breast with bubble & squeak; chestnut terrine with cappuccino cream. **Details:** www.ritchers.co.uk; 9.30 pm; closed Sun; no Amex.

WEST HALLAM, DERBYSHIRE   5–3C

The Bottle Kiln   **£ 14**   A

High Lane West DE7 6HP   (0115) 932 9442

"You may have to queue", such are the attractions of the "home-cooked pies" and "tempting cakes and puds" at this "good informal lunch venue", attached to an art gallery. / **Sample dishes:** Stilton & walnut quiche with salad; cheesecake. **Details:** L & afternoon tea only; closed Mon; no smoking; no booking; children: not permitted in garden.

WEST MERSEA, ESSEX   3–2C

The Company Shed   **£ 12**   ★★

129 Coast Rd CO5 8PA   (01206) 382700

"It has to be tried", say fans of this "small" BYO (bread as well as wine) seaside "shack", which sells "wonderful", "real", "fresh" seafood in ultra-"basic" surroundings. / **Sample dishes:** fish platter. **Details:** no credit cards.

WESTERHAM, KENT   3–3B

Tulsi   **£ 25**   ★

20 London Rd TN16 1BD   (01959) 563397

Some find it a mite "cramped", but "better than average" curries make this "welcoming" Indian a favourite nonetheless.
/ **Details:** 11.30 pm.

WESTFIELD, EAST SUSSEX   3–4C

Wild Mushroom   **£ 34**   ★

Westfield Ln TN35 4SB   (01424) 751137

"A blessing in a desert"; this "well-kept local secret" – a restaurant housed in a former boozer – is well worth seeking out if you're thinking of dining in these parts. / **Sample dishes:** red pepper & tomato soup; chicken with mushrooms, capers & mash; tropical fruit sorbets with jasmine syrup. **Details:** www.wildmushroom.co.uk; 9.30 pm; closed Mon & Sun D; closed 3 weeks in Jan; no smoking in dining room; children: 8+ prefered in evening.

WETHERBY, WEST YORKSHIRE   5–1C

La Locanda   £33
Wetherby Rd LS22 5AY   (01937) 579797
"Bustling and busy", this "cheerful" trattoria is a "well-run" place
where "not-bad cooking, friendly service and footballer-spotting
possibilities add up to an enjoyable overall experience".
/ *Sample dishes:* fried calamari with salad; beef Stroganoff; chocolate fudge cake.
Details: www.lalocanda.co.uk; 11 pm.

WEYBRIDGE, SURREY   3–3A

Colony   £33
3 Balfour Rd KT13 8HE   (01932) 842766
"Very average, considering the price" – even those who say it serves
"great food" are becoming less and less impressed by the value
on offer at this rather "formal" Chinese of long standing. / *Details:* on
A317; 10.30 pm.

WEYMOUTH, DORSET   2–4B

Perry's   £34
4 Trinity Rd, The Old Harbour DT4 8TJ   (01305) 785799
This quayside spot has a "cosy" style that can seem a touch
"dated"; all feedback, though, attests that it's a "solid" place,
with "fresh fish", "a good view" and "nice service".
/ *Sample dishes:* chicken & bacon terrine with apple chutney; fillet steak with
tarragon cream sauce; pear sorbet & brandy snaps.
Details: www.perrysrestaurant.co.uk; 9.30 pm; closed Mon L & Sat L (& Sun D
in winter); no smoking area; children: 5+.

WHITBY, NORTH YORKSHIRE   8–3D

Magpie Café   £26   ★★
14 Pier Rd YO21 3PU   (01947) 602058
"Fantastic" fish and chips – "like we'd never tasted before" – and a
"huge menu" of other "sophisticated" piscene fare have made this
unpretentious café the North East's most commented-on culinary
destination; "arrive early", though – "the queues are getting worse".
/ *Sample dishes:* grilled tuna with courgette fritters; cod & chips; sticky sultana
loaf. *Details:* www.magpiecafe.co.uk; opp Fish Market; 9 pm; no Amex; no smoking;
no booking at L.

Trenchers   £15   ★★
New Quay Rd YO21 1DH   (01947) 603212
"Ignore the prices – the quality is fantastic, and amenities include
marble-clad loos", raves one fan of this "unique" chippie; there are
even those – whisper it softly – who claim it's "better than the
Magpie"! / *Details:* opp railway station, nr marina; 9 pm; no smoking area;
need 7+ to book.

The White Horse & Griffin   £34
Church St YO22 4BH   (01947) 604857
A "romantic olde worlde pub", with a "cramped", "bistro-style"
restaurant; fans say it's hearty fare can be "excellent", but others
say it's "not that special". / *Sample dishes:* Caesar salad; char-grilled
steak & chips; plum & almond pizza. *Details:* www.whitehorseandgriffin.co.uk;
centre of old town, on Abbey side of river; 9.30 pm; no Amex; no smoking area.
Accommodation: 11 rooms, from £60.

WHITCHURCH, HAMPSHIRE   2–3D
Red House Inn   £32   𝔸★
21 London St RG28 7LH   (01256) 895558
"Ambitious", "restaurant-grade" food delights local fans of this
modernised and "atmospheric" coaching inn, owned by Californian
chef Shannon Wells. / **Sample dishes:** Parmesan-crusted langoustine; fillet
steak in bacon with Stilton sauce; lemon tart & strawberry coulis. **Details:** 9.30 pm;
no Amex; no smoking; booking essential; children: D 12+.

WHITEBROOK, MONMOUTHSHIRE   2–2B
The Crown at Whitebrook   £39   ★
NP25 4TX   (01600) 860254
"Sparkling" cooking makes this restaurant-with-rooms a "hidden
gem", for most reporters; its "old-world" atmosphere can seem
surprisingly "unmemorable", though, despite an "attractive location"
in a "steep-sided wooded valley". / **Sample dishes:** venison carpaccio; roast
monkfish & foie gras with red lentil purée; caraway parfait with fig sponge.
Details: www.crownatwhitebrook.co.uk; 2m W of A466, 5m S of Monmouth;
8.45 pm; closed Mon L; no smoking in dining room; children: 12+.
Accommodation: 11 rooms, from £90.

WHITEHAVEN, CUMBRIA   7–3C
Zest   £32   ★
Low Rd CA28 9HS   (01946) 692848
"Never anything short of brilliant", insist fans of this surprisingly
"modern" brasserie; most reports are of "delicious" cooking.
/ **Sample dishes:** chicken liver & whisky cream pâté; spice-coated chicken with
curried new potatoes; apple tarte Tatin with green apple sorbet. **Details:** 9.30 pm;
D only, closed Sun-Tue; no Amex; no smoking in dining room.

WHITLEY, WILTSHIRE   2–2B
The Pear Tree Inn   £34
Top Ln SN12 8QX   (01225) 709131
Even some fans say it's "slightly overpriced", but this "great food
pub in a lovely area" still generally gets the thumbs-up.
/ **Sample dishes:** wild mushroom & tarragon risotto; lamb cutlets with creamed
leeks & caper jus; green fig tarte Tatin with panna cotta. **Details:** 9 pm; no Amex;
no smoking in dining room. **Accommodation:** 8 rooms, from £80.

WHITSTABLE, KENT   3–3C
Crab & Winkle   £34   ★
South Quay, Whitstable Harbour CT5 1AB
(01227) 779377
"Great seafood on the harbour" wins continued popularity for this
"real treasure"; it's "excellent for families" too. / **Sample dishes:** oysters;
baked crab with garlic butter & Cheddar; treacle sponge & custard.
Details: www.crab-winkle.co.uk; 9.45 pm; no Amex.

Wheeler's Oyster Bar   £29   ★★
8 High St CT5 1BQ   (01227) 273311
"Like granny's front room, but with amazing food and offering
incredibly good value"; this "tiny caff" ("effectively at the back of a
shop") offers "the cheapest and freshest oysters you'll find", as well
as other "fresh" and "vibrant" dishes, using "top-quality produce".
/ **Sample dishes:** skate ravioli; baked cod with spinach & curried mussels; date &
chocolate sponge. **Details:** 7.30 pm; closed Wed; no credit cards.

Whitstable Oyster Fishery Co.   **£41**   𝔸★

Horsebridge CT5 1BU   (01227) 276856

"London prices and fellow diners" are defining features of this *"quaint"* and *"simple"* seafood establishment – a *"worst-kept secret"* destination, where refugees from the Smoke can *"eat while overlooking the beach"*; many reporters feel it has *"emerged from its recent ropey phase"*, but some concerns persist, in particular about *"mediocre"* service. / **Sample dishes:** rock oysters; char-gilled mackerel with roast tomato sauce; chocolate truffle cake with raspberries. **Details:** www.oysterfishery.co.uk; 9 pm, Sat 10 pm; closed Mon (& Sun D Sep-May). **Accommodation:** 30 rooms, from £40.

WILMINGTON, EAST SUSSEX   3–4B

Giant's Rest   **£26**   ★

The Street BN26 5SQ   (01323) 870207

"Home cooked, traditional British food" from *"locally-sourced ingredients"* induces uniformly upbeat feedback on this inn on the Downs. / **Sample dishes:** avacado & prawns; home-made fish cakes; fruit crumble. **Details:** www.giantsrest.co.uk; from A22 at Polegate take A27 towards Lewes, after 2m left at crossroads; 9 pm; no Amex; mainly non-smoking; booking: max 12. **Accommodation:** 1 room, at about £40.

WILMSLOW, CHESHIRE   5–2B

Chilli Banana
Kings Arms Hotel   **£27**   ★

Alderley Rd SK9 1PZ   (01625) 539100

Fans continue to hail *"excellent"* food at this relaxed Thai, behind a pub. / **Details:** www.chillibanana.co.uk; 11 pm; closed Mon, Tue L, Wed L & Thu L.

WINCHCOMBE, GLOUCESTERSHIRE   2–1C

5 North Street   **£40**   ★★

5 North St GL54 5LH
(01242) 604566

"A brilliant newcomer"; reporters all speak in superlatives when it comes to Marcus Ashenford's (the chef who established Chavignol, now RIP) *"very special"* latest venture, hailing his *"original"*, *"considered"* and *"finely judged"* cuisine; the ambience is *"homely"* and *"friendly"*, too. / **Sample dishes:** roast scallop with sautéed foie gras & cauliflower purée; chump of lamb with haggis & baby vegetables; chocolate brownie with vanilla ice cream & butterscotch sauce. **Details:** 9 pm; closed Mon, Tue L & Sun D; no smoking.

Wesley House   **£42**   𝔸★

High St GL54 5LJ   (01242) 602366

"Magical, from the rustic fireplace in the entrance to the stunning food" – most reporters speak only well of this *"really friendly"* establishment, where *"first-rate"* contemporary food is served in a *"beautiful"* ancient, half-timbered building. / **Sample dishes:** red snapper terrine with saffron potatoes; seared duck with pickled apples & Calvados cream; iced toffee & pistachio parfait. **Details:** www.wesleyhouse.co.uk; next to Sudeley Castle; 9.15 pm; closed Sun D; no smoking in dining room. **Accommodation:** 6 rooms, from £70.

WINCHESTER, HAMPSHIRE   2–3D

Chestnut Horse   £ 38   ★
Easton Village SO21 1EG   (01962) 779257
*This "very attractive, upmarket pub" is hailed by all reporters as a
"splendid" place – the cooking can be "excellent" (and there's
a good wine list).* / **Sample dishes:** *fresh crab; rack of lamb; sticky toffee
pudding.* **Details:** *no Amex; children: 14+.*

Hotel du Vin et Bistro   £ 43   Ⓐ★
14 Southgate St SO23 9EF   (01962) 850676
*"A winning formula" – this original branch of the growing boutique
hotel chain established the "stylish" look that underpins its success
(and of course the "amazing choice of wines"); the food has
traditionally played second fiddle, but this year reporters judged
it "excellent" and "so consistent".* / **Sample dishes:** *moules marinière;
salmon pavé with mussel ragoût; lime panna cotta with melon.*
Details: *www.hotelduvin.com; 9.45 pm; booking: max 10.* **Accommodation:** *23
rooms, from £105.*

Loch Fyne   £ 30
18 Jewry St SO23 8RZ   (01962) 872930
*"A solid formula, but it's not exceptional" – in a city without any fish
places of note, however, this chain outlet can make a useful option.*
/ **Sample dishes:** *pan fried sea bass with scalloped potatoes.*
Details: *www.loch-fyne.com; 10 pm; no smoking area.*

Old Chesil Rectory   £ 52   ★★
1 Chesil St S023 0HU   (01962) 851555
*"Really top-quality food" – created by Philip Storey with "genuine
knowledge, talent and enthusiasm" – makes this historic Tudor
building a culinary destination of considerable note; the atmosphere
can seem a bit "sombre", though, despite the efforts of the
"accommodating" and "courteous" service.*
/ **Sample dishes:** *twice-baked Roquefort soufflé; duck with parsnip purée & lime
vanilla sauce; melon sorbet with ginger shortbread.* **Details:** *8.45 pm, Sat 9.15 pm;
D only Tue-Fri, closed Mon & Sun; no smoking area.*

Wykeham Arms   £ 34   Ⓐ
75 Kingsgate St SO23 9PE   (01962) 853834
*"The epitome of a good unspoilt pub", this famous inn – between
the College and the Cathedral – is "as reliable as ever", and hugely
popular; the food doesn't try too hard, but it's "hearty",
and complemented by a "great" wine list.* / **Sample dishes:** *mushroom,
walnut & Stilton pâté; roast monkfish with red onion & cherry tomato salad;
orange & maple cheesecake.* **Details:** *between Cathedral and College; 8.45 pm;
closed Sun D; no smoking area; booking: max 8; children: 14+.*
Accommodation: *14 rooms, from £90.*

WINDERMERE, CUMBRIA   7–3D

Gilpin Lodge   £ 46   Ⓐ★
Crook Rd LA23 3NE   (01539) 488818
*"It's just so relaxing and pampering", say fans of this "quietly
refined" Edwardian country house hotel, which enjoys a "beautiful"
Lakeland setting; the odd gripe of "diminishing portions", aside,
most judge the cooking as "very, very good".* / **Sample dishes:** *smoked
haddock pavé; roast lamb with truffled potato & garlic sauce; Greek yoghurt sorbet.*
Details: *www.gilpin-lodge.co.uk; 9.15 pm; no smoking in dining room; children: 7+.*
Accommodation: *14 rooms, from £200.*

Holbeck Ghyll £60 Ⓐ★
Holbeck Ln LA23 ILU (01539) 432375
"Terrific and inventive" French cuisine and "a great location"
(overlooking Lake Windermere) help win some rave reviews for this
former hunting lodge; the occasional doubter finds it a mite "stilted".
/ **Sample dishes:** veal ravioli with morels; salmon with tomato fondue; pear &
praline parfait. **Details:** www.holbeckghyll.com; 3m N of Windermere, towards
Troutbeck; 9.30 pm; no smoking; children: 8+. **Accommodation:** 20 rooms,
from £190.

Jerichos £39 ★
Birch St LA23 IEG (01539) 442522
A "friendly" family-run restaurant in the town-centre, where almost
all reporters praise "interesting, and good-quality food" and "a very
good wine list"; (the menu is "limited" though, and one great former
fan senses "a loss of direction"). / **Sample dishes:** smoked haddock, spring
onion & Cheddar risotto; pork tenderloin with roast parsnips & Madeira jus;
butterscotch toffee crème brûlée. **Details:** 9.30 pm; D only, closed Mon; no Amex;
no smoking; children: 12+.

WINDSOR, WINDSOR & MAIDENHEAD 3–3A

Al Fassia £25 ★
27 St Leonards Rd SL4 3BP (01753) 855370
"A family-run Moroccan that's worth a visit", especially in this under-
served locality; some find the ambience "a little too café-ish",
but the place is unanimously applauded for its "tasty" food and
"very reasonable" prices. / **Details:** 10.30 pm, Fri & Sat 11 pm; closed Sun;
no smoking.

WINKLEIGH, DEVON 1–2D

Pophams £32 Ⓐ★
Castle St EX19 8HQ (01837) 83767
"Intimate" to an extent rarely experienced, this "tiny" BYO, 10-
seater offers "a super experience", "like visiting friends", and the
food is "great"; do note the very limited opening hours.
/ **Sample dishes:** baked goats cheese with spicy chutney; lamb in puff pastry with
mushroom pâté; orange tart with apricot sauce. **Details:** off A377 between
Exeter & Barnstaple; open only Thu & Fri L; closed Feb; no credit cards; no smoking;
children: 14+.

WINTERINGHAM, NORTH LINCOLNSHIRE 5–1D

Winteringham Fields £72 Ⓐ★★
DN15 9PF (01724) 733096
"I want to live here, it's so good"; with its "inspired" cooking,
"immaculate" service and "wonderful" ambience, Annie and
Germain Schwab's 16th-century manor house has established
a huge reputation as a "really special" destination – thank heavens
they decided against selling up! / **Sample dishes:** pan-fried langoustines;
veal with wild mushrooms & veal jus; chocolate & macadamia nut mousse.
Details: www.winteringhamfields.com; 4m SW of Humber Bridge; 9.30 pm; closed
Mon & Sun; no smoking; booking: max 8. **Accommodation:** 10 rooms, from £115.

WITHERSLACK, CUMBRIA   7–4D
Old Vicarage   £41   𝔸★
Church Rd LA11 6RS   (01539) 552381
*This "very agreeable" Lakeland country house hotel produces impressively consistent feedback, on the basis of some "excellent" cooking. / **Sample dishes:** oyster tempura with horseradish cream; seared smoked venison with sweet potato purée; star anise syrup sponge.*
Details: *www.oldvicarage.com; from M6, J36 follow signs to Barrow on A590; 9 pm; D only, except Sun open L & D; no smoking.* **Accommodation:** *14 rooms, from £65.*

WOBURN, BEDFORDSHIRE   3–2A
Birch   £34
20 Newport Rd MK17 9HX   (01525) 290295
*Most (if not quite all) reporters are impressed, by the "excellent grills" served at this rural pub; it's "more of a restaurant", these days. / **Sample dishes:** cod carpaccio with gazpacho sauce; pork with apple & black pudding stuffing; honey crème brûlée with orange shortbread.*
Details: *www.countrytaverns.fsbusiness.co.uk; 9.30 pm; closed Sun D; no smoking in dining room; booking: max 8, Fri & Sat.*

Market Place   £31   𝔸★
19 Market Pl MK17 9PZ   (01525) 290877
There's "always something to surprise" – not least "a wine list where most bottles come from the USA" – at this "special" town-centre restaurant (and banqueting venue), which offers "ever-changing" and "well-realised" Californian cuisine.
*/ **Sample dishes:** asparagus tempura; organic beef fillet topped with mushrooms; Marco's classic cheesecake with mango & passion fruit.* ***Details:*** *9 pm; closed Mon & Sun D; no Amex; no smoking.*

Paris House   £63
Woburn Pk MK17 9QP   (01525) 290692
Fans say "it has a lovely setting" (a half-timbered house in a deer park) and praise the "good" French cuisine at this "cosy" fixture; the "time warped" ambience doesn't suit everyone, though, nor does the food (which detractors describe as simply "atrocious").
*/ **Sample dishes:** prawn & crayfish with mango; roast brill with Noilly Prat sauce; raspberry soufflé.* ***Details:*** *www.parishouse.co.uk; on A4012; 9.30 pm; closed Mon & Sun D; no smoking area.*

WOLVERHAMPTON, WEST MIDLANDS   5–4B
Bilash   £36   ★
2 Cheapside WV1 1TU   (01902) 427762
*Sitab Khan's town-centre Bangladeshi is "the best" according to its fans; it's not cheap, but the fare on offer is both "good" and "different". / **Details:** www.bilash-tandoori.co.uk; opp Civic Centre; 11 pm; closed Sun; no smoking in dining room.*

WOODBRIDGE, SUFFOLK   3–1D
Captains Table   £27
3 Quay St IP12 1BX   (01394) 383145
*Reports span the whole range from "delightful" to "awful", but the middle view is that if you're looking for "an efficient meal, plainly cooked and served", this long-established town-centre restaurant is worth remembering; NB despite the name, there's no great emphasis on fish. / **Sample dishes:** twice-baked spinach soufflé; slow-roast duck with red wine sauce; hot toffee pudding.* ***Details:*** *www.captainstable.co.uk; 100 yds from theatre; 9.30 pm, Fri & Sat 10 pm; closed Mon & Sun D; closed 2 weeks in Jan; no Amex; smoking in bar only.*

Seckford Hall Hotel £ 30 A ★
IP13 6NU (01394) 385678
"Maintaining and improving its long-established standards",
this "delightfully situated" Elizabethan house in Constable country
remains very popular with more mature reporters; notably
reasonable prices add to its appeal. / **Sample dishes:** salmon roulade;
monkfish with pasta & wilted greens; champagne mousse with strawberries.
Details: www.seckford.co.uk; 9.30 pm; closed Mon L; no smoking; children: 6+ after
7 pm. **Accommodation:** 32 rooms, from £120.

WOODCOTE, OXFORDSHIRE 3–3A

Highwayman £ 42 A
Exlade Street RG8 0UA (01491) 682020
A "charming old pub" with "loads of character"; its small fanclub
says the cooking is "great", too (you can eat in the bar, or the "quite
upmarket" restaurant). / **Sample dishes:** pan-fried pigeon breast; seared
cannon of lamb with potatoes; glazed lemon tart. **Details:** 9.30 pm; no shorts;
no smoking area. **Accommodation:** 4 rooms, from £65.

WOODSTOCK, OXFORDSHIRE 2–1D

The Feathers Hotel £ 48
Market St OX20 1SX (01993) 812291
Most reporters find it a "lovely" experience to visit this luxurious
hotel (converted from a number of town houses) at the heart of this
famous Cotswold village; the sometimes "quiet" dining room can
seem "pretentious", though, and "expensive for what it is", so the
bar may be a "better-value" option. / **Sample dishes:** confit chicken with
fig marmalade; lemon sole with rocket soufflé; nougat glacé with mango & chocolate
sauce. **Details:** www.feathers.co.uk; 8m N of Oxford on A44; 9.15 pm; no smoking.
Accommodation: 20 rooms, from £225.

WORCESTER, WORCESTERSHIRE 2–1B

Brown's £ 49 ★
24 Quay St WR1 2JJ (01905) 26263
Most (if not quite all) reporters find this ambitious river-view
establishment – which is absolutely no relation to the ghastly chain –
absolutely "excellent". / **Sample dishes:** devilled lambs kidneys with polenta;
roast duck with minted pea mousseline; bitter chocolate ice cream. **Details:** near
the Cathedral on riverside; 9.45 pm; closed Mon, Sat L & Sun D; no Amex;
no smoking; children: 8+.

WREXHAM, WREXHAM 5–3A

Pant Yr Ochan £ 27 A
Old Wrexham Rd LL12 8TY (01978) 853525
Part of a small local group of pub/restaurants ("though it doesn't
feel like a chain"), this popular outfit – set in an "historic" house
of some charm – offers a menu that's quite "adventurous", for the
locale. / **Sample dishes:** mushroom ravioli; red bream & olive potatoes with
asparagus; apple tart with cider custard. **Details:** www.brunningandprice.co.uk;
1m N of Wrexham; 9.30 pm; no smoking area; booking: max 14; children: before
6 pm only.

WRIGHTINGTON BAR, LANCASHIRE   5–1A

Mulberry Tree   £36   ★
9 Wrightington Bar WN6 9SE   (01257) 451400
This "converted pub with a modern feel" incorporates both
a "bar and a more formal restaurant"; its cooking, from a Gavroche-
trained chef, sets "a good standard, particularly for the area".
/ **Sample dishes:** pea & ham soup with Parmesan croutons; baked cod with
cheese & basil crust; rice pudding with apricots. **Details:** 2m along Mossy Lea Rd,
off M6, J27; 9.30 pm; no Amex; no smoking.

WYE, KENT   3–3C

Wife of Bath   £40
4 Upper Bridge St TN25 5AF   (01233) 812540
"Maintaining standards under new owners" (and with the chef
unchanged), this "eccentric" (going on "twee") restaurant in a
converted village house remains quite a "classy" choice.
/ **Sample dishes:** goats cheese & pickled quail egg salad; sea bass with lime &
coriander salsa; sticky toffee pudding. **Details:** www.wifeofbath.com; off A28
between Ashford & Canterbury; 9.30 pm; closed Mon & Sun; no smoking area.
Accommodation: 5 rooms, from £75.

YARM, CLEVELAND   8–3C

McCoys at Yarm   £35
44 High St TS15 9AE   (01642) 791234
The McCoys – of Tontine fame – have yet to work their magic
at the premises formerly known as Stricklands; no reports suggest
that the place is in any way exemplary, and some accounts just say
it's plain "disappointing". / **Sample dishes:** smoked haddock fishcake with
French bean salad, poached egg & hollandaise; braised lamb shank with Spanish
black pudding, roast tomatoes & wet polenta; Eton mess.
Details: www.mccoysinyarm.co.uk; 9.30 pm; no smoking at L.

YATTENDON, BERKSHIRE   2–2D

Royal Oak Hotel   £39
The Square RG18 0UG   (01635) 201325
On limited feedback, there are gripes about "London prices" at this
elegant and attractively-situated village inn, where corporate
ownership seems to have done little for what was once
an establishment of some note. / **Sample dishes:** lobster ravioli on seasoned
spinach; roast lamb with celeriac gratin; praline soufflé.
Details: www.corushotels.co.uk; 5m W of Pangbourne, off B4009; 9.30 pm;
no smoking; children: 6+. **Accommodation:** 5 rooms, from £130.

YORK, CITY OF YORK   5–1D

Bettys   £27   Ⓐ
6-8 St Helen's Sq YO1 8QP   (01904) 659142
"The only problem is being spoilt for choice", say fans of this
"very popular café" (formerly Taylor's), which is now an outpost
of the famous Harrogate institution – it offers a similar cakes-and-
savouries formula, but is not quite so highly rated overall.
/ **Sample dishes:** Swiss rosti with bacon & cheese; Yorkshire rarebit with apple
chutney; Yorkshire curd tart. **Details:** www.bettysandtaylors.com; down Blake
St from York Minster; 9 pm; no Amex; no smoking; no booking.

Blue Bicycle £ 40
34 Fossgate YO1 9TA (01904) 673990
*Anthony Stephenson bought the most commented-on destination
in York after our survey closed, so let's hope for a return to form –
the place was notably "inconsistent" in the dying days of the old
régime. / **Sample dishes:** spicy salmon hash with lime salsa; Aberdeen Angus beef
with green bean stir-fry; passion fruit & Campari rice pudding.
Details: www.bluebicyclerestaurant.com; 10 pm, Sun 9 pm; no Amex; no smoking;
booking: max 8. **Accommodation:** 1 room, at about £150.*

Café Concerto £ 32
21 High Petergate YO1 7EN (01904) 610478
*"Still York's best place of its kind", this "relaxed" and "friendly"
café/bistro by the Minster "maintains high standards" – "arrive
early, as there are often queues". / **Sample dishes:** grilled halloumi with
pomegranate molasses; pork chops with root vegetable mash; Irish coffee jelly
with amaretti biscuits. **Details:** www.cafeconcerto.biz; by the W entrance of York
Minster; 9.30 pm, Fri & Sat 10 pm; no Amex; no smoking; no booking at L.*

City Screen Café Bar £ 22 A★
Coney St YO1 9QL (01904) 541144
*"Friendly service, lovely cheap sandwiches, a pleasant atmosphere
and superb views over the river Ouse" – such are the attractions
of this large-windowed café, on the top floor of a modern cinema.
/ **Sample dishes:** Parma ham & Mozzarella salad; smoked salmon & scrambled
eggs; lemon cheesecake. **Details:** www.picturehouses.co.uk; 9 pm; no Amex;
no smoking area; no booking; children: before 7 pm only.*

Durham Ox £ 34
Westway, Crayke YO61 4TE (01347) 821506
*The "small and intimate dining room" of this restaurant-with-rooms
just outside York offers "superb" food, and very much appeals
to some locals – others, however, complain of "small portions" and
"London prices". / **Sample dishes:** baked queens scallops; breast of duck
on roast butternut squash, wilted greens & fondant potato; warm chocolate fondant
souffle with hazelnut ice cream. **Details:** www.thedurhamox.com; 9.30 pm;
no smoking.*

Melton's £ 35 ★
7 Scarcroft Rd YO23 1ND (01904) 634341
*"No laurel-resting here!" – this "upmarket bistro/café" maintains
a very broad following with its "innovative and creative" cooking and
its "top-value" wine list; a shop-conversion in a "nondescript terrace,
just outside the City walls", it achieves an atmosphere of "well-
judged informality", rather than anything more.
/ **Sample dishes:** Jerusalem artichoke soup; braised oxtail with chervil mash; apple
crêpes with cider sorbet. **Details:** www.meltonsrestaurant.co.uk; 10 mins walk from
Castle Museum; 10 pm; closed Mon L & Sun; no Amex; no smoking area.*

Melton's Too £ 28
25 Walmgate YO1 9TX (01904) 629222
*Mixed reports on Melton's bistro-style offshoot confirm the
conclusion that it's "not as good as the original"; the flexibility of all-
day opening, however, is a plus. / **Sample dishes:** pork rillettes with
Cumberland sauce; Merguez sausage with couscous & lemon oil; Yorkshire curd tart.
Details: www.meltonstoo.co.uk; 10.30 pm; no smoking in dining room.*

Middlethorpe Hall £ 48
Bishopthorpe Rd   YO23 2GB   (01904) 641241
It has a glorious location – part of a country house hotel and spa, in a 200-acre estate right on the fringe of the city – but this grand dining room continues to inspire somewhat mixed reviews.
/ **Sample dishes:** *oxtail terrine with horseradish cream; pike fillet with Bayonne ham; aniseed parfait with roast pears.* **Details:** *www.middlethorpe.com; next to racecourse; 9.45 pm; jacket & tie required; no smoking in dining room; children: 8+.* **Accommodation:** *30 rooms, from £160.*

Rish £ 40
7 Fossgate   YO1 9TA   (01904) 622688
These Edwardian store premises were revamped a few years ago along "clean, modern lines", and serve a menu that's "quite innovative (for York)"; even fans who say the place is "consistently good", though, say it has "become a little overpriced".
/ **Sample dishes:** *beetroot-scented gravadlax; roast lamb with olive mash & salsify; pear Bakewell tart with Calvados sorbet.* **Details:** *www.rish-york.co.uk; 10 pm, Fri & Sat 10.30 pm; smoking in bar only.*

UK MAPS

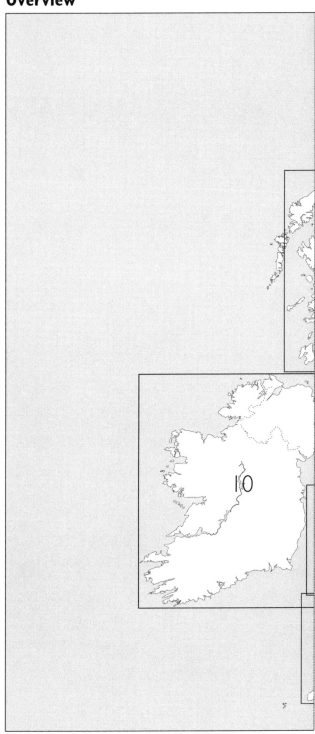

10

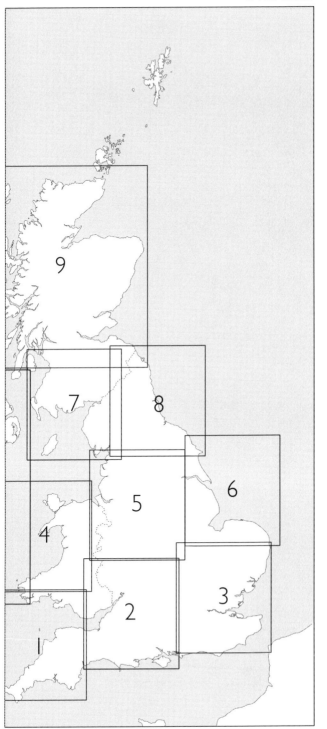

Map 1

Map 1

Map 2

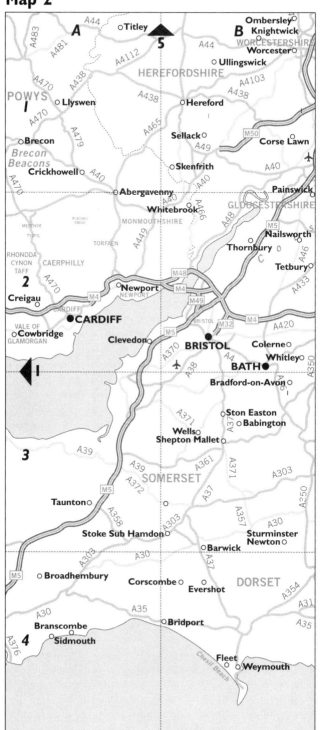

Map 2

Map 3

Map 3

Map 4

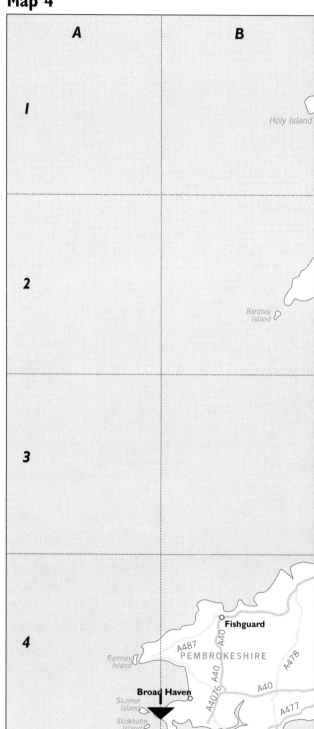

Map 4

Map 5

A

B

8

○Lancaster

○Hetton

_A6_

LANCASHIRE

○Sawley

Clitheroe○

○**Cowling**

_A6068_

_A585_

_A6_

_1_ **Blackpool**○

○**Longridge**

_A59_

Langho○

_M55_

Preston○

_M65_

_A646_

_A59_

Todmorden○

○**Cheesden**

_A58_

Southport○

**Bispham
Green**○

_M6_

Ramsbottom○

_M66_

_M62_

_A570_

_A59_

Wrightington Bar○

_M61_

_A58_

Bolton○

_A58_

Lydgate○

Oldham○

_M58_

MANCHESTER●

LIVERPOOL●

MERSEYSIDE

_M62_

_M63_

_M56_

_M67_

_2_ ○**Hoylake**

Birkenhead○

_A57_

Hale○

Mellor○

_M53_

_M62_

Nether Alderley○

Wilmslow○

_A548_

Parkgate○

Knutsford○

Prestbury○

_A537_

_M56_

CHESHIRE

Chester○

Great Barrow○

_M6_

_A50_

_A54_

FLINTSHIRE

Cotebrook○

4

_A494_

_A55_

_A41_

_A51_

Astbury○

_A534_

○**Aldford**

_A49_

Llandegla
○

○**Wrexham**

_A525_

_A525_

WREXHAM

_3_ ○**Llangollen**

_A5_

_A51_

_A53_

Cheadle○

STAFFORDSHIRE

_A5_

Oswestry○

_A495_

_A49_

_A53_

_A41_

_A51_

_A483_

_A5_

_A518_

_M6_

_A34_

Shrewsbury○

_A442_

_A458_

SHROPSHIRE

Iron Bridge○

_M54_

_A458_

○**Norton**

_A483_

_A458_

Wolverhampton○

_A49_

_A489_

_A458_

_4_

Stourbridge○

_A442_

Leintwardine○

Ludlow○

○**Cleobury
Mortimer**

Clent○

_M5_

2

**Chaddesley
Corbett**○

_A488_

_A49_

_A456_

_A449_

_M5_

Presteigne○

○**Brimfield**

Map 5

Map 6

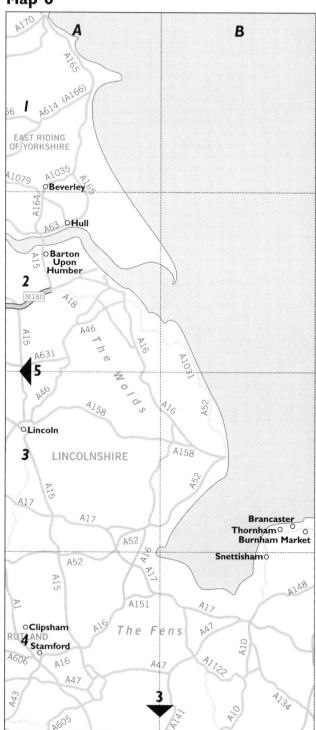

Map 6

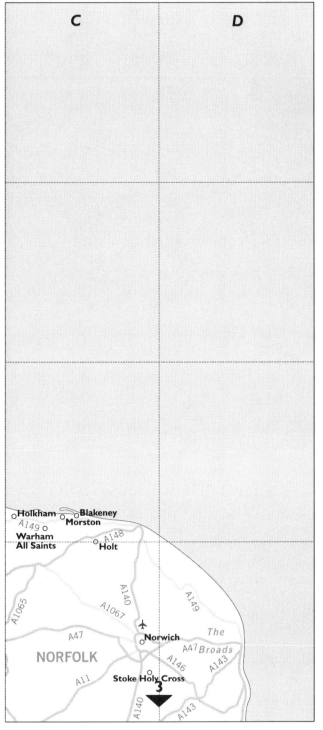

C

D

Holkham °—° Blakeney
A149 ° ° Morston
Warham
All Saints ° Holt
A148

A1065

A140
A1067

A149

A47

Norwich

The

NORFOLK

A47 Broads

A146 A143

A11

A140

Stoke Holy Cross

3

A143

Map 7

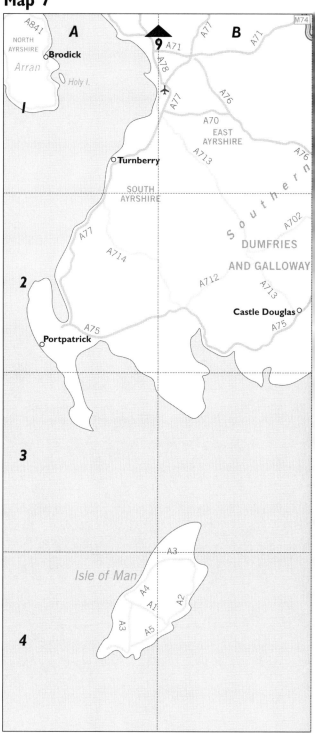

Map 7

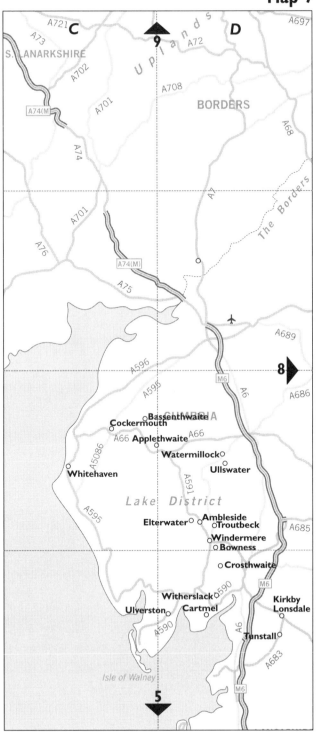

Map 8

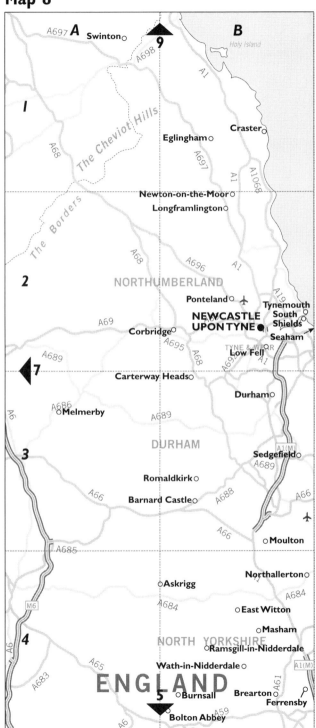

Map 8

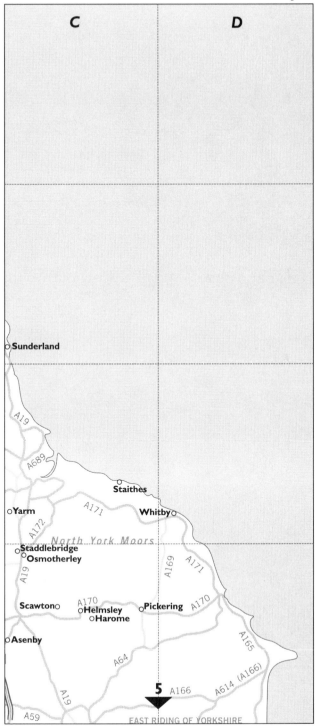

Map 9

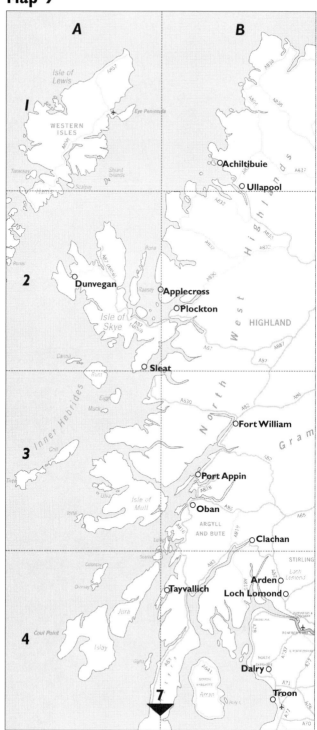

Map 9

Map 10

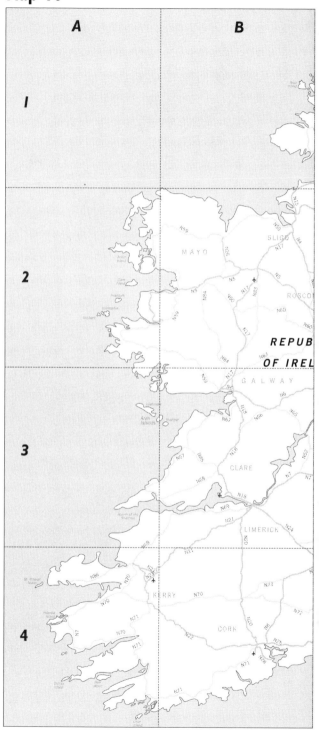

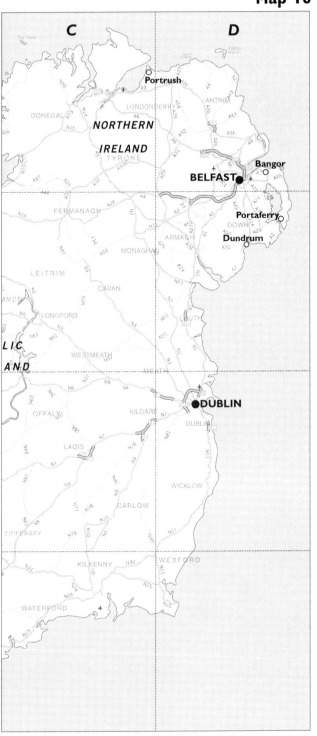

Map 10

ALPHABETICAL INDEX

ALPHABETICAL INDEX

ALPHABETICAL INDEX

ALPHABETICAL INDEX

ALPHABETICAL INDEX

ALPHABETICAL INDEX